A New Approach
To Contemporary Kurdish Issue
From The Chinese Perspective

Tang Zhichao

liber

LIBER PUBLICATIONS INTERNATIONAL

London - Berlin - Istanbul - Santiago

This edition is an authorized translation from the Chinese language edition, published in cooperation with **Social Sciences Academic Press**, Beijing, China.

We thank Canut Intl. Publishers for their cooperation in this publishing project.

A New Approach To Contemporary Kurdish Issue From The Chinese Perspective
Authored by Tang Zhichao
Chinese Title: 中东库尔德民族问题透视 (Kurdish National Question From The Middle East Perspective, ISBN: 978-7-5097-4397-3)
Copyright © Social Sciences Academic Press, China, 2013

Liber Publications International
33 Holmlea Rd. Reading, RG8 9EX, United Kingdom
Copyright © Liber Publications International, 2016

ISBN: 978-605-9914-38-3 (Paperback)

Printed in UK
Lightning Source Ltd. UK
Chapterhouse, Pitfield Kiln Farm
MK11 3LW
United Kingdom
www.canutbooks.com

About the Author

Tang Zhichao, born in 1970, graduated from School of International Studies, Peking University, he received doctorate degree from China Institute of Contemporary International Relations (CICIR). His Phd dissertation was on the Kurdish Issue in the Middle East. He was Deputy Director of Middle East and Africa Studies in CICIR between 2008-2012. He is currently senior research fellow and Director of Middle East Studies in the Institute of West Asian and African Studies attached to the Chinese Academy of Social Science (CASS). He was guest researcher at the Leiden University in Netherlands. Has presided over and participated in a number of national, provincial and ministerial level research reports. His main works are: "The Nationalities of Jordan" (monograph), "The War on Cancer" (translation), "International Terrorism and the Fight against Terrorism" (co-author), "Global Change: the Iraq War" (co-author), "New Generation Arab Politicians" (co-author), "Global Religious Issue - A Macroperspective" (co-author), "Global Ethnic Issues - A Macroperspective" (co-author), "An Insight into the Contemporary Third World" (co-author), "India's Modern Development Path" (co-author), "Contemporary National Political Systems: South Africa" (co-author), "Extremist Forces in Asia" (co-author) and others. He has written numerous research articles, which were published in the Journal of West Asian and African Studies, and other academic journals on Kurdish issue, Iran Nuclear issue, Regional Security, Energy issues, Turkey, Iran, and Israel. His short articles were published in the "People's Daily", "Global Times", and "World Knowledge" and other newspapers.

Contents

Abbreviations

AI	Amnesty International
AKIN	American Kurdish Information Network
AKP	Justice and Development Party (Turkey)
ARGK	Kurdish People's Liberation Army (Turkey)
AYOD	Ankara Association of Higher Education
BDP	Peace and Democracy Party (Turkey)
CIA	Central Intelligence Agency
CHAK	Halabja Anti-Anfal and Anti-Genocide Kurdish Center
DDKD	The Eastern Revolutionary Democratic Cultural Associations (Turkey)
DDKO	The Eastern Revolutionary Eastern Cultural Center
DEHAP	Democratic People's Party (Turkey)
DEP	Democratic Party (Turkey)
DISK	Confedaration of Revolutionary Workers Union
DTP	Democratic Socialist Party (Turkey)
ECHR	European Court of Human Rights
ERNK	Kurdish National Liberation Front
EU	European Union
EUTCC	EU Turkish Civic Council
GAP	Southeastern Anatolia Project (Turkey)
HADEP	People's Democratic Party (Turkey)
HAK-PAR	Rights and Freedom Party (Turkey)
HEP	People's Labor Party (Turkey)
HPG	People's Defense Army (PKK)
HRK	Kurdistan Freedom Brigade (PKK)
ICP	Iraqi Communist Party
IGC	Iraqi Governing Council
IKF	Iraqi Kurdish Front

IMK	Islamic Movement of Kurdistan (Iraq)
INC	Iraqi National Congress
JITEM	Gendarmerie Intelligence and Anti-terrorism Forces (Turkey)
J.K (Komala)	Kurdish Recovery Committee (Iran)
KADEK	Kurdish Freedom Democratic Congress (Turkey)
KCK/KKK	Kurdish Community Union (Turkey) / Kurdish People's Assembly
KDP	Kurdish Democratic Party (Iraq)
KDPI	Kurdish Democratic Party of Iran
KDPT	Kurdish Democratic Party of Turkey
KDSP/PCDK	Kurdish Democratic Solution Party (Iraq)
KGK/Kongra-Gel	Kurdish People's Assembly (Turkey)
KHRP	Kurdish Human Rights Project (English)
KIU	Islamic Union of Kurdistan (Iraq)
KNC	Kurdish National Council (Syria)
KON-Kurd	Federation Kurdish Associations (Europe)
KRG	Kurdistan Regional Government (Iraq)
MEK	People's Mujahidin
MGK	National Security Council (Turkey)
MIT	National Intelligence Agency (Turkey)
NATO	North Atlantic Treaty Organization
NGO	Non-Governmental Organization
ODP	Freedom and Solidarity Party (Turkey)
OHAL	Emergency Management (Turkey)
ONW	Northern Observation Operation (Iraq)
OPC	Comfort Offer Operation (Iraq)
PJAK	Kurdistan Free Life Party (Iran)
PKDW	Kurdish Assembly in Exile
PKK	Workers' Party of Kurdistan (Turkey)
PSK	Kurdistan Socialist Party (Turkey)
PUK	Patriotic Union of Kurdistan (Iraq)
PYD	Democratic Unionist Party (Syria)
SNC	Syrian National Council
TAK	Kurdistan Freedom Eagles (Turkey)
TAL	Transitional Government Law (Iraq)
TCK	Turkish Criminal Law
TESEV	Turkish Economic and Social Study Fund
TMY	Turkish Anti-terrorism Law (2006)
TSK	Turkish Armed Forces

Publisher's Note

Kurdish national issue, is one of the most complex and tragic issues in the Middle East, still unresolved. The Kurds, whose origins lay in classical antiquity, are the only native, stateless nation in the Middle-East, longing for independence and political freedom. They have suffered greatly from colonialism, pan-nationalisms, faced with the betrayals and the self-centeredness of world's big powers, since the World War I. Their status have progressed remarkably in the last decades, but there is still long way to go, and many challenges lie ahead. This is one of the primal messages of the book.

We are honored to publish this valuable work, from renown Chinese scholar Tang Zhichao. He has passionately studied the Kurdish issue for more than 15 years, and created one of the most comprehensive, voluminous and thought provoking books of the Chinese academy, in this field. Since 1990s, globally, books written by the academy, on the Kurdish issue has increased geometrically, but translations from Chinese studies have been rare. Thus, English readers will be able to experience and examine a Chinese perspective, the first ever, that has been translated into English.

The regions where the Kurds live is divided by the borders of four different countries, thus the author has examined the unique natures of the issue in the four countries in detail, paying equal importance to all; besides particularities and universalities are dialectically combined, and the author focuses on the key areas which are most central to explain and grasp,the general regularities of the Kurdish national movement, and tries to answer, both why the issue is not resolved for nearly a century, and its possible future prospects. On the other hand these findings on the general regularities, has been re-examined in each of the four parts. At the same time, the book also contains abundant information, chronology, maps and informative appendixes and facts, for those who desire to know more about Kurds and their protracted national freedom struggles.

Tang Zhichao, underlines the long course, that Kurdish national movement needs to consummate before an ultimate favorable solution can be achieved. This is mainly due to external interventions and uncertainities, surrounding the issue: "although the Kurds have not yet fully controlled their own destiny, their capacity to control their fate is is growing gradually and there exists great possibility for them to do so. However, for achieving their long-cherished national aspirations, Kurds do not only need to develop and expand their own strengths, their achievements will also depend on the progress of modernization, democratization and policy adjustments of the relevant countries in the region, the changes in the international and regional patterns, as well as the Kurds' relations with the outside world. Tang Zhichao also emphasizes that, both international, cross-border characteristics have been the most prominent characteristics of the Kurdish issue, just from the beginning.

Therefore, in this book, the readers will also be able to examine the application of Marxist International Relations theory into the issue, throughout great power struggles and wars of the 20th century, and national interest conflicts. We are thankful to the Chinese editor of the book Ms. Gao Mingxiu and the foreign relations director of Social Sciences Academic Press in Beijing, and Canut International-Istanbul who have very cooperatively helped us in realizing this book project.

L. M. Walker
Liber Publications Intl.
London-Britain
February, 2017

Preface

Having heard associate research fellow Tang Zhichao was absorbed in studying the Kurdish national issue in the Middle East, I'm glad to be informed that his research finding "An Insight into the Kurdish National Issue in the Middle East" is about to be published. As a researcher who is engaged in the study of Middle East affairs for long years, I would like to extend my sincere congratulations to him, because in my opinion, the forthcoming publication of this book will satisfy people's requirements for an in-depth understanding of Middle East issues and realize another commendable progress of China's research in this regard.

The Middle East, a cradle of ancient civilizations in the world and also a hot spot of international politics filled with continuous wars and conflicts, has witnessed the rise of many great powers and meanwhile ruined much of their brilliance. Since the end of the Cold War, the Middle East has remained unstable and a lot of local wars including the Afghanistan War, the Iraq War and the Libya War broke out during the new century. Throughout the ages, complex national and religious relations which demonstrated themselves as collisions and fusions of various civilizations are one cause of the complexity of the issue. The sequel of the past and current fierce hegemonic competition among leading world and regional powers and the strategic interests they are pursuing, as well as political and economic conflicts among different countries result in deep-rooted factors associated with turmoil and complicated international relations in this region. The underlying causes of unrest in this area and the path to peaceful prospects are still a Gordian Knot without a clear answer being offered yet.

There seems no shortcut for cracking such a major issue. Without being confined to a general observation about Middle East issues, we have to carry out profound analysis on the fundamental issues in this region and uncover the interactive relationships among them. Only in this way can we gradually approach a correct understanding of the turmoil and peace in the Middle East.

The Kurdish national issue is exactly a fundamental issue worthy of in-depth analysis which influences the overall picture of international relations in a specific region. Over a century since the disintegration of the Ottoman Empire during the First World War, this issue used to be so serious that it dramatically affected domestic politics of some countries and their international relations with neighbors. Under the rapidly changing situation in the Middle East today, this fundamental issue surfaces again with an increasing impact on the relevant countries. Issues of Syria, Iraq, Iran and Turkey that people are currently showing great concern over are all closely associated with the Kurdish national issue. However, despite the rapid political changes in the Middle East, the Chinese research on the Kurdish national issue and particularly the influence, which this issue exerts on the international relations in the Middle East appear to lag behind.

By virtue of his research finding, Dr. Tang Zhichao has made a profound study of the Kurdish national issue as well as its impact on international relations of the Middle East. Based on the existing research results, he presents the national origin of the Kurds, illustrates the origin and development of the Kurdish national issue and discusses the effect of this issue to relevant countries in the Middle East coupled with the attitude that great powers hold towards it. Furthermore, he proposes clear and bold point of views about the definition of this issue, the underlying root why it hasn't been resolved yet and its prospects in the future. The publication of his study provides a more comprehensive and insightful pondering over this issue, broadens the horizon of other researchers who observe the constant changes which take place in international relations in the Middle East and adds a valuable research result to the disciplinary construction of Middle East research.

I wish the publication of his study would promote the research on the Kurdish national issue and international relations in the Middle East. I also hope that there will appear more profound research findings on the fundamental issues of the Middle East and our academy would develop an in-depth understanding of and undertake further probe into the Middle East issues with great endeavors.

Yang Guang

Director of the Institute of West Asian and African Studies
of the Chinese Academy of Social Sciences
Director of the Chinese Institute of Middle East Studies
June 11, 2013

CHAPTER ONE

The Rise of Kurdish Nationalism and the Formation of Kurdish Issue

Along with the decline and disintegration of the Ottoman Empire[1] during the late 19th and early 20th century, the First World War (1914-1918) gave rise to dramatic changes worldwide and a great surge of nationalist movements in Asia, Africa and Latin America. We can say that the nationalist movement in the Middle East was the most remarkable one among them. Kurdish nationalism appeared almost simultaneously with the Arab nationalism, Turkish nationalism, Persian nationalism and Israeli nationalism (Zionism). Yet, the renounce and indifference of the Western European big powers as well as the spread of nationalism in three major nations, such as Turkey, Arab and Persia have shattered Kurdish nationalists' dream of founding an independent state. Hence the Kurdish issue came into being. Kurdish people are the only nationality divided among five major nations in the Middle East which has not established its own independent national state. Since the First World War, the Kurds in all parts of the Middle East have been struggling for national rights, self-determination and national unity. When we look into the current situation, we can easily see that the Kurdish issue has become more and more intense and henceforth it is evaluated as a hot issue plaguing many countries across the globe and seriously threatening the security and the stability of Middle East.

---

1   The Ottoman Empire (1299-1922), also known as the Turkish Ottoman Empire, was established by the Turks in the 13th century and named after its founder Osman I. Ottoman Turks first settled in the east of Minor Asia (1071), then middle Anatolia where they built the Seljuk Empire and worshiped Islam as their state religion. Afterwards, they migrated towards West, grew increasingly powerful there, they then set up the Ottoman Empire in Bursa, whose powers, in its prime, reached the three continents of Europe, Asia and Africa. After the First World War, this empire was dismembered because of the defeat and perished later with most of its territory gaining independence and imperialist dominance. The Republic of Turkey which was established in on its native land of Asia Minor in 1923 is considered to be its successor.

1.1 The Kurdish People and Kurdistan

1.1.1 The Origin of the Kurds

The origin of the Kurds has remained an unsolved mystery for too long. As opinions vary, no unanimous conclusion about it can be drawn. One vital cause is the lack of solid historical data, and another significant reason lies in the fact that the Kurdish national culture contains a large number of ethnic and cultural elements from neighboring peoples. Specifically, there are several arguments about it, which can be illustrated as follows.

1. Theory of Descendants of the Medes[2]

Currently, the Kurds tend to identify themselves as the descendants of the Medes, one of the most ancient peoples in the Middle East. Some experts verified this view from the perspective of language similarity. Soviet orientalist Vladimir Minorsky (1877-1966) demonstrated that there was a "language-geographical commonality" between the contemporary Kurds and the ancient Medes from the angle of "history, language and literature". However, a lot of scholars were opposed to the above standpoint. For example, Garnik Asatrian argued, the Kurds didn't enjoy any special affinity with the Medes based on genes. David Neil MacKenzie, an authority on the Kurdish language, thought that the Medes spoke a northwestern Iranian language, while the Kurdish people speak Kurmanji which is also a northwestern Iranian language. He argued that the contemporary Kurdish language, which is closer to Farsi, actually has a big difference from the language used by Medes.[3]

2. Theory of Descendants of the Carduchi

Fisher and other experts of Iranian studies have argued that the Carduchi, who used to be active in Mesopotamia in as early as the 4th century BC, were the ancestors of the Kurds,[4] and the word of Kurd most probably stemmed from Carduchi.

3. Theory of Descendants of the Cyrtians

Being a branch of the Persians, the Cyrtians "Carduchi" once widely spread to the Zagros Mountains. Dandamayev claimed that the Cyrtians were forefathers of the Kurdish people.[5] The Cyrtians were warlike tribes

---

2 The Medes established the powerful Medean Empire in the Iranian plateau during the 6th century BC to the 8th century BC.

3 Antonio Panaino, Sara Circassia, the Scholarly Contribution of Ilya Gershevitch to the Development of Iranian Studies: International Seminar, Mimesis, 2006, pp.71-72.

4 Ilya Gershevitch & William Bayne Fisher, The Cambridge History of Iran: the Median and Achamenian Periods, Cambridge University Press, 1985, p.257.

5 "Carduchi", http://www.iranicaonline.org/articles/ Carduchi-latin-form-of-greek-kardokhoi.

which occupied in antiquity the mountainous country along the upper Tigris near the Assyrian and Median borders.

4. The Theory of Mixture

The prestigious Kurdish scholar Izady objected to the analysis made merely from the linguistic point of view, thinking that the Kurds had existed long before the emergence of the Medes and the contemporary Kurdish people are actually a mixture composed by more than one tribe including many indigenous inhabitants. Their relationship is just like the one between the ancient Romans and the present Italians who are known not to be the pure descendants of the former.[6]

He also mentioned that the Kurdish ethnic culture includes the cultural genes of at least five periods: Halaf culture which came into being 8,000 years ago, Ubaid culture, Hurrian culture, Aryan culture and Semitic and Turkic culture.[7] This argument is supported by many scholars.

Encyclopedia of Islam writes that the Kurdish people are a complex race, composed of various ethnic groups.[8] *Encyclopedia Britannica* points out that the Kurds are descended from people who settled down in Kurdistan long time ago and their ancestors are the Guti, the Hattians, the Kassites, the Mitanni, the Mannai, the Mushku, the Zila, the Khaldi, the Medes and the Adiabene.[9]

3

Although Famous Dutch scholar Martin van Bruinessen held that the Kurdish people have heterogeneous origins, he emphasized as well that although many peoples lived in Kurdistan during the past thousands of years they had almost entirely disappeared as a nation or a language group and the tribes in the Kurdistan region were not homologous. *Dictionary of International Affairs* published by China Commercial Press in 1982 also notes that the Kurds are "a nation which developed after the ancient Medean tribe (namely, the Medes) and that the Iranian tribes had infiltrated the region of Kurdistan."

The author is inclined to suggest the latter viewpoint of mixture.[10]

6   Prof. M. R. Izady, "Are Kurds Descended from the Medes?", June 19, 2008, http://www.kurdistanica.com/?q=node/78.
7   Mehrdad R. Izady, "Exploring Kurdish Origins", Apr. 30, 2009, http://www.kurdistanica.com/?q=node/74.
8   "Kurds, kurdistan", http://www.brillonline.nl/subscriber/entry?entry=islam_COM-0544>.
9   "The Kurds", http://www.kurdistanica.com/english/history/origine.html.
10   Dictionary of International Affairs, Commercial Press, 1982, p.276.

1.1.2 The Kurdish Population

There has never been an accurate statistics about the Kurdish population, for it not only involves the lack of census, but also certain political reasons. Official data released by relevant governments have deliberately downsized the Kurdish population or simply did not recognize the existence of the Kurds as an ethnic group, whereas the data given by Kurdish sources are likely to be exaggerated. As a result, it is difficult to judge which statistics conform to the reality.

Recognized by various statistics, the recent 100 years has witnessed a dramatic growth in the Kurdish population. The beige book published by the French government in 1892 said that there were 3,012,897 Kurdish people in the world. The data released by the Committee of Mosul Issue affiliated to the League of Nations in 1925 revealed that there were approximately 3.2 million residents in Kurdistan, 1.5 million living in Turkey, 700,000 in Iran, 500,000 in Iraq and 300,000 in Syria and other countries.[11]

In 1948, some Kurdish intellectuals submitted a memorandum to the UN which said the Kurdistan population had reached 8 million in total and demanded the UN to endow the Kurds with an independent state.

C.J. Edmonds, the former adviser of Iraqi Interior Ministry and writer of the book *Kurds, Turks and Arabs* estimated that there were all together 4 to 4.5 million Kurdish people in the year of 1950 including the 2 million resident in Turkey, 1.1 million in Iran and 900,000 in Iraq. *The Great Soviet Encyclopedia* published in 1952 said the Kurdish population had reached to about 7.2 million, including 2 to 3 million living in Turkey, 2 to 2.5 million in Iran, 1.2 million in Iraq, 300,000 in Syria, 200,000 in Afghanistan and Pakistan and 45,866 in the Soviet Union. During the 1960s, there were more than 10 million Kurds in the world. Czech experts on the Kurdish issue claimed in 1965 that the global Kurdish population was about 10.45 million with 4.6 million living in Turkey, 3 million in Iran, 1.4 million in Iraq, 400,000 in Syria and 1 million living outside the region of Kurdistan (for example, 300,000 in other districts of Iran, 200,000 in Afghanistan and 59,000 in the Soviet Union as well as some others living in such big cities as Baghdad, Damascus, Istanbul and Ankara).[12]

The Kurdistan File published by the Kurdish Institute at Brussels in 1988 declared that there were 25 million Kurds around the world, among whom 20 million resided in Kurdistan region (10 million in Turkey, 6 million in

---

11 It refers to an international commission of inquiry set up by the League of Nations after World War I to solve the attribution problem of Mosul province. Detailed information can be found in chapters about the Iraqi Kurdish issue.

12 Abdul Rahman Ghassemlow, Kurdistan and the Kurds, Publishing House of Czechoslovak Academy of Sciences, Prague, 1965.

Iran, 3 million in Iraq and 800,000 in Syria) and 5 million in other regions (500,000 in Europe, 350,000 in the Soviet Union, 150,000 in Israel, 100,000 in Lebanon and approximately 4 million in Istanbul, Baghdad, Tehran, Damascus, Ankara, Aleppo and other big cities).[13]

David McDowall, an expert of the Kurdish studies, announced in 1987 that the Kurds across the globe were around 19.7 million with 9.6 million living in Turkey (accounting for 19% of the total Turkish population), 5 million in Iran (10% of the Iranian population), 3.9 million in Iraq (23% of the Iraqi population) and 900,000 in Syria (8% of the Syrian population) as well as 30,000 in the Soviet Union. In the year of 1991, he increased the figure to 22.5 million with 48% living in Turkey, 24% in Iran, 18% in Iraq and in 4% Syria.[14]

At present, the statistics about the Kurdish population differ sharply around the world. Salah Aziz, an expert of the Kurdish studies from Florida State University, argued that the global Kurdish population reached about 25 million to 30 million.[15]

In 2009, CIA predicted there were around 13.82 million Kurds dwelling in Turkey, 9.48 million in Iran and 3.86 to 5.79 million in Iraq, which added up to 26 to 28 million. The US Congressional Research Dept. issued a report in October 2010 and held that the total Kurdish population arrived at 20 to 25 million.[16] The Kurdish Language Association pointed out the number was actually 40 million[17], which is too high to be regarded as true. The author believes there are approximately 30 million Kurdish people all over the world.

The vast majority of world's Kurdish population live in Kurdistan, of whom about 55% live in Turkey, of whom about 20% live in Iraq and in Iran respectively and about 5% live in Syria (see Fig. 1-1). In consideration of population concentration status, the Kurds are the second biggest nation in Turkey, Iraq and Syria and the third rank in Iran where Persians and the Azerbaijani ethnic group hold the first and the second rank respectively. Besides, in some regions outside of Kurdistan there are a large number of Kurdish people. According to the estimation made by the Kurdish Institute of Paris, currently one-third of the Kurdish people are living outside Kurdistan, which seems a bit exaggerated.

5

---

13 The Kurdistan File, the Kurdish Institute at Brussels, 1989.
14 David McDowall, A Modern History of the Kurds, I. B. Tauris, 1991.
15 "Kurdish Studies Program at Florida State University", http://www.xs4all.nl/-tank/kurdish/htdocs/announce/KSF.html.
16 Kenneth Katzman, "The Kurds in Post Saddam Iraq", October 1, 2010, RS22079, https://opencrs.com/document/RS22079/2010-10-01/.
17 "Kurdish Unified Alphabet", http://www.kurdishacademy.org/?q=node/2.

In the Middle East, a great many Kurds stay in such big cities as Istanbul Izmir, Adana and Mersin of Turkey, Baghdad of Iraq, Tehran and Tabriz of Iran and Aleppo and Damascus of Syria. There are three million Kurds only in Istanbul, which becomes a city with the largest Kurdish population. About one million Kurds reside in Khorasan of northern Iran. Baghdad, Damascus and other metropolises which contain abundant number of Kurdish communities. In many other countries of Middle East dwell a lot of Kurds, including Lebanon, Jordan, Yemen, Kuwait and Israel. For example, 80,000 Kurds live in Lebanon[18], who account for 1% of its total population and mainly stay in Beirut. Allegedly, Lebanese-Druze community[19] leader's the Jumblatts tribe of Kurdish descent, whose ancestors were Ayyubids of the Saladin period and moved from Syria to southern Lebanon during the 15th and 16th century. In the contemporary political history of Lebanon, Kamal Jumblatt (1917-1977) and Walid Jumblatt (1949-) from the Jumblatt tribe are well-known Lebanese politicians and the Progressive Socialist Party led by them is the main political force in Lebanon. There are approximately 233,500 Kurds in Kuwait, most of them coming from Iraq.[20] And about 100,000 Kurdish people live in Israel.[21]

6

---

18   "The Kurdish Diaspora", Institut Kurde de Paris, 2006, http://www.institutkurde.org/en/kurdorama/.
19   As a minority sect distributed in Syria and Lebanon, the Druze belong to the Ismaili branch of Shia Islam, whose religious beliefs, social habits, customs and traditions differ from conventional Muslims sharply: no zakat paying, not fasting, no circumcision, no pilgrimage, being monogamous and rarely marrying people from other ethnic groups, thus being regarded as heretics by some other Muslims. The Druze are brave and rebellious enough to once resist the invasion launched by the Ottoman Empire for a long term and joined anti-imperialist uprisings more than once after their land was aggressed by British and French people in World War I.
20   http://www.worldstatesmen.org/Kuwait.htm.
21   Lokman I. Meho, "The Kurds and Kurdistan: A General Background", Kurdish Culture and Society: An Annotated Bibliography, Greenwood Press, 2001, p.4.

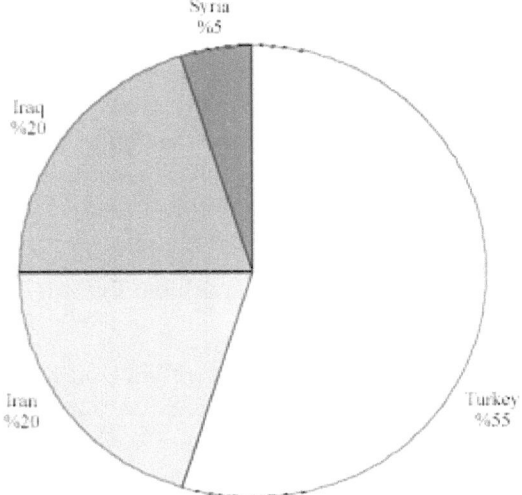

Figure.1-1 Global Distribution of the Kurds

Source: A. Arnaiz-Villena, J. Martiez-Lasoa and J. Alonso-Garcia, "The Correlation between Languages and Genes: The Usko-Mediterranean Peoples", Human Immunology, No. 9, 2001, p.1057.

Today, hundreds of thousands of Kurds are dwelling in the Caucasus and Central Asia. Among them, 150,000 live in Azerbaijan,[22] 34,000 to 60,000 in Georgia (mainly stay at Tbilisi and believe in Yazidi belief),[23] approximately 42,139 in Armenia,[24] 40,000 in Turkmenistan[25] and 200,000 in Afghanistan[26]. And some parts of Caucasus also belong to the geographic scope of "Kurdistan".

Europe is the place where Kurdish immigrants gather most. At present, about one million Kurds settle in Western Europe.[27] Among them, there are 600,000 to 650,000 Kurds in Germany.[28] 85% of European Kurdish immigrants came from Turkey and most of the rest originated from Iraq. A report

---

22   "The Kurdish Diaspora", Institut Kurde de Paris, 2006, http://www.institutkurde.org/en/kurdorama.

23   "Kurds in Georgia", Eurominority: Portal of European Stateless Nations and Minoritie, Quimper, France: Organization for the European Minorities, 2006, http://www.eurominority.org.

24   "The Kurdish Diaspora", Institut Kurde de Paris, 2006, http://www.institutkurde.org/en/kurdorama; based on another saying, there are 750,000, http://www.khrp.org/country/armenia.htm.

25   Ibid.

26   Ibid.

27   "Demographics of the Kurdish People", http://en.wikipedia.org/wiki/Demographics_of_Kurdish_people.

28   "The Kurdish Diaspora", Institut Kurde de Paris, 2006, http://www.institutkurde.org/en/kurdorama/.

released by the European Commission said that there were 1.3 million Kurds in Western Europe. The Confederation of Kurdish Associations (KON-KURD) announced that there were as many as 1.5 million Kurdish people.[29] The figure estimated by the Kurdish Institute of Paris is even bigger: 800,000 to 1,000,000 Kurds live in Germany; 200,000 in the Netherlands, 120,000 to 180,000 in France, 100,000 to 150,000 respectively in Britain, Switzerland and Sweden, 80,000 to 100,000 in Belgium, 50,000 to 80,000 separately in Greece and Finland, 60,000 in Denmark, 50,000 to 60,000 in Austria, 40,000 to 60,000 in Norway, 50,000 in Italy.[30]

Besides, a number of Kurds live in Russia and Eastern Europe and there are nearly 100,000 living in Russia.[31]

Approximately 30,000 Kurdish people dwell in North America, of whom 15,000 to 20,000 settle down in the U.S and 6,000 to 7,000 in Canada.[32] The largest Kurdish communities in the US are Nashville of Tennessee and San Diego of California. Another assertion claims that there are all together 100,000 Kurds in the US and 50,000 in Canada.[33]

In the Asian-Pacific region, there are about 15,000 Kurds residing in Australia, and many Kurdish people have immigrated to Australia via Indonesia during recent years. A few Kurds live in Japan, where Kawaguchi City of Saitama enjoys the largest number of Kurds. But over the years, the Japanese government hasn't granted them refugee status.[34]

Beluchistan region of Pakistan witnesses a lot of Kurds. Born into a rich Kurdish tribe from Isfahan of Iran, the mother of Benazir Bhutto, former Pakistani Prime Minister, is of Kurdish descent.

There are a small number of Kurds in Somalia and Eritrea of Africa. Most Kurds living in Somali are the Kurds who used to stay in Iraq and were sent to exile during the Saddam Hussein regime.

---

29   "EU Urges Turkey to Find Political Solution to Kurdish Issue", Mar.31, 2012, http://www.ekurd.net/mismas/articles/misc2012/3/turkey3865.htm.
30   "The Kurdish Diaspora", Kurdish Institute of Paris, http://www.institutkurde.org/en/kurdorama.
31   Lord Russell Johnston, "The Cultural Situation of the Kurds", Council of Europe, July 2006, http://assembly.coe.int/Main.asp?link=/Documents/WorkingDocs/Doc06/EDOC11006.htm.
32   "The Kurdish Diaspora", Institut Kurde de Paris, 2006, http://www.institutkurde.org/en/kurdorama/.
33   http://en.wikipedia.org/wiki/Kurdish_people#Diaspora.
34   "Japan: Kurd Refugees Hopefuls' Ally Speaks out", Japan Times, Jan. 15, 2009.

1.1.3 Kurdistan — Homeland of the Kurds

The Kurds have settled in a place named "Kurdistan" (Kurdistān in Arabic and Kordestān in Persian; the suffix of "stan" means "place-land" in Persian). As a Persian concept of cultural geography, Kurdistan means "the land of the Kurds" in the literal sense. *Encyclopedia Britannica* describes Kurdistan as "a region mainly inhabited by the Kurdish people in the past".[35]

It is difficult to delineate the boundaries of Kurdistan in an accurate way, but it is roughly located at 37-38 °N and 33-40 °E with about 1,000 km from north to south, almost 750 km from east to west in its northern tip and approximately 200 km from east to west in its southern end. It reaches Bākhtarān (the previous Kermanshah) of Iran in the east, Kirkuk of Iraq in the south, Yerevan of Armenia in the north and Aleppo of Syria and the upstream of the Euphrates of Turkey in the west. Geographically, it appears a narrow arc zone covering eastern Turkey, western Iran, northern Iraq and northeastern Syria as well as a small region of Armenia. Therefore, Kurdistan "remains a multinational humanly and geographical district only with an estimated scope but without clear boundaries"[36].

As for the region of Kurdistan, there is much controversy. Five specific versions are illustrated as follows: first, Kurdistan extends in an area of 392,000 square kilometers with 190,000 in Turkey, 125,000 in Iran, 65,000 in Iraq and 12,000 in Syria (refer to Figure 1-2);[37] second, 409,650 square kilometers with 194,400 in Turkey, 124,950 in Iran, 72,000 in Iraq and 18,300 in Syria;[38] third, 518,000 square kilometers;[39] fourth, 500,000 square kilometers;[40] fifth, *Encyclopedia Britannica* states that Kurdistan only covers an area of 191,660 square kilometers.[41]

Close to the second one, the first figure is currently believed to be the most representative. It is worth mentioning that the title of Kurdistan has not been recognized in the official maps of the countries in the Middle East yet. Iran officially admits Kurdistan which however only refers to its Kurdistan Province. The Kurds usually regard the Kurdish part of Turkey as Northern Kurdistan, that of Iran as Eastern Kurdistan, that of Iraq as Southern Kurdistan and that of Syria as Western Kurdistan. Various parts of Kurdistan enjoy different

---

35 "Kurdistan", http://www.britannica.com/EBchecked/topic/325241/Kurdistan.
36 Encyclopedia of China (Vol. 13), Encyclopedia of China Publishing House, the Second Edition, 2009, p.148.
37 http://www.encislam.brill.nl/data/EncIslam/C4/COM-0544.html.
38 Abdul Rahman Ghacsemlon, Kurdistan and the Kurds, Publishing House of Czechoslovok Academy of Sciences, Prague, 1965.
39 Anthony C. Lobaido etc., Asian Kurds, translated by Zheng Xinyang, China Water Conservancy and Hydropower Press, 2004, p.4.
40 The Kurdistan File.
41 "Kurdistan", http://www.britannica.com/EBchecked/topic/325241/Kurdistan.

political statuses and administrative divisions in relevant countries. Turkey does not recognize the existence of an independent Kurdistan and generally claims it as Southeastern Anatolia or "Eastern Region". Although Iran acknowledges Kurdistan and has set up the Kurdistan Province, its area only covers a very small part of the Kurdish region in this country. Iraq also admits the Kurdish district and has established the Kurdish Autonomous Region, but the central government disagrees sharply with the Kurds in the range of Kurdistan.[42] Syria does not recognize the Kurdish region either.

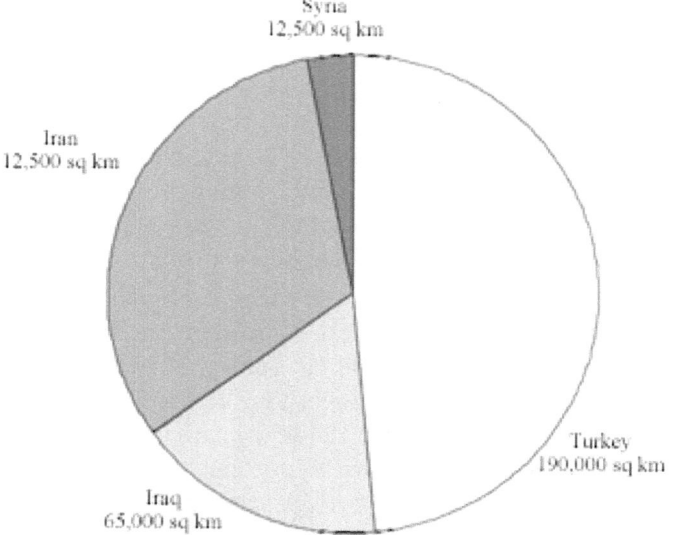

Figure. 1-2 Distribution of Kurdistan

Source: http://www.encislam.brill.nl/data/EncIslam/C4/COM-0544.html.

---

42   Encyclopedia of China (Vol. 13), p.148.

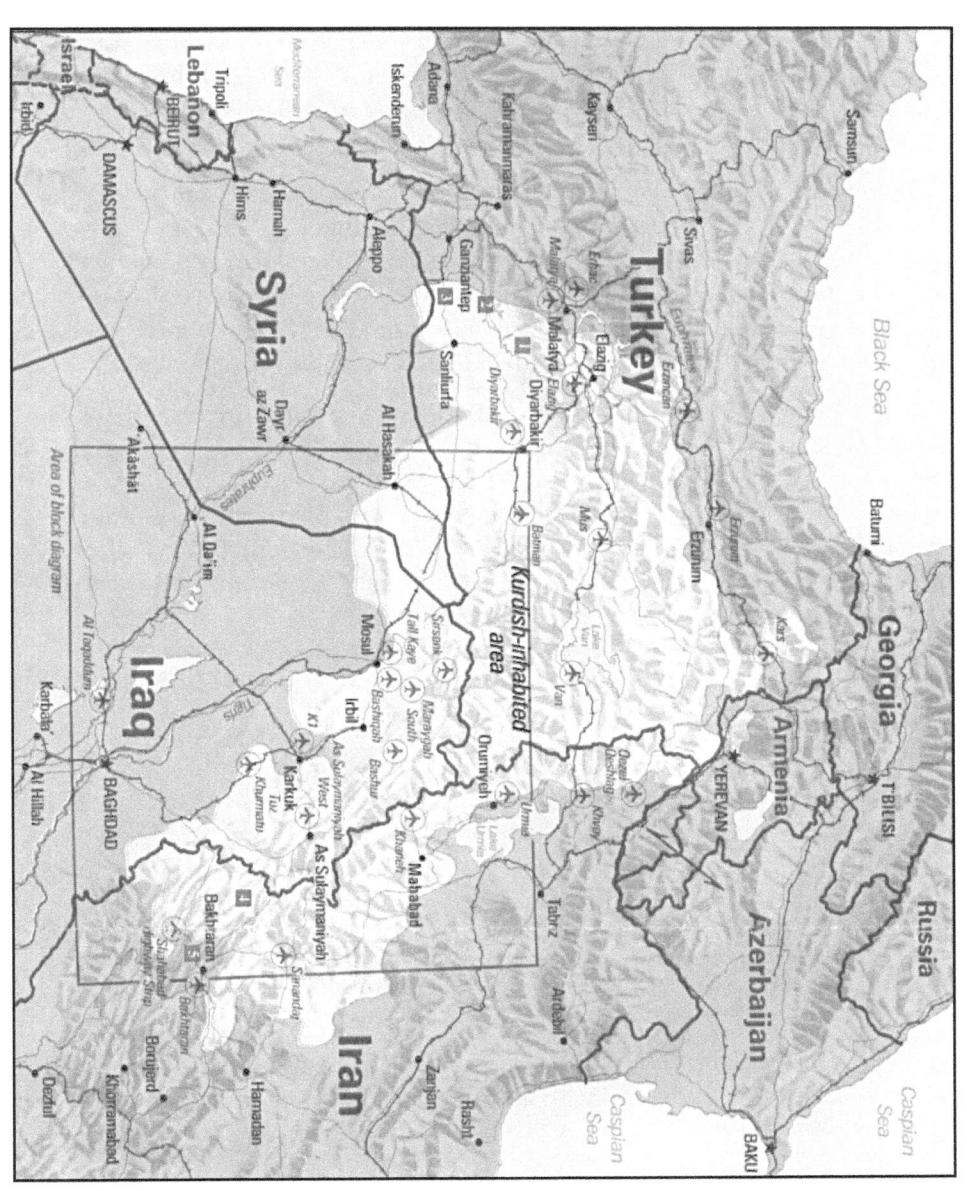

Fig. 1-3 Map of Kurdistan

*Source: Perry Castaneda Library
Map Collection at The University
of Texas at Austin: http://www.
lib.utexas.edu/maps/middle_east
and_asia/kurdish_lands_92.jpg.*

Most residents living in Kurdistan, where there are also a certain number of Arabs, Jews, Armenians, Turkmen and Assyrians[43], are Kurdish people, who stay in major cities including Diyarbakir, Bitlis and Van of Turkey, Arbil, Mosul and Kirkuk[44] of Iraq, Kermanshah of Iran and Qamishli of Syria.

Dominated by mountains and plateaus geographically, Kurdistan has less plains and a freezing climate. With an average altitude of 1,000 to 1,500 meters, Southern Kurdistan holds a sub-tropical climate. In its hot and dry summer, the annual precipitation is about 200 to 400 mm. Yet, its low altitude regions such as valleys receive abundant rainfall with an annual precipitation of about 700 to 2,000 mm and even 3,000 mm occasionally.

It has plenty of valleys, forests and rivers. Almost gathering all the plains of Kurdistan, Southern Kurdistan is regarded as one of the granaries in Iraq. Going from the middle to the north, the climate turns to an arid continental climate. During the severely cold winter, the average temperature is 4 C° and the annual rainfall is 300 to 500 mm. Some higher parts of the mountains are covered by snow for about seven months a year. The dramatic temperature swing can reach as high as 80 C°. The temperature in the winter of some regions of Northern Kurdistan like Karaca Dağ is as low as -40 C°, whereas the temperature in the summer of Southern Kurdistan reaches up to 40-45 C°.

Characterized by a network of endless mountains, Kurdistan enjoys north-to-south Zagros Mountains in its east and east-to-west Taurus Mountains in its north. Zagros Mountains are the largest mountain range inside Iraq and Iran. Located in the southwest of the Iranian plateau, its north-south main

---

43 Assyrians who are now settling in the region of Mosul, in Iraq are about 50,000 in number and believe in Christianity. They claim that their ancestors are the ancient Assyrians. However, some experts say they actually originated from Hakkari Province of the Kurdish region in Turkey. During the regime of the Ottoman Empire, Europeans saw them as their potential ally within the Ottoman territory. Around 1870, there were about 97,000 Kurds in Hakkari. For supporting the Allies, Assyrians were slaughtered throughout World War I. British people transferred the rest—approximately 20,000 Assyrians to the Kurdish region of Iraq. Assyrians have accused the Kurds of being the accomplices who helped the Ottoman government massacring their compatriots. During the British mandate in Iraq, British people treated the Assyrians as an important ally and set up an army mainly composed of Assyrians to suppress the Kurdish rebellions. Therefore, later the Kurdish people and Arabic officers from the Iraqi army killed a large number of Assyrian officers jointly, which led to the collapse of the Assyrian Legion. After the Gulf War, many Assyrians emigrated to Europe and America. Today, about 50,000 Assyrians reside in Iraq. Assyrians have established Assyrian Democratic Movement (ADM) and participated in political activities in the Iraqi region of Kurdistan.
44 A large number of Kurds live in Kirkuk Province and the city of Kirkuk, but whether it is a Kurdish city remains uncertain and the Kurds, Arabs, Turkmen and the Turkish government have a big controversy on this issue, which also becomes one of the major contradictions between the local Turkmen (Turkey supported) local leaders/governments of Iraq and the Iraqi central government coupled with the Turkish government.

body winds from Northwestern Turkey and Iran-Iraq borders to the Persian Gulf and the Strait of Hormuz, stretching about 1,500 kilometers long, over 300 km wide and an average of 3,000 meters high. Being high in the west and low in the east, its peak Mount Ararat lies in Turkey with an elevation of 5,156 meters. Zard Kuh (4,548 meters above sea level) is the peak of Zagros Mountains inside Iran, and Ibrahim (3,549 meters above sea level) is the highest mountain within the borders of Iraq. This mountain chain gradually lowers from the northwest to the southeast. Valleys and foothills in its parallel western mountains have a high altitude and a mild climate, thus being one of Iran's major populated regions.

As the major mountain ranges in south-central Turkey, Taurus Mountains are situated at the edge of the Anatolian Plateau, extending from Lake Eğirdir in the north of Antalya to the upper reaches of the Euphrates and the Tigris in the west, and have an average altitude of more than 2000 meters with a 3,756-meter peak. In addition, famous mountains include Alborz Mountains and Pontiac Mountains. The highest mountain in the Kurdish district inside Iraq is Damavand Mountain, which is as high as 5,771 meters. Extending from Diyala to Kirkuk of Iraq, the Hamlin Mount is treated as a natural dividing line between the Iraqi Kurdistan and the Arab region. The Great Rift Valley of Anatolia in Northern Kurdistan is an active seismic fault line, where earthquakes often take place. For instance, the big earthquake in 1939 took away the lives of more than 30,000 people. Over thousands of years, the Kurdish people have inhabited big mountains, therefore being referred to as "people of mountains". There is a proverb popular with the Kurds—"Except mountains, the Kurdish have no friends"—which vividly illustrates the special meaning mountains have for the Kurds. Judi Mount and Ararat Mount are two highest mountains in Turkey (5,156 meters above sea level) play vital roles in the Kurdish folk legends. Judi Mount is the most important mountain in the legend, while Ararat Mount is the place where the Noah's Ark docked after the Great Flood according to the Old Testament of Genesis.

1.1.4 Resources in the Kurdish Region

The Kurdish region is famous for its water and hydrocarbon resources, which are the natural wealth of the Kurds. Kurdistan is a region which boasts the most abundant water resources and functions as the most crucial water source in West Asia. With sufficient rainfall around the place, some mountains are covered by snow throughout the year. Furthermore, there are numerous lakes and rivers, including the two noticeable rivers in the Middle East, the Euphrates and the Tigris, as well as many other rivers which originate from Kurdistan. The Euphrates and the Tigris jointly gave birth to one of the oldest civilizations in the world—the Mesopotamian civilization (also known as the Two Rivers Civilization; Mesopotamia is what the ancient Greeks call the two rivers) and meanwhile have nurtured local residents like Arabs and Kurds. The Euphrates and the Tigris both stem from Kurdistan inside Turkey. Being less than 80 kilometers apart, rivers of Euphrates and Tigris flow southward through Syria and Iraq, converge inside Iraq and eventually reach the sea at the Persian Gulf. The Euphrates River is about 2,800 km long and the Tigris River is approximately 1,900 km in length. The two rivers are usually divided into three segments: the upper reaches gradually go downward from the source at the altitude of 1,830-3,050 meters and flow amid the eastern mountains and valleys of the Anatolian Plateau, the middle reaches pass between the northern highland of Syria and the highland of Iraq with an elevation of 366 meters to 52 meters on the top of the delta; the lower reaches are alluvial plains caused by both of the two rivers. They converge and form the Shatt al-Arab at Al-Qurnah and finally flow into the Persian Gulf. In addition, other rivers originating from Kurdistan are: the Ceyhan River (509 km long; in south-central part of Turkey,), the Kura River (1,515 km) and Aras River (also named the Aras River which flows through Turkey, Armenia, Iran and Azerbaijan into the Caspian Sea and has a total length of 1,072 km, being one of the longest rivers in the Caucasus) in Turkey; the Karun River, the White River and the Halil River (390 km long) in Iran; the Great Zab River (400 km long; coming from Van Golu (Van Lake) in the Taurus Mountains of Turkey and converging with the Tigris at Mosul of Iraq), the Little Zab River (400 km long; stemming from the Zagros Mountains of Iraqi part of Kurdistan and converging with the Tigris in Iraq) and Shatt al-Arab (190 km long; being situated at southeastern Mesopotamia Plain and caused by the convergence of the Tigris, the Euphrates and the Karun; the lower reaches lie in the boundary rivers of Iran and Iraq, which hold controversy on the belonging of this river) within the borders of Iraq; the Khabur River in Syria (405 km; Syria's longest river; a tributary of the Euphrates; flowing through the territory of Syria; the alluvial Khabur Delta formed by this river is a vital irrigated agricultural field in Syria). With numerous lakes, Kurdistan is the place which hosts the most intensive water areas in West Asia. Its major lakes are: the Van Lake in Turkey (Turkey's largest lake and also the world's fourth largest freshwater lake with an area of 3,755 sq km), Lake Urmia in Iran (being called Lake Rezaiyeh and Lake Chichast in the past and the largest saltwater lake in the Middle East as well as the world's third largest saltwater lake with a surface area up to 5,000 sq km) and Lake Dukan (the largest lake in the Kurdistan part of Iraq with a surface area of about 270 sq km), Duhok Lake and Zariwar in Iraq.

Oil is the greatest wealth that the Kurds possess. The Persian Gulf-Zagros Basin is a place with the richest oil and gas resources in the world. According to relevant statistics, the oil and gas reserves of the Zagros Basin and the Persian Gulf Basin respectively account for 42.6% and 24.7% of the world's total.

In terms of the equivalent weight, the oil and gas reserves that have been proven in the two basins account for 34.6% of the world's total.[45] Oil and gas resources of the Kurdish region are mainly distributed in the Kurdish areas inside Iraq and Iran as well as Syria. The Kurdish region within the borders of Iraq enjoys the richest oil resources, which were discovered by the British people in the early 20th century and became a significant reason why the Kurds could not have established their own independent country. The Iraqi government announced that 30 billion barrels of oil had been discovered in its Kurdish region. However, the Kurdish regional government in Iraq said there were about 45 billion barrels of oil and 100 trillion to 200 trillion cubic feet of natural gas there (1 cubic foot is equal to 0.028 cubic meter).[46] Oil of the Iraqi Kurdish region is mainly stored in the central foothills of the Western Zagros Mountains. Meanwhile, its natural gas reserves are also abundant. The Iraqi Kirkuk Oil Field is situated at the Zagros Basin. Being one of the largest oil fields in the world, it was discovered in 1927 with a reserve of 232.88 million tons.[47] The abundant oil and gas resources have endowed the Kurds with great wealth and also changed their fate. As the major oil-producing area, the Kurdish region inside Syria boasts oil resources too, but they are relatively small in number. Among its various oil fields, The Suwaidiyeh was known to the world in 1959 with 20.55 million tons of oil reserves.[48]

Mountainous areas in the Kurdish region enjoy rich forest resources. With 16 million hectares of forests covering 160,000 sq km land, it mainly possesses firs, cypresses, cedars, oaks and sycamores as well as plane trees, willows, euphrates poplars, white poplars and chestnuts. Yet, due to the long-term deforestation, forests are declining in number each year. Remote mountains of Northern Iraq are covered by dense forests characterized by plenty of white poplars and oaks. In low lands and valleys there grow a lot of walnut, fig and almond trees. Besides, iron ore, chrome ore and other mineral resources are also very rich.

---

45 Bai Guoping ed.. Geological Features of Oil and Gas in the Hydrocarbon Fields of the Middle East, China Petrochemical Press, 2007, p. 133.
46 Oil Temptation in the Kurdish Region, China-Iraq Economic and Trade Network, September 2, 2011, http: //www.china.iraq.org/news_detail.asp key = A00770027 & id = 4449.
47 Bai Guoping ed., Geological Features of Oil and Gas in the Hydrocarbon Fields of the Middle East, p. 134.
48 Ibid.

1.1.5 Cultural Features and Lifestyles of Kurds

As a mixed culture influenced by the Kurdish historical tradition and other ethnic cultures also existing in this region, the Kurdish culture possesses both its uniqueness and diversity. The biggest external factor impacting the Kurdish cultural identity has been the Persian culture. These two cultures share similarities in language, religion, customs, festivals, etc.

The Kurdish region is one of the birthplaces of the oldest civilizations in the Middle East, such as the Two Rivers Civilization. In 1994, people found Göbekli Tepe in Eastern Turkey, which dated back to at least 12,000 years ago. Göbekli Tepe is the oldest human remains in the world, being much older than Stonehenge (3,000 BC) of England and the pyramids (2,500 BC) of Egypt. Some scholars claim that it is probably the Garden of Eden mentioned in the Bible. This region is also the cradle of agriculture, for it is the place where the human's first transition from gathering to farming took place. The most primitive grains such as ryes and oats were also planted here. The world's first pigs, sheep and cattle were domesticated in Eastern Turkey.[49]

1.1.5.1 Language

A significant sign of distinguishing the Kurds, Arabs, Persians and Turks is their language. Despite being Muslims like their neighbors, the Kurds differ from them largely because they speak Kurdish. The language of Kurdish is an indispensable factor that leaders of the Kurdish movements in the 20th century as well as ordinary Kurds have used to define their Kurdish characteristics and that makes the Kurds most cohesive. The Kurdish language belongs to the Indo-Iranian family of Indo-European languages. The Indo-Iranian language family is mainly divided into Indo-Aryan branch and Iranian branch which is composed of Persian, Kurdish, Balochi, Pashto, etc.

The number of people who speak Kurdish is only second to Persian. The word order of Kurdish is basically the same as that of Persian, which takes on the structure of Subject-Predicate-Object. The Kurds enjoy a long history, but the Kurdish language is rarely mentioned in literature. It officially came into being during the 15th to the 17th century. Maurizio Garzoni, an Italian missionary who used to live in the Kurdish region for 18 years, published the first linguistic book about the Kurdish language in the year of 1787 which was the first professional Kurdish book in the history of the Kurds, therefore being respectfully addressed as "Father of the Kurdish Linguistics"[50]. At present, no unified standard has been set for the Kurdish

---

49　Many Mysterious Huge Stones Have Been Discovered in Turkey and Suspected of Being the Ruins of the Garden of Eden, http: //news.xinhuanet.com/tech/2009-03/06/content_10954134.htm.

50　Mirella Galetti, "Kurdistan and Its Christians", World Congress of Kurdish Studies, Sept. 6-9, 2006.

language yet, which has many dialects and non-uniform spoken and written language. There are now two major dialects respectively in the north and south—Kurmanji and Sorani. The Kurdish people living in Iraq and Syria as well as Northern Kurdistan of Iraq and Iran mostly speak Kurmanji. Their compatriots who dwell in Southern Kurdistan of Iraq and somewhere of Kurdistan in Iran mainly speak Sorani. From the perspective of linguistics or grammar, the difference between the two is just similar to that between English and German. Kurmanji has both "genders" and suffix changes, whereas Sorani has neither of them.[51] It is hard for people speaking the two languages to communicate in the reality.[52] Without uniform letters, the Kurdish language mainly has three writing systems: Arabic alphabet used by Sorani, Latin alphabet used by Kurmanji and Cyrillic alphabet employed by the Kurds who live in the former Soviet Union. Some Kurds who stay at Iran still utilize the Persian alphabet. The Kurdish broadcasts made by the Voice of America (VOA) and the Kurdish TV stations in Iraq both adopt Kurmanji. Historically, many Kurdish writers wrote in Persian, Turkish and Arabic. In view of this fact, some Kurds are trying their best to promote the unification of the Kurdish language. The Kurdish Association of Language (KAL) believes that the diverse Kurdish writing forms are extremely unfavorable to the development of the Kurdish nation and thus a uniform way of writing is urgently demanded. It has revised a new alphabet called Yekgirtú on the basis of Kurmanji letters and popularized it as a unified Kurdish alphabet. It is worth mentioning that the use of the Kurdish language is a major mark in determining the Kurdish people. However, some controversy exists about the definition of the Kurdish language. Seref Han, a historian in the 16th century, defined the Kurds as people who speak Kurmanji, Sorani, Lur and Kelhur, claiming they are all dialects of the Kurdish language. Nevertheless, Turkish thinker Ziya Gökalp thought that they are different languages rather than diverse dialects of a certain language. As for the issue of the Zaza language and the Zaza people, most experts treat the Zaza people as the Kurds and the Zaza language as a dialect of Kurdish. This view has been opposed by many other people, but the vast majority of Zaza people see themselves as part of the Kurdish people.[53]

The Kurdish language is treated differently in different countries. In Iraq, as one of the official languages in the Kurdish region, it has been allowed to use. In Turkey, it used to be banned for a long term and many people were punished for using the Kurdish language; after 1991, the government began to gradually permit the use of the Kurdish language; when the Justice

51   Philip G. Kreyenbroek, The Kurds: A Contemporary Overview, Routledge, 1992, p. 68.
52   J. N. Postgate, Languages of Iraq, Ancient and Modern, British School of Archaeology in Iraq, 2007, p. 139.
53   Servet Mutlu, "Ethnic Kurds in Turkey: A Demographic Study", International Journal of Middle East Studies, 28 (1996), p. 519.

and Development Party came to power in 2003, education and broadcasting have been allowed in Kurdish and some schools have begun teaching Kurdish courses including post-graduate study in some universities. In Iran, the Constitution recognizes the Kurdish minority status and permits the use of Kurdish, so the public use of Kurdish is not taboo.[54]

Yet, public schools cannot impart the Kurdish language,[55] and therefore many Kurdish people in Iran go to Iraq for learning Kurdish.[56] In Syria, the Kurdish language is officially banned and prints are prohibited from publication, but there is no limitation for the personal use of Kurdish.[57] The use and study of the Kurdish language were encouraged in Armenian Republic of the former Soviet Union and the current Republic of Armenia.

1.1.5.2 Religion

The ancient Kurds believed in Zoroastrianism. Though there are few Zoroastrians now, Zoroastrianism still plays a vital role in the conventional Kurdish culture. After being conquered by the Arabs in the 7th century, the Kurds began to convert to Islam. Currently, more than 95% of the Kurdish people believe in Islam. About 75% of them worship the orthodoxy of Islam—the Sunni belief and most believe in Shafii school. Approximately 15% of them who mainly live in Iraq believe in Shiite, the minority sect of Islam. Some other Kurds belong to such denominations as Alawite which live in Turkey.[58] The mysterious Sufi sect is also popular in the Kurdish region.[59]

The Kurds remain less loyal to Islam than the Arabs and Persians due to the following three reasons: first, the Kurds originally believed in Zoroastrianism and many of them are still influenced by the traditional Zoroastrian heritage; second, the Kurds have always been conquered by alien nations who believe in Islam, thus bearing some resentment against Islam,[60] and different from Arabs and Turks who belong to the Hanafi Islamic school, most Kurds in Turkey worship Shafiism of the Sunni sect; third, the Kurds have resided in deeply mountainous areas, thus having

---

54   Graeme Wood, "Iran Bombs Iraq: Meet the Kurdish Guerrillas Who Want to Topple the Tehran Regime", Slate Magazine, June 12, 2006.
55   Amir Hassanpour, The Language Policy of Iran from State Policy on the Kurdish Language: The Politics of Status Planning, University of Toronto, 1992.
56   "Neighboring Kurds Travel to Study in Iraq", http://www.npr.org/templates/story/story.php?storyId=4528599.
57   "Repression of Kurds in Syria is Widespread", Amnesty International Report, March 2005.
58   Alawite, also known as al-Nusairiyyah, is one faction of Islamic Shiite and Shia Ismaili and mainly distributed in Turkey, Syria and Lebanon. Alawite has stayed in a dominant position in Syria for a long time.
59   "The Kurds and Islam", International Turkey Network, July 3, 2007, http://web.archive.org/web/20070703230947/http://www.itnet.org/kurds_islam.html.
60   Ibid.

a lower degree of civilization, and as a Turkish proverb says, "Only by comparing with an infidel (Christian) can the Kurdish be considered as a Muslim".[61]

In addition, a few Kurdish people believe in Christianity, Catholicism, Judaism, Yezidis,[62] Bahaism and Ahl-i Haqq,[63] and Zoroastrianism, etc. Yezidis is also a sect that the ancient Kurdish people believed in. Since they are confident that they are uniquely created by the God and different from other people, they live in isolation from the outside world and prohibit their children from marrying people with other religions who are also not welcome to join them.

Disciples who are in violation of the canon will be sent into exile or even sentenced to death. "Thousands of people murdered a girl by throwing stones" in Iraq in April 2007, because she eloped with a Sunni man regardless of the opposition of her clansmen. Due to this incident, from August 2007, Sunni extremists launched a series of frenzied retaliation against Yezidis followers who reside in Northern Iraq. On August 14, 2007, a habitation of Yezidis followers at the outskirts of Kahtaniyye, a small Iraqi town, was attacked by suicide bombers driving four trucks, resulting in the death of more than 400 people and became the bloodiest violence after the US invasion into Iraq in 2003. Western countries criticized the attackers of this violent assault as an "ethnic cleansing". Yezidis enjoy 500,000 to 700,000 disciples in total, most of whom live in the Kurdish region of Northern Iraq and few of whom settle in Armenia, Germany, Russia and other places. The majority of Yezidis followers speak Kurdish.[64] Cosmology of Ahl-i Haqq group is similar to Yezidis and Alawite. There are about 500,000 followers of Ahl-i Haqq around the world, who are distributed in Syria, Armenia, Georgia, Turkey, Iraq and Iran. 100,000 followers reside in the Kurdish region of Iraq and gather around Mosul. The Kurdish people have believed in Christianity for a long term. During the Arabic conquest, Arabs destroyed close to 40,000 churches, synagogues and Zoroastrian temples at Kurdistan. In the 10th century, Arabic geographer al Masudi once mentioned tribes of Christian Kurds.[65] During the late 18th century, Christianity has revived in the Kurdish region. In 1910,

19

61　The Kurdistan File, p.15

62　Yezidis, also known as the Yazidi, is an ancient and unique religion which integrates teachings of Polytheism, Zoroastrianism, Christianity and Islam. Its disciples worship Archangels in the image of peacocks and believe there is a supreme god, but they deny the dualism of good and evil and the existence of hell and the devil. Thus, they are regarded as "Devil Worshipers" in the eyes of Christians and Muslims.

63　Ahl-i Haqq, also known as Yaresan and translated as "believers of the truth" and "admirers of the truth", was founded in Northwestern Iran, Northern Iraq, Southeastern Turkey, Azerbaijan and other Kurdish districts in the 14th century. Scholars usually consider it to be a variant of Sufi.

64　"Yezidis", http://zh.wikipedia.org/wiki/%E9%9B%85%E5%85%B9%E8%BF%AA

65　Anthony C. Lobaido etc., Asian Kurds, p. 24.

the Christian missionary Assembly was held at Edinburgh, which decided that Lutheran Church should be responsible for preaching Gospel around the Kurdish region and establishing LOMS. Immediately, LOMS sent the first mission to Mahabad of Iran, set up several Kurdish fellowships and translated New Testament into Kurdish. LOMS did its missionary work in Iraq until the Iraqi Revolution in 1958. It stayed active in Iran till the Islamic Revolution occurred in 1979. After the Iraqi war in 2003, Kurdish Christians as well as Christian churches have grown dramatically. Many Kurdish people who live in the West become Christians. There are about 100,000 Jewish Kurds settling in Israel, who are both Jews and Kurds and the largest non-Muslim group except Jews in Israel.

1.1.5.3 Tribalism

The Kurdish people are deeply impacted by tribalism. They often use Arabic term—Ashiret to refer to tribes. According to legends, all the Kurdish tribes originated from two tribes in the ancient time, namely, Milan and Zilan. There are various sayings about the number of Kurdish tribes. It is claimed that there are more than 800 Kurdish tribes, which are divided into many sects and tribe groups. And some tribes share one clan, while some are composed of more than one clan.[66] Purportedly, there are approximately 60 tribes in Iran, of which 15 are large ones; there are 22 major tribes and 54 small ones in Iraq; there are 12 tribes in Syria. Tribal leaders generally fall into two categories: the first is Agha who works as the tribal leader and takes charge of managing internal affairs of the tribe in accordance with tribal customs and law; the second is Sheikh who functions as the religious leader. Under most circumstances, Agha and Sheikh is the same person. Agha usually sets up a place for receiving guests and holding public events. Tribalism is one of the core cultures that the Kurdish people adhere to. Almost every Kurdish person has a tribal identity, whether he or she lives in an urban or rural area, in Kurdistan or Europe. Tribes have exerted a wide and far-reaching influence on the Kurdish political, economic and social life. Kurdish parties and Kurdish national movements are characterized by a strong tribal property. Some Kurdish parties and organizations have been established on the basis of tribes. For example, the Iraqi Kurdistan Democratic Party mainly depends on the Barzani tribe which is led by Mustafa Barzani. The Kurds are very loyal to their tribes and clan leaders. Some even remain more loyal to them than to the nation or the country. The tribal property has both positive and negative effect on the Kurdish movements. For instance, tribal consciousness hinders the formation of national consciousness and nationalist ideology, and frequent strife inside the tribes hampers national unity and cooperation. Some governments and elite intellectuals accuse leaders of traditional tribes of being

---

66   Ibid.

backward in thoughts and life styles and setting obstacles to modernization. However, many leaders of Kurdish national movements are actually tribal Aghas or Sheikhs, such as the Barzani tribe. Since the 20th century, the conventional tribal life of the Kurdish people has gradually changed, because an increasing number of them abandon their traditional nomadic life, settle down and engage in industrial and agricultural production; thus, tribes are disintegrating. This detribalization process is not only propelled by the internal economic and social development, but also deliberately driven by the governments of relevant countries. Turkey, Iran, Iraq and Syria have all been implementing detribalization programs in varying degrees, which take into consideration both ethnic factors and political factors of promoting economic and social development as well as modernization and urbanization in underdeveloped areas. All in all, the Kurdish tribal property is getting increasingly weak. During the 1960s, about 60% of people at the Kurdish region of Iraq claimed they belonged to tribes, but now this situation has transformed.

The Kurds who live in plateaus and mountains are agile, brave and martial. Wearing swords is a habit of Kurdish men. There are a lot of well-known Kurdish warriors in the history. Saladin, famous anti-Crusade hero, is a Kurd. The Kurds account for a large part in both the cavalry led by Saladin and the cavalry established in the later period of Ottoman Empire. Since the 20th century, the Iraqi Kurdish people have founded an armed organization called Peshmerga (which means "people who face death"). The martial culture plays a crucial role in maintaining Kurdish national survival and promoting the Kurdish national movement.

The Kurds pay much attention to their families. In a traditional family, father is the head and mother takes care of children and completes housework. Marriage is one of the most important family matters. Girls live in their parents' houses before marriage and do not need to be renamed after they get married. In the past, the Kurds usually married people of their clans and marriage was arranged by their parents, but this situation has changed significantly now. Playing a vital role in a family, sons usually inherit their fathers' work, and they must maintain the family honor and protect their sisters from bullies. The Kurds attach great importance to the honor of the clan or family. Events of "honor killing" which often take place in the Islamic world occasionally happen in the Kurdish society. The so-called "honor killing" refers to the phenomenon that a murderer kills tribe members who "lose virginity" or are "profligate" so as to "defend the honor of the clan or family". Victims are mostly women who are raped, are suspected of adultery, dress fashionably, refuse arranged marriage or ask for divorce. If a girl has a dirty reputation, male members of the tribe will murder her to protect the reputation of the family. "Honor killing" has cruel measures, including shooting, stoning, burning, burying alive, suffocating, stabbing and so on. According to the statistics released by the UN Human Rights Office, "honor killing" is widespread throughout the world, especially in the Middle East and South Asia, and 5,000 women die of this type of homicide each year. In February 2010, a 16-year-old Kurdish girl at Southeastern Turkey dated with her boyfriend and "humiliated" her family, and her father buried her alive to death. Bliss, the masterpiece and full-length novel of prestigious Turkish writer O.Z. Livaneli, told a story that after being raped by the uncle who is the tribe leader, a 15-year-old Kurdish girl is forced to suicide by her father but refuses, and later her father orders his son to kill her.

Costume is a significant feature of the Kurds. Costume differs around Kurdistan. Yet, the traditional Kurdish costume is that a man wears a jacket, trousers that are tight in the waist and ankles and a dagger on the belt which is a symbol of being a man and warrior. Many Kurdish people like wearing weapons in front of their chests. Women's clothing is diverse. Most of them wear headscarves, wide belts and long-sleeved clothes, but do not wear veils. The Kurdish costumes are colorful, and both men and women like to wear jewelry. The jewelry of the Harki tribe is most famous. Some Harki women wear jewelry even weighing several pounds. Some are fond of decorating their scarves with coins. Kurdish women in Syria like to tattoo their faces, necks and hands. The younger tattoo their cheeks, while the elder have tattoos below mouths and on cheeks.

1.1.5.4 Kurdish Festivals

The Kurdish people usually celebrate birthdays, weddings and other important festivals. The most important festival is the Regional New Year (Nowruz or the Persian New Year), which proves the long-term inseparable relations between the two nations. Nowruz means New Year in the Kurdish language and is celebrated on the annual spring equinox (March 22 or 23). The celebrations last for several days. The most enthusiastic celebration is made on the day before Nowruz, when the whole tribe or the entire village people sing and dance around a bonfire and pray for good luck in the upcoming year. In a few weeks before the festival, they put up a special table, where seven different items (vinegar, vegetable, gold, candy, fruit, hyacinth and garlic) are placed and each represents a desire. Since the Kurds consider 13 as an unlucky figure, the Kurdish families often go camping and undertake games on the thirteenth day after the festival to avoid unluckiness. A few years ago, the Kurdish celebration of New Year was banned in Turkey and Syria and often attacked by the police, which led to clashes, but such events have become rare in recent years.[67] Islamic religious holidays are also an indispensable part in Kurdish festivals.

67 Ibid., p. 45.

Kurdish women enjoy a high social status. Being confined to fewer social constraints, they usually wear no veil and are allowed to talk with guests freely and engage in various occupations. Plenty of Kurdish women have been active in political, military and commercial fields. In the Ottoman period, some Kurdish regions were dominated by women.[68] It is said that during 100 BC, women at Western Kurdistan rebelled against the Roman army. In Turkey, there are a lot of female guerrillas inside the Kurdistan Workers' Party (PKK) and the Iraqi Kurdish Armed Forces. The latter specially set up an army of women in 1996. In addition, the Kurdish person Asenath Barzani (1590-1670) was the first female rabbi in the Jewish history. Like other women living in the Arabic countries, the Kurdish underage females also receive "female genital mutilation/cutting, FGM/C"[69] to remain chaste.

From the perspective of the economic forms, the Kurds were nomadic tribes traditionally, but now this situation has changed considerably. The Kurdish people in mountainous areas live on nomadic basis, raising sheep, goats, cattle and horses, weaving carpets, cutting timbers and producing leather; the Kurdish people in plains live by agriculture, mainly planting barley, wheat, corn, rice, tobacco and cotton and managing orchards. Since the 1950s and 1960s, industrialization and urbanization have promoted an increasing number of Kurds to migrate into cities and towns. The large-scale development of the oil industry in Iran and Iraq drive a large number of Kurds to become oil workers. The Kurds are good at weaving carpets and doing other handicrafts. Kurdish carpets are very famous and historic. Being tightly and strongly knit, they are hand-woven in wool with Turkish buckles, rich colors and beautiful patterns of birds, stars, moon, flowers, animals, etc. Carpets with patterns of gardens and "spark" petals produced during the late 19th and the early 20th centuries are well-known for their bright wealthy colors.

---

68   Encyclopaedia of Women & Islamic Cultures, Brill Academic Publishers, 2003, p. 359.
69   According to WHO, female genital mutilationcomprises all procedures involving partial or total removal of the external female genitalia or other injury to the female genital organs for non-medical reasons (for purely traditional) reasons", which is prevalent in some countries of Africa and the Middle East.

1.2 Historical Evolution of the Kurdish Nation

The formation of the Kurdish nation has undergone a long process. Although the existence of the Kurdish people as a nation in the Middle East is an indisputable fact, it remains a hard job to construct a complete history of Kurdish nation. *The Encyclopedia of Kurdistan* states that the reconstruction of Kurdish history is a very difficult task, for two major reasons: first, there is no "beginning" of the Kurdish history and nation—it remains unclear about the origin of the Kurdish people; second, there is a lack of historical documents written by the Kurdish people themselves and official records were mostly made by dominant aliens in the region.[70] However, the Kurds have inhabited Kurdistan for thousands of years and played an important role in the human history and the big family of nations in the Middle East. Such a fact has been recognized widely.

The Kurdish historical stages lack clear boundaries. Generally speaking, several signs can be used as a reference in this regard, including Aryanization, Islamization, two world wars and the two gulf wars.

The prehistoric period (about 10000-4000 BC). The Kurdistan region is one of the earliest cradles of human civilization. Through archaeological excavation in this region, archaeologists found that this region once witnessed the earliest civilization in human history, which is over 7,000 years, earlier than the Mesopotamian civilization (4000 BC). Czech archaeologists unearthed the oldest settlement ruins of human history in 2010.[71]

The ancient times (4000 BC-7th century). Before 6000 BC, the Hurrians dwelled in Lake Van of Kurdistan, who might be the earliest inhabitants there and established the Mitanni Kingdom (1550 BC-1308 BC) that saw its best days in the 14th century BC. Around 2500 BC, Akkadians who belonged to the clan of Semitic people went into Mesopotamia and founded Akkad Kingdom (about 2371 BC to about 2230 BC), which was located in southwest of the kingdom of Assyria and north of the Sumerian Kingdom. This kingdom existed for a short time and was destroyed by the Gutian people in about 2191 BC. Living in the Central Zagros, the Gutian people ruled the Mesopotamian plain in 2150 BC and established Gutian Kingdom (also known as Gutian Dynasty) which lasted about a century. In 2050 BC, the Third Ur Dynasty ended the Gutian regime and united Southern Mesopotamia. In addition, the Assyrians moved into this district around 2500 BC and then flourished gradually. They built up the giant Assyrian Empire, whose capital Nineveh separated from Mosul only by a river, and

24

---

70 "History", http://www.kurdistanica.com/?q=node/1.
71 Czech Archaeologists Have Discovered the Oldest Human Settlements in Northern Iraq, Henan Museum Website, http://www.hawh.cn:82/gate/big5/www.hawh.cn/html/20100310/373675.html.

dominated this region for as long as over 1000 years. In 850 BC, the Kurds began to speak Indo-European language, which marked the beginning of the Aryan culture. In 615 BC, the emerging kingdom of the Medes (founded in about the 7th century BC) captured the Arrapkha of the Assyrian empire (the current Kirkuk). Subsequently, it conquered Nineveh together with the Kingdom of the Neo-Babylonian in 612 BC, so the powerful Assyrian Empire collapsed. Speaking Indo-European language, the Medes used to be nomadic people living in tribes of Central Asia and later founded the Medean Kingdom after their conquest of the Iranian plateau. Their land reached the east of Asia Minor and the north of the Persian Gulf when it arrived at its zenith. In 550 BC, Cyrus rose in rebellion against the Medes and established the Persian Empire (550 BC-330 BC), leading to the destruction of the Medean Kingdom. From the 9th century BC, the Kurdish region was conquered successively by the Assyrians, Medes, Persians (referring to the Persian Empire), Greeks, Parthians, Romans, Iranians (Sassanian Dynasty, 226-650 AD). During the Seleucid Dynasty (312-64 BC)[72], a large number of Kurdish people joined armies at Western and Southwestern Anatolia and fought against the Romans. According to historical records, thousands of Kurds took service at the army of Antiochus III. In the early 3rd century, the Kurdish people had a serious conflict with the Sassanid Dynasty and were defeated. After that, the Sassanid people forced the Kurds to move outside into Kerman and Baluchistan of Southeastern Iran.

Generally speaking, the Kurdish national community emerged during the 6th-7th century BC, which was jointly formed by the local indigenous people and tribal people who spoke Iranian languages and moved to this region. They dispersed in mountains of Kurdistan and won a relatively independent status because of being closed. The Medes were considered as their ancestors by the current Kurds.[73] Local residents in the Kingdom of Medes worshiped various gods and natural forces, of which the most significant ones were Minerva, Apollo, Arethusa and Isis, offered sacrifice to gods and worshiped sacred flame at temples. During about the mid-7th century BC, Zarathustra (628-551 BC) who was born to a noble knight family at the Kurdish region under the jurisdiction of the Kingdom of Medes founded Zoroastrianism, which later became the state religion of the Persian Empire and the major religion of the Kurds.

---

72   The Seleucid Dynasty is a dynasty founded by Seleucus I, a military officer under the command of the Great Alexander, after the collapse of the Alexander Empire, which was centered by Syria and included Iran and Armenia. Its territory reached Asia Minor, Syria, Mesopotamia in the west and the vast region of India in the east. The Seleucid Dynasty was one of the most important countries of the Hellenistic period.

73   The Kurdistan File, p. 18.

During the 7th century, the Arab Empire rose and occupied Kurdistan. Accordingly, the Kurds turned to believe in Islam and enter the period of Islamization, in which the word of "Kurd" began to be used.[74] Kurd means "heroic people". The word of "Kurdistan" first appeared in the 12th century. The famous Kurdish writer Al-Dinawari (828-889) composed a book entitled *Ancestry of the Kurds*. When being conquered by Arab armies, Kurdish vassal states yielded to the Sassanian Dynasty and worshiped Zoroastrianism as well as Christianity. After that, they began to believe in Islam. In 637, the Kurds first met Arab armies which marched northward. In 641, Arab armies occupied the semi-independent Kurdish kingdom Adiabene (which was located near Arbil with residents mainly believing in Christianity). During 639-644, the Kurdish people assisted the Sassanid Empire in resisting Arab Muslim armies, but it was of no avail. With the demise of the Sassanid Empire, Kurdish vassal states surrendered to the Arab Empire one by one. It took a short time for the Arabs to conquer the Kurds, and this process also underwent not too strong Kurdish resistance. After the conquest, various Kurdish kingdoms continued to pay tribute to the empire. During the later period when the empire was declining, there were occasional events of Kurdish rebellion against the central government. In Kurdistan arose some semi-autonomous Kurdish vassal states, such as the Shaddadids (951-1174) in the district of Caucasus and Armenia, Merwanides (990-1096) centered by Eastern Anatolia, the Rawadids (955-1221) in the Azerbaijan region of Northwestern Iran, the Hasanwayhids (959-1015) at the middle part of Zagros Mountains, Fadhilwayhids and Ayyarids. The Hasanwayhids were located in Kermanshah of Western Iran with Dinawer being the capital, which dominated the west of today's Iran as well as the Mesopotamian plain. It was founded by Hasanwayh bin Husayn, the leader of the Kurdish tribe named Barzikani. In his reign, the Hasanwayhids successfully resisted the attack launched by the Buyid Dynasty.[75] He signed an agreement with the dynasty which allowed the autonomy of the Hasanwayhids, whose territory once covered the present Kirkuk, Ahwaz, Asadabad, Borujerd, Ilam and other places. Nevertheless, after the death of Husayn, his sons struggled for power and conflicts took place inside; therefore, it soon became a subsidiary to the Buyid Dynasty. In 1006, the Hasanwayhids clashed with the Annazid (990-1116), another vassal state of the Kurdish Kingdom, and the King Emir died in battle in 1014. This state was finally destroyed by the Seljuk Turks in 1047. The land of the Annazid covered Kermanshah, Ilam, Hurevin, Dinawer of today's Western Iran and Norma, Mandalay, Daskara

---

74   Some experts say that the word of "Kurd" officially appeared in Assyrian literature around 1000 BC and the Assyrians regarded the Kurds who lived near Lake Van as Kurti.
75   Established by the Daylami people who came from the southern coast of the Caspian Sea, the Buyid Dynasty ruled Western Iran as well as Iraq during the 10th and 11th centuries. It conquered Baghdad in 945 and Caliphate became a puppet of the Buyid tribe. When Seljuks went into Baghdad in 1055, the Buyid Dynasty ended.

and other places of the current Southeastern Iraq. After eight generations of Emirs, this country was also destroyed by the Turks in 1116. During the first half of the 10th century, the Aishanid (912-961) dominated the north-central region of the Zagros Mountains. Generally speaking, there were five major Kurdish kingdoms in Kurdistan throughout the second half of the 10th century: the Shaddadids and the Rawadids in the north, the Hasanwayhids and the Annazid in the east, the Marwandis in the west. In the late 12th century, a new Kurdish kingdom named Hazaraspid (1148-1424) rose at the south of Zagros Mountains and Luristan, the west of Iran. It conquered Khuzestan, Isfahan and so on in the 13th century and annexed Basra and other places in the 14th century, having seen its best days. Furthermore, the 12th century also witnessed the greatest national hero Saladin Yusuf Ayub (1138-1193) in the Kurdish history. His father was a Kurdish who worked as an official in the Sulalah Zangidwhich lay in today's Northern Iraq. Saladin not only overthrew the Fatimid Dynasty, a Shiite kingdom of Egypt, but also led the Arab armies to win the famous war against the invasion of the Crusaders and set up a stronger Sunni dynasty—the Ayyubid Dynasty (1171-1250).[76]

The establishment of the Ayyubid Dynasty made Egypt return to the big family of Sunni Islam and reunified Egypt as well as the wide district of Western Asia. Because Saladin was a Kurdish and his dynasty covered a land including most of the Kurdish region, the Ayyubid Dynasty has also been called as the Kurdish Kingdom. Saladin is not only a Kurdish national hero that the Kurds have been most proud of since the cavalry led by him was most composed of Kurdish people, but also a national hero in the Arab and Islamic world for he defeated the Crusaders and recaptured Jerusalem from the Christians.

Since the 11th century, Kurdistan has entered a new period of alien subjugation and domination. The Seljuk Turks who came from Central Asia invaded the Western Asia and part of Anatolia and established the Seljuk Dynasty (known as the Seljuk Empire, 1055-1157). During its heyday, it covered an area of Iran, Mesopotamia, Asia Minor (Anatolia) and most of Syria (including Palestine) and other places, which included the northern region of Kurdistan like Mosul. In 1055, the Seljuk Empire captured Baghdad and exterminated Buwayhids (945-1055, some Kurds believe that the Buwayhid people who controlled Khalifa were actually Kurds from Persia). Around 1150 AD, Ahmad Sanjar, Sultan of the Seljuk Empire, ordered to set up a Kurdistan Province whose capital was Bahar (which means spring), a village close to Ecbatana (the current Hamadan of Iran),

---

76   Sulalah Zangid (1127-1262), also known as Nur or Zengid, is an Islamic dynasty established by the Turks in the north of Syria and Iraq, whose territory covered the three big cities of Aleppo, Haran and Mosul and which later surrendered to Saladin's Ayyubid Dynasty.

the capital city of the Medean Kingdom. It reached Sinjar and Shahrazur in the west and Hamedan, Kermanshah and Dinawer in the east. During the 13th century, the Mongols entered Kurdistan. Guyug, the son of Ögedei—the eldest son of Genghis Khan was appointed as Khan in the spring of 1246. He died less than three years after being on the throne, and Mongka, the younger son of Genghis Khan, succeeded to the throne. Mongka ordered his sixth brother Hulagu Khan to march towards the West. Hulagu captured Baghdad, the capital of Abbasid Empire, in 1258 and Damascus in 1260. The Kingdom of Ilkhanate (Ilhan state) was built subsequently, extending to Amu Darya River in the east, the Mediterranean in the west, the Caspian Sea as well as the Black Sea and the Caucasus in the north and the Persian Gulf in the south. The present Iran, Iraq, Azerbaijan, Georgia, Armenia and Turkmenistan were under the direct rule of Ilkhanate. After the death of Ghazan Khan in 1304, Ilkhanate fell into chaos and many small states were set up everywhere. Among them, Jalairid Dynasty (1336-1411) occupied Iraq, Azerbaijan, Mosul; Sarbadars state (1245-1389) ruled parts of Herat and Khorasan; Muzaffarids state (1313-1393) dominated Fars, Kermanshah and Kurdistan. Ilkhanate was destroyed by the Timurid dynasty (1370-1507), which was founded by Timur (1336-1405)—a descendant of the Turkic Mongol nobility in Central Asia and whose capital city was Samarkand. From the beginning of 1380, Timur led a powerful army composed of Turkic nomads from Central Asia to launch a campaign of massive expansion, successively capturing Iran, Afghanistan and Mesopotamia. His army conquered Armenia and South Caucasus during 1389 to 1395, invaded Asia Minor in 1399 and seized Damascus of Syria in 1400. In 1402, his army defeated the troops of the Ottoman Empire at the northeast of Ankara city and captured Sultan Bayezid, whose armed forces were completely annihilated. During the 30-odd-year reign of Timur, the Timurid Empire with a vast territory was established, which reached the Euphrates River in the west, the Syr Darya and Delhi in the east, Caucasus in the north and the Persian Gulf in the south. After Timur's death, the kingdom was caught in civil strife and various local forces got rid of the central control. Iran's western territory was occupied by Black Sheep and White Sheep Dynasties successively. The Timurid Empire fell in 1507.

During the reign of the Ottoman Empire (1299-1922) and the Safavid Dynasty of Iran (1502-1736), Kurdistan was divided into two. The Ottoman Turks originally belonged to the Kai tribe of Western Turkic Oghuz people along Amu Darya in Central Asia, who were nomadic and migrated to wherever water and grassland available. In the early 13th century, Mongolians made a massive invasion into Central Asia, so Ertuğrul Gazi, the leader of Kais, was forced to migrate the tribe westward into Anatolia. After surrendering to Sultanate of Rum built by Seljuk Turks, he separated the Kais off it gradually and founded the Ottoman Sultanate in 1324, which then embarked on the road of a massive expansion. This country first expanded westward, occupying Constantinople (Istanbul) in 1453 and destroyed the Byzantine Empire (395-1453, also known as the Eastern Roman Empire, located in Eastern Europe and covering Western Asia and Northern Africa and also incorporated Malta, Creata islands, Syria, Palestine, Egypt and the Mediterranean Coast of North Africa in its heyday with its capital being Constantinople). It began to expand eastwards in the early 16th century and grew into a giant empire ruling the roost across the three continents of Europe, Asia and Africa in the mid-16th century.

Meanwhile, in Iranian plateau rose the Safavid Dynasty, which is also called Safi Dynasty for its founder was Safi ad-Din (1252-1334 on the throne). At the end of the 13th century, Safi ad-Din set up Safi Mission at Ardabil of Azerbaijan, and his descendants have been Sheikhs of the mission for generations and enjoyed a high prestige among the Shiite masses. In 1502, Ismail I (reigning from 1502 to 1524) defeated the Aǧ Qoyunlu Dynasty, conquered Tabriz, made himself king and built the Safavid Dynasty. He announced Shia to be the state religion, not only enabled Iran to convert to Shia which differs much from the mainstream Islam and planted seeds of long-term confrontation against Iran and Saudi Arabia where Sunni is popular, but also became the ancestor of a great number of Shiite Kurds inside Iran.

The two empires respectively treated Sunni and Shiite as orthodox and were largely composed of Turks and Persians respectively. They fought with each other fiercely for the domination over Kurdistan mainly in the battlefield of Kurdistan for as long as over a century. Both of them once seized some territory of each other. In 1502, the two had conflicts for several times. The Ottoman Empire occupied Kurdistan and Armenia during 1514 to 1536. In the reign of Selim I (through 1512-1520), the Ottoman Empire waged a long-term war against the Safavid Dynasty so as to seize Iraq, Kurdistan and South Caucasus which were under the control of the latter. They fought a bitter battle at Chaldiran, a place in the northeastern part of Lake Van in 1514. Consequently, the Safavid cavalry was defeated by the Ottoman army which boasted artillery and guns. Later, the Ottoman army captured Tabriz—the capital of the Safavid Dynasty as well as some places of Kurdistan and Azerbaijan. This battle was of historic significance, basically marking the failure of the Safavid Dynasty. In 1517, the Ottoman army entered Syria, Palestine, Egypt, Mecca and Medina without meeting any resistance. Troops of Selim I first attacked Kurdistan. To win the support of Kurdish tribal chieftains, Selim I put famous Kurdish scholar Idris Bitlis (?-1520) in an important position and appointed him to negotiate with them in order to offer amnesty and enlistment to rebels and gain victory without battle. Idris made it and persuaded about 16 semi-autonomous Kurdish emirates to surrender to the Ottoman Empire, which allowed them to retain their current status, establish governments and relieve taxes. These emirates covered approximately 30% of the Kurdistan region and this situation was maintained until the mid-19th century. The rest of Kurdistan was subsequently controlled by the Ottoman Empire, and about 20 Sanjaks (equivalent of provincial administrative regions) were founded, some of which were still under hereditary rule and some were directly ruled by the central government. Sanjak-bey (Bey was governor, only inferior to Pasha) was the administrative and military governor in Sanjak districts, and some Sanjak-beys were directly accountable to Istanbul.

Suleiman I the Magnificent (reigning through 1520-1566) waged a massive attack on the Arabian Peninsula and North Africa. He captured Baghdad, Tabriz, the Mesopotamia plain and Azerbaijan in 1534. The Safavid Dynasty launched a war against the Ottoman Empire in 1553, which made a counterattack immediately and then conquered the east of the Euphrates River in 1554. The two sides signed a peace treaty in 1555, determining the Zagros Mountains as the boundary line. From 1578, the Ottoman Empire launched strikes against the Safavid Dynasty for continuous years when it fell into civil strife, and seized Azerbaijan and the Kurdish region at Western Iran. After Abbas held power of the Safavid Dynasty in 1587, it first signed a peace treaty with the Ottoman Empire, built up strength secretly and then waged a war again in 1603. Being busy with the war against Austria, the Ottoman Empire lost a large area to the Safavid Dynasty. During 1609 to 1610, the army of Abbas besieged Dimdim, the capital of the Kurdish emirate Baladusit on the west bank of Lake Urmia, for more than six months and ultimately captured the city and killed all the defenders inside. This tragic event of heroic resistance against invasion has become one of the Kurdish national epics. In 1612, the two empires made peace and confirmed the land which was newly occupied by Safavid belonged to it. After the death of Abbas in 1629, his grandson Shah Safi succeeded to the throne and the dynasty decayed ever since. Taking advantage of this weak point, the Ottoman Empire captured Hamadan in the middle of Persia in 1630, Yerevan and Tabriz in 1635 and Baghdad in 1638. In 1639, the Safavid Dynasty was eventually forced to sign The Treaty of Zuhab with the Ottoman Empire, announcing most areas of Kurdistan belonged to the latter and the rest land of about 20,000 square kilometers was owned by the former. This treaty has exerted a far-reaching influence upon the Kurdish national history as well as the emerging Kurdish nationalist movements. Before this treaty, Kurdistan was mainly under the rule of one regime, but since then, it has been divided into two parts and maintained so legally.

In the eyes of the Kurds, the contention for hegemony over Kurdistan made by the two empires was an important stage when Kurdistan descended to the most backward region in the Middle East and the Kurdish society fell into a lagging development. On the one hand, Ottoman and Safavid empires had long-term battles in the Kurdish region, which made the wartorn Kurds have no means to live; on the other hand, the rise of the Ottoman Empire caused the "Silk Road" which connected the East and the West to decline continuously and forced Europeans to start looking for a new route. The "Geographical Discovery" historically transformed the traditional international trading route. The Kurdish region which used to be situated along the vital East-West road was caught in plight, and the Kurds were gradually reduced to isolated "People Living in High Mountains".

Whether under the domination of Persians, Arabs or Turks, maintaining their autonomy as much as possible while yielding to the central government only nominally have always been an enduring theme in the Kurdish political life.[77]

Under the rule of the Ottoman Empire and the Safavid Dynasty during the 16th century to the mid-19th century, Kurdish regional lords were no longer as free as before, but the two empires did not govern this region in a direct way, so Kurdish emirates still enjoyed freedom and autonomy to a certain degree. When the two empires fought against each other, the Kurdish people changed their object of dependence from time to time and always chose to rely on the winner. They originally allied with the Safavid Dynasty to jointly deal with the Ottoman Empire. However, after the War of Chaldiran, most Kurdish tribal leaders turned to support the Ottoman Empire. Thereafter, the Ottoman Empire set up a special position called Hukumet Sanjaks which was assumed by hereditary Beys, and meanwhile sent the Janissary army group to central towns. In the Ottoman reign, the Kurdish people enjoyed a highly "autonomous" status, which was largely related to the struggle for hegemony between the two empires. Persians always wanted to annex the Kurdish region that belonged to the Ottoman Empire, which then used the Kurds to make defense and counter-attack and thus reduce control on the Kurds in its policies. The Ottoman Empire defeated the Persians in 1514, largely because it was supported by many Kurdish tribal chiefs. Its Sunni property played a role in drawing the Kurdish people who mainly believed in Sunni over to its side. The Ottoman Empire and the Kurdish emirates reached an unwritten agreement that the former officially recognized the relatively independent status of the 16 Kurdish principalities and 50 Kurdish fiefs which were under its rule in the Kurdish region. At that time, Diyarbakır Province was divided into 11 Ottoman districts, 8 Kurdish districts and 5 hereditary fiefs. In Southern Kurdistan, powerful

77   David McDowall, A Modern History of the Kurds, I. B. Tauris, 1991, p. 21.

Kurdish regional lords enjoyed almost independent status, who could coin money and not pay tribute to the Sultans on the condition that they must neither oppose the Ottoman Empire nor adjust borders. The Kurds lived in inhospitable and remote mountains. It was Kurdish tribal chiefs in place of the government that managed the emirates. They were allowed to conduct freely and inherit ruling power. In turn, they were obliged to organize armed forces to for fighting so as to support Ottoman armies, especially against Persia.

Sharaf Khan (1543-1603), emir of Bitlis Emirate located in today's Bitlis of Turkey, completed *Sharafnama* in 1596—the most significant book at that time, which depicted the history of Bitils Emirate and another five Kurdish emirates in detail. To concentrate on writing this book, he resigned sovereign authority to his son in advance.

Being sturdy, brave and fierce, the Kurdish people who were nomadic in peace times and went out to battle at wartime were an important manpower for the Ottoman army. In November 1890, Hamid II (1842-1918) imitated Russia's Cossacks and formed a cavalry mainly composed of the Kurdish people—Hamidiye (meaning "belonging to Hamid"), which reached once up to 50,000 soldiers and was deployed in the eastern region for the purpose of "restricting the nomads in the region and requiring the Kurdish tribes to be loyal to the central authority". In fact, this cavalry was employed mainly against the revolts of Kurds, Armenians and Assyrians.[78] It was originally deployed at the junction of the Ottoman Empire and Russia's Caucasus, namely, Erzurum, Bitlis and Van Province. Being put in a vital position, the Kurdish cavalry enjoyed a high prestige in the local area and even killed and pillaged. The local government was helpless, and some local officials said the eastern region had become Hamidiehlan.[79] Ibrahim Pasha[80] with the title of "uncrowned king of Kurdistan" was appointed as the commander of the Kurdish cavalry by Sultan. Hamid II who came into power on August 31, 1876, was known for his cruelty. He carried out bloody repression policies against all the revolts launched by minorities under the rule of the empire, which included the massacre of Armenians and Kurds, thus getting the nickname of "Bloody Sultan". Armenians claimed that Ottoman Turks slaughtered nearly 1.5 million Armenians at that period. The Turkish government denies the massacre. Parliaments of the Europe and the US as well as other Western countries passed resolutions on the Armenian Massacre more than once and even repressed Turkey, which resulted in tense

---

78   Richard G. Hovannisian, The Armenian Question in the Ottoman Empire, 1876-1914, New York: St. Martin's Press, 1997, p. 217.
79   Janet Klein, The Margins of Empire: Kurdish Militias in the Ottoman Tribal Zone, Stanford University Press, 2011, p. 87.
80   Ibrahim Pasha (?-1908) was a leader of the Kurdish Milan tribal alliance who remained loyal to the Ottoman Empire. When the Young Turks staged a coup in 1908, he raised an army to support Sultan, but was defeated.

relations between Turkey and Western countries. He sent the Kurdish cavalry to fight with Western Europe and Russia and also employed the Kurdish armed forces to suppress domestic resistance including the revolt launched by the Kurds, Armenians and Arabs. For example, he suppressed the Kurdish uprising in Demsep and Southern Kurdistan and the uprising made by the Arabs in the Ottoman Empire. The Kurds played an important role in the suppression of Armenians. During the Armenian revolt in 1894-1896, the Kurdish cavalry participated in the war for the first time and engaged in the crackdown. Hamid II authorized the Kurdish chiefs to deal with Armenians.[81] In April 1997, the Kurdish Parliament in Exile passed a resolution to recognize the genocide against Armenians and Assyrians and meanwhile announced that the Kurdish cavalry was a criminal companion of the Ottoman Turkish government.[82] The Turkey's Kurdish Liberation Party also stressed that Kurdish feudal lords were involved in the Armenian massacre as a conspirator of the Ottoman Turkey.[83] In 2008, the Turkey's Kurdish Democratic Society Party made an apology to Armenians for the massacre that took place in 1915. The Young Turk party dissolved the Kurdish cavalry after they came to power in 1908. However, Turkey reorganized the Kurdish cavalry in the independent war after World War I, which was called achiret hafif suvari alayları (tribal light cavalry regiments). Some Kurdish light cavalry regiments became major tools for the central government of Persia to maintain its rule during the second half of the 19th century. Impacted by Russia's Cossack cavalry, Persia also established a Cossack cavalry in 1878 which was composed of many Kurdish people besides the Cossacks.

1.3 The Rise of Kurdish Nationalism

The Kurds have a long history of rebellion against the Persian Empire and the Ottoman Empire, but this is not a true nationalist struggle. The rise of the Kurdish nationalism in the true modern sense emerged between the end of the 19th century and the beginning of the 20th century, which reflected the new trend of political development in the Middle East and other regions of the world in the late 19th century and was directly related to the decline of the Ottoman Empire and Persia. In modern times, Western European countries represented by Britain and France grew into prosperity and launched a global colonial expansion and plunder, which caused the two eastern empires even more shaky. Furthermore, Ottoman, Turkish, Arab, Persian and Kurdish nationalism rose one after another, launching attempts so as to seek a way out for their empires or nations.

81   Sébastien de Courtois, Forgotten Genocide: The Eastern Christians, The Last Arameans, Gorgias Press LLC, 2004, p. 138.

82   "Kurdish Parliament in Exile Recognizes Genocide", http://www.cilicia.com/armo10i_kurdistan.html.

83   "Final Declaration of the First Party Congress of the PRK/Rizgari (Liberation Party of Kurdistan) 1999", http://www.mirakweissbach.de/News/TorosSarian/TorosSarian.html.

Owing to the rise of Western Europe and twelve Russo-Turkish Wars[84] which lasted 241 years as well as the long-term internal strifes, the Ottoman Empire has become quite weak in the early 19th century. On the one hand, a great deal of its territory was occupied by colonists from Western Europe and Russia. Egypt was captured by France in 1798 and occupied by Britain in 1882. France controlled Algeria in 1830 and ruled Tunisia in 1881. The Austro-Hungarian Empire annexed Bosnia-Herzegovina in 1908. Italy occupied Libya in 1912. Through successive wars, Russia grabbed a vast land of the Caucasus and the Black Sea region. On the other hand, the oppressed people on the lands of the Ottoman Empire gradually embraced nationalism. In 1805, Muhammad Ali established a regime in Egypt. Greece declared independence in 1822. After that, nationalism in Balkans and Eastern Europe which attempted to separate from the Ottoman Empire was surging. In 1875, Serbia, Montenegro, Wallachia and Moldova declared to be independent from the Ottoman Empire. Due to spreading of the nationalist ideology originating from Western Europe, the decline of the empire, the empire's attempt to strengthen central control over local districts,[85] the sufferings of the Kurdish region for being long-term battlefields of the Russo-Turkish War and the Turkish-Iraqi War, the rise of nationalism in various countries under the control of the empire and other causes, the Kurdish nationalism was strongly promoted in the late 19th century.

During the 18th century, the Kurds experienced a peak of literary, cultural and artistic prosperity and development, and a variety of thoughts emerged in that period. At Bitlis, Hakkari and other districts, capitals of many Kurdish emirates grew into significant cultural centers, where a lot of poets, musicians and scientists gathered. In Istanbul, some Kurdish poets and writers gained high reputation, such as Fuzûlî, Nabi and Nef'i. Some experts called that period of time as the Kurdish renaissance and also the golden age of the Kurdish feudal society.[86] However, at that time the Kurdish nationalism had not emerged. The narrow-minded view of power held by Kurdish regional lords, the profound influence of traditional religion and the divided state of the Kurdish society all hindered the formation of the Kurdish national consciousness. The nomadic economy taken as the main economic form and the tribe structure taken as the main social structure by the Kurdish region has become a major obstacle.

---

84 The Russo-Turkish War refers to the 12-year war between Russia and the Ottoman Empire for the control of the Caucasus, the Balkans, the Crimea, the Black Sea and other places, of which 12 battles were important. This war severely shook the rule of the Ottoman Empire, becoming a vital factor that caused its decline.

85 After holding power in 1789, Selim III implemented a new policy, and one of the main content was to strengthen the centralization of power, expand his power and suppressed the tendency of regional isolation. During the reign of Mahmud II (1808-1839), he continued this policy. Tanzimat Decree was enacted in 1839 to further increase centralization and conduct Europeanized reforms. In 1864, the Ottoman Empire enacted a decree which divided the entire country into 27 provinces and provincial governors were appointed by Sultan.

86 Gérard Chaliand, A People Without a Country: The Kurds and Kurdistan, p. 15.

Some new factors and new situations arose by the 19th century. Firstly, with the declining control over its territory in Europe, the Ottoman Empire began to strengthen the control of the eastern region and meanwhile levied a large number of troops there. Therefore, the Kurds became the major source of recruitment, which was resisted by Kurdish feudal lords. In 1889, the Ottoman Empire expelled the Kurdish Hamewand tribe located in Sulaymaniyah which revolted against the central government to the Adana region and Tripoli of Libya. Secondly, by sending missionaries, opening consulates and setting up schools, the West increasingly penetrated into this region and also promoted the development and spreading of new thoughts and education. Thirdly, throughout the 19th century, the Kurdish region was the main battlefield of the Russo-Turkish War (1828-1830, 1877-1878) and the Ottoman-Persian War, which seriously damaged its production and social life and evoked the Kurds' dissatisfaction with the Ottoman Empire. Fourthly, the modernization reforms as well as the two constitutional revolutions that took place in the late period of the Ottoman Empire played a certain promoting role in the birth of the Kurdish nationalism, which not only brought a relatively relaxed political and social environment, but also prompted the revival of thoughts and educational development in the Kurdish society. Under this background, the Kurdish nationalist ideas began to sprout.

Famous Kurdish poet Haji Qadyr Koyi (1817-1897) was one of the earliest initiators of Kurdish nationalism. He put forth that only by means of pens and swords could the Kurds realize the founding of a state. He called for the development of written Kurdish language and establishment of newspapers and journals. He himself wrote a large number of poems themed by Kurdish nationalism, which motivated many young Kurdish intellectuals at that time.[87]

With the support of the New Ottomans, Abdul Hamid II ascended to the throne on August 31, 1876. He followed a dual policy, gave both rewards and penalties to the Kurdish people. On the one hand, he strengthened control and suppressed resistance; on the other, he drew his potential supporters to his side. Overall, he imposed much more tolerant policies on the Kurds than on the Armenians. For example, he appointed Bahri Bey, son of Bedir Khan, court consultant, the descendants of Abdurrahman Pasha to senior posts in the administration and the university and Sheikh Abdul Qadyr, son of Ubeydullah, to become President of the Senate and President of the Council of State. A lot of local Kurdish leaders spent a dignified exile life in Istanbul. Furthermore, in 1892, Hamid II founded ashiret mektepleri (tribal schools) in Baghdad and Istanbul, mainly recruiting children of Kurdish and Arab tribal chiefs and instilling the thought of being loyal to Sultan-the caliphate system. These schools nurtured plenty of Kurdish

---

87   Michael M.Gunter, Historical Dictionary of the Kurds, Scarecrow Press, 2011, p. 168.

intellectuals equipped with advanced ideas, many of whom became leaders of the Kurdish national movements in the future. Fifthly, during the reign of the Ottoman Empire, the Kurds enjoyed a high degree of autonomy inside the empire, which was largely related to the fierce competition between the Ottoman Empire and Persia. The day by day declining Ottoman Empire started an attempt to regain its authority over local districts and strengthen its centralization. This move has threatened the privilege enjoyed by Kurdish tribal chiefs for a long time. Under this background, the Kurds began to refuse to pay tribute or donate troops and waged revolts.

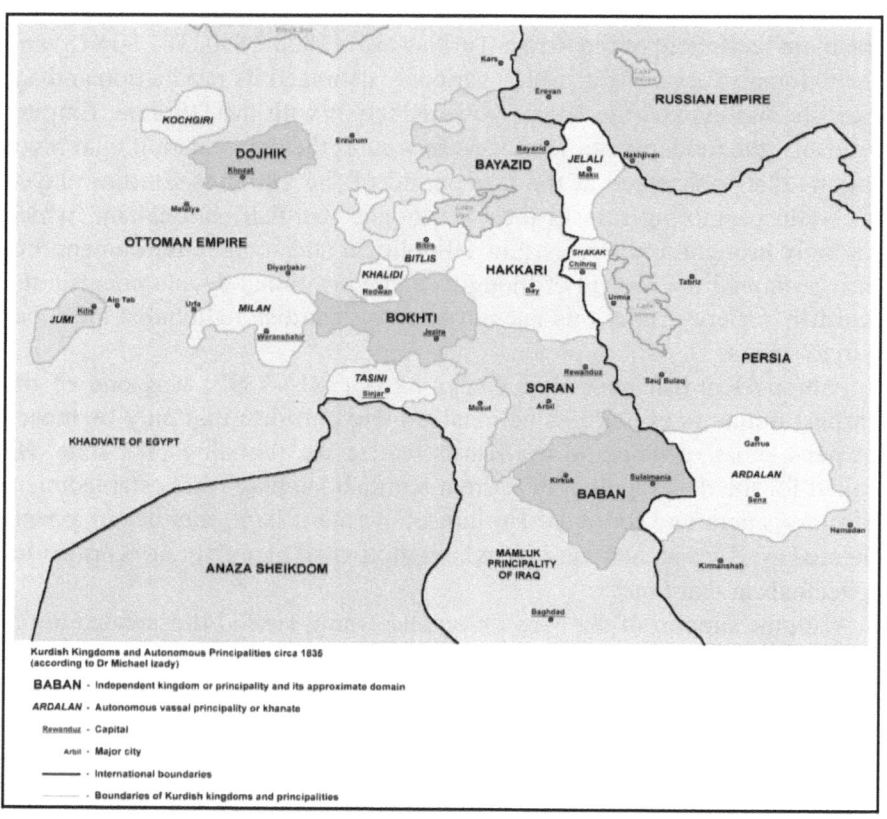

**Fig. 1-4 Major Kurdish Kingdoms in Kurdistan
during the Early 19th Century**

*Source: Website of the Kurdish Institute of Paris
http: //www.institutkurde.org/images/cartes_and_maps/kurdish_independent_kingdom.jpg.*

In the 19th century, the Kurdish people unceasingly launched revolts against the rule of the Ottoman Empire and Persia so as to maintain and expand their rights. These revolt activities promoted the awakening of the Kurdish national consciousness. About 50 uprisings broke out in Kurdistan between 1804 and 1878.[88] The main leaders were Muhammad Pasha, Bedir Khan and Yezdan Sher. The modernizing and centralizing efforts of the Ottoman Sultan Mahmud II antagonized Kurdish feudal chiefs. As a result two powerful Kurdish tribes rebelled against the Ottomans around 1830s. Bedr Khan of Botan rose up in the west of Kurdistan, around Diyarbakır, and Muhammad Pasha of Rawanduz rebelled in the east and established his authority in Mosul and Arbil. The earliest Kurdish revolt broke out in 1806 under the leadership of Emir Abdurrahman Pasha of the Baban Emirate[89]. The events have followed such a course that after the Emir of Baban Ibrahim Pasha Bebe died, the Ottoman Sultan intended to appoint Khalid Pasha from another Kurdish tribe to assume the Emirate leadership. This move encountered opposition from the people of Baban, thus the Kurdish revolt broke out. Ibrahim's nephew Abdurrahman Pasha defeated the Ottoman army and killed the local governor. The revolt lasting about three years, was finally suppressed by the Ottoman army in 1850 and Abdurrahman Pasha took refuge in Persia. Soon, Mir Mohammed[90], Emir of Soran—another Kurdish fiefdom, also waged an uprising with the intention to establish a Kurdish Kingdom, and he soon controlled the entire Southern Kurdistan region. He established a regular army which contained 10,000 cavalrymen, 20,000 infantries and established armaments factories that could produce rifles and even cannon. He also tried to build alliances with various Kurdish principalities in Persia and other districts, but was rejected. The Ottoman Empire sent troops of Rashid Pasha as well as armies in the two provinces of the Ottoman Empire namely Mosul and Baghdad, but the attacks were all defeated by Mir Mohammed forces. In October 1835, the uprising Kurdish forces marched towards the Kurdish region in Persia and kept fighting until they reached the border of Southern Azerbaijan. The Persians were forced to seek assistance from Russia. The rebels defeated the Ottoman army again in July 1836. The helpless Ottoman Empire started to play the religion card, and tried to gain the support of local mullahs and sew dissension among among the Kurds. A mullah named Khati released a fatwa (religious decree), claiming that any person or group fighting the troops of the Caliph, namely Ottoman forces, would be infidel. This religious fatwa had a big effect and hindered the Kurdish anti-Ottoman activities. Under these

---

88   The Kurdistan File, p. 22.
89   Baban Emirate (1550-1850) was located in today's Northern Iraq, whose capital was moved to city of Sulaymaniyah in 1785. It was a long-term competitor of the Kurdish kingdom Ardalan, which was situated inside Iran.
90   Equivalent to Emir/Amir, Mir is the title of leaders of emirates in the Middle East.

pressures, Mohammed and his forces have surrendered. He and his family were sent to a prison in Istanbul and later they were assassinated when they returned to Kurdistan from Istanbul. Bedir Khan Bey (1802-1868)[91], Emir of the Bokhtan or Botan Emirate[92], which was located in today's Southern Turkey, also launched an uprising. The family of Bedir Khan Bey was one of the biggest families in the Kurdish region, which had been the chieftains of the Bokhti tribe and rulers of Bokhtan Emirate since the 14th century. Bedir Khan Bey succeeded to the throne in 1821 and then built an army. He also established an alliance with Nurulah Bey from the Hakkari Emirate and Mahmoud Khan of Mukus Emirate in Central Kurdistan. In 1840, his influence extended to whole part of Kurdistan that was under the rule of the Ottoman Empire and meanwhile he formed an allience with the Kars Emirate in the northern tip of Kurdistan and the Ardalan Emirate in the Persian Kurdistan. Under his rule, the Kurdish region maintained in peace and happiness and became one of the most secure regions in the empire. Yet, this situation did not last long. Soon after the Ottoman army forces attacked the emirate and the two fighting sides carried out a seesaw war. In this war Britain and France have also supported the crackdown of Kurdish uprisings by the Ottoman authorities. The first Ottoman force sent against Bedir Khan was defeated, further encouraging him to celebrate his power and independence from capital Istanbul, supposedly even minting coins in his name. The second invasion force however was much larger and managed to eject Bedir Khan and his forces from the capital at Djazireh (today Cizre). The Ottomans were able to beat out the Botan Emirate both by numbers and being able to surround and cut off its source of supplies. He later went through an eight month siege at a nearby fortress at Eruh/Dihe, north of Djazireh, but soon capitulated. Bedir Khan, along with his family, was sent into exile first at Varna city in Ottoman Bulgaria, and later to the island of Crete. Owing to the betrayal of Yezdan Sher, his nephew in1847, Bedir Khan Bey has surrendered, then was exiled to the island of Crete and finally died in Damascus in 1868. His children would however go on to do important things—indeed the name Badrkhan would come up many times in the Kurdish struggle. Soon afterwards the campaign against Bedir Khan evolved into a larger one that would essentially end the Kurdish emirates.

---

91   It is hard to explain the accurate definitions of Bey and Khan, which had different meanings in different periods of time and were only honorary titles in most occasions. The title of Bey was originally used by chiefs of larger tribes and was simply added to the name. Later, Sultan of the Ottoman Empire appointed the supreme commanders of a certain region as Bey. The title of Khan was generally used in the same way.

92   The Bohtan or Botan Emirate existed over centuries in Southern Turkey. Its ruling (emir) family claims that they originated from the family of Islam prophet Muhammad's famous general Khalid Ibn al-Walid. The capital city was Cizre of Sirnak Province in today's Turkey. In the mid-19th century, this emirate reached its heyday under the leadership of Emir Bedir Khan Bey, but declined immediately. The current Kurdish nationalists often call the southeastern Turkey as Bokhtan or Botan (which refers to the region around the city of Diyarbakir).

His allies in Van were put down and the leader there, Khan Mahmoud of Mukus, was captured and later killed from torture. In Bitlis, Sherif Bey was defeated and put into exile. Nurulah Bey, the Mir of Hakkari who had called on Bedir Khan in the first place, was exiled. Other lords in the region were eventually made to surrender to the Ottoman Empire as it set out to end the 'instability' in the region, ending with the Baban Emirate at Sulaymaniyah, where it stood down without a fight in 1850. Beginning with the Baban revolt of Abdurrahman Pasha at the opening of the 18th century, the Ottoman attempts to assert themselves finally over the Kurdish kingdoms had taken about 40 years. As a result, the Bokhtan Emirate had perished. Bedir Khan Bey is still regarded by the Kurds as one of the representatives who first advocated Kurdish nationalism and his historical role is highly appreciated in the Kurdish national history. Because of him, the Bedir family has played a vital role in the political history of the Kurdish people.[93] Ottoman Sultan immediately appointed Yezdan Sher (God Lion) as the governor of Hakkari Province. He was so ambitious that he was interested in founding an independent Kurdish kingdom and become "King". Knowing his intention, the Ottoman Sultan removed him from office in 1850. During the Russo-Turkish War in 1853, a large number of Kurdish people resisted Sultan's order and refused to participate in the war. Yezdan Sher took advantage of this opportunity and waged a revolt around Hakkari provinces. In the spring of 1855, he took military action to expel the new governor, has conquered the Bitlis region and has appointed a new governor. He then occupied Mosul and captured the local armory. After that, he immediately marched towards Siirt (today in Turkey), the political and military center of Kurdistan in the Ottoman Empire. Within several months, he achieved to get the control of the vast region from Baghdad to Lake Van and Diyarbakir[94].

93   Allegedly, Bedir Khan had a lot of wives. Among his dozens of sons, Uthman and Husayn led the revolt against Ottoman Turkey in 1879; Midhat published bilingual journal of Kurdistan which was printed in Turkish and Kurdish in 1898; Kamil and Abdurrazzaq were appointed as governors of Erzurum and Bitlis by Tsraist Russia; Emin Ali was one of the founders of Kurdistan Revival and Advancement Association; the other three brothers Emin Ali Thurayya (1883-1938), Jaladet (1893-1951) and Kamuran (1895-1978) were important leaders of the Kurdish nationalist movements in the later period of the Ottoman Empire. Emin Ali was put to prison for many times for engaging in campaigns of Kurdish nationalism. After the coup launched by Young Turks in 1908, he resumed the publication of the magazine "Kurdistan" in Istanbul and was one of the early members of "Khoybun" (Independence), a Kurdish nationalist organization. Jaladet used to serve as the first president of Khoybun and began the efforts to latinize the Kurdish alphabet. As a famous Kurdish writer, Kamuran taught Kurdish at the university of Paris and once worked as spokesman of Mullah Mustafa Barzani in the UN in the 1960s.
94   The city of Diyarbakir has a long history. The castles in this city were built by the Byzantine Empire as early as the year of 349 A.C. It has been a central city of the Kurdish region in Turkey and regarded as the unofficial capital of Turkish Kurdistan by Kurds in modern Turkey, which has a similar status as Arbil in the Iraqi Kurdish region. The name of Diyarbakir city among Kurdish people is Amed and today the city has about one million residents.

Kurdish people had actively supported and fought in his army. His troop had increased from the initial number of 2,000 to 100,000 in the summer of 1855. With winter approaching, the Russian army fighting against Ottomans began to retreat and the Russo-Turkish war had ceased temporarily. Due to the worry that Kurdistan would become a puppet of Russia after its independence, Britain and France took the initiative to mediate the dispute between the Ottoman Empire and the Kurds. At the end of 1855, the British government sent the emissary Nimrud Rassam to visit tribal chiefs in Kurdistan with a large amount of cash and other gifts and persuaded Yezdan Sher to resolve the war conflict through negotiation. Some Kurdish tribal chieftains and big families accepted bribes and quitted from the uprising. Because the special envoy which Yazdan Sher sent to Russia did not get a positive reply for the request of assistance, this time he had turned to Britain for support. He personally went to Istanbul with the British emissary and intended to negotiate with the central government, but he was arrested once he arrived at Istanbul, which marked the failure of the Yazdan Sher uprising.

For decades thereafter, the uprising made by Sheikh Ubeydullah was the largest in scale. Kurdish tribal chief Sheikh Ubeydullah launched a revolt in 1880 with an intention to unify the entire Kurdish region and his troop was composed of thousands of people. Some experts said, the uprising made by Ubeydullah was the first Kurdish nationalist movement in modern times, since he proposed the requirement for the independence of Kurdistan and the establishment of Kurdistan and also stressed the Kurds must no longer be interfered by the Ottoman Empire and Persia.[95] Ubeydullah's father Sheikh Taha enjoyed a very high religious status in Kurdistan and was known as the "greatest spiritual leader of the Kurds." After his death, Ubeydullah succeeded to the throne and also became a "spiritual leader of Kurdistan". In December of 1872, the Persian government required the two Kurdish regions of Urmieh and Khoy to pay taxes and was refused by the Kurds for they had already paid taxes to Sheikh Ubeydullah. As a result, the Persian government took military actions, but unsuccessfully. The Russo-Turkish War broke out primarily in Northern Kurdistan during 1877 to 1878, which devastated people's life there. The uprising took place continuously in places like Hakkari and local people called for Ubeydullah to resolve the crisis. In this case, he took the opportunity to fill the power vacuum, build troops and prepare for revolt. He also sent emissaries to Mecca and Cairo for support and associated with Russian consulates in Erzurum and Van provinces. However, Russia had just ended the Russo-Turkish War and paid no attention to the Kurdish people. The British vice-consul in Van

95   Hakan Ozoglu, Kurdish Notables and the Ottoman State: Evolving Identities, Competing Loyalties, and Shifting Boundaries, State University of New York Press, 2004, p. 75, http://en.wikipedia.org/wiki/Sheikh_Ubeydullah.

Province visited Ubeydullah in 1879, promising to provide him with arms and ammunition. In August 1880, about 220 Kurdish elders held a meeting and decided to launch a revolt and establish an independent country of Kurdistan. Sheikh Ubeydullah determined to wage a war against Persia first, requiring Persia to admit the Kurdish country and his rule over it. The war began in October, and the troops composed of 80,000 Kurds occupied Mahabad and other places soon and got close to Tabriz (today in Iran). The Persian government asked the Ottoman government to restrict the Kurds on its territory. The Ottoman Empire was also worried about the expanding influence Ubeydullah had upon the Kurds; thus, it cooperated with Persia to deal with Ubeydullah and meanwhile drew some Kurdish tribes over to its side to fight against him. Soon the uprising failed and Ubeydullah was imprisoned in Istanbul. He fled from Istanbul in August 1882 and attempted to make a comeback, but was arrested again that October and exiled to Mecca. He died in 1883. The largest Kurdish revolt in the late period of Ottoman Empire failed. Before this, most revolts were led by Kurdish tribal chieftains for the purpose of fighting for turfs and maintaining their own interests, whereas Ubeydullah was the first one to propose that uprising should be made for the Kurdish national cause and hope to establish an independent Kurdish national state.[96]

He made it clear in the letter addressed to the local Christian missionaries that "The Kurdish nation, consisting of more than 500,000 families is a people apart. Their religion is different, and their laws and customs distinct.... We are also a nation apart. We want our affairs to be in our hands, so that in the punishment of our own offenders we may be strong and independent, and have privileges like other nations.... This is our objective.... Otherwise, the whole of Kurdistan will take matter into their own hands, as they are unable to put up with these continual evil deeds and the oppression, which they suffer at the hands of the Persian and Ottoman governments."[97]

---

96 "Sheikh Ubeydullah", http://en.wikipedia.org/wiki/Sheikh_Ubeydullah.
97 Wadie Jwaideh, The Kurdish National Movement: Its Origins and Development, Syracuse University Press, 2006, p. 79.

The early 20th century uprisings

In the early 20th century, the Kurdish uprisings were more obviously characterized by nationalism. When the armed revolution led by the Young Turks[98] broke out in July 1908 in Istanbul, Hamid II was forced to restore the 1876 Constitution and reconvene the parliament. The Young Turks launched a coup again on April 27, 1909, and deposed Hamid II. After Young Turks had risen to power, they vigorously promoted the Ottomanism doctrine, repressing national movements of minorities and banned all non-Turkish associations, clubs, schools and publications. Many Kurdish nationalist leaders were either imprisoned or sentenced to death. Under such circumstances, some Kurdish political activities had gone underground. Some leaders, including the family of Bedir Khan Bey, chose to live in exile. Kurdish uprisings broke out in Dersim and Mosul. Immediately after the Dersim uprising was suppressed at the end of 1909, a revolt led by Sheikh Mahmoud Berezendji took place in Mosul, which won the support of tribes of Barzani and Zebari. Rebels demanded that the Ottoman Empire withdraw its troops and administrative bodies from the district so as to found an autonomous Kurdish regime. The empire sent two corps to repress the uprising, which destroyed 40 villages, but could not defeat the rebels completely. Eventually, the empire compromised and appointed a relative of the Sheikh's as the governor of Sulaymaniyah Province to relieve the conflict. Few months later, Turkish partisans prohibited the activities held by the Kurdish nationalists, so the Barzani tribe launched another revolt under the leadership of Sheikh Abdusselam. The rebels defeated the imperial army which came there to suppress the revolt. In the early 1910, the revolt extended to the entire Southern Kurdistan. Yet, the Kurdish leaders did not take further significant actions to build a political body, what they did was only expelling the Turkish troops from their territory. Meanwhile under the leadership of Sheikh Shahabeddin, Selim Ali and Mullah Selim, another Kurdish uprising occurred in Bitlis, but was suppressed quickly for being isolated and that it could not get help from other Kurdish forces.[99]

---

98   In May 1889, under the leadership of Ibrahim (Ethem) Temo, students of Istanbul Medical School secretly set up the Ottomanist organization called as the Committee of Union and Progress , which was generally named as the "Young Turks" by Europeans. Soon, many young students, military officers, intellectuals and exiled personages participated in this association. It represented both the interests of bourgeoisie and the liberal landlords and advocated maintaining the territorial unity of the Ottoman Empire; meanwhile, it opposed autocracy and demanded the restoration of the 1876 Constitution. In 1895 The Young Turks movement joined with other opposition groups in Europe and jointly organized the Ottoman Progressive and United Association in 1895 and led a bourgeois democratic revolution in the early 1909. After they got the ruling power, they implemented the "big Ottoman doctrine", suppressed national movements inside the empire territories and pursued a pro-German foreign policy. It changed its name to the United Progressive Party in 1913. After the outbreak of World War I, it joined the German-Austrian war alliance and was defeated. In November 4, 1918, the Party announced its dissolution.
99   Gérard Chaliand, A People Without a Country: The Kurds and Kurdistan, p. 28.

During the 19th century, the Kurdish resistance movements lacked political organization, clear political programs and strong national consciousness. The Kurdish nationalist ideology had not formed yet. It was not until the end of the 19th century that the Kurdish intellectuals in the modern sense began to appear. Most of the earliest Kurdish intellectuals, came from noble families. Many of them were sons of Kurdish regional lords or heirs of tribal chieftains who were exiled to Istanbul. They studied in local Islamic schools (Madrasas) (tribal schools established and allowed by the current government) or Ottoman empires's military schools (which enrolled Kurdish students only after 1870). At that time, Istanbul was an intellectual center of many enlightened people and oppositional figures and there were also a group of Kurdish regional lords, tribal chieftains, intellectuals and young people with national consciousness. They began to form Kurdish publications, clubs and cultural associations. The first daily Kurdish newspaper was published in 1897. In the following year, Midhat Bedir Khan, Emir of Kurdish Bokhtan Emirate, founded the first Kurdish magazine—"Kurdistan", which included articles and news both in Turkish and Kurdish. Kurdistan mainly promoted Kurdish education and culture. It functioned as the catalyst for Kurdish nationalist movements and provided a platform for Kurdish nationalists. Bedir Khan's brothers worked as editors. Due to changes in the political climate, this magazine was issued in London, Geneva, Folkstone and Cairo from time to time. By the early 20th century, the nationalist consciousness further grew among the Kurds. Sheikh Abdul Qadyr founded "Hetawe Kurd" (The Kurdish Sun) in 1908. In the autumn of 1908, the Kurdish Research Council opened a Kurdish school in Istanbul. After the coup, launched by the Young Turks in 1908, a large number of Kurdish leaders expressed their support for the new regime, hoping to gain its support offor Kurdish national rights. Taking advantage of this relatively liberal atmosphere, Emir Ali Bedir Khan Bey, General Sherif Pasha and Sheikh Abdul Qadyr (son of Ubeydullah and Speaker of the Parliament of the Ottoman Empire) co-founded the the Kurdistan Teali Djemiyeti (Society for the Rise of Kurdistan) and published the Kurt Teavun we Terakki Gazetesi (Kurdish Solidarity and Progress Gazette). This was the first legal Kurdish publication. It widely discussed Kurdish culture, language, national unity and other issues and was soon popular spread among the Kurds in Istanbul. However, this association couldn't be considered as a full-fledged political organization, for it lacked an advanced structure, program and strategy and was only a mixture of various Kurdish elites, who differed in their thoughts and goals; yet it played a vital role in the formation of Kurdish nationalism as well as the development of Kurdish national political movements. Later, internal strife plaqued the association and leaders rivaled fiercely for power. There were three main groups of Bedirkhanites, Sheikh Abdul Qadyr and his clan of Sayyeds of Nihiri, whom denounced one another as "traitor to the nation".

Some researches assert that the Bedir Khan family was secession-ists while the Sayyids of Nihiri were autonomists. These differences se-riously weakened the Kurdish national movements. Some young Kurdish local officers and intellectuals established Kurdish clubs in major Kurdish cities like Bitlis, Erzurum, Muş and Mosul. At the end of 1908, Bitlis Club was initially founded with 700 registered members while gained thousands of members in a few months time. Most of these clubs imitated the Young Turks and had the nature of military organization to some extent. At the end of 1912, Kürdistan Mahibbur Djemiyeti (Society for the Friends of Kurdistan) was set up in Istanbul which actively introduced the Kurdish issue to the public. At the end of the same year, deputy in the Ottoman Parliament and Kurd Lutfi Fikri has founded Mujedded Fırkası (Renewal Party), which stemmed from İttihat ve Terakki Djemiyeti (Society for Union and Progress) of the Young Turks, whose predecessor was İttihad-ı Osmanî Djemiyeti (Society for Ottoman Union) founded in 1889 and which advo-cated and promoted the Turkish constitutional revolution and transformed into the political organization of the Young Turks in 1906. Before its split, it advocated secularization (the separation of state from religion), latinization of the alphabet, abolition of honorary titles such as (paşa, bey, şeyh etc.) and gender equality, it attracted a large number of Kurdish intellectuals. Its main publication was Idjtibat (Point of View). Many of its views were adopted and implemented by Mustafa Kemal Atatürk later. The founda-tion of the above associations and clubs showed that the Kurdish people began to establish preliminary modern political organizations and were preparing to launch a modern type of organized political struggle. In 1910, some Kurdish students and intellectuals set up a secret organization named Hiwa Kurdish Association (Kurdish Hope Society) and made it legal in 1912. This was the first Kurdish political body which was more maturely organized. It was led by senators of the Ottoman Parliament Khalil Hassan Motki, Omer, Kadri, Ekrem Djemil (Cemil) as well as Fuad Zade and Zeki Zade from Van Province. Mehmet Şükrü Mehmed Sekban was its spiritual leader, but later in 1933 he wrote a book in which a statement was included that said: "Kurds are essentially 'Turks'". Targeting the Kurdish workers and young people, this organization expanded its influence in Kurdistan and published "Roja Kurd", a bilingual newspaper in Turkish and Kurdish. Its name was changed into Kurdish Sun in 1914 and it positively promoted the reform of Kurdish alphabet and Kurdish nationalist ideology.

During this period, there emerged some cultural activities related to Kurdish nationalism. In 1909, Lutheran Christian Church missionar-ies opened the first school for the Kurds in Mahabad (Iran). In 1912, fa-mous Kurdish leader Simko Shikak (from Shekak tribe) published the first Kurdish journal "Kurdistan" (monthly) and opened a Kurdish school in the city of Khoy. During 1919 to 1922, he also founded "Roja Kurd" as the official publication of the Kurdish government under his leadership, when he launched the uprising. By summer 1918, Simko had established his authority in the region west of Lake Urmia. After this, he organized his forces to fight the Iranian army in the region and managed to expand the area under his control to nearby towns and cities such as Mahabad, Khoy, Miandoab, Maku and Piranshahr in a series of battles.

All in all, before the outbreak of World War I in 1914, the climate of Kurdish political movements and the Kurdish nationalist awareness had taken shape, and Kurdish intellectuals grew increasingly active. During the First World War and the early postwar period, Kurdish nationalism developed further and the Kurdish issue became more visible.

1.4 Formation of the Kurdish Issue

WWI broke out on August 2, 1914. As one major member of the Allies, the Ottoman Empire joined the war in October 29th of the same year. This war alliance of by the Ottoman ruling class (at least one part of it) contributed the most fatal blow to this declining empire and resolved the long-term "Eastern Problem" in the interests of the big powers of Europe" through the disintegration of the empire.[100] During the War, a variety of ethnic groups or nations under its rule gained independence but the Kurdish issue—the largest minority within its territory remained unsolved.

During the First World War, Kurdish nationalism had further developed. The Ottoman authority mobilized the Kurds to fight against the Allied Powers Countries, especially against the Tsarist army. The Kurds held a complex attitude towards the WWI.

Generally speaking, they responded positively to the call made by the Ottoman Caliph for the WWI and Hamidiye cavalry still remained faithful to the Ottoman Sultan. The Ottoman Empire initially deployed 30 Kurdish cavalry battalions in the eastern front. When the war broke out, Russia quickly captured the Iranian Kurdish region adjacent to Armenia and armed Armenians to fight against the Ottoman Empire, while the Ottoman Empire immediately mobilized the Kurds to deal with the Armenians. Bitter battles took place between the Kurds and the Armenians. It is worth mentioning that the Assyrians were also slaughtered by the Kurds. In 1914, the Assyrians who settled in Eastern Turkey and some districts of Iran declared war against the Ottoman Empire. Eventually, the Ottoman army defeated

---

100   There were a series of international issues caused by the struggle among modern European powers in their quest to control and divide the Ottoman Empire among themselves. From Europeans' point of view, since the Ottoman Empire was located in their east, so it was referred to as the "Eastern Problem". It was the problem about "how to deal with Ottoman Empire", which was one of the important themes of Europe's foreign policy throughout the 19th century and also one reason for the WWI.

the Assyrian uprising troops with the help of the Kurds. Still some Kurds, particularly the Kurds living in Southern Kurdistan and Dersim refused to engage in the war. In Northern Kurdistan, a small number of Kurds cooperated with the Tsarist Russian army to fight against the Ottoman army. In response, the Ottoman government conducted a fierce reaction. Jacob Künzler, a Swiss missioner working in the Urfa Church Hospital, in his memories recorded that the Young Turks had carried out an ethnic cleansing targeting both the Armenians and the Kurds. He depicted clearly that a great number of Kurds in Erzurum and Bitlis were forced to migrate during the winter of 1916.

At that time, a part of Kurds was considered as Russia's "fifth column" inside the Ottoman Empire. As a result, the government deported a large number of Kurds. Approximately 300,000 Kurds were forcedly deported to Urfa, Maras (Maraş) and Aintab (the name of which was changed to Gaziantep in 1922). During the summer of 1917, many Kurdish people were deported to Konya in Central Anatolia. At the end of WWI, about 700,000 Kurds were forced to migrate, where half of whom died because of homelessness[101] According to another record, 600,000 Kurds were killed in Eastern Turkey during 1915 to 1918.[102] The figure was also said to be 700,000.[103]

During the wartime, Tsarist Russia occupied the east of the Ottoman Empire and popularized the national ideology of self-determination among the Armenians and the Kurds, while promoting the independence of Armenia, which also stimulated the Kurdish national movements to some degree. At that time, Iran declared its neutrality.

In fact, since the Iranian constitutional revolution in 1907, the Kurds were basically free of the central government's control. Before and after WWI, a vast land of Iranian Kurdistan was captured by the Ottoman Empire and Russia (the Ottoman Turkey attacked Iran in 1908 and Russia had conquered the Iranian territory respectively in 1911 and 1917). Kurdish people in Iran made use of this political turmoil to arm themselves. The October Revolution broke out in Russia in 1917 and a new socialist regime was established. On December 3, of the same year, the Soviet government announced that it would not recognize unequal treaties signed by (Tsarist) Russia with the Ottoman Empire and Iran. In those days, a riot erupted inside the Russian army which was deployed to Iran. The Kurds took advantage of this opportunity and launched an attack, killing Russian military

---

101   G. S. Harris, Ethnic Conflict and the Kurds, the Annals of the American Academy of Political and Social Science, 1977, pp. 118-120.
102   Edgar O'Balance, The Kurdish Revolt: 1961-1970, London: Faber and Faber Limited, 1973, p. 19.
103   The Kurdistan File, p. 23.

officers and forcing Russia to withdraw its troops. The region fell into a state of anarchy.

Britain, France and Russia as well as other European powers had coveted the dying Ottoman Empire for a long time and speeded up their efforts to grab its territories during WWI. The Tsarist authority promised to give the Kurds substantial assistance, but, in fact, it was preparing to annex Kurdistan once the Ottoman Empire collapsed. During the First World War, big powers constantly discussed about how to get the control of Arab, Armenian and Kurdish territories under the rule of the Ottoman Empire. Britain and France had reached a secret agreement on this issue on May 16, 1916. Since the draft of this agreement was written by British Middle East expert Mark Sykes and French diplomat François Picot, it was known as "Sykes-Picot Agreement". In September of the same year, Tsarist Russia also joined and signed this agreement in Petrograd. The main content of the agreement was as follows: Syria, Southern Anatolia and Iraq's Mosul would belong to France (Mosul was later agreed to be controlled by Britain); Southern Syria and Southern Mesopotamia (most areas of today's Iraq) would be within the British sphere of influence; the southeast coast of the Black Sea, the Bosphorus and the Dardanelles Straits would be under the control of Tsarist Russia. This agreement later became the basis of Treaty of Sèvres which carved up the Ottoman Empire, while it exerted a vital impact on the division of boundaries and later border disputes in this region. Syria under the French control was later divided into Lebanon and Syria; in regions like Iraq, Kuwait and other countries the British mandate emerged. Many state borders were artificially drawn with a ruler and a pen. It has brought about a series of future national conflicts and issues such as the Kurdish and Palestine issue.

The Ottoman Empire was defeated. It signed the Armistice of Mudros with the representatives of the Allied Powers Countries (mainly UK and France) in the town of Mudros on October 30, 1918, thus announced unconditional surrender. Armistice stipulated the following: the Bosphorus and Dardanelles Straits (water ways) would become completely open to the vessels of all countries; the Allied Powers Countries would be able to commandeer merchant ships, seaports, railways and other facilities of the Ottoman Empire; the Ottoman Empire was forced to break off diplomatic relations with other allies; the Ottoman Empire would dissolve its armed forces and transfer its warships to the Allied Powers Countries; the Ottoman army would withdraw to the borders regulated by the Treaty of Berlin in 1878. In addition, this treaty specifically stipulated that if any riots occurred in the eastern provinces of the defeated empire, the victor Allied Powers Countries would be free to send troops and suppress them; they would also be able to deploy troops in vital militarily strategic cities of Turkey, when they felt their interests were threatened.

On April 22, 1920, the Allied Powers countries invited the Ottoman Empire to the peace conference held in Paris. Former Prime Minister Ahmed Tevfik Pasha represented the Empire in the conference. He believed some terms of the peace treaty were too harsh and thus refused to continue the peace talks. Consequently, the empire replaced him with Prime Minister Damat Ferid Pasha. On July 22 of the same year, Ferid Pasha brought the draft back to Ottoman capital. The ruler Sultan, Mehmed VI immediately convened a Cabinet meeting and ratified it. Treaty of Sèvres as a component of Paris Conference was signed on August 10. (See Appendix for full explanation.)

The treaty mainly stipulated the following: Independence of Hejaz Province and Armenia would be recognized; Iraq and Palestine would be under the British mandate; Syria and Lebanon would be under the French mandate; the Kurds would be allowed to be autonomous; the Ottoman territories in Europe especially Dodecanase islands would be transferred to Italy and Greece; Bosphorus and Dardanalles Sea straits would be managed jointly by the international community; and the armed forces of Ottoman Turkey would be limited within 50,000 troops. Ottoman Turkey's finance and economy was put under the supervision of victors; war reparation and indemnity demands of the Allied Powers Countries would be paid through the state taxes to be collected. After this agreement was signed, the Allied Powers Countries began to invade and occupy the territories of the Ottoman Empire. They sent their troops to capture several regions of Turkey. Greece began to invade West Anatolia and prepared to advance towards inner Anatolia. France and Italy entered the Anatolia respectively from the South and the East. Britain had already occupied Mosul and Kirkuk as early as 1918.

Treaty of Sèvres is one of the most important international treaties concerning the fate of the Kurds in the history. It consisted of 433 articles, of which No. 62, 63 and 64 were about the Kurds. Article 62 mentioned the establishment of a tripartite committee composed by the representatives of British, French and Italian governments for the purpose of implementing autonomy in the Kurdish region within the following six months after the Treaty was signed.

This Kurdish region was evaluated as the region where the Kurds accounted for the majority of the population, namely, from the east of the Euphrates River—the south of Armenia country which was about to be founded to the north of conjunctions of the boundaries of Turkey, Syria and the Mesopotamia plain. If the tripartite committee could not agree on the autonomy program, they would let their governments make the final decision. While the Kurds enjoyed autonomy, they had to ensure the benefits and rights of Assyro-Chaldeans (who believed in an ancient kind of Catholicism) and other religious and ethnic groups in the autonomous region. The treaty also stipulated that a committee composed of British, French, Italian, Iranian and Kurdish representatives would be set up to investigate this region and discuss whether or not to adjust Turkish-Iranian borders. Article 63 stipulated that the Ottoman government must implement the decisions made by the above two committees within three months. Article 64 stipulated that in one year after the implementation of the treaty, if most people living in the Kurdish region demanded independence, they could submit an application to the League of Nations and demand formal discussions on the issue. If the League of Nations would decide that the Kurds in the region had the capacity for independence, major Allied Powers Countries would not oppose Kurdish independence, and the Ottoman government would have to obey such suggestion of the League of Nations' renunciation decisions for Kurds. The detailed provisions for such renunciation by Turkey will form the subject of a separate agreement between the Central Allied Powers and Turkey.

Allied Powers, if and when such League of Nations renunciation takes place, no objection will be raised by the Central Allied Powers to the voluntary adhesion to such an independent Kurdish State of the Kurds inhabiting that part of Kurdistan which has hitherto been included in the Mosul vilayet (province).

Treaty of Sèvres first admitted that the Kurdish people had the right to self-determination and agreed that they could establish an independent state, which was of great significance in the modern Kurdish history and provided a great impetus for Kurdish national movements. Nevertheless, the treaty was not flawless. First, the Treaty of Sèvres was an imposition on Kurds where their views were not taken into consideration. Second, the conditions for autonomy or particularly independent state which the treaty stipulated were too hard and the Kurds had to dance after others' pipe. Third, the treaty divided Kurdistan artificially and severely restricted the Kurdish nation and its overall development as well as Kurdish unification. Fourth, despite the demands of the Kurdish people, Kurdistan was directly placed under colonial rule: Bitlis and south of lake Van would belong to Armenia; the Arab and Iraqi regions which were originally owned by the Ottoman Empire were carved up by Britain and France and new protectorates were founded. France obtained Syria and some areas of Southeastern Anatolia including Gaziantep, Urfa and Mardin (today's Turkey). A vast land from Silesia (including Adana and some areas of Central and Eastern Anatolia) to Sivas and Tokat in the North was announced to be put under the French influence. Qamishli and south of Mardin were incorporated into Syria; South of Mosul was put under the control of Iraq. Fifth, the territory of Kurdistan was greatly reduced in general. And finally, although the victor Allied Powers signed the treaty, they were not sincere enough to fulfill it, trapped by their narrow interests, which later shattered the dream of independence longed by the Kurds.

Participants of Sèvres Conference were the Britain, France, the United States, Italy (observer), Japan, Armenia, Belgium, Greece, Hijaz, Poland, Portugal, Serbia-Croatia, Serbia (the future Yugoslavia) and Turkey. The Kurdish people formed a delegate to participate in its sessions when the Kurdish and Armenian issues were discussed. The Kurdish representative Sherif Pasha (1865-1951) resolutely defended the Kurdish cause and submitted two memos to the conference (on March 22, 1919 and March 1, 1920). However, the Kurdish leaders among themselves had much controversy over the borders of Kurdistan.[104]

In the eyes of Sherif Pasha, Kurdistan within the Ottoman Empire covered: Ziven (Zivin) of Caucasus in the north, Erzurum and Erzincan, Kemah in the west, Mount Sinjar, Arbil, Kerkuk, Sulaymaniyah, Harran and Tel Asfar in the south and Ravandiz, Bashkale, Vezirkale and the Mount Ararat in the East.[105] This geographical concept offered by him caused much controversy among Kurdish nationalists, for Lake Van was not incorporated and Armenians were also claimed sovereignty. Emin Ali Bedirkhan thought that Kurdistan should include Lake Van as well as Hatay in the west. With a former name of Sanjak of Alexandretta (Hatay Province), located in the Southern Turkey bordering with Syria, had two major cities—Antioch (today's Antakya) and Alexandretta (today's Iskenderun). When it was incorporated into Syria in 1920, Turkey finally protested to the League of Nations in 1936. And three years later, France has left Hatay city to the rule of Turkey.

On November 20, 1919, the Kurdish and Armenian delegations resolved their disputes and reached an agreement which was signed by General Sherif Pasha and Boghos Nubar Pasha. In the joint declaration issued by both parties, the Kurds gave up territorial claims regarding Erzurum and Sason but retained sovereignty over Agri (Ağrı) and Muş. This joint declaration aroused a great disturbance both among the Kurds and Armenians. Sheative in the conference. Yet, these proposals had not been adopted by the Allied Allied Powers Countries and the regions of Kurdistan mentioned in the treaty was basically limited with the regions of the Ottoman Turkey.

104   Hakan Ozoglu, Kurdish Notables and the Ottoman State: Evolving Identities, Competing Loyalties, and Shifting Boundaries, p.38.
105   Serif Pasha, "Memorandum on the Claims of the Kurd People, 1919", http://en.wikipedia.org/wiki/Treaty_of_S%C3%A8vres#cite_note-12.

Treaty of Sèvres imposed by the victor Allied Powers, pushed the Turkish nation into a critical juncture of life and death. Turkish nationalists represented by Kemal believed that this treaty seriously damaged the interests and sovereignty of the Turks; hence they did not recognize it and undertook a vigorous initiative to protect the national rights of their country.

Under the leadership of Kemal, the 1919-1923 anti-aggression struggle finally brought the victory of the Turkish national liberation movement. The Allied Powers countries invited representatives of the Ottoman Empire and the new revolutionary Turkish Grand National Assembly based in Ankara to negotiate in London during February 21 to March 12, 1921.

The representatives of the new Turkish Grand National Assembly proposed the abolition of Treaty of Sèvres; the proposition was declined. In that September, the Turkish army defeated the aggressor Greek army, so France and Italy immediately announced that they gave up insisting on the Treaty of Sèvres and made peace with the Turkish Grand National Assembly. France signed an armistice agreement with Turkey on October 20, 1921. Article No. 6 of this agreement stipulated that the new government of the Turkish Grand National Assembly should solemnly recognize the rights of minorities in the National Convention.

Turkey won the decisive victory in the war against Greece in 1922, and therefore, the Allied Powers agreed to repeal the Treaty of Sèvres and re- open peace talks in Lausanne, Switzerland. On July 24, 1923, Turkey and the Allied Powers countries signed theTreaty of Lausanne, which provided that the Allied Powers countries restored peace with Turkey; the Allied Powers recognized the independence and the territorial integrity of Turkey in Asia Minor and confirmed Turkey's official borders from the Black Sea to the Aegean Sea and Iran. According to the Treaty of Lausanne, Eastern Thrace and Izmir would be returned to Turkey, and those regions where Armenians and the Kurds, as well as other ethnic groups lived would be part of Turkey; the sovereignty of Mosul city would be solved in the future; Turkey renounced its territorial claims over Egypt, Tunisia, Morocco, Libya and other places and admitted Britain's claims over Cyprus and Italy's claims over Dodecanese Islands; the mutual parties gave up waive claims; Turkey repaid partial debts owned by the former Ottoman Empire; all the parties announced the cancellation of extraterritoriality as well as fiscal and customs supervision rights, and Turkey's customs became autonomous; demilitarization was implemented in the sea strait regions, and all the parties declared their agreement on the principle of free passage in the sea and air of the strait region. Indeed for Turkey, Treaty of Lausanne was quite fair. Though Turkey lost its Arab populated regions and Cyprus, it still retained Eastern Thrace and managed to hinder the Kurdish independence or autonomy. According to the Treaty, Turkey agreed to recognize the minority status of non-Muslims such as the Greeks, Armenians and Jews, but refused to admit the same status for the Muslim Kurdish minority. This treaty was a terrible news for the Kurds. Treaty of Sèvres had been the only treaty that was not implemented and hence completely abandoned from among various treaties signed in the frame of the Paris Peace Conference. The Treaty of Lausanne not only ignored the Kurdish autonomy or independence, but, also, emphasized the maintenance of the territorial integrity and the unity of the New Turkey. Because Western European colonists contradicted themselves in words and deeds, the Kurds missed their best chance in the history for their national independence.

During the time from the outbreak of the WWI to the Turkish War of Independence occurred the best opportunity for Kurdish independence. During that time, Turkey was faced with a total vacuum in its internal politics. The Ottoman Sultan could not extend its authority outside the capital Istanbul, and its army was disintegrated and the government could not deal with the Kurds. Externally, Britain and France had pledged to support Kurdish independence. During the war, British and French troops withdrew from Gaziantep and Urfa. Iran was also caught in turmoil and its weak central government had to put aside the Kurdish issue. Tsarist Russia which used to covet Kurdistan had undergone a socialist revolution. Instead of being aggressive, the new Soviet regime was sympathetic and supportive to national and democratic revolutions. Yet, the Kurds failed to seize the golden opportunity to achieve the goal of founding an independent country. There are many causes accounting for this outcome. The most important one is that the Kurdish nationalism was still in its early infancy, while the sense of national independence had not formed yet and the national power was limited for its lack of internal unity. In the first place, the Kurds did not have powerful national leaders like Kemal who could take the burden of founding an independent state and uniting the people. Most Kurdish leaders were feudal tribal chieftains, who held backward views, narrow vision and insufficient modern national consciousness under the deep influence of religious and tribal thinking. The establishment of a national country was far beyond their capacity. At this period of time, the Kurds did not have such leaders who led them to revolt decades ago as Bedir Khan and Yezdan Sher. In the second place, during the late 19th century and the early 20th century, after the strong control of the central authority, the Kurds lived in the traditional order of tribal rule once again. And the Kurdish community divided and each tribe fought only for itself. Furthermore, the Kurds did not have a powerful political organization which could lead the national independence movement. The most influential Kurdish organization at that time was the Kurdistan Teali Djemiyeti, which was set up in 1918 and whose members were renowned Kurdish political leaders and tribal chieftains, including Ekrem Djemil, Fikri Gani Zade Reshad and Djerdjis Zade. In its first general meeting, Sheikh Abdul Qadyr was elected as chairman, Emin Ali Bey, son of Bedir Khan, and General Fouad Pasha as vice chairmen, and General Hamdi Pasha as secretary-general. A call was published by the meeting. The leaders of its branch in Istanbul were Mullah Said Mikisli, Khalil Hayali and Hamza Motki Bey, who founded the publications "Life" and "Kurdistan". This organization actively promoted what US President Woodrow Wilson proclaimed about the principle of national self-determination and even sent delegations to visit American, British and French embassies in Turkey to express their demands of independence.

However, there was a serious disagreement about the independence issue inside the organization. Young activists advocated complete independence, whereas nobles represented by Sheikh Abdul Qadyr supported only autonomy. Qadyr said, "If we abandon the Turks, when they are in urgent need and declare the Kurdish independence, it will give a fatal blow to them, and we should not do such a thing to hurt our honor as Kurdish people. I suggest that we should help them out. In addition, you know, the Turks have agreed to establish a Kurdish autonomous region. You also know, if they do not keep their promise, the Kurdish people can also realize this goal with the use of force." He advocated that the Kurds should fight against the Turks to achieve the autonomy goal.[106]

Ironically, the new Turkish government did not fulfill their past commitments, and the Kurdish armed revolt attempt failed. Sheikh Abdul Qadyr was hanged by the Kemal government. The people who supported the autonomy eventually split up with those in favor of independence.

The latter group founded a new organization named Kurdish Social Committee. They launched an independent movement in 1919. It was suppressed by the Kemal government in March 1921 and 110 people were sentenced to death. Under the request of Kurdish tribal chieftains of Dersim, Kemal government of Turkey pardoned many of them.

In fact, it was because Kemal felt he was not powerful enough and still needed the support of the Kurds. Another organization which behaved actively during this period was the Freedom of Kurdistan led by Seyd Abdurrahman, son of Sheikh Abdul Qadyr. It mainly appealed for the Kurdish independence in the diplomatic circles. At the end of 1922, Soureya Bedir Khan Bey and some Kurdish congressmen like Yusuf Ziya and Halit Bey established the Kurdish Independent Committee in Erzurum and meanwhile set up branches in Bitlis, Siirt and other places. The members included many intellectuals, artists and businessmen as well as General Ihsan Novry and such tribal chiefs as Sheikh Sait, Sheikh Sharif of Palu and

106   Gérard Chaliand, A People Without a Country: The Kurds and Kurdistan, p. 33.

Sheikh Abdullah of Meilkan. After the establishment of the committee, its members decided to prepare for an armed uprising. The Kurdish Club also became active again and its policies were roughly the same as those of the Kurdish Independence Committee. With hundreds of members, it initially engaged in cultural activities and later embarked on a strategy of armed campaigns. In November 1920, the Kurdish tribe Kochgiri in West Dersim province of Turkey which believed in the Alawite belief which was led by tribal chief Alishan Bey (grandson of Mustafa Pasha) launched an uprising against Kemal's national army. Neither supported by the Sunni Kurds nor by Alawite Kurds living in the other regions of Turkey, the revolt was suppressed in April 1921.

In this way, from Treaty of Sèvres to Treaty of Lausanne, the chance or opportunity of independence expected by the Kurdish people was lost, and Kurdistan under the rule of Ottoman Empire was divided into three parts: Northern Kurdistan in Turkey, Southern Kurdistan in British Iraq and Western Kurdistan in French Syria. Treaty of Lausanne officially carved up Kurdistan for the second time in history. Along with Eastern Kurdistan which was incorporated into Persia in the 17th century, Kurdistan was divided into four blocks. This four blocks pattern has mainly remained till today.

During the subsequent years, continuing to fight for national self-determination and to establish a Kurdish state has become the common dream living in the hearts of all Kurdish people around the world. While Kurdish nationalism develops deeper and further, governments of the countries where the Kurds live implement big-nation chauvinism or ethnic assimilation policies in varying degrees and they discriminate, limit and cancel Kurdish national rights. Under these circumstances, the Kurdish issue has kept intensifying and the Kurdish struggles for national rights, autonomy or independence has occurred one after another, and grown as a crucial problem which affects national security of several countries, their territorial integrity and regional stability in the whole Middle East. Kurdish issue became a vital political and social problem that seriously threatened the security and national unity of Turkey.

Summary

As one of the indigenous inhabitants in the Middle East, the Kurds have a time-honored history and unique culture as well as a wealth of natural resources (oil and water which are their two most valuable assets). Being a mixture in terms of cultural genes, the formation of the Kurdish nation depends on various factors. Its special geographical location and ongoing alien invasion have played a key role in its national formation. During quite a long time, the Kurds were controlled and divided by the Ottoman Empire and Iran, but they still maintained considerable autonomy. However, being one of the five major ethnic groups in the Middle East, the Kurdish nation is the only one that has not built an independent state.

Nationalism as an ideology originating from Western Europe was one of the catalyzers for Kurdish nationalist ideology, but Western European colonialists were the main initiators of the Kurdish tragedy. The Kurdish national consciousness and Kurdish nationalism has formed through a gradual process, which accelerated by the decline of the Ottoman Empire and the spread of Western nationalist ideology. The outbreak of WWI as well as the disintegration of the Ottoman Empire, caused by this war directly led to the emergence of the Kurdish issue. It was also this very time when Kurds, missed the utmost historical opportunity to establish an independent state. We can say that the Kurdish nationalism was not mature enough at that time and, eventually, grew full-fledged in the process when the Kurdish people developed their national struggles during the later epochs.

CHAPTER TWO

The Kurdish Issue in Turkey

The Kurds in Turkey suffered from the most severe discrimination and the most humble position among the four major countries where the Kurds dwelled. After the establishment of the Republic of Turkey in 1923, a vigorous assimilation policy was followed, and the Kurds, whose national identity and minority status were not recognized, were discriminated in all spheres of life. As a result, the Kurds had carried out struggles for national identity, rights, autonomy or independence immediately after the foundation of the Republic of Turkey. Their national struggle is only second to that of the Iraqi Kurds. In 1984, the Kurdistan Workers' Party (PKK) launched an armed guerrilla warfare. The three-decade conflict has led to huge casualties and property losses, so the Kurdish issue became a vital political and social problem that seriously threatens the security and national unity of Turkey. With the end of the Cold War after the 1990s, the accelerated process of Turkey's access into the EU as well as the elevating status the Kurds enjoyed in the neighboring country of Iraq made the Turkish government gradually adjust its Kurdish policies and relaxed the restrictions imposed on the Kurdish national identity in terms of language and culture. Yet, in this country a relatively thorough solution of Kurdish issue, still has a long way to take.

2.1 The Situation of Turkish Kurds

With many mountains and plateaus, the Kurdish region in Turkey is traditionally known as Northern Kurdistan, accounting for almost 40% of the entire Kurdistan and covering an area of about 190,000 sq km. Located on the edge of the Anatolian Plateau, the Taurus Mountains are a mountain range in central and southern Turkey. Their east reaches Lake Eğirdir, north of Antalya, and the west extends to the upper reaches of the Euphrates and the Tigris. Another big mountain range is the Zagros Mountains, which border with Iran. The Famous Grand Ararat is 5,156 meters above the sea level, thus being the highest peak in Turkey. The second highest peak on this piece of land is Little Ararat, which is 3,925 meters above the sea level. Northern Kurdistan boasts abundant forests, rivers and lakes, which are the sources of many big rivers in the Middle East, including Tigris, Euphrates, Khabur, Ceyhan, Kura and Aras. Lake Van is the largest lake in Turkey and also the fourth largest freshwater lake in the world. Most Kurds live in mountainous geographic regions, so they were regarded as the "People in Big Mountains" by the Turkish government. Since Northern Kurdistan is situated in Eastern and Southeastern of Turkey, the Kurdish issue is also known as the "Eastern Issue".

Despite being a country including various ethnic groups, Turks are the dominant national group in this country. There are many sayings about the number of minorities in Turkey. The first one claims that there are all together 72.5 ethnic groups in Turkey.[1] Another saying gives a number of 47.[2]

Historically, the Ottoman Turkish authorities only recognized non-Muslim minorities as ethnic groups and thus Muslim Kurds were not included among the minorities. But the Kurds are certainly the second biggest minority in Turkey, with the largest population in Kurdistan regions divided among four countries. In 1935, Turkey had released an official statistics about the Kurdish population—1,480,200, but the figure was reduced to 1,362,900 in 1945. According to UN Demographic Yearbook, Turkish Kurd population was 1,476,562 in 1945 and 1,854,569 in 1950. Scholar S. Mutlu thought that there were 3,130,390 Turkish Kurds in 1965, accounting for 9.98% of the total Turkish population, and the figure increased to 7,046,200 in 1990, accounting for 12.6% of the population. During 1965 to 1990, the Kurdish population increased by an average of 3.24% annually (the total Turkish population increased by 2.31% in the same period).

---

1   Servet Mutlu, "Ethnic Kurds in Turkey: A Demographic Study", Int. J. Middle East Stud., 28 (1996), pp.517-541.
2   Peter Alford Andrews, "Catalogue of Ethnic Groups", Ethnic Groups in the Republic of Turkey, Wiesbaden: Dr. Ludwig Reichert Verlag, 1989, pp.53-178.

If the growth rate remains so, the Turkish Kurds would be 9.74 million in 2000, which was 13.8% of the Turkish population.[3]

Nezan Kendal pointed out that there were 8.5 million Kurds in Turkey in 1975 and that was 23.6% of the Turkish population.[4] However, the figures in the early 1990s were quite different, ranging from 7 to 15 million.[5] Famous Dutch Middle East expert Martin Von Burenesen believed, the Kurdish population in Turkey was 7.5 million in 1975 and reached 10.45 million in 1990, if being calculated with an average annual growth of 2.21%. Kurdish expert David McDowall claimed that the figure was 9.6 million in the late 1980s and accounted for 19% of the total in Turkey.[6] Izady, thought there were 13.65 million Kurds in Turkey in 1990, accounting for 24% of the total Turkish population.[7] In December 2006, a survey made by KONDA, a Turkish research organization, demonstrated that there were 11,445,000 Kurds in Turkey, who accounted for 15.7% of the Turkish population, and the Kurdish people who spoke Kurdish as their mother tongue reached 11.97%.[8] Turkey's National Security Council estimated the Kurdish population in Turkey was 12.6 million in 2008.[9] In 2012, CIA estimated that there were about 13.82 million Kurdish people dwelling in Turkey and that was 18% of the total Turkish population (which was 79.75 million in July 2011).[10] In spite of all these figures, the Kurds believe, there are 20 to 25 million Kurdish people living in Turkey.

59

3   Servet Mutlu, "Ethnic Kurds in Turkey: A Demographic Study", Int. J. Middle East Stud., 28 (1996), pp. 525, 527, 532, 534, 541.
4   Nezan Kendal, "Kurdistan in Turkey", in A People Without a Country: The Kurds and Kurdistan, pp.47-48, 102-103.
5   Mortan Abramowitz, "Dateline Ankara: Turkey After Ozal", Foreign Policy, 6 June, 1993, p.174; Christopher Dickey, "A Game of Kurdish Roulette", Newsweek, 12 July, 1993, p.33; Michael M. Gunter, The Kurds in Turkey: A Political Dilemma, Westview Press, 1990, pp.6-8.
6   David McDowall, "The Kurdish Question: A Historical Review", in The Kurds: A Contemporary Overview, Routledge, 1992,p.32.
7   Mehrdad Izady, The Kurds: A Concise Handbook, Crane Russak, 1992, pp.113-119.
8   http://www.milliyet.com.tr/2007/03/22/guncel/agun.html.
9   http://www.milliyet.com.tr/default.aspx?aType=SonDakika&ArticleID=873452.
10   "The World Factbook:Turkey",https://www.cia.gov/library/publications/theworldfactbook/geos/tu.html.

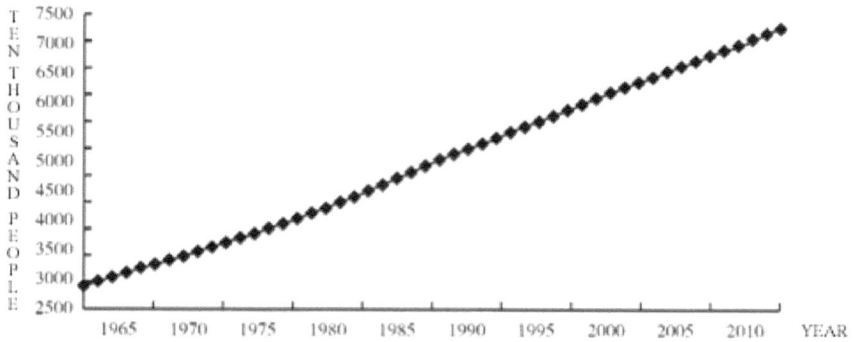

Fig. 2-1 Increase of the Turkish Population

Source: Data FAOSTAT, year 2010, http://faostat.fao.org/site/550/
DesktopDefault.aspx?PageID=550#ancor (last updated 23 June 2011)

Compared with Iraq, Iran and Syria, the Kurds in Turkey had the worst social status and suffered the most systematic discrimination. Their national identity was not recognized and their language and cultural rights were strongly suppressed. Martial law and military control were often imposed in the Kurdish region. Besides, they are the poorest. Through their long-term struggle, the Turkish government gradually realizes in recent years that the Kurdish issue has turned to be the most serious problem in the country. While continuing to stop the armed struggle of the separatist PKK, it has begun to lift the ban on Kurdish language and culture and explores a possible solution to this issue by means of political dialogue.

Tab. 2-1 Population Distribution in Turkey according to Mother Tongue

Year	Turkish	Kurdish	Total
1935	13899073	1480246	16157450
1945	16598037	1476562	18790174
1950	18254851	1855169	20947188
1955	21622292	1679265	24064763
1960	25172535	1847674	27754820
1965	28289680	2370233	31391421
Growth Rate (1935-1965) (%)	2,26	1,58	2,12

Unit: Person

Source: Servet Mutlu, "Ethnic Kurds in Turkey:
A Demographic Study", Int. J. Middle East Stud., 28 (1996), p.520.

Due to geographical, historical and cultural factors, the Kurdish region has traditionally been the most underdeveloped region in Turkey. Compared with the prosperous west, the east has long been marginalized economically.[11]

For a long time, the Turkish government has attributed the Kurdish disunity and discontent to economic underdevelopment and social and cultural backwardness in the east, considering the Kurdish issue as only an economic and social problem. Income, education, health and other indicators in this region are the lowest across Turkey. In 1985, the illiteracy rate was 35.5% in the east and 44% in the southeast, ranking in the bottom. The per capita income in the Kurdish area was only a quarter of the Marmara region which lies in the west.[12] In 1990, the rates for doctors and private cars (6 per hundred people) were both lower than the national average. According to a report made by the UN's Human Development Index (HDI), Turkey's HDI was 0.778, whereas the Kurdish region was 0.585, highly below the national average.[13] The economic structure in this region was dominated by agriculture, and the husbandry and agricultural occupation accounted for the 64% of the total population, while this rate in the central region of Turkey was 46.8%.[14]

Infrastructure is also poor, lacking investment. Turkey implemented its first five-year plan in 1963, and its investment orientation changed with more emphasis being put on regions which would achieve better economic benefits like coastal districts rather than on "backward areas".[15]

After the 1980s, the Turkish government conducted the GAP agricultural water-supply project in the Kurdish region and invested much to construct hydropower stations and develop irrigation so as to eliminate poverty of the Kurds and relieve the national separatist pressure, but its effect was limited. A report released by the Turkish Confederation of Young Businessmen in 2000 pointed out that although the government had invested 20 billion dollars in the GAP project during the past two decades, the GDP in this region was still lower than 40 years ago. GAP Regional Director Mehmet Açıkgöz noted: "one of the special purposes of this project was to resolve economic and social problems in the region", and he stressed that "there remains only the issue of economic development in this region, ethnic issue is an illusion." Alp Mehmet Kaya, chairman of Chamber of Commerce, pointed out,

---

11   Paul J.White, "Economic Marginalization of Turkey's Kurds: The Failed Promise of Modernization and Reform", Journal of Muslim Minority Affairs, Vol.18, Issue 1, 1998.
12   Servet Mutlu, "Economic Bases of Ethnic Separatism in Turkey: An Evaluation of Claims and Counterclaims", Middle Eastern Studies, Vol.37 (2001), No.4, p.103.
13   Amikan Nachmani, Turkey: Facing a New Millennium, Manchester University Press, 2003, p.41.
14   Smuru Altug, Alpay Filiztekin, "Productivity and Growth, 1923-2003", The Turkish Economy: The Real Economy, Corporate Governance and Reform, Routledge, 2006, p.45.
15   Servet Mutlu, "Economic Bases of Ethnic Separatism in Turkey: An Evaluation of Claims and Counterclaims", Middle Eastern Studies, Vol. 37 (2001), No. 4, p.110.

"If the country doesn't take measures to address the (ethnic) problem here, it will only get worse. It is both an economic and political issue". However, Professor Ali Kaklu from Sabanci University, Istanbul, said that the political reform is needed to solve the Kurdish problem: "The mere economic reform is far from enough, and unless more substantive political and cultural reforms are carried out...the completion of GAP dam and irrigation project with billions of dollars being spent will be useless".[16]

Over the years, the Turkish government has attributed the Kurdish issue to economic and social backwardness, and feudal influence in the region. In fact, the problems that the Turkish Kurds mainly face are that they are deprived of their national rights and national and cultural discrimination, besides the current political-government system and state ideology of Turkey which cannot satisfy their political, economic and cultural requirements.[17]

During recent years, Turkey has adopted measures to improve the living conditions of the Kurds. The UNHCR issued the Assessment Report on Turkish Kurds in December 2003, which said that the life of the Kurdish people in Turkey had improved, but they still suffered severe discrimination and the resolution of the Kurdish issue was confronted with serious obstacles.[18]

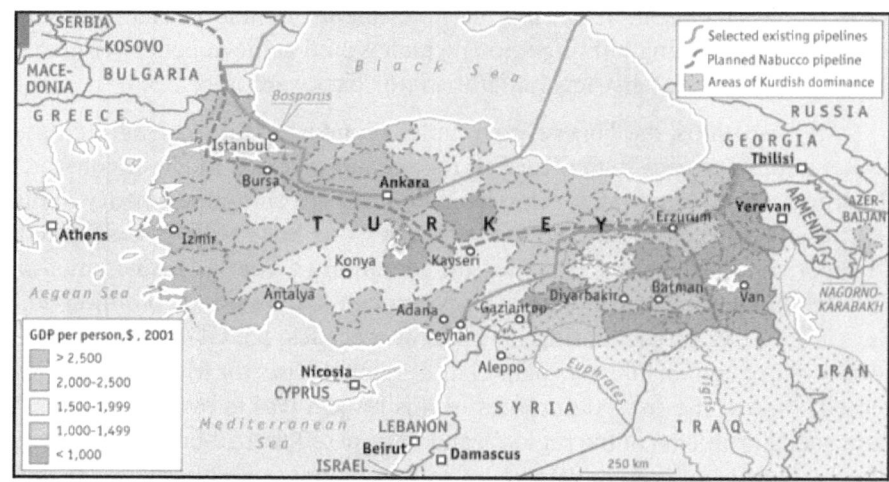

**Fig. 2-2 Comparison of Economic Situation
in Various Regions of Turkey**

*Source: "Anchors Aweigh", Economist, Oct.21, 2010,
http://www.economist.com/node/17276440?story_id=17276440.*

16 "Turkey Revives Stalled MYM32 Billion GAP Dam and Irrigation Project", The Christian Science Monitor, May 28, 2008, http://www.csmonitor.com/World/Europe/2008/0528/p12s01-woeu.html.
17 "The Root Causes of Turkey's Kurdish Challenge", Today's Zaman, Feb.9, 2010, http://www.brookings.edu/research/opinions/2010/02/09-turkey-kurdish-taspinar.
18 "Minorities at Risk Project, Assessment for Kurds in Turkey", Dec.31, 2003, http://www.unhcr.org/refworld/docid/469f3add1e.html.

Tab. 2-2 Distribution of Turkish Kurds in 1965 and 1990 (Proportion of Local Population)

Year	Marmara Sea Area	Aegean Sea Area	Mediterranean Sea Area	East and Southeast Area
1965	1,24	0,36	4,98	81,80
1990	6,09	3,93	8,95	65,22

Unit: %

Source: Servet Mutlu, "Ethnic Kurds in Turkey:
A Demographic Study", Int. J. Middle East Stud., 28 (1996), p.532.

Tab. 2-3 Development Comparison between the Kurdish Region and Other Regions in Turkey

Year	1985	1990	1991	1979	1986
Project / Region	Illiteracy Rate (%)	Private Cars per Hundred	Doctors per Thousand People	GNP per capita	GNP per capita
East region	35,5	6,4	4,0	34,4	29,2
Southeast region (Kurdish region)	44,0	6,4	4,0	34,4	29,2
Aegean Sea region	18,6	11,0	9,0	100,0	100,0
Black Sea region	24,7	6,3	5,0	56,2	47,4
Central region	18,3	21,6	12,0	53,8	2,1
Marmara Sea region	14,2	46,5	12,0	100,0	100,0
Mediterranean Sea region	22,1	8,7	5,0	69,1	61,6

63

Source: Servet Mutlu, "Economic Bases of Ethnic Separatism in Turkey:
An Evaluation of Claims and Counterclaims", Middle Eastern Studies, Vol.37 (2001), No.4, p.103.

2.2 The Kurdish Issue during the Single-Party Rule of CHP (RP Party)

This period mainly refers to the time from 1923, when the Republic of Turkey was founded to 1950 when the single-party rule of the Republican People's Party (CHP)[19] ended. During this period, "Father of the Nation" M. Kemal Atatürk died in 1938; and in 1946 after the World War II, Turkey began to implement a multi-party system led by CHP (RP Party) leadership; after the second national elections the Democratic Party came to power in 1950 and one-party system ended.

Guided by Kemalist doctrine, the Turkish government paid great efforts to establish a homogeneous Turkish nation-state in this period by systemically implementing Turkization policies, assimilating the Kurds and repressing Kurdish anti-government insurgencies harshly.[20]According to statistics, eighteen armed insurgencies broke out during this period, among which sixteen were waged by Kurdish people. There were three large-scale Kurdish revolts which exerted far-reaching influence: the uprising made by Sheikh Said in 1925, Mount Ararat uprising between 1927 and 1932 and Dersim uprising from 1936 to 1939.

The Kurdish revolt made in this period shows, to a certain extent, the nostalgia of autonomy the Kurds enjoyed in the Ottoman Empire ages as well as their misunderstanding they had towards the new-born social system of Turkey. Under the reign of the Ottoman Empire, the ethnic-national policies were generally tolerant. Its pan-Islamist policies did not cause national discrimination against the Kurds who were also Muslims and meanwhile these pan-Islamist policies allowed them to maintain their national identity and thus relatively led an autonomous social life.

On the contrary, the new-born Republic of Turkey was obviously characterized by pan-Turkism and extreme nationalism, which made the Kurds fear. Article 39 in the Treaty of Lausanne stipulated that Turkey would not restrict the use of non-Turkish languages in private communication, commerce, media, publications, conferences, etc., but this clause was not complied with. After the establishment of the new republic, the Turkish government banned the Kurdish language. It also removed many Kurdish senior officials in the east region from office, revoked all maps and official documents containing the words of "Kurd" and "Kurdistan" and

---

19   CHP was established by Mustafa Kemal on September 9, 1923 and initially named as "People's Party". On November 10, 1924, its name was changed into CHP. As the oldest political party in Turkey's history, it has played a vital role in the political life of Turkey. Its fundamental ideology is Kemalism, besides other thoughts.

20   Svante E. Cornell, "The Kurdish Question in Turkish Politics", Orbis, Vol. 45:1 (Winter 2009), p.77.

replaced Kurdish names of eastern cities and towns even villages with Turkish names. Furthermore, most Kurds believed in Sunni Islam belief and highly worshipped the title Caliph leadership, which enjoyed a lofty and sacrosanct status in the eyes of the Kurds. The Republic of Turkey was founded in 1923 and announced the abolition of the caliphate institution of the Ottoman empire in March 1924, which shocked the conservative Kurdish people. Kurds have believed that the national independence war was launched in order to save the Ottoman Sultanate regime, but to their surprise the new-born Turkish government has adopted the policies of radical secularism and nationalism to eliminate certain remnants of the Ottoman Sultanate regime and disrupted the Islamic life of people. It can be said that the political and cultural revolution launched by Kemalist practices has failed to get the support of the broad masses.[21] The caliphate system was abolished by Kemal in 1924, which played a key role in triggering the Kurdish revolt.[22] Some experts have argued that the uprising led by Sheikh Said was actually a religious resistance instead of a national one.[23]

After the establishment of the Republic of Turkey, the Turkish government continued to strengthen its centralization and strengthened local controls, which has violated the interests of Kurdish tribal chiefs. Therefore, the Kurdish insurgencies in the early stage after Turkey won national independence had the nature of resisting the said centralization to a large extent.[24]

2.2.1 The Sheikh Said Uprising in 1925

On March 3, 1924, the Turkish government announced the abolition of the Sultanate system and required Caliph Mehmed VI (Vahdettin) as well as his royal family to leave the country within 24 hours. The government announced in April that the legislative power belonged to the Grand National Assembly (TBMM) in capital Ankara; former departments in charge of religious and church property affairs were cancelled; independent religious schools were closed; religious courts were repealed. In 1925, the government banned all kinds of ascetic groups and closed their residences, temples and mausoleums. The series of moves amazed all Turkish people including the Kurds, and subsequently, several campaigns took place across Turkey for the restoration of the caliphate system. In 1924, the Kurdish Independent Commission launched an uprising in Bitlis, but it was soon repressed. In February 1925, Sheikh Said, a Kurdish tribal chieftain of Piran, waged a revolt and appealed to the Kurds to overthrow the secular government through jihad and restore

---

21 Ibid.
22 Ibid.
23 Mehrdad R. Izady, The Kurds: A Concise Handbook, Taylor & Francis, 1992, p.38.
24 Svante E. Cornell, "The Kurdish Question in Turkish Politics", Orbis, Vol. 45 (Winter 2009/1), p.79.

the caliphate system. He pointed to Mohammed Selim Effendi, the eldest son of Sultan Hamid, as the new Caliph. Rebels established a supreme committee, whose members were Hazham Kalabek Pasha, former commander in chief of the Ottoman eastern corps, and Yusuf Beg, former commander of the Ottoman Kurdish cavalry. Leaders of the uprising mostly came from a Kurdish nationalist organization named Azadi, whose headquarters were located in Erzurum, such as Khalid Beg (?-1925), leader of the Jibran tribe. Said enacted a decree on February 14, declaring that Darhini to be the provincial capital of "Kurdistan". The uprising army only spent one month to occupy 1/3 of the Kurdistan region. In mid-March, the rebellion army captured Bingol, North Siirt and other places. It soon grabbed 14 provinces, and Kurdish tribes at Lice, Mush (Muş) and other regions also participated in the uprising one after another.

The Turkish government immediately ordered the martial law to be implemented in the eastern regions of the country. On March 3, TBMM passed the Security Law which endowed the government with two-year martial law powers and meanwhile set up a Special Court in Ankara that could implement faster trials and immediate death sentences, which would be responsible for trialing Kurdish rebels.[25]

The Turkish government declared that Sheikh Said and his followers were "religious fanatics". It condemned that their rebellion was made contrary to state sovereignty and national interests and revealed that they intended to separate from Turkey and unite with Iraqi Kurds.[26]

While mobilizing troops to suppress the uprising, the government endeavored to win certain Kurdish tribes over to its side and tried to trigger divisions among Kurds from within. In early April, the Turkish army launched the general offensive. Owing to the betrayal of other leaders, Said and other 24 important leaders including Sheikh Ali, Sheikh Abdullah, Rashid Bey, Sheikh Hazem Ismail were arrested. Many other leaders who joined the uprising fled to such countries as Syria. The Turkish government founded an independent court (which was established in 1923 to punish the opposition in a fast and severe way) to judge the rebels. Said and his 52 companions were hanged on June 30. During the uprising, approximately 206 villages and 8,758 houses were destroyed, and 15,200 people were killed. The Said uprising was the first large resistance struggle made by the Kurds after the establishment of the Republic of Turkey and exerted a far-reaching influence upon the Kurdish national movements in Turkey as well as future Kurdish policies of the Turkish government.

---

25 After the Kurdish revolt was suppressed, the Turkish government abolished the Security Law and the special court in March of 1927.
26 Quanan Ha & Shuqing Zhou, Research on Political Democratization in Turkey, Shanghai Joint Publishing, 2010, p. 28.

After the suppression, the Turkish government paid great attention to Kurdish separatist activities and took a series of measures to restrict them. First, the central government further strengthened its control over the Kurdish region. A troop with about 80,000 soldiers was stationed in this region and a long term martial law was implemented. Second, the Turkish government began to remove the Kurds to southwestern regions. From 1925 to 1928, about one million Kurds were forced to migrate and tens of thousands of people died on the way.[27] Third, the Turkish government adopted a series of harsh measures to crack down the Kurdish nationalist activities. During the Kurdish uprising, the government enacted the Order Restoring Act, which endowed local city governments with the power to deal with any activity that endangered national stability or social order. All organizations and publications that were harmful to national security were banned; labor unions were prohibited from being established; the Republican Progressive Party[28] and various Kurdish organizations were banned; wearing traditional Kurdish costumes was banned. The independent courts (Istiklal Mahkemeleri) were closed in 1927, before which all together 7,400 Kurds were arrested and 660 were executed to death (some sources give higher figures). On June 25, 1927, TBMM (The National Parliament) passed the Law No. 1164, set up the inspectorate-general governing status in the Kurdish region and authorized it with the right to approve court decrees, protecting local security and expelling local residents if necessary. In November 1928, Turkey declared the Latin alphabet reform and the Arabic alphabet was repealed. Meanwhile, it embarked on the campaign of purifying spoken Turkish language from other languages and popularizing Turkish writing and speaking. The Turkish Language Association (TDK) was founded in 1932 with an aim to promote Turkish, purify the Turkish language and eliminate alien words. While purifying the Turkish language, it removed a large number of Arabic and Persian words that were being used by the population. Fourth, the uprising made some impact on the Mosul city problem which is now in Iraq. The suppression of Kurdish uprising caused many Kurdish tribes in Mosul to decide to remain in Iraq rather than moving to regions in Turkey, which influenced the reports released by the Mosul Commission of the League of United Nations.[29] Fifth, after the uprising, the Kurdish movements in Turkey greatly lost their religious and revivalist Ottomanist features and gained pure nationalist characters.[30]

---

27   Gérard Chaliand, A People Without a Country: The Kurds and Kurdistan, p.54.

28   The Republican Progressive Party (Terakkiperver Cumhuriyet Partisi) consisted of famous generals and officials who participated in the Independent War of Turkey. It was a conservative party which advocated more liberal approach about secularism and was mildly critical against Kemal government. On June 3, 1925, the Turkish government announced it was illegal and outlawed it.

29   Mehrdad R. Izady, The Kurds: A Concise Handbook, p.38.

30   Ibid.

Sixth, a large number of Kurds have fled to Syria and settled down there, resulting in the problem of "stateless Kurds" of Syria.

2.2.2 The Mount Ararat Uprising (1927-1932)

Kurdish nationalists around the world held a conference in Lebanon in August 1927 and established the National Kurdish League. The participants came from the Kurdistan Revival Association, the Kurdish Independent Committee (Khoybun)[31] and the Kurdish Social Committee. The uprising won the support of Armenian nationalist organization Dashnak and the Soviet-backed International Minority Movement. The conference decided to launch an uprising at Mount Ararat which was near the border of Armenia and Ihsan Nuri Pasha (1896-1976) from Bitlis would serve as the general commander. The uprising army declared that Kurdistan was independent. It occupied the region surrounding the Lake Van like Van and Bitlis in 1928. In the following year, the rebel army controlled a vast area from Mount Ararat to the north of Lake Van and Bitlis and founded a government led by Ibrahim Pasha. From May 1930, the Turkish government mobilized its troops with over 60,000 soldiers and 100 aircrafts to attack Mount Ararat. The uprising was soon suppressed. Nuri Pasha fled to Iran (and died at Tehran in 1976). Many leaders were arrested and executed. About 100 Kurdish intellectuals were wrapped with sacks from feet and sunk into the Lake Van. In August 1930, Turkish Prime Minister Inönü[32] publicly declared: "Being instigated by foreign forces, this rebellion in our East region has lasted five years, but now it is on the decline. Only the Turkish nation is entitled to ethnic and national rights in this country, which cannot be enjoyed by other ethnic groups."[33] In the meantime, Turkey cooperated with Iran. Turkey promised to return the Eastern part of Mount

68

---

31   Being also known as Independence, it was a Kurdish nationalist organization which was founded at Lebanon in October 1927. Its members were mainly Kurdish intellectuals with artistic background in Turkey. Jaladet Bedir Khan was the first president. Its headquarters lay in Aleppo of Syria.

32   As a Turkish military strategist and politician, Ismet Inonu (1884-1973) was the second President of Turkey (1938-1950) and the second figure in the Republic of Turkey during Kemal's period. He was born in Izmir and graduated from Military Academy of Istanbul. Being a faithful disciple of Kemal, he participated in the national liberation war led by Kemal in 1920 and worked as the congressman of TBMM and chief of the general staff of the government army. He served as Minister of Foreign Affairs in 1922. After the establishment of the Republic in 1923, he was elected Prime Minister twice. After the death of Kemal in 1938, he became President and lifelong Chairman of CHP. CHP failed in the general election held in 1950 and he became the leader of the opposition party. After the military coup in 1960 which overthrew the regime of Menderes' Democratic Party, Inonu organized and unified the cabinet for three times (1961-1965) and implemented the plan of economic construction. He was overthrown by Bülent Ecevit, quitted the CHP and died of illness on December 25, 1973.

33   Newspaper Milliyet, Aug.31, 1930.

Ararat which used to be owned by Iran back to this country. In exchange, Iran allowed the Turkish army to enter into its territory to besiege rebels and cut off their retreat routes to Iran. These two countries signed a border treaty on January 23, 1932, eventually determining the their historical boundaries up to date. They also signed a treaty of friendship and a treaty of arbitration on the same day.

During the uprising, the Turkish government restored the Security Law and the special courts. It also enacted the Law No. 1850, which stipulated that "any behavior made by any organization and individual in the uprising regions for the purpose of hunting and killing rebels would not be considered as a crime and thus not be punished" from June 20 to December 10, 1930. It actually allowed the army forces to slaughter the Kurds. IOS (International Socialist Organization) passed a resolution on August 30, 1930 and condemned the massacre targeting Kurds: "The cruel repression is far beyond what is required to restrict the actions undertaken by the Kurdish people for freedom". It appealed to various countries in the world to be concerned regarding the "massacre" being conducted by the Turkish government.[34] Indian nationalist leader Nehru also criticized the Turkish government, saying: "The Turks who just fought for their independence are now suppressing the Kurds who demand independence. How strange! A self-defense type of nationalism turns to be aggressive".[35]

After this uprising, Turkey accelerated its implementation of assimilation policies. On May 5, 1932, the Turkish government passed a law to deport the Kurds and divide Kurdistan into four districts. "Due to health, material, cultural, political, strategic, public order and other reasons, a secured zone" was established in the fourth district, and all the Kurdish people should leave this zone.[36] According to the law, a large number of Kurds were forced to migrate into other parts of Anatolia; meanwhile, a population of Turkish people would immigrate to Kurdish regions. Furthermore, Kurdish immigrants would not exceed 1/10 of the local population where they were relocated. Ethnic groups speaking non-Turkish languages as mother tongues could neither establish their own villages, towns and cities nor found any artisan associations and labor unions. In the winter of 1932, millions of Kurds were displaced from their homes under the escort of Turkish soldiers. This law had a great impact on population structure, social system and especially affected the traditional tribes (families) in Kurdistan and weakened the roles of Kurdish tribal chieftains and Sheikhs. Since the day when the law was enforced, the Kurdish people were regarded as "Turks

34   Gérard Chaliand, A People Without a Country: The Kurds and Kurdistan, p.57.
35   Jawaharlal L.Nehru,Glimpses of World History,Vol.2, Allabad,1935, p.1108.
36   Hawar, No.8, 1934.

in Mountains" or "Eastern Turks" in the official documents.[37] After that, speaking Kurdish mother language in the public was fined. Each spoken word was worth five kurush (monetary unit in Turkey).

2.2.3 The Dersim Uprising (1937-1938)

The Kurdish people in Dersim had the tradition of being resistant against the central government. A report released by the Turkey's Ministry of the Interior in 1926 emphasized it was necessary to take tough measures in the region. In accordance with the 1932 Migration Act, Dersim was declared as a province where the Kurdish people should be forced to migrate. TBMM (National Assembly) passed the Resettlement Act on June 13, 1934 and speeded up the assimilation and relocation process. On December 25, 1935, Act No. 2884 (Administrative Law related to Tunceli Province) renamed Dersim to be Tunceli. The Turkish government launched a campaign of opening new schools, building roads, setting military guard posts and deporting the Kurds to other parts of the country, which was strongly opposed by the Kurds in Dersim. On June 6, 1936, the Turkish government appointed a general prosecutor in this province for strengthening control there. President Kemal delivered a speech in TBMM on November 1, 1936, saying the Kurdish issue in Dersim "has become the most important interior problem of Turkey".[38]

In March of 1937, due to an event that a Turkish soldier raped a Kurdish woman, a serious conflict broke out in Dersim. Subsequently, the government mobilized an army to repress the protests. Local tribes (families) elected Sheikh Seyid Riza as the leader of the uprising. The uprising army soon controlled a region of about 200 square kilometers, including Dersim, Bingol and Elazig provinces.

In May 1937, the Turkish air forces bombed the rebels. Sheikh was arrested in September, he and his two sons as well as several tribal chieftains were hanged after the trial in November. During February to September, 1938, the Turkish army completely annilihated the rest of the Kurdish militants in this region. Minister of the Interior announced at TBMM that "We no longer have the Kurdish issue, since these bandits have learned their lessons, our army has achieved that..."[39] The Turkish government ordered to deport all Kurdish people who engaged in this uprising to other cities and provinces. According to the official report given by the fourth prosecutor, Turkish troops killed a total number of 13,160 civilians and expelled

---

37 The Kurdistan File, p.29.
38 M.A. Hasretyan, Türkiye'de Kürt Sorunu (1918-1940), Berlin: Wesanen, Instituya Kurdi, 1995, p.262.
39 The Kurdistan File, p.29.

11,818.[40] According to some other experts about 40,000 people were killed.[41] The Kurdish sources have claimed that the figure was 70,000.[42] Many tribal leaders were shot after their surrender, and women and children were burned to death.[43]

On August 11, 1937, two Iraqi Kurdish politicians Imam Qasim and Ismaili Hakki called on the Iraqi government and foreign governments to interfere in the deportation policy enforced by Turkey against the Kurds. He accused Turkey of using poisonous gas to deal with the Kurds and meanwhile required the international community to send a committee composed by the representatives from neutral countries and investigate the Dersim massacre. Many Kurdish people defined the Dersim event as a genocide. On October 14, 2008, the Kurdish PEN passed a resolution, which said Turkey committed genocide when suppressing the Dersim uprising.[44] However, the Turkish government has considered, this evaluation of the event was greatly exaggerated. A Turkish court gave a ruling in March 2011 that the Dersim event was not genocide.[45] Some scholars believed that, in accordance with international law, this event was ethnocide because it aimed at destroying the Kurdish language and national identity.[46] But a few months later the Turkish Prime Minister Tayyip Erdogan made a public apology for the Dersim event on behalf of Turkish government in November, 2011, saying that the Turkish army had killed 13,806 Kurdish people from 1936 to 1939.[47]

After the Dersim uprising, the Kurdish armed insurgencies in Turkey experienced a long period of silence under the strict control and repression of the government. During WWII, Kurdish tribal chieftain Said Biroki in the Eastern border region of Turkey launched a revolt in July 1943, demanding autonomy, but it was suppressed in less than one month. Thereafter, the Kurdish armed resistance movements did not resume until the 1980s.

During the Independence War of Turkey, Mustafa Kemal has recognized the existence of the Kurds as a nation, saying that the Ottoman country and the New Turkey was the common homeland of Turks and Kurds and even mentioned the possibility of a Kurdish autonomy, but that declaration

40   Radikal Newpaper, November 19, 2009.
41   David McDowall, A Modern History of the Kurds, I.B.Tauris, 2002, p.209.
42   "Dersim 38 Conference",http://www.pen-kurd.org/almani/haydar/Dersim-PresseerklC3A4 rungEnglish.pdf.
43   "The Suppression of the Dersim Rebellion in Turkey (1937-38)", www.hum.uu.nl/medewerkers/m.../Dersim_rebellion.pdf.
44   "Dersim 38 Conference", http://www.pen-kurd.org/almani/haydar/Dersim-PresseerklC3A4 rungEnglish.pdf.
45   "Turkish Prosecutor Refuses to Hear Dersim 'Genocide' Claim", Hürriyet Daily News, Mar.14,2011.
46   George J. Andreopoulos ed., Conceptual and Historical Dimensions of Genocide, University of Pennsylvania Press, 1994, pp.141-170.
47   "Turkish PM Apologizes over 1930s Killings of Kurds", Associated Press, Nov.23, 2011.

mainly aimed to win their support during the war of independence.[48] After the establishment of the new Republic, M. Kemal soon changed his attitude towards the Kurds. While suppressing the Kurdish insurgencies, his government embarked on a large-scale systematic Turkization.

His understanding of the Kurdish issue has laid a solid foundation for the Kurdish policies which were followed by the Turkish government for the future 90 years and also determined their core content. Kemal's personal understanding regarding the building of the newborn Turkish nation as well as the policies set by him to build a modern Turkey was a key factor that contributed to the Kurdish policies, at the core of which was the Kemalist doctrine.

In the view of Mustafa Kemal and his followers, the decline and collapse of the Ottoman Empire resulted from its backwardness compared to western civilization. Lacking cohesive elements and force for the nation-building and having manifold religions and ethnicities in the society were major obstacles to the progress of Turkey. To achieve the Turkish modernization and its deserved position among civilized nations in the contemporary times, Turkey had to construct a secular, republican and homogeneous nation-state. Sovereignty had to be enjoyed by all citizens and national identity must be established in the new country without ethnic, national and religious differences. Only in this way could Turkey enhance its cohesion and maintain its territorial integrity and unity. Such a homogeneous nationality or nation state had to be achieved as Turkish people being at the core, which forms the majority. As a result, Turkization became to be the core of the government policies and the assimilation of uncivilized Kurds who were the largest minority in Turkey became the key element for the success of these policies. Consequently, the government should re-write the history of Turkey, popularize Turkish language and promote Turkish culture. The Turkish Historical Society (TTK) as a research society was set up in 1925 to re-construct the history of Turks and incorporate Kurds and other minorities into the framework of the Turkish national history. In its great efforts to construct the history of the Turkish nation, the Turkish government constructed the concept that the Turkish nation was civilized and Kemalist elites and supporters of Kemalism were the leaders of civilization. Naturally, the Kurdish people were marked as an uncivilized nation and needed to be civilized. The Kurdish revolt further pushed Kemal to accelerate the construction of a national state and new anti-Kurdish education deepened Turkish elites' perceptions on the Kurds: they were a savage, economically poor and religiously fanatical nation which abided by the old and backward traditions of tribal society, and Kurdistan was a barren turbulent land where thieves, bandits and feudal superstitions prevailed, so their

---

48   David McDowall, A Modern History of the Kurds, I.B.Tauris, 2000, p.196.

such uncivilized existence was an internal threat to the territorial integrity of Turkey and only through tough measures could the Kurds and Kurdistan could be civilized.

In 1925, Minister of the Interior of Turkey submitted a report on the rebellion led by Sheikh Said—The Eastern Report, which suggested governing the Kurdish regions in the colonial way and Turkizing them by forced resettlement. Kemal had a famous saying, which goes: "Those uncivilized nations are destined to be trampled underfoot by the civilized ones"[49]. Kemal's best friend and successor Ismet Inonü publicly stated, "We're sincere nationalists and nationalism is the only factor that unites us together. No other factor enjoys such great influence in the country where Turks account for the majority of the population. No matter what happens, our responsibility is to Turkize non-Turks living in Turkey at any cost. We'll destroy all the those who oppose Turks or Turkism." Mahmut Esat Bozkurt, leading thinker of Kemalism and Minister of Justice had explained the official stance clearer: "My friends and opponents must listen. This is my firm view: Turks are the only God and the sole owner in our country. Those non-genuine Turks only have one right in Turkey, which is to be servants and slaves."[50]

In order to make the Kurdish people forget their national identity, the Turkish government took a series of measures, among which the major one was refusing to recognize their minority status and endeavoring to eliminate their national memory and undermine their Kurdish characteristics in Kurdistan. In the official discourse, the Kurds existed no longer as a special ethnic group, nor a "brother nation", but "Turks in Mountains". The Turkish government ordered historians to reconstruct history for the Kurds and incorporate them into the Turkish nation as well as its historical framework. The new historical view claimed that the Kurdish people was actually a group of "Turks in Mountains" who had "forgotten" their original Turkish characteristics and needed to be told the truth.[51] *The Turkish Dictionary* which was edited by the Institute of Turkish Language and published in 1936 defined the Kurds in the following way: the title "Kurds" refers to people who live inside Turkey, Iraq and Iran and originate from a group of Turkish nation or members of this group; many of them have changed their language and who now speak an incomplete Persian language. Meanwhile, the Kurdish language, traditional costumes, folk music and other Kurdish cultures were forbidden. The word "Kurdistan" which was widely

---

49   "Atatürk's Speech in the Turkish Hearth Association (Türk Ocağı) in Akhisar on 10 October, 1925", Atatürk, 2006, p.668.
50   Milliyet, Sept. 16, 1930.
51   Robert Olson ed., The Kurdish Nationalist Movement in the 1990s, The University Press of Kentucky,1996, p.13.

recognized and used in the Ottoman period was removed from all the maps and official documents. Kurdish names of towns and villages were replaced by Turkish ones. Historical sites and monuments which displayed the existence of the Kurds were destroyed. After the founding of Turkey, a large number of place names were changed. In most cases, those places where minorities dwelled were renamed in Turkish, especially in Eastern Turkey and eastern coastal areas of the Black Sea. Some experts have asserted that numerous places were renamed in Turkey. Among them, 4,200 ones used to be originally Greek names, 4,000 Kurdish, 3,600 Armenian, 750 Arabic, 400 Assyrian, 300 Georgian, 200 Laz and 50 names from other languages.[52]

According to the statistics released by Turkey's official agency Special Committee of Geographical Name Change, all together 12,211 place names were changed, including villages, towns, cities and settlements.[53] Tunceli (formerly Dersim)[54], Gaziantep (formerly Dolok), Urfa (formerly Riha), Hakkari (formerly Colemêrg), Diyarbakir (formerly Amed), Batman (formerly Êlih) and other provinces were endowed with Turkish names. A region, which was known as Piran, in history, was renamed as Dicle.[55] The government launched a massive campaign with such slogans as "I am honorful for being a Turkish", "One Turkish individual is equal in strength to the whole world" and "One language, one nation, one flag".

2.3 The Kurdish Issue in the Turbulent Era of Turkish Democratic Reforms

This era mainly refers to the historical period during 1950s to the late 1980s. Its characteristics can be summarized as follows: Turkey entered a turbulent phase of democratization and the multi-party democratic system which objectively and subjectively offered some opportunities for the Kurdish political activities, but the Turkish government did not change its Kurdish policies and official ideology; in the Kurdish political movement, the old generation of Kurdish tribal or religious leaders were replaced by a new generation of young political activists who were highly educated and lived in cities, and the latter became representatives and leaders of the Kurdish national movements. Details of these developments will be examined further in this chapter. In this new era the Kurds carried out their

52 Sevan Nisanyan,"Hayali Coğrafyalar: Cumhuriyet Doneminde Türkiye'de Degistirilen Yer Adları", Istanbul: TESEV Demokratikleşme Program,2011, retrieved 12 January 2013. http://en.wikipedia.org/wiki/Geographical_name_changes_in_Turkey.
53 Proceedings of the second International Symposium on Islamic Civilization in the Balkans, Tirana, Albania, 4-7 December 2003,Istanbul: Research Center for Islamic History, http://en.wikipedia.org/wiki/Geographical_name_changes_in_Turkey.
54 The Turkish parliament resumed the name back to Dersim through the law in 2012.
55 Geographical name changes in Turkey, http://en.wikipedia.org/wiki/Geographical_name_changes_in_Turkey#cite_note.Proceedings_of_the_second-26.

national movements and expressed their demands through joining various Turkish reformist and left-wing political organizations, merging into the Turkish democratization process and following other peaceful political means. Consequently, all kinds of modern type of Kurdish political groups and organizations which were deeply influenced by socialism and the Soviet Union sprang up. Their political ideas were greatly dominated by "left-wing" ideas. And in the preliminary phase, Kurdish organizations got actively involved in the domestic political violence during 1975-80, but then turned to armed struggle in the 1980s and many militants of the former groups were forced to join the PKK led by Ocalan.

After the death of Kemal Atatürk in 1938, the successor President Inönü did not have the personal charm that could be compared to his predecessor, and CHP (RP Party) was losing popularity due to its authoritarian rule. Industrialization and agricultural modernization of Turkey had encountered profound changes and the demand for political participation and democratization grew rapidly. The principle of "one party, one nation, one leader" which had been implemented since 1923 began to be challenged seriously. Amid the global wave of democratization after the WWII, Turkey started its process of democratization and embarked on historical changes. In November 1945, President Inönü announced that democracy would be expanded and the opposition would be allowed. In the early 1946, a batch of opposition parties like the Democratic Party and the National Development Party were established. In July 1946, a national election was held in Turkey, and CHP won the first elections and gained 391 seats in the National Assembly. The Democratic Party proposed expanding democracy, promoting individual freedoms, developing the liberal private economy and revision of anti-democratic articles in the Constitution and laws, thus won 61 seats. This election marked the turning point that Turkey reformed its one-party dictatorship into a multi-party democracy. After the election, the CHP government adopted a series of measures to improve the image of the ruling party and please its supporters. For instance, it promised to allow Kurds returning back to their hometowns in the east, expand democracy and freedoms and endow local governments with greater powers.[56] The second general election occurred in May 1950. This time, the Democratic Party gained a landslide victory by winning 408 seats and became the ruling party, whereas CHP suffered a surprising defeat and won only 69 seats. Democratic Party leaders Celal Bayar and Adnan Menderes respectively became President and Prime Minister. This general election determined future political history of Turkey, and practically ended CHP's one-party rule, opening the new era of multi-party democracy.

---

56 Quanan, Ha & Shuqing, Zhou, Research on the Political Democratization of the Republic of Turkey, p. 88.

In the process of democratization, the end of one-party system and the implementation of ideological pluralism and electoral politics activated the political participation and social atmosphere in Turkey, which provided a relaxed environment for the Kurdish political activities and stimulated the Kurdish national movements. Different from the previous stage, Kurdish movements during this period expressed indirect demands by taking part in parties and public group activities rather than raising any direct slogan of national autonomy or independence. According to statistics, free associations organized by citizens in Turkey from 1950 when the Democratic Party came to power to 1960 had reached to a number of 18,000 in number, eight times more than the past period.[57]

In the election, both CHP and the Democratic Party proposed relieving cultural constraints imposed on the eastern region and reducing brutal acts that military police made there. Most Kurdish voters supported the Democratic Party, which co-opted a large number of influential Kurdish figures as candidates and they were elected as deputies. It is worth noticing that the external environment during this period also had a significant impact on the Kurdish issue in Turkey. During the 1950s and 1960s, changes in the international political environment and especially vigorous development of national and democratic movements in Asia, Africa and Latin America as well as the wide spreading of socialist ideology in the Third World exerted a significant influence upon the Kurds in Turkey. The new-generation Kurdish intellectuals were deeply influenced by left-wing thoughts. In addition, after the Iraqi Kurdish people waged an uprising in 1961, the Turkish media had reported a lot on it. People in the Kurdish region of Turkey even could listen to the radio broadcasting of the Iraqi Kurdish Democratic Party which resisted against national oppression. These had some effect on the enlightened Kurds from various classes, including upper classes and intellectuals in Turkey.

After the second half of the 1950s, the Democratic Party exercised a dictatorial type of governance, sharpened inner conflicts with the opposition and also the political, economic and social crisis deepened in Turkey. On May 27, 1960, the Turkish military launched a coup, overthrew the government of the Democratic Party and set up the "National Unity Committee". From 1965 on, Turkey gradually entered a period of political turmoil, the struggle between parties has intensified and with the year 1968 the political violence between the left and extreme rightist youth intellectual organizations as well as terrorist activities gradually increased. Taking advantage of this political instability in the 1960s, the Kurds demanded reforms for national rights and conducted some demonstrations and protests. However, the Turkish governments failed to adjust their original Kurdish policy and relax its suppression against the Kurds. In the early 1960, the military regime leader General Cemal Gürsel

76

---

57   Ibid.

declared in Diyarbakir, "(Our) country does not have Kurds. If anyone dares to say he/she is a Kurdish, I'll spurn him in public." He also praised high the historical book which claimed the Kurds originated from the Turks.[58]

He even warned that if any rebellion broke out in the Kurdish region, the army would bomb cities and villages without any hesitation.[59] After the coup, the "National Unity Committee" banned any political activity in the Kurdish cities and 484 eminent Kurdish persons were arrested; 49 famous Kurdish intellectuals were put on trial for propaganda and inciting riots; 55 local Kurdish landlords (Aghas) were deported to western provinces.[60] In the same year, Forced Resettlement Law (Law No. 105) was issued, which stressed the necessity to eliminate the social order of the medieval times in the East, such as chiefdom and religious leadership system so as to promote the social reform progress. In 1961, the military announced the establishment of the National Security Council (NSC), which comprised of ten members including President, Chief of Staff, Armed Forces Commander, Defense Minister, Foreign Minister, Minister of the Interior, etc. Its main responsibility was to check the elected governments according to the new Turkish Constitution of 1961 and deal with internal and external security threats, but later its powers were expanded and conflicts occurred especially between it and the right wing parties and governments due to constitutional checks by the former.

Political Parties Law was passed in 1964, which prohibited the establishment of ethnic-based political parties and banned the recognition of the existence of different ethnic groups and languages in Turkey. In 1965, the former domestic security organization attached to Interior Ministry was formally reorganized as the National Intelligence Agency (MIT), which was responsible for security and intelligence work inside and outside and was especially tasked to strictly investigate communists even leftists, ethnic separatists and extreme right Islamic activists. It has played a crucial role in repressing the Kurdish national movement.

During the 1960s, the Kurds joined or founded a variety of political organizations and actively participated in Turkey's political process of democratization and liberalization. Therefore, the Kurdish national consciousness has further developed. Joining the left-wing political parties and organizations became one important feature in this phase. The Turkish Workers' Party (TIP) was established in 1961 and became the first socialist party

---

58   Christopher Anderson, "Kurds in Turkey: Building Reconciliation and Local Administrations", March, 2009, http://beyondintractability.colorado.edu/case_studies/kurds_in_turkey.jsp?nid=6825.
59   David McDowall, A Modern History of the Kurds, I.B.Tauris, 2000, p.404.
60   Henri J. Barkey and Graham E. Fuller, Turkey's Kurdish Question, Carnegie Corporation, 1998.

which won 15 seats in the Turkish parliament. TIP has made a great impact on the political stage after 1964 and led the worker and peasant movements and left-wing movements in Turkey throughout the 1960s till 1971. It was banned twice respectively in 1971 and 1980 and merged with the exiled Communist Party of Turkey headquartered in East Berlin into the Joint (United) Communist Party of Turkey in 1988.

In the parliamentary election held in 1965, this socialist party supported by the pro-Soviet exile party has won 3% votes and 15 seats. With a reform oriented interpretation the party believed in Marxism and opposed class oppression, besides mildly opposed the national oppression of the Kurds. Immediately after its entry into the parliament, it mildly brought the "Eastern Issue" (Kurdish Issue) onto the political agenda of Turkey.

The TIP and another left-wing organization Confederation of the Revolutionary Worker Unions (DISK) contained a lot of Kurdish members and leaders. The left-wing Revolutionary Workers Union (DISK) was established in 1967. Also some Kurdish enlightened land-lords leaders had entered the parliament through the lists of TIP. Influenced by the Iraqi Kurdish Democratic Party and under the leadership of Faik Bucak (1919-1966)—a Kurdish lawyer-writer and poet from Urfa, the Kurdish Democratic Party of Turkey (KDPT) was founded in November 1965. But Faik Bucak was assassinated in July, 1966, and Serafettin Elçi (1938-2012) became his successor. Subsequently, this party split into two mutually hostile factions and fled to Iraq, inside which it undertook political activities. Its new leaders Dr. Shivan and Said Elçi were both assassinated in Iraq in 1971.[61]

The Kurdish Democratic Party of Turkey was basically a mouthpiece of the Iraqi Kurdish Democratic Party. Its ideological line and program has copied its Iraqi counterpart, and it has disappeared without playing a vital role in Turkey.[62] A radical organization separated from this party in 1970s was called PPKK or Vanguard in English and Pesheng in Kurdish. In the period between 1965 and 1980, the left-wing Revolutionary Workers Union (DISK) organized a lot of strikes, protests and demonstrations. While DISK led a "Labor Day" Parade in Istanbul in 1977 together with communist and left-wing parties a tragedy occurred which resulted to 37 deaths, probably behind the mass shooting attack was a covert state organ.

The famous Turkish left-wing militant youth organization "DEV GENC" was founded in 1969. It was composed of both Turks and Kurds and its members were mainly middle school and college students. It nurtured

---

61   Who was the assassin maintained a mystery. It is said the national intelligence agency of Turkey or Mullah Mustafa Barzani made it.
62   In September 1992, Turkey established the Kurdish Democratic Party (PDK/Bakur), also known as the Kurdish Democratic Party of Northern Kurdistan, and it was listed as one of twelve terrorist organizations and three major Kurdish separatist agencies.

plenty of radical left-wing organizations like PKK, DEV YOL,[63] DEV SOL,[64] THKP-C, TIKKO, THKO. Abdullah Ocalan who became the leader of PKK had been deeply influenced by THKP-C. A famous liberal journalist also declared that Ocalan was a member of a nationalist/Islamist/anti-Western organization named The Great-East inspired by a famous ideologue and poet Necip Fazıl Kısakürek, whose poems are loved by Tayyip Erdogan.

It was also banned after the military coup of 1971. The Eastern Revolutionary Cultural Center (DDKO) was set up in Istanbul and Ankara in 1969, and later its branches were established in Kurdistan cities. It advocated reforms demanding improvements of political, economic and cultural rights for Kurds. This was the first new-type Kurdish political association.[65] It believed that the nature of the Kurdish issue had changed, turning to be a problem of a nation oppressing another nation and a problem of national class struggle instead of being an underdevelopment problem in a certain region, and only a progressive power could rescue Kurdish nation from the double chains.[66] This organization played a vital role in arousing the class and national consciousness among the Kurds.[67]

In October of 1970, many of its leaders were arrested and trialed in Istanbul. During this period, the Kurdish nationalist ideology was characterized by diversity. There were two major schools: the first one believed in Marxism-Leninism, holding that only socialism could solve the Kurdish issue, and the Kurdish nationalism, like its counterparts in other countries, was the natural ally of the international socialist-communist movement; the latter rejected Marxism, but was "left-wing democratic" in its thought and practice, such as the Kurdish Democratic Party.

Under the relatively free political environment in the 1960s, a trend of "Easternism" thought which was named "Doğuculuk", emerged in the Turkish society among Turkish intellectuals. Its main idea was not to ignore the remote and underdeveloped area in the east and demanded that the government should attach importance to its social and economic development. The east actually referred to Kurdistan, and the use of it resulted from the fact that the words of "Kurd" and "Kurdistan" were still politically

---

63   It was founded in 1976 and banned in 1980.
64   It was founded in 1978. It assassinated former Prime Minister of Turkey Nihat Erim, which directly led to the military coup in July 1980. At present, some of its fractions still maintain active in Turkey.
65   After it was banned in 1971, DDKD was established. And then it split during the mid-1970s and "Freedom Trail" was founded, which changed its name to be the Turkish Kurdistan Socialist Party in 1979.
66   Philip G. Kreyenbroek, Stefan Sperl, The Kurds: A Contemporary Overview, Routledge, 1992, p.101.
67   The Kurdistan File, p.32.

taboos in Turkey. This trend of thought lasted about ten years, directly or indirectly stimulating a large number of Kurdish intellectuals to enter the road of Kurdish nationalism. From 1967 to 1969, a lot of protests broke out in Kurdish cities and towns, appealing for civil, economic rights, demanding people's livelihood and cultural rights. For example, they demanded increasing investment in education, schools, roads, bridges and factories and agricultural mechanization at the Kurdish region, also dissent against landlord oppression and demand for land were important demands.

These demands were not exclusively nationalist or separatist in nature, but they were all various forms of national separatism in the eyes of the Turkish government, which accordingly continued to take repressive measures. The Turkish extreme right-wing leader Alparslan Türkeş who was also involved in the 1960 coup publicly threatened to carry out "final solution" to the Kurds, which was similar to what was done to the Armenian people in 1915. He claimed, "If the Kurds dream of founding their own country, they should face the destiny of disappearing from earth. Turkey has been established at the cost of countless blood and labor of the Turkic nation, which is able enough to deal with those people coveting the Turkic land. She has cleared the Armenians on her own land in 1915 and the Greeks in 1922". The Kurdish region was placed under military control and martial law was implemented there. In 1969, Special Forces (Kommandos) were set up by the Turkish army, which were led by the Ministry of the Interior and responsible for seizing weapons and "hunting insurgents and bandits" in the Kurdish region.

From 1969 to 1970, Turkey faced a serious political unrest. Massive workers', peasants' and students', teachers' movements broke one after the other, and political meetings, parades, mass protests as well as some leftist terror acts has emerged in an endless stream. On March 12, 1971, the Turkish army launched a coup again and meanwhile imposed martial law in 11 provinces and banned all left-wing political parties and Kurdish organizations across the country. Furthermore, "in order to safeguard national unity and eliminate terrorism", it arrested a lot of Kurdish activists. Hundreds of Kurdish intellectuals, workers and peasants were put in jail during 1971 to 1973. Deniz Gezmiş (1946-1972), leader of the left-wing Marxist-Leninist THKO, and 2 other leaders of this organization was hanged with the charge of "overthrowing the regime by armed struggle" in 1972. Gezmiş was a young Kurdish student leader and one of the idols worshiped by the PKK leader Ocalan in his early political career. In this historical context, the Kurdish movements gradually became more radical between 1974-1980, and these activists desired to eliminate feudalism and religious influence, change the underdeveloped status of the Kurdish region and demanded the free use of Kurdish language in publishing, broadcasting and education.

After the 1971 coup, dozens of Marxist and leftist Kurdish organizations appeared within a short time, which participated in the fierce fight between left-wing and right-wing youth organizations across Turkey. These Kurdish left organizations were organically combined with the Turkish Marxist organizations but later after 1976 a political and organizational separation occurred. The split line was the strategic priority issue, whereas Kurdish Marxist and Kurdish left organizations advocated the national liberation as the first priority and accused the Turkish Marxists for the ignorance of the national issue. Kurdish Marxist and Kurdish left organizations held that there was a great revolutionary power and potential hidden in the Kurdish issue which could revolutionize whole Turkey and even the whole Middle East region, thus should be the key priority in the revolutionary strategy.

After DDKO was banned in 1971, DDKD was founded in 1975 as the successor and continued to undertake covert propaganda. Ocalan, before organizing his own political party criticized this organization as the advocator of "national-chauvinism" and accused its members as "national reformists". This was the period when he was rather affected by the Marxist-Leninist thoughts and his national liberation idea was ambiguous.

Throughout the 1970s, Turkey fell into crisis especially owing to Cyprus Invasion War (1974), and with frequent changes of government, economic downturn, serious social and income gaps, constant student and workers' protests, union and peasant movements, flooding violent and terrorist activities. Cyprus Invasion War had deteriorated Turkey's relations with the West, economically, politically and militarily. Besides, Soviet influence over the Marxist parties, left and democratic intellectuals, unions and among CHP deputies had greatly increased between 1976-80 which was led by East Berlin based TKP (Communist Party of Turkey). In 1973-74, CHP led by B. Ecevit embraced a left course, with the hope of launching a democratic-left change similar to Portugal, Greece and Spain.

In the late 1970s, Turkey was actually caught in multiple crises of ideology, politics, economy and security. Kurdish leftist radicals seriously criticized that the Turkish government ignored the fundamental rights of the Kurdish nation and strongly demanded that the political and economic rights of the Kurds should be recognized. They separated from the left-wing Marxist organizations of Turkey which advocated armed struggle such as THKP-C originally[68] (later split and took the names as Dev-Yol and Dev-Sol and KURTULUŞ and HALKIN YOLU as 4 separate parties the last

---

68   Its leader was Mahir Çayan (1946-1972), well-known student leader of the 1960s and founder of the Party in 1971-72 and one of the important model figure for Abdullah Ocalan. For being involved in kidnapping Israeli ambassador to Turkey, he was arrested. Soon he escaped and passed to rural areas to organize armed struggle, but soon he and his comrades was shot in Kızıldere in the fight with armed forces on March 30, 1972.

one being Maoist), THKO (Turkish People's Liberation Army), the Maoist TKP-ML (its armed wing as TIKKO). Consequently Kurdish Marxist-Leninist left-wing groups or parties, including the Kurdistan Democratic Party, PKK (Kurdistan Workers' Party), DDKD, SPTK (Socialist Party of Turkey's Kurdistan)[69] the KUK, the Pioneer Workers Party of Kurdistan, RIZGARI,[70] ALA RIZGARI[71] and KAWA and DENGE-KAWA were formed, the last two being Maoist parties.[72]

In the eastern region, the Kurdish leftist organizations developed vigorously. In the 1960s and 1970s, leftist organizations in Turkey including Kurdish ones, nearly all pursued the ideas of "people's war and armed propaganda." Through active armed campaigns, they attacked state agencies to awaken the masses, attract public attention and show the state's inability and weakness to protect itself.[73]

In September of 1979, Turkish Navy Commander Bülent Ulusu said that the eastern region was "boiling", where "Communists and Kurdish people are conducting a comprehensive cooperation". Bülent Ecevit, the liberal social democrat leader of the CHP who acted as the Prime Minister twice in the 1970s, also held a tough stance, insisting that there was no Kurdish issue in Turkey, but only a problem of economic and social development.[74]

69   It was founded in 1974 with the name of SPTK and it changed its name into PSK in 1992. Its leader Kemal Burkay (1937-) was an Allawi follower. Being a relatively moderate socialist, this party opposed violent revolution pursued by the PKK. It proposed a two-step strategy: the first one was to achieve the Kurdish autonomy under the federal framework of Turkey; the second step would be to realize socialism in the unified Kurdistan. Kemal Burkay established a magazine entitled Road to Freedom in 1975 and a newspaper named Roja Welat in 1977. After the 1980 coup, he fled to Sweden and continued his political activities and was deprived of Turkish citizenship. After an agreement with the Erdogan government he returned back to Turkey and re-established a socialist-nationalist party named as Rights and Freedoms Party (HAK-PAR)

70   It was a Kurdish Marxist party which was established in 1976. It emphasized in its program: "Since the Kurdish nation is under the colonial rule of Turkey, we cannot expect the Turks to liberate Kurds and only through a socialist revolution led by the Kurdish proletariat freedom of Kurds will be won." It split in 1979 and was banned in 1980.

71   It separated from the left-wing Marxist Turkish organization "KURTULUŞ" (Liberation) which upheld Marxism-Leninism, whose political line was similar to Trotskyites of the Soviet Union and which basically pursued non-violence with a rather flexible political stance. It was banned in 1980.

72   Being established in 1976, they were "Maoist" left-wing radical parties, adhering to armed revolution and being anti-Soviet, pro-China. It was split in 1978 due to the "Three Worlds Theory" raised by the CPC, and was prohibited after the military coup in 1980.

73   Michael M.Gunter, Historical Dictionary of the Kurds, p.40.

74   Bülent Ecevit (1925-2006) was a politician and the former Prime Minister of Turkey. He served as the Prime Minister of Turkey twice in the 1970s, during which he sent troops to Cyprus in 1974 when he ruled a coalition government with the Fundemental Islamic Party of Erbakan. He became the Prime Minister of the joint government with the Motherland Party and Extreme Nationalist party (MHP) in 1999, but failed in the renewed national election of Nov. 3, 2002 after the coalition government was dissolved by the MHP.

The 1980s was a period when some Kurdish left parties grew, with PKK being the prominent and dominant among them, and re-stepped on the road of violent resistance. A military coup took place again in Turkey on September 12, 1980, a few days after a demonstration by Islamic radicals in Konya. Chief of the Staff, General Kenan Evren[75] was the leader of the military coup. The pretext declared was the "massive armed conflicts between left and right wing organizations, massive terror acts, and the two major parties being ineffective to bring a joint national political solution due to their alliances with the extremist parties of the left and right."

After arresting the leaders of political parties and banning their political activities, he announced the dissolution of the parliament and Cabinet, set up the National Security Council of five military leaders and established a government of civilian politicians from above. Since he became the head of the state, he established a pro-military government, which banned all political parties and arrested a large number of politicians, unionists, huge number of leftist activists and left-wing intellectuals plus activists of the extreme right wing party. On November 7, 1982, a new Constitution drafted by the military government was passed in the national referendum, which restricted political activities, slightly strengthened the presidential authority and strengthened the executive authority used by the Cabinets and limited the power of the Parliament (legislative organ) and the judiciary power.

83

After Evren officially became president, he enacted a new law of political parties and a new electoral law in the first half of 1983, which stipulated the following: "civil associations, professional organizations must not engage in political activities and cooperate with political parties; political parties must not found youth, women and other affiliated organizations; only political parties that can obtain the 10% of national votes could enter the parliament; a new political party must have branches in 34 out of 67 provinces across the country." The regulation of 10% was specifically set for Kurdish and extremist parties and specifically election coalitions among

75   General Kenan Evren was the seventh and the last president of Turkey (1982-1989) with an army background. He was born at Alaşehir County of Manisa Province in 1918 and graduated from the Artillery School in 1940 and Higher Military Academy of Istanbul in 1949. During 1958 and 1959, he served as director and chief of staff of military operation and training in the Turkish Brigade which was stationed in the South Korea. He was promoted as the brigadier general in 1964, major general in 1967, lieutenant general in 1970, admiral in 1974 and chief of staff of the Turkish armed forces in March, 1978. He led the military coup on September 12, 1980. Taking over the state power, he appointed himself as head of the state and established a pro-military government. He officially became President on November 7, 1982. He insisted on the establishment of a secular state following Kemalism, opposed Islamic interference in politics, strengthened the supreme authority of the state and legal authority, encouraged the development of private enterprises and advocated strengthening of relations with the United States and the European Community and was loyal to NATO alliance of Turkey.

small parties were prohibited. Under the new law, though there were more than 20 political parties in Turkey, only the Motherland Party, the National Democratic Party and the Populist Party were allowed to take part in the general election held in November of 1983, among which the latter two were designed and tasked by the military. By a surprise, the Motherland Party led by Turgut Ozal[76] (former leader of an influential businessman association and World Bank expert) won the election obtaining 211 seats and established the civilian Cabinet, but was strongly supported and checked by the President Kenan Evren who represented the political influence of the military forces.

During this period, the Kurdish struggle for national rights has transformed from political struggle into armed revolt. After the establishment of PKK in 1978, it immediately carried out assassinations and sabotage acts a part of which targeted other rival Kurdish Marxist organizations so as to monopolize the movement around itself. After the coup, PKK headquarter and guerilla training camp was moved to Syria, with the help of Syrian government. On August 15, 1984, PKK attacked Siirt and Hakkari, killing three people and wounding eleven, which opened a prelude to its guerrilla warfare. From August 15, 1984 to 1991, about 2,500 people were killed. The fight between PKK and Turkish security forces as well as village guards employed by the government dragged the Kurdish region into a kind of civil war, which caused heavy casualties and property losses. Apart from PKK, many other Kurdish organizations carried out armed struggle during the same period. On June 10, 1988, eight Kurdish organizations including the Banner of Liberation, KUK-Se, Parrhez, PDK-RN, PPKK, PSKT, SK and YSK announced the establishment of TEVGER at Brussels, capital of Belgium and declared that they would launch armed struggle in Kurdistan.

After the 1980 coup, Turkey's repression and assimilation policies targeting the Kurds had reached its peak. The military regime stressed that Kurdistan had become a special threat for the national unity, so more strict measures were employed. The new measures included the following:

---

76 Turgut Ozal (1927-1993) worked as advisor of the State Planning Organization, member of Coordination Board of the European Community, special projects advisor of World Bank, economic advisor of Prime Minister and vice-chancellor of the State Planning Organization after 1976. He became Deputy Prime Minister and Foreign Minister in May 1983. In May of 1983, he established the Motherland Party and served as the chairman (1983-1993). In December of the same year, he became Prime Minister. The Motherland Party won for the second time in the general elections of November 1987, and he continued to be the Prime Minister. He was elected as the eighth President of Turkey in November 1989 until he died. The hospital announced he died of heart failure, but his wife insisted her husband was poisoned. In October 2012, Turkish prosecutors decided to open the coffin and examined the corpse to determine the cause of his death.

First, adhering to and strengthening of the assimilation policies. The Turkish government resolutely eliminated all Kurdish organizations, prohibited the use of Kurdish language and banned the expression of Kurdish national identity. After the 1980 coup, 81,000 Kurds were arrested. Article 89 of the 1982 Constitution prohibited any political party from defining itself as an organization of defending, developing and disseminating non-Turkish language and culture. Article 28 stipulated that "publishing and broadcasting industries are prohibited from using languages banned by law".

In October 1983, Turkey enforced the Law on the Use of Non-Turkish Languages (Article No. 2932) and banned the public usage of Kurdish language. By 1986, 2,832 out of 3,524 villages in Adiyaman, Gaziantep, Mardin, Siirt and Diyarbakir were renamed in the Turkish language. Law of Population Registration (Article No. 3080) which was modified and passed on November 15, 1984, prohibited parents naming their newborn babies with Kurdish names. In December 1982, the Minister of Education warned the city governors that Kurdish folk songs must be only sung in Turkish to prevent people being influenced by ethnic separatists. In 1988, several Kurdish deputies as members of the CHP were disqualified for their public support of the report issued by the European Commission which said Kurdish was an ethnic language and the Kurdish issue existed in Turkey.[77] In April of 1990, the Turkish government enacted the Article No. 413, endowing regional governors with greater powers, such as the power to ban any news and publication if they "falsely reflect the regional (Kurdish region) conflicts or events and make false reports or commentaries".

Second, enforcing state of emergency (OHAL) in Kurdistan region and stationing troops in a large-scale, which reached 200,000 soldiers by the early 1990s. The population in the city of Tunceli was only 19,000, but there was a troop composed of 55,000 people. After the 1980 coup, Turkey imposed a martial law across the country. In April 1987, Turkey applied to join the European Union. To please EU, Turkey cancelled the martial law in four provinces on July 19, 1987, but announced to enforce OHAL in these areas and set up a position called regional governor (all known as super governor). National Intelligence Agency official Hayri Kozakcioglu was appointed as the first regional governor, who ruled eight provinces where PKK carried out active campaigns. The power of regional governor mainly included: directing the security and special forces; controlling the National Intelligence Agency; promoting officers and raising wages; emptying or merging village and pastorals; supervising civil trials against security agencies; leading provincial governors.

---

77   Kemal Kirisci and Gareth M. Winrow, The Kurdish Question and Turkey: An Example of a Trans-State Ethnic Conflict, London: Frank Cass Publishers, 1997, p.112.

Third, continuing to expel the Kurds. Merely in the first month of 1987, people of 234 Kurdish villages in Tunceli were expelled to western regions, and 275 villages in Erzurum, Erzincan and Kars were emptied. Article No. 413 of 1990 endowed regional governors with the power of forced eviction. Within a few months, Kurdish people and villages that were expelled increased dramatically. According to the investigation about eastern migrants made in 1987, though economic factors played an important role in the westward migration of the Kurds, political and security factors were the most crucial ones behind.[78]

Fourth, implementing the village guard system to make the Kurds deal with the Kurds. To deal with the PKK and enhance security in the east, the Turkish government amended Village Guards Law in April 1985, allowing the government to raise fund and recruit local Kurds to fight against armed forces of the PKK. Thus, the village guard system was officially introduced. Village guards were similar to Hamidiyeh cavalry in the Ottoman Empire and Jash[79] in Iraq, and all of them were Kurdish armed forces that were pro-government. Due to poverty and high unemployment rate in the Kurdish region, many villagers were attracted to join village guards. The annual income per capita in poverty-stricken regions was less than US $ 400 in 1992, whereas the monthly salary offered to the guard members was up to $ 230. Driven by the government, the number of guard members kept growing from 20,000 in 1990 to 35,000 in 1993 and even reached as high as 100,000. Being familiar with local conditions in the Kurdish region, they were good at collecting intelligence and dealing with the PKK. Their existence threatened the PKK severely. As a result, the PKK treated them as a target of attack. The establishment of the village guard system exacerbated the conflict in the Kurdish region, deteriorated the security situation and sharpened the internal contradiction among the Kurdish people. A survey among the Kurdish migrants revealed that 70.3% of them left home because of the village guard system.[80]

Fifth, in order to enhance international support and strike the PKK bases in Iraq with cross-border operations, Turkey made an agreement with Iraq in October 1984 about the control of the Kurds on respective territories and allowing cross-border operations to attack and hunt rebels. Turkey made use of this agreement for its operations against the PKK. On May 26, 1983, 15,000 Turkish troops marched as deep as 40 kms into the Iraqi territory. In October 1984, Turkish army launched the "Sun Action" against the PKK

78 Ibid., p.134.
79 Jash is translated to be "little monkey" and thus has a slanderous meaning. It refers to Kurdish (village) guards which are employed by the government.
80 "Post-Conflict Reconstruction and Humanitarian Consequences of the Village Guard System", Evren Balta, Fall 2004.

forces in Iraq. On August 15, 1986, it bombed northern Iraq and sent special forces to fight against the PKK. On March 4, 1987, thirty fighter jets bombed PKK targets in Iraq, causing 170 injured and 12 deaths. 1986, it bombed northern Iraq and sent special forces to fight against the PKK. In 1985, Turkey built a barbed wire wall along the border regions with Syria to prevent the PKK from infiltrating. The Turkish Prime Minister Turgut Ozal requested to cooperate with Iran in terms of border security in February 1988, but Iran did not respond positively. In 1992, Syria closed the Mazlum Korkmaz Camp of the PKK at Beqaa Valley of Lebanon.

In the late 1980s, the international community paid more attention to the Kurdish issue in Turkey. On February 11, 1988, the US State Department mentioned in its annual report of the world's human rights that Turkey should recognize the minority status of the Kurds and criticized that there were abundant and serious phenomena of torture in Turkey. This report caused strong resentment by the Turkish government and was accused by the Turkish media. At the same time, use of the Kurdish language as a taboo began to be broken in Turkey and first open debates about Kurdish insurgencies took place in the Turkish society. The mainstream view claimed that the only language that the Kurds understood was violence and tougher policies had to be adopted, but an increasing number of politicians became aware that military means would not solve the problem of "hearts and minds" in the Southeast region. In 1978, Sherafettin Elçi, Minister of Public Construction at the Ecevit Cabinet, declared publicly, "I'm a Kurdish. There are Kurdish people in Turkey". After the military coup, for saying this, he was sentenced to two years and three months in prison on the charge of "separatist propaganda"[81].

In February 1986, the SHP (successor of the CHP) claimed that the entire southeastern region was like a concentration camp, where citizens were treated as suspects and suffered from oppression, torture and humiliation.[82]

On January 19, 1988, Mehmet Ali Eren, Kurdish deputy from the SHP (Social Democratic Populist Party) said that there was the Kurdish nation in Turkey, which should not be ignored and publicly demanded that the Turkish parliament should solve the issue. Like a bombshell dropping into the Turkish political arena, it immediately hit the headlines of the main newspapers. Right-wing organizations and deputies condemned it one after another. Conflict also broke out inside the SHP, but the party chairman defended that Eren had something wrong in his expression and what he only

---

81   "At last: Kurdish classes in Turkish schools", Hurriyet Daily News, June 3, 2010, http://www.hurriyetdailynews.com/atlastkurdishclassesinturkishschoolsaspx?pageID=238 &nID=23008&NewsCatID=411.
82   Martin Van Bruinssen, "Between Guerilla War and Political Murder: The Workers' Party of Kurdistan, PKK", Middle East Report, No.153, July-Aug.,1988, p.42.

intended to illustrate was that there were different languages in Turkey.[83] Some Kurdish deputies of the Motherland Party showed their concern over the Kurdish policies in 1988 and one deputy was dismissed for openly raising the Kurdish issue in the parliament. In the autumn of 1989, seven Kurdish deputies of the SHP were dismissed, because they participated in the International Conference on "Kurdish National Identity and Human Rights" in Paris. Many other Kurdish deputies resigned to protest it. In the same year, Aksoy, a congressman of the SHP (Social Democratic Populist Party), mentioned that the Kurdish deputies had made a mistake by meeting the deputies of the European Parliament and thus was expelled from the party. This event accelerated the division of the party. In June 1990, several Kurdish deputies left the Social Democratic Populist Party and founded the People's Labor Party (HEP).[84]

It was the first legal Kurdish party in the Turkish parliament. Since then, the Kurds have had a political party in the parliament to represent them and voice their demands. In July 1990, the Social Democratic Populist Party published a lengthy report on the southeastern problem and gave suggestions about how to solve it, which included the following: to allow the free expression of Kurdish national identity; to allow the free use of the Kurdish language; to abolish the village guard system and regional semi-military enforced governor system; to cancel the state of emergency law related to Kurdish cities; to formulate and implement a plan of regional social-economic development. In addition, a part of the mainstream media criticized the government's policies. Renowned reporter Mehmet Ali Birand has argued that continuing to deny the existence of the Kurds was actually an "ostrich" policy, which should be changed. Meanwhile, the Kurdish people were constantly wakening. In March 1990, families of the PKK militants who were killed held a public funeral for them, which developed into mass protests. The government had to enforce a curfew in 11 cities and towns including Mardin and Siirt. The security forces shot at the protesting masses and more than 100 people were killed on March 20.

---

83   The Kurdistan File, p.41.
84   This party was the source of other Kurdish parties in the Turkish parliament. After it was banned, new successor Kurdish parties were established immediately, including HEP (founded in 1990 and banned in 1993), DEP (founded in 1993 and banned in 1994), HADEP (founded in 1994 and banned in 2003), DEHAP (founded in 1997 and merged with the Democratic Social Movement into DTP in 2005), DTP (founded in 2005 and banned in 2009) and BDP (Peace and Democracy Party founded in 2008) latest being the HDP (Peoples' Democratic Party).

2.4 The Kurdish Issue in the 1990s

The years from 1991 to 2002 witnessed a major change in the landscape of the Middle East and even the whole world. The disintegration of the Soviet Union and the fall of many socialist states including the SU urged the world's nationalist movements to gain a separatist nature. The start of the peace process in the Middle East in 1990, the Gulf War in 1991 and the "9/11" incident caused Turkey to face a new situation in the Middle East and the Kurdish issue became even hotter. To enter the EU soon, Turkey implemented a series of reforms and made some minor adjustments to its Kurdish policies in a symbolic sense. The Turkish government publicly acknowledged the existence of the Kurdish issue and relaxed the original limitations on the political activities of the Kurdish parties and the use of the Kurdish language. At the same time, armed activities undertaken by the PKK showed and increasing trend, till it encountered a big setback after the capture of PKK's Chairman Ocalan in 1999. In December 2003, United Nations HCR agency issued the Assessment Report on Turkish Kurds. It pointed out that their social and political circumstances had improved during the recent years: constraints on the Kurdish language were relaxed; Kurdish parties were allowed to be founded and engage in political activities under certain legal restrictions; some Kurdish artistic and cultural centers were allowed to perform. Yet, the Kurdish people in Turkey were still discriminated greatly and the resolution to the Kurdish issue still faced big obstacles.[85]

The most serious impact that the Kurdish issue brought to Turkey in the 1990s was the Gulf War. On August 2, 1990, Iraq outrageously invaded Kuwait which shocked the entire world. After a heated debate on September 5 of 1990, the Turkish parliament authorized the government to send troops to Iraq and allowed foreign US troops to be stationed in Turkey and pass through its territory. Present Turgut Ozal expressed his support of the US's dispatching troops to Iraq and willingness to provide military logistics for the western powers. After the outbreak of the Gulf War in January 1991, the problem of Iraqi Kurdish refugees immediately became the toughest issue confronting Turkey, which also revealed the Kurdish issue of Turkey to the international community.

By the support and instigation of the US, the Iraqi Kurds took this opportunity of Gulf War to wage an uprising against Saddam, but the uprising was soon suppressed by the Iraqi government and a large number of refugees flooded over the borders into Turkey. The first batch of Kurdish refugees entered into Turkey on the March 31, 1991, and about 700,000 refugees

---

85 "Minorities at Risk Project, Assessment for Kurds in Turkey", Dec.31, 2003, http://www.unhcr.org/refworld/docid/469f3add1e.html.

flocked there by mid-April, which posed a difficult problem for the Turkish government. Turkey was unwilling to accept Kurdish refugees, but their tragic situation as well as the massive humanitarian disaster caused it to change its conservative stand. This was the first time for the international media to focus on Iraq and Kurdish refugees in a large scale.

Western television screens were filled with scenes of Kurdish refugees. The reports by various kinds media outlets and social media exerted a tremendous impact on the western public and imposed a huge political and moral stress on Turkey. If Turkey didn't open the borders and didn't help, the Turkish Kurds would also demonstrate anger against the government. However, accepting a large number of Kurdish refugees was an unbearable economic and social burden for Turkey and could frustrate its vulnerable economy and bring about serious political and security issues. Iraqi Kurdish refugees swarming into and staying for a long time could not only transform the structure and scale of Turkish population, but possibly radicalize the Turkish Kurds and lead them to imitate the struggle way of the Iraqi Kurds. Besides, the armed forces of the PKK which is based in Northern Iraq (Qandil) might enter Turkey hiding among refugees and take this opportunity to increase their armed attacks. Therefore, the Turkish government initially did not allow those refugees to enter Turkey and emphasized that there would be intractable logistic and financial problems, if it accepted them. Yet, with this problem getting more and more serious and the international community showing great concern over it, the Turkish government began to change its attitude. On April 2, the Turkish government called for the UN Security Council to discuss about this issue and take actions. On April 4, Turkey submitted a resolution draft to the Security Council, agreeing to provide military bases for Cooperation Provide Comfort (OPC) while condemning Iraq and meanwhile requiring the international community to provide assistance for it. On April 5, the UN Security Council passed Resolution No. 688, which condemned the crackdown made by the Iraqi authorities against the Kurds and established a safety zone. Turkey announced to open its borders and allow 20,000 refugees, mainly the elderly, children and pregnant women, enter. President Ozal said on April 7 that the establishment of safety zone in Northern Iraq was "a fresh idea", which means Turkey had changed its attitude towards the Kurdish policies of Iraq as well as its own Kurdish policies and relaxed its long-standing policy of opposing the split of Iraq and would tolerate a status quo change in the region. Turkey knew that, although the West said the establishment of a safety zone was a temporary solution, actually it was probably to exist permanently as the refugee camp in Palestine and threaten the sovereignty of Turkey. As for Turkey, the acceptance of this safety zone meant that it must admit the autonomy of the Iraqi Kurds and allow them to became a quasi-state in Iraq. It was British Prime Minister John Major who first proposed the founding of a safety zone in Northern Iraq, and that was later supported by the US President Bush. On April 10, Turkey announced that it had dispatched troops to control the refugees in Iraq. After the US ground forces entered Northern Iraq on April 17, British and French troops also arrived successively. They founded the "safety zone". By the end of April, about 17,000 Allied soldiers entered Iraq, and by mid-June, all refugees were returned to Iraq. In the short term, Turkey was successful in the issue of refugees. Since then, there has been a Kurdish "safety zone" at Northern Iraq, which brought many new challenges to the politics, diplomacy and security of Turkey.

The outbreak of the Gulf War and particularly the establishment of a safety zone at Northern Iraq created a golden opportunity for the PKK. It took advantage of the favorable situation that the Iraqi government lost control of the north to expand its influence there and strengthen its attacks on Turkey. From 1991 to 1992, the conflict between the PKK and the Turkish security forces resulted in 17,500 deaths.[86]

For this reason, Turkey waged cross-border air raid and ground assault on Iraq, which was criticized by the international community and caused worries among its neighboring countries. Some countries doubted the intention of Turkey, thinking it coveted Iraqi territory and attempted to annex Kirkuk, Mosul and other oil-producing regions. The EU expressed its opposition, and Syria and Iran also suspected Turkey for the fear of its hegemony in the region. As a result, Turkey sent special representatives to make explanation to Syria and Iran. Representatives from the three countries held a conference at Istanbul on November 14, 1992, promising to maintain the territorial integrity of Iraq and respect its sovereignty. In May 1997, the Turkish army launched a massive offensive in Northern Iraq. Iraqi Foreign Minister Al-Sahaf sent letters to UN General Secretary Kofi Annan and the Security Council, requiring the UN to intervene and stop Turkey from violating Iraq's territory.

At the same time, the Gulf crisis made Turkey's leadership represented by President Ozal realize the significance of recognizing the Kurdish issue in Turkey and that in Iraq. After the war, a Kurdish entity would be founded at Northern Iraq under the protection of the West and this trend was unstoppable. Therefore, Turkey must take the initiative to participate in this process and win the right to speak; otherwise, it would only play the role of an envious spectator. The development of the Iraqi Kurdish regional government not only had a direct impact on solving the problem of the PKK, but also possibly stimulated the Kurds in Turkey as a model. Thus, Turkey felt necessary

---

86 http://en.wikipedia.org/wiki/15_August_1984_PKK_attacks.

to establish relations with the Kurdish autonomous government in Iraq and persuade it to break its relations with the PKK. Ozal began to revise Turkey's traditional Kurdish policy. On March 11, 1991, Ozal announced that officials of Turkish Foreign Ministry and National Intelligence Agency had held talks with the Iraqi Kurds in accordance with his instructions and said that this move was made for the sake of friendship. The Kurdish leaders invited to participate in these talks were Jalal Talabani, the leader of the social democratic Kurdish Patriotic Union and Muhsin Sezhay, a heavy weight leader of the Iraqi Kurdish Democratic Party (led by Barzani). This contact was criticized by the main opposition party in Turkey. Ozal also encouraged people to discuss the Kurdish issue openly and broke certain taboos in Turkey. He submitted a bill to the TBMM (National Assembly) in February 1991, requesting to amend the Act No. 2932 and allow the use of the Turkish language in regions except broadcasting, publishing and school education. In April 1992, Turkey officially lifted the ban on the Kurdish language, allowed the use of Kurdish in broadcasting and TV and permitted the teaching of Turkish as a second language at schools. In 1992, Ozal made another bold proposal: to grant amnesty for PKK militants.

He acknowledged, the PKK was a participant in the political system of Turkey and said that "The Republic of Turkey is facing an unprecedented threat. A social earthquake will cut away part of Turkey and we'll be buried below".[87] In February 1993, Ozal wrote a letter with six pages to prime Minister Demirel[88], in which he mainly talked about the growing influence of the PKK, the increasing isolation of the Kurds from the government and the PKK's long-term threat to the Turkey's territorial integrity. He proposed reconsidering the policy of mass expulsion of the Kurds so as to win their hearts.[89] Ozal not only had a great influence on the military, but enjoyed a reputation among the Kurds, so he was an appropriate person for solving the Kurdish issue in the political way. Ozal represented the radical faction in Turkey, whereas the conservative faction led by Demirel opposed to do so and considered it contrary to the Constitution.

---

87 The Independent, Nov.13, 1993.
88 Süleyman Demirel (1924-2015) a major politician in Turkey, who served as Prime Minister for seven times and became the 9th President in 1993. He graduated from the Civil Engineering Department of Istanbul Technical University in 1949 and studied in the United States. He worked as director of the State Water Conservancy Bureau during 1955 to 1960, joined the Justice Party in 1962 and was elected as chairman of this party in 1964. He became Deputy Prime Minister in 1965 and Prime Minister in October 1965. After the military coup he was arrested but later he became the chairman of the True Path Party in 1987. In November 1991, he won the national elections and set up the cabinet and served as Prime Minister of the coalition government of the True Path Party and the Social Democratic Populist Party. On May 16, 1993, he was elected to be the 9th President of Turkey.
89 The Independent, Nov.13, 1993.

Ozal died unexpectedly on April 17, 1993,[90] and Demirel became President.[91] After the inauguration, he made clear that he would never negotiate with the PKK or make any compromise and he planned to increase troops in the Kurdish region to 300,000 people. However, he acknowledged that "Turkey has admitted the Kurdish reality". In the 1990s, Kurdish political organizations publicly stepped on the political arena of Turkey and actively participated in local and national elections. They spoke at the parliament on behalf of Kurdish people and required to expand ethnic and cultural rights of the Kurds and improve their human rights as well. In the general election held in October 1991, the True Path Party led by Demirel won with 27.3% of the votes and established a Cabinet with the Social Democratic Populist Party (20.8%) together. The People's Labor Party (pro-Kurdish) and the Social Democratic Populist Party jointly participated in the election. The former made impressive achievements in Kurdistan and won 22 seats elected by the region's voters. During the election, it promised to abolish the emergency state and the village guard system. The new government proposed carrying out a series of liberalization reforms and did not raise the Kurdish issue directly, but it mentioned there existed different ethnic groups in Turkey which should be given rights to express and develop their cultural identities and meanwhile it stressed such an attempt would enhance rather than undermine the national unity.[92]

On November 6, 1911, when new deputies took the oath of office, some radical Kurdish deputies like Leyla Zana[93] refused to read "The state and the nation are inseparable". Leyla Zana wore a traditional Kurdish headscarf and "swore on behalf of brother Turks and Kurds", causing a strong resentment among the right-wing parities. Since the coalition government announced to extend the Emergency Law for another four months in March 1992, 14 congressmen of the People's Labor Party quitted from the parliament to show their protest. Famous Kurdish intellectual Musa Anter was assassinated in September 1992. In 1993, Mrs. Tansu Ciller[94] became the Prime Minster.

90   A conspiracy theory said that Ozal was assassinated by ultra-rightists who were worried about his radical Kurdish policy.
91   Four candidates engaged in the ninth presidential election, including Demirel nominated by the True Path Party, and Kamran Inan (1929-), a Kurdish candidate elected by the Motherland Party. Kamran Inan was a politician and diplomat of Turkey. He was a parliamentarian at TBMM and once served as the ambassador of Turkey to the UN. He was often quoted by the government to show that the Kurds did not suffer discrimination.
92   Kemal Kirisci, Gareth M. Winrow, The Kurdish Question and Turkey: An Example of a Trans-State Ethnic Conflict, Routledge, 1997, p.137.
93   Leyla Zana (1961-) is the first female Kurdish parliamentarian at TBMM and one of the most well-known Kurdish political activists in the contemporary times.
94   Born in 1946, Tansu Ciller was a politician in Turkey and the first female Prime Minister of Turkey. After the party leader Demirel assumed the Presidentship of the Republic in 1993, she served as chairman of the True Path Party and established a cabinet. Her government collapsed in 1995, and then she joined the Erbakan administration, which

At first, she was relatively moderate in dealing with the Kurdish issue, but soon she became increasingly tough. The pro-Kurdish People's Labor Party was banned in July 1993. Subsequently, some members set up the DEP as its successor, and the Constitutional Court even disqualified an elected Kurdish deputy named Fehmi Isiklar.[95]

In March 1994, Leyla Zana and other 12 DEP deputies were deprived of their legislative immunity and were jailed. On June 16, the Constitutional Court outlawed the Democratic Labor Party and arrested several leaders of this party. In the same month, several deputies of this party established the new party HADEP. In September, Mehmet Sincar, a deputy of the DEP was assassinated. In December 1994, Leyla Zana and other six democratic deputies as well as one independent deputy were sentenced to 15 years on the charge of supporting the PKK. Some former Democratic Labor Party deputies who had fled to Europe set up the Kurdish Parliament in Exile (PKDW), at Hague of the Netherlands on April 12, 1995 and held the first conference. The former leader of the Democratic Labor Party Yasar Kaya worked as the chairman, and the former vice chairman Remzi Kartal worked as the chairman of the Executive Committee. They declared that this organization would aim at strengthening the national liberation struggle to end the alien occupation of Kurdistan, defend the political, cultural and social rights of the Kurds and "achieve self-determination of the Kurdish nation".[96]

---

fell down in 1997. Following her failure in the general election held in 2002, she announced to withdraw from the political arena.

95   He was the founder and chairman of the People's Labor Party.

96   PKDW comprised of 65 representatives and the Executive Committee of 15, with seven boards below. In the first conference, PKDW proposed a 35 point program and its main contents were: to establish a free national assembly of Kurdistan; to sign a voluntary unity agreement with neighboring nations/ethnics of the region; to strengthen the national liberation struggle to end the alien occupation of Kurdistan; to take plans to defend political, cultural and social rights of the Kurds; to implement provisions in the Geneva Convention of 1947 and 1977 and to achieve common ceasefire; to submit the Kurdish issue to the UN, the OSCE, the European Council, the European Parliament and other international institutions; to enable Kurds to obtain the observer status in the international institutions mentioned above; to persuade the international community to enforce political, military and economic sanctions on Turkey; to try to achieve the unity of all Kurdish parties, institutions, organizations, associations and important figures; to end Kurdish partisan struggle in Iraq; to draft constitutional and legal provisions related to civil rights as well as civil, criminal and environmental issues; to establish Kurdish schools and universities; to persuade the Kurdish youth, not to serve in the enemy army, instead serve in the Kurdish National Army; to build friendship with other nations, including Turkish people. This organization claimed to represent all Kurdish people, but was generally regarded as the mouthpiece of the PKK. Thus, United Kingdom, United States, France and Germany refused to recognize it. Kurds in Iraq and other places also did not admit its representative authority, thus it was dissolved in May 1999, and the Kurdistan National Congress (KNC) was founded.

Its headquarters was set in Brussels. The pro-Kurdish People's Democratic Labor Party (HADEP) participated in the general election of December 1995, which was the first time that a Kurdish party was permitted to take part in the election. This party won 4.17% votes and won the highest votes in some Kurdish provinces, but failed to enter the parliament due to the 10% threshold. The Islamist political party—the Welfare Party[97]—gained more votes than it in the Kurdish region.

In July 1996, the Welfare Party characterized by the main ideologies of Anti-Turkism (Turkish Nationalism) and Pro-Ottomanism and Fundemental Islamism came to power, and its leader Necmettin Erbakan became the Prime Minister. Erbakan believed that it is necessary to admit the existence of the Kurds, cancel the emergency state enforced in southeastern Kurdish regions and lift restrictions on the Kurdish language. He declared to solve the Kurdish issue by enhancing the unity among all Muslims of Turkey, he said: "Kurds, Turks we are all brothers and sisters of the same belief." Yet, he did not attempt any progress in this problem when he was in the office. In June 1996, the People's Democratic Party hang the flag of the PKK instead of the national flag of Turkey, and all of its leaders were arrested. During 1998 to 1999, the Turkish Constitutional Court attempted to ban this Kurdish party for several times, but failed. In this context, some members of this party set up the DEHAP on October 24, 1997. In the general election held in April of 1999, the People's Democratic Party won 4.75% of the votes, which had only increased by 0.58% compared to the previous elections, but still could not enter the parliament. It obtained mayors' seats in over thirty cities of the southeastern region. In January 2000, Mesut Yilmaz,[98] chairman of the Motherland Party and important minister of the coalition government, declared that the path between Turkey and its accession to the EU passed through Kurdistan (solution of the Kurdish issue), and he emphasized that if the Kurdish issue was not resolved in a democratic way, Turkey would not be accepted by the EU.

---

97   The Welfare Party was founded in 1983 and formed a coalition government with the True Path Party in 1996. Due to its Islamist policies which challenged the specific Turkish secularism, it encountered severe conflicts with Turkish military and Kemalist bureaucracy. The Constitutional Court outlawed the Islamist Welfare Party in January 1998. In May of the same year, the party members founded the successor Moral Party (Fazilet Party).
98   Mesut Yilmaz was the chairman of the Motherland Party, a center-right political party. It was founded on May 20, 1983 by T. Ozal. It obtained 9.65% of the votes in the general election in December 1995 and became the second largest party in the parliament. However, in the general election held in April 1999, it became unpopular and ranked as the fifth largest party. It established a coalition government with the Democratic Left Party of Ecevit and the Democratic Turkish Party in July 1997 and another coalition government with the Democratic Left Party and the Nationalist Action Party in June 1999. Mesut Yilmaz served as Prime Minister twice (March to June of 1996 and June of 1997 to January of 1999) and as the Deputy Prime Minister in Ecevit administration (1999-2002).

During this period, many Kurds established Kurdish cultural associations and human right organizations. The Mesopotamian Cultural Center (MCC or MKM) was founded in 1991 and the Kurdish Institute in 1992. Both of them devoted to spreading Kurdish language and culture and made a lot of achievements in promoting Kurdish language and culture, thus being oppressed and banned by the government. In May 1997, the branch of the IHD was closed by the police and many members were put in jail. At the end of the same year, the Urfa branch of the MCC was closed by policemen who also arrested some people. In addition, Kurdish politician Serafettin Elci set up the DKP in 1997, which advocated that the Kurdish issue should be solved through democratic means. Holding that the PKK was a result rather than a cause of the Kurdish issue, DKP called on the government to admit the Kurdish characteristics, establish a new national system and enforce federalism. It was banned in February 1999. Furthermore, the Turkish government also abolished many Kurdish journals and newspapers in the 1990s, such as Facing 2000 (1992), Agenda (1992-1993), Free Agenda (1993-1994), Free Land (1994-1995) and New Policy (1995).

In the 1990s, the armed conflict between the PKK and the Turkish security army intensified, and the eastern regions almost fell into a civil war. The PKK strengthened its guerrilla battles and treated Syria and Iraq as a springboard to penetrate into the Kurdish region of Turkey. It expanded its attack targets and scopes and meanwhile established underground regimes in some towns and counties. Its armed forces reached a peak of 10,000 to 15,000 active fighters with 50,000 to 75,000 backups by 1994.[99]

From 1991 to 1995, the armed conflicts led to at least 15,000 deaths, six times compared to 1990. The deteriorating security situation forced a large number of Kurdish people to immigrate from their villages and towns to bigger cities and western cities. According to the report issued by the Turkish Ministry of the Interior, during 1992 to 1994, there were 5,210 schools that were closed for security reasons in the eastern region. A mass of immigrants made cities expand dramatically (see Tab. 2-4). A report of the Turkish government pointed out: "PKK, weakened in south-eastern Turkey, had changed tactics and started to move its recruitment and terrorist activities into urban regions with high concentrations of Kurdish immigrants.[100]

By the late 1990s, the Turkish government had attained a major breakthrough in its fight against the PKK. Ocalan, leader of the PKK, was arrested and this organization suffered a heavy blow in 1999.

99　"Terrorism: Middle Eastern Groups and State Sponsors, Kurdistan Workers' Party (PKK)", Global Security CRS Report, Aug. 27, 1998.
100　Kemal Kirisci and Gareth M. Winrow, The Kurdish Question and Turkey: An Example of a Trans-State Ethnic Conflict,p.136.

Tab. 2-4 Population Change in Major Kurdish Cities due to Increase of Domestic Immigration

Year / City	1990	1994	1996
Batman	148	260	--
Diyarbakır	380	950	1300
Hakkari	38	100	--
Urfa	276	650	--
Van	153	300	500
Total	995	2260	

Unit: One Thousand People

Source: The data were sorted by the author.

The Turkish government continued to adopt harsh polices and crack down on the insurgencies, which were demonstrated as follows:

(1) It imposed pressure on the countries in support of the PKK and forced them to cease their support at the threat of violence. Turkey stationed armies on the border of Syria in October 1998, threatening Syria to stop supporting the PKK, close the PKK camps inside Syria and hand over Ocalan. Under the coercion of Turkey, Syria had to close the PKK camps and expel Ocalan. After being deported, he fled to various European countries and eventually was arrested in Kenya on February 15, 1999, for no country accepted his application for asylum. This was the biggest victory that Turkey won in attacking the PKK and also a significant turning point in the development of the PKK. The arrest of Ocalan was a heavy blow to the PKK, which subsequently changed its strategies and tactics. Ocalan declared a ceasefire, gave up armed struggle and required for a peaceful resolution while more widely mobilizing the world opinion to put pressure on Turkey. Furthermore, Turkey waged military operations on the PKK targets inside Iraq.

(2) It continued to increase military presence in the Southeast and took new anti-guerrilla strategies. By the end of 1994, coupled with the police, Special Forces and village guards, the Turkish security forces in the southeastern region increased to 300,000 people, including soldiers, gendarmeries and policemen and Special Forces, all of which engaged in the counter-terror battles in the region. The mountainous geography of Kurdistan was convenient for the PKK to carry out guerrilla warfare. As a result, the Turkish government cut down and burned out forests in the east and also

emptied villages in some regions. In July 1995, a Turkish minister admitted that at least 2,664 villages were emptied and about 2 million people had become homeless.[101] In the summer of 1999, villages that were emptied exceeded 3,500 in number.[102] A research report released by the Turkish Human Rights Association in 1995 said: "90% of the respondents claimed to leave their homes under the government's pressure and 88.7% believed they were expelled just because they were Kurdish. And this policy was extremely harsh for the people." Only agricultural production losses in 1994 had reached up to $ 350 million. Livestock production fell by 50% and forest areas were reduced by 60% around the Diyarbakir city.[103] Once President Ozal had also thought that the best way to solve the Kurdish problem was to remove the Kurds into the west, because their separatist sentiments could weaken if they enjoyed a better life there. Yet, he stressed immigration must be done in a careful and planned way.[104]

(3) It made use of such right-wing organizations as the Kurdish Hezbollah to fight against the PKK and assassinate Kurdish politicians. Founded in late 1970s, the Kurdish Hezbollah was a radical religious organization which opposed secularism, Marxism-Leninism and Kurdish parties that worshiped these thoughts like the PKK. Since it conducted brutal struggle against the PKK, it was regarded as the "Betrayer Party of the Kurds" by the PKK. Sunni Hezbollah was supported by the military and intelligence agencies of Turkey. In the 1990s, it was suspected of killing 500 Kurdish rebels and executing 5,000 mysterious deaths in the region. Although the Turkish government denied its support of or relationship with the Hezbollah, an objective fact was that Hezbollah had never attacked the police and soldiers and the latter had never attacked Hezbollah either.[105] Caglar, former Cabinet Minister of the Turkish government, said the Turkish army not only employed the Hezbollah members, but funded it. He claimed that the government had made the decision to support Hezbollah and allow it to deal with the PKK as early as in 1985. Arif, a retired colonel from the Turkish army, admitted that he participated in the establishment of Hezbollah for the purpose of cracking down the PKK and added that the organization's initial name was Hizbul-Kontr.[106] A report made by the Parliamentary Investigation Committee of Turkey pointed

---

101 Milliyet, Nov. 19, 1994; Milliyet, July 25, 1995.
102 David McDowall, A Modern History of the Kurds, I. B. Tauris, 3. Revised edition, 2004, p. 440.
103 Ibid.
104 Kemal Kirisci and Gareth M. Winrow, The Kurdish Question and Turkey: An Example of a Trans-State Ethnic Conflict, p. 135.
105 The Scene behind Turkey's Fight against Hezbollah, Yangtze Evening News, Jan. 30, 2000.
106 Turkey Officer Says He Created Local Hezbollah Group, Star Says", Bloomberg News, Jan. 18, 2011, http://www.bloomberg.com/news/2011-01-18/turkey-officer-says-he-created-local-hezbollah-group-star-says.html.

out in 1993 that Hezbollah had a training camp in the Batman region, where it obtained political and military training as well as funding from the Turkish security forces. However, it began to struggle against the government after the late 1990s.[107]

During this period, Ozel TIM and JITEM were also actively involved in the assassinations, causing many people missing. Vedat Aydin, chairman of provincial branch of the People's Labor Party, was assassinated in July 1991. Many members of this party were assassinated in 1994. Three Democratic officials of Marash (Maraş) Province were assassinated in December 1995. Three Kurdish politicians were shot to death in June 1996.

(4) It continued to implement the village guard system and the state of emergency. In spite of facing a powerful voice which required abolishing the village guard system, the number of guards increased from 18,000 people in 1990 to 63,000 in August 1994. The village guard system played a vital role in helping the government to fight against the PKK, but it brought a lot of problems as well. For example, the Kurdish community was divided; brothers killed each other; besides village guards were suspected of being involved in a variety of criminal activities. The Political Murders Investigation Committee of the Turkish parliament accused village guards of selling weapons, slaughtering rivals indiscriminately, participating in murders, trading drugs and doing other illegal things. One member of the committee said that misdeeds made by these village guards pushed many Kurds towards the PKK, which expanded the influence of the PKK. The government continued to enforce the state of emergency status. In July 1987, Turkey began to impose the state of emergency status in 11 cities, including Bingol, Diyarbakir, Elazig, Hakkari, Mardin, Siirt, Tunceli, Van, Bitlis, Mus and Adiyaman, where governors ruled the region in a semi-militarily way.

Later, Batman and Sirnak were added, so the number increased to 13. From 1994, Turkey began to gradually reduce the number of places in which the emergency state was enforced, and finally abolished it in November 2002. In June 2002, the TBMM (National Assembly) decided to completely cancel the emergency state in the Kurdish region since November 30. On that day, the Turkish government officially cancelled the emergency state imposed upon Diyarbakir and Sirnak provinces, marking the complete end

---

107   In January 2000, the Turkish authority carried out a nationwide campaign against Hezbollah. On January 17, the Turkish security forces launched a lightning attack on a villa at Istanbul where Hezbollah was possibly to hide, and they shot its leader Vellioglu to death and captured its two key members alive. Subsequently, the Turkish police conducted a carpet search around the country. According to statistics, approximately 3,300 members of this organization were arrested in Turkey and a mass of weapons were seized. Through research on various documents and weapons captured, a large number of unclear cases in the history came to light.

of this law which lasted 15 years in the Kurdish region of Turkey. The Turkish Interior Minister Aksu said, the cancellation symbolized that Turkey's southeastern regions have restored the normal social order.

Fig. 2-3 The Southeastern Region of Turkey where the State of Emergency Status Was Enforced during 1987-2002

Source: Kermanshahi, "OHAL region in Turkey 1987-2002",
http: //en.wikipedia.org/wiki/File: OHAL.png.

(5) It enacted a tougher anti-terrorism law. A new anti-terrorism law was formally enforced on April 12, 1991, in which the most crucial Article No. 8 made it possible that any scholar or reporter in open support of Kurdish rights and cause would face the charge of favoring terrorism. The new definition of terrorism was not only broad in content, but ambiguous in meaning, thus being very easily abused. The new anti-terrorism law was criticized severely inside and outside Turkey. A report released by the Turkish Human Rights Committee in 1994 said that 95 intellectuals, politicians and scholars were arrested for violating the anti-terrorism law. A scholar was sentenced to stay in prison for 200 years, as his publication breached this law. Besides, the law entitled the authorities to greater power and caused them to be involved in a large number of mysterious murders. In the 80ies, there were only 11 unsolved homicide cases in Turkey, but the number went up dramatically: 31 in 1991, 362 in 1992, 467 in 1993, 400 in 1994 and 92 in 1995.[108] In September 1992, famous Kurdish writer Musa Anter was assassinated.[109] Akin Birdal (1948-), well-known Kurdish human rights activist and chairman of the Turkish Human Rights Association, got

108 Kemal Kirisci and Gareth M. Winrow, The Kurdish Question and Turkey: An Example of a Trans-State Ethnic Conflict, p. 129.
109 The European Court of Human Rights alleged that the Turkish government should be responsible for this case and fined it 28,500 euros.

injured in an assassination that happened in May of 1998.[110] In October 1995, under internal and external pressure, Turkey amended the Article No. 8 in the anti-terrorism law: narrowing the scope, reducing the punishments and shortening the prison terms.

2.5 The Kurdish Issue in the Erdogan Era

From 2003 to date, four major events have exerted significant impact on the Kurdish issue, namely, the Adalet ve Kalkınma Partisi (Justice and Development Party) winning the general elections in 2002, the outbreak of the Iraq War in 2003, the EU starting to negotiate with Turkey about its entry in 2005 and the "Arab Spring" that started in 2011.

The new Turkish government led by Erdogan accelerated to reconsider the Kurdish issue and adopted some measures to improve the situation of the Kurds and recognize the Kurdish national identity, but in breaking through the old conceptual and policy framework, it did not make significant progress. Meanwhile, the government still continued the armed suppression targeting the PKK as its main policy. On August 14, 2001, the AKP with Islamist tendency which was born out of the Welfare Party and the Moral Party was established.[111] In the Turkish general election held on November 3, 2002, the AKP stood out and won two-thirds (363) of the total seats in the parliament, which brought it the opportunity to form a single party cabinet, thus the era of multi-party coalition cabinets in Turkey since 1987 was left behind. In the local council election in 2004, this party obtained a second victory, winning 1,750 local councils with 42.185% votes. Subsequently, the party won the general elections in 2007 (341 seats) and in 2011 as well as the local elections in 2009. Turkey had a stable elected government which was a rare state since the 1960s.

101

After AKP came to power, positive changes took place in the Kurdish policies. The Turkish government still insisted in harshly cracking down on the PKK as well as separatism and terrorism, but it began dialogues with the arrested leader of PKK, Abdullah Ocalan, and took practical measures to improve the situation of the Kurds, expand their national rights and accelerate the economic development of the Kurdish region. Thus, there appeared a "Kurdish Spring" for a while. AKP had a quite different attitude and policies on the Kurdish issue compared with the previous ruling parties, which is demonstrated in the following four aspects: first, the Kurdish government used to simply attribute the Kurdish issue to economic (or eastern),

---

110   He was sentenced to prison being accused of "inciting ethnic hatred" in the public in September 1996. Amnesty International listed him as political prisoner.

111   Immediately after the Moral Party (Fazilet Partisi) was banned in June 2001, its members founded the Felicity Party (Saadet Partisi). Tayyip Erdogan and some other members quitted the Felicity Party and founded the AKP.

terrorist or security reasons, while AKP considered it as a comprehensive issue involving political, economic, social and security factors and admitted the discrimination against the Kurds existed for a long run; secondly, AKP publicly acknowledged the Kurds and the existence of the Kurdish issue, emphasized ethnic and cultural diversity of Turkey and gave up the "Turkization" policy which had been implemented for 80 years; third, AKP no longer adopted the simple assimilation policy, counter-terrorism and military means, but instead emphasized integrated solutions and proposed dealing with it fundamentally, such as stressing the common Islamic identity, expanding democracy, enhancing efforts to develop economy and allowing ethnic groups to express their unique characteristics; fourth, AKP treated the PKK with both soft and hard tactics: making certain dialogues with it while continuing to attack it, which was also a major breakthrough.

Directing at the Kurdish issue, the party program of AKP pointed out frankly in 2005: "Unfortunately, this issue is a realistic one confronting Turkey, which is said to be the Kurdish issue or a terrorist problem. Our party recognizes that cultural diversity actually exists in this region (the east and southeast). As long as Turkish remains the official and educational language, we believe allowing non-Turkish languages to undertake cultural activities (including broadcasting) will be a benefit, which will strengthen rather than undermine the unity and territorial integrity of our country. Terminating terrorism requires the government to adopt policies to respect fundamental rights and freedom and also have new ideas to treat economic development and security as a whole. Every citizen of the Republic of Turkey is a binding agent that unites our society together."[112] The party program not only recognized the existence of the Kurdish issue, but proposed new ideas to solve the problem. It emphasized a civil society approach to the issue—the civic nature of solution—instead of Turkization or assimilation—which was promoted in the past. In August 2005, chairman of the AKP Erdogan[113] openly said: "there is a Kurdish problem in Turkey and more democracy should be needed," and meanwhile he swore to solve it and promote and establish a "democratic republic". He stressed, "The Kurdish issue was a problem of all of us and particularly a problem of mine".[114] He became the first Turkish Prime Minister who admitted the government made mistakes

---

112　"AKP Party Program, 2.6. The East And The Southeast", http://eng.akparti.org.tr/english/partyprogramme.html.

113　Recep Tayyip Erdogan (1954-) was born in Istanbul and later joined the Welfare Party and was elected as mayor of Istanbul in 1994. In 1998, the State Security Court of Turkey deprived him of the right to engage in politics and sentenced him to 10 months in prison for he issued "speech that incited religious hatred". He established the AKP in 2001 and has served as chairman since then. In 2002, the AKP won the general election. Since March 2003, he has served as Prime Minister.

114　Umit Cizre ed., Secular and Islamic Politics in Turkey: The Making of the Justice and Development Party, New York: Routledge, 2008, p.97.

in the Kurdish issue. In May 2009, the state president Abdullah Gul from AKP[115] emphasized the Kurdish issue was the "most urgent thing in Turkey and there now comes a historic opportunity to resolve it". He added, "No matter what you call it: a terrorism issue, the issue of Southeastern Anatolia or the Kurdish issue, it is the first priority for Turkey and must be solved".[116] In November 2011, Erdogan made a public apology for the slaughter of thousands of Kurds made by the government forces in Dersim in the 1930s, saying that "I apologize for the incident in the name of the state" and this violence was "one of the most tragic and painful events in our modern history". He appealed to the ruling Republican People's Party (CHP) to make an explanation for this event and criticized it "is not courageous enough to comment on this dark chapter in the history".[117]

In July 2009, the Erdogan government enacted a policy entitled Kürt Açılımı (Kurdish Opening). In mid-August, Erdogan called on deputies of various parities to support his plan and pointed out that "if Turkey hadn't spent so much energy, budget, peace and youth on the issue of terrorism, if Turkey hadn't been in conflict for the past 25 years, what kind of life we would have led today?"[118] Interior Minister Atalay held dialogues with various political parties, unions and business groups on this issue. The government launched the "Kurdish Plan" in September, which would restore the Kurdish names of Kurdish villages, expand freedom of speech, resume civil rights of Kurdish refugees, expand the power of local governments and conduct an amnesty for PKK members. After being released, this plan received a positive response among the Kurdish people as well as the international community. Ocalan also praised this plan. On November 12, Interior Minister stressed democracy was the only way to solve the Kurdish issue and under this framework the government would take six steps: 1. An independent human rights institution would be established to supervise behaviors of violating human rights; 2. A committee would be founded to assess discriminatory policies and behaviors directed at minorities;

---

115   Abdullah Gul (1950-) is one of the main leaders of the AKP and his status was second only to Prime Minister Erdogan. After the AKP won the general election in 2002, it was Gul who initially served as Prime Minister, because Erdogan was not qualified at first by the old establishment. After Erdogan became the Prime Minister, Gul worked as Deputy Prime Minister and Foreign Minister. Abdullah Gul was elected as the 11th President of Turkey on August 28, 2007. He held a moderate attitude toward the Kurdish issue, thinking that Islamism is a way to solve this problem. Admitting that the Kurds used to be discriminated, especially in language, he then stressed that their current reforms have improved the situation significantly.

116   Andy Hilton and Marlies Casier, "Road Maps and Roadblocks in Turkey's Southeast", Joost Jongerden, Oct. 30, 2009, http://www.merip.org/mero/mero103009.

117   "The First Apology and Its Consequences", Hurriyet Daily News, Nov. 24, 2011, http://www.hurriyetdailynews.com/n.php?n=thefirstapologyanditsconsequences-2011-11-23.

118   Today's Zaman, Aug. 12, 2009.

3. The UN Convention on Anti-torture would be approved of by the parliament and a national preventive and follow-up mechanism would be set up; 4. An independent oversight body would be established to investigate cases that security forces were accused of making torture or ill-treatment behaviors; 5. Names of towns and villages would be changed in accordance according to the demands of local communities; 6. Candidates of political parties would be allowed to communicate in non-Turkish languages during election campaigns.[119]

This policy was widely welcomed both at home and abroad. Iraqi President Jalal Talabani said the Kurdish regional government of Iraq supported the Kurdish Opening policy enacted by the Turkish government and urged the PKK to cease fire. Foreign Minister of the Iraqi Kurdish regional government claimed, "any positive suggestion about this issue (the Kurdish issue) will obtain our praise. We'll ensure our territory not to be treated as a platform from which attacks are launched on our neighbors".[120] Nevertheless, this policy was strongly opposed inside Turkey. The opposition condemned the AKP as surrendering to terrorists and PKK. The CHP (Republican People's Party) accused the government of showing weakness to PKK.[121] The National Movement Party (MHP)[122] connected the government's behaviors with Ocalan, condemning the government cooperated with terrorists.[123] Not long after, the policy was enacted, the implementation of it met setbacks, for the Turkish Constitutional Court decided to ban the DTP in December 2009 and arrest many of its members, Kurdish riots broke out in several cities of Turkey and the PKK announced resuming the war situation.

The most important change during this period was lifting the ban on the Kurdish language and culture. Before the AKP government, the Ecevit government (from May of 1999 to November of 2002) enacted those decrees in August 2002, which allowed radio and television to use local languages and private schools to teach non-Turkish languages. Both of the two decrees were passed by the parliament. The former one obtained 267 votes and the latter 235. After the AKP came to power, the two decrees were formally implemented. On June 7, 2004, TRT-6 attached to the TRT TV officially started broadcasting in Kurdish. On March 8, 2006, Turkey began to allow private radio stations to broadcast in Kurdish. The Radio and Television

---

119   Hurriyet, Nov. 13, 2009.
120   Today's Zaman, Aug. 12, 2009.
121   "PKK Leader Abdullah Ocalan Challenges Omission from Peace Initiative from His Prison Cell", Terrorism Monitor Volume, Issue 37, Dec. 3, 2009, http://www.jamestown. org/single/?no_cache=1&tx_ttnews%5Btt_news%5D=35799.
122   Being founded on February 9, 1969, it is a right-wing nationalist party of Turkey and has some tendencies of pan-Turkism and great Turkish chauvinism.
123   Hurriyet, Nov. 13, 2009.

Supreme Council (RTÜK) approved two TV channels called Gün TV and Söz TV as well as a radio station named Medya FM to use the Kurdish language. Yet, these TV stations could only broadcast 4 hours a week or 45 minutes a day and radio stations only 5 hours a week. Besides, cartoons and teaching of Kurdish were forbidden.

Afterwards, on January 1, 2009, TRT-6 TV began broadcasting in Kurdish 24 hours a day. Prime Minister Erdogan personally delivered a speech to congratulate on its shows. In September 2009, the Turkish Supreme Council of Radio and Television decided to further relax the Kurdish restrictions on private radio and television stations. Under the new regulations, private TV stations could broadcast in Kurdish 24 hours a day just like TRT-6. Meanwhile, the provision that there must be Turkish subtitles in the bottom of the screen was cancelled. However, the new regulations still didn't allow private radio and television stations to teach non-Turkish languages and dialects. At the same time, huge changes were made in the education of Kurdish language. Many Kurdish schools were opened. Plenty of universities at Mardin, Hakkari, Muş, Tunceli and Bingöl set up courses to teach Kurdish. In 2009, Ataturk University at Mardin Province became the first university in Turkey which set up postgraduate Kurdish teaching. The Eastern Language Institute of this university established the Kurdish Language and Literature Department in 2011, which became the first undergraduate teaching body of Kurdish language in Turkey. Southeastern regions of Turkey decided in 2010 to adopt the Kurdish language besides Turkish in water-electricity bills, marriage certificates and building and street and road signs as well as social and cultural notifications. Friday prayers hosted by the mosques started to use Kurdish and shopping malls began to write Kurdish in price tags. Kurdish satellite channels of the Middle East and Europe could be watched casually in Turkey. In virtual space, Kurdish was also widespread in blogs, social media (Facebook) and online forums. At present, the use of Kurdish in non-public places and the discussion of the Kurdish issue in public have been almost free and legal, which is a major breakthrough. However, the use of Kurdish still faces some obstacles:

Firstly, the ban on the use of Kurdish in public places and institutions has not been lifted completely. Kurdish is confined to only private life. Secondly, although private schools are allowed to teach Kurdish, basic education institutions cannot do so. The Turkish Constitution regulates that the fundamental education system in Turkey must employ Turkish. The Kurdish alphabet has not been recognized yet. Kurdish names including the letters of X, W and Q that the Turkish alphabet does n0t have are forbidden. In 2007, Kurdish politician Osman Baydemir[124] was charged by

---

124   He is a Kurdish political and human rights activist and member of the Democratic Society Party and was elected as mayor twice in 2004 and 2009 respectively.

the prosecution for writing the letter "W" on the New Year greeting cards which were made in Kurdish by him. Thirdly, the start of Kurdish education and schools is often impeded deliberately. Fourthly, some people are still persecuted for using Kurdish.

The AKP government also took a series of measures to promote democratization. Due to the great progress it made in cracking down on the PKK and the strong desire to join the EU as soon as possible, Turkey lifted the Emergency Law in December 2002 which had been enforced in the southeastern region since 1987. At that time, only Diyarbakir and Sirnak still implemented this law and had regional governors (Gokhan Aydiner was the last governor). On April 11, 2010, Turkey modified the law of political parties, allowing them to use non-Turkish languages including Kurdish to carry out election campaigns. On June 29, Parliament passed a new anti-terrorism law, which made some progress compared with its counterpart in 1991. For example, it prohibited the prosecution of minors under the age of 18; it reduced punishment on illegal demonstrations and rallies; it released minors who were found guilty according to the previous anti-terrorism law. However, the new law expanded the scope of criminal behaviors of "terrorists", incorporating drug and human trafficking, public transport hijacking, document forgery, etc. into the range of terrorism. The new law also imposed a number of new restrictions upon the news media. This law was enforced on July 25. In addition, the AKP actively amended some articles of the 1982 Constitution made by the military and bureaucratic elite. Erdogan repeatedly stressed that if Turkey didn't carry out a thorough reform on the Constitution and didn't keep pace with the EU in terms of basic human rights and democracy, it would be impossible to achieve the nation's goal of joining the EU. The Turkish parliament passed a catalogue of bills on the constitutional revision in May 2010: modifying the structures of the Constitutional Court and the Committee of Supreme Judge and Prosecutor; allowing people to appeal to civil courts about decisions made by the Supreme Military Council; establishing a government agency to investigate officials' misbehavior and corruption; eliminating discrimination against women, children, veterans, the disabled and the elderly. But the bill on "the ending of dissolution and banning of political parties" was rejected by the parliament. On September 12 of the same year, a referendum about revising the Constitution was held in Turkey, which was approved "by 58.2%-Yes" votes. Erdogan delivered a speech, saying Turkey "has undergone a historic turning point towards democracy".

During this period, the peaceful Kurdish political movements had been greatly developed. Kurdish parties which were considered to be pro-PKK were permitted to engage in political activities, participate in parliamentary elections and led local governments. Politicians actively called for a peaceful solution to the Kurdish issue rather than simply asking for Kurdish language and cultural rights in the past. In the general election held in November 2002, the DEHAP obtained 6.22% votes, an increase of 1.49% over what the HADEP got in 1999. Voters were mainly concentrated in the Kurdish region. It obtained over 40% votes in big Kurdish provinces, but still failed to meet the 10% requirement for the entry into the parliament. On February 11 of the same year, Kurdish politician of Turkey Abdul Melik Firat[125] established Hak ve Ozgürlükler Partisi (HAK-PAR).[126] The DEHAP was banned by the Constitutional Court on March 13, 2003. The Law of Reintegrating into the Society was passed by the parliament on August 5, which provided the PKK militants who were willing to lay down their weapons with an opportunity of reintegrating into the society. In April 2004, the Ankara State Security Court sentenced Leyla Zana and other three former DEHAP deputies who had been in prison for as long as ten years to 15 years in jail on the charge of "implementing the instructions of PKK leaders and inciting separatist activities at home and abroad". Under an enormous pressure from the EU, the Supreme Court of Appeal announced the release of these four deputies on June 9. Shortly after being released, Zana declared to found the DTH party. On August 17, 2005, the DTH and some members of the older DEHAP jointly formed the DTP. About the charge that this party supported the PKK, its leader Ahmet Türk publicly stated more than once that the armed struggle of the PKK hurts the Kurdish people as well, but he refused to consider the PKK as a terrorist organization, openly. In December 2005, 56 Kurdish city mayors jointly made a petition by writing to the Danish Prime Minister, requesting him not to close the Kurdish TV station Roj-TV. But they were charged for this petition letter. More than 600 candidates of the Democratic Socialist Party participated in the general election which was held on June 22, 2007, with independent status (without open party affiliation), winning 5.2% of the total votes and 27 seats and became the third largest opposition party. In July, the same year, Zana, one of the leaders of this party, called for transformation of the Turkish state-political system, implementation of a federal system and autonomy of the Kurdish region, claiming that doing so would not lead to separation but enhance national unity and coexistence of all ethnic groups. She pointed out that since Ocalan was arrested, the Kurds had taken new policies of not separating from Turkey, but the unchanged policies enforced by the Turkish government since 1998 could not meet the requirements of the Kurds, and

125 Abdul Melik Firat (1934-2006) became a parliamentarian of the Democratic Party in 1957 and was put in jail in 1960. He was elected as a parliamentarian of the Right Path Party in 1991 and later quitted from it. Subsequently, he was jailed again. He established the Right and Liberal Party in 2002 and retired owing to health reason in 2006.
126 This party enjoys some voice in the Turkish political community and is one of the major Kurdish parties. In 2012, Kemal Burkay, former leader of the Kurdistan Socialist Party, who exiled abroad for almost 40 years, joined this party and became its leader.

the government always took one step forward and two steps backward.[127] On November 5, 2007, the DTP required to write the implementation of autonomy in six Kurdish provinces into the party program. On November 11, 2007, Nurettin Demirtas[128], leader of this party, appealed to all Turkish parties to hold a "Democratic Summit" and discuss about the Kurdish issue.[129] When giving a speech in April 2008, Zana deemed Ocalan, Massoud Barzani and Talabani as three major leaders of the Kurds, thus being sentenced to two years in prison by the Turkish court. In the local election held on March 29, 2009, the DTP won 5.41% votes. The provincial governors controlled by it increased from 4 to 8, and mayors from 32 to 51, including majors of nine provincial capitals.[130]

The newly elected mayor of Diyarbakir Osman Baydemir was sentenced to 10 months in prison since he called the PKK guerrillas as "guerrilla fighters". The DTP and the HAK-PAR were banned by the Turkish Constitutional Court on December 11, 2009. Chairman of the DTP Ahmet Türk and former chairman Nurettin Demirtas as well as other 35 people were sentenced to five years in prison and banned to join any political party. While the DTP was banned, some of its members established the BDP in 2009 and 19 DTP members who worked as deputies declared to join in the BDP. The BDP held a party congress in February 2010 and about 2000 delegates participated. Nurettin Demirtas and Gulten Kisanak[131] were elected as co-chairman and co-chairwoman. Immediately after this party was founded, the Turkish public prosecutor embarked on investigating it and arresting Kurdish politicians across the country. On December 24, 2009, the Turkish police carried out a large-scale operation simultaneously in 11 cities and seized more than 30 Kurdish politicians, among whom at least 7 were city mayors, one of them was a famous politician and 2 were human rights activists. The BDP appealed to a boycott of the referendum of constitutional revision proposed by the AKP, condemning that the AKP failed to satisfy the demands of the Kurdish people. Chairwoman Gulten Kisanak said in a statement that they opposed "the existing fascist constitution", but "we will not support the new fascist Constitution either". Because of the boycott, the vote rate in the Kurdish region was far below the national average (70.01%), and the vote

127 "Pro-Kurdish Politician Zana: Time to Divide Turkey into States", Today's Zaman, http://www.kurdishaspect.com/doc072307TZ.htm.
128 Born in 1973, Nurettin Demirtas is a Kurdish politician and lawyer of Turkey. He advocated undertaking disobedience campaigns and encouraged Kurdish doctors, teachers and students to use the Kurdish language.
129 "PM Erdogan Recep Tayyip Says DTP Headed Down Deadend Street", Today's Zaman, July 14, 2007. http://www.todayszaman.com/tz.web/detaylar. do?load=detay&link=127053.
130 "Ruling Party Main Loser in Local Ballot", http://www.hurriyet.com.tr/english/domestic/11326291.asp.
131 She was born in 1961 and was a female Kurdish journalist.

rate in Hakkari was only 9.05%, Sirnak 22.5% and Diyarbakir 34.8%.[132] In the general election held in June 2011, 37 political parties were allowed to participate. The BDP united another two small Kurdish parties—the Participatory Democracy Party (KADEP)[133] and the Right and Freedom Party to take part in the election. They nominated 61 candidates all together, and finally, Kurdish people won 36 seats in the parliament with 11 being obtained by women. Zana was elected successfully again. Hatip Dicle[134] was disqualified by the Supreme Electoral Council after he obtained a seat in the parliament, and he was replaced by a candidate of the AKP who ranked only 6th. On June 22, the Supreme Council announced disqualifying the 9 deputies, among whom 6 were members of the BDP, 2 were from the Republican People's Party and one from the Nationalist Movement Party. As a result, deputies of the pro-Kurdish BDP boycotted the opening of the parliament. The new parliament opened on June 28, and 170 members including the Kurdish ones belonging to opposition parties declared a boycott and chose to be absent in the conferences. In May 2012, a Turkish court sentenced Leyla Zana to ten years in jail on the charge of being a PKK member and engaging in separatist propaganda.

---

132   Government of Turkey, Supreme Election Board (YSK) (12 September 2010), "Official Results-12 September 2010 Constitutional Referendum", http://www.ysk.gov.tr/ysk/ReferandumSecimSonucServ?bilmece1=.

133   It was founded in December 2006 and its leader was the famous Kurdish politician Serafettin Elci.

134   Hatip Dicle used to be the chairman of the Democratic Party in 1993. In 1994, his immunity was disqualified and sentenced to 15 years in prison. Under the pressure imposed by the EU, he was released in June 2004, but was sentenced to 20 months in jail for he talked about the Kurdish issue when being interviewed in 2007. In April 2010, he was arrested again for being involved a case related to the PKK.

Party	Seat
AKP	327
CHP(RP Party)	135
MHP /Nationalist Movement Party)	53
Independent Kurdish Deputies	35

**Tab. 2-5 Seat Distribution of Parties at the TBMM
(National Assembly) in the June of 2011**

Source: it was sorted out by the author based on relevant documents.
"Turkish general election, 2011", http://en.wikipedia.org/wiki/Turkish_general_election,_2011.

The AKP government also stressed to encourage the new investments in the Kurdish region. It submitted a policy report to the TBMM (National Assembly) on August 30, 2007, pointing out that "we'll continue to promote the supply of state's public goods and services in the eastern and southeastern regions which have been ignored for years, mainly in terms of education, health, justice, road construction and especially in drinking water".[135] The government announced on May 27, 2008, that it would invest further $ 32 billion in the Southeastern Anatolia Project (GAP).[136] By the end of 2010, 30.6 billion Turkish liras had been invested, accounting for the 72.7% of the total (42.1 billion liras). The Turkish government planned to complete this project by 2012. Since 2002, economic development and foreign trade in the GAP region cities grew rapidly. The export was $ 689 million and the import was $ 773 million in 2002, but the export increased to $ 4.166 billion and import $ 3.167 billion in 2010. Since 2004, this region has become a net exporter.[137] Electricity production also went up. In 2010, electricity production reached 22% of the national energy consumption. Irrigated area doubled and crop yields increased substantially. Over the past eight years, cotton production grew from 140,000 to 400,000 metric tons.

135 "AKP Government Program", http://www.akparti.org.tr/programm.doc.
136 "Turkey Revives Stalled MYM32 Billion GAP Dam and Irrigation Project", The Christian Science Monitor, May 28, 2008, http://www.csmonitor.com/World/Europe/2008/0528/p12s01-woeu.html.
137 http://includes.gap.gov.tr/files/ek-dosyalar/gap/gap-son-durum/Son%20 Durum-2010.pdf.

These policies implemented by the AKP helped it win many votes of the Kurds, thus pro-Kurdish parties faced a shrinking trend in winning votes. In the general election of 2002, HADEP has won a wide voter support, but this situation has changed in the election of 2007, six out of ten national assembly deputies from the Diyarbakir Province was won by the AKP candidates and four by the DTP, and the votes of the two parties has increased to 88.6%, leaving a quite small space for other parties.[138] The AKP won 54% in 13 Kurdish cities, whereas the DTP only won 24%. This outcome might be caused by the proper election strategies that the AKP adopted, and meanwhile it reflected the Kurdish voters had recognized or sympathized with the AKP government to a certain degree. Erdogan has begun to claim that the AKP government was the best representative of the Kurds, because it had 75 Kurdish deputies.[139]

During this period, the Turkish government continued to crack down on the PKK and its armed organisations. Though there was temporary cease-fires, armed conflicts did not cease. However, compared with the 1990s, the armed conflicts became fewer both in intensity and scale. The policies enforced by the AKP won the support of many Kurdish people. With the Kurdish people's life improving constantly, the mass base and support for the PKK's armed struggle diminished. From September 1, 1999 when Ocalan declared a ceasefire up to June 1, 2004, when he again announced the suspension of the cease-fire, it was basically peaceful and armed conflicts had reduced sharply. After 2004, battles were underway. Northern Iraq became the major stronghold of the PKK. Therefore, the Turkish army took military actions in Northern Iraq repeatedly and thus contradicted with the US policies, the Iraqi government and the Kurdish regional government, respectively. In 2007, in retaliation for terrorist attacks, the Turkish army fought against the PKK for several times by crossing the national border and bombed its camps. On February 21, 2008, the Turkish army started a large-scale military operation coded as "Operation Sun" and went across the border into the north of Iraq. The Headquarters of the General Staff of the Turkish army said that a total of 230 PKK members were killed and 27 Turkish soldiers martyred. With 452 affirmative votes and 23 negative ones, the TBMM (National Assembly) passed the bill submitted by the government on the extension of the one-year time limit of attacking the PKK bases abroad on October 6, 2009. On August 17, 2011, the Turkish army launched several air strikes on the PKK camps in Northern Iraq, bombed 132 targets. The six-day air raid killed nearly 100 PKK militants and injured at least 80. On October 20, the Turkish army mobilized 22 battalions to start

138 "A Sea Change in Cultural Politics", Turkish Daily News, July 24, 2007, http://www.turkishdailynews.com.tr/vote2007/article.php?enewsid=56.
139 "Is the Representative of the Kurds the AKP or the DTP?", Radikal, Nov. 8, 2007, http://www.radikal.com.tr/haber.php?haberno=238214.

the cleaning-up in five regions along the Turkish-Iraqi border, shooting 21 PKK members to death.

In addition, a new Kurdish armed organization the Kurdistan Freedom Falcons (TAK) appeared in July 2004. It waged bomb attacks and other terrorist incidents on some cities of Turkey. For example, it launched a bomb attack on a tourist city along the western coast in July 2005, resulting in 20 casualties; it struck a bus station at Istanbul in March 2006, killing one person; it attacked an office at Istanbul on April 5, 2006; it set Ataturk International Airport on fire on May 24, 2006; it made bomb attacks on Antalya, Istanbul and another coastal tourist cities from August 27 to 28, 2006, killing 3 people and injuring over 20; on August 30, 2006, a bomb attack occurred in the city of Mersin and one person was injured; in June 2010, it attacked a military vehicle and killed 4 people; it launched a suicide bomb in Istanbul on October 30, 2010, which injured 32 people; TAK bombed Ankara on September 30, 2011, causing 3 deaths and over 30 injuries. The Turkish government did not evaluate it as an independent terrorist organization, but regarded it as a branch led by the PKK. On January 10, 2007, the US announced to list it as a terrorist organization. It has also been considered as a terrorist organization by Britain as well as the EU. Nevertheless, the PKK claimed it had nothing to do with this organization. This organization didn't have many members, and it was said that there were only dozens of people in it and its headquarters was located in Kandil Mountains of the Iraqi Kurdish region.[140]

Year	Turkish Security	PKK	Civilian	Total
2008	143	657	49	849
2009	44	78	67	189
2010	80-150	60-130	20	160-300
Total	267-337	795-865	136	1198-1338

Tab. 2-6 Data of Deaths in Conflicts Estimated by ICG during 2008 to 2010

Source: http://en.wikipedia.org/wiki/Kurds_in_Turkey.

It is worth noticing that impacted by the "Arab Spring" in 2011, the Turkish Kurds also carried out peaceful protests. On February 28, 2011, three PKK soldiers were shot to death when they attempted to enter Turkey

---

140 "Kurdistan Freedom Falcons", http://en.wikipedia.org/wiki/Kurdistan_Freedom_Falcons.

from Northern Iraq, so the BDP launched a large-scale protest action. The funeral of the three PKK guerillas held in Nizip on March 14 led to a big conflict and then turned to be a large-scale riot. Ultimately, more than 700 people were arrested. The riot was subsequently extended to neighboring cities and towns. There were 15,000 people in Sirnak participating in the protest, which caused 5 people to be killed, 80 people to be injured and 155 to be arrested. When the Kurdish New Year arrived on March 21, protests and riots were spread further, and strikes, sit-ins and demonstrations continued everywhere. On March 24, the BDP publicly declared that it would immediately implement the "Civil disobedience struggle tactic". Leader of the protest and congressman Demirtas said that the BDP decided to launch the "Civil Disobedience Resistance" in the entire Kurdish region. Kurdish leader Ahmet Turk condemned that Erdogan allowed the use of unproportional force against Kurdish protestors while being tolerant against the Islamist protestors of the Arab Spring, in the region. On the morning of April 25, the Turkish police took actions simultaneously at 17 provinces to remove tents of "democratic solution" erected by the protestors and arrested hundreds of them. According to incomplete statistics, the Turkish government arrested all together 2,506 protesters from March 24 to May 10. Two protestors were dead and 308 injured.[141]

Targeting the increasingly growing protest actions made by the Kurds, the Turkish media warned that the "Arab Spring" was leading to the "Kurdish Summer". The success of the Arab protests stimulated the Turkish Kurds to some extent. They have been increasingly courageous to challenge the government through democratic protests. Their actions have revealed that the new national consciousness of the Kurds has awakened, which would make a significant influence upon the Kurdish issue in Turkey.

Facing new situations both at home and abroad as well as the dying "Kurdish Democratic Initiative", Erdogan decided to re-start the "Kurdish Democratic Initiative". On June 12, 2012, Erdogan announced in the parliament that public schools would be allowed to teach Kurdish. "If there are enough students, Kurdish can be taught as an elective course." He said this was "a historical step" and emphasized that the AKP held an open attitude towards the discussions made by various political parties about the Kurdish issue.[142]

If this was achieved, it would be the first time in the Turkish history to have Kurdish courses in public schools. At the same time, the CHP which insisted on the hard-line stance in the Kurdish issue also turned to hold a positive attitude. On June 4, 2012, the CHP leader made a ten-point proposal about the issue: the CHP recognized that the Kurdish issue was the

---

141   "Thousands Detained in Eastern Turkey since March", Hurriyet, May 16, 2011.
142   http://www.aljazeera.com/news/europe/2012/06/2012612133656956705.html.

most important issue confronting the country; the history had proved that the Kurdish problem could not be resolved through security-centered policies; other policies should be implemented without any hesitation to deal with this issue and democratic means should be applied; the parliament should become the proper arena where the solution to the problem can be discussed and decided; to resolve this problem, a comprehensive consensus must be reached; the new solutions should bring security, peace and confidence to the Turkish society; the main objective was to set up a platform where various political parties could make direct and regular dialogues to achieve maximum consensus; the TBMM (Nation Assembly) should establish a social consensus committee which would be composed of eight equal members from various political parties, and meanwhile it should establish a civil elite group to discuss the Kurdish issue.[143] For a long time, the CHP had treated the Kurdish policies enacted by Kemal Atatürk as something that should not be changed and had always criticized the Kurdish policies enforced by the AKP. Nowadays, the CHP has made a turn and began to make some positive proposals and explicitly expressed that the previous policies should not be maintained any more, which can be seen as a major shift. On June 6, leaders of the CHP and the AKP held a conference which specially discussed the Kurdish issue. Kurdish parties spoke highly of the new initiatives made by the government and particularly praised the proposals given by the CHP.

Overall, an increasing number of people in the Turkish political and elite communities realized that the Kurdish policies which had been implemented for a long time actually failed and believed that it was necessary to seek a new solution. In March 2007, former President Evren who used to hold a tough attitude toward the Kurdish issue surprisingly said that federalism could be used as a way to solve the Kurdish problem and meanwhile claimed that his previous endeavor to ban Kurdish in public was a mistake. The Erdogan government had made some breakthroughs in dealing with the Kurdish issue, but hadn't broken some major principles for it faced many obstacles inside. Some of its reforms were regarded as "one step forward and two steps back".[144] Therefore, it still has a long way to go to thoroughly resolve the Kurdish issue.

The responses to those new policies and to the measures adopted by the current government have been different inside Turkey. A survey conducted by Konda public survey company across Turkey in 2007 showed that only 34.9% of interviewees approved entitling the Kurds the right to learn their

---

143   "This is the CHP's Kurdish initiative", http://www.habermonitor.com/en/haber/detay/this-is-the-chp39s-kurdish-initiative/179128/.
144   Semra Polat, "Turkey's Kurds: One Step Forward, Two Steps Back", Le Monde diplomatique, Nov. 2011, http://mondediplo.com/blogs/turkey-s-kurds-one-step-forward-two-steps-back.

mother tongue was a correct way to solve the Kurdish issue and the rest disapproved. Interviewees who supported Kurdish media broadcasting only accounted for 36.4%. About 39% approved of abolishing the 10% threshold of entry into the parliament (the Kurds believe this election law was especially set to prevent them entering the parliament as a political party). 42.4% of the interviewees supported the government's efforts to preserve and promote the Kurdish culture and traditions. 48.3% thought it was a must to expand the power of local governments and local autonomy. 80.3% claimed only the discarding of terrorism by PKK could end the Kurdish issue.[145] In December 2008, the liberal association Economic and Social Studies Foundation of Turkey (TESEV) released a report about how to solve the Kurdish issue supported by an extensive investigation—the report included suggestions and demands from the region to the government. It stressed that the Kurdish issue was actually an issue of human rights rather than a security issue which was claimed by the government. That the government deprived the Kurds of their ethnic characteristics and assimilated them was the major reason for the Kurdish issue. Though the PKK carried out a large number of violent activities, the government resorted to more violence. The report required the new Constitution to have a bigger inclusiveness, offer an unconditional amnesty for the PKK, endow the Kurds with language rights and abolish village guards. A report about the progress in Turkey published by the EU in 2007 said that there were 57,000 village guards in Turkey. When the Minister of the Interior answered questions in the parliament on March 20, 2009, he said that the figure was 71,907. This organization still exists at present. That report required the government to sweep out land mines in the Kurdish region and ensure the legitimate political rights of the DTP. It also desired that economic reforms that aimed at enhancing the new investments in the Kurdish region must be coordinated with political reforms. Chairman of the foundation said: "unless Turkey solves the Kurdish issue, it cannot reach social peace and join the EU.[146]

In 2009, Turkish Political, Economic and Social Research Foundation (SETA) and Pollmark survey company carried out an opinion survey titled as "Public Perception of the Kurdish Question in Turkey" and the survey results reflected the current social understanding of this issue to a certain degree (see Tab. 2-7). First, most people in Turkey thought the Kurdish issue was the most significant political issue confronting Turkey and the behavior in the past 25 years to regard it as a mere security issue was mistaken. The masses expressed a strong support for the Kurdish policies pursued by the Erdogan government, and most people were discontent with the hard-line policies of the CHP and the MHP. Second, the Turkish nation

145 "Turks Lukewarm to Broader Rights for Kurdish Minority", Mar. 25, 2007, http://www.ekurd.net/mismas/articles/misc2007/3/turkeykurdistan1116.htm.
146 Michael M. Gunter, Historical Dictionary of the Kurds, pp.288-289.

and the Kurdish nation had achieved national integration to a large extent. About one-third of Turks had a Kurdish friend, relative or neighbor, and about two-thirds of Kurds had a Turkish friend, relative or neighbor. No serious hostility or direct confrontation between the two peoples was deeply recorded in their historical memory. The most important factor that contributed to the united Turkish society was that both of them owned the nearly same belief and values. According to the survey, unless the Kurdish issue was resolved, the current national integration and unification in the Turkish society would collapse. Third, on how to resolve the Kurdish issue, the two nations had political divergences and misunderstandings. 71.3% Turks believed the Kurds hoped to establish an independent state and feared that Turkey would be split. As a result, they resisted the articles written in the Constitution about the recognition of the Kurdish national identity and the abolition of restraints imposed on the Kurdish language as well as the formation of a more democratic constitution. On the contrary, 59% of the Kurds said that they didn't want to establish an independent state and separation was not their ultimate goal. Fourth, as for the "Kurdish Opening" plan promoted by the Turkish government, nearly 43% of Turks expressed their support, but close to 40% opposed. However, only 19% supported the opposition parties together with their anti-government initiatives. As many as 62% people were against their policies. SETA Secretary-General pointed

out that the most crucial feature of the current Kurdish issue was it was considered to be a political issue instead of a security one by an increasing number of people. Due to the emergence of many new factors, the Kurdish issue has turned out to be extremely complex. Nowadays, we have to discuss it under a brand new framework rather than the previous discourse system.[147]

---

147 "In your opinion, do the Kurds want to have a separate state?" (Poll report), Public Perception of the Kurdish Question, Turkey: Foundation for Political, Economic and Social Research (SETA) and Pollmark, 2009, p.63, http://www.setav.org/Ups/dosya/8504.pdf.

Tab. 2-7 Survey on People's Opinions of the Kurdish Issue

Views on the Kurdish Initiatives Made by the Erdogan Government		
Category / Attitude	Turks	Kurds
Positive	42.77	75.77
Negative	40.88	13.99

Attitudes Toward the Official Kurdish TV Station TRT-6			
Category / Attitude	Turks	Kurds	Total
Supportive	47,9	67,1	51,0
Opposed	41.4	25,0	38,0

Whether to Agree to the View that the Effort Made by Prime Minister Erdogan and the Government May Promote Separatism							
Category / Attitude	Turks	Kurds	Total	AKP	CHP (RP PARTY)	MHP	DTP
Yes	28,3	9,0	25,0	12,2	43,8	44,7	19,0
No	55,9	79,1	60,0	75,0	53,4	42,6	19,0
Have no idea	15,9	11,9	16,0				

Whether the Recognition of Kurdish Cultural Rights Threatens Territorial and National Unity of Turkey			
Category / Attitude	Turks	Kurds	Total
Yes	47,3	18,8	42,5
No	42,6	74,6	47,9

Whether to Approve Lifting the Ban on the Kurdish Language

Category / Attitude	Turks	Kurds	Total
Yes	37,2	78,2	44,0
No	52,0	14,4	45,8

Whether the Constitution Should Recognize the Kurdish Identity

Category / Attitude	Turks	Kurds	Total
Yes	15,5	67,3	65,2
No	73,9	22,1	24,1

Whether the Kurds Have The Desire to Establish An Independent Country

Category / Attitude	Turks	Kurds	Total
Yes	71,3	30,3	64,4
No	17,9	59,0	24,0

Whether Öcalan and the PKK Can Represent The Turkish Kurds

Category / Attitude	Turks	Kurds	Total
Yes	37,1	38,1	37,4
No	51,8	42,7	50,1

Whether Political Views of the DTP Represent Turkish Kurds			
Category / Attitude	Turks	Kurds	Total
Yes	36,4	46,4	38,1
No	51,9	41,0	50,0

Whether to Mind Having Kurdish or Turkish Labor Colleagues		
Category / Attitude	Turks	Kurds
Yes	21,0	9,0
No	74,0	88,5

Whether You Have Close Turkish or Kurdish Relatives, Friends or Neighbors		
Category / Attitude	Turks	Kurds
Already Have Such Relatives	33,8	69,9
Already Have Such Friends	59,4	83,6
Willing to Make Friends	75,5	92,0
Already Have Such Neighbors	54,1	70,0
Not Minding Having Such	78,3	90,5

Proportions of Political Party Members Who Have Intimate Kurdish Relatives, Friends or Neighbors			
Category / Attitude	Have Kurdish Relatives	Have Kurdish Friends	Mind Having Kurdish Neighbors
AKP	35,8	56,8	15,4
CHP (RP Party)	33,8	64,9	16,8
MHP	31	58,9	23,4
Pro-Kurdish DTP	74,1	84,7	13,6

Unit: %

Source: "In your opinion, do the Kurds want to have a separate state?" (Poll report),
Public Perception of the Kurdish Question, Turkey: Foundation for Political, Economic and
Social Research (SETA) and Pollmark, 2009, p.63, http://www.setav.org/Ups/dosya/8504.pdf.

2.6 Case Analysis: the PKK and Its Role

Now and then, the PKK, has changed its names such as the "Kurdish Freedom and Democracy Assembly" (KADEK), "Kurdish People's Congress" (Kongra-Gel) or "Kurdish Democratic Union"/"Kurdish Social Union" (KKK/KCK)[148], but it is traditionally known as PKK. Ideologically, PKK initially upheld Marxism-Leninism and socialist thoughts. Later it has encountered changes in its thoughts, reduced its socialist color and increased nationalist and western liberal democratic thought elements. It initially aimed to liberate the Kurdish people and establish an independent Kurdish state which would include the four parts of Kurdistan, divided by borders. After Ocalan was arrested in 1999, it proposed programs of autonomy and federalism instead of a separate state. In terms of the struggle mode, it had initially emphasized armed revolution and mainly conducted protests, riots, assassinations, kidnappings, bombings, sabotages, armed attacks and guerrilla warfare targeting the Turkish military and economic facilities as well as infrastructures and civilians. After the arrest of Ocalan, it renounced upholding armed struggle and made more emphasis on political struggle, but both struggle modes still co-existed. In the new period it used armed struggle as a bargaining chip so as to be recognized as a legal political actor. Besides

---

148   KCK is a pan-Kurdish organization led by the PKK and has no big difference from PKK. In addition to the PKK, the alliance also has the Kurdish Free Life Party in Iran, the Democratic Union Party (PYD) in Syria and the Kurdish Democratic Solution Party (PCDK) in Iraq.

Turkey, PKK has been listed as a terrorist organization by many countries and international organizations such as the US, the EU, the NATO, Canada, Australia, Israel, Iran and Syria.

The period from 1978 to 1984 witnessed the establishment of the PKK and its military preparations. During the time, the PKK mainly tried to win the support of the masses and recruit new members. It adopted tactics like ambushing police, conducting sabotage activities, creating disturbances, launching protests and holding anti-government demonstrations. Their major targets included military police, Kurdish "traitors" and other left-wing organizations.Its founder Abdullah Ocalan was born in Urfa Province on April, 4, 1948. Deeply influenced by left-wing thoughts when he studied at the Political Department of Ankara University, he was actively involved in the fierce political struggle and student movements in Turkey. Ocalan was one of the leaders of the Marxist-Leninist-led university student mass organization (Ankara Democratic Higher Education Association) which was established in 1974.[149] The "Apocular group" first concentrated its activities in the capital Ankara, but later decided to shift their activity focus to Kurdistan in 1975 and co-opted new members in the Kurdish cities, such as Urfa, Tunceli, Gaziantep, Kahramanmaraş and Elazig, advocating Marxist-Leninist ideas and Kurdish nationalism. In 1977, PKK decided that "enemies of the Kurdish People" were fascists, official agencies, other left-wing Kurdish organizations and those individuals that cooperated with the government, the Turkish Marxist left organizations and the Kurdish landlords. On November 27, 1978, this organization issued a "Declaration of Independence", officially declaring its changed name as PKK and claiming to carry out a Marxist-Leninist proletarian revolution, overthrow the bourgeois rule and ultimately achieve communism in Turkey. At that time, landlords who occupied 3% of the local population enjoyed a great influence in Kurdistan and worked as right hands of the central government in controlling this region. Therefore, the PKK decided to start from the landlords and establish its fame as anti-feudalist. In August 1979, the PKK assassinated a reknown ashiret leader Mehmet Celal Bucak, also a leading member of the Justice Party in Urfa, and accused him of "as a feudalist exploiting peasants" and "cooperating with the government". This was the first assassination attempt by the PKK, but had failed. Subsequently, the PKK frequently engaged in assassinations, sabotage, disturbance and protests, gradually gaining a violent reputation. The violent conflicts between 1979 and 1980 had caused 5,241 deaths and 14,152 injuries, among which 21% of the deaths were executed by the PKK. This period was the heyday of violence and activities undertaken by the PKK were one of the microcosm.

---

149   The six people were Kesire Yildirim (who later married Ocalan), Cemil Bayik, Haki Karaer, Kemal Pir, Mehmet Sevgat and Mehmet Karasungur. Other ten founders came from AYÖD.

In November 1979, Demirel became the Prime Minister and made greater efforts to crack down on the PKK. On November 28, 1979, the Turkish government arrested 242 PKK members in Silvan and Siverek. A military coup occurred in Turkey in 1980, and about 1,790 PKK members were arrested. Ocalan and his key companions crossed the border and fled to Syria. With the help of Syria, the first training camp of the PKK was founded at the Bekaa Valley. In July 1981, the PKK held its first national congress, in which it decided to establish a united front, stop attacking other Kurdish Marxist leftist organizations and meanwhile build relationships with Iraqi Kurds so as to found a base in Northern Iraq. The PKK used to criticize the Iraqi Kurdistan Democratic Party (KDP) as following conservative and defeatist policies and limiting itself with demand of autonomy rather than independent state, but then it changed its past attitude and wished to cooperate with the KDP. At that time, the Turkish government openly supported Iraq and Iran to deal with the Kurds. In May 1983, the Turkish army crossed the border and attacked the Kurds in Iraq, and in July, Mustafa Barzani agreed to cooperate with the PKK and allowed it to use the northern territory of Iraq. From August 20 to 25 of 1982, the PKK held its second national congress and formulated a three-phase strategy: defensive phase, stalemate phase and counterattack phase.The preliminary phase was characterized by a guerrilla war against the government forces, and the last phase aimed to expel the Turkish army from Kurdistan with regular armed forces and battles. The PKK stressed it was in the first phase and its major strategy was not to fight against the Turkish army directly but to work jointly with Marxist left-wing armed organizations of Turkey and build a united front.

The period from 1984 to 1999 was the guerrilla war phase. From 1984, the PKK embarked on the armed actions and launched frequent attacks on the government army in the form of guerrilla war. It used to make sporadic assassinations, but now it waged a large-scale guerrilla war. Targets further expanded, including military police as well as infrastructure and civilians associated with the government. Muslum Durgun nicknamed Dr. Baran and Semdin Sakik led the guerrilla forces in the Tunceli region. On August 15, 1984, the PKK established the Kurdistan Freedom Brigade (HRK) as its armed organization and launched attacks in two places on the same day. Its attack on President Evren and killing of three guards opened the prelude to the long-term civil war in Turkey. Duran Kalkan[150] was the leader of the HRK. In March 1985, the PKK established the Kurdish National Liberation Front (ERNK), which conducted propaganda and organizational activities

---

150   Duran Kalkan was one of the main initiators of the PKK. In the mid-1980s, he led the HRK. In 1988, he left the PKK for having contradiction with Ocalan. He was put in jail in Germany in 1989. After being released, he joined the PKK again. During the mid-1990s, he entered the Political Bureau of the PKK and became one of the members of the PKK Chairman Committee and also a member of the KKK Executive Committee.

in cities and whose main tasks were to recruit members, raise funds, gather intelligence, develop communications and make agitation and publicity. The ERNK was a screen for the PKK and its members had cover identities, such as doctors, teachers, students, staff, tailor, shopkeepers and peasants. Before the mid-1990s, it gathered 50,000 members. Mazlum Korkmaz[151] and Mustafa Karasu[152] were its main leaders. To improve its military operations, the PKK decided in its third national congress which was held in October of 1986 to found the Kurdistan People's Liberation Army (ARGK) and treat it as its specialized forces of armed guerrilla. The ARGK mainly worked on mountains and in countryside to build communication lines, collect intelligence, set up bases and attack cities. The militants wore military uniforms and abided by strict disciplines. They once reached to 10,000 including women. On December 15, 1984, the PKK signed cooperation agreements with the Turkish Labor Party, the Turkish Communist Labor Party, the Turkish Communist Party, Kurdistan Socialist Party of Turkey and the Turkish Socialist Labor Party. In the spring of 1985, the PKK attacked the government forces fiercely in Siverek, killing 60 people including Turkish soldiers, PKK members and civilians which shocked the whole country.

By August 1985, this organization had launched about 70 attacks and killed approximately 200 people, producing a horrible climate in the southeastern region. Village guards system against PKK were set up in Turkey from 1985, which posed a big threat to the penetration and sabotage made by the PKK. Since 1987, the PKK had waged harsh strikes on village guards. Between 1987 and 1988, the PKK almost eliminated all village guards at Mardin, Siirt and Hakkari provinces, and even the families of people who led and participated in village guards were all killed. Under the threat of the PKK, members of village guards dropped from 20,000 to 6,000 in 1987. In September 1989, the PKK declared a list of 13 Kurdish tribes which should be targeted and attacked. The cruel blows made by the PKK also gave rise to a lot of negative consequences: pushing many tribes to the side of the government and village guards; Turkish security forces and village guards took more ruthless retaliation against the PKK; the Iraqi Kurdish Democratic Party decided not to cooperate with the PKK anymore. Massoud Barzani said, "The PKK is getting a resentful and disgusting reputation among all

---

151   Mazlum Korkmaz was one of the main leaders of the PKK and the first commander of the ERNK. He died in a battle in 1986. It was said that he was a figure who was second to Ocalan in the PKK guerrilla army. After his death, the PKK named the training camp at the Bekaa Valley as the Mazlum Korkmaz Camp.
152   Mustafa Karasu, also known as Huseyin Ali, was one of the main leaders of the PKK. He was put in jail after the 1980 coup. In the 1990s, he led the ERNK and entered the PKK Politburo. After the arrest of Ocalan in 1999, he became a member of the PKK Chairman Committee.

the Kurdish people". It is said that the leader of the HRK Duran Kalkan had opposed Ocalan also for this reason. In such context, Ocalan announced to dissolve the HRK in 1986. In the early 1991, Ocalan declared not to attack the local Kurds and meanwhile to forgive pro-government village guards who would lay down their weapons.

Due to the disintegration of the Soviet Union in the late 1980s and the early 1990s, the PKK lost the Soviet support and thus made some ideological adjustments. It attached more importance to nationalism and also added Islamist color. To crack down on the PKK, the Turkish government vociferously advocated that the PKK believed in communism, atheism and secularism and was an "anti-Islamic devil" and meanwhile funded such Kurdish Islamist organizations as the Kurdish Hezbollah to fight against it. This publicity had some effect on the Kurdish people and Kurdish Islamic groups. Hezbollah replaced leftist Kurdish organizations to be the major competitor of the PKK in the local regions. The two parties conducted brutal struggles. Under this circumstance, the PKK began to change its attitude towards Islam, promote social freedom under the framework of Islam and strive for the support of mullahs. It also established shadow agencies including the Kurdistan Islamist Party (PLK) and Islamist Movement to resist the government. In terms of strategies, the PKK also desired to win the support of Iran. In the New Year speech delivered by Ocalan in March 1990, he specially praised the positive significance of the Islamic revolution.[153]

The Iran-Iraq war provided an opportunity for the PKK to carry out activities in Northern Iraq and it could penetrate into Turkey from the Iraqi-Turkish border and launch attacks since then. The Iraqi Kurdistan Democratic Party allowed the PKK to be active in regions under its control as well as the southern region of the Iraqi-Turkish border. In the late 1980s, The Iraqi Kurdistan Democratic Party gave up its support and cooperation with PKK, and the latter had to cooperate with the democratic socialist Kurdish Patriotic Union. The two sides reached an agreement in May 1988. In 1988, the Iranian government which is generally in rivalry with Turkey allowed the PKK to build camps in its border regions close to Turkey and sold weapons to it via Iran's Revolutionary Guards. In 1989, Ocalan's brother leader Osman Ocalan[154] set up an office in Iran for the organization of Iran branch of the PKK named PJAK. From August 2 to October 5 of 1991, the Turkish army waged the "Operation Northern Iraq" and entered the north of Iraq by crossing the border, killing 1,551 PKK members and arresting 1,232. This military action was supported by the Kurdish armed forces in Iraq. This failure shook the leadership of Ocalan and many members have left the PKK.

---

153   David McDowall, A Modern History of the Kurds, I. B. Tauris, 3 Revised Edition, 2004, p.436.
154   Osman Ocalan later in left the PKK due to political differences during 2000s.

Before and after the Gulf War, the PKK made positive responses to President Ozal's reconciliation initiatives and speeches. Ocalan declared in April 1990 that there was no "such issue of separating from Turkey" and that "our people need Turkey, and we cannot be separated for at least 40 years".[155] In March of 1991, the PKK spokesman hinted that it might welcome a federal solution. When being interviewed in November, Ocalan expressed his willingness to accept federalism, saying "undoubtedly, this has been what we want to see". This indicates that the PKK didn't insist on its past belief of establishing an independent state. One month later, Ocalan proposed ceasefire and negotiation to the Turkish government on condition that all the PKK prisoners were released; secret wars in the Kurdish region were stopped; political activities were allowed freely; the Turkish government ensured its ceasefire. On March 13, 1993, Jalal Talabani, leader of the Iraqi Patriotic Union of Kurdistan, claimed that Ocalan told him he had prepared to give up armed struggle and made a series of requirements: to condemn terrorism, renounce confrontation and solve problems via negotiation; to agree that Kurdish congressmen rather than PKK members negotiate with the government on behalf of the Kurdish people; to promise to maintain the unity of Turkey and reject separatism; to promise to abide by legitimate democratic procedures.

On March 17, Ocalan issued a statement that the PKK would have a unilateral ceasefire from March 21 to April 15. He extended the cease-fire on April 16, and proposed new demands: to endow the Kurds with cultural and Kurdish broadcasting rights; to abolish the village guard system; to lift the state of emergency; to take appropriate steps to deal with unsolved covert murders of Kurdish patriots; to recognize political activity rights of Kurdish organizations.[156]

He didn't mention Kurdish autonomy demand. Nevertheless, Ozal died of a heart attack on the following day, and Demirel who held a tough stance was elected as President. Demirel saw Ocalan's ceasefire as a sign of weakness and thus continued to take repressive actions without showing any intention of having dialogues. Within a few weeks after his inauguration, the government army killed more than 100 PKK members and civilians. On May 24, 1993, the PKK attacked a military vehicle in Bingol Province, killing 35 people. The war broke out subsequently, and the PKK declared to abort the unilateral ceasefire. From May 24 to early October of 1993, the conflict led to over 1,600 deaths. The PKK also frequently attacked Turkey's diplomatic and commercial organizations in Europe. It waged a series of strikes against Turkish targets in Western Europe in November.

---

155 The Independent, Apr.7, 1990.
156 Turkey Briefing, Vol.7, No.2, Summer, 1993.

During this period, the PKK penetrated into the Kurdish region of Turkey and established an underground organization there. By the end of 1993, over 10,000 people were the victims of Kurdish conflict in Turkey. The power of the PKK reached peak in 1994 with 10,000-15,000 armed men and 50,000-75,000 militias.[157] A Turkish general died in a strike made by the PKK in 1994, which stimulated a shift of policy in the Turkish government. The Turkish government decided to entitle the army with greater powers in fighting against the PKK. In the spring of 1994, the PKK's activities were undermined to some extent and the security situation of the Kurdish region had improved. Its activities decreased significantly in 1995. In March 1995, the Turkish army mobilized a troop composed of 35,000 soldiers to combat the PKK inside Iraq. At the same time, the PKK was busy with attacks on Turkish embassies and business organizations in Europe. In July, the Turkish government mobilized a 30,000-people troop to fight against the PKK inside Iraq again. The PKK had to declare a unilateral cease-fire on December 15, 1995. In May 1996, the PKK aborted the ceasefire. During this period, the Turkish government adopted a new anti-guerrilla strategy. Its two important policies were "Two Lights Policies": burning and chopping down all the forests and emptying all the villages so that the PKK had nowhere to hide. Under the tough attack of the government, the PKK grew increasingly passive from 1996. In 1996, Ali Haydar Kaytan[158] led the Central Command of the Kurdish People's Liberation Army to enter Iraq. After 1997, the Turkish army entered Northern Iraq and combated the PKK on a regular basis and 30,000-soldier troops were permanently stationed in the Turkish-Iraqi border. In 1998, the Turkish government thought it had already defeated the PKK and thus declared to lift the emergency state in four provinces. Ocalan announced a unilateral ceasefire on August 1, 1998.

In October 1998, Turkey unexpectedly put an army of 100,000 soldiers on the northern border of Syria, requiring Syria to expel the PKK and extradite Ocalan to Turkey. Under the pressure of Turkey, Syria was forced to terminate PKK activities on its land. It signed a common security treaty with Turkey, prohibiting the PKK from taking actions along the Turkish-Syrian borders. However, Syria didn't extradite Ocalan, but he had to leave Syria for Russia, which failed to accept him due to the pressure from Turkey. He went to Rome with a false passport to seek asylum on November 12. Italy rejected Turkish request of extradition for it didn't abolish death penalty and wished to extradite him to Germany, but Germany refused. In mid-January of 1999, Ocalan went to Russia again and applied for political asylum.

---

157 "Terrorism: Middle Eastern Groups and State Sponsors, Kurdistan Workers' Party (PKK)", Global Security CRS Report, Aug.27, 1998.
158 Ali Haydar Kaytan, also known as Fuat, was one of the founders of the PKK. He was once put in jail in Germany. In the 1990s, he entered the Politburo of the PKK. After the arrest of Ocalan, he became one member of the PKK Chairman Committee.

Left-wing parties in the Russian Duma (parliament) agreed to offer Ocalan political asylum, but this proposal was rejected by the government.

When receiving an interview, Ocalan pointed out that Russia and Turkey had made an agreement and Turkey would provide Russia with economic aid and cooperate with it on the issue of Chechnya, so he had to leave Russia.[159] The Dutch government also rejected the asylum application made by Ocalan. By the end of January, he went to Greece, which could not dare to accept him either. The Turkish media wrote: "Ocalan is rolling around like a ping pong ball."[160]

Ocalan fled to Kenya on February 1, 1999 and later planned to fly to South Africa. On his way from the Greek embassy in Kenya to the airport on February 15, he was captured by Turkish intelligence agents and escorted back to Turkey. The capture of Ocalan was helped by the CIA.[161] On February 16, the Turkish government held a press conference and Prime Minister Ecevit personally announced the capture of Ocalan. This event aroused massive protests by the Kurdish people worldwide. In Berlin, Kurdish people protested and besieged Israeli Embassy in Germany, giving rise to serious conflicts and causing three Kurds dead and 16 people injured. The PKK armed forces also retaliated. The Kurdish organization named "TAK" which defines its mission as revenge organization set fire in Istanbul and killed 13 people. Ocalan was sentenced to death on June 29.[162] The arrest of Ocalan made the PKK lose its most significant leader. It became a historic turning point in the development of the PKK, which exerted a vital impact on the Kurdish issue in Turkey.

159   "Fugitive on the Run: Ocalan's Mysterious Tour", Feb.16, 1999, http://news.bbc.co.uk/2/hi/europe/280473.stm.
160   Ibid.
161   Tim Weiner, "U.S. Helped Turkey To Find and Capture Kurdish Rebel", New York Times, Feb.20,1999, http://query.nytimes.com/gst/fullpage.html?res=9E03E3D8143DF933A15751C0A96F958260.
162   After the verdict, his defense lawyer submitted the case to the European Court of Human Rights. On December 15, 2000, the First Chamber of the European Court of Human Rights declared to accept and hear the appeal. Turkey abolished death penalty in September 2002, and the State Security Court commuted his death sentence to life imprisonment. On March 12, 2003, the European Court of Human Rights made a verdict and condemned unfair judgment made on him. In 2005, this court made another verdict, claiming Turkey violated Article No. 3, No. 5 and No. 6 of European Convention on Human Rights and Ocalan did not receive a fair trial and his right to appeal was not guaranteed.

Tab. 2-8 Casualty Statistics of Turkish Security
Forces Caused by PKK Attacks
(From August 15 of 1984 to November 13 of 1998)

Category \ Casualty	Death	Injury
Officer	259	580
Non-combat Officer	232	567
Soldier	3440	7294
Police	166	502
Village Guard	1217	1703
Total	5314	10646

Unit: Person

Source: PKK Terrorism, Ministry of Foreign Affairs,Ankara,December 1998, p.44.

Tab. 2-9 Statistics of Civil Servant Casualties Caused by PKK Attacks
(From January 1 of 1984 to November 13 of 1998)

Category \ Casualty	Death	Injury
Prosecutor	2	--
Judge	1	--
Warden	1	2
Professor	111	32
Imam	32	7
Mufti	1	1
Lecturer	1	--
Engineer	9	2
Nurse	1	2
Mayor	7	3
Guard	4	--
Village Government Leader	105	11
Doctor	6	--
Lower Government Officer	59	43
Total	340	103

Unit: Person

Source: PKK Terrorism, Ministry of Foreign Affairs,Ankara,December 1998,p.45.

Tab. 2-10 Statistics of Civilian Casualties Caused by PKK Attacks
(From August 15 of 1984 to November 13 of 1998)

Casualty / Category	Death	Injury
Men	3579	4028
Women	528	787
Children	523	634
Total	4630	5449

Unit: Person

Source: PKK Terrorism, Ministry of Foreign Affairs, Ankara, December 1998, p.43.

The time from 1999 to today is the third development stage of the PKK. After the arrest of Ocalan, strategies and tactics of the PKK had changed greatly. Being a refugee in Italy in November 1998, Ocalan issued a statement through his lawyer, condemning terrorism and violence and proposing a seven-point peace plan to end the civil war which had lasted 14 years. He expressed his wish to imitate the mode of the Irish Republican Army in Northern Ireland and the Basque in Spain so as to achieve autonomy and freedom, respect Kurdish language and culture and attain the same democracy as in Europe. His seven-point peace plan included the following content: ceasing military operations against Kurdish villages; allowing Kurdish refugees to return to their villages; abolishing the village guard system; achieving the Kurdish autonomy under the national framework of Turkey; entitling the Kurds to the same democratic rights as the Turks; officially recognizing the Kurdish national identity, language and culture; realizing religious freedom and pluralism.[163]

Akif Hasan, representative of the European division of ERNK, said that both of this organization and the PKK agreed to Ocalan's peace proposal. After being arrested, Ocalan changed the policies of the PKK in a series of talks with the Turkish authorities and proposed a peaceful resolution to the Kurdish issue while maintaining the territorial integrity and unity of Turkey. In February 1999, the PKK changed the name of ARGK into HPG, withdrew a large number of its armed forces from Turkey to Iraq and meanwhile dissolved ERNK. The Turkish State Security Court put Ocalan on trial on May 31, 1999. He expressed penitence in the courtroom, mourned and apologized over the death of 5,000 soldiers during the 15-year civil

163 "Abdullah Ocalan Proposes 7-Point Peace Plan", Nov., 1998, http://kicadam.home. xs4all.nl/pers/oud/propose.html.

war, claiming the emergence of the PKK was a mistake and he was willing to cooperate with the government to end the struggle. He said, if his life was spared, he would make efforts to stop bloodshed and achieve peace.[164]

Subsequently, the PKK issued a statement to support Ocalan's appeal for peace. On September 1, 1999, Ocalan declared a ceasefire in prison again. Later, the PKK withdrew its armed forces from Turkey and founded a new base at Kandil or Qandil Mountains[165] of Northern Iraq. In February 2000, the PKK officially announced the end the civil war, claiming that it would change its strategies, give up armed struggle and attain goals through peaceful means. In April 2002, the PKK changed its name into the Kurdish Freedom and Democratic Congress (KADEK) and Ocalan was elected as the honorary president. He said the PKK had completed its historical mission and would carry out activities as a pure political organization.[166]

Its main intention was to suddenly transform the tarnished image and former violent identity into a legal political party in Turkey so as to conduct political work for the promotion of Kurdish democratic and cultural rights. In October 2003, the KADEK was dissolved and a new organization named the People's Congress of Kurdistan (KONGRA-GEL) was established. Though this organization changed its names more than once and claimed to renounce armed struggle, it didn't change its major members and Ocalan remained as its nominal leader. Turkey, the United States, Israel and Europe still considered the KADEK and the KONGRA-GEL as a terrorist organizations and didn't legalize them for the new changes. After Ocalan was arrested, the actual leaders of the PKK were Zübeyir Aydar[167], Murat Karayilan[168] and Cemil Bayik.

130

164   Life or Death: Ocalan's Trial Entered its Second Day, Evening News, June 2, 1999, http: //news.sina.com.cn/world/9906/060248.html.
165   The mountain is situated on the Iraqi side of the Iraqi-Iranian border region and in the 50 kilometers south of the junction of Iraq, Iran and Turkey. With about 3,000 meters above the sea level, it belongs to the Zagros Mountains. This mountainous area is geographically isolated and inaccessible, so it is difficult for troops to enter in a large scale. The PKK controls the territory of approximately 50 square kilometers around the mountain. Turkey often sends air force to bomb it. The Free Life Party, Iranian anti-government armed forces, has also long been entrenched here.
166   "PKK/KONGRA-GEL and Terrorism", http://www.ataa.org/reference/PKK/PKK.html.
167   Zübeyir Aydar is one of the founders of the PKK and was born in Elazig Province in 1951. When studying at the Language and Literature Department of Ankara University, he made the acquaintance of Ocalan and later established the PKK with him. He has long been regarded as the second most important figure of this party and led the ARGK. After Ocalan was arrested, he became one member of the PKK Chairman Committee (composed of eight to ten people) and also one of the 12 members of the KCK. During the trial, Ocalan criticized he lacked military competences. The current PKK leader and Zübeyir Aydar are evaluated as the "conservatives" of the party.
168   Murat Karayilan, also known as Cemal, entered the Politburo in the 1990s and led the ARGK. After the arrest of Ocalan in 1999, he became one of the members of the PKK Chairmanship Committee. He has now become the most important leader of the PKK and chairman of the KKK.

The party was split in 2003. The radical "innovationists"[169] led by Hikmet Fidan declared to separate from the party and founded the Kurdish Patriotic Democratic Party (PPDK/PWD) in Mosul, Iraq. The PPDK said that Ocalan was a figure similar to Stalin or Hitler who ordered the assassination of many party members that held different views from him. This party announced that it opposed armed struggle and supported to solve the Kurdish problem by means of democracy and federalism. It is said that this new party cooperated with Osman Ocalan, brother of the leader, and Osman Ocalan now leads this party.

In 2004, Fehman Huseyin served as leader of the ARGK attached to Kongra-Gel, which now has about 5,000 members and is active mostly in Northern Iraq.[170]

During this period, the Turkish government continued to crack down on the PKK and other Kurdish armed forces. Though there was temporary cease-fire, conflicts were underway soon. However, compared with the 1990s, the conflict decreased in both intensity and scale. Policies enforced by the AKP won the support of plenty of Kurdish people and the living standards of the Kurds improved; thus, the mass base for the armed struggle of the PKK was weakened. From September 1, 1999, when Ocalan declared a ceasefire to June 1, 2004, when he announced the suspension of the ceasefire and resumed the armed struggle, it remained basically peaceful and conflict reduced sharply. The Turkish government said the PKK didn't stop its attacks during the time and what they did was only reducing the attack scale, but the PKK said that they were forced to defend itself and condemned the Turkish government waged about 700 strikes. Although the PKK declared a ceasefire, its radicals didn't comply with the agreement and even joined forces with other Kurdish militants to launch attacks.

On May 29, 2004, the PKK issued a statement that in view of the aggressive and destructive operations made by the Turkish government within the past three months, the ceasefire with Turkey would end on June 1 and armed forces of the PKK would wage new attacks on the Turkish army. Compared with the 1990s, the PKK changed its strategies and tactics dramatically. Losing the support of Syrian government, it couldn't launch large-scale attacks anymore and then turned to take small-scale actions, such as ambushing, laying mines and sniping. "Its action teams have decreased from 15-20 to 6-8 people and meanwhile bases and underground forces are no longer founded."[171] In these days,

131

169   Innovationists were represented by Kani Yilmaz, Osman Ocalan (Abdullah Ocalan's brother) and Nizamettin Tas. Kani Yilmaz used to be the third most important figure of the PKK. He was assassinated in Sulaymaniyah of Iraq on February 11, 2006. Ocalan claimed in 2008 that the PKK tried to assassinate him twice but failed.
170   "PKK/KONGRA-GEL", http://www.mfa.gov.tr/pkk_kongra-gel.en.mfa.
171   "PKK Changes Battlefield Tactics to Force Turkey into Negotiations", Jamestown, Oct.24, 2007.

during its 2005 Congress, PKK approved its fifth party flag, the Congress approved a red flag with red star placed in a yellow circle. The flags were changed due to ideological evolution and certain practical-political reasons. On April 13 of 2009, the PKK declared a ceasefire for the sixth time, and Ocalan demanded stopping of the military operations in preparation for peace. But, the pro-Kurdish party DTP was banned at the end of the year, which reignited the armed conflicts. According to the figures released by the Turkish government in June 2010, armed conflicts between the Turkish security forces and the PKK led to death of 4,015 Turkish soldiers, 217 police officers and 1,335 village guards as well as 2,904 PKK members from 1984 to the end of 2009.[172]

In addition, the Turkish government made secret contacts with the PKK. In October of 2010, the Turkish government confirmed that it had a dialogue with Ocalan's representatives.[173] It was reported that the place was in Oslo and the dialogue was similar to the secret negotiation between Palestine and Israel which was held in Oslo.[174] When Ocalan received an interview in March 2011, he still held an optimistic attitude toward a political solution to the Kurdish problem, claiming that the AKP was the biggest obstacle to peace and called on the Turks and Kurds to put pressure on this party and take actions to solve the Kurdish issue. He said the dialogue with the government continued and he still wished it would yield to a good result. He expressed that "we're trying to formulate a resolving program for the Kurdish issue on the basis of a democratic constitution" and restated that "my theory of democratic solution is the most important in the world". He hoped to establish a national democratic front, which involved minorities, green movements, workers, leftist organizations and labor unions.

Meanwhile, Ocalan suggested that the Kurds should undertake a new wave of protests and put up tents at the squares of the city centers and suggested the Kurdish parties to rename the squares as "Square of Freedom" and make them centers to protest against the Turkish government. He emphasized, "If we want to launch opposition movements similar to those in Egypt, Tunisia, Libya and Iraq, we'll have the potential to do so and even obtain more support and power".[175]

The two sides resumed the interrupted negotiation in 2012 and announced a peace agreement to end the war in early 2013. In March 2013,

132

---

172   Milliyet, June 24, 2011.
173   http://www.freedom-for-Ocalan.com/english/download/AbdullahOcalan-TheRoadMap-Summary.pdf.
174   "End to Turkey's Kurdish Conflict Fades from Sight", The Daily Star, Mar. 23, 2012,http://www.dailystar.com.lb/News/Middle-East/2012/Mar-23/167766-end-to-turkeys-kurdish-conflict-fades-from-sight.ashx#ixzz1qOuVOqPP.
175   "Abdullah Ocalan Remains Optimistic in search for Political Solution to Kurdish Question in Turkey!", Mar. 9, 2011,http://hevallo.blogspot.com/2011/03/Abdullah-Ocalan-remains-optimistic-in.html.

Ocalan declared the war was ceased and the PKK armed forces could be withdrawn from Turkey in batches. In May, the PKK declared it had embarked on the withdrawal process.

Fig. 2-4 Party Flag of the PKK during 1978 and 1995

Fig. 2-5 Party Flag of the PKK during 1995 and 2002

Fig. 2-6 Party Flag of the PKK during 2002 and 2003

Fig. 2-7 Party Flag of the PKK during 2003 and 2005

Fig. 2-8 Party Flag of the PKK from 2005

Ocalan read a lot of books about western social theory in prison, claiming his ideal society idea was the one of "democratic confederation" and considered Nietzsche as "Prophet". He issued "Manifesto of Kurdistan Democratic Confederation" in March 2005, wishing to establish a "free non-state confederation" in Kurdish regions of Turkey, Syria, Iraq and Iran. Three legal systems would be adopted in this region: the EU law, the Kurdish law and the law of Turkey, Iraq, Iran and Syria. This manifesto of Democratic Confederation was added into the PKK program in April 2005. On September 28, 2006, Ocalan issued a statement to call on the PKK to cease fire and seek peace with Turkey, saying that "it is very important to set up a democratic alliance between the Kurds and the Turks and thus a road to democratic dialogue should be taken". In August 2009, he said he would announce his comprehensive proposal of peace, namely, "Road Map to Peace", on the 25th anniversary of the Kurdish uprising.[176]

The "Road Map to Peace" proposed by Ocalan, also known as "The Road Map to Democratization of Turkey and Solution to the Kurdish Question", criticized the two traditional solutions to the Kurdish issue—The Solution Plan of Traditional Policy of Denial and Annihilation and the Federalist and Nationalist Solution Plan and thirdly put forward to his own alternative as "Democratic Solution Plan". This plan was divided into three phases. The first was to cease hostilities and ensure non-provocation, strict constraints on armed forces and effective mass work.

135

---

176   http://www.freedom-for-Ocalan.com/english/download/AbdullahOcalan-
TheRoadMap-Summary.pdf.

In the second phase, the Truth and Justice Commission would be established after being proposed by the Turkish government and approved by the TBMM with the aim to help remove various obstacles in the sphere of legislation and make concrete suggestions for the new legislations. The commission should propose an amnesty concept and system to the TBMM (National Assembly) the PKK would withdraw its armed forces from Turkey and accept the supervision of a committee co-founded by the US, the EU, the UN, the Kurdish government of Iraq and Turkey.

In the third phase, with the formulation of democratized Constitution and the implementation of relevant legislative steps, activities of the KKK would be legalized and the PKK would be dissolved. The Kurdish people who exiled for many years would gradually return to their homeland (including the PKK members, Kurds losing their nationalities and Kurdish refugees). Ocalan said that as "the democratization of and solution to the Kurdish issue", this program reflected the Turkish history and reality, which not only meant that the development of Turkey would be more independent, but also showed that people in the Middle East were taking a more democratic, equal and free path.[177]

Summary

136   Compared with the Iraqi Kurds, Turkish Kurds have a weaker national consciousness, which is partially caused by their residence in deep mountains and backward economic, social and cultural development and also attributed to the Turkization policy implemented by Turkey for a long run. Sheikh Said's grandson and Congressman Abdul Malik Firat pointed out: "Oppression of the Turkish government on the Kurds played a much bigger role in arousing the Kurdish national consciousness than PKK's propaganda."[178]

Since the 1990s, national consciousness of the Kurds has grown rapidly. The assimilated Kurds began to emphasize their Kurdish national identity, which became a developing trend. This fact proves that the policy of denying the existence of the Kurds and assimilating them that the Turkish government has enforced is going towards a dead end.

After the Cold War, Turkish Kurds have undertaken national struggle in two routes: the first is setting up political parties and engaging in political activities with legal status; the second is the armed struggle typically

---

177   "Abdullah Ocalan: The Road Map to Democratization of Turkey and Solution to the Kurdish Question",http://www.freedom-for-Ocalan.com/english/download/AbdullahOcalan-TheRoadMap-Summary.pdf.
178   Kemal Kirisci, Gareth M. Winrow, The Kurdish Question and Turkey: An Example of a Trans-State Ethnic Conflict, p.112.

followed by the PKK. The PKK's armed struggle for national rights has limited effect and is doomed to failure, but has given rise to three major objective influences: first, it cultivates national feelings of the Kurdish people and awakens their nationalist awareness; second, it severely damages national and social stability of Turkey, brings heavy political and economic burden to it and meanwhile results in such negative consequences of inharmonious ethnic relations and poor external image for the country; third, it makes the Kurdish issue in Turkey attract more attention from the international community, which promotes the Turkish government to care about and resolve this problem. The policy transformation by the PKK has achieved success to some degree and obtained some public support and sympathy inside and outside Turkey.

Since the 1990s and especially with the AKP government, the Turkish government has greatly changed its policies in dealing with the Kurdish issue and the life and status of the Kurds have improved. This phenomenon has been caused by many factors. Among them, the following four are most important:

First, a political upheaval takes place in this region, which results from changes in international and regional patterns as well as the international development trend, including the end of the Cold War, the re-emergence of democracy and nationalism, the big transformation in Iraq, the establishment of the Kurdish autonomous region in Iraq and the "Arab Spring".

Second, political, economic and social development brings dramatic changes inside Turkey, democratic elements keep increasing, and the legacy of Kemalist doctrine encounters challenges in various aspects. Third, Turkey's process of joining the EU exerts a significant impact on the development of the Kurdish issue.

Fourth, the long-term armed struggle of the PKK objectively pushes the Turkish government to try to solve the Kurdish issue. In the spring of 2013, the Turkish government finally reached a historic peace agreement with Ocalan. Yet, this new process still faces many obstacles coming from the government's ideology, law and policies as well as the public opinion to eventually solve the Kurdish issue. The future is not that optimistic.

CHAPTER THREE

The Kurdish Issue in Iraq

In contrast, the Iraqi Kurds have won and enjoyed the highest status among the countries where Kurds reside. Their national identity has been basically recognized and they gained the autonomous government right in 1970 after a long-term struggle. After the Gulf War in 1991, they achieved autonomy in Northern Iraq and established "a state within a state". After Saddam Hussein's regime was overthrown in 2003, the Kurds further elevated their status and became one of the three major political forces in Iraq, and meanwhile the Kurdish regional government turned to be a "quasi-state". In fact, their current status was not easily won. Their struggle for national rights was the largest in scale, the most fierce in intensity and of course has won the most fruitful results among the four countries of Turkey, Iraq, Iran and Syria. Since the World War II, the Iraqi Kurdistan has maintained to be the center of the Kurdish national movements in the Middle East. The development of its future will also be the main wind vane of the trend of the Kurdish issue in the entire area.

3.1 Kurdish Struggle in Iraq

Kurdistan in Iraq is traditionally known as "Southern Kurdistan". It neighbors with Syria in its east, connects with Turkey in its north, borders Syria in its west and links with Iraq's Arab region in its south, thus being the core of Kurdistan. In the late Ottoman Empire, it belonged to Mosul Province in terms of administration and managed three sub-provinces: Mosul, Kirkuk and Sulaymaniyah. Southern Kurdistan is most fertile and richest area in the entire region of Kurdistan, with vast fecund plains and abundant water resources. Such rivers as the Euphrates River, the Tigris River, big and small Zab rivers and the Sheva River go through it. It boasts abundant rainfall and the average annual precipitation is 375 to 724 mm. Therefore, it enjoys the fame of Iraq's "barn". Furthermore, possessing extremely rich oil resources, it is the most fortunate area containing oil reserves in Iraq. Its proven oil reserve reaches as many as 43.7 billion barrels (the figure in the entire Iraq is 102 billion barrels) and its potential oil reserve arrives at 25.5 billion barrels. Besides, its oil production accounts for nearly half of the country.[1] Kirkuk[2] Oilfield is one of the largest oilfields in the world and Mosul is one of the largest petrochemical cities in Iraq.

The current Iraqi Constitution calls Southern Kurdistan as "Kurdish region". This title can be traced back to the 1970s. In 1970, the Iraqi government reached an agreement with the Kurdish people and allowed them to achieve autonomy in the Kurdish region. Accordingly, Southern Kurdistan became the "Kurdish Autonomous Region", and the Kurdish Autonomous Government was renamed to be the "Kurdish Regional Government" (KRG). In 1976, the Iraqi government readjusted administrative divisions of the country and set up 18 provinces, among which Arbil, Sulaymaniyah and Duhok were all located in Kurdistan and constituted the Kurdish Autonomous Region. The Kurds believed that Nineveh, Diyala, Wasit (it was called as Kut Province before 1976 and its capital was Kut) and other provinces also belonged to Kurdistan and thus Kurdistan in Iraq covered seven provinces. However, the Iraqi government dissented from the Kurds in this regard. The area of Southern Kurdistan is about 29,000 square miles (about 80,000 square kilometers), covering 17% of the land in Iraq. Tamim Province where Kirkuk lies has the largest area (7,622 square miles), which is followed by Arbil (5,973 square miles), Sulaymaniyah (4,677 square miles) and Duhok (3,804 square miles). In addition, the area of 4,300 square miles of Nineveh, 2,150 of Diyala and 350 of Wasit was also owned

---

1   "Energy", http://knowkurdistan.com/about/energy.
2   Kirkuk is the capital of Tamim Province and the main industrial and oil city in Northern Iraq. Oil fields were discovered in 1929 with a reserve of 2.2 billion tons. By the end of 1975, 44% had been mined. Kirkuk Oilfield was discovered early and contains a large reserve of oil. There are five pipelines leading to Lebanon, Turkey and Syria.

by Kurdistan. Arbil (formerly known as Hewler) is the center of Southern Kurdistan and also the capital of the Kurdish region, with a population of about 1.3 million (2009). Sulaymaniyah is the second largest city in the Kurdish region with a population close to 825,000, and it is regarded as the cultural capital of the Kurdish region in Iraq. Compared with the ancient city of Arbil, Sulaymaniyah was built late and used to be the capital of the Emirate of Emir Baban in 1785. It was named after Buyuk Suleyman Pasha (governor of Baghdad during 1780 and 1802) who worked as its governor at that time.

The Iraqi Kurds account for about 20% of Iraq's total population. According to the forecast made by the British government in 1919, the population of Basra, Baghdad and Mosul provinces was 2.75 million and that of Mosul was 788,000. A census was held in Iraq in 1957 and the result showed that the entire population was 6.5 million, of which there were 5,018,962 Arabs living in 14 provinces of the country, 1,042,774 Kurds mainly in 4 provinces and 236,806 people from other minorities. The Kurdish people thought it had been the most honest and authentic census ever in the Iraqi history, so they insisted this figure should be treated as the foundation for the solution to problems of Kirkuk and other mixed areas in the March Agreement in 1970.[3] By May 31, 1975, the Kurdish population of Iraq was 2.8 million, of which 564,000 were in Arbil, 653,000 in Sulaymaniyah, 168,000 in Duhok, 641,000 in Kirkuk and 800,000 in other provinces.[4] Data provided by the UN's "Oil-for-Food" plan[5] in 2002 showed that the Kurdish population of Iraq was 3,757,058. The figure given by the Kurdish government in May 2010 was 4.7 million, among which 1,713,461 dwelled in Arbil, 1,800,769 in Sulaymaniyah and 1,176,709 in Duhok.[6] The report released by the American Club revealed that there were 4 to 4.5 million Kurds in Iraq.[7] Taking various data into consideration, the author believes the current Kurdish population in Iraq is 5 million and accounts for about 20% of the country's total. In 1957, the Kurds accounted for the 27.2%, and the rate dropped to 26.07% in 1965 and to 25% in 1975.[8]

3 Mustafa Barzani and the Kurdish Liberation Movement, Palgrave Macmillan, 2003, p.159.

4 Gérard Chaliand, A People without a Country: The Kurds and Kurdistan, p.142.

5 This plan was made in 1995 according to Resolution 986 of the UN Security Council and was officially enforced in December 1996. Its basic content was using oil export revenues of Iraq to purchase necessary food, medicine and other basic supplies to alleviate the humanitarian crisis. It was officially discontinued in 2010. In accordance with relevant statistics, during this period, the oil export revenue of Iraq was $ 65 billion, of which approximately $ 46 billion was used to exchange for food.

6 "The People of the Kurdistan Region", May 20, 2010,http://www.krg.org/articles/detail.asp?rnr=141&lngnr=12&smap=03010400&anr=18657.

7 Kenneth Katzman, "The Kurds in Post-Saddam Iraq", October 1, 2010, RS22079, https:. //opencrs.com/document/RS22079/2010-10-01/

8 Gérard Chaliand, A People without a Country: The Kurds and Kurdistan, p.142.

Travel Guide to Iraq published by the Iraqi government in 1975 said, Kurds accounted for 15% of the total population of Iraq in 1975. Yet, the US State Council stated they occupied 15% to 20% (in 2012).[9] The figure released on the website of the Chinese Foreign Ministry is 18%.[10]

Historically, the Kurds migrated in a large number from rural to urban areas due to government policies. From the 1970s to 2001, at least 600,000 Kurdish people were forced to leave their hometowns. In November 1991, 100,000 Kurds were expelled from Kirkuk. According to the UNDP, 66% of the population in Duhok province was forced to migrate to avoid war, and the figure was 31% in Sulaymaniyah and 7% in Arbil.[11]

Residents in the Kurdish autonomous region are mainly the Kurdish people and there are also some Arabs, Assyrians, Chaldeans, Turkmens[12] and Armenians. By 2010, there were 100,000 to 200,000 Turkmens and 50,000 Assyrians in the three provinces of the Kurdish autonomous region. The population in this region was highly young. The population aged 0 to 14 accounted for 36% and the elderly aged over 63 only occupied 4%. The average age of the Kurds there was about 20 years old, which meant close to 50% people were less than 20.[13] The urban population accounted for about 80%, while rural population only 20%.

The Kurdish language is an official language in Iraq and has been allowed to be used in education, publishing and other industries. The official languages of the Kurdish regional government are Arabic and Kurdish. Kurdish in Iraq, also known as Southern Kurdish Kelhuri and Sorani differs from Kurmanji spoken by Turkish Kurds and uses the Arabic alphabet as its writing system. Sorani is mainly employed in Arbil and Sulaymaniyah, whereas Kurmanji is used in Duhok. After the autonomy of the Kurdish region, the regional government greatly promoted Kurdish, and at present, residents can basically listen to and speak the two major Kurdish dialects.

Most Iraqi Kurds believe in Sunni Islam and some worship Shia. After the fall of Saddam Hussein, the Kurdish people who believe in Christianity as well as Christian churches increased in number at the northern part of Iraq. There are Syrian Catholicism, Syrian Orthodox, Armenian Orthodox,

9   http://www.state.gov/r/pa/ei/bgn/6804.htm.
10   Country Profile of Iraq, July 2011, http: //www.fmprc.gov.cn/chn/pds/gjhdq/gj/yz/1206_39/.
11   "The People of the Kurdistan Region", 20 May, 2010,http://www.krg.org/articles/detail.asp?rnr=141&lngnr=12&smap=03010400&anr=18657.
12   Turkmen is the third largest ethnic group in Iraq with a population of 500,000 second only to Arabs and Kurds. However, the Turkish government said there were 2 to 3 million Turkmens in Iraq, which may be exaggerated. Turkmens mostly live outside the Kurdistan region.
13   "The People of the Kurdistan Region", May 20, 2010, http://www.krg.org/articles/detail.asp?rnr=141&lngnr=12&smap=03010400&anr=18657.

etc. In recent years, communal conflicts against Christians often took place in Northern Iraq. Furthermore, about 70,000 to 500,000 Kurds pursue Yazidi and such people concentrate on west and northwest of Mosul.[14] It is worth mentioning that most Yazidi followers come from Iraqi Kurdistan.

The Kurdish region in Iraq has abundant farmland and forests. Residents there live a sedentary life and this region is most urbanized in Kurdistan, which may be relevant to its vast fertile plains and arable land and also caused by its economic development and especially the rise of its oil industry since post-1970s. In the 1980s, the Saddam government destroyed more than 4,000 Kurdish villages and forced villagers to migrate into cities and towns. Currently, some villages have been reconstructed. With the help of UN agencies and NGOs, the Kurdish regional government has rebuilt 2,620 villages since 1991, which accounts for 65% of the ones that were destroyed.[15]

Nevertheless, tribes still function as a vital social structure in this region. Although the influence that tribal chieftains enjoy declines a bit, it remains great. Major tribes in this region include: Barzanis, Zebari, Surchi (which neighbors Barzanis and discord with it for a long run and had joined the pro-government Kurdish armed forces), Rawanduz, Bhotan, Herki, Dolameri, Jirki, Sindi, Mendikan and Kharmawend. The well-known Barzani tribe is located in Barzan. Bordering with Turkey and lying on the left bank of the Small Zab River and the edge of Shirin Hill, this region is mountainous and inaccessible. Barzani migrated here around the mid-19th century. Barzani people are religiously fidel, brave and skillful in battle, and from them there appeared a large number of famous figures in the modern history of Iraq, such as Sheikh Ahmed Barzani (1896-1969), Sheikh Abdul Salam Barzani II (1882-1914) and Mullah Mustafa Barzani (1903-1979).[16] This tribe had made tremendous contributions to Iraq as well as to the national cause of

143

---

14   http://en.wikipedia.org/wiki/Yazidi.
15   "The People of the Kurdistan Region", May 20, 2010, http: //www.krg.org/articles/ detail.asp rnr = 141 & lngnr = 12 & smap = 03010400 & anr = 18657?.
16   Barzani tribe tree is illustrated roughly as follows: Massoud→Said→Tajal-Din→Sheikh Abdul Rahman→Sheikh Abdullah→Sheikh Abdussalam→Mohammad. Mohammad had five sons: Shiekh Abdul Salam, Sheikh Ahmed, Mohammed Siddique, Babo and Mustafa Barzani. Sheikh Ahmed, also called as Khudan and the elder brother of Mullah Mustafa, worked as the tribal chieftain and Sheikh of Barzani and enjoyed the fame as the designer of the modern Barzani. During his tenure, he expanded the population and area of Barzani. From the 1920s to 1930s, he led the struggle of Barzani against the government. His younger brother Mullah Mustafa Barzani was the leader of the contemporary Kurdish national movement and the founder of the Kurdish Democratic Party. The sons of Mullah Mustafa Barzani were Massoud Barzani (current chairman of the Kurdish regional government) and Idris Barzani. Massoud Barzani has five sons and three daughters. One of his sons Masrour Barzani takes charge of security agencies of the Kurdish regional government. Idris Barzani's son Nechirvan Barzani is the vice-chairman of the Kurdish regional government.

the Kurds in the entire region. According to statistics, this tribal area was destroyed by the government army for 16 times in the 20th century.[17] About 8,000 Barzani members were rounded up by the government army and a great number of Barzani men were executed in 1983.

Women enjoy a high status in Southern Kurdistan. Being highly educated, they don't wear veils and can talk with visitors freely. Many of them even participated in the Kurdish armed forces against the Iraqi government. And some now hold posts in the autonomous government.

3.2 The Period of British Mandate and Faisal Dynasty

This period spans from the end of the First World War in 1918 to the outbreak of "July Revolution" in Iraq in 1958. During the time, the country of Iraq was just founded and basically under the British mandate. The Kurdish nationalism was in the embryonic stage and the struggle was in its infancy. Although Britain did not fulfill its international obligation to grant the Kurdish autonomy, British Kurdish policies were relatively tolerant under the colonial rule and the Kurds were not assimilated systematically. Discrimination against them was mainly shown in the national political rights sphere.

There emerged Kurdish emirates of varying scales in Southern Kurdistan in different periods of time, most of which were semi-independent. In 1831, the Ottoman Empire which kept declining and faced secessionist threat began to rule this region directly so as to strengthen its central control. This situation lasted until the end of the World War I. At that time, Iraq was not a complete country and its land was roughly divided into three provinces: Basra, Baghdad and Mosul. During the World War I, Britain and France reached a secret agreement to put Mosul under the French mandate. Due to the discovery of oil in Mosul later, France agreed to make concession and put it under the British mandate. Since then, Southern Kurdistan has been part of Iraq. How to ensure the Kurdish national status and rights in the country of Iraq has become the basic content of the Kurdish national movements.

While the Kurdish nationalism formed gradually in the late 19th and early 20th century, the Arab nationalism also rose, which set off the first struggle wave and a climax for national rights. After the outbreak of the WWI, Arab nationalist leaders represented by Mecca Sheriff Hussein Ibn Ali aimed to take the advantage of the Ottoman decline to achieve national independence and thus actively strove for the support from the Allied Powers

---

17   Michael M.Gunter, Historical Dictionary of the Kurds, p.52.

countries. Meanwhile, the Allied Powers countries desired to encourage Arabs to launch an uprising against the Ottoman Empire by using the bait of supporting the establishment of an independent Arab country. On October 15, 1915, Mecca Sheriff Hussein wrote a letter to Britain, requesting to found an Arab country which included the "Fertile Crescent", the Arabian Peninsula and provinces of Baghdad and Basra but didn't include Mosul Province. Britain replied on October 24 and agreed to this proposal on the condition that the Arabs waged an uprising.[18]

The Arab uprising began in June 1916, and the Arabs soon captured a vast land of Jeddah, Mecca, Taif, Aqaba and Damascus and established the Arab Kingdom. However, the colonists said one thing and actually did in the opposite way. To divide up the territory and possessions of the Ottoman Empire, the Allied Powers countries made a series of secret diplomatic activities. In May 1916, Britain and France reached a secret agreement about the division of Arab provinces of the Ottoman Empire, namely, Sykes-Picot Agreement. Under the agreement, Britain would obtain the control over the current Jordan, Southern Iraq and Haifa, whereas France gained the control over Southeastern Turkey, Northern Iraq, Syria and Lebanon. This agreement broke the promise made to the Arabs. Hussein declared himself King of Arabia in October 1916, but Britain, France and Italy only recognized him as the ruler of Hejaz.

On March 7, 1920, the Syrian National Assembly declared independence of Syria and put Hussein's son Faisal on the throne, but Britain and France refused to recognize it. In April, the same year, the San Remo Conference placed Syria (including Lebanon) under the French mandate and meanwhile put Iraq under the British mandate. As a compensation for France which had to give Mosul, it obtained the 20% stake of the Turkish Oil Company. France occupied Damascus of Syria in July. The Ottoman Turkey government was forced to sign the Mudros Armistice Agreement with the Allied Powers countries on October 30, 1918. Subsequently, Britain, France and Italy sent troops to occupy vast territories of Turkey, including the Straits, vital ports along the Black Sea, southeastern and southwestern Anatolia and important towns along the railway. The British army grabbed the Mosul Province.

In accordance with the secret agreement reached by Britain and France, Mosul Province was put under the French mandate. During the WWI, Iraq became the battlefield for British and Turkish armies. The British army occupied Basra in March 1914, Baghdad in March 1917 and Kirkuk in May 1918. After the armistice which was made on October 31, 1918, the British army grabbed Mosul in November. After the war, Britain grabbed

---

18   This series of letters are also called as "Hussein-McMahon letters".

the mandate of Basra, Baghdad and Mosul. Iraq was designated under the jurisdiction of the British colonial authority in India. The British government appointed Sir Arnold Wilson as the highest commissioner of Iraq.

In October 1920, Sir Percy Cox replaced Wilson to become the highest commissioner. In November 1920, a government was being set up in Iraq, and its 21 Cabinet members came from Basra, Baghdad and Mosul provinces, among whom Sunni Arabs were dominant. In August 1921, Britain enabled Hussein's son Faisal to take the throne of Iraq and the Kingdom of Iraq was established. King Faisal said in his inaugural speech, "When we speak from the position of Patriots, the words of Muslims, Christians, Jews and Kurds are meaningless. We only have one country, and that is Iraq."[19]

Iraq is considered to be the Arabic translation of the Greek word Mesopotamia. Yet, some others believe it stems from the ancient Arabic word, which means "vessel" and refers to the network of the two rivers which looks like a human blood vessel. In October 1922, Britain and the Faisal Dynasty signed the Iraqi-British Treaty of Alliance, which recognized the British control over Iraq's political, economic and military areas as well as certain British privileges in Iraq for a period of 20 years. In 1924, a Constitution was issued and parliamentary monarchy was started in Iraq. The first parliamentary election was held in 1925, and the country was divided into three constituencies. The first session of parliament began after the general elections.

In principle, Kurdish nationalists supported Arab nationalists in establishing their state, Iraq, but opposed to a pan-Arab nation-state, and meanwhile they solemnly pointed out that any attempt to ally Iraq with other Arab countries would lead to the "establishment of an independent Kurdish state".[20]

When Arab nationalists wanted to establish an Arab country, the Kurdish people proposed founding an independent Kurdish country. On December 1, 1918, Iraqi Kurdish leaders met Sir Arnold Wilson, British commissioner in Iraq, appealing to establish an independent and unified country of Kurdistan under the British support. However, the British had no intention to do so. Coveting at the oil-rich province of Mosul, they desired to incorporate Mosul into the territory of Iraq. Sir Arnold Wilson recalled in his memoir that "The Kurds neither want to be ruled by the Turks anymore, nor hope to be controlled by the Iraqi government. In Southern Kurdistan, 80% people support Sheikh Mahmud Barzanji's (1878-1956) plan to found an independent Kurdistan, and the idea that Kurdistan belongs to the Kurds

---

19　Gertrude Bell, http: //baike.baidu.com/view/4600359.htm.
20　Introduction to the World Nations, Publishing House of Minzu University of China, 1993, p. 394.

is very popular and almost each Kurd is eager to cut off relations with Turkey".[21] In April of 1919, Sir Arnold offered advice to the British government that the country of Iraq which was about to be established should include the Kurdish region and Mosul, and this region, especially the entire Zab area, should not belong to the newly established Armenia.

As for the issue of Kurdish autonomy, he suggested that "the best way is to give solutions in accordance with our own judgment and we should do everything possible to ensure that this issue will not be brought up for discussion in (Paris) Peace Conference".[22]

Another colonial officer Major Edward Noel also advocated the establishment of an independent Kurdish state or the Kurdish autonomy under the British rule. Based on his own experience in Iraq, he specifically wrote Diary of Major Noel's Special Mission from June 14 to September 21 of 1919. Yet, this British proposal was not adopted in the Paris Peace Conference. In the Treaty of Sèvres with the Ottoman Empire which was signed in August 1920, the Kurds were entitled to independence. The Article No. 64 of the Treaty of Sèvres stipulated: "The Kurds who live in the Kurdish region of Mosul Province should enjoy the right to join the country of Kurdistan in the future". However, Britain didn't comply with this article. On August 23, 1921, the British High Commissioner Sir Cox announced that Faisal has become the King of Iraq, which included Mosul province. In his official report submitted to the Mandate Territory Committee of the League of Nations, he pointed out that the Kurdish people were worried that Faisal's Baghdad controlling Iraq's all industries and economy, their interests would be damaged. Kurds felt that they were deceived. Kurdish people in Sulaymaniyah had decided not to participate in the Iraqi general elections. They almost unanimously rejected any form of Iraqi rule and demanded the establishment of their self-government. King Faisal was also not recognized in Kurdish Kirkuk. At this time, Iraq government actively demarcated the boundaries of Iraq. The British senior official in Iraq, Miss Gertrude Bell who was involved in the formation of the Kingdom of Iraq and helped the determination of Iraqi territories wrote in the letter to her father on December 4, 1921, "I happily drew out the damarcation demarcation line of the southern desert of Iraq in my office this morning."[23]

21   A.Wilson, Mesopotamia1917-1920, London, 1931, pp.103,127,129,134,137.
22   Ibid., p. 117.
23   Female genius who demarcated the national boundaries of Iraq, http://www.china.com. cn/chinese/zhuanti/310513.htm. Gertrude Bell (1868-1926) was a British adventurer, writer and diplomat. She she began forming what became the Baghdad Archaeological Museum, later renamed the Iraqi Museum. She used to travel extensively in the Middle East and served as one of Britain's top experts. She wrote many books about archeology, architecture and culture of the Middle East. During the First World War, she helped British intelligence agencies to instigate the Arabs to resist the Ottoman rule. In 1921, she assisted Britain in founding the Kingdom of Iraq. She worked as director of an Antiquities museum in Baghdad from 1918 to her death.

147

In July 1923, Kemal of Turkey finally defeated Britain, France and other Allied Powers countries and forced them to abolish the Treaty of Sèvres and sign the Treaty of Lausanne. Allied Powers countries gave up the idea of setting up a Kurdish country in the Kurdish region of Turkey. Kemal also required the British to return Mosul. In this context, Britain and Iraq issued a joint declaration on December 24 of 1922 that they both allowed the Kurds to found an autonomous government in Iraq. The declaration said, "His Britannic Majesty's Government and the Government of Iraq recognize the right of the Kurds who live within the frontiers of Iraq to establish a Government within those frontiers. Our two Governments hope that the various Kurdish groups will reach some mutual agreement as quickly as possible to the form they wish this Government to take and as to the boundaries within which they wish to extend its authority. These groups will send responsible delegates to negotiate their future economic and political relations with His Majesty's Government and the Iraqi Governments". However, the Kurds in Sulaymaniyah were not satisfied with it, for they still wished to establish an independent and free state of Kurdistan.

From 1919 to 1924, Sheikh Mahmud Barzanji, a prestigious Kurdish leader in Sulaymaniyah, waged two uprisings and established the Kingdom of Kurdistan, i.e. the Kurdish government. Barzanji was Sheikh of a Sufi tribe in Sulaymaniyah and the most influential Kurdish leader in Southern Kurdistan. In the beginning of the British control, he was appointed as governor of Sulaymaniyah for the purpose of British covert control of the Kurdish region. On May 22, 1919, he launched the first anti-British uprising in Sulaymaniyah and ordered to arrest all British officials in this area. He controlled Arbil and Mosul subsequently. He then announced the independence of Kurdistan and declared himself as the Emir of the entire Kurdistan. In June of 1919, the British army mobilized two brigades to suppress the uprising and sent the Royal Air Force to bomb this area. The uprising was suppressed. Sheikh was injured and arrested. He was later sentenced to death and finally exiled to India. In July 1920, 62 tribal chiefs in the region called for Kurdish independence under the British mandate, and this appeal was refused by the British government, for fearing it would cause a chain reaction and lead to the fight for independence in Basra and Baghdad. With the war situation between the Allied Powers countries and Turkey changed, Iraq was impacted soon. In the spring of 1922, the Turkish army entered Northern Iraq and marched toward Sulaymaniyah to occupy Mosul and Kirkuk. Under such circumstances, the British decided to release Barzanji and support Kurdish autonomy so as to make the Kurds fight against the Turkish army. Sir Cox even quarreled with Colonial Secretary Winston Churchill in the release issue. Cox favored the release, claiming that Barzanji was the only hope to resume the British prestige in this region and maintain stability there. Eventually, Barzanji was released and sent back home. The British wished he would set up a Kurdish army to battle Turkish troops. In September 1922, the British government appointed him governor, but he refused and launched uprising again. On October 10, he announced the establishment of the Kurdish nation and declared himself King of Kurdistan. On December 24, 1922, Britain and the Iraqi government issued a joint declaration and agreed to Kurdish autonomy, but he rejected and continued to lead the uprising and fight against the British army. With the support of the British army, Iraqi troops occupied Rawanduz in April 1923 and then moved into Sulaymaniyah, so the British regained the control over this region. In July 1923, Barzanji made an agreement with the Iraqi government and accepted the Iranian-British Joint Declaration. Meanwhile, the Iraqi government agreed to the Kurdish autonomy under the Iraqi framework. However, the agreement did not last long before the conflict was underway. The uprising was eventually suppressed in July 1924.

Meanwhile, the British government tried to solve the increasingly serious problem of Mosul and strove to make it part of Iraq. Britain fought against Turkey in terms of Turkish-Iraqi border for several years. According the Article No. 3 of Treaty of Lausanne of 1923, "the border between Turkey and Iraq should be finally determined by the League of Nations". Britain and Turkey held a special conference in Istanbul in 1924 to discuss the issue of Mosul, but they failed to reach an agreement and submitted this issue to the League of Nations. The International Investigation Commission of Mosul Problem was set up on July 16, 1924. The League of Nations roughly determined the "Brussels Line" on October 29, 1924 (along the northern border of Mosul Province). From January to March 1925, the commission conducted a field work in Mosul. On July 16 of the same year, it released an investigation report in Geneva. The report said that most people in Mosul were Kurds. From the perspective of lifestyle, they belonged to Indo-Europeans, neither Arabs nor Turks. Their national consciousness was constantly increasing. Except a small number of educated Arabs in Mosul, the Arab national awareness in this region had not formed yet. The report finally suggested "if a racial standpoint is taken, it is bound to conclude that the best way is to establish an independent Kurdish state, because the Kurds account for 5/8 of the population of Mosul Province. If this program is considered unrealistic, Yazidis and Turks can also be counted, for Yazidis are actually the Kurds and Turks can also be gradually assimilated into Kurds, then the Kurdish people will account for 7/8". The report stressed, "to ensure the Iraqi economy can survive," it was better to put Mosul into Iraq, but two conditions must be satisfied: Iraq must continue to accept the mandate of the League of Nations for 25 years; Iraq must respect the

Kurds' aspirations, and administrative, judiciary and educational sectors in this region should be in the charge of the Kurds. Kurdish should be treated as the official language and educational institutions should be allowed to use Kurdish. Besides, the report also suggested Britain to take measures to protect local Assyrians and Chaldeans (who believed in Christianity).

In September 1925, the Council of League of Nations discussed the report in Geneva. It made a verdict in favor of Britain on October 16, which placed Mosul into Iraqi territory and demarcated the boundaries between Turkey and Iraq. At the same time, it made the following requirements: 1. The British government should submit suggestions to the Council of the League of Nations about how to ensure the Kurds enjoying a local administrative power; 2. The British government should submit the treaty made between Britain and Iraq to the council, which should provide that the mandate duration would be limited to 25 years or until Iraq entering the League of Nations. Iraq welcomed this verdict. As demanded by the League of Nations, Britain and Iraq signed a treaty in October 1925. The British government promised to help Iraq enter the League of Nations and extend the mandate time limit to 25 years or until Iraq entering the League. The British-Iraqi treaty was ratified by the Iraqi parliament in January 1926. Turkey initially opposed the resolution and threatened to prevent its implementation by taking all necessary measures, including military means. However, Turkey eventually accepted the verdict. On June 5, 1926, Britain, Turkey and Iraq reached a tripartite agreement, namely, Treaty of Ankara. According to the treaty, Turkey gave up its claim to the sovereignty over Mosul and agreed to recognize Mosul's being under the Iraqi control; Iraq agreed to offer 10% oil interests of Mosul to Turkey for the next 25 years. In addition, the first article of the treaty provided that the Iraqi-Turkish border was 331 km long (from the boundary intersection between Turkey and Iran in the east to the border between Turkey and Syria in the west). Article 10 required establishing a border area with 75 km wide and provided that both sides should take measures to ensure the Kurds on each other's territory was under control. Turkey ratified the treaty in July 1926. Since then, Iraq had been officially incorporated into Iraq. The commission completed the work of demarcation of Iraqi-Syrian border in 1933.

After resolving the problem of Mosul, the Iraqi government enacted "Law on Local Languages" in 1926, allowing Kurdish elementary schools in Sulaymaniyah and some regions of Arbil to teach the Kurdish language and meanwhile allowing Kurdish publishing houses to publish private books. The central government also appointed Kurdish people to be ministers. Yet, the Kurds were still unsatisfied. Barzanji returned to Iraq and launched an uprising again at the end of 1926. The government sent troops to suppress it in March of 1927 and Barzanji retreated to Iran. In the summer of 1927, the Iranian army took military actions against the rebels led by Barzanji, who then had to go back to Iraq and got arrested there. In 1928, Iraq thought the Kurdish issue had been basically solved, for Kurdistan was controlled by the government forces and remained calm. Thousands of Kurds served in various government agencies as well as military and police teams. The Kurdish uprising in Turkey in 1925 didn't exert a big influence upon the Kurds in Iraq. During the election of Lower House held in 1928, 16 Kurdish people entered the parliament. Though several Kurdish deputies required for Kurdish autonomy, their appeal was not valued. In the general election held in Iraq in 1929, many Kurdish people resisted it and even protests broke out in the Kurdish region.

In June 1930, Britain ended its mandate and Iraq declared its independence. They signed a new British-Iraqi treaty, but actually Iraq was still under the British control. The new treaty didn't mention Kurdish autonomy, which aroused strong dissatisfaction among the Kurds. Barzanji escaped from house arrest in September, and waged an uprising together with some Iranian Kurdish tribes and attacked the Iraqi army. In the same month, Kurdish strikes and demonstrations took place in the city of Sulaymaniyah to support the uprising led by Barzanji. Protestors included workers, students and businessmen, which marked a significant change in the development of the Kurdish national movement from rural to urban areas and also the vital shift of leaders from religious and tribal chiefs to the urban petty bourgeoisie.[24]

The Iraqi government tried to crack down on the uprising, and Barzanji led his armed forces in hiding in the mountainous areas. In March 1931, he launched another revolt, but it was eventually suppressed in May, 1932.[25] Barzanji was regarded as one of the first generation of Kurdish national leaders in the 20th century, and revolts led by him exerted a far-reaching influence on promoting the Kurdish national consciousness in Iraq and stimulating the vigorous Kurdish national armed struggle in the future.

While Barzanji launched uprising, the Barzani tribe, one of the largest tribes (families) in Iraqi Kurdistan, also rose up in arms. The leader of this tribe was Sheikh Ahmed Barzani, whose younger brother was Mullah Mustafa Barzani (he is referred to as Mullah or Mullah Mustafa hereinafter). Barzani brothers were young and promising. Taking advantage of the turbulence, they expanded their influence widely. By 1927, they defeated many surrounding Kurdish tribes (families) and made the tribe of Barzani one of the most important Kurdish forces. Initially, the Barzani tribe cooperated

---

24   Introduction to the World Nations, Publishing House of Minzu University of China, 1993, p. 395.
25   Subsequently, Barzanji was arrested and exiled to Nasiriyah in Southern Iraq. He was released and returned home in 1941, and died in 1956.

with the Iraqi government. The government stationed a troop in the area controlled by Barzani and set up the first police office in Balzan town in 1927. In 1929, the Barzani tribe required the government to establish a Kurdish province in Northern Iraq. After the end of the British mandate in 1930, the Kurds revolted one after another. Barzani brothers waged the first big revolt in 1931. Under the support of the British Royal Air Force, the Iraqi government forces attacked, but the attacks were repelled. One month later, the government army attacked again and finally defeated the forces led by Barzani brothers. Ahmed surrendered to the Turkish army in June 1932, but Mullah Mustafa and another brother Mohammed Sadiq continued to fight.

In 1933, taking the advice given by Ahmed, Mustafa surrendered to the Iraqi government and was placed under house arrest. Later, according to the agreement reached by Britain, Turkey and Iraq, Ahmed Barzani and his tribe were allowed to return to Iraq. They were first put under house arrest in Nasiriyah and then in Sulaymaniyah. During 1934 to 1935, the Barzani tribe revolted again. Within a few months, they repeatedly repulsed the attacks by Turkish and Iraqi troops. At the end of 1935, the uprising was suppressed. In the same period, an anti-government Kurdish tribal forces were active in the border area between Sulaymaniyah and Iran. It was led by Said Mohammed, who penetrated into Iraq from Iran time and again and carried out armed attacks. Being besieged by the Iraqi army forces, he surrendered to the government in August of 1935 and was forgiven.

During this period of time, the Middle East became the battlefield of the Germany led Axis countries and the Allied countries, and Iraq was also a place which Britain and Germany fought fiercely. Pro-British and pro-German forces inside Iraq were in a serious conflict. Because the Rashid Cabinet held a pro-German stance, the British army occupied Baghdad and Basra in May 1941 and overthrew the Rashid government. Iraq announced war against the Axis powers in 1943. In this turbulent situation, Mullah Mustafa Barzani escaped from the house arrest in June 1943 and waged uprising in his home town Barzan. In October, the Iraqi army was too exhausted to abandon Arbil and other places. Since the war developed unfavorably to Britain, the British government hoped to resolve this problem and urged the Iraqi government to negotiate with Mullah. In December 1943, Nouri Saeed restructured the government and appointed three Kurds to be the members of the Cabinet. Among them, Kurdish person Majid Mustafa served as Minister of State, responsible for solving the Kurdish issue. On January 7, 1944, the Iraqi government sent him to investigate the Kurdish region and negotiate with mullahs. Besides, some unpopular local officials were dismissed and a Kurdish was appointed as governor of Sulaymaniyah. Mullahs proposed conditions for negotiation: to dismiss or transfer government officials in the Kurdish region who were suspected of corruption and abuse of power; to establish Kurdish Province, which included Kirkuk, Sulaymaniyah and Arbil as well as some Kurdish areas in Mosul and Diyala; to recognize Kurdish as an official language in the Kurdish region; to appoint a Kurdish deputy minister in each ministry of the Cabinet; to set up a new department in the Ccabinet which took charge of the Kurdish affairs and appoint a Kurdish as a minister; to compensate for the the the damages and losses which the Kurds had encountered in the conflict; military, financial and diplomatic power of Kurdish Province would belong to the central government; hospitals, schools and roads should be constructed vigorously in the Kurdish region.[26]

Subsequently, the government troops withdrew from the area, which was then put under the control of Barzani tribe again. After hearing the report made by Majid Mustafa, the Iraqi government made a decision on January 25, 1944: appointing new officials in the Kurdish region and set up liaison offices there; resetting up police stations in Barzan; constructing roads linking various police stations; deporting Mullah Mustafa outside Balzan; allowing Sheikh Ahmed to go back to Balzan; ordering the Kurds to hand in their weapons; agreeing in principle to grant amnesty except government officials and soldiers who participated in the uprising. The government also began to distribute food in this region. Sheikh Ahmed was released and returned to Barzan in February. And later, mullahs visited Baghdad and negotiated with the government. Prime Minister Nouri Saeed personally inspected the Kurdish region, met Kurdish leaders and made some promises in May. However, the government failed to fulfill many promises made to the Kurds, which aroused their discontent. The Nouri Saeed government collapsed in June, and the new government was founded, in which two Kurdish people served as Minister of Justice and Minister of Economy respectively. Unwilling to meet the promises made in the previous agreement, the new government began to take tough policies on the Kurdish people. In July, the armed forces of Mullah Mustafa attacked police offices.

153

He led and established the "Freedom Committee" in January 1945 and meanwhile developed a program: to liberate Kurdistan from oppression and injustice; to form armed forces to defend Kurdistan; to promote domestic national reconciliation; to build relationships with all patriotic progressive parties and organizations in Kurdistan; to reveal and explain the sufferings of the Kurds to the Iraqi people and public opinion through embassies in Iraq; to uncover anti-Kurdish policies enforced by the Iraqi government via mass media; to call for the implementation of the 1943 Agreement and treat it as the basis of ceasefire.[27]

---

26 Massoud Barzani, Mustafa Barzani and the Kurdish Liberation Movement, p.65.
27 Ibid.,p.73.

He also submitted his request for Kurdish autonomy to the British ambassador in Iraq and the Iraqi government. In March, the British ambassador in Iraq met with Mullah Mustafa, wishing him not to challenge the Iraqi government army and to obey the orders of the Iraqi government and meanwhile suggested Kurdish officials who were transferred from the Defense Department reassume these positions. These suggestions and advices were rejected by Mullah. The Iraqi government announced in March that Mullah Mustafa once more attacked the Kurds cooperating with the Iraqi army in February of 1944. In May 1945, Mullah Mustafa sent envoys to meet Soviet officials in the Iranian Kurdistan for seeking support. The Soviet Union sent two military officers to meet Mullah Mustafa. They reached an agreement with Mullah and expressed their support for the Kurda' anti-aggression struggle. An uprising broke out in August. The Iraqi government issued an order on August 8, which accused Mullah Mustafa of undermining peace and security and authorized the Department of Defense to take measures to bring him to justice. On August 19, the Iraqi government announced to implement martial law in Arbil and Mosul provinces. It not only sent troops to oppress the uprising, but also offered bribes to tribes (families) like Zebari, Baladusti and Surchi tribe which were hostile to Barzani. The British Royal Air Force carried out the bombing. The Turkish government closed the border between the two countries. On October 11, Mullah and some of his followers fled to Mahabad in the Iranian Kurdistan. According to statistics, about 9,000 people fled to Mahabad with Mullah, among which 3,000 are armed members. He was involved in the establishment of the Iranian Kurdish Democratic Party and led the foundation of the Republic of Mahabad, but he failed soon for being suppressed by the Iranian government. He fled to the Soviet Union in June 1947 and wasn't invited back home until the outbreak of the Iraqi Revolution of 1958.

Since then till the 1960s, there had never been any large-scale Kurdish uprisings in Iraq and the Kurdish regions were mainly peaceful. In the 1940s and 1950s, the Kurdish political and cultural activities started to grow again. The Kurdish nationalist political movements developed and the modern political organizations started to be set up. The Iraqi Kurdish organizations were mainly influenced by two thoughts: one was the communist and socialist party while the other was Pan-Arab nationalism. The most influential one was the former. Many Kurdish activists opposed Pan-Arabism and set up left leaning organizations. During this period, many organizations were set up in Bagdad, Arbil, Sulaymaniyah, Kirkuk and other cities, such as Komalay Lawan (set up in 1930 in Bagdad), Komalay Brayati (acted between 1938 and 1943 in Sulaymaniyah), Shoresh (a Kurdish Communist party organization set up in 1943. The name of the party magazine was also Revolution), Rizgari Kurd (a Kurdish branch of

Iraqi Communist party set up in 1945. It once appealed to the UN for allowance to set up the Kurdistan), DARKAR (a left wing organization which was active in Sulaymaniyah), Hewa (or Hiwa) and ICP (set up in 1934).

There were two organizations which were most active and influential currently. One was Hewa—a left wing organization. It was set up in 1941 by some advanced Kurdish intellectuals and officials in Kirkuk (It was also said to be set up in 1939). It had branches in Bagdad, Mosul, Sulaymaniyah and Arbil. Then the headquarters moved to Baghdad. Many members were officials of the Iraqi government and officers. The Party magazine Azadi ("freedom" in Kurdish) mainly propagandized communist and socialist ideas. Its strategy was to realize the Kurdish autonomy, complete recognition of Kurdish national rights and oppose fascism. Its leader Rafiq Hilmi was an urban intellectual, and the organization became popular among the urban petty bourgeoisie. Its members were mainly students, doctors, priests, lawyers, and landlords, tribe leaders in the rural areas, it had also some members with Arab origin.

This organization established good relations with the Turkish, Iraqi and Syrian Kurds, which played a crucial role in the inspiration of the Kurdish nationalist emotion.[28] This organization was closely linked to Molla Mullah Mustafa and supported Mullah's uprising, which played an important role in inspiring the broad masses' support for the Barzani uprising,[29] but the uprising was severely suppressed by the government. In March 1945, this organization handed in a petition with other Kurdish organizations to Loy Henderson, the US ambassador in Iraq, emphasizing that the US should not forget the Fourteen Points Plan of the President Wilson and asked help from the US to set up an independent Kurdistan. The other was Iraqi Communist Party which regarded itself as the representative of suppressed classes, which recognized the Kurdish nationalist rights and supported the Kurdish nationalist cause. Many of its members were Kurds. Its General Secretary Halid Bakdash (1912-1995) was a Syrian Kurd. Later, this party gave up its support for the Kurdish independence, emphasizing the Kurdish issue was an issue of minorities in Iraq. This organization had some influence in the urban Kurdish intellectuals, such as Jalal al-Talabani, Ibrahim Ahmad, Hamza Abdullah, Salih Heydari and others. In 1944, the Soviet Union sent an ambassador in Iraq. After the establishment of the relationship between the Soviet Union and Iraq, the Iraqi Communist Party started its activities legally and set up branches named as "Free the Kurds" in the Kurdish regions.

---

28   Mahir A. Aziz: The Kurds of Iraq: Ethnonationalism and National Identity in Iraqi Kurdistan, p.66.
29   Massoud Barzani, Mustafa Barzani and the Kurdish Liberation Movement, p.63.

Meanwhile, Mullah Mustafa was preparing to establish his own political party. On January 15, 1945, Mullah decided to set up the "Free Committee" and declared the foundation officially on February, 12. Many members were officials, governmental officers and college professors. He declared the aim of the party was to promote the unity of Kurdish tribes in Barzan and then realized the unity among the tribes in the Kurdish regions. On August 16, 1946, in the second day of the conference which convened in Bagdad, the establishment of the new KDP[30] was declared. The 32 delegates of the first Congress elected a central committee with Hamza Abd Allah as secretary-general, Shaykh Latif and Kaka Ziyad Agha as vice-presidents, and Barzani as president-in-exile.

The representatives presented in the 1st Congress of the KDP included the participation of five organizations or groups: "Hope", "Revolution", "Liberation group" (Rizgazi, which advocated to the liberation and unification of the Kurdistan), "Free the Kurds" and the Iraqi branch of the KDP. The party program pointed out the Kurdish nation was under pressure and splitting. It should fight for the realization of national self-determination.

The new KDP was not a Marxist political party, representing Kurdish workers, peasants, employees, craftsmen and revolutionary intellectuals. Its current targets were to turn over feudal dynasty, realize a popular Iraqi democracy and liberate it from imperialism. The Kurdish autonomy should be realized in a united Arab-Kurdish state. This party emphasized that the situation of Iraq differed from Iran and believed that its aim should be to realize Kurdish autonomy. The monthly journal of the party was Rizgari. In March 1951, KDP held the 2nd congress secretly in Bagdad, strengthened the leadership and organization. After the collapse of the Mahabad republic in early 1947, Ibrahim Ahmad, previously the Sulaymaniyah representative of the Iranian KDP (KDP-I), joined the Iraqi KDP. Ibrahim Ahmad was a highly influential Leftist intellectual, who had succeeded to win most of

156

---

30   One of the Kurdish political parties with the longest history and also the core leader of the Kurdish national activities. Its organizational structure was: President, Vice President, Political Bureau and Central Committee in Central Leadership; four levels in base organizations: Lq (24 in total. It has 4 branches in Iraq, Europe, the US and Canada in addition to the 20 branches in Iraq), Nawcha, Rek-khraw and Shana. Till 2010, this party had held 13 Party Congresses (first time in Baghdad on August 16, 1946; second time in Baghdad in March 1951; third time in Kirkuk on January 26 1953; fourth time in Baghdad in October 1958; fifth time in Baghdad in May 1960; sixth time in Kaladizha in July 1964; seventh time in Kirkuk on November 15 1966; eighth time in Duhok on July 1 1970; ninth time in December 1979; tenth time in December 1989; eleventh time in Arbil on August 16, 1993; twelfth time in Arbil in October 1999; and thirteenth time in Arbil in December 2010). At the 13th Congress, a new 15-members Political Bureau was elected. Massoud Barzani was selected as the President. His nephew Nerchivan Idris Barzani who also was a son of Idriss, was elected as Vice President. In addition, KDP set up youth and women and other mass organizations.

the Iraqi Kurdish leftist-nationalists to KDP in 1951. KDP took this opportunity to convene a second Party Congress and duly elected Ahmad as the secretary-general (practically as the acting Chairman.)

Throughout the late 1940s and early 1950s, the KDP and the Kurdish members of the Iraqi Communist Party steadily increased their working relationship – in many cases fielding joint candidates. The ICP campaigned directly against the aghas (tribal elders) and won the support of the workers in the cities of Arbil, Duhok, and Sulaymaniyah – while the KDP reassured the aghas that the ICP was ultimately under their control.

On January 26, 1953, the KDP held the 3rd Congress and changed its name into Kurdistan Democracy of Iraq, emphasized that its represented people from all walks of life in Iraqi Kurdistan, and not only the Kurds but other nations in the region. The Congress also decided to set up all kinds of people's groups and professional groups. It changed the name of the journal from Rizgari to Xebat. Because Mullah Mustafa was exiled for a long time, the situation of the KDP was chaotic. The party had a lot of inner conflicts, an ideological rift developed in the KDP between the intellectual and leftists Ibrahim Ahmad and Jalal Talabani on the one hand, and Mullah Mustafa Barzani on the other. Mullah Mustafa "talked freely, with a bitterness amounting to hatred, against the intellectual rudeness of the some other KDP leaders, and especially attacked Ibrahim Ahmad for his particular dislike". While Ibrahim Ahmad complained of Mullah Mustafa's "selfishness, arbitrariness, unfairness, tribal backwardness and even acuused him as his dishonest." But while each wanted to reduce the others' influence in the KDP, each also knew that the other was indispensable in securing the loyalty of their respective supporters – the tribal villagers and nomads as the supporters of Barzani, and the urban and educated people as the supporters of for Ahmad and Talabani.[31]

In the 3rd Congress in 1953, Hamza Abdullah was expelled from the party, who later set up the Kurdistan Democratic Party-Progress Front. The Third Congress of 1953 changed the name of the party to the Kurdistan Democratic Party as a gesture towards nationalism, and adopted a leftist program calling for agricultural reform and recognition of peasants' and workers' rights. Later in 1956, Hamza and his followers were invited back to KDP.

---

31   Ibrahim Ahmad (1914-2000), one of the main leaders of KDP, had graduated from Law, University of Baghdad and joined in KDP in 1947. In 1951, he motivated a great number of Left Wing Kurds to join in KDP and served as the General Secretary. From 1953 to 1964, but due to his radical attitude and pro-Soviet Union stand, he was not in harmony with Mullah Mustafa Barzani, he left the KDP and began to set up a new Party in 1964. In 1975, he set up the PUK (Patriotic Union of Kurdistan) with his son-in-law the current Iraq President Jalal al-Talabani. Later Ahmad was exiled to Britain but continued the Kurdish nationalist struggle.

In 1954, KDP split again and changed its name into UDPK. Ibrahim Ahmad served as the General Secretary and Mullah Mustafa was again the President. Ibrahim Ahmad was a socialist with advanced thoughts and was pro-Soviet Union. He kept a close relation with Iraqi Communist Party. Ibrahim Ahmad originally opposed the establishment of Iraqi KDP, regarding this ran against the unity of the Kurdish nation. He entered into fierce political conflicts with Hamza Abdullah and won at last. Some conservative Kurdish tribe leaders were dissatisfied with KDP and Iraqi Communist Party. In 1956, they sent people to talk with the British consulate in Mosul, and proposed that they wished to set an "anti-communist Kurdistan" in north Iraq and asked for arms and finance.[32]

During a period of time, KDP and Iraqi Communist Party were two major cooperating political parties in Iraqi Kurdistan. Both the two parties were generally left leaning but one believed in Marxism-Leninism, they generally recruited members from the same social classes, trying to have more members in the Kurdish regions. In 1945, Iraqi Communist Party set up the Kurdish branch. Leader of the Iraqi Communist Party, Muhammad Aziz (1933-) was a Sunni Kurd. He had been the leader of Iraqi Communist Party since 1963 to the 1990s. Till 1960, the condition of ICP was much better than KDP. Iraqi Communist Party criticized KDP as a petty bourgeois party and refused to join a united fight with it. In the eyes of Iraqi Communist Party, KDP followed the "petty bourgeoisie Kurdish nationalism, and demanded the oil reserves of Kurdistan."

So, Iraqi Communist Party aimed to restrict the activities of KDP. The KDP complained that the ICP refused to admit the existence of the Kurdish nation, criticized that it was a "severe mistake" to take the Kurds, Turkmens, and Armenians as minorities as stipulated in the Article No.10 of the ICP program.[33]

KDP argued that the Kurds were the second largest nation in Iraq and also the major nation which should have self-determination. In 1956, the 2nd ICP congress passed the resolution within which the 1st article was as follows: the land where Iraqi Arab nation lived is one as the disintegrated part of the whole Arabic nation. Iraq is an Arabic nation and the main member of the big Arabic tribe. The 2nd article emphasized: "within the borders defined by imperialism, Iraq included the Kurdistan". The 3rd article pointed out: "Iraq is consisted of two nations of Arabs and Kurds. "Iraqi Kurdish nation is one part of the Kurdish nation which has all the internal features as a nation, i.e., the common history and territory, common language and common national economy which motivates it to national liberation and national unity".

32 David McDowall, A Modern History of the Kurds, London: I.B. Tauris, 2007, p.300.
33 Massoud Barzani, Mustafa Barzani and the Kurdish Liberation Movement, p. 201.

Although differences, both two parties cooperated to a certain degree. In 1956, the two parties had reached agreement: the ICP admitted the identity of Kurdish nation and its national self-determination right; the Kurdistan was able to build up a national and democratic political party; Arab and Kurds should be united to fight against imperialism and avoid conflicts with each other; both parties will recognize self-determination and the legitimacy of longing for freedom and national unity demand of each other.[34] The KDP led by Ibrahim Ahmad also proposed to overthrow the feudal Iraqi dynasty to set up a People's Republic, which had shocked many conservative Kurdish tribes.[35]

From the failure of Mustafa's uprising to the1960s, the Iraqi Kurdish national movement was in a low ebb.

But in Iran the Kurdish revolution occurred (1946) and the Mahabad Kurdish Republic was set up in Mahabad Iran. Although the Iraqi Kurdish national movement was in a low ebb, many Iraqi Kurds participated in the revolution of Mahabad. To hinder this support the Iraqi government sent its troops to Sinjar region and helped Iran.

In 1947, the Mahabad Republic failed, most of Mullah Mustafa's soldiers escaped back to Iraq. Iraqi government army attacked Barzan region and allocated the lands and wealth of the Barzani tribe to those Kurdish tribes (families) which cooperated with the Iraq government. In turn, Barzani tribe and its allies launched an uprising under the leadership of Mahmud Khaled, son of Sheikh Ahmed Barzani, but was suppressed soon. In September 1950, Iraqi prime minister Nuri as-Said inspected the Kurdish regions, promising to cancel the restrictions on the migrations of tribes (families). In 1951, the Iraqi Baghdad TV Station started to broadcast in Kurdish. During this period, generally the Kurds were prohibited in Iraqi political life, but some Kurds had enjoyed certain high positions, such as Bekr Sidqi, the Chief of the General Staff of Iraqi army who launched a political coup to overthrow the Ccabinet of Hashemi in October 1936.[36] The Cabinet of Hikmat Sulayman (Turkmen) set up in the same year which expanded the political participation of Shiite Arabs and the Kurds. In 1953, the Kurdish leader Said Gazhazi was assigned as the Minister of the new Cabinet. In the new Cabinet composed in December 1957, the population of Sunni Arabs, Shiite Arabs and Kurds were six, six and three respectively.

159

---

34   Massoud Barzani, Mustafa Barzani and the Kurdish Liberation Movement, p.202.
35   David Mc Dowall, A Modern History of the Kurds, London: I.B. Tauris, 2007, p.299.
36   Bekr Sidqi (1890-1937) was Kurd, but not a Kurdish nationalist. He joined in Ottoman Army in early years and once studied in Staff College, Istanbul. He felt sorry for Arab nationalists and joined in the Arabic uprising. During the British mandate, he was constantly promoted and studies in British Military School and became a Brigadier General in 1933. In October 1936, he launched political reform and set up military government. On August 12 1937, he was assassinated in Mosul.

In March 1958, there were two Kurds in the Cabinet of Said-Nuri. In May 1958, a Kurdish leader, Ahmad Mukhtar Baban became the Prime Minister of Iraq as the head of the Cabinet.[37]

During this period, the Kurdistan was generally peaceful. Mullah Mustafa was expelled to the Soviet Union and Sheikh Ahmed was in house arrest. In 1956, Barzanji passed away. The power of the Kurdish political organization was weak and was under severe suppression. It was forced to work secretly and had difficulties due to abundant domestic political disputes. After the WWII, the Iraqi government invested more in the infrastructure, roads, and schools and so on. However, the economic and social development of the Kurdish region still lagged far behind.

Meanwhile, there were also disputes among the ruling political class of Iraqi. Nuri as-Said had pointed out in his resignation letter in 1944: "there are three major types of Kurds: chiefs of tribes whose living style is close to federalism rather than a united system. They have no special political goals and mainly concern about how to promote and protect their own regions, tribal power and tribal influence; businessmen always hope to have a government to completely obey orders and worship peace to protect and promote their business profits; intellectuals whose ranks are expanding hope to develop education, improve citizens' social level, desire the building of new and more roads, improve sanitary conditions. They desire to be responsible for the local governmental affairs so as to weaken the influence of the tribe leaders. But when it comes to build an independent Kurdistan, most of them do not believe in the realization of this political ideal, this is why 80% of the Kurds prefer to live abroad, if no foreign big power supports them. As Iraqis, the Iraqi Kurds do not have any special demands. They only hope to see some reforms made by the governmental reforms, related to education, health, roads,etc. These issues, including the improvement of life, should be urgently solved by Iraq soon or later."[38] Therefore, he suggested urgent reforms, increase productivity, develop resources and establish a solid and proper stand in our Kurdish policy.[39] He specially emphasized that some foreign super powers hoped to take advantage of the Kurdish issue for their own interests. Therefore, Iraq should carefully handle the Kurdish issue."[40]

160

---

37 Ahmad Mukhtar Baban (1900-1976), was the last Prime Minister of Iraqi Kingdom. He became the Prime Minister on May 18, 1958, but this cabined was abolished by a military coup. Baban was arrested and sentenced to death, but the sentence was suspended.
38 Massoud Barzani, Mustafa Barzani and the Kurdish Liberation Movement, p. 228.
39 Ibid., p. 70.
40 Ibid., p. 70.

During this period, the Iraqi Kurdish issue was nearly forgotten by the international society gradually. In 1931, a large group of the Kurdish nationalists submitted a written petition to the League of Nations, which demanded establishing an independent Kurdistan. On January 28, 1932, the relevant committee of the League of Nations declared that this minorities issue of Iraq was out of its responsibility. On July 8, 1937, Iraqi government signed Saadabad Treaty with Turkey and Iran with the purpose of protecting regional peace and security in the Middle East. In February 1955, Iraq signed treaty with Turkey to resist the domestic and foreign threats it faced. Later Britain, Pakistan and Iraq joined in the Treaty and "Baghdad Pact Treaty" was formed, including Turkey. The Kurds thought Saadabad Treaty (1937), Turkey-Iraq Treaty (1946) and Baghdad Pact Treaty (1955) were all international arrangements to restrain the national ambitions of the Kurds.[41]

3.3 The Cold War Era: A Period of Fierce Struggles

This period is from 1958 to 1990 and can be divided into three stages: the first stage is from 1958 to 1970; the second stage is from 1970 to 1975 and the third stage is from 1975 to 1990. The situation in Iraq changed greatly in this stage and significant historical events occurred one after the other, such as "July Revolution", the establishment of the Iraqi Republic, establishment of Baath Party regime, the two Iraqi Wars, invasion of Kuwait by Iraq and the Gulf war. During this period, the Iraqi Kurdish national movements rose and have made a peak with the fiercest struggles and forming the most violent period. During this period, Arab nationalism had become quite strong and became the leading ideology. It threatened the existence and status of the Kurds and became the main root of national conflicts and contradictions in the Middle East. And during this period, through a long term struggle, the Kurds gained a nominal authority or autonomy in 1970.

In the first half of the 20th century the Iraqi nationalist movements were in the peak, they fought against British colonialism, Faisal Dynasty rule and explored the ways for national independence which can be defined as the main steps. On July 14, 1958, the "Free Officers" organization led by Abd al-Karim Qasim followed the example of Nasser, Egypt and began the "July Revolution", aiming a radical political reform. The "July Revolution" overthrew the Faisal Dynasty and declared the establishment of Iraq Republic. The new government with Qasim as the prime minister banned the Monarchy, confiscated the loyal property, promulgated an interim Constitution, declared the new land reform law and promised a policy of national peace. On March 24, 1959, Iraq declared to quit from Baghdad Pact Treaty and Sterling currency Area.

---

41   Massoud Barzani, Mustafa Barzani and the Kurdish Liberation Movement, p.159.

The revolution launched by Qasim won the support from all the opposition factions including the KDP. Qasim emphasized Iraqi nationalism and development of democracy, recognized the dual-nationalist feature (Arab and Kurdish) of Iraq. Qasim wisely recognized the national feature of the Kurdish issue. Therefore, Qasim thought that the improvement of the political status of Kurds would be the key to realize peace and cooperation between Arabs and Kurds. But, he strongly rejected the disintegration of Iraq and held a cautious attitude towards the Kurdish autonomy, and was hopeful that the Arab nations would unite surpassing ideological and national differences.

On July 27, 1958, Qasim declared: "Arabs and Kurds are the partners of our nation... Their national rights will be recognized by the Iraqi state." The newly issued interim Constitution stipulated the following: Arabs and Kurds are the partners of the nation. The Constitution also ensured all the ethnic-national rights of peoples in Iraq. For the first time Iraqi Constitution recognized the national rights of Kurds. But the Constitution emphasized that Iraq was part of the entire Arab nation. After the July revolution, the Central Committee of KDP immediately sent a congratulation and support telegram and called on the Kurds to support and defend the July Revolution. On July 16, the KDP issued the Declaration to the Kurdish People, which said: "The Kurdish nation has also longed the overthrow of the corrupt dynasty, we support the new regime and its separation from the Baghdad Pact Treaty."

This meant KDP had decided to protect the unity of Iraq and its stability and prosperity. To achieve this goal purpose, "all the members of our KDP and our supporters should be freedom fighters to protect the Republic of Iraq and struggle against imperialism and its the collaborators and agents.[42]

After the success of the revolution, Qasim's first move was to free Sheikh Ahmed Barzani who was in house arrest and decided to invite Mullah Mustafa who was in exile to take a leadership position in the new government of Iraq.

In August 1958, Mullah Mustafa Barzani who had been living in the Soviet Union for eleven years was in Romania for a visit and sent a telegram to Qasim, expressed his congratulations for the success of revolution and asked to return back to Iraq. On August 29, Mullah Mustafa, wrote a second letter to Qasim, from Czechoslovakia, praising his leadership and emphasized the past uprising of Barzani's tribe was one part of the long-term anti-imperialist and anti-feudal struggle against the Faisal Dynasty of the whole Iraq, repeated his desire to return back.

---

42 Massoud Barzani, Mustafa Barzani and the Kurdish Liberation Movement, p.175.

On September 2, Qasim replied back, showed his welcome, stating that he had arranged necessary conditions, for the freedom of Mullah Mustafa and his companions in Iraq. On September 10, Mullah Mustafa replied to show his gratitude, expressed he would be honored to join the great cause of defending Iraqi people, the new Republic of Iraq and its progress. Molla Mustafa, had included the slogans "long live the Republic of Iraq", "long live Qasim" and "long live the brotherhood of the Kurds and Arabs" in his letters.[43]

In those days, the renowned Kurdish leader Ibrahim Ahmad had visited Mullah Mustafa in Prague with a delegate. In early October, Mullah Mustafa met the Egyptian prime minister Nasser in Cairo. In the evening of October 6, Mullah Mustafa returned to capital Baghdad. The government arranged millions of people to participate the official welcome ceremony. On October 7, Mullah Mustafa when visiting Qasim in his office made an apology and defined "himself as a soldier of the July Revolution and expressed his readiness to accept the command of the leader (Qasim)". Qasim was also very polite to Mullah Mustafa.

Qasim provided an accommodation, a car, and high salary for Mullah Mustafa. His return to Iraq had significant meanings, on the one side, it reflected the sincerity of the new Iraqi regime on the Kurdish issue; on the other side, the return had increased Mullah Mustafa's status and paved the way for the improvement of the Kurds' status in Iraq. However, the domestic and international reactions against the new Iraq regime and towards Mullah Mustafa's return was quite different. The Soviet Union, the socialist camp and Egypt supported Mullah Mustafa's return, but Turkey and Iran was worried. There was also a domestic opposition: Sir Wright, British ambassador in Iraq, in his secret telegram wrote: "many Iraqi intellectuals hold a cautious and a worrisome attitudes towards Mullah Mustafa's return, they believe it will be an unwise move to support his return, thus give an opportunity to those who advocate to keep close relations with the Soviet Union and pave the way for the Kurdish independence. Some people even think Qasim's move is inspired by the Iraqi Communist Party.[44]

The Iraqi "Revolution" of 1958 signified three trends in Kurdish history in Iraqi Kurdistan. Firstly, for the first time the Kurds of Iraq were officially recognised as a partner in Iraqi state and their cultural and political rights were recognised. Before that the Kurds had never enjoyed an official status. This paved the way for the growth of 'mass Kurdish nationalism' and gave the Kurds a hope that one day they would be able to enjoy their cultural and political rights.

43   Ibid., pp. 180-181.
44   Massoud Barzani, Mustafa Barzani and the Kurdish Liberation Movement, p.184.

Secondly, the Iraqi "Revolution" of 1958 signified a new phase in Kurdish revolt in Iraqi Kurdistan. A revolt which was no more tribal alone but supported by the different classes in Kurdish society such as teachers, merchants, students and so on. Thirdly, the Iraqi "Revolution" of 1958 created new lines of division within Kurdish insurgency. This time the division was not only based on tribal line, but on ideological basis and differences of opinions that has continued to the existing day.

But we can say that the honeymoon of the Qasim regime and Kurds encountered a turning point in September 1961 and conflicts arose. In order to show sincerity, the new regime hailed that Arabs were the "partners" of the Kurds, recognized the legal status of KDP and other Kurdish political parties and freed many Kurdish leaders who were prisoned. In first day of the revolution, it was declared that the supreme committee who won the revolution will assume full authority and form a government including the three stakeholders of Iraq, the Sunni Arabs, Shiite Arabs and the Kurds, already Khalid Naqshinbandi, a Kurdish leader was in the supreme committee.

Among the 13 ministers of the new government, there were two Kurds: Sheihbaba Ali Mahmud (Communication Minister) and Muhammad Salih. The KDP, Baath Party, Independent Party, National Democracy and other Iraqi political parties were all invited to join and support the government. On August 19th, 1958, Ibrahim Ahmad the leader of KDP asked the government to permit the publication of the party's central newspaper Conflicts, but was refused. However, his request of openly celebrating the Newroz— the New Year of the Kurds (March 22) as an official day was accepted. In September, the Vice President Abdussalam Arif made an inspection tour to the Kurdish region, promising to implement the land reform and enable the allocation of land to peasants. In February 1959, Qasim re-designed the cabinet. Now, the former Kurdish figures were substituted by new Kurdish names as Hassan Talabani and Fuad Arif. Surprisingly, on April 4, 1959, the newspaper Conflicts was allowed to be published. The government allowed 14 Kurdish magazines in total, including the two magazines of the KDP, the Conflicts and the Kurdistan and Life (Jin), also the official magazine of the Kurdish Branch of the Iraqi Communist Party, the Hetaw and Freedom was also allowed to be published. Between October 4 and 7, 1959, the KDP held its 4th Congress in Baghdad. Mullah Mustafa Barzani participated in the Congress for the first time and his leadership was officially confirmed. On January 6, 1960, Iraq promulgated the law of political parties, and KDP obtained legal status which was the first in the KDP's history. In early May 1960, the KDP held its 5th congress in Baghdad, which elected Barzani as the Chairman of the party. This was first time for KDP to hold its congress legally.

In return, the Kurds also supported the Qasim regime and cooperated with him in his policy to attack and restrict the Nasserism trend which praised Pan-Arabism and Iraqi Communist Party. In March 1959, in Mosul Iraqi Communist Party organized strong protests against the government, and Mullah Mustafa supported the government's suppression and called on the Kurds to oppose the Iraqi Communist Party.

ICP had mobilized a quarter of a million people in Mosul, many of them armed, to suppress a coup by Nasserites and counterrevolutionary officers. This triggered several days of street fighting in which Communist-led workers and soldiers mopped up the conspirators and their bourgeois backers, arresting many and hanging others from lampposts.

The KDP also supported the government's suppression of Nasserism, Baath Party, and some dissident Kurdish tribes (families). Since the land reform had given a hard blow to Kurdish feudal forces, an 1959, uprising by the Bradost tribe had occurred in Lolan which is the border area near Turkey, Iran and Iraq, in the spring of 1959. Molla Mustafa accepted Qasim's order to organize its peshmerga army to suppress the uprising. The leader of the uprising was Sheikh Reshid and he escaped to Iran. At the same time, Mullah Mustafa supported the government to suppress the uprising of another Kurdish tribe in Pisdar, which was involved in some severe bloody incidents, faced by Mullah Mustafa's attacks thousands of people had escaped to Turkey and Iran as refugee. In July 1959, in agreement with the Qasim and his comapanions, KDP officially split with the Iraqi Communist Party and their cooperation agreement was ended.[45]

However, Qasim neither supported the Kurds' demand for autonomy, nor fulfilled the promises he made on the Kurdish issue. In the early days of his reign, Qasim needed Kurds' support to resist the Nasserists and the Iraqi Communist Party. Once their alliance was not urgently needed, Qasim became intolerant against the Kurds.[46] After Mullah Mustafa Barzani's return to Iraq and his leadership had strengthened, he also demanded urgent Kurdish autonomy, which aroused the dissatisfaction and doubts of Qasim. Frightened by Barzani's increasing power Qasim set up a popular militia (PRF), to suppress the polirical forces which he suspected.[47]

---

45   On November 10, 1958, the two party had signed an agreement and formed the supreme committee of cooperation between the two parties and other joint cooperation organs, committees. Then, KDP had joined the "New United Front".

46   In October and December 1958, Nasserrists who supported Pan-Arabism, the vice-President Arif and Rashide al-Gailani were arrested. In October 1959, Baath Party organized an assassination plot targeting Qasim but had failed. With this event, Qasim began to suppress the Baath Party.

47   According to the No. 989 Military order issued on July 22, 1958, the Popular Resistance Force (PRF) was set up by Qasim. This armed activity of PRF militants soon went beyond the scope of militia activities and this force became "a state within the state".

As early as July 17, 1958, General Secretary of KDP, Ibrahim Ahmad, had proposed the Kurdish autonomy when meeting Qasim but was refused. In June 1959, taking advantage of the conflicts between the Kurdish tribes, the governmental army went into Barzan (where Barzani tribe ruled) and attacked the militia ruled by Barzani. In July 1959, severe conflicts broke out between the Kurds and Turkmen people living in Kirkuk. Over 100 Turkmen were killed, which shocked Qasim. By the end of 1960, Qasim's governing power was quite consolidated, therefore, he became more confident and neglected the Kurds' demands for autonomy, instead, he formulated a regional development and adopted measures to restrict the activities of KDP.

Qasim gave special privileges authority to the Governor of Arbil and to the head of Mosul police department with privilege to keep the peace and security of the two provinces. The government also started to arm the neighboring tribes (families) against the Barzani tribe to restrict Mullah Mustafa Barzani's power, such as Zibari, Surchi, Bradost, Elijani and so on. Also the relation between Qasim and Mullah Mustafa Barzani had become a cold relation. In the spring of 1960, Zibari tribe attacked Barzani and armed conflicts between the two sides broke out. Mullah Barzani asked Qasim to set up a neutral investigation commission for this event.

In May 1960, many KDP members were arrested and many of the local party branches were banned. By September, only Baghdad and Sulaymaniyah branches were functioning, and in other places KDP had to work secretly. In the same month, Mullah Mustafa Barzani went to meet Qasim in Bagdad, where he once more declared his support for the "July Revolution" and Qasim government.

But the situation continued to worsen. In November 1960, the KDP party General Secretary, Ibrahim Ahmad was arrested by the government with the pretext of instigating national conflicts. Several other leaders of the party were arrested, many of them had to go underground activities. Subsequently, the Kurdish newspapers and magazines were cancelled one by one. By the end of 1960, the situation between the two parties had become very sensitive. The government had ceased the implementation of all the policies it had promised after the July revolution, and started to dismiss the staff and officials in the government and military army who had Kurdish origin. Qasim also used the well known tactic of divide and rule. He contacted and met with those feudal families which had conflicts with the Barzani tribe, such as the Herki tribe and the Zibari tribe and provoked them to disturb Barzanis.

With these adverse developments as the background, Mullah Mustafa Barzani and Kurdish Democratic Party (KDP) began to adopt some de facto measures towards autonomy and increased the pressure on the Qasim government.

On November 3, 1960, Mustafa Barzani was invited to take part in the commemoration event of the 1917 October Revolution in Moscow, and he used this opportunity to meet several senior leaders and officials of the Soviet Union, including Khrushchev. He asked them for help, to exert some pressure on the Iraq government, for Kurdish autonomy. But in those days, the relation between the Soviet Union and Iraq was getting closer and the Soviet government did not want to press and offend Qasim.[48]

In February 1959, Iraq government and the Soviet Union signed a seven-year economic and technological cooperation agreement, which included a 550 million ruble loan for the development of 43 industrial projects in Iraq. In March the same year, Iraq announced its withdrawal from the Baghdad Pact Treaty. In 1960 the Soviet Union provided a second loan of 180 million rubles and granted an education facility for 800 Iraqi students, in Moscow.

Iraqi government was disturbed by Barzani's this last step and took to back the house and the car assigned to Mullah Mustafa Barzani, and increased its support to those Kurdish tribes rivaling Barzani. Therefore, Mullah Mustafa Barzani speeded up his efforts to organize Kurdish militias in the northern Iraq and intensified anti-government publicity in the region as preparation to attack the pro-government Kurdish tribes.

In February 1961, the armed conflict between Mullah Mustafa Barzani militia and pro-government Shekak tribe broke out. Mullah Mustafa Barzani militia executed the leaders of the rival Shekak tribe, Sheikh Sadiq and Osman Nouri, this event further consolidated Barzani's leadership in the region.

In March 1961, Mullah Mustafa Barzani left Baghdad and returned to his headquarter in Barzan, he had become wary of the intention of the Qasim's regime. On March 22, Iraqi government ordered to ban the only circulating Kurdish newspaper Struggle. In June 1961, KDP filed a petition to Qasim, asked for the freedom of the party newpaper, opening of the Kurdish schools and proposed to share the profits of Kirkuk and Mosul oil fields with the government. As the requests were denied by the government, in June, KDP issued a severe ultimatum. In August, KDP issued a second

---

48   In February 1959, Iraq signed a seven-year Economic and Technological Cooperation Agreement with the Soviet Union. The Soviet Union offered Iraq 0.55 billion rubles to assist 43 industrial projects in Iraq. In March the same year, Iraq declared to quit from „Baghdad Pact". In 1960, the Soviet Union offered 0.18 billion rubles to Iraq again and allowed 800 Iraqi students.

ultimatum again, which declared Qasim's regime as dictatorship, accused the regime for ignoring the autonomy demand of Kurds, arresting KDP's leaders and expelling Kurdish officials and monopolizing the state powers.

Qasim government as the first step preferred to agitate the Kurdish tribes hostile to Barzani to fight him, as a preparation for the war. The full-scale fighting began when the Arkon (Arkou) detachment led by Sheikh Abbas Muhammad, a tribe allied to Barzani, angered by the government's land reform law, attacked a government force between Kirkuk and Suleimaniyeh, where 23 soldiers were killed. The government retaliated by bombarding Barzani villages. Barzani forces retaliated by occupying army's frontier posts, Kurdish villages and towns. Therefore, a full-scale war the "Great September Revolution" began on 11 September 1961.[49]

Subsequently the government army forces launched a large-scale attack against the Kurds, on September 13, Qasim ordered air forces to strike Barzan district and on September 23, declared the banning of the KDP officially. On September 25, Central Committee of KDP decided to join the battle against Qasim government. The period from the eruption of the war in September 1961 to the cease-fire agreed on March 1970 is called as "the First Kurd-Iraq War".[50]

Kurdish forces revolted vigorously, attacked police stations, frontier posts of the army, and expelled all the local officials, ambushed police and army forces, established their control over most of the Kurdish districts. Qasim ordered the Second infantry division to reinforce the attacking forces and re-gained regained some districts from Barzani forces with the help and cooperation of the Jash armed forces.[51]

By October 10, Qasim declared the ending of the military offensive, since the army had gained the full control of the war situation. A great number of Kurdish people were killed, hundreds of Kurdish villages were destroyed and tens of thousands of people lost their homes or were forced to migrate. On November 16, 1961, the Central Committee of KDP wrote and

168

---

49   Massoud Barzani, Mustafa Barzani and the Kurdish Liberation Movement, p. 232.
50   Michael G. Lortz, "The Kurdish Warrior Tradition and the Importance of the Peshmerga", pp.39-42, http://etd.lib.fsu.edu/theses/available/etd-11142005-144616/unrestricted/003Manuscript.pdf.
51   Jash or Josh, the word referring to Iraqi Kurdish nationalist and Kurdish armed forces which cooperated with the government, means „little monkey". It came into usage in 1960s. But the Iraqi government called these pro-government tribe armies as „Furan Salah al-Din", meaning „Salaadin Knights" or „Light Brigades". Most of these tribes (families) were the rivals of the Barzani tribe. By the summer of 1986, the scale of these type of army forces reached to 150,000 to 250,000. These forces were also used by the Iraqi government to fight against Iran and Kurdish national Peshmerga forces. After the Gulf War in 1991, most of the above pro-government armed forces turned against the Saddam government and fought on the side of Kurdish national forces.

sent a letter to the Secretary General of the United Nations, accusing Iraqi army for massacring the Kurdish people and asked for the establishment of an international investigation commission that would visit the region.

With the approach of winter, the snow blocked the mountains, the government army was forced to retreat due to the difficulties in completing the military operation, in turn the Kurdish forces utilized this opportunity to regain the control of most districts of the North Iraq region. In March 1962, Mullah Mustafa Barzani forces launched another spring attack targeting the government armies and the pro-government Kurdish tribes. Kurdish attackes have killed and injured more than 3,000 men of the pro-government Kurdish tribe militia. In the same month, Qasim declared an amnesty possibility to revolting Kurds who would surrender their weapons.

On April 20, Mullah Mustafa Barzani declared: "A cease fire can only be possible, if the self-determination right of the Kurds is recognized, the notorious Qasim government should be replaced with the establishment of a new democratic government." He also emphasized that the aim of Kurds was to realize the Kurdish autonomy within the Iraqi sovereignty rather than seeking an independent Kurdish state. This declaration was favored and support of many Arab state leaders in the region, and some outstanding Arab leaders declared their sympathy to Mullah Barzani's position.

The Iraqi Communist which had initially supported Qasim's military offensive against Barzani, changed its position and assumed an opposing stand. ICP's "Report On The Just Solution for The Iraqi Kurdish National Issue" held a double criticism and said: "Qasim government has neglected the Kurdish issue and denied the existence of Kurdistan", but also accused "the Kurdish bourgeoisie has put its national interests above the common interests of Iraq, thus put its national cause into danger and isolation." But the report favored the Kurds: "In the current situation, the only reasonable solution is to realize an Arab-Kurdish partnership and true democracy through establishing an autonomous government in Iraqi Kurdistan within the united framework of Iraq". On January 25, 1963, Arabic Iraqi launched a petition, which demanded that Qasim government should negotiate with the Kurds.

During the summer of 1962, both the two sides did not attempt any large-scale military actions, the government army forces army was mainly stationed in Arbil, Kirkuk and other smaller Kurdish cities, and ninor armed conflicts occurred. Mullah Mustafa Barzani declared that they killed and injured more than 1,000 men of the government army during April and June, Mullah Mustafa Barzani took the opportunity to suppress the rival Kurdish tribe. In July 1962, Sheikh Ahmed Barzani a prominent leader of Kurds (Mustafa Barzani's brother) conducted secret negotiations with Qasim, but failed. Nevertheless Qasim agreed to an amnesty and post-war economic re-construction, but still rejected the Kurdish autonomy.

On January 10, 1963, Qasim gave another promising declaration: "If the Kurds can surrender within 10 days, they will get an amnesty." Later, he delayed the surrender date to the end of month, but the Kurds did not respond. By September 1962, Peshmerga (meaning "facing death") forces had increased to over 15,000 men and together with other fighting forces, the fighters controlled by Mullah Mustafa Barzani had increased to over 40,000 men which equaled to nearly half of the Iraqi army forces. The districts controlled by the rebel Kurds had expanded to 13,500 square kilometers, have established a government-like structure and also issued a series of laws for the region.

During this period, the regions controlled by the rebel Kurds were mainly divided into two parts: the North was mainly controlled by Mullah Mustafa Barzani while the Southern party was a smaller area controlled by the KDP activities. In the North, KDP led four headquarters, one of which was near the Iran border and commanded by Ibrahim Ahmad and others were led by Jalal Talabani (Ibrahim Ahmad's son-in-law). The army led by Talabani was well trained and disciplined. It had good contacts by the local Kurds and had seen a rapid development.

During the period, Qasim adopted a pro-Soviet policies and quitted the "Baghdad Pact", which had worsened the relations between Iraq and the West, Iran and Turkey. Qasim blamed Britain and the US for providing arms to the Kurdish rebels. He declared that the government had cracked down a British spy net in Iraq and discovered that British embassy had spent 400,000 Pounds to instigate the Kurdish revolt.[52] Iraq also accused Pahlavi led Iran regime for supporting Mullah Mustafa Barzani and providing arms.[53]

Meanwhile, the relation between Iraq and Turkey had worsened and frequent border conflicts occurred. Turkey had built a 12-kilometer-wide restricted zone along the border of Turkey, under its control, so as to reinforce border patrols. On July 9 and 16, 1962, two Iraqi fighters attacked a Turkish military position, which had led to the death of 2 Turkish soldiers, and on August 16, Turkish air forces shot down an Iraqi fighter plane. Iraqi

---

52 Edgar O'Balance, The Kurdish Revolt: 1961-1970, p. 76.
53 In December 1959, Qasim regime declared the abolition of the 1973 Agreement with Iran and border conflicts occurred between the two sides. According to the 1973 Agreement, the main river route of Shatt al-Arab belonged to Iraq. The waters of 8 square kilometers of Abadan, the Iran port, belonged to Iran. Iranian warships could enjoy the right to sail in and out of Abadan Port through the Shatt al-Arab. Qasim required re-division of the said river route and its usage. In 1961, Iraq government officially re-named the Persian Gulf as the Arabic Gulf, which aroused the dissatisfaction of Iran.

government also protested Turkey for supporting Kurdish revolt Turkey firmly denied the accusation and declared to retreat its ambassador of Iraq on August 23.

As the Iraqi civil war had entered into a deadlock, a political crisis occurred within the Iraqi government. Qasim had underestimated the organization and resisting abilities of the Kurds. The Iraqi army was also distressed and frustrated due to military setback, which triggered the political crisis further. The frustration in the army ranks had gradually increased and had caused to an organization anti-Qasim Free Officers Movement which was in contact with the Baath party secretly.

Before the state coup, the Baath Party had actively sought to get the support of Kurds to overthrow the Qasim government and contacted the KDP General Secretary Ibrahim, who expressed willingness to cooperate but asked them to accept the Kurdish autonomy. The Baath party finally agreed in the negotiations and offered to allocate six ministerial positions for Kurds in the future government, which meant Baath party was more generous than the Qasim government. The political cooperation honeymoon between the Kurds and Baath Party had thus began before the 1963 coup.

The clashes between the Kurdish forces and the Qasim army had continued until he was overthrown in February 1963. War stopped between the government and Kurdish forces only when Qasim was removed from power in a coup led by the Baathists and General Abd al-Salaam Arif. Qasim was gradually isolated in the domestic politics and losing public support. On February 8, 1963, under the leadership of Ali Saleh al-Saadi, the anti-Qasim forces launched a state coup. They arrested and executed Qasim and established the Revolutionary Commanding Committee. Abdussalam Mohammed Arif Aljumaily served as the President and the Baath Party controlled the Revolutionary Commanding Committee as the latter had become stronger in the contest against the former.[54]

In a power struggle between the Baathists and General Arif, the Baathist had become over-powered compared to General Arif by November 1963. Initially, the new Iraqi government led by Arif was not in a position to fight the Kurds. The Iraqi leaders were more concerned to consolidate their positions against their political rivals. The Kurds too refrained from attacking the weak government forces hoping that the new government would recognise their rights. The Arif government ignored Kurdish autonomy, but as a

54 Abdussalam Mohammed Arif Aljumaily, 1921-1996, was one of leaders of the July Revolution in 1958, which overthrew the Faisal Dynasty and established the Iraq Republic. He was dismissed from key positions due to his differences with Qasim. In February 1963, he served as the President after the 1963 coup. He died in a helicopter crash on April 13, 1966. His brother Abdul Rehman Mohammed Arif Aljumaily succeeded him as the President.

gesture of good will he had appointed two Kurds, Baba Ali Sheikh Mahmud and Brigadier Fuad Arif, to his cabinet.

The day the political coup succeeded, the new authority issued a communiqué, calling on the Kurds to stop the revolt. The government army started to end the besiege of the Kurdish regions areas and eventually the retreat had begun. Mullah Mustafa and KDP welcomed the overthrow of the Qasim government and declared a cease-fire. After the cease-fire, the Kurds assigned Jalal Talabani as their representative to negotiate with the government. On February 19, the negotiations started. The forces behind the new government denied their promise of autonomy agreement before the political coup, and the negotiations entered into a deadlock.

On February 28, Talabani declared on in his news conference that the Kurds had strictly observed the conditions of the cease-fire in order to give a chance and an opportunity to the new government since its formation. He clearly expressed that the new Iraqi government should recognize the autonomy right of the Kurds, emphasizing that the Kurds would accept the central control of the whole Iraqi armed forces and national diplomacy, but insisted that all other issues should be controlled by Kurdish regional autonomous government. He also proposed that a Kurdish citizen might be the vice-president of Iraq as the best solution.

At the end of April, the negotiations started again, but this time Kurds proposed higher demands: in addition to Arbil, Kirkuk, and Sulaymaniyah, they also demanded to include the provinces which had more Kurdish population, such as the Mosul and Diyala, into the Kurdish region; the Kurdish region should have the right establish a regional legislation and judicial institutions; the establishment of regional armed forces; plus expressed their desire to share the 1/3 of the total oil revenues of the country; appointment of Kurdish leader as Vice-President; 1/3 of the ministerial positions in the government; have a fixed quota for the leading army positions and the post of Deputy Chief of the General Staff, and so on.

These heavy handed demands had made the new government feel highly and caused the latter change their attitude.

The President Arif was ready to compromise on cultural and language issues, but didn't want to comment and talk about the Kurdish autonomy issue. He soon gave the indication that like his predecessor Qasim he was not interested in the Kurdish autonomy. Tensions soon grew and clashes began between the government and Kurdish forces.

On 10 June 1963, the Iraqi army started its 'Second Offensive'. The Kurdish nationalists were labeled as a group of gangs by the government. On July 2, 1963, Lieutenant General Saleh Mahdi Ammash, the Defence

Minister, denied that there was war going on between the Kurds and the government forces.

The fighting intensified; on April 5, 1965, and on May 4, 1966 the Iraqi army began their 'Third and Fourth Offensives'. During the 'Fourth Offensive' Abd al-Salaam Arif died in a helicopter crash and his brother General Abd a-Rahman Arif replaced him

In May, the government stared to mobilize its troops to Northern Iraq. By the end of May, 3/4 of the whole Iraqi forces were stationed around the Kurdish regions, and started to block the main roads and built fortresses, which meant the army was preparing for a military offensive.

On May 23, Iraq government declared curfew rule in the "mixed districts" where Kurds and Arabs lived together. Mullah Mustafa Barzani once more contacted to the Prime Minister Bekr, with the hope of not to cease negotiations.

Between 16 May-June 3 1963, Talabani visited Egypt, asking for Nasser to persuade the Iraq government for compromises and help Kurds, but failed. In early June, Arif government sent an ultimatum to the Kurdish leadership, which accused Kurds for demanding "unfeasible and hard" conditions and required them to surrender within three days. The Kurdish leadership did not respond. On June 10, Iraq government mobilized 12 brigades which besieged the region and marched deeper from multiple directions, Iraqi side issued an order that all the enemy elements should hand over their weapons and surrender within 24 hours. The government also attacked Mullah Mustafa Barzani as the "enemy of revolution" who collaborated with the communists, who also attacked the state, police and army, who robbed the villagers and villages and offer a 100,000-Pound reward was offered for Mullah Mustafa Barzani, dead or alive.

The government also established an emergency court which would trial the rebels and their leaders, which would easily issue harsh punishments including death penalties, the government also issued a secret decree to destroy any village supporting or sheltering the rebels.

On the same day, the government arrested the Kurdish leaders who had participated in the negotiation. On June 11, the government issued another order, which required that the residents in the Northern provinces should handover their weapons immediately, and also started an all-day curfew rule in the cities of Kirkuk, Arbil and Sulaymaniyah.

Baath Party also started an Arabization program in Kirkuk, which included deporting Kurds and transferring Arabs to the city and its surrounding districts and villages. Baath Party ordered the Kurds who had migrated to Kirkuk after 1985, to return back to their original towns. On June 20, two

Kurdish ministers resigned from the Arif government. Meanwhile, many Kurdish officers and government officials were dismissed from their duties. But the military offensive was soon repelled.

In February 1964, Arif and Mullah Mustafa Barzani held a secret meeting and reached a cease-fire agreement and two parties declared the cease-fire. The agreement reached included a new permanent Iraqi constitutions which would recognize national rights of Kurds and a general amnesty for the Kurds, but the agreement did not mention the autonomy issue. Mullah Mustafa Barzani did not report the agreement to the Political Bureau of KDP which was opposed to the cease-fire, which had led to a split in the party.[55]

In early July 1964, KDP held six plenum meetings in which the leadership issue and the inner-party crisis was debated deeply and heatedly. During the meetings the party decided to expel 14 leaders including Ibrahim Ahmad and Jalal Talabani from the party. Since then Mullah Mustafa Barzani has been controlling the KDP without any contest. In the past, Political Bureau faction led by Ahmad was once forced to go to a border town of Iran by the party, but later they had returned to party ranks. On November 15, 1966, KDP held its seventh National Congress, which emphasized further reinforcing the unity and solidarity within the party.

On March 4, 1965, the two sides embraced warring again, and on 4 May 1966 the Iraqi army began their 'Third and Fourth Offensives'. During the 'Fourth Offensive' Abd al-Salaam Arif died in a helicopter crash and his brother General Abd a-Rahman Arif replaced him.[56]

The new President continued the military offensive against the Kurds. In May 1966, the Iraqi army encountered a complete defeat in the mountainous district of Handlin and its whole brigade was annihilated.[57]

---

55   The radical wing within the KDP which was led by Ibrahim Ahmad and his son-in-law Jalal Talabani is also known as the KDP-Politburo. Its members were generally leftist and socialist intellectuals. They spoke the Sorani Kurdish, whereas Mullah Barzani faction had a more conservative and traditional position with intensive tribal culture colors. Its members mostly spoke Kurmanji Kurdish. Besides significant differences in their views, education and origins, the two factions had emerged in different regions, and lived up with the latter. Since the headquarter of the Political Bureau was in a small town Mawat in the northeast of Sulaymaniyah city, Mullah Barzani sometimes accused the Political Bureau as leading the "Mawat Empire."
56   Abdurrahman Arif Aljumaily was born in 1916. In 1958, he supported and joined the military coup, which overthrew the monarchy. After the 1963 coup, he served as the Chief of the Staff of the Army and became the third president of Iraq in 1966. After the revolution in July 1968. Arif was sent into exile and hosted by Turkey and died on August 24, 2007 in this country.
57   G.S. Harris, Ethnic Conflict and the Kurds, pp. 118-120.

After this battle, the two sides started a negotiation and affirmed the two-nation nature of Iraq Republic, full autonomy of the Kurdish nation was agreed, the Constitution of the Iraq Republic would have Kurdish as the official language in Kurdish regions, investments in the Northern Iraq would be increased, plus a cease-fire was agreed in the negotiations. On June 15, 1966, Iraq government announced the cease-fire, subsequently a 12-point Peace Plan was declared. On June 29, the two sides had reached agreement. But soon after, there occurred a change in the cabinet, by which Kurdish military led hard-liners had gained the upper hand, which led to another war.

On July 17, 1968, the Arab Baath Socialist Party led by Ahmad Hassan Bekr accomplished a succesfull coup d'état started ended the Abd a-Rahman Arif government.

After the coup d'état Ahmad Hassan Bekr became the President, and Saddam Hussein the vice president. Soon Revolutionary Command Council possessing which the highest authority was established, the new regime started a large-scale elimination of the dissidents. Since then, Iraq entered the historical period of Baath Party rule which lasted for 35 years. In those days, the inner party contest for leading power was quite fierce within the Baath Party, and the new government was busy with power consolidation and leadership arrangements, which meant that it could not spare enough time to deal with the Kurds.

Therefore, Ahmad Hassan Bekr had assigned a special negotiator group to hold secret talks with Mullah Mustafa Barzani, the talks were themed as "fulfilling the 1966 Agreement." Soon after the coup the new government had included three Kurds into the cabinet, two from the KDP and one minister from the Political Bureau faction of the KDP. In August, the two KDP ministers resigned to show their dissatisfaction with the government.

In autumn, the conflict between the two warring parties erupted. In December, the conflict intensified, and the government forces began to bomb the Kurdish region. Iran supported the Barzani forces and sent two divisions into Iraq. From the end of 1968 to early 1969, a series of principles were agreed during the Seventh Regional Conference of Arab Baath Socialist Party, the resolution recognized the Kurdish language and cultural rights of Kurds; establishing a systematic framework for the development of Kurdish culture; allowing the utilization of Kurdish language in school teaching, research institutions, universities, teacher training institutions, military academies and military institutions; promoting Kurdish poets and novelists; establishment of television stations broadcasting in Kurdish language and in particular the creation of Kurdish-language television programs in Kirkuk and increase in the number of Kurdish TV programs; promulgation of laws and decrees which would expand the powers of local government organs; the establishment of a Kurdish Academy in Sulaymaniyah; establishment of new residential zones in the Kirkuk region and a general amnesty for all civilians and soldiers who have participated in the revolts. The Revolutionary Command Council regarded this resolution as a milestone on the road "to achieve the coordinated development of Arab and Kurdish nations."

After a long period of negotiations, on March 11, 1970, the new Iraq government and KDP finally reached an agreement as follows: the Iraqi government agreed to grant Kurds a broad autonomy, they would establish special administrative regions where Kurdish have majority population; the Constitution would be amended so as to include the two nations as the pillars of the country; Kurds would be supported so that they will be able to return to their homes and would be economically compensated; vice-president would be from the Kurdish people and Kurds would hold appropriate positions in the ruling cabinet; Kurdish would be one of the official language of the state and officers, Arabic and Kurdish as the official language of the Kurdish autonomous regions; Kurdish armed forces would be integrated into the Iraqi army; Kurds would suspend their relations with the Iran government; Kurds will transfer their secret radio station and heavy weapons to the government; Kurdish education and cultural undertakings would be further developed; to promote Kurds in establishing student, youth, women and teachers' organizations; resolution stipulated that the relevant administrative regulations would be re-adjusted in accordance with the other articles of the resolution. The resolution also stipulated that, the provisions regarding the Kurdistan autonomy, in the resolution, would be implemented, latest before March 11, 1974. The Iraqi Revolutionary Command Council issued a communique which said: "the two parties have agreed to the terms of the solution and Kurdish autonomy, and are determined to put into practice." In history this agreement is known as the "March agreement of 1970."

Following the penning of the agreement, the government invited Kurdish representatives to participate in the ceremony in Baghdad.

President Bekr declared publicly that "our nation, Arabs and Kurds have been united again, restored the unity. Our solidarity and fraternity is more solid than ever and will no longer be weakened." Mullah Mustafa Barzani also appreciated the "wisdom" of the leaders of the Arab Baath Socialist Party and his son Idris Barzani promised to Bekr that "the Kurds support the Arab nation's just war against its enemies". The Kurds cancelled the government agency they had established in 1964, in turn the central government included five Kurds into cabinet and also set up the Ministry of North to deal with Kurdish issues.

A member of the Standing Committee of the Political Bureau of KDP, Mohammad Abdul Rehman became the minister of Ministery of North. The government also appointed several Kurdish leaders to serve as administrative officials and governors of the Kurdish regions. In July 1970, Iraqi government issued the Interim Constitution, which ruled that Iraq was the unity of Arabs and Kurds the Interim Constitution declared Iraq's goals as "achievingsocialism and union of Arabs as a nation." On July 1, KDP held its Eighth National Congress which was themed as "Conference of Peace and National Unity." Eighth National Congress invited many non-party public figures in order to to unify the various opinions within the Party.

Thus thefour-year transitional period of Kurdish autonomy started. However, the high level committee which was made up jointly by the Baath Party and KDP being responsible for carrying out of the "March Agreement" soon faced a series of problems, also as: the scope of Kurdish autonomy; the powers that should be given to regional autonomous government, sharing of the state budget, the division of country's resources, issues regarding the Kirkuk Referendum (according to a former regulation, the census (Article 14) for disputed areas and Kirkuk was planned be done before March 11, 1971 and a referendum would follow the census. Mullah Mustafa accused the government of resettling Arabs in the contested areas, Kirkuk, Khanaqin and Sinjar, and told the government he would not accept the census results if they indicated an Arab majority.

In the government cabinet, although five Kurds served as ministers, they did not have real power. Revolutionary Command Committee had the final say on major decsions. In 1971, primary schools in the Kurdish region started to teach in Kurdish, but the junior high schools were excluded from the new practice. Kurdish becoming the official language was not still in force. Meanwhile, government kept promoting the Arabization policy.

In November 1971, Mullah Mustafa accused thatthe Iraq government for enforcing Arabization process in Kirkuk, and emphasized that Kirkuk would always belong to the Kurds. In addition, both in September 1971 and July 1972, there were two assassinations attempts against Mullah Mustafa. The Kurds accused the Iraq Security Agency for these assassinations.

In February 1973, Iraqi army bombed the Kurdish villages in the Sinjar region which is adjacent to the border of Iran, which resulted great numbers of Kurdish refugees, who flowed into Iran. Between March and June, people many Kurds were forced to migrate from Kirkuk districts.

At the end of 1973, the Iraqi army bombed Kurdish villages. In February 1974, Government organized the Eighth Army Division to be stationed in Arbil city and its surroundings. Meanwhile, Kurdish workers and technicians laboring in the Kirkuk oil fields were dismissed in large numbers and more than 400 Kurdish families were forced to leave Kirkuk. On February 8, residents of 15 Kurdish villages around Kirkuk were forced to migrate. On February 24, the Revolutionary Command Committee issued the Order No.176, which banned all the political organizations which had not joined the "National Progressive Front". The Front included KDP Political Bureau faction organized as the Kurdistan Democratic Party, Iraq Communist Party, Iraq Arab Socialist Baath Socialist. Barzani's KDP was not in the Front.

On June 6, 1974, KDP handed in the report "The Kurdish Issue in Iraq" to the Secretary General of the U.N. In June and July the same year, in UN organized an international meeting of United Nations International Conference on the Rights of National Minorities in Yugoslavia, KDP handed its above Report to the UN Conference. In this report, KDP accused the Baath rule for implementing a "terrorist horror policy" and listed a series of discriminatory operations of the Baath rule.

On January 17, 1974, Kurdish representatives started another round of negotiations with the government on the issue of Kurdish autonomy. Soon, disputes on some key issues appeared between parties and negotiations ceased again. On March 3, Iraq government declared they would prepare and issue a Kurdish autonomy law by themselves rather than negotiating it with the Kurdish representatives.

This was in fact against the spirit of the "March Agreement". On March 8, Vice-President Saddam Hussein met with Idris Barzani in Baghdad. Idris suggested that the government should postpone the announcement of its unilateral autonomy law and extend the one-year transition period of the "March Agreement" to March 11, 1975.

But on March 11,1975, at the end of the transition period of the"March Agreement", Baath Party government announced its unilateral Kurdish Autonomy Law (the Decree 33), according to which, Kurdish region in the north was granted autonomy while being an integrated part of Iraq. Arbil was stipulated as the capital of Kurdish Region; the Kurdish Regional Legislative Assembly and the regional administrative departments would be established through elections; Iraqi president would be qualified to appoint or remove the Chairman of the Kurdish Regional Administrative Council, would also be qualified to dissolve the Kurdish Legislative Assembly;

the central government was given the sole control of the army, oil and financial budget; regional justice, finance should be kept in accordance with that of central government; both Kurdish and Arabic would become official languages; Kurdish language would be allowed to be used in school teaching, but Arabic would be taught as the compulsory language; the boundaries of the Kurdish regions would be determined according to the 1970 "March

Agreement" and according to the census results of 1957; the rights of minorities living within the Kurdish autonomous regions should be observed.

This law in fact practically denied KDP's complete autonomy goal and demand. On March 11, the government sent an ultimatum to Mullah Mustafa, asking him to accept the unilateral law within 15 days. Kurds refused this ultimatum and the war started again. In the same day, five Kurdish ministers in the Iraqi government resigned from their positions. Kurdish rebels resumed military hostilities against the government on March 12, 1974. Eleven members of the KDP were executed by the government in Arbil on April 11.

On March 12, the report titled "Overview of the Kurdish Autonomy Demands by KDP" delivered by the Political Bureau revealed the course of negotiations with the governments and explained the disputes on important issues. In April 1974, Iraqi government started to implement its autonomy law unilaterally Iraq president Bekr refused to accept the Kurdish candidate—Habib Karim—which was nominated by the KDP as Vice-President,[58] but nominated an ex-diplomat who was also Kurd, named Taha, and the government unilaterally declared the establishment of the KRG.

The government's argument was that Karim belonged to the Fayli Kurds (a famous Kurdish tribe) and was Iranian. Shia Kurds amount to about 150,000 people, who originally lived in Kermansah region of Iran, the Ottoman Empire had gradually deported them to Iran and to some regions of Iraq due to their Shia Muslim belief. The Baath government refused to recognize the Fayli Kurds as Iraqis and did not grant them Iraqi citizenship. In the late 1970s, about 50,000 Fayli Kurds were deported to Iran and became refugees. In 2009, the Iraqi government announced that it would grant the Fayli's citizens the Iraq citizenship.

On October 5, 1974, the Kurdish Regional Assembly was opened. The vice-president Taha came to the opening congratulated the opening on behalf of president Bekr of Iraq. There were 80 deputy members in the Regional Assembly within which 72 of them were appointed by the President. The spokesman of the Regional Assembly was the pro-government figure Barbar and the chairman of Executive Committee was Hashimi who was at the same time the minister of Local Affairs in the Iraqi central government. In the same month, the first administrative committee (cabinet) of the Kurdish Region was set up. The Iraqi government also amended the

---

58   Kurdish, Habib Karim, was nominated by KDP as the candidate for Vice-President, but rejected due to being a Fayli Kurd. There were about 150,000 Fayli Kurds who originally lived in Kermansah region in Iran, The Ottoman Empire gradually annexed it to Iraq. Baath Party government refused to accept this tribe was Iraqi and did not give them citizenship. In the late 1970s, about 50,000 Fayli Kurds was deported from Iraq to Iran and became refugees. In 2009, Iraq government declared to grant citizenship to Fayli Kurds.

1970 Constitution of the country, and included the laws which reflected the new status of the Kurdish autonomy. In these days other pro-government Kurdish groups joined the National Progressive Front. By 1976, the number of political organizations in the National Progressive Front reached to six. Its leadership body included 8 members from Baath Party, 3 from the Iraq Communist Party and 3 independent figures.

In 1977, within the Revolutionary Command Committee and cabinet ministers of the central government, Kurds accounted for the 16%, and the population in Kurdish autonomous region in 1977 was 1,482,588, where the Kurds were the majority nation, besides Kurdish population in Iraq amounted to 18% of the whole Iraq population.[59]

In August, 1974, Iraqi army started an offensive towards the Kurdish mountainous areas and a full-fledge war broke out. Kurds in Iraq were supported by Iran and US. During this period, KDP occupied 1/3 territory of Kurdish autonomous region zone and the number of its guerrillas reached up to 45,000. In order to prevent Iranian support to Kurds, Iraq decided to conduct border negotiations with Iran.[60]

In October 1974, the Vice-President of Iraq Saddam Hussein sent his message to Iran via Egypt and Algeria. In those days, the US was aiming to promote a peace agreement between Egypt and Israel. Both the US and Egypt wanted to gain the support of Iraq for the peace negotiations. Iran proposed that if Iraq stopped its open hostile policies against Iran and can make concessions in the Persian Gulf territory issues, it would be willing to give up the plan of supporting the Kurds.[61]

On March 6, 1975, Iran and Iraq leaders conducted side-line negotiations in a summit conference of the OPEC (Organization of the Petroleum Exporting Countries) in Algiers which was mediated by the Algerian president Boumediene, where two sides reached an agreement. Iraq and Iran issued a joint communique, which included the sentence "parties are ready finalize the land boundary issue between the two nations" and the water border between Iraq and Iran in Shatt al-Arab will be the centerline (Thalweg) of it. Both sides guaranteed that they would "commit themselves to maintain close and effective supervision over their common boundary

---

59   Concise Encyclopedia Britannica, China Encyclopedia Publishing House, 1985, p. 829.
60   Historically, border disputes had existed between the 2 countries. There were two main reasons: one was the land border disputes. The land border between the two nations was over 1100 kilometers long, with some disputes on setting landmarks. The second one was the waters boundaries issue. The main issue was the division of Shatt al-Arab. The South part of Shatt al-Arab (about 100 kilometers) was the water boundary of the two nations and also the marine outfall. The disputes of the water boundary had existed for years. The two nations plagued in military conflicts on the issue of water boundaries.
61   L'Express Newpaper, March. 8-14, 1976.

to end insidious nature intrusions from every possible source. Both sides also declared that "any external interference should be eliminated from this area." Iraq declared to accept the plan of division of Shatt al-Arab and Iran government stopped its support to KDP and blocked the border passages between Iran and Iraq.

On March 17, Iraq and Iran signed the protocol settling the boundary disputes. The protocol stated that "the two countries undertakes re-mark the border." On June 13, Iran and Iraq signed Treaty of "Iraq-Iran international borders and good neighborly relations" which involved a lot of parts about conflicts between them and the placement of the borders and its changes. (Protocol on Re-marking of the Land Boundary, the Protocol on the Boundary of Waters, the Protocol on Border Security and the Annexation.)

On March 18, KDP held an enlarged conference of its Political Bureau and military arm, which decided to stop the warring and retreat to Iran. In turn, Iraq government launched large-scale offensive and soon occupied the Kurdish region. Thousands of Kurdish militants surrendered to the government forces while some others went underground and continued the fight. This war from 1974 to 1975 had caused 60,000 casualties including injury and death, the destruction of 40,000 houses of 700 villages and 300,000 refugees.[62] According to the communiqué of the Supreme Command Council of Iraq, this war had caused a death of 1,640 men and 7,903 injuries in the government forces (including 66 army officers).

There are a number of reasons that effected the failure of the Kurds in this war.

First, the huge strength difference between the warring sides.

Iraq's financial and military capacities had increased due to remarkable increase of its oil revenues. The scale of Iraqi army had reached to 200,000 by 1974. At the start of the war, Iraq government mobilized 120,000 soldiers in 8 brigades, 700 to 800 tanks (the total number of Iraqi tanks was 900) and the whole air force was mobilized. But the Kurdish fighters were no more than 50,000 while their weaponry was much weaker, lacking arms and ammunition and possessed very limited food supplies.

Secondly, Kurdish leaders followed some mistaken strategy and tactics.

They underestimated the fighting ability of the Iraqi army. They refused to concede to the government and ceased the negotiations too early at the immature stage, and over-estimated the support of foreign powers such as US and Iran.

---

62   Dilip Hirom, The Essential Middle East, Carroll and Graf Publishers, 2003, p. 287.

During this period, internal conflicts appeared in the KDP. Mullah Mustafa began and finally established his complete arbitrary authority. He attacked those who did not obey as "alien forces" also expelled and executed many left wing members of the party, thus weakened his own ranks.

In 1964, some KDP members who opposed Mullah Barzani's arbitrary conducts had quit from the KDP and had established the Kurdish Revolutionary Party (KRP) led by Abd as-Sattar Tahir Sharif.

Due to dissatisfaction with the attitudes and policies of Mullah Barzani, who sought cooperation with the US, Iran and Israel, many senior leaders of KDP, including Mullah's son Ubeydullah stood on the side of Iraqi government and joined the "Progressive National Front". They accused KDP for betraying socialism. Thirdly, Iraq government won a remarkable international support, especially the military support from the Soviet Union. In June 1964, the Soviet Union had signed a military cooperation agreement with Iraq. Soviet Union had provided Iraq with a large amount of arms and ammunition. On May 1969, both signed a new military cooperation agreement which showed that the Soviet Union continued to offer arms and military aid to Iraq and also SU sent military consultants to train the Iraqi army. On April 9, 1972, a 15-year Treaty of Friendship and Cooperation was signed between the Soviet Union and Iraq which meant an important diplomatic victory for Iraq.

Since then, Iraq's isolation in the Arab world was broken. In addition, Iraq also actively gained Turkey's support through its positive oil trade dealings. As a reward, Turkey closed its border to the Kurdish fighters during the war.

After the Algiers Agreement was signed, many Iraqi Kurds fled to the border of Turkey, but Turkey refused to accept them.[63]

Fourthly, the Kurds led by Barzani depended too much on the external help. US and Iran betrayed the Kurds, which was a fatal blow to Kurdish national struggle. Initially, Kurds had sought help from the Soviet Union, but the Soviet Union had chosen to keep the Kurds at bay.

So, they decided to seek help from the US and Iran to get military assistance from Iran. In order to counter the Soviet Union expansion, after Iraq and the Soviet Union signed the 15-year Treaty of Friendship and Cooperation, in April 1972, the US President Nixon visited Iran on May 30.

In this meeting Shah Pahlavi suggested that the US should "support and help the Kurds".[64] Nixon agreed to the plan of assisting the Kurds with 16 Million dollars and CIA was commissioned to carry out this plan.

---

63 See Appendix of our book Algiers Agreement.
64 W. Safire, "Mr. Ford's Secret Sell-out", New York Times, Feb. 5, 1976.

A CIA memo on March 22, 1974 stated that Pahlavi only suggested his plan of assisting the Kurds as a strategic trump card to compete with Iraq.

"We believe that the King will not welcome the establishment of a Kurdish independence. Both US should aim that this (Kurdish) issue should remain unsolved" so as to have weaker Iraq.[65]

Considering the suggestions offered and put forward by the US and Iran, Mullah Barzani had refused the plan proposed by the Soviet Union to solve the disputes between the government and the Kurds. On March 6, 1975, Iran and Iraq had reached agreement in Algiers. Hence Iran stopped its support to KDP. This decision was also supported by the US. Eight hours after the Algiers Agreement, Iran government started to transport back, the formerly delivered arms and ammunition, and even food, thus betrayed the Iraqi Kurds.

Algiers Agreement in 1975 was an important turning point, after which Iraqi Baath Party government started to carry out a large scale Arabization. Many Arabs were transported to the North (Kurdish) region, especially to Kirkuk. From 1978 to 1979, about 600 villages were burned and 200,000 Kurds were forced to moved to other places.[66] The government built a 15-kilometer wide "epidemic quarantine zone" along its borders between Iran and Syria.

Thus from 1975 onwards, situation in Kurdish region has begun to change significantly. The revolt had mainly ceased, only minor-scale guerrilla forces continued to implement underground activities. Iraqi government led a pro-government Kurdish autonomous government according to its unilateral autonomy law.

In 1980, Election Law of Kurdish Autonomous Region was passed and regional Assembly elections were held in September 1980, August 1986 and September 1989.

Kurdish was promoted as the official language in Kurdish autonomous region. areas. From those days to the Gulf War in 1991, autonomy of the Kurdish region was just on paper.

After 1975, government has increased investments in the Region and by 1976, the government had pledged over $ 1.1 billion loans to Kurdish Region in order to be invested in the construction of industrialization, water conservation, education, sanitation, road and communication facilities. In June 1975, the Revolutionary Command Committee passed the decision to

---

65   Gregory Andrade Diamond. ed., The Unexpurgated Pike Report: Report of the House Select Committee on Intelligence, 1976, Mc Graw-Hill, 1992.
66   M. Farouk-Sluglett, P. Sluglett, J. Stork, "Not Quite Armageddon: Impact of the War on Iraq", MERIP Reports, July-Sept. 1984, p. 24.

carry out land reform in the North of Iraq and promoted the establishment of peasant cooperatives.[67]

In July 1979, president Bekr quit due to illness and Saddam Hussein took over the position as president. Saddam under his rule reinforced domestic authoritarian rule. At the beginning of the same year, the Islamic Revolution broke out in Iran and the pro-US, Pahlavi Kingdom collapsed.

The relations between Iran and Iraq worsened and a fierce competition appeared on the issues of territorial disputes, ideological and leadership competition in the Middle-East.

On September 17, 1980, Iraqi President Saddam Hussein declared the abolition of the 1975 Algiers Agreement and started the war against Iran on September 22. The Iraq-Iran war changed the destiny of Iraqi Kurds again. During the war, Iran used the Kurds in the war against Iraq, offered arms to DKP and helped them fight back. The war greatly weakened the Iraqi government's and control on the Northern region. Iraq was forced to reduce its military presence in the Kurdish region. Iranian army once entered the North region, which enabled the Kurdish guerrilla forces to become active in the North again. KDP set up a base along the border of Iraq and Iran, took the control of about 103.060 square kilometers which it had liberated. The Patriotic Union of Kurds led by Talabani also formed a base area along the borders of Iraq-Iran and Iraq-Turkey.

After 1975, Iraqi Kurdish Resistance Movement showed certain different characteristics compared to the former period. Firstly, tribal and religious colors of the leadership has weakened. In the past, generally Kurdish leaders were mostly elders, tribe leaders or landowners tribe while after 1975, they came mainly from among urban intellectuals. Secondly, core leaders who had led the movement for a long term were lost.

On March 1, 1979, Mullah Mustafa Barzani died in the US[68] His son Massoud Barzani[69] and Idris Barzani[70] continued to lead the KDP.

---

67   Huang Xingmin, General History of Middle East, Iraq Volume, the Commercial Press, p. 286.
68   Mullah Mustafa Barzani was originally buried in Iran after his death. In 1993, his tomb was transferred to his hometown Barzin.
69   Massoud Barzani was born in Mahabad, Iran on August 16, 1945. In 1958, he returned to Iraq after being exiled to the Soviet Union with his father. In 1971, he was elected to the Central Committee of the KDP and later entered the Political Bureau of the Party. After the Kurdish defeat in 1975, he had to flee to Iran with his father and later went to US in 1976. After Mullah Mustafa Barzani's death in 1979, he returned to Iran and took over the KDP leadership. Since the Iraq War in 2003, he has served as the president of the Kurdish regional government till today. He can speak Arabic, Persian, and Kurdish and read English. He has eight sons.
70   Idris Barzani was born in 1944 and died in 1987 due to a heart attack. He was the consanguineous brother of Massoud Barzani. After Mullah Mustafa Barzani died in 1979, he and Massoud Barzani became joint presidents of KDP. He had strong analysis capacity and strategic thinking.

In December 1979, KDP held its Ninth Congress at the border area join-ing the 3 countries Iran, Iraq and Turkey. This Congress was held in a criti-cal historical time when KDP was facing a difficult turning point. Massould Barzani called it "the most difficult and hardest Congress".[71]

The Congress re-organized the leadership body of the party and select-ed a new Political Bureau. Massoud was selected as the Chairman of the party, but the prestige of 34-year old Massoud could not be compared by his father. Thirdly, the Iraqi Kurdish movements in the 1950s and 1960s were practically led by the KDP alone, but after 1975, KDP was repeat-edly split which greatly decreased its strength and broke its domination over the movement. On June 1, 1975, Jalal Talabani quit KDP and set up the PUK. In December 1976, another group around former leading aide of Mullah Mustafa, Dr. Mahmud Osman left the KDP formed the new KDP/ Preparatory Committee. In addition, another group around Party General Secretary, Hachem Hassan also split from the KDP, advocating to "expand Kurds' national rights in Kurdish region" under the leadership of Baath Socialist Party and advocated his position a achieving a new peace on the basis of March Agreement of 1970, finally Dr. Mahmud Osman joined the ranks of "National Progressive Front" in 1975. This group around Dr. Mahmud Osman was mainly made up by the leaders of tribes and influen-tial regional figures.

In 1981, Muhammad Abdul Rahman (1932-2004), whose nickname was "Sami" left the Kurdistan Kurdish People's Democratic Party (KPDP) and set up KPDP Abdul Rahman, the member of Provisional Command Committee of the KDP since 1975, took a progressive stand and criticized the KDP as being too conservative and having to strong tribal colors.

In addition, many small political parties and organizations had appeared making the movement dispersed, and fragmented. For instance, three new Kurdish Islamic parties, were formed which was supported by Iran, and two Christian political parties and some small left wing parties were formed. In 1979 Kurdish Islamic Movement (Sunnit) was set up as a coalition of 3 Kurdish Islamic parties, such as the Kurdish Hezbollah led by Shaikh Mohamed Khalid Barzani (son of Shaikh Ahmed Barzani), and the Kurdish Union of Clergy led by Mullah Hamdi. The leaders of the coalition mainly came from Halabja.

This movement was supported by Iran and its leader Sheikh Osman Aziz declared the goal of establishing an Iran like Kurdish Islamic state in the Northern Iraq.

---

71 See brief information on the party congresses of the KDP, http://www.kdp. se/?do=congress.

Fourthly, the ideologies of Kurdish political parties have gradually diversified. Their left wing colors started to fade, especially within the KDP. Fifthly, guerrilla warfare became the main form of Kurdish national struggle. Each organization had its own self-controlled areas which they called "liberated area" and had its own militia. Among them, KDP and PUK were in the largest parties and each had 10,000 fighters. Small parties, such as the Islamic Party possessed only few hundred armed men. Sixthly, the increase in the numbers of political parties caused internal conflicts and frequent armed fights among them. The competition between the KDP and PUK was fierce and constant armed conflicts occurred between them. In 1982,the two parties reached an agreement allowing each one to use another's controlled area, but the agreement was not implemented. During this period, while PUK made some cooperation alliances with the Iraqi Government, the KDP mainly allied with Iran, when fighting against each other. Until the end of Iran-Iraq War, different Kurdish parties managed to form a Kurdish United Front.

The rise of Talabani's PUK meant that this party had become one of the two main forces within the Kurdish nationalist struggles, which was a significant character of this period.

Within KDP, there were long-standing disputes around the issues such as ideology, struggle forms, policies to follow, and attitude towards the Soviet Union and US and on many other issues, main disputing factions were formed around Ibrahim Ahmad, Jalal Talabani and Mullah Mustafa Barzani. In March 1975, Mullah Mustafa fled to Iran while Ibrahim Ahmad and Jalal Talabani chose Syria.

On June 1, 1975, PUK was established in Damascus-Syria which was formed mainly by 4 groups Kurdish Labor Alliance, Kurdish Socialist Movement, Social Democratic Movement, Nawshirwan Mustafa's clandestine Marxist-Leninist group Komala, their joint communique ascribed the collapse of the revolt to "the inability of the feudalist, tribalist, bourgeois rightist and capitulationist Kurdish leadership" which severely criticized Mullah Mustafa's line.[72]

In 1977, Talabani returned to Iraq and set up the PUK's headquarter in the west of Kurdish region in the Silemani Saldash which was near to the border between Iran and Iraq. PUK possessed a Leadership Committee similar to a central committee which was composed of 32 people and a Political Bureau with 11 people. During the Iran- Iraq War, this PUK used this opportunity to develop its influence in Sulaymaniyah and other districts. Following the death of Mullah Mustafa Barzani fierce competition

---

72 "Patriotic Union of Kurdistan", http://en.wikipedia.org/wiki/Patriotic_Union_of_ Kurdistan. See Appendix of our book for program.

between Talabani and Massoud Barzani has continued which formed a complex partner-rival relationship.

During the Iran-Iraq War, Kurdish region became an important battle field. Kurds regarded this war as a good opportunity to actively develop the anti-government activities and fought against the Central Government with Iran's support.

In November 1980, Kurdish rebels and anti-government organizations and other opposition forces formed a patriotic national front in Damascus, Syria. With the support of Iran and Syria, Kurds began another revolt against the Saddam rule. In Summer 1983, Iranian army attacked Kurdish region of Iraq with the assistance of KDP guerrilla forces, which caused Iraq government lose its control in a part of Kurdish region. In order to change the adverse situation, Iraq government was forced to conduct a negotiation with PUK, seeking to utilize the struggle between KDP and PUK, thus cease-fire with PUK was declared. Later Iraq was able to deal separately with KDP and Iran side to its advantage.

In 1982, Baath Party leadership included Kurdish figure for the first time. In January 1984, the government and PUK declared a mutual cease-fire and held negotiations.

The negotiations mainly included the aim of a stable cease-fire, exchange of war prisoners; the government promised expanding the Kurdish Autonomy; integration of Talabani militia into Iraqi army while transforming it into Iraq's border force; Government also proposed to invest 30% of the oil revenues into the Kurdish regions.

The cooperation between Talabani and the Iraqi government has affected the war situation in the North of Iraq, the cooperation positioned PUK against KDP, thus Iraqi government could solely focus on the war against Iran. The threat in the North was partially relieved by Iraq.

But in 1985, the relation with PUK and the Iraq government became hostile again. Saddam refused to grant greater autonomy to Kurds and rejected concessions regarding Kirkuk. Following this disruption of relations, PUK turned to Iran for support. Iran tried to find a common ground between PUK and KDP and provided heavy weapons to them. In November 1986, the two parties, PUK and KDP decided to reinforce their cooperation. In May 1987, PUK and KDP and other Kurdish parties decided to set up united front against the Saddam government.

In July 1987, PUK and KDP in principle agreed to establish the Iraqi Kurdish Front and in May 1988 the foundation of the IKF was declared, which also included other six smaller Kurdish parties. The Six small parties included: Socialist Party of Iraqi Kurds, Kurdistan People's Democratic

Party, led by Mohamed Abdul Rahman, the Socialist Party of Kurdistan (PASOK), the Kurdish branch of the Iraqi Communist Party led by Aziz Mahmoud (Kurdish), the Assyrian Movement for Democracy, and the Kurdish Workers' Party. But the Kurdish Islamic Movement did not take part in the foundation of Iraqi Kurdish Front.

The IKF declared its purpose as the overthrow of the Saddam rule and setting up a true democratic government in Iraq and also aimed to fight for the strengthening the status of Kurds in the North of Iraq. Jalal Talabani and Massoud Barzani would serve as the two joint Chairmen of the front. The establishment of the front depicted demonstrated that the Kurds were gradually re-uniting their forces and resuming their former strength in the negotiations of autonomy with the Iraq government after it was weakening following the Gulf War. From December 12, 1989 to December 17, 1989, KDP held its Tenth Congress, which emphasized the national unity and accordingly decided to promote the strengthening of the Iraqi Kurdish Front.

During the late period of the Gulf War, in order to punish the Kurdish "traitors" who hit the Iraq Nation from the back, the Iraqi Government carried out a large-scale suppression campaigns against Kurdish fighters.

In March 1987, the Government began a massive offensive targeting the Kurdish region and conducted a barbarous bombing, 80,000 Kurds were deported to a "Model Village" in the border areas near Saudi Arabia and Jordan, set up a 30-kilometers wide no man zone along the Northern border. Iraqi forces destroyed a great number of villages and forced Kurdish guerrillas to flee to Iran and Syria. From February 23, 1988 to April 23, 1989, Iraq mobilized 200,000 troops to launch another large scale military offensive, which was called the "Anfal Operation".The Center of Halabja against Anfalization and genocide of the Kurds wrote that 182,000 men and women with minority origin were killed.[73]

Amin, Iraqi Human Rights minister revealed that there were over 5,000 Kurds who were either died because of the conditions that they had been forced to live or executed between 1987 to 1988. Iraqi Army used chemical weapons against Kurds. On March 16, 1988, Iraqi army began the Halabja massacre and more than 5,000 people were killed by chemical weapons.[74]

---

73   David McDowall, A Modern History of the Kurds, I.B. Tauris, 2004, p. 359; William Ochsenwald & Sydney N. Fisher, The Middle East: A History, McGraw Hill, 2004, p. 659. The word "Anfal" comes from the title of the 8th chapter of the holy Muslim book Quran, meaning „The Spoils of War" which also implies "repudiation."
74   Halabja is an Iraqi Kurdish town along the frontier of Iran with the population of about 70,000. During the Iran-Iraq, Iranian army together with Talabani's PUK had occupied Halabja. On March 16, 1988, after the war, Iraq government in order to take a revenge, started an aggression and used biochemical weapons, resulting 50,000 people's death.
Later, Kurds established the NGO called the The Center of Halabja against Anfalization and

According to the analysis by the International Human Rights Organization, KRW Law, during the "Anfal Campaign", Iraq government has murdered 50,000 to 100,000 Kurdish residents, and destroyed about 4,000 villages, which amounted to 90% of the whole villages in the Kurdish region.

From April 1987 to August 1988, 250 towns and villages were attacked by chemical weapons, 1754 schools, 270 hospitals, 2400 mosques and 27 Christian churches were destroyed.[75] "Anfal Campaign" was the darkest page in the Iraqi Kurdish history. At that time, Massoud Barzani wrote to the U.N., asking to stop Saddam from using chemical weapons. Nr. 620 Resolution of the U.N. Security Council condemned and criticized Iraq for using chemical weapons on August 26, 1988. The Council then encouraged the Secretary-General Javier Pérez de Cuéllar to carry out investigations into allegations of the use of chemical and biological weapons by any Member State that may constitute a violation of the Geneva Protocol of 1925.

Yet the International community did not respond much. After the western forces attacked and invaded Iraq, Saddam was forcedly sent the trial in August 2006, prosecutor of the UN's Iraq Special Court charged Saddam Husein for 14 crimes, including: first, executing more than 140 Shia Islam citizens in the in the village of Dujail in 1982, as a retaliation for a failed attempt of assassination; second, ordering the "Anfal Campaign" an intentional plan for ethnic cleansing targeting the Kurdish region. Saddam faced the allegations of war crimes, crimes against humanity and ethnic cleansing; third, ordering of chemical weapons to attack Halabja in 1988, which caused the death of about 5,000 Kurds and injury of 10,000; fourth, invading Kuwait in 1990 and occupying it for over seven months; fifth, repressing Shia Muslim revolt in the South of Iraq, related to this crime, in

genocide of the Kurds (CHAK) to defend human rights against ethnic massacres including all other minorities in the Middle East. The NGO set up branches in the US, Britain, Holland, Canada, Germany, Switzerland, Denmark, Norway and the Kurdish Region in Iraq.
75   In December 2005, Hague UN Tribunal arbitrated "Anfal Agression" was an "ethnic genocide." In June 2006, Iraq Special Court declared Saddam and other six defendants (former Director of Iraqi National Intelligence: Sabir Abdul Azez Duri (former Minister of Defense: Sultan Hasjim Ahmad, former provincial governor of Mosul,Taher Tawec Hany; former Commander of Republican Guards, Hussein Rashed Muhammad; former Principle of Military Intelligence of Eastern Region, Farhan Multaq Salih and the cousin of Saddam, Ali Hasan Majed should be charged for the Anfal Massacre and were trialed in August the same year. In December, 2006, the same year, Saddam was executed for his crime of ethnic cleansing. In June 2007, cousin of Saddam, Ali Hasan Majed, (a brutal figure). He was accused of commanding "Anfal Agression " when serving as the regional Secretary of Baath Party in the North Region and intentionally using biochemical weapons. Since then, he was nicknamed "Chemical Ali" and other two defendants were accused of committing war crimes and crimes against humanity, and ethnic cleansing and was sentenced to death. The two other defendants were sentenced to life in prison, January 2010, Majed was also sentenced to death.

May 2003, a "huge mass grave of corpses" was discovered in the central region of Iraq. As estimated by the locals, 15,000 men might be buried there; sixth, "the Plan of Arabization" was implemented since 1991, and Kurds were to migrate and their lands were confiscated, thousands of Kurds were forced to move into Iran; seventh, for ordering the massacre of 8,000 people belonging to the Barzani tribe; eighth, destroying the wetlands in the South of Iraq; ninth, ordering the shelling of the oil city Kirkuk; tenth, executing five Shia religious leaders; eleven, ordering the assassination of anti-government political activists, only during ten years after the Gulf War over 500 journalists and writers were killed in Iraq by security forces,; twelve, ordering the persecution and repression of non-religious groups; and thirteen, persecuting and repressing various dissident political groups.[76]

3.4 The Period after the 1990s: A New Historical Phase

This period can be divided into two stages: the first stage, from 1991 to 2003 and the second starting from the second Gulf War in 2003 till today. In the first stage, the Kurds established autonomous regions within the no-fly zone secured by western forces including Turkey and prepared to achieve true autonomy, but the internal conflicts among Kurdish forces had not ceased, and Saddam used these conflicts to interfere and attack from time to time, which meant that the Kurdish region was not peaceful.

Later, Saddam rule was overthrown by the US led western coalition. Kurds took the opportunity to establish their autonomy in the North and have gained a high positions in Iraq's national politics, which meant a historical turn in the Kurdish national movement. The new Iraqi Constitution clearly stipulated the federal state principle for Kurds, and they gained a quite high level of autonomy with comprehensive democratic rights, proportional state power sharing, and veto right to block any major decision of the central government unfavorable to their interests, which meant they have become stake holder in the future destiny of Iraq.

In this postwar Iraq, the Kurdish region became a peaceful oasis, and the Kurds not only won regional governance power, but also became shareholder in the military, diplomatic, financial affairs of Iraq, including oil revenues, which mean that Kurdish region has achieved a "quasi-state" status. In the face of internal divisions and foreign interference by various external forces, and a weak central government, the Kurds due to self-confidence also occasionally declare their intention of or threaten their partners to build an independent state.

---

76   Saddam Was Trialed for "Anfal Campaign", China Daily, August 21, 2006.

On August 2, 1990, Saddam's Iraq launched aggressive war against Kuwait and annexed Kuwait into Iraq as its 19th province. The aggression and annexation was condemned by numerous nations of the world. On November 29, 1990, the U.N. Security Council passed the Resolution 678, authorizing the U.N members. to force Iraq to withdraw from Kuwait by all means. On January 17, 1991, multinational armed forces authorized by U.N. and led by US, launched a large-scale military operation named "Desert Storm" targeting Iraq, which ended on February 25, and Iraq army was forced to retreat from Kuwait. The outbreak of the Gulf War related to Kuwait invasion radically changed the destiny of Kurds, and offered the Iraqi Kurds the best opportunities to truly really their own destiny.

After the Gulf War, KDP leaders were able to freely return back to the region. On February 15, 1991, the US President George W. Bush called on the Iraqi people to rise and overthrow the Saddam dictatorship, which were severely oppressed by the Iraqi government, this move by the US inspired the Shia political movement in the southern Iraq to launch a revolt against the government.[77]

And in early March 1991 the Kurds in northern Iraq launched an anti-government uprising, attacked government buildings, the Baath Party offices, military bases and police stations, occupied Kirkuk and the surrounding oil fields, within a few weeks they won control over the 3/4 of the Kurdish autonomous region and captured more than 9,000 government troops.

On March 4, another Kurdish uprising broke out in a small town of Lanchi in the Northeast region, followed by the uprisings in Sulaymaniyah and Arbil on the 6th and 7th, respectively. On March 11, Dohuk also joined the uprising.

On March 21, Kurdsoccupied Kirkuk. The storm was so strong that "the Jash Kurds", i.e. Kurdish fighter groups, which had cooperated with the government also joined the uprisings. "Iraqi Kurdish Front" declared a general amnesty for the former Jash tribes. Kurdish rebel army forces moved towards the highway connecting Baghdad and Kirkuk. In those days Massoud Barzani commented: "the uprising was initiated by the masses". "This was out of our expectation".[78]

On March 26, Iraqi Government fought back the Iraqi Republican Guards gained back the Kirkuk city on March 30. The US and other western powers did not interfere at this moment, thus Kurdish revolts were quickly suppressed and Kurds lost over 20,000 fighters and more than 1 Million ended up as refugees that fled to Turkey. This caused a large-scale

---

77 February 15, 1991, The US President Bush asked the Iraqi people to overthrow the dictator.

78 David McDowall, A Modern History of the Kurds, London: I. B. Tauris, 2007, p. 372.

humanitarian crisis which has attracted great global attention. Under huge pressure raised by the international public the US and Britain decided to form a secured zone for Kurds in the Northern Iraq, following the suppression of the Kurdish revolts.

On April 5, 1991, U.N. Security Council passed the Resolution No. 688, condemning the Saddam government for the suppression of Shia Muslims and Kurdish civilians, and for threatening the peace and security in the Middle East region. The resolution called on the Iraqi Government to immediately stop repressions of the whole Iraqi people including those in Iraqi Kurdistan and respect human rights of its population. The Council insisted that Iraq allow access by international humanitarian organizations to the areas affected, requesting the Secretary-General to report on the Iraqi and Kurdish populations affected by repression from the Iraqi authorities, using all resources possible to address the needs of the population. It also demanded Iraq co-operate with the Secretary-General and international organizations to assist in humanitarian aid efforts. France, the United Kingdom, and United States used Resolution 688 to establish Iraqi no-fly zones—about 9325 square kilometers and extending from the 36th parallel northwards—to protect humanitarian operations in Iraq, although the resolution made no explicit reference to no-fly zones.[79] This was a historic decision favoring the Kurds, as this was the first time the UN Security Council documents included the phrase "repression of Kurds."

Subsequently, following the UN Resolution the US, British with other western nations militarily attacked Iraq to implement the "Operation Provide Comfort" (which was later renamed as Operation Northern Watch" and formally declared a no-fly zone. About 16,000 international soldiers participated in the military operation under the pretext of providing security to Kurds. Yet, security zone did not include Sulaymaniyah, Kirkuk and other important Kurdish cities. In mid-April, Iraqi government declared a cease-fire. In May, about 1 million refugees returned home, but the conflicts between the government forces and Kurdish insurgents continued. Due to the failure in the negotiation between Kurds and the government, Iraqi army forces and government officers withdrew from the Kurdish region on October 23, 1991.

Thus North of Iraq factually began to be administered by Kurds. In order to make up the political vacuum after the retreat of the government forces; Kurds decided to hold elections and set up an autonomous government.

---

79 Mahir A. Aziz, The Kurds of Iraq: Ethno-nationalism and National Identity in Iraqi Kurdistan, p. 83.

On May 19, 1992, regional assembly election was held in the Kurdish region, KDP won 50.22% of the votes and 51 seats, while PUK received 49.77% votes and 49 seats. Both parties failed to gain enough votes to form a single-party government thus they had to form a coalition. Apart from KDP and PUK, Kurdish Islamic Movement (5.1% of votes) and Assyrian political party also won five seats (from 105 total seats).

The election competition for regional government chairmanship between Massoud and Talabani was very intense, their votes were 466.819 and 441.057 respectively, none of them could reach the legal requirement for chairmanship. Sheikh Osman Abdulazez from the Kurdish Islamic Movement also participated in the regional government chairmanship competition and received 4% of the votes.

Then, the two main parties reached a co-habitation agreement, which can also be defined as the "50/50 power sharing system". On June 4, on the First assembly of the Parliamentin Arbil, KDP and PUK served as President and Vice President respectively. On July 4, the regional government was set up under the leadership of prime minister Fuad Masum from PUK[80] while the deputy prime minister was appointed from KDP. According to the achieved political solution Massoud Barzani and Talabani did not take any direct positions in the government or in regional assembly. On October 14, Kurdish Assembly declared Kurdistan as the federal regional government of Iraq. However, neither Kurdish Parliament nor government was formally recognized by the Iraqi central government.

In the 1990s, the US's containment, embargo policies against the Saddam rule provided Kurds a golden opportunity for the Kurdish autonomy. During this period, due to the establishment of no-fly zone, Iraqi government almost lost all the control of the Kurdish Region. Under the protection of the West, Kurdish region de facto became "the state within the state".

Soon after the Gulf War in 1991, Saddam appointed Taha Yasin Ramadan, as the vice-President, declared a general amnesty to Kurdish insurgents and offered to re-start negotiations for a peaceful solution. He also invited Massoud Barzani and Jalal al-Talabani to negotiate in Baghdad. The Iraqi Kurdish Front decided to negotiate and in August, 1991, both sides agreed to start the negotiations based on the 1970 "March Agreement". Kurds proposed their conditions, as the complete autonomy, legalization of Kurdish peshmerga army forces, joint control of army and police forces of the central government. In order to prevent national secession, Saddam agreed to most of their conditions. In late August 1991, both the sides reached a draft

---

80   Fuad Masum was a technician-bureaucrat, he quit his position in March 1993 and gave his position to Khosla Rasoul from the PUK party. Currently, he still plays an important role in Iraq and Kurdish politics.

treaty which contained: autonomy to be implemented in the five provinces in the North, while the central government would continue to be responsible for diplomatic affairs and national defense; Kurdish to become one of the two the official languages; KRG would cease to pay taxes to the central government; Kurdish parties would be legalized and Kurds would be allowed to participate in administrative, legislative, and judicial powers; Kurds would be able to have independent army. The government would release all Kurdish political prisoners.[81] In September 9, the Iraqi National Assembly legalized all opposition parties that defend Iraq, support the revolutions of 1958 and 1968, are not based on race, regionalism, sectarianism, or express anti-Arab positions.

Subsequently, Kurdish refugees abroad returned home. But at the last moment, the Kurdish parties held a meeting to discuss the draft treaty and put forward some additional conditions, such as obtaining the sovereignty of oil rich city of Kirkuk, KRG's full control over the regional defence, customs management of the region and diplomatic autonomy in foreign policies etc. As these additional demands were refused by the Iraqi government, negotiations failed.[82] In October 1991, the central government further withdrew its military arms and administrative organs institutes and staff from the Kurdish region and began to implement an economic sanctions and stopped the wage payments for the civil servants working in the North, in these days transport of food supplies to Kurdish areas was ceased by the central government.

On October 2, 1992, Kurdish Regional Assembly declared implementing of federalism. In this period, while neither of the two sides resorted to a large-scale military offensive, Kurds and other Iraqi anti-government forces began to conduct partial attacks and guerilla activities and assassinations, and small-scale conflicts continued in Iraq. Iraqi government tried to take advantage from the internal conflicts among the Kurdish political forces, using one faction against the other in order to suppress the Kurds. During this period, Iraq government imposed an economic blockade on the Kurdish region and cut the supply of oil and food, Iraq's blockade policy coupled with the United Nations' sanctions previously adopted, the Kurdish region was actually faced with double sanctions, which caused a serious humanitarian crisis, there.

Kurds started to blame both Saddam and Iraqi Kurdistan Front, proposing "we only want bread and butter damn with Saddam or the Iraqi Kurdistan Front". Massoud Barzani realized the situation and warned the KDP: "our government has been paralyzed... IKF is facing an important crisis".[83]

---

81   Huang Xingmin, General History of Middle East, Iraq Volume II, the Commercial Press, p. 335.
82   Introduction to World Nationalism, p. 400.
83   David McDowall, A modern History of the Kurds, London: I.B. Tauris, 2007, p. 385.

The Oil-for-Food Program (OIP), established by the United Nations Security Council in April 14, 1995—under the Resolution 986—was established to allow Iraq to sell oil on the world market in exchange for food, medicine, and other humanitarian needs for ordinary Iraqi citizens without allowing Iraq to boost its military capabilities. This meant that Iraq could only export 13% of its oil production. This program slightly improved the economic situation of the Kurdish region. Later, Resolution No. 1153 by the Security Council on February 20, 1998 increased the above oil export ratio.

From 1997 to 2001, benefiting from the oil-for-food program Kurdish region could have a revenue 4.6 Billion US. Dollars, the rest was used by the central government.

As of 2003 before the outbreak of the war in Iraq, 8.35 Billion US. Dollars were allocated to Kurdish region in total while 4.0 Billion US. Dollars of the revenues had remained unused.[84] During this period, Iraqi Government had practically lost the control of the North, only maintained a nominal sovereignty. In the parliamentary elections of Iraq in 2000, only 30 seats out of 250 were reserved for the Kurds, and candidates were directly appointed by the president Saddam Hussein.

Even though Kurds had established regional autonomy after the war, the differences and conflicts between KDP and Talabani's PUK did not cease or weaken, which formed a division and confrontation between the Northern and Southern Kurdish regions. KDP controlled the Northern provinces and cities with Arbil as its center while Talabani's PUK controlled Southern provinces with Sulaymaniyah as its center.

Although both the regional Assembly and a government were there, they were in fact in fact fragmented as two governments, two armed forces and two security forces. According to the power distribution agreement between the two main parties, the official positions in government organs and agencies, even number of polices and teachers were shared between them. This demonstrated the severe competition and conflict for power between the two parties.

Control of Habur border crossing point with Turkey was a great conflict object between the two parties, it was estimated Habur border point generated a revenue of 0.15 Million US. Dollars per day (some even estimated the revenue reached to 1 Million US. Dollars). The revenue was practically controlled by the KDP and the PUK was greatly frustrated about it.

---

84   "Iraqi Kurdistan", http://en.wikipedia.org/wiki/Iraqi_Kurdistan.

In December 1993, two sides entered into a small-scale armed conflict, and Kurdish Islamic Movement party supported KDP, this meant that alliance between Talabani's PUK and the Kurdish Islamic Movement party was broken. After these crises, in the early days of 1994, the coalition behind the Kurdish Regional Government collapsed and after this collapse a conflict broke out. On May 1, 1994, a large-scale conflict led to the deaths of more than 1,000 men.

Turkey invaded Iraqi Kurdistan in order to stamp out the Turkish-Kurd PKK (People's Workers Party) rebels. Iraqi Kurdish groups initially condemned the invasion and charged that civilians were being targeted. Estimates of Iraqi Kurd refugees caused by the attack ranged from a few hundred to several thousand.

In December 1994, PUK occupied the Arbil city. Later, with international mediating efforts the two Kurdish parties reached an agreement, they agreed to increase the number of government ministers from 10 to 15 with 7 to each party and one ministry was allocated to Kurdish Islamic Movement (IMK). In March 1995, conflicts re-appeared once again due to differences of position in the fight against Saddam government, with this division Kurdish region was divided into two hostile parts. Although the provinces controlled by the KDP shrank to 1/3, but because of Iraq's illegal oil exports passed through, KDP controlled region, Massoud Barzani could accumulate finance for the purchase of weapons and ammunition. Under these conditions Talabani's PUK chose to form alliance with Iran, Syria and Ocalan's PKK to strengthen its position. On the other side Turkey supported Barzani's KDP to fight against PKK.

From August 9 to August 11, 1995 and from September 12 to 15, 1995, with the brokerage of the US, two sides carried out peace negotiations in a small town of Drogheda near Dublin, Ireland, but PUK and KDP leaders failed to reach a peace agreement in meetings.

They had sharp disputes on the issues of demilitarization of Arbil and customs income of border pass points, another dispute was whether to prevent PKK's (Ocalan's Party) attacks against Turkey

In August 1996, fierce war erupted between the 2 sides, Iran supported the PUK and sent its army into the Kurdish region and KDP sought help from the Iraq Government. Iraq government took this opportunity to send 30.000 troops into the Kurdish region and rapidly captured Arbil and PUK controlled areas.

At this point US started missile strikes against Iraqi government forces. Subsequently, with the support of Iran, the Kurdish Patriotic Union started a successful counterattack to regained Arbil city.

Although frictions continued between the two factions, in October 1996, with the arbitration of US, Britain and Turkey, KDP and PUK reached a ceasefire agreement and formed a supreme Council which would will supervise the cease-fire. I can say that from 1994 to 1998, due to the power fights between KDP and PUK, Kurdish region was plunged into a full-fledged civil war. As a senior Iraqi Kurdish statesman said: "they (Massoud Barzani and Jalal Talabani) distrust each other. When you meet one of them, the only thing he speaks about is the other. They are trapped in the fight for power. They can't formulate a common strategy, other than eliminating and destroying each other, they have no other strategy".[85] This situation between the two seriously detrimental for the US strategy which aimed of to turn the Kurdish Region into an anti-Saddam fighting base. The US many times failed to mediate between the two parties, the CIA trained army forces in the region was forced to leave and went to US. and the US could no longer provide financial support to Kurds.

During the second term of Clinton administration (1996-2000), the United States stepped up its action to overthrow Saddam Hussein's regime, and greatly supported Iraqi opposition forces.

US as the first priority tried to persuade the Kurds to achieve reconciliation. On September 17, 1998, with the help of US, KDP and PUK reached an agreement in Washington D. C., declared a cease-fire reinforced cooperation and unity. In December 1999, the joint coalition government was formed again and the region entered a period of peace. On October 5, 2002, Kurdish regional assembly resumed its normal work after many years and promulgated a "regional Constitution" which set Kirkuk as the "capital" of the Kurdish region. This aroused a strong reactions from Turkey. Turkish prime minister Bülent Ecevit warned that the Kurdish parties' behaviors "has passed the red line". This was in the period when the joint system of KDP and PUK coalition was set up.[86]

---

85   David McDowall, A Modern History of the Kurds, London: I. B. Tauris, 2007, p. 385.
86   In 1992 the Iraqi Kurdistan Front had promulgated two documents: Kurdistan Liberation Front Law No. 1 of 1992, issued April 8 1992, which called for the election of a Kurdistan National Assembly (KNA), and Kurdistan Liberation Front Law No. 2 of 1992, Leader of the Kurdistan Liberation Movement, which called for the election of a "Leader of the Kurdistan National Movement" (hereafter referred to as President) and defined the powers and duties of this figure, with the election to be held coincidentally with the KNA election provided for under Law No. 1. Law No. 1 was promulgated by "political leadership of the Iraqi Kurdistan Front": Masoud Barzani of the KDP, Jalal Talabani of the PUK, Sami Abdul Rahman of KPDP, as well as the leaders of PASOK, KSP, KCP, ADM, and the Kurdistan Toiler's Party, but in 1993 Sami decided to re-join the Kurdistan Democratic Party.

Fig. 3-1 The Iraqi Civil War and Distribution of Power In the 1990s

Recourse: "Iraq: Country Profile" [map], CIA, January 2003,
http://www.lib.utexas.edu/maps/iraq.html.

In this period, PKK began to be active in the North of Iraq, and also established a base in Qandil. In August 1994, a severe armed conflict between PKK and KDP broke out. In March 1995, Turkish army exercised an operation against the PKK forces where they penetrated 40 kilometers deep into Iraq. In May and September 1997, to attack PKK, Turkish army marched into the North of Iraq and eliminated all the guerrilla forces of PKK. On October 15, 1997, Turkey unilaterally announced its intention of setting up a "security zone" in the North of Iraq, which aroused severe opposition both from Iraq and other Arab nations. In October and November 1998, Turkish army crossed the Iraq borders twice, in order to eliminate the guerrilla forces despite severe oppositions from Iraq. In addition, in October, ten thousand Turkish troops have moved to the Syrian border, the Turkish air force was set onto the red alert, and RF-5 and F-16 jets were constantly buzzing along the border. And Egyptian President Hosni Mubarak has spent the week shuttling between Ankara and Damascus. Turkey demanded from Syria that Ocalan, leader of PKK should be expelled from Syria. During this period the Iranian army had once entered the territory of Iraq.

Meanwhile, Kurdish areas became an important bridgehead for the United States to promote the anti-Saddam regime and an important for the Iraqi opposition camp. In June 1992, promoted by US, various anti-government organizations of Iraq held meetings in Vienna and established a broad-alliance, the Iraqi National Congress "INC" to unite against Saddam with the purpose of overthrowing Saddam and establish a democratic federal Iraq. KDP, PUK and IMK joined in this organization and immediately becoming the most important forces.

In October 1992, INC held a second conference in Salahuddin near Arbil where it was officially announced and selected an administrative organ (executive committee). Shiite leader Ahmad Chalabi[87] served as the executive committee chairman, and was responsible for the daily works of the organization. The INC would have "a three-man presidency" (a Shia, a Sunni and a Kurd) including Massoud Barzani and two other leaders (one senior Shiite cleric and one general from the Arab Sunnis) formed a three-man presidency. The leader of the Kurdish Islamic Movement, Sheikh Usman was one of the six members of the INC's executive committee.

The headquarter of INC was in Salahuddin-Kurdish Region which became an important base of anti-Saddam forces. The US government, especially CIA offered great help to the INC and in March 1995, the forces led by this organization launched an attack against the Iraqi government forces with the support of CIA, but failed. The Clinton administration withdrew support at the last minute, and it (along with the attempted coup) the revolt was crushed by Iraqi troops at the same time that Turkish troops invaded

---

87   Ahmad Chalabi (1944-), a Shia Iraqi statesman, graduated from the University of Chicago, Department of Mathematics, and received his doctoral degree, there In 1977, he entered into the banking industry, he also participated in the struggle against the Saddam regime, he had good relations with the US government.

In 1992, he served as the President and founder of the INC supported by the US and received a great amount of financial support from the US.In April as US forces took control during the 2003 Invasion of Iraq, With allied troops, Ahmad Chalabi entered into the southern town of Shatrah. In September 2003, he served as the chairman of Provisional Governing Council of Iraq. From April to May 2005 and December 2005 to January 2006, he served as the Minister of Oil of Iraq government. From May 2005 to June 2006, he served as the deputy prime minister of Iraq. In December 2005 he lost in the general election, failed to enter the parliament. He has long been accused of corruption. He held a positive attitude towards Kurds.

Iraq from the north. I should note that Kurdish Democratic Party had not joined the Kurdish revolt. In September 1996, invited by KDP, Iraqi government marched into the Kurdish Region and severely suppressed the anti-government activities of INC.

Meanwhile, Saddam Hussein was able to play off the fratricidal rivalry between the two main Kurdish organizations-the Patriotic Union of Kurdistan (PUK), headed by Jalal Talibani, and the Kurdistan Democratic Party (KDP), headed by Massoud Barzani. With Iranian backing, Talibani's forces attacked the KDP forces. Failing to get US support, Barzani requested assistance from Saddam Hussein, who promptly invaded northern Iraq, taking over areas controlled by the PUK (and then quickly withdrawing). Surviving remnants of the Iraqi National Congress were forced to flee in a panic along with their CIA backers. Not only did attempts by the CIA to use the "safe haven" as a staging ground for "regime change" fail miserably, they increased the vulnerability of Kurds to both Iraqi and Turkish attacks and exacerbated inter-Kurdish factional rivalry.

96 members of the INC were sentenced to death and INC headquarter was forced to flee to London. In October 1998, Liberation of Iraq Act was passed in the U.S Congress, which stipulated the termination of Saddam rule and allocated 97 Million US Dollars to foster the opposition factions and promote Iraqi democratic movement. In February 1999, Clinton government identified seven Kurdish organizations to fund, including KDP, PUK, and IMK. The Liberation of Iraq Act required the US. government to offer fund in different aspects, including military aid (training and equipment), broadcasting, radio and television propaganda, and humanitarian aid. This act later became one of the direct basis of US government's intention for launching the Iraq War.

The "9/11" incident became the turning point for the fate of Kurds and Iraq. On September 11, 2001, Washington, the Capital of the US, New York and other cities were violently attacked by Al-Qaida resulting in huge financial losses and casualties. Since the "9/11" incident, there occurred a significant change in the US foreign and national security strategies. After the 9/11 terrorist attacks, the Bush administration decided to overthrow Saddam regime as their first step in the democratic transformation of the Middle East.

Hence, the US further increased its support for the INC and other Iraqi opposition forces. In August, 2002, the US government invited Massoud Barzani, Jalal Talabani and Ahmad Chalabi, the President of INC and other leaders of the opposition faction forces—six groups—to attend a meeting in Washington for the plan of overthrowing Saddam. In September, the spokesperson of the US State Department, R. Boucher said that the

US planned to expand the aid of military training and assistance for opposition factions in Iraq. In December, promoted by US, dozens of Iraqi opposition organizations, including KDP, PUK, attended a meeting in London to discuss the future situations, post-war arrangements and post-war power distribution. The General Assembly in London established the political principles and framework for the two-year transitional period following the overthrow of Saddam Hussein and decided to establish a coordinating committee of 65 members, the majority of whom were occupied by Shiites and Kurds.

Talabani, the leader of PUK delivered a speech, stating: "we welcome the participation of US to eliminate the Saddam regime" On March 19th, 2003, regardless of the strong opposition from the international public US unilaterally gave start to military attack which was dubbed Operation Iraqi Freedom by the United States.

On April 2, Iraqi president Saddam wrote to Talabani, leader of PUK, asking the Kurds in the North of Iraq to fight against the US+UK led coalition forces together. In the meantime, KDP was fighting against Iraqi government under the shield of US air-strikes. On April 9th, Saddam's rule was overthrown. In this war since Turkey had refused to offer US forces cross-border passage from its territory at this critical time, this has made Iraqi Kurds become the most important ally of the US on the northern front in the Iraq War. The Kurds actively participated in Iraq War and played a crucial role in overthrowing Saddam regime.[88]

Before the war, Kurdish opposition had closely cooperated with the CIA, and US Special Forces in US's fight against the anti-US Kurdish Radical Islamic Military Organization, "Ansar al-Islam"[89] And to persuade the US military to open up the northern battlefield, the two sides also cooperated to discover a chemical weapons site in Iraq. Kurdish armed forces' activities also forced the deployment of the Fifth Army of the Iraqi government in the north of Iraq, which divided Iraq's military forces. During the Iraq War, Kurdish guerrilla forces and the US army worked together, and after

88   Michael Garrett Lortz, "Willing to Face Death: A History of Kurdish Military Forces-the Peshmerga-From the Ottoman Empire to Present Day Iraq", http://etd.lib.fsu.edu/theses/available/etd-11142005-144616/.

89   Ansar al-Islam, also called "Islam supporters", was set up in September 2001. Most of its members were from "IMK". It was the Iraqi Kurdish Islamic radical group and was listed as a terrorist organizations by the US. After the Iraq War, this organization became active and launched frequent terrorist attacks in Iraq. In addition, on February 18, 2001, Frasno Hariri, the member of Political Bureau of KDP and Provincial Governor of Arbil was assassinated by "Tawhid" which was an extremist organization led by Abu Musab al-Zarqawi. In April 2002, this organization attempted to assassinate Salim, a prominent leader of PUK, but had failed. The Islamic Army in Iraq (IAI) was a Sunni Islamist militant organization created in 2003 with the aim of expelling foreign troops from Iraq. From 2003-2011, the group primarily targeted US forces in Iraq.

the War they took the responsibility to maintain the security and order in the North. The US also helped PUK to establish the Anti-Terrorist Intelligence Unit (CTG), which was nominally part of the Kurdish regional government but remained under the control of the Kurdish Patriotic Union, in order to fight against the Ansar- al-Islam. Iraq War was a landmark in the Iraqi Kurdish History.[90]

Since then, the status of the Kurds has improved greatly. Kurdish autonomy was consolidated and transformed into a quasi "independent kingdom". This regional government in Iraq Kurdish also became an example model for Kurds living in other countries of the Middle-East, encouraged and inspired them to fight for and expand their struggle for their national rights.

Following the Iraq War, Kurds participated in Iraqi political affairs more equally for the first time in history, on equal footing with the Arabs.

They joined in CPA (Coalition Provisional Authority led by US and later took part in the Interim Governing Council of Iraq (that existed from July 13, 2003 to June 1, 2004). By July 2003, five of the 25 members in this Iraqi Governing Council were Kurds, including Jalal Talabani, Massoud Barzani, Salahadin Mohammed Bahaddin (General Secretary of the Kurdish Islamic Union), Dara Nur al-Din (the independent Judge of the Court of Appeal of Iraq of Iraqi) and Mahmud Osman (an independent statesman).

Among them, Jalal Talabani, and Massould Barzani both served as the presidents of the Interim Governing Council of Iraq. In February 2004, the establishment of Kurdish regional government was proposed by the US, while Kurds participated in making the Iraq's Provisional Constitution and proposing it to US government. The main contents of the Provisional Constitution related to Kurdish autonomy were: Kurdish autonomous region should be expanded including Nineveh, Kirkuk and Diyala, keeping of the Kurdish armed forces, and transform them into the Kurdish National Guard; Natural resources of the Kurdish region to belong solely to Kurds; Fiscal issues and taxes would be effective after approved by the Kurdish Regional Assembly; Iraq's permanent Constitution should enter into force after a referendum in the Kurdish region and with the support of the majority of people.[91] On March 8, 2004, with the US leadership Transitional Government of Iraq Act (TAL) was put into effect and Iraq's transitional

90   It nominally belonged to Kurdish regional government, but was practically under the control of PUK. It was one of the three major security agencies in the Kurdish region. Its leader was Lahur Talabani, nephew of President Talabani.
91   Brendan O'leary, John McGarry, Khaled Salih, The Future of Kurdistan in Iraq, Universiy of Pennsylvania Press, 2005, pp. 309-313.

Constitution was promulgated and Iraq's transitional government was formed. In June, Hoshyar Zibari, the assistant of Massoud Barzani began to serve as the Minister of Foreign Affairs.[92]

In accordance with the transitional Constitution and TAL, Iraqi Kurds kept their autonomous status; Kurdish regional government would continue to operate and Kurds would retain a 75,000-men army. Kurdish language was allowed to be one of the two official languages (Arabic and Kurdish) in Iraq. This new Act did not include Kirkuk as part of the Kurdish Region but stipulated that Kurds who were forced migrate during the Saddam period might return home.

Meanwhile, despite strong opposition from the Arabs, Kurds was able to add another article to the Act which was a success: in the case of an opposition from three provinces of Iraq, the promulgation of the Iraq's permanent Constitution might be vetoed. This article practically gave the Kurds a veto right against any constitution, which they disagreed, because three provinces of Iraq were Kurdish provinces. On September 1, 2004, Iraq's Provisional National Assembly, was established, with 100 seats within which, 40 belonged to Shi'ites, 25 seats were allocated for Sunnis and Kurds, respectively. The rest 10 seats were divided among Turkmens, Christians and other ethnic groups. Kurds were unsatisfied with Paul Bremer,[93] the highest US authority in Iraq, he was criticized for putting too much pressure on the Kurds and reluctant to make proper concessions to the Kurds at the level of self-government, regarding the Kurdish armed forces, oil revenue rights of the region and border checkpoints. During Constitution debates

---

92   Hoshyar Zibari, a Zebari tribe descendant,was born in 1953 and studied in Britain, He had long fought against Barzani tribe and participated in pro-government Kurdish army. In order to end the conflicts between two tribes, Mullah Mustafa married Hamayl Zibari from the Zebari tribe and Massoud Barzani was born from this marriage. Hoshyar Zibari was Massoud's uncle. Hoshyar Zibari was the member of the Political Bureau of KDP and one of the spokesmen of Foreign Affairs Department. In 1990s, he was the representative of KDP in Britain. In September 2003, he was assigned as Minister of Foreign Affairs of the Interim Governing Council. In June 2004, he began to serve as the Minister of Foreign Affairs of the Iraqi transitional government.

93   Paul Bremer (1941-), Administrator of the Coalition Provisional Authority of Iraq, was an experienced diplomat and anti-terror expert. He had served in the US State Department for 23 years and was the assistant of both ex-Secretaries of the State, Mr. Rogers and Mr. Kissinger. From 1983 to 1986, he was the US ambassador to Holland; from 1986 to 1989, he was the ambassador-at-large, responsible for the Anti-terror Department of the US State Department. In 1999, he was appointed as the President of the Anti-terror Committee by the two parties for two terms. On May 6, 2003, he took over Lt. General Jay Garner to serve as the highest Civilian Post, responsible for the re-building of Iraq in the post-war era. He resigned on June 28, 2004. As he has been considered successful but was criticized disbanding the Iraqi army, the police, and enabling the non-renaissance party to take part in the government. After resigning, he wrote My Year in Iraq: The Struggle to Build a Future of Hope.

Kurds vigorously struggled for their autonomous rights. The Provisional Constitution adopted in March 2004, stipulated "in the future referendum to determine the permanent Constitution of Iraq, as long as there are three provinces opposing it, the permanent Constitution can be rejected, which includes Kurds-controlled northern three provinces".

Grand Ayatollah Ali Al-Sistani, leader of Shiite Muslims, had strong reservations about this veto provision. He issued a statement which called the U.N. not to endorse the TAL (transitional constitution). UN Security Council Resolution 1546, considered Ali Al-Sistani's opposition and omitted any mention of the TAL.

In May 2004, the leader of an US envoy to Iraq told the Kurdish leaders that the Kurds will not be able to become President or prime minister of Iraq. On June 8, 2004, U.N. Security Council passed a new resolution (Resolution 1546) on the Iraqi issue, which recognized the Iraqi Provisional Government and finalized the resolution stating that "Acting under Chapter VII of the United Nations Charter, the Council welcomes the assumption of responsibilities and authority by the Iraqi interim government by 30 June 2004 and the end of the occupation and Coalition Provisional Authority (US and Britain).

This UN resolution stipulated that Iraq would become a federal republic but ignored the Kurdish demands on the method of ratification of the Iraq's Interim Constitution. This stipulation made Kurds very dissatisfied. On June 9, Minister of Public Affairs of the Provisional Government of Iraq, Mr. Nisrin Bawrwari commented that the new UN resolution on Iraq by the U.N. Security Council had "rejected the proper demands of the Kurdish autonomy. The Kurdish members of Provisional Government are determined to resign, if the Kurdish leadership asks us to resign from the central government, we will do this to show our determination."

Before voting for the draft of the new resolution, the draft was debated in the Interim Governing Council, during this debate Iraqi Kurdish leader, Talabani and Barzani threatened the Council, that the Kurdish members might withdraw from the Iraqi Provisional Government, and also Kurds might block the 2005 elections campaign of 2005.

Nisrin Bawrwari also commented that the Iraqi Provisional Constitution has neglected the rights of all minorities in Iraq including Kurds. After intense and long negotiations with the Kurds, Allawi, Iraqi prime minister announced on June 10 that they had solved the disputes over the Kurdish autonomy, and avoided internal divisons on the issue of central Iraqi government.

In January 2005, Iraq held its first post-war general election and voted for the Transitional National Assembly, the Provincial Council and the Kurdish National Assembly (KNA). The KNA, KDP, PUK and other small Kurdish parties including Kurdistan Democratic Patriotic Alliance, (DPAK), the Kurdish Labor Party and Kurdish Communist Party also participated in the election.

Democratic Patriotic Alliance of Kurdistan led by Talabani and Barzani had gained 2,175,000 votes, 26% of the total votes, thus 75 seats out of total 275 seats. On April 6, Chairman of the PUK, Talabani was elected as the Iraq President. This was the first time a Kurdish figure became the President of Iraq which was a major breakthrough, reflecting the historical change in the status of Kurds.

In the provincial assembly elections other than the three Kurdish provinces, Kurdish party also won the most votes in Nineveh and Diyala where the majority population was Sunni Arabs.

The main responsibility of Transitional National Assembly, was to prepare and pen a permanent Constitution. In October 2005, Iraq held a referendum on the permanent Constitution and was adopted with a 78% approval rate, most of the Kurds voted yes in the referendum.

The new Constitution defined the basic system of the new State, which stipulated that Iraq is an independent federal state with complete sovereignty, with parliamentary representation; Islam being the religion of the state ; defined Iraq as the founding member and full member of the League of Arab States; oil and gas resources as the common property of the whole Iraqi people, that the federal government and the local government should jointly manage oil and gas resources, oil revenues should be shared in accordance with the size of the population in each province region proportionally and equally. The new Constitution recognized the Kurdish region as the stake holder of the federal power.[94]

On December 15, 2005, Iraq officially held General Parliamentary elections, in which Kurdish Alliance won 53 seats of 275 seats with voting rate of 19.3%. From April to May 2006, new Iraqi government was formed according to new Constitution, and on April 22, Talabani was once more elected as the President of Iraqi, while Zebari remained in the cabinet as the minister of Foreign Affairs in the new government.

Barham Salih, as one main leader leader of PUK, began to serve as one of the deputies together with Salam al-Zaubai and Rafi al-Issawi as the Deputy Prime Minister of Iraq.[95]

94 Liu Yueqin, Iraq, Social Sciences Academic Press, 2007, p. 196.
95 Barham Salih, was born in 1960 and joined PUK in 1976. He was the vice general secretary of the PUK. In 1979, he fled to Britain to avoid persecutionby the Iraqi government received his Phd. at the Liverpool University. In 1985, he became the spokesman

On March 7, 2010, new Iraq held another National elections, Kurds participated this election through the "Kurdistani List" consisting of 11 Kurdish political parties led by KDP and PUK. This coalition of Kurds received 14.37% of the total votes. In the National Assembly KDP was represented by 26 seats, PUK with 17 seats, Gorran Movement with 8 seats, Kurdish Islamic Union with 4 seats and Islamic Movement of Kurds with 2 seats. In November 2010, Jalal Talabani was elected as the President of Iraq again.[96]

Tab. 3-1 Seats of Kurdish parties after the Kurdish Regional Assembly Elections of 2009

Province	KDP	PUK	Alliance Kurdistan List	Total Seats in the Province
Diyala	0	1	1	13
Dohuk	8	1	9	10
Arbil	8	2	10	14
Kirkuk	2	4	6	12
Nineveh	6	2	8	31
Sulaymaniyah	2	6	8	17
Compensatory Seats	0	1	1	7
Total	26	17	43	325

Source: "Kurdistan", http://en.wikipedia.org/wiki/Kurdistan_List.

of PUK in Germany, and in 1991, he served as spokesman of the PUK in the US. From January 2001 to July 2004, he served as the vice chairman of the Kurdish Patriotic Union (PUK), and later served as the deputy Prime Minister of Iraq until the 2009 presidential elections. After the provincial elections in 2009, he became the prime minister of Kurdish autonomous government.

96   Gorran Movement ("revolution" in Kurdish), whose members were mainly PUK. Its leader Nawshirwan Mustafa was one of the founders of the PUK. The slogan of this party was to eliminate corruption, disclose financial dealings, reform election law, establish professional civil servants, and end the long monopoly of KDP and PUK. It was a welcoming movement for the youth. The party won 25 seats in the Kurdish regional Parliament in 2009.

**Tab. 3-2 "Kurdistani List" votes in different
provinces of Iraq after the election of 2010**

Province	Votes of "Kurdistani Alliance List"	Percentage (%)	T.Votes of province
Babil	1,167	0,21	556,123
Baghdad	19,732	0,93	2,129,557
Dohuk	332,951	76,23	413,964
Dhi-Qar	334	0,06	557774
Diyala	47,749	9,33	469087
Arbil	458,403	67,02	648,924
Kirkuk	206,542	38,10	472,453
Al-Muthanna	1,432	0,64	222,851
An-Najaf	524	0,14	378,854
Nineveh	239,109	20,52	1,013,635
Al-Qadisiyah	805	0,23	353,086
Selahaddin	21,776	4,82	451,509
Sulaymaniyah	350,283	42,22	769,302
Total	1,681,714	14,37	10,813,216

207

Source: "Kurdistan", http://en.wikipedia.org/wiki/Kurdistan_List.

Generally, Kurds maintained a cooperative relation with the Iraqi Central government. From 2003 to 2008, Kurds also carried out good relations with Shi'ite political parties, such as the Islamic Dawa (Cause) Party led by Minister Nouri al-Maliki, and Supreme Council for Islamic Revolution of Iraq, led by Hakim. Both sides fought against Sunnis and Kurds also supported the Maliki government who tried to suppress the radical Shi'ite organization led by Muqtada Al-Sadr. However, from 2008, the relation between Kurds and Maliki government became tense because of the issue of Kirkuk, on the sharing of oil revenues of Kirkuk and oil revenues of Kurdish region, fiscal budget issues, level of autonomy and juridical issues, which led to a division between the 2 parties. The Iraq central government's worry was the gradual strengthening of Kurds which would cause the collapse of the complete system of power sharing. The Kurds often blamed Maliki for "monopolizing" power, while Maliki accused Kurds by attempting to dismiss "constitutional" policies, such as deploying Kurdish troops outside the Kurdish region and seeking to open diplomatic missions in some foreign countries. In November 2008, Massoud Barzani criticized Maliki publicly for his "monopolizing" power.

In the beginning of August 2009, prime minister Maliki made a special trip to Arbil to meet with Barzani to resolve their differences. This has been the first official visit to Kurdish autonomous region by Maliki since he was in office as the prime minister. The meeting focused on some unsolved issues that bothered both the central government and Kurds. Following the meeting, Maliki declared that central government and Kurdish regional government would set up a joint working committee in order to settle the existing disputes between both sides. After the meeting Maliki emphasized: "one important result of this meeting is that the Central government and Kurdish autonomous region will remain in contact in all levels and settle disputes and differences through this working committee." He also declared: "both sides have made great efforts to discuss and resolve their differences, including setting up a liaison office in the Kurdish region with the representatives of the Kurdish autonomous region and the central government" and invited the Kurdish delegation to visit the capital Baghdad. Massoud Barzani also regarded the talks as "very successful" and exclaimed that Kurds will maintain negotiations with Maliki to resolve the differences.

However, issues were not settled. In the national elections in January 2009, the number of voting Kurds in the provinces of Diyala and Ninaweh fell sharply as the result of the actively mobilized participation of the Sunni Arabs in the elections, which led to an armed conflicts between Kurds and Arab Sunnis and between Kurds and government forces.

In August 2009, General Raymond Odierno, the US military commander in Iraq, suggested and put forward his conflict resolution plan which offered to set up a US military force in Baghdad, as a buffer between the two sides, this buffer force would restrict the two sides and avoid the escalation of conflicts and confrontations. Odierno thought that the conflicts between the Kurds and Arabs mainly emerged from border issues and distribution of oil resources or revenues,which in the future would certainly negatively impact the national stability of Iraq and poses the biggest threat to the stability of power sharing.

.In December 2010, KDP's Congress convened where Massoud Barzani in his speech said, "self-determination of Kurds" was a "just right" and it would be "discussed and negotiated" among the relevant parties.

Agence France-Presse reported that this was the first time Massoud Barzani talked on the concept "self-determination by Kurds" in a KDP Congress, publicly. At the end of 2011, Minister Maliki ordered the arrest of Sunni vice-president Hashemi on suspicion of terrorism and murder. Thus the conflict between Shi'ites and Sunnis became intensified, here Kurds assumed a neutral position. USA Today had reported in December 2006 that Hashemi was involved in forming a multi-sectarian alliance to replace the government of Prime Minister Maliki, with the encouragement of US President George W. Bush, to counter the political influence of Muqtada al-Sadr. At a meeting with Turkish Prime Minister Recep Tayyip Erdogan in 2007, Hashimi had said that the Iraqi government was prepared to cooperate with Turkey in its fight against the PKK.

Hashemi fled to the Kurdish Region and denied the charges declared that he should be trialed in the Kurdish region due to safety concerns and higher possibility of fair trial.

Maliki asked the Kurdish regional government to hand Hashemi, emphasizing that "we demand the Kurdish regional government to take responsible position and hand in Hashemi to Iraqi Justice, We can't accept any interference to Iraq's judicial process. President of Kurdistan Massoud Barzani declared in March 2012 that the Kurdistan Regional Government would not hand over Hashimi to Iraqi authorities because Kurdish ethics prevented them from doing so.

On April 1, 2012, Hashimi was allowed by the authorities in Kurdistan to travel to Qatar to meet with Sheikh Hamad bin Khalifa Al Thani, on what the Qatari administration described as an official diplomatic visit. Iraqi deputy prime minister Hussain al-Shahristani denounced the visit as unacceptable on Qatar's part and called for Hashimi to be immediately handed over.However, Qatar refused the request of the Iraq government to extradite Hashimi, stating that extradition would be against diplomatic norms. Later, Hashimi went to Saudi Arabia and met with Saudi Foreign Minister Prince Saud Al Faisal. Then, on April 10, Hashimi travelled to Turkey, and was given refuge with his tribe.

On the same day April 1, 2012, Kurdish regional government stopped its exports of oil through the pipeline controlled by the Iraq central government, and accused the central government has been in payment arrears of $ 1.5 billion regarding oil revenues, since May 2011, this incident has led to further deterioration of relations between the two sides. Massoud Barzani spoke in public that the Iraqi leadership is heading towards "dictatorship" and that he will inform the Kurdish people about this "reality" so that they could make their own decisions.[97]

---

97 "Iraq Kurd Leader Accuses PM Maliki as 'Dictator'", AFP, Apr. 8, 2012, http://web. krg.org/articles/detail.asp?lngnr=12&smap=02010200&rnr=73&anr=43534.

Here, it was worth mentioning that Fred Eckhard, the Spokesman for the UN Secretary-General, confirmed, on December 22, 2004, that the U.N. had accepted a petition, through its special envoy officials to Iraq in January 2005. This Petition was written and given by a Kurdish group, asking for establishing an independent Kurdistan which was signed by more than 1.7 Million Kurds in the name of South Kurdistan [northern Iraq] representing 6 million Kurds.

The petition asked for a referendum which would decide whether Kurdistan should be independent from Iraq or not and whether establishing an independent Kurdistan. It emphasized: "Kurds are a unique nation, racially, culturally and philosophically different from Iraqi Arabs." "Kurds were compelled to be part of Iraq, without being asked their choices and demands, during the past 80 years, Kurds have been suppressed, enslaved and slaughtered by the Iraqi regime." The Petition stated that since 1991, "under the protection and support of international community, Kurds have enjoyed de facto independence... Kurds do not wish to be controlled by an Arab dominated Iraq." The petition demanded that the U.N. send a special commission to Kurdish Region and investigate "the true aspirations of the Kurds... and take effective measures to arrange a referendum which would allow Kurds to exercise their right of self-determination". A Californian businessman, the coordinator of the "Kurdish referendum movement", Ardi Rashidi said in an interview: "Of course that is the current position of the UN. On the other hand, the UN charter gives people the right for self-determination. So we are trying to respect the current applicable law" but at the same time we seek independence by peaceful means."[98]

During this period, ethnic and culturel relations in Iraq were tense between Arabs and Kurds, between Turkmens and Kurds too, but occasional terrorist acts happened between the two sides, on the other side the most prominent conflict was between Sunni and Shi'ite Arabs which led to bloody bombings.

Major terrorist attacks and conflicts were: On February 1, 2004, the two suicide bomb attacks targeted the office buildings of the KDP and PUK in Arbil. The blast killed at least 50 people and wounded more than 200 people, many of whom were senior officials of the local government, including Mohamed Abdul Rahman, the deputy prime minister of the regional government, the governor of the Arbil governorate, including several regional government ministers. This was the most devastating terrorist attack in the Kurdish region. On May 19, 2007, a group of armed men wearing Iraqi army uniforms attacked Hamid village near the border between Iraq and Iran in Diyala province, killing 15 Shi'ite Kurdish villagers. On July 6,

98 Iraqi Kurds Submitted a Petition of Independence to the U.N., Beijing News, December 26, 2004, http://news.sina.com.cn/w/2004-12-26/00594628100s.shtml.

2007, a Kurdish village near Diyala province bordering Iraq and Iran was hit by a suicide car bomb. 26 people were killed in the attack and at least 33 others were wounded. It was reported that most of these bloody attacks were implemented by the Kurdish Sunni extremist organizations, such as the "Ansar al-Islam."

Here it is worth mentioning was that the Iraqi Kurds continued to offer shelter for the PKK. In 2002, Kurdistan Democratic Solution Party (KDSP/PCDK) was established which was regarded as a pro-PKK political organization working in Iraq. Turkey often made military attacks against the PKK bases in the North of Iraq. In July, 2004, the chief of the staff of the Second Army of Turkey, Ilker Başbuğ declared that as long as the PKK guerrillas continued their operations in the North of Iraq, Turkish Army would not withdraw its forces from the region. On October 17, 2007, the Turkish Parliament passed a government motion to allow the Army forces to conduct cross-border operations targeting the PKK guerrillas in the North of Iraq. Followed by the approval of the motion Turkish ground forces continued to send troops to Iraq border areas.

Under the pressure from the Turkish government, the Kurdish regional government publicly condemned PKK's violent terrorist activities, and took some measures to curb its activities, asking them not to attack Turkey from the northern Iraqi territory. Under the pressure of Turkish military forces, on the November 3, 2007, the Kurdish regional government announced the closure of the PKK offices in the three cities of the Kurdish region and on November 5, Kurdish regional government cut off the PKK's arm supply lines in the region, also ordered the Kurdish armed forces to establish checkpoints on the roads leading to the border areas, blocked all the facilities PKK might use to continue its fight. Under numerous pressures and restrictions, the PKK reduced its armed forces in Iraq, and gradually transferred its forces to Iran.

This is one of the strategies of the PKK, when they face a threat of repression in a neighboring country, they move their bases to another country. In addition, Kurdish Regional Government prohibited the pro-PKK Kurdistan Democratic Solution Party to take part in the regional election in July 2009, and closed all the offices of this party. However, this party continued its activities in the North of Iraq. In August 2012, according to a report by the Iraqi Kurdish media, the Kurdish regional government and Turkey reached an agreement to jointly combat against the PKK in order to prevent any terrorist organization to take advantage of the power vacuum in Syria, this war torn country. But KDP leader Masoud Barzani soon issued a statement denying that news and commented: "the KDP's principle not to participate in any military operations in the region that would to undermine or injure any element of Kurdistan's national struggle," … "The permanent policy of ours is insistence on a peaceful solution to the Kurdish problem and Kurdish rights, through dialogue, in all regions of the country."[99]

3.5 Case Analysis: The Kurdish Regional Government in Iraq

Only after long and hard struggle Kurds living in Iraq have won the right for national autonomy. "March Agreement of 1970" marked the first official success, Kurds' right to self-government. In March 1974, the Kurdish Regional Government was formally recognized and established by the Government of Iraq through the Autonomy Act and its implementation. However, from 1951 to 1991, all the autonomy practices by Kurds were in fact rather nominal, the Kurdish regional government was not able to determine its own affairs, the regional officers and government leaders and regional affairs were still mainly determined by the central government. After the 1991 Gulf War, with the support of the United States and the no-fly zone measure, Kurds finally achieved genuine autonomy and made their autonomous region a "state in the state." After the 2003 Iraq war, with the establishment of the federal state in Iraq, the Kurdish autonomy was further consolidated, and the Kurdish region has achieved political stability, economic development and regional security.

On October 15, 2005, new Iraq held a referendum on its permanent Constitution which was approved by its people. The new Constitution stipulated that Iraq would implement the federal system the Kurds have always longed for and legally recognized Kurds' existing autonomy. Article 113 of the permanent Constitution recognized the Kurdish regional government constituted by the three provinces of Arbil, Sulaymaniyah and Dohuk as "Kurdish provinces" legally.

In accordance with the Federal Constitution, an autonomous "region" has the right to maintain local security forces, have the right to modify the local legislations which do not meet the local conditions. Article 117 provides that "regions" may also establish representative offices abroad. Local governments have legislative, executive and judicial powers and the right to establish regional security organizations such as the police, security forces and agencies and guards. Article 3 of the Constitution also stipulates that the Arabic and Kurdish are the official languages of Iraq. This Constitution provided legal guarantees for the self-governance of the Kurdish people and upheld the true rights that the Kurds had won since the Gulf War.[100]

99　"KDP, Denies Agreement with Turkey to Attack PKK", Aug.7, 2012, http://www. shafaaq.com/en/news/3195-kdp-denies-agreement-with-turkey-to-attack-pkk.html.
100　Liu Yueqin, Iraq, p. 196.

Compared with the 1974 law, Kurdish autonomy greatly expanded, not only determined the affairs of the region, but also benefited Kurds in the military, diplomatic fields and oil revenues. When we look at their external relations, as of October 2010, Kurdish Autonomous Region set up about 20 foreign reperesentative offices, including representative offices in the United States and the United Kingdom.

Militarily, the Kurds resisted those demands to disban their armed forces, thus the Kurdish armed forces remained under their self-control, although the Kurdish armed forces became part of the common Iraqi army and part of the Iraqi National Guard, it still maintained its autonomy and independence as a complete system, without being disrupted, besides its equipment and training was greatly improved. At present, the Kurdish armed forces have more than 100,000 fighters, with about 200,000 militia. There are also reports which estimate it to lead 270,000 men.

Currently stationed in Mosul, the Iraqi army second division is basically composed of Kurdish troops. Kurdish regional government has also promulgated a national flag and national anthem. The Kurdish National Anthem is a poem by the famous Iraqi Kurdish poet and historiographer. Yonis Reuf (also known as Dildar, 1917-1948), in 1938, "Hey, Enemy."[101] In Kurdish language, "Ey Reqip", (See Appendix).

The Kurdish National Anthem as a song was adopted in 1946 by the Republic of Mahabad, the first short-lived Kurdish state as the national anthem, since then has been used among all parts of Kurdistan. The PKK originated in Turkey also uses it as a party song. In fact, the Kurdish region has become a reality as a "quasi-state" or "de facto State".[102]

---

101   The lyrics of Kurdish anthem was "Hey, Enemy" composed by Yonis Reuf (also known as Dildar, 1917-1948) in 1948. The anthem "Ey Reqip"was composed by Shivan Perwer.
102   http://en.wikipedia.org/wiki/iraq_Krdistan. The Kurdish Region representative in Britain was Sami Abdul Rahman who was the daughter of Minister Mohammad Abdul Rahman of the former Kurdish region. The representative in the US was Qubad Talabani, the son of the President Talabani. He was born in Damascus and then went to study in Kingston University in Britain. After graduation, he worked in the office of PUK in Washington. After Saddam government was overthrown, he worked in Iraq and played an important role in the PUK, helped drafting the Iraqi Interim Constitution and led the communication and coordination between the US army forces and the Kurds. In 2004, he went back to the US and served as the representative of the PUK and the government of Kurdish region. His wife is Jewish.

Fig. 3-2 The National Flag of the Kurdish Regional Government

Political structure of the Kurdish autonomous region is basically parliamentary representative system and a multi-party democracy. The President of the regional government is directly elected by the voters, who is the head of the regional government and government, also the commander in chief of the Kurdish armed forces. In addition to the President, there is also a deputy-President. The Prime Minister exercises executive power under the leadership of the President. The cabinet consists of the majority of the parties that has won the election and this majority party appoints the prime minister. The cabinet led by the prime minister, and the deputy prime minister and consists of 19 cabinet ministers. Kurdish National Assembly, is elected once every four years, and the regional President has the veto right to decide on any bill approved by the Assembly.

In accordance with the separation of powers rule, and traditional power sharing regional president, vice-president, prime minister and deputy-prime minister posts, are appointed by the Kurdish Democratic Party and the Kurdish Patriotic Union respectively.

Since the war in Iraq, the Kurdish autonomous region has basically achieved political stability and the regional government has been operating well. The Kurdish Democratic Party and the Kurdish Patriotic Union have reserved and shelved internal differences and cooperated well, and the violent wars among them as in the 1990s have been avoided. In January 2006, Talabani and Barzani put aside their ideological differences, formed the Kurdistan Alliance (KAL) and headed to Baghdad with all their eggs in a unified basket. The KAL has proven to be a disciplined force in both regional and national politics, with Talabani agreeing to stay in Baghdad and work with the GoI and Masoud Barzani assuming the mantle of KRG President, thus the Kurdish Democratic Party and the Kurdish Patriotic Union reached an agreement to strengthen bipartisan cooperation on the basis of partnership, equality and consensus principles to consolidate the Kurdish regional government and other regional institutions to promote the political, economic and social development in the Kurdish region. The main contents of the agreement were:

Kurdish Patriotic Union, will assume the post of the vice-president, and assume the post of deputy-commander-in-chief of the Kurdish Regional Armed Forces. The prime minister is traditionally the head of the legislative body but also shares executive powers with the president. The president of Iraqi Kurdistan is also the commander-in-chief of the Peshmerga Armed Forces, these posts are occupied by the KDP. The Prime Minister and Deputy Prime Minister posts are determined by the elected National Assembly members, and approved by the President.

Till the end of 2007, the Assembly Speaker post was assumed by the Kurdish Patriotic Union, the post of cabinet prime minister was assumed by the Kurdish Democratic Party.

After the next election of 2009, the post of cabinet prime minister would be assumed by the Kurdish Patriotic Union, and the Assembly Speaker post will be assumed by the Kurdish Democratic Party.

These two governing posts are rotated in every two years, and if any of the ministers in the cabinet resigns, the entire cabinet has to resign. Ministry of Internal Affairs, Justice, Education, Public Health, Social Affairs, Religious Affairs, Water, Transport, Reconstruction, Planning and Human Rights ministeries are assumed by the Kurdish Patriotic Union, on the other side Finance, Kurdish Armed Forces, Higher Education, Agriculture, Martyrs, Culture, Electricity, Natural Resources, Municipal Works, Sports and Youth, Regional domestic affairs and other ministerial positions are assumed by the Kurdistan Democratic Party.

Budgets are distributed equally and proportionally among the governing institutions and equally distributed among the provinces according to the proportion of population. Under the supervision of the regional Presidentship organ, the regional Supreme Council is responsible for institutionalizing prosecutorial and security institutions of the Kurdish region. The foreign representatives of the regional government is appointed by the Prime Minister and the Deputy Prime Minister.

The two parties established a joint bipartisan committee to solve the problems encountered in the Kurdish region and on May 7, 2006, the two parties finally completed the merger of administrative organs.[103]

Even then, unification of certain key ministries – namely Justice, Interior, Finance, and Peshmerga – was postponed, with final unification to occur one year later, but was successful.

215

103   Mahir A. Aziz. The Kurds of Iraq: Ethnonationalism and National Identity in Iraqi Kurdistan, pp. 169-170.

Since 2003, many elections have been held successfully in the Kurdish region, electing of Regional President, and National Assembly. In 2005, the 2nd National Assembly Elections was held, in which the number of seats in the National Assembly was increased from 105 to 111.

13 parties and organizations participated in the election (see Tab. 3-3).

In the Kurdish Regional Assembly elections, "Democratic Patriotic Alliance of Kurdistan List" led by KDP and PUK won 104 seats out of the 111 seats with the vote rate of 89.55%.

The distribution of 104 seats among the Democratic Patriotic Alliance was as follows: Kurdish Democratic Party 40 seats, Kurdish Patriotic Union 38 seats, the Kurdish Islamic League 9 seats, Turkmenistan Democratic Movement 4 seats, 3 seats for the Kurdish Communist Party, the Kurdish Social Democratic Party 2 seats, 2 seats for the Assyrian Democratic Movement, the Chaldean Cultural Association 1 seat, Chadin Democratic Alliance Party 1 seats, Bet–Nahrain Democratic Party (Assyrian) 1 seat, Farmer Movement party 1 seat, Kurdistan Democratic National Union 1 seat, Nouri Talabani 1 seat.

And, the Kurdish Islamic Organization outside the Democratic Patriotic Alliance the won 6 seats and Kurdish Labor Party and the independent candidates won 1 seat (see Tab. 3-3). And the new parliament met for the first time on June 4, 2005, with Adnan Mufti member of the Political Bureau of PUK as speaker.

In June 2005, Regional Parliament elected Massoud Barzani as the President of Kurdish Regional Government. After a bargain of half a year, on December 15, the Regional Government was set up. Nawshirwan Barzani, nephew of Massoud served as the Prime-Minister of the government. In the election of committee members of different provinces in 2005, KDP had won in Arbil and Dohuk and PUK had won in Sulaymaniyah. Within the three provinces, despite PUK won 43.4% of the votes, this party only gained 48 seats, while KDP won 42% of the votes and gained 14 seats more than PUK, since KDP had majority in Nineveh and Kirkuk.[104]

216

---

104   Nawshirwan Barzani was born in 1966. He is the nephew of Massoud Barzani and son of Idris Barzani. He worked in the high positions of the KDP. In 1989, he was elected to the Central Committee of the party. In 1993, he was elected into the Political Bureauin the 11th Party Congress. He was once responsible for intelligence department of the KDP and served as deputy-minister of the regional government. In 2006, he served as the Prime Minister of Regional Government. Afterthe election of July 2009, he was elected as one of the two deputy-Presidents of the Kurdish Regional Government. He is regarded as the heir of Massoud Barzani together with Masrour Barzani. Nawshirwan Barzani is married and has two children. He is fluent in Kurdish and Persian and also masters Arab and English. He is fond of Kurdish and Persian poetry.

Tab. 3-3 Votes of Different Parties in the Kurdish Regional Assembly in 2005

Party	Votes		Seats
	Number of Votes	Proportion (%)	
DPAK, including movement for change	1,570,663	89.55	104
Kurdistan Islamic Union	85,237	4,86	6
K. Toilers' Party and Independent Canditates	20,585	1,17	1
Kurdistan Democratic Labor Party	11,748	0,67	0
K. Peoples Democratic Party	10,953	0,62	0
Independent List	10,262	0,59	0
Iraqi Republican Group	9,499	0,54	0
Kurdish Democracy Attainment	9,081	0,52	0
Iraqi National Union Front	8234	0,47	0
Kurdish Democrats Movement	6,69	0,38	0
Kurdistan Conservative Party	5,506	0,31	0
Iraqi National Brotherhood Party	3,422	0,20	0
Kurdish National Movement	2,018	0,12	0
Total Votes	1,753,919	100	111

Source: http://www.kurdistan-parliament.org/default.aspx?pa ge=sitecontents&c=Parliament-History2005.

On July 25, 2009, National Assembly and Regional Presidential elections were held. According to the new law, the region's President would be no longer elected by the National Assembly, but by the voters directly. 5403 polling stations were placed in the Kurdish Regions whereas five in Baghdad. There were total five candidates, and Massoud Barzani once again won the Presidentship by 69.6% of the votes (see Tab. 3-4).

Nawshirwan Barzani and Kosrat Rasul were appointed as deputy-Presidents of the Region Government. The Deputy President assists the President in his or her duties and in the President's absence is the acting President. According to the Law of the Presidency of the Kurdistan Region, the President may delegate some of his powers to the Deputy President.

Barham Salih from PUK was appointed as the prime- Minister of the regional government. The new government was consisted of 19 ministers. This election reflected a deep change in the political landscape of the Kurdish Region, as the competition between the KDP and PUK had further increased and a new Kurdish political power had emerged, the Gorran (change) group. In the Assembly election, 509 candidates from 25 parties had competed where there were two major lists. One was the "Kurdistani List" led by KDP and PUK and the other major was the "Change List" led by the former leader and second man of the PUK, Nawshirwan Mustafa (1944-).[105]

218

While the social and electoral base of the former older parties was the rural population wheras the Gorran has its basis in the urban Kurdish youth. As a result, the "Kurdistani List" won 59 of the 111 seats[106]; the "Change List" won 25 seats gaining 24% of the votes. The "S&R List" a coalition with the Kurdistan Islamic Union, Kurdistan Socialist Democratic Party and the Future Party, called the Service and Reform List, won 13 seats. The rest 3 seats were won by smaller parties, among which "Islamic Movement List" won 2 seats, and the "Social Justice and Freedom List" 1 seat.

---

105   This movement was established in 2009, also known as "Change Movement" or "Goran". Its members were mainly from PUK. Nawshirwan Mustafa (1944-) was one of the founders of PUK and was only secondto Jalal Talebani insidethe party. In 1970, he was sentenced to death by the Iraqi government and fled to Europe. In 1991, he had led the Kurdish uprising which liberated Kirkuk. On December 5, 2006, he quit his position of General Secretary in the PUK and founded the "Change Movement". The aims of this newsparty wereto eliminate rampant corruption, campaigns against patronage in politics, reform election laws, establish professional civil servants and break the long-standing political monopoly of the KDP and PUK as established parties. Movement was popular among the youth. Gorran movement won 25 seats in the 2009 elections. And in March 2010, the "Movement" won 8 seats in the Iraqi GeneralAssembly elections.
106   There were 11 seats reserved for the minorities, 5 seats for Assyrians, 5 seats for Turkmens and 1 for Armenians.

The leader of KDP, Kamal Kirkuki served as the Speaker of the Assembly. In the Regional Presidential elections, there were four other candidates (see, Tab. 3-4) apart from Massoud Barzani, Kemal Mirawdily won a 25.3% of the votes. Massoud Barzani only won 30% in Sulaymaniyah, whereas there in this city Mirawdily won 60%. As can be seen the traditional Kurdish parties were faced with a new rival and KDP was gradually weakening.[107] On the other hand, PUK was also weakening due to its split in 2006 (Gorran Movement). Democratization of the Kurdish political landscape and diversification increasingly obvious trend which meant that the two-party system was transforming into a multi-party system, consequently the current number of active parties in the Kurdish region has exceeded more than a dozen. What is worth mentioning is that the role of the Assembly has become increasingly important. In 2007, the Kurdish cabinet for the first time complaint against the supervision of the Assembly, this means its supervision on the government activities has increased. The content of debates in the Assembly has been more substantial and intensive, thus KDP and PUK face great challenges. More parties have joined in the competition of political power, which means the traditional two-party system has made a major progress.

Tab. 3-4 Presidential Elections in the Kurdish Regional Government in 2009

Candidates	Votes	Vote Rate (%)
Massoud Barzani	1,266,397	69,6
Kemal Mirawdily	460,323	25,3
Halow Ibrahim Ahmed	63,377	3,5
Ahmed Mohammed Rassoul	18,89	1,4
Hussein Garmijani	10,665	0,6
Total	1,819,652	100%

Source:https://en.wikipedia.org/wiki/President_of_Iraqi_Kurdistan

107   Currently, Massoud Barzani serves as the Chairman, Ali Abdul as the deputy-Chairman. The Political Bureau consists of 8 members, and the central Committee 20 members and the Central Committee has 9 alternate members.

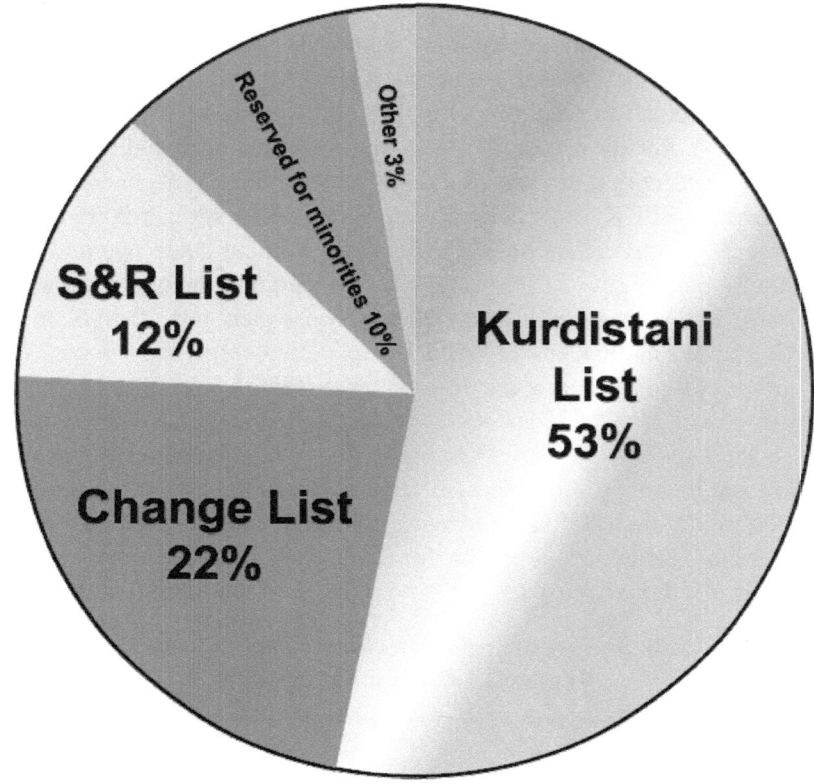

Fig. 3-3 Allocation of Seats in the Kurdish Regional Elections in 2009

Source: https://en.wikipedia.org/wiki/Iraqi_Kurdistan_parliamentary_election,_2009.

From March 2007 to June 2007, Kurdish studies researchers have conducted a field survey among 450 students from three universities in the Kurdish Region between the ages of 18 to 25. The survey results have demonstrated that after 20 years autonomy, Kurdish youth's comprehension of the Kurdish issue has greatly altered, and this will make a significant effect on the future of Kurds and Iraq state. This generation did not experience the brutal war years and political struggles, nor has received a systematic Arabic education, and mostly live in the relatively peaceful Kurdish region. The survey has revealed that most of them are proud of being Kurds, believe that they are non-Iraqi people and vast majority of them support the Kurdish independent statehood. The results are shown in Table 3-5.[108]

---

108   Mahir A. Aziz, The Kurds of Iraq: Nationalism and Identity in Iraqi Kurdistan, pp. 118-147.

Tab. 3-5 An Opinion Survey among College Students in the Kurdish Region in 2007

Do you feel Kurdish or an Iraqi ?	
Kurdistani	%73.11
Kurd	%17.33
Iraqi Kurd	%1.33
Kurdistani not Iraqi	%5.11
Iraqi not Kurd	%0.89
More Iraqi than Kurdish	%2.22
Are your faithful to Kurdistan ?	
Extremely yes	%87.11
Yes	%7.56
Not so much	%4.89
Not at all	%0.44
Factors beneficial to the unity and consolidation of Kurdish national characteristics	
National Factor	%35.8
Territory Factor	%24.2
Language Factor	%19.8
Political Factor	%19.1
Educational Factor	%0.7
Economic Factor	%0.4
Do you feel related to Iraq?	
Very much	%13.33
Not too much	%69.78
Extremely yes	%4.0
Not at all	%12.89
Are you proud of being Kurdish?	
Very much	%88.89
Not too much	%5.78
Not at all	%4.89
Are your proud of being an Iraqi?	
Very much	%12.7
Not too much	% 7.8
Not at all	% 3.6
I'm not Iraqi.	%76.0

What is your opinion on the nature of the Iraqi War in 2003?	
Agressive	%10.22
Progressive war of liberation	% 64.67
Aggressive but finally beneficial for the Kurds	% 25.11
Do you support the idea of Kurds establishing an independent state?	
Kurdistan should be independent from Iraq.	% 90.0
Kurdistan should be independent from Iraq and the other three parts of Kurdistan should merge	% 1.6
Kurdistan should remain as a part of Iraq but have its own parliament and more federal powers.	% 8.2
Kurdistan should remain as a part of Iraq without having its own parliament or federalism.	% 0.2

Unit: %

Source: Mahir A. Aziz, The Kurds of Iraq: Ethnonationalism and National Identity in Iraqi Kurdistan, pp. 118-147.

After the war in Iraq, generally Kurdistan became the safest area in Iraq, with fewer terrorist attacks and violence. On February 1, 2004, in the northern Iraq city of Arbil, Kurdish Democratic Party and the Kurdish Patriotic Union office buildings were attacked by two suicide bombings. The blast killed at least 50 people and wounded more than 200 people, many of whom were senior officials of the local government, including Mohamed Abdul Rahman, the deputy prime minister of the regional government, the governor of the Arbil governorate, several regional government ministers were also injured. This was the most devastating terrorist attack in the Kurdish region. At the same time, the regional economy has experienced the fastest growth epoch in its history, also culture, education and other aspects of social saw a rapid development. After the war, with the abolition of international sanctions, the northern region was relatively stable and the gradual resumption of oil production and expansion of the Kurdish region's economic prosperity, an average annual growth rate of 10% was accomplished.

In 2011 November, the Prime Minister of the regional government Ali Saleh predicted that in 2012 the region's economic growth rate would reach 12%. Kurdish regional budget in 2012 has increased by 30%, and reached 10 billion US Dollars.[109]

In July 2006, in order to promote investment, the Kurdish region passed a new Investment Law and founded Investment Committee to attract foreign investment. In September 2007, Kurds passed the Oil and Gas Law. In 2006, Iraq's first post-war new oil well began drilling in the Kurdish region, in cooperation with a Norwegian energy company DNO. The government also uses the slogan "Kurdistan: The Other Iraq" to vigorously promote the Kurdish region to attract investment. The government has announced that the region had attracted 16 billion US. Dollars in investment by the end of 2011, only Sulaymaniyah received 6.4 billion. Consequently 6500 of the 4,500 Kurdish villages that were destroyed in the war have been rebuilt.[110]

The region is the region with the lowest poverty rates in Iraq. The country's population below the poverty line is 23%, but only 3% in Sulaymaniyah and highest poverty is 49% in the southern province of Muthanna.[111]

According to the World Bank Statistics of 2006, GDP of the Kurdish Region reached to 2.200 to 2.500 US dollars, 20%-25% higher compared to the rest of Iraq. Constructions of roads and airports are highly supported, two international airports has been built in Arbil and Suleimaniyah. Refugees are resettled. It is worth mentioning that, in accordance with the provisions of the Iraqi constitution central government allocates 17% of the budget revenues to the Kurdish autonomous region each year.

From the perspective of social development, the Kurdish region's urbanization level is rapidly rising, the tribal consciousness is declining, and civil society is emerging. According to an opinion poll in 2007, 84.2% of college students believe and think that they do not belong to a tribe.[112]

Education in the region has undergone a major development. At present the Kurdish autonomous region has more than 10 universities, in addition to Saladin University which was built in 1968, other universities were established after 1992, such as the University of Dohuk (1992), Soran University, University of Sulaimani (founded in 1992), University of Koya (founded in 2003), University of HalabjaMedical University, Sulaimani Polytechnic University SPU, Sulaimani; University of Zakho, Zakho;

109   "Kurdistan Economy to Grow by 12% Next Year", 29 November, 2011, http://www.iraq-businessnews.com/2011/11/29/kurdistan-economy-to-grow-by-12-next-year/.
110   "Kurdistan: The Other Iraq", http://www.theotheriraq.com/.
111   "Nearly 25 Percent of Iraqis Live in Poverty", MSNBC, May 20, 2009, http://www.masnbc.msn.com/id/30849286/.
112   Mahir A. Aziz, The Kurds of Iraq: Ethnonationalism and National Identity in Iraqi Kurdistan, p. 139.

Duhok Polytechnic University DPU, Duhok; Arbil Polytechnic University, Arbil; University of Garmian, Kalar; University of Kurdistan Hawler (founded in 2006), American University of Iraq (Sulaymaniyah, founded in 2007) (Private), University of Sabis (private) and University of Ishik (Işık) also private.

In response to the low status of women, the Kurdish regional government took active measures to improve the status of women and adopted a series of laws on the prohibition of domestic violence, also prohibited female circumcision and the "honor murders" In 2007, the Parliament passed the Act on Prohibition of Female Circumcision, and in June 2011 adopted the Domestic Violence Act. Iraqi ambassador to the United Nations, has commented that the Kurdish region has become a model for other parts of Iraq in terms of political, social development, human rights and religious tolerance.[113]

However, there are also many problems waiting to be solved in the Kurdish region, such as bipartisan political monopoly, corruption, nepotism, unemployment and so on. The Daily Star, published in Lebanon on November 18, 2005, wrote that the Barzani tribe had accumulated about 2 billion USD wealth since the 1991 Gulf War. Some Western institutions also often criticize the Kurdish security agencies for violating human rights. In April 2009, Amnesty International published a report on the situation of human rights in the Kurdish region, criticizing the Kurdish security agency Asayesh, which infringes the laws and often abducted or arrested political prisoners, tortured with electric shocks, political prisoners were not allowed to sleep, tied up and other abuses was recorded. The report criticized the regional government that it can not effectively control the special security agencies attached to the two established parties. And in March 2012, an university professor Abdul Mashhavar Barzani, the cousin of Massoud Barzani, who often criticized the government, was abducted by the security services.[114]

In early 2011, after the outbreak of the "Arab Spring" and due to its sympathetic effect, in the spring of 2011, tens of thousands of Kurdish people took the streets for demonstrations, protests against corruption, against

---

113 http://www/cfr.org/iraq/bakir-kurdistan-model-iraq/p145687.
114 Asayish is the primary security and anti-terror agency of the regional government, possessing extensive power and playing an essential role in the regional security and intelligence which is led by Masrour Barzani the oldest son of the President Massoud Barzani. Masrour is also the leader of the Parastin, the intelligence agency of the KDP. Masrour Barzani was born in 1969 and spent his childhood in Iran. He studied in the US and Britain and got a bachelors degree of International Relations from Washington University. In 1998, he returned to the region and was elected to the Central Committee and Political Bureau in the 12th Congress of the KDP. He is regarded as a strong contender for the future Kurdish regional government presidency.

unemployment and price inflation in the region. One reason behind is that according to statistics, the region's 18 to 25-year-old unemployment rate is around 50% to 75%.

On February 17, 2011, protesters in the Sulaimaniya city, demanded reforms against corruption, which led to clashes with the police forces, resulting in nine casualties. On April 17, the same year, protests erupted in the city again causing 35 casualties.

The Kurdish region has been a "quasi-state" in political, economic, military, diplomatic and other fields. The Voice of Germany had commented that the conditions for the Iraqi Kurds' self-determination are ripe and they already have all the essential elements of a state ruled by law, including the executive, legislative and the judiciary aspects. With the economic take-off, many Kurds optimistically wish to realize the long-standing dream of building an independent Kurdish state. A renown political analyst Akif Hassan also said that the Kurds have already established check and balance systems of powers and that now the belongs to different institutions of the regional political system.

On September 27, 2012, a former Kurdish Iraqi central government minister, Sarbast Permeni said: "I cannot understand why a nation cannot live in its own independent state. The Kurdish people have struggled for more than a century, their dream was to fight for freedom, fairness and autonomy."[115]   225

However, the future developments related to Kurds' self-government still bear many uncertainties, especially due to Kirkuk problem with the central government, and control of oil resources, and other issues related to autonomy which will have a significant impact.

For decades, Kirkuk and Diyala, Nineveh and other provinces where Kurds have substantial population were controlled by the central government which is the most controversial issue as one focus of problems between the two sides. Kirkuk is an important province with abundant ethnic diversity in the northern part of the country, and rich in oil. The Kirkuk population mainly consists of Kurds, Turkmens and Arabs. In Kirkuk, historically, the distribution of population was manipulated and relocated politically in different periods.

According to the 1947 census, the Kurds accounted for only 25% of the population of the city districts of Kirkuk and 53% of the population of the whole Kirkuk province.

---

115   See, news "Turkmen Front Delegation in New York, Turkmens Demand Special Status for Kirkuk", The New Anatolian, June 29, 2007.

But, by 1958, Kurdish population in Kirkuk had decreased to less than that of Turkmens. At the time of the 1965 census, there were new changes in the population of Kirkuk: 71,000 Kurds, 55,000 Turkmens, and 41,000 Arabs. After 1975, the Iraqi government has implemented the policy of Arabization in Kirkuk, a large number of Arabs were settled there, while a large number of Kurds were forced to move out. The Iraqi government, then had also renamed the Kirkuk province as the Tamim province, which means "nationalization" which was also intended to celebrate the successful nationalization of oil in 1972.

Kifri, Daquq, Muqdadiyah, Jalawla, and Saadiyah have significant Turkmen minority populations, where Kurds form the majority,and Tuz Khormato (also known as Tuzhurmatu in Turkish), along with Altun Kupri, Amerli, Bashir, Bustamli, Mahalabiyah, Qarah Tappah, Sulaiman Bek, Tal Afar, Taza Khurmatu, and Yankjah, make up the largest Turkmen-majority cities in Irak where Kurds live.

In Saddam period, due the further Arabization, the Kurds were no longer the majority in Kirkuk. During the Iraq war in 2003, the Kurds, with the help of US troops, seized Kirkuk and actively settled the previously deported Kurds back home. The Kurds desire and aim to include—those provinces where Kurds are largely populated—under the Kurdish control, these provinces are Mosul, Kirkuk and Nineveh, Diyala, but they are opposed by local Assyrians, Turkmens and Arabs, also Iraq central government and Turkish government also oppose their aims.

During the Ottoman Empire era, Kirkuk belonged to Mosul province. In 1921, when Iraq was founded under the British mandate, Kirkuk voted against Faisal becoming king of Iraq during the referendum.

The new founded Turkish government also claimed sovereignty over Kirkuk, but in 1926 the League of Nations in its final decision stipulated that Kirkuk belonged to Iraq.

In the 1960s and 70ies, Kirkuk's control became one of the focus of the disputes between Kurds and the central government of Iraq. Mustafa Barzani refused to compromise on the issue of Kirkuk. After the overthrow of Saddam Hussein's regime, the issue remained unresolved. The new Iraq Constitution, stipulated that the final borders of Kurdish regions or provinces would be determined by a series of referendums before the end of 2007. Among them, the Kirkuk problem is the most controversial, which involves all kinds of interest differences. The Kurds have stressed that Kirkuk has historically always been a Kurdish city and demanded its inclusion into Kurdish autonomous region, but was rejected by local Arabs and Turkmens. Turkmens demand that Kirkuk should have a special status.[116]

---

116   see, news "Turkmen Front Delegation in New York, Turkmens Demand Special Status for Kirkuk", The New Anatolian, June 29, 2007.

The Iraqi central government advocates that Kirkuk remains a multi-ethnic hybrid city. Turkey is also very concerned about the status of Kirkuk, and argues that Turkmens have strong marks in the history of this city, consequently the Turkish government feels responsible to protect the rights of local Turkmens due to common Turkic origins. The Turkish government is strongly rejects referendum as a solution to the issue.

Since Kirkuk possesses 10% of the Iraq's proven oil reserves, both Turkey and the Iraqi government are concerned that Kurdish control on Kirkuk would lead to Kurds' economic self-reliance and cause a separation from Iraq. During the reign of the Iraqi Baath party, the two sides had agreed that the status of Kirkuk would be determined by a referendum.

After the overthrow of Saddam Hussein, the Kirkuk issue was put on the agenda again. Article 140 of the new Constitution of Iraq established the principle of vesting in the referendum and the referendum was initially planned for November 15, 2007, but was delayed first to December 3, and then by a further six month.

The report by "Iraq Study Group" of the US issued in 2006 had proposed to postpone the referendum, due to concerns that the Kirkuk problem would cause civil unrest in Iraq, then. The Kurds accused the report and the US attitude as a betrayal. Under pressures from the United States, the Kurds agreed to postpone the referendum to 2008. The United Nations Assistance Mission for Iraq (UNAMI) formed in 2003 is a specialized agency to solve the sovereignty issues of Kirkuk and Diyala, Nineveh and other Kurdish provinces. In June 2008, the UNAMI issued a report which recommended that Akra District of Ninawa Governorate and the Makhmur District of Kirkuk Governorate be incorporated into Kurdish region but that the al-Hamdaniya area of Ninawa Governorate and the Mandali area of Diyala Governorate would be directly under the control of the central government. These recommendations were rejected by the Council of Representatives of Iraq.

In April 2009, the United Nations issued another report on the situation of Kirkuk, suggesting that either the central government of Iraq and the Kurdish regional government should share the disputed territory on an equal basis or they should allow Kirkuk to become a semi-autonomous region, and urged Kurds not to rush for the referendum.

In July 2009, Massoud Barzani stressed that the disappointed Kurds will never compromise on the sovereignty of Kirkuk. In December 2010, Masoud Barzani reiterated that "Kirkuk City's Kurdish identity is unquestionable" and added that "Kirkuk is a model of peaceful coexistence". And in May 2012, the Kurdish Regional Government issued a presidential statement on prime minister Nouri al-Maliki's visit to Kirkuk, which criticized Maliki which said: "He failed to even make any mention of Article 140 and in order to appease some chauvinists, he attempted to determine the identity of Kirkuk," "If Mr. Maliki wants to resolve the status of the disputed areas, he needs to implement Article 140 and allow the people of Kirkuk to determine their fate," continued the statement. "The identity of Kikruk cannot be determined through deployment of military forces from Baghdad. Kirkuk is an Iraqi city with a Kurdistani identity."[117]

The Kirkuk issue in the period after Saddam's fall

According to the Article 140 of the Iraqi Constitution, before the 2007 referendum, the Government should take measures to address the problems brought by Arabization policies during the Saddam Hussein reign, i.e. the expulsion of the Kurds and a large number of Arabs being settled to Kirkuk by the government.

In those days the Kurds were helped to return to their hometown, and the central government led by Maliki ordered the establishment of the Normalization Committee for Kirkuk's Status to promote the reversal of "past Arabization policies." In February 2007, this Commission adopted the following plan:"The government will fund those Sunni Arabs who willingly desire to leave Kirkuk and return to their original homes with 15,000 US dollars per head, and they will be given the corresponding plot of land for their living."But soon this Normalization Commission was paralyzed due to certain difficulties.

228

Many western media outlets have reported that the Arabs and Turkmens are being forced to leave Kirkuk by various means, including violent attacks by Kurdish militia. New York Times has reported on June 20, 2004 that almost every day Kurdish families appear living in simple tents and later build their houses, which grab the lands inhabited by Arabs.

Jeffrey Fleishman, wrote in Los Angeles Times, "Kirkuk is a benchmark for how most Kurds would define their legitimacy in Iraq," said Barham Salih, prime minister for the Patriotic Union of Kurdistan, one of two main political parties controlling the Kurdish autonomous zone in northern Iraq. "We have a claim to Kirkuk rooted in history, geography and demographics.... This is a recipe for civil war if you don't do it right." Violence so far has been sporadic. But many Arabs fear retribution and street battles—like a firefight in December that left four dead and dozens wounded—and have fled. Said Akar, an Arab member of the Kirkuk City Council, said: "The people are worried and they're leaving because Kurdish militias are coming to their houses and threatening them."[118]

---

117 "Presidential Statement on the Visit of Prime Minister Maliki to Kirkuk", May 9th, 2012, http://www/krg.org/articles/detail.asp?rnr=223&lngnr=12&smap=02010100&a nr=43873.
118 Iraqi Melting Pot Nears Boiling Point: In "Oil-rich Kirkuk, Kurds, Arabs and Turkmens Compete for a Place in the New Order", Los Angeles Times, Jan. 26, 2004.

Besides, there are about 10,000 Kurds living in the suburbs of Kirkuk supported by the Kurdish RG, who are determined to grab the lands of Arab residents.

Although the Iraqi interim constitution is expressly prohibited, but some Kurdish officials still in the new encirclement of the land Some Kurdish officials said the expulsion of Arabs was part of their plan to expand the Kurdish-controlled areas, and the Mayor of Mehmoor, re-occupied by the Kurds, a member of the Kurdish Democratic Party "We have to make sure that no Arab is left here... we have not yet stopped south, and we have to take back more land," Belaf said. "An unnamed US official said that there are about 10 million Arabs from the northern Iraqi region to escape the Iraqi central area."[119]

Turkmens, also accuse the Kurds for following certain "Kurdization". A senior Iraqi Defense Ministry official told Reuters: "The official said the KRG would not invade Kirkuk after the US leaves but would seek to displace Arabs. He said the Kurd population had soared from 150,000 to 350,000 since 2003."[120]

Another major contradiction between the Kurdistan RG and the Iraqi central government is the oil wells development and the distribution of oil revenues which is a highly controversial problem. Kurds desire to enjoy a larger share of the oil revenues, and a higher say in the planning and imple- mentation of oil projects, oil field development projects and related facili- ties, within the government departments.

However, there are major differences between the two sides on the is- sue of oil quotas arrangements, proportion of export, production etc. and regarding control of oil related investments.

Iraqi oil production is mainly concentrated in the southern Shi'ite region and the northern Kurdish region, while the production in the central Sunni Arab region is lesser. Sunni Arabs insist that oil is a common national re- source and oppose the distribution of oil revenues by regional quotas. And many Sunni Arabs are worrisome that the Kurds will get more quotas and control the North's regional energy investments, which will enable them get rid of their dependence to the central government, that would lead to Kurdish independent state. Kurds also demand to use those earnings/rev- enues which are generated by their own investments. Soon after the war, the Iraqi government has started to design new oil laws, but because of the Kurdish opposition, the introduction of new laws were delayed, or blocked.

---

119   The Kurds Moving to South Iraq Faces Disruption, World News, June 26, 2004, http://mil.news.sina.com.cn/2004-06-24/1628206243.html.
120   "Kurds Give Warning Signals as US Withdrawal Nears", Reuter, July 31, 2011.

In February 2007, the Iraqi government prepared a new draft bill on the issue of oil and gas revenue distribution among the regions, but soon failed due to Kurds' resistance, the event was followed by intensive discussions, frictions and political divisions, consequently in June 2007, the draft bill regarding the oil revenue distribution agreement, was amended. In fact Council of Ministers' February 2007 approval of the draft hydrocarbon (oil-gas) framework legislation has been an important step forward. However, the draft legislative package remains the subject of intense scrutiny from Iraqi and international observers: the draft framework law is imprecise on key issues, including contract terms and revenue sharing.

In July 2007, the Iraqi government proposed a framework law and had forwarded the bill to the Council of Representatives for consideration, the bill raised discussions again and Kurds withdrew their support. Since in the central parliament, Kurds hold numerous seats, without the support of Kurdish deputies, no bill can passed, so the presentation of the draft bill to the parliament was blocked. In December 2007, CRC Chairman Humam Hamoudi requested and received a further six-month extension. In January 2008, the chairman of the parliament's Energy Committee stated that, "the Parliament awaits for the government's approval of any of the draft law's four copies

In late 2007, the KRG finalized its own regional oil and gas investment law and signed new production sharing agreements with several international companies, which can be evaluated as an interim solution between the two sides amid ongoing tensions.

According to a draft of the revenue sharing law published by the Kurdistan Regional Government on June 20, 2007, the federal Iraqi government would be empowered to collect all oil and gas revenue, with the stipulation that all funds be deposited into external and internal accounts based on their source. The Iraqi federal government would have priority to allocate the funds in the accounts to support national priorities such as defense and foreign affairs, "provided that this does not impact the balance and needs of the governments of the Regions and the Governorates which are not organized in a region." The remainder of the revenue accounts would be distributed to regions and governorates automatically, on a monthly basis, based on agreed population-density-based percentages until a new census can be completed. The Kurdistan Regional Government would receive a 17% share of the remaining funds deposited in two accounts at the Central Bank of Iraq branch in Arbil.

Although Kurds are partially satisfied with the current distribution practice of oil revenues, argue that the new draft bills proposed by the central government gives the INOC (Iraqi National Oil Company) too much power to control the nation's oil resources and that could lead to the loss of Kurdish self-government and loss of KRG's control of oil resources in the Kurdish region.

On August 28, 2011, the Iraqi central government once again prepared a revised draft bill, and submitted it to parliamentary discussions, but so far the Parliament has not approved it.

This oil and gas issues have not only become a major challenge in the relationship between the Kurds and the central government, but also one of the key obstacles to post-war Iraq's economic development, especially development of the oil industry. A former minister of the Iraqi central government, Mr. Pembeni elected from the Kurdish quota commented on the issue: "This contradiction will lead to a split of the country."

According to a draft of the revenue sharing law published by the Kurdistan Regional Government on June 20, 2007, the federal Iraqi government would be empowered to collect all oil and gas revenue, with the stipulation that all funds be deposited into external and internal accounts based on their source. The Iraqi federal government would have priority to allocate the funds in the accounts to support national priorities such as defense and foreign affairs, "provided that this does not impact the balance and needs of the governments of the Regions and the Governorates which are not organized in a region." The remainder of the revenue accounts would be distributed to regions and governorates automatically, on a monthly basis, based on agreed population-density-based percentages until a new census can be completed. The Kurdistan Regional Government would receive a 17% share of the remaining funds deposited in two accounts at the Central Bank of Iraq branch in Arbil.

In August 2007, the Kurdish Regional Government enacted and passed the revenue sharing law, regional Oil and Gas Law of the Kurdistan Region (IRAQ, Law No. 22-2007) which consists of 61 articles. Although it is a law promulgated by the Kurdish Regional Assembly the Article 3 of the Law stipulates that: "First: Petroleum in the Region is owned in a manner consistent with Article 111 of the Federal Iraq Constitution. The Regional Government is entitled to a share from the revenues from producing fields, consistent with the share of all Iraqi people, in accordance with this law and Article 112 of the Federal Iraq Constitution."

Article 3 goes on stipulating: Third: The Regional Government shall, together with the Federal Government, jointly manage Petroleum Operations related to producing fields according to the provisions of Article 112(1) of the Federal Constitution. Fourth: The Regional Government shall oversee and regulate all Petroleum Operations, pursuant to Article 115 of the Federal Constitution and in a manner consistent with Article 112 of the Federal Constitution. The Minister may after obtaining the approval of the Regional Council license Petroleum Operations to third parties to maximize timely returns from the Petroleum resources of the Region. Fifth: The Regional Government shall oversee and regulate the marketing of the Regional Government's share of the extracted Petroleum from the Delivery Point where that Petroleum has been extracted from Petroleum Operations, and may license the marketing of that share to third parties.

Under this Law, the Kurdish Regional Government has signed oil and gas drilling contracts with more than 20 foreign oil companies. But the Iraq central Government believes that the Kurdish Regional Government has by-passed the central Government as signing these contracts and evaluates them as void invalid.

The Iraqi oil ministers have criticized these contracts as "void" and threatened the foreign oil companies for imposing sanctions against them. Kurdish Regional Government has also bypassed the central Government by cooperating with Turkey to build an oil pipeline to independently export oil through Turkish territory, which has also frustrated the Iraqi central Government and led to conflicts with Turkey.

In June 2009, the Kurdish Regional Government began exporting crude oil from the two oil fields in northern Iraq at a rate of 100,000 barrels per day. But exports halted only after few months, since the central Government refused to pay the relevant production costs of the co-producer foreign oil companies, which cooperated with Kurds in the region.

In July 2012, Iraqi government spokesman Jawad Aldabbagh said in a statement: "The oil exported from the Kurdish Region to and through Turkey is illegal and can harm the relations between Baghdad and Ankara. Jawad Aldabbagh stressed that the Kurdish Region's oil revenues belongs to all Iraqis, which means the said revenues should flow through and be controlled by the Iraqi central Government.[121]

---

121   Iraq: Export of Oil May Damage Turkey-Iraq Relations, July 16, 2012, http://www.trtchinese.com/trtworld/zh/newsDetail/ aspx?HaberKodu=ae8ea5d3-06bd-4791-aea8-b4c21017569a.

Summary

Compared to the other three countries where Kurds live, Iraqi Kurds enjoy the highest national status. National identity is recognized, the Kurdish language is not only allowed to use, but Kurdish has become the official language. In 1970 Kurds also gained regional autonomy, and after the Gulf War, the Kurdish Regional Government is established and has become "a state in the state" enjoying rights and authorities far beyond the usual autonomy cases we have seen in the world.

Before the regional autonomy, the proportion of Kurds was not very low among the ruling posts—ministerial level or above—of the Iraqi government. Between 1948 and 1958, the Kurds held the 19% of the ruling posts of the Iraqi government, while Sunnis held 44%, and Shiites held 33% of them.

Between 1958 and 1968 the rate has diminished, the proportion of the Kurds were 11%, Sunnis 54%, Shi'ites 30%.[122]

Compared with the other three countries, the Iraqi Kurds' struggle for national rights has been the most vigorous, most violent one and they have made greater sacrifices. For a long period of time, Iraq has been the center of Kurdish national struggle in the region and has become a model for other parts of Kurdistan. The current higher status of the Iraqi Kurds is the fruit of their protracted struggle, but this historical gain has more to do with the effect of the external factors including the dramatic changes in the international and regional situation, the dictatorship and militarist adventurism of Saddam Hussein government, the worsening relations between Iraq and the international community, especially the changes in the friendly relations between the United States and Iraq, which make up the external factors behind the success story of the Iraqi Kurds, as the most important factor.

In the meantime, the struggle of Iraqi Kurds have encountered ups and downs in its development course, they were several times encouraged but later betrayed by the foreign forces and lived severe defeats, and they were even made "pawns" for intervening Iraq, and the Middle East. It can be said that the changeof historical fate of Iraqi Kurds is largely due to two Iraqi wars led by the US.

In the arduous and long struggles between the Iraqi central government and the Kurds, heavy casualties, human disasters and property losses, and serious damage to national unity and construction has occurred, which has offered abundant experiences and lessons to be learned from.

The lessons point that the Iraqi government bears the primary responsibility, with its aggressive Arabization ideology and policies, often acted half-heartedly on this issue of Kurdish autonomy. But the Kurds also bear

---

122   See, Huang Minxing: General History of the Middle East, Volume of Iraq, p. 285.

some responsibility, they have proposed unrealistically high handed demands related to power sharing and have led those strategies which emphasized seeking external support, even they have felt the opportunistic demands of these foreign forces. Mullah Mustafa and his son Masoud Barzani have also admitted that they had made such mistakes, in this regard.

At present, the Iraqi Kurds have entered the most glorious period in their history, and achieved equal status with the Arabs. Their control in the Kurdish Autonomous Region is almost a "quasi-state" status, but still there are some uncertainties related to the future of the KRG. Evaluating from the current circumstances, it is difficult to reverse or shake the Kurdish autonomy, but its future prospects to a large extent depends on the development of Iraqi politics. The rule of the game presents itself as such: if the Central government is strong, then the KRG would be weakened, and vice versa. However, if the relations between the Central Government and the KRG are not handled properly, the possibility of full Kurdish independence cannot be ruled out.

CHAPTER FOUR

The Kurdish Issue in Iran

Kurds are the third largest ethnic group of Iran, after the Persians and Azerbaijanis. Their overall quality of lives are better than the Kurds in Turkey and Iraq. They were not subjected to any large-scale systematic persecution and assimilation. Since the social development of the Iranian Kurds relatively lags behind and since Iran has long been maintaining unified multi-ethnic social life, the autonomy or independence demand by Iranian Kurds has not been prominent. During the early years of post-WWII period, Iranian Kurds have founded the Kurdish Republic of Mahabad under the support of the Soviet Union, which became the peak of the Kurds' fight for national self-determination and also marked an important page in the broad history of Kurdish nation.

4.1 The Iranian Kurdistan

Compared with Iraq and Turkey, the Kurdish issue in Iran has not been prominent, the Kurdish national movements and insurrection demanding autonomy or independence and the domestic and international impacts of the struggle has been marginal in scale. The main reasons are as follows: Firstly, Kurds has been enjoying a rather higher status in Iran. The status of ethnic minorities are recognized in this country and Kurdish language can be freely used.

Second, historically, Iran has been a unified multi-ethnic country, the relations between ethnic groups are more harmonious. Iran is the most multi-ethnic country in the West-Asia region, there are more than 40 nationalities in this country, the main ethnic group Persians account for only about 60% of the total population, there are Azerbaijanis, Kurds, Baluchis, Arabs and many other ethnic groups. Robert Kaplan, a noted history expert in the US, has commented: "Iran is rather a miscellaneous, multi-ethnic empire than a country."[1]

In Turkey and Iraq, the Kurds are the second largest ethnic group, it can be said that they are double-national states, within which other ethnic minorities are almost negligible. In Iran, the Kurdish nationality ranks the third, accounting for about 10% of the population, not only far less than the Persians, but also lesser than Azerbaijanis (about 16%). In Iran, the relationship between the various ethnic groups is relatively harmonious, ethnic oppression is not prominent, ethnic groups basically enjoy equal status, many ethnic minorities including the and Kurds have similar circumstances. Neither the Kurds nor other ethnic minorities basically claim further ethnic-national rights such as autonomy or independence.

Ethnic composition of Iranian political ruling class is also quite diverse and various nationalities of Iran have enjoyed the state power, different from Turkey and Iraq where Turks and Arabs have ruled for centuries and implemented large scale Turkization and Arabization policies.

Third, Iran has a history of more than thousand years of history, Iran is home to one of the world's oldest continuous major civilizations, with historical and urban settlements dating back to 7000 BC, the current Republic enjoys strong cohesion.

Both Turkey and Iraq are newly established countries in the 20th century, comparatively shorter histories and different degrees of concern about Iran's fragmentation from their respective countries. In contrast Iran has similarities with the Chinese history and culture, enjoying a unified national history and cultural traditions, which have a long history and a long tradition. All

---

1 Anne-Marie Slaughter, "Power Shifts", The New York Times, October 5, 2010.

ethnic groups living in Iran identify themselves as part of the Iran nation. The situation in Turkey and Iraq is different, ethnic groups have difficulties to co-exist and face hardships to match up with the outside world to form a country, some groups' lack of national identity is obvious.

Fourth, from the aspect of racial, language, cultural, customs characteristics and many other aspects, Kurds have deep similarities with Iran people, especially with the Persians, we can say there is a sense of affinity. Relatively speaking, Kurds are closer to the Persians than to Arabs and Turks in their kinship, language, and culture, and they lack similarities (in addition to Islam) to the Arabs and Turks. "Unlike the Turks and Arabs, the Persians are closely related to the Kurds. This ethnic affinity has probably to moderate Kurdish national demands in Iran."[2]

Iran's Kurdish region which is also known as "East Kurdistan", is adjacent to the border with Turkey, and Iraq's Kurdish regions which extends from the northern Azerbaijan to the south where Khuzistan is located, which covers an area of about 124,950 square kilometers, accounting for the 25% of the entire Kurdistan.

Iran's Kurdish region which is also known as "East Kurdistan", is adjacent with Turkish border, and Iraq's Kurdish regions which extends from the northern Azerbaijan to the south where Khuzistan is located, which covers an area of about 124,950 square kilometers, accounting for the 25% of the entire Kurdistan.

Iran's Kurdish regions mainly include the Kordestan province (with its capital Sarandaghi), the Kermanshah province (formerly known as Bākhtarān province) which was later renamed in 1996 as Kermanshah province; Ilam Province and also includes some parts of West Azerbaijan (with its capital city Urmia, the famous city of Mahabad is also located in this province. Kordestan was set up in 1961, is the only region (province) named after Kurds, meaning "land of Kurds", a region with an area of 24,998 square kilometers.

In the West it is bordered with Iraq and its capital is Sarandaghi. Kurds of Iran mostly enjoy the Sunni Islam belief. Kermanshah city as the capital Kermanshah province, with a population of about 1.5 million, is the largest Kurdish city in Iran.

The main Kurdish tribes in this province are Guran, Kalhur, Jawanrud and Sanjabi. In addition, the northern Khorasan where half a million Kurds are inhabited, across the Iran-Turkmenistan border, mainly speak the Kurmanji-Kurdish language. They were moved from north west of Iran after the 1610 war between Kurds and the Safavid Empire. After the Safavids massacred a large number of Soorani and Kurmanj Kurds in the 1610 war, a large number of them were moved by force to Khorasan, in the eastern part

---

2   Michael M. Gunter. Historical Dictionary of the Kurds, p. 21.

of Iran, in order to weaken and divide them. There are many Kurdish settlements in other parts of Iran, such as the northern Albuzi mountains, Guilan, West Luristan, southeast of Sistan and Baluchistan provinces. Also, Tehran, Tabriz and Shiraz are the large cities of Iran where many Kurds live.

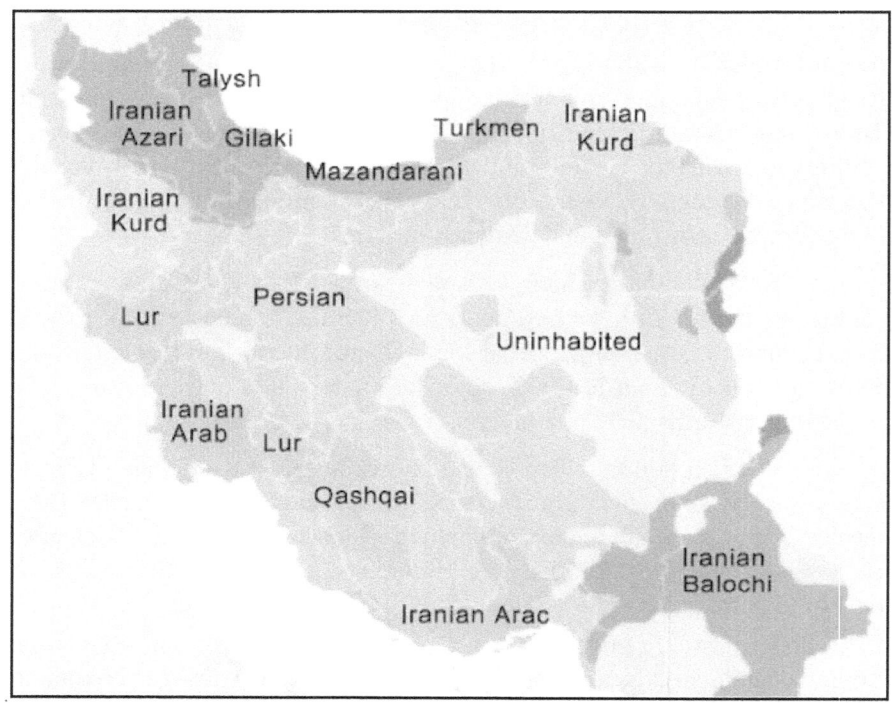

Fig. 4-1 Distribution of Main Ethnic Groups of Iran

Reference: http://en.wikipedia.org/wiki/File: Iran-Ethnicity-2004.PNG.

Unlike the Iraqi Kurdish region, the terrain of Iran's Kurdistan is mountainous and plateau-less plain. Iranian Kurds live in the Zagros Mountains. Zagros is one of the largest mountainous region of Iran, which extends from the northwest of Turkey and forms the Iran-Iraq border. Zagros mountains extend towards the south and reach the Persian Gulf and the Strait of Hormuz, a total distance of about 1,500 km, and more than 300 km. wide. Zagros mountains are rich in oil resources, Iran's main oil field is located in the western part of the Zagros mountains in the central hilly foothills. Dena acme point is the highest point of the Zagros mountains in Iran. One of the western parallel to the valley between the foothills, and with high altitude, having a milder climate, constitute Iran's most populated provinces.

Kurdish region in Iran has many rivers, such as the Aras River (also known as the Aras River, which flows through Turkey, Armenia, Iran and Azerbaijan, with a total length of 1072 km, and a drainage area of 102,000 square kilometers), Karun, Iran's largest river, the only navigable river, with a total length of 720 km, eventually reaches the sea at the Persian Gulf. White River, Iran's second largest river, with a total length of 670 km, reaches the Caspian Sea. Halil River with a length of 390 km. Lake Urmia of is the largest lake in Iran and the Middle East, which is the largest saltwater lake, the world's third largest, with a surface area of about 5200 square km.

Iran's Kurdish population accounts for the 9-10% of the total population, about 7.5 million. And as of March 2011, the Iranian census commission announced the national population as 75,161 Million, and according to the 2012 forecasts of the CIA, Iran has a population of 78.86 million.[3]

According to Amnesty International 's 2008 report, there are 12 million Kurds, or 15% to 17% of Iran' s population.[4]

It seems that the Iranian Kurds' population has grown faster than other ethnic groups. In 1925, the Mosul Committee established by the League of Nations has estimated that the Iran Kurds accounted for only about 700,000.

In 1952, the Great Soviet Encyclopedia wrote that the population of the Iranian Kurds was 2 to 2.5 Million. In 1991, researcher David McDowall has predicted the population of Iranian Kurds as 5.5 million making 10% of the Iran population and 24% of the global Kurds as of 1991.[5] Compared with in other Iranian provinces and ethnic groups, the Kurdish population is younger, the youth below the age of 15 makes the 42% of the total Kurds.[6]

Iranian Kurds mostly live a settled and semi-settled life, but a small part of them still live a nomadic life. Tribal social system still exists, and has a great impact on the individuals' social life. The major Kurdish tribes in Iran are: Mukri, Bilbas, Shakaki, Qur'an, Sinjabi, Krkhor, Shikak, Zarza, Mama Mangul, Shabankara and so on. The Mukri tribe is a powerful tribal community living in the southern and western parts of Lake Urmiya. In 1623, this tribe helped the Safavid dynasty to capture Baghdad from Ottomans, and served as the cavalry of the Safavid dynasty for a long period. By 1900, this tribal community has split into two major tribes: Dehbokri and Mamaš (Mamash). The Iranian Kurds living in northern Khorasan are mainly two tribes known as Zafalanglu and Shadulu.[7]

---

3 "Iran's Population Passes 75 Million", http: //www.payvand.com/news/11/mar/1262. html; https://www.cia.gov/library/publications/the.world-factbook.
4 "Report on Iran: Human Rights Abuses Against the Kurdish Minority", Amnesty International Publications, 2008, p. 6.
5 Amir Hassanpour, "A Stateless Nation's Quest for Sovereignty in the Sky", the Frei Universitat von Berlin, Nov. 7, 1995.
6 "The Status of Girls and Women in Kurdistan Province of the Islamic Republic of Iran", UNICEF, 1998, p.137.
7 Book by Zhao Jinyuan and Dai Peili, History of Nations in the World (Vol.1), Central University of Nationalities Press, 2000, p. 401.

By region, the Iranian Kurds can be divided into four groups: the Kurdish and North Kurdish people of Azerbaijan in the northwest; second group living around the Lake Urmiye, Kurdistan mountains, including the Kurdistan province and the Khorasan region between Mahbubani Kurds; third group of Iranian Kurds live in Paveh, Saqqiz and the Sanandaj regions which are adjacent to Iraq; border; fourth group are the Kermanshah Kurds living between the Zagros Mountains and the Khuzestan plains. In addition, the Lurs ethnic group of Iran is also seen as a branch of the ancient Kurds.[8]

The Lurs ethnic group which have strong affinity with Kurds live in the southwestern province of Luristan and in parts of the Kurdistan province of Iran. They also consider themselves as the descendants of the ancient Medes. The Lurs and the Kurds have some similarities in language and culture, and have a population of 2.6 million to 4.7 million.[9]

70% of the Lurs belong to Shi'ite belief, 20% belong to the Ahl-e Haqq belief involving a belief in successive incarnations combined with ancient rites. However, the Lurs do not think they are part of the Kurds. Luri language is a mixture of Kurdish and Persian, within which most of the words are Kurdish origin. Fayli ethnic people which are also known as part of the Kurds, live in northern Lorestan province. The appearance of Fayli people and Lur people are similar, but there are significant differences in language. The founder of the famous Zand Dynasty, Karim Khan, was from the Fayli people. In the southwestern mountains of Iran, there are also a Bakhtiyari minority, whose language and culture are close to the Kurds.

They are mainly divided into two groups: Chahar lang (English: Four Legs) with 24 tribes and Haft Lang (English: Seven Legs) including 55 tribes. The renown prime minister of the Pahlavi dynasty, Shapur Bakhtiar, was a member of this tribe. Iran's people mainly believe the Shi'ite Islam, which is the state religion of this country which is based on the "twelve Shiia Imam teaching". Iranian Kurdish people believe also in Islam, of which about half of them believe in Shia Islam, and Shia Kurds mainly live in the Kermanshah province, West Azerbaijan province and province of Khorasan and also in Iraq. This division of faith also affects Kurds' attitude towards the government. After the outbreak of the Islamic revolution in 1979, many Sunni Kurds have opposed to the new Islamic Shi'a regime of Homeyni, and mostly the Sunni kurds have played an important role in this regime change.[10]

240

8   Falaomalqi: Travel Guide of Iran, Ye Yiliang (translated), World Knowledge Press, 2000, pp.8-9.
9   "Lurs", http://en.wikipedia.org/wiki/Lurs.
10   Kurt Greussing, Religion and Politik im Iran, Frankfurt am Main: Syndikat, 1981, pp. 372-409.

Generally speaking, the Iranian Shi'ite Kurds do not demand autonomy, and those who demand autonomy are mainly the Sunni groups. In addition, there are also some Kurds who believe in the Sufi, Baha'i, Ahl-e Haqq belief and others.[11]

Iranian Kurds mainly speak a Kurdish dialect of Sorani, written with Arabic alphabet. Some Kurdish regions close to the Turkish border speak Kurmanji-Kurdish. A small number of Kurds speak the Iranian Gorani dialect. Local Kurdish men are used to wrap their head in a large scarf, wearing tight and narrow ankles of coarse cloth clothes, women wear trousers and bright colored scarves, and prefer tight-fitting dresses with brocade fabric.

Iran's Kurdistan province is economically poor, with higher unemployment and inconvenient transportation, one of the poorest regions of Iran. The economy mainly depends on agriculture, animal husbandry and handicraft industry, while industry and service industry is underdeveloped. During the mid-1970s, about 30% of the Kurdish families lived below the poverty line, while 21% of the Kurdish families have lived below the poverty line dwelling in the central Iran regions.[12]

In 2008, Amnesty International published the report titled as "Iran: Human Rights Abuses against the Kurdish Minorities", which has stated: "The Constitution of Iran stipulates that all citizens are equal before the law and discrimination against minorities is not allowed, but this is not the case. Although Kurdish language is allowed in schools, radio stations and some publications, and Kurdish cultural expressions such as clothing and music are respected, in contrast the Iranian Kurds have long been discriminated in political, economic, social and cultural fields and their rights and demands in these fields are suppressed. Some leaders of a Kurdish human rights association involved in human rights work and national identity issues, have faced the threat of imprisonment." The report has listed a series of aspects of discrimination against the Iranian Kurds such as the religion, culture, employment, education, housing. "As to religion, the Sunni Kurds are discriminated, Sunni religious sites and religious practices face severe difficulties, in contrast the Shi'ite religious sites and practices are encouraged and supported. Government restricts the construction of new Sunni mosques, and there is no Sunni mosque in the capital Tehran. Sunni clerics are often subjected to maltreatment. As of 1998, there were only two rural secondary schools in the Kurdish province, both of which were operating in the Shi'ite towns. The central government does not allow the parents who desire to give names carrying certain meanings, such as freedom, struggle, flag, equality, tears and so on to their newborn children. As to the employment issue, the Kurdish people

---

11　David McDowall, A modern History of the Kurds, I.B. Tauris, 1996, p. 270.
12　Akbar Aghajanian, "Ethnic Inequality in Iran: An Overview", Int. Journal of Middle East Studies, May 15, 1983.

who are admitted to public posts are forced to swear allegiance to Islam and the Islamic Republic. The government investments in the Kurdish regions are marginal and job opportunities are extremely limited. The government also acts very slowly in cleaning up the land-mines laid in the Kurdish region during the Iran-Iraq war, which restricts the economic-trade activities. As to the housing, during the Iran-Iraq war a large number of Kurdish dwellings were destructed, besides the forced relocation and other factors including lack of government support for housing have added to the poor conditions in the Kurdish region. As to the education, the only official language of Iran government is Persian, although no restrictions of speaking in other minority languages, the education system has not seen any reform policies and measures to encourage the use of Kurdish and other minority languages in education sphere. The government has restricted and banned a number of Kurdish educational facilities. In February 2007, Kurdish students studying at the University of Tehran have demanded the use of Kurdish language in the educational system, but many of them were arrested." The Amnesty International report has called on the Iranian government to "take effective measures in eliminating human rights discrimination regarding the ethnic minorities, including Kurds, amend or abolish those laws and regulations which include discriminative contents" and Amnesty International has demanded "immediate release of all political prisoners."[13]

4.2 The Kurdish Issue in the Pahlavi Era

Historically, we cannot ignore that Kurds have been fighting against the Iranian government, in fact, between the two sides, there was a struggle between control and counter-control. This struggle has never ceased. The earliest account of the conflict between the Kurds and the Persians was probably the conflict between the Kurds and the Sassanian Empire. In the 10th and 12th centuries, there were two Kurdish vassal states in Kurdistan: Hasanwayhids (959-1015) and Ayyarids (990-1117).

In the 12th century, the Turkic Seljuk Empire was established in the Kurdistan province, Sultan Sanjar created a province called "Kurdistan" centered at Bahar, located to the northeast of Hamadan. This province included Hamadan, Dinawar, Kermanshah, Sanandaj and Sharazur. It was ruled by Sulayman Shah, the nephew of Seljuk leader Sultan Sanjar. In 1217, Kurds of Zagros defeated the troops of Ala ad-Din Muhammad II, the Khwarazmid King, who were sent from Hamadan.

In 1271, the Iranian Kurds have defeated the Khwarazmid Kingdom (1077-1231), which had dominated most parts of Iranian Kurdistan for a long time. During the Persian Safavid period, the Safavids tried to control

---

13 "Iran: Human Rights Abuses Against the Kurdish Minority", Amnesty International Publications, 2008, p.6.

Iran's Kurdish region. There were many semi-independent Kurdish Emirate states in the region, such as Mukriyan emirate, centered in Mahabad, secondly Ardalan emirate which was centered at Sinne, and the Shikak Emirate around the lake Urmiye.

The Kurds tried to resist against the rule of the Safavids and fought to maintain their semi-independence. This led to a series of bloody confrontations between the Safavids and the Kurds. The Kurds were finally defeated, and as a result the Safavids decided to punish rebellious Kurds by forced relocation and deportation in the 15-16th century. This policy began under the reign of the Safavid King Tahmasp I (ruled between 1514–1576).

The Kurds were forced to migrate to Khorasan, the Alborz mountains and as well as the heights in the central Iranian Plateau. From 1609 to 1610, the Kurdish tribes around the Urmiya lake region and the Safavid dynasty engaged a major bloody war, and the Kurds were defeated, and were massacred. Safavid Shah Abbas ordered a general massacre in Beradost and Mukriyan (reported by Eskandar Beg Turkoman (Turkmen), Safavid historian, in the book Alam Aray-e Abbasi) and resettled the Turkish Afshar tribe in the region while deporting many Kurdish tribes to Khorasan.

In 1639, the Safavid dynasty and the Ottoman Empire have split the Kurdish region after a long war which ended with the "Zuhab Treaty", defeated Safavid was forced to give Baghdad and this traty finally settled the Ottoman–Persian frontier, with Iraq permanently ceded to the Ottomans. Mesopotamia, which had formed an important part of various Persian empires from the time of the Achaemenids, was thereby irrevocably lost.

In the early 18th century, the Kurds used the opportunity of the invasion of Iran, Afghanistan, launched a rebellion, occupied Hamadan and other places. In 1722, the Afghans exterminated Safavid, which ruled Iran for 220 years.

In 1724 after a civil unrest in Iran, the Ottoman Empire and the Tsarist Russia made the Treaty of Constantinople and partitioned the Iranian territory. Thus, the annexed Iranian lands located on the east of the conjunction of the rivers Kuroush (Kur) and Aras were given to the Russians, comprising the provinces in northern mainland Iran (Gilan, Mazandaran and Astrabad) as well as the lands in Dagestan, while the lands on the west went to the Ottomans, comprising large parts of Iranian Azerbaijan (incl. Ardabil, Hamadan, and Tabriz), Kermanshah, and much of the rest of Iranian-ruled Transcaucasia (encompassing modern-day Georgia and Armenia).

The treaty furthermore specified that if Safavid Iran, at that time led by the regime of King Tahmasp II, would refuse to accept the treaty both Imperial Russia and the Porte would take common action against Iran and install a puppet ruler.

However, the gains for both Russia and Ottoman Turkey proved to be very brief, for the 1732 Treaty of Resht and 1735 Treaty of Ganja returned all territories taken by Russia back to Iran, while the Ottoman–Persian War (1730–35) decisively returned all Ottoman annexed territories back to Iran.

In 1727, the Ottoman Empire and the Afghan Hotaki Dynasty signed the Treaty of Hamedan which confirmed Ottoman sovereignty over all the western and northwestern parts of Iran and, in return for Hotaki ruler Ashraf's giving up of his territorial claims, gave him official recognition as Shah of Persia with rights of minting coins and sending annual pilgrimage caravans to Mecca. From 1736 to 1747, Afsharid dynasty founded by Nadir Shah defeated the Afghans, deposed the last member of the Safavid dynasty and proclaimed himself the Shah of Iran. During Nader's reign, Iran reached its greatest extent since the Sassanid Empire,

He also defeated the Ottoman Empire, saved the Iranian regions occupied by the Ottoman Empire and In 1736, the Nader Shah army forced the Ottoman Empire to sign the Treaty of Constantinople, the Ottoman Empire was forced to return the Iranian territory which she occupied for more than a decade, the border between the warring parties resumed to the status of the 1639 "Zuhab Treaty" (Qasr-e Shīrīn in Arabic). In 1747 after Nader Shah was assassinated, Iran once again fell into anarchy.

In 1748, the Kurds and Turkmen tribes supported Nader's young son Shahrukh for the Iranian throne but the state was actually in a split state.

1751-1753, Kurdish Zand tribes led by Karim Khan and Bakhtiyar tribes entered into a battle, the Kurdish Zand attacked the central Iranian city of Isfahan and nearly captured most parts of the southern Iran. The Zands also defeated the Afghans led by Azar, and Karim Khan established his rule at Shiraz by 1757. He was able to win over Qajar officers with bribes and because Muhammad Hasan Khan quarreled with other Qajar leaders. Karim imprisoned the last Safavid Isma'il, who died in 1773. After promoting building and commerce in Shiraz, Karim Khan returned to Isfahan in 1764 and ruled western Iran until he died in 1779. Preceded, surrounded, and followed by cruel warlords, Karim Khan was renowned for ruling peacefully and justly in a violent era. Zand Dynasty ended in 1794 after 37 years.

During this period, the Qajar tribes in northeastern Iran gradually rose up and fought against the Zand dynasty. In 1786, they established the Qajar dynasty with Tehran as its capital Tehran, Qajar defeated the Zand dynasty forces in 1794 and destroyed it. Iran was under the rule of Qajars between 1794-1875. In 1796 Hajji Ibrahim and other Qajar chiefs expanded the Qajar dynasty. Under the Qajars the shah usually appointed governors who contributed the most money, and governors in turn got their positions by selling local tax-collecting. This left most of the people with little savings for investment. Many peasants worked by sharecropping for their landlords. The Persian army mostly depended on tribal forces that were motivated by the opportunity to plunder. The central government maintained control by dividing opposing tribes, giving pensions as bribes, and by taking hostages from prominent families. Islamic law (shari'a) was used for tribe issues, wills, contracts, and religious laws, while criminal cases and rebellion against the state were usually handled by magistrates. Commercial litigants could choose between religious or secular courts. Very little printing was done in Iran, though from 1851 the government published the weekly Iran Journal that became the official report of government orders and was required reading for officials.

In the early period of the 19th century, Qajar Dynasty began to decline, under the external pressures and threats posed by colonialism of Britain, Russia and the Ottoman Empire and was reduced to a semi-colony state. A series of border incidents in the 1830s again brought Qajars and the Ottoman Empire to the brink of war. Britain and Russia offered to mediate, and a second Erzurum Treaty was signed in1847. This treaty divided the disputed regiosn between Iran and the Ottoman Empire and provided for a boundary commission to delimit the entire border. Traaty abandoned the Sulaimaniya sovereignty requirements, and the Ottoman Empire got, Sulaymaniyah western Zuhab, east of Zuhab and Kürend river and other areas including Muhammere port, Hızır island and Şattülarab were left to Iranian Qajars.

This Erzurum Treaty was very crucial because both countries relied on the Silk Road for trade. Those wars between the two states devastated the two countries and weakened their integrity alongside the economy of war that made both states poor. Russians and Europeans meanwhile used this opportunity to capture and take control of disputed regions including Caucasia. The Qajar court soon became infected with foreign spies' meddling in country's affairs and concessions were taken at the expense of the nation.

At this time, the Iran had internal problems and fell into disarray and uprisings and rebellion, between 1849-1850 occurred the Babi people's uprising. On 5 May 1850 the Babis of Zanjan rose in arms against the Qajar governor of the town. Led by a charismatic cleric known as Hujjat-i Zanjani, two thousand Babi fighters with their families held part of the town against a much larger government army. Nine months later, when the army captured the last ruined houses held by the Babis, fewer than a hundred Babi fighters survived to face execution.

Until the middle of the 19th century, most of the Kurdish regions were divided by many Kurdish emirates, which enjoyed considerable autonomy. After Qajar Iran and Ottoman started centralization reforms Kurdish vassal emirates were frustrated and began to resist against centralization and direct control. In 1880, the Kurdish leader Sheikh Ubeydullah of Nehri launched a revolt against the Qajar Iranian government, but was suppressed.

Before and after the First World War, colonial and semi-colonial Iran's crisis deepened, and gradually anti-feudal, anti-colonial nationalism thought trend formed. Between 1905-1911, the constitutional revolution erupted in Iran, but has finally failed. The constitutional revolution also played an important role in promoting the formation of Iranian Kurdish nationalism. In 1914 World War I broke out, although Iran declared to be neutral, the Kurdish region under the control of Russia became the battlefield of Tsarist Russia and the Ottoman Empire.

In December 1914, 70,000 troops of Tsarist Russia captured the northern part of Iran and the western part of the border regions adjacent to the Ottoman Empire, after the Ottoman Empire troops marched into this region, the two sides have engaged a battle. In November 1914, the British army in order to protect its oil interests also entered Iran, occupied the south of Mesopotamia and marched northward against heavy Turkish opposition.

By the end of World War I, although Iran did not face a partition and disintegration as the Ottoman Empire, Iran's whole territory was basically occupied by Russia and the British army. During this period, the Iran lived a domestic chaos, the central government lost the control of many regions, consequently in the northern Iran a pro-Soviet state was established. Thus the Persian Socialist Soviet Republic (widely known as the Soviet Republic of Gilan) was a short-lived Soviet republic in the Iranian province of Gilan that lasted from June 1920 until September 1921. It was established by Mirza Koochak Khan, a leader of the Constitutionalist movement of Gilan, and his Jangali (Foresters Movement) partisans, with the assistance of the Soviet Red Army.

Many Kurdish chiefs also took this situation of Iran as an opportunity for revolts, attempting to establish Kurdistan, the most prominent leader of the revolting Kurds was Ismail Agha or Simko. He led the most effective, largest and longest uprising which was simultaneous with the Sheikh Saed uprising in Turkey, and the Mahmud Barzanji uprising in Iraq (1921-22).

During the latter part of the First World War, the Shikak tribal chief, Ismail Agha (Simko), used the weakness of the central government and actively expanded its territory, defeated other Kurdish tribes and local Assyrians and Azerbaijanis, and established Shikak's authority in the western regions of the lake Urmiya.

In 1919, Ismail Agha established a Kurdish government in Urmiya region and set up a Kurdish armed force of 20,000 men. Subsequently, he led his army to expand Shikak territories, repeatedly fought against Iranian government forces and defeated them. By 1922, the regions controlled by the Shikak forces had greatly expanded from the west to the south of the Urmiye, as far as Mahabad, Khoy, Miandoab, Maku and Piranshahr. In 1921 a coup d'état was achieved by Iranian army officer Reza Khan Mirpanj (later Reza Shah Pahlavi) who rapidly prepared forces to suppress the Kurdish rebels.

At this time, government in Tehran tried to reach an agreement with Simko on the basis of limited Kurdish autonomy. But Simko had organized a strong Kurdish army which was much stronger than Iranian government forces. Since the central government could not control his activities, he continued to expand the area under his control and by 1922, cities of Baneh and Sardasht were under his administration. In the early 1922, Reza Khan sent Iran troops to suppress the Kurdish rebels, but was once again defeated, the Iranian army commander was killed.

In the battle of sari Taj in 1922, Simko's forces could not resist the Iranian Army's onslaught in the region of Salmas and were finally defeated and the castle of Chari was occupied. In 1922 the strength of the Iranian Army forces led by Reza Khan against Simko was 10,000 soldiers. Simko and one thousand of his mounted soldiers took refuge in nearby Turkey, so then they were forced to lay down their weapons, and later entered into the territory of Iraq.

In 1930, Simko was invited by the Iranian government to return to the negotiations, but on his way to negotiations he was ambushed by government troops. Simco's failure had many reasons.

First, in the later period of Kurdish uprisings, Iranian regime was strengthened, the chaos situation was overcome. Reza Khan who came to power was an experienced long-term military men, he did not only have military experience, but organizational, skills thus he established a modern army, in contrast Kurdish armed forces lacked proper training, advanced weapons and equipments.

Second, the Kurds failed to establish alliances and unity, the internal disputes among different factions could not be diminished, even Simco's own tribe was divided into three factions. The repression of the Iranian government was also supported by some Kurdish tribes, who were worrisome to be annexed or subordinated by Simco.

Simco, although vigorously upheld the banner of Kurdish nationalism, lacked the proper ideology and could not lead systematic propaganda, also failed to establish a proper organizational leadership which could mobilize and organize the Kurds.

Although Simco was an ambitious tribal leader, he did not have an advanced national thought. In October 1921, when the army led by Simko had captured Mahabad, the army had massacred the local Kurds.

In those days, compared with Turkey and Iraq, national ideology was not yet prevalent among the Iranian Kurds has not yet reached to the stage of propaganda and mobilization.

Thirdly, Simco led revolts lacked foreign support. Simco had initially sought the support of Britain and the Soviet Union, but his efforts had failed.

Failure of Simco led struggle marked the end of the Iranian civil strife situation. Reza Han (later Reza Shah Pahlavi) Pahlavi, after the successful coup, in 1921, gradually took the control of the state and domestic situation. In 1922, the British and Soviet troops withdrew from Iran, thus the long colonial yoke over Iran had ended. In 1925, Pahlavi was declared as king, and in April 1926 he was formally crowned, thus the Pahlavi dynasty was established. After Reza Shah Pahlavi came to power, he drew on Mustafa Kemal's reforms in Turkey, and actively promoted the modernization and secularization reforms, in order to strengthen his ruling power.

Between June 16 to July 2, 1934, Reza Shah Pahlavi visited Turkey, together with a mission of high-ranking officials, among which General Hassan Arfa, at the invitation of Mustafa Kemal Atatürk. Several regions in Turkey were visited and attempts at close friendship and cooperation between the two leaders were made.

This visit further strengthened bilateral relations and also strengthened the military and security relations, and Iran more vigorously followed Turkish model in its modernization drive. Iran focused on the economic development, the building of factories and mine openings, strengthened tax collection system, speeded the construction of the railways and roads network which would connect the whole country. In the social sphere Iran promoted a secularization reform, also implemented reforms related to modern judiciary, religion, education, culture, clothing reform and others. Iran under Reza Shah Pahlavi's rule cultivated nationalism with Persian nationalism as its core, enforced the centralization of the state power and maintained the use of traditional Iranian dating in order to strengthen the national identity.

In 1935, Reza Shah Pahlavi officially changed the name of the country from Persia to Iran.

Reza Shah Pahlavi's reforms, especially the strengthening of centralization, and his fight against local forces which resisted to centralization, the elimination of backward natural and nomadic economies, and his reform measures related to the social and political structure of the society has made a significant impact on the Kurds.

Firstly, Iran sent troops to suppress the revolts across the country. Between 1922 and 1925, he sent troops to Azerbaijan, Kermanshah, Fars, Luristan, Khorasan and other places where there were resistance and revolts, which included the Kurdish revolts (Azerbaijan and Khorasan).

Secondly, Iran re-arranged and reformed administrative divisions of the state. "In 1938, the 49 major and minor provinces (ayalat and valayat) were reduced to 11 geographically and economically viable ostans, each with further divisions into šahrestans, and bakses, and all leading officials were appointed by the central government. Thus in the modern history of Iran the state organization was—for the first time—extended beyond the scope of capital Tehran and even covered the towns and the villages."[14]

Thirdly, the power of tribal chiefs was restricted. The influence of the traditional tribal leaders was weakened by means of taxation, compulsory military service, land reform and forced settlement, which broke the old tribal social structure. Any attempt by local forces targeting the central authority was severely suppressed. Hundreds of tribal chiefs were expelled and forced to live far from where their tribe was located. Many tribal chiefs were put under house arrest in the capital, Tehran, and their landed property was confiscated. Some of the tribal chiefs were expelled to Turkey.

In 1933 a mandatory settlement policy was started, the government restricted the nomadic living habits of certain tribes through the establishment of checkpoints along the borders and other measures were put into force to restrict free migration. In 1934, the new electoral law was promulgated which abolished all tribal constituencies, weakening the impact of tribal leaders.

Fourthly, the governance and control on the Kurdish regions were strengthened and the policy of Persianization was vigorously implemented. The government established a number of military bases and checkpoints in the Kurdish regions at the strategic locations, increased military presence and appointed army generals to monitor the tribes. A network of roads were constructed to facilitate control and exchanges. The Persian language was forcedly promoted, followed by the prohibition of education, publishing and public use of the Kurdish language. Many Kurdish schools were closed. Also European-style clothing attitudes were imposed to Kurds and other Iranians. Kurdish names of the geographical locations even village and street names were renamed with artificial ones, i.e. the city was renamed from Orumiyeh to Rezaiye, Kurdistan was changed as West Azerbaijan. Turkey's ideological trick as Kurds being "the Turks living in mountainous places" was also adopted by Pahlavi, and Iran began to emphasize the

14   Ha Quanan, History of Middle East (610-2000), Vol.1, Tianjin People Publishing House, p. 414.

use of "mountain Iranians" to replace the Kurds, but the word "Kurd or Kurdish" was not officially banned.[15]

Pahlavi's reform and repression measures have greatly achieved the determined goals. After the accomplishment of the land registrations, many tribal leaders became landlords, and tribesmen became peasants, dependence on tribal and tribal chiefs has weakened, and the implementation of the tax system has enhanced the national consciousness. The Government also confiscated the lands of a large number of tribal chiefs, and by the implementation of the forced immigration policy, many Kurdish tribes were deported from their original settlements to other regions. The government has also restricted the free movement of the tribes by closing the borders and forbidding the annual move of tribesmen and their flocks to pass through certain areas, the Kurdish tribes were forced to settle down and get accustomed to permanent settling or semi- permanent settling. These measures and restrictions have increased the number of settled Kurdish villages and weakened the traditional tribal social relations, and large tribal communities were divided into numerous smaller tribes. When Pahlavi ascended to the reign of Iran, tribal population accounted for about 25% of the population, in 1932 it fell to 8%, in 1941 further decreased to 7%, with a population of 1,000,000.[16]

From 1930 to 1931, small-scale Kurdish uprisings broke out in Azerbaijan and Hamadan, but were quickly suppressed. Since then, until the end of World War II, the Iranian Kurdish region under the strict oppression of the government has remained calm. Compared to Turkish and Iraqi Kurdish insurgencies, the Iranian Kurdish opposition or revolts during this period were not vigorous and smaller in scale. On July 8, 1937, Iran and Turkey, Iraq and Afghanistan, four foreign ministers signed a five-year non-aggression treaty in Tehran, also known as the Treaty of Saadabad (Saadabad Is the royal palace of Pahlavi in Tehran), the main contents of the treaty include non-aggression, non-interference in each other's internal affairs, respect for border and agree to use consultation when resolving international disputes concerning common interests, and cooperation in strengthening regional security. On June 25, 1938, the Treaty was ratified and In 1943, the treaty was automatically extended for further 5 years.

After the outbreak of World War II, Iran and Turkey declared neutrality in 1939, but Pahlavi had followed a pro-German policy, causing strong dissatisfaction of rival camp. On August 25, 1941, the Britain and the Soviet Union simultaneously marched into Iran and occupied Tehran, Pahlavi was forced to abdicate, the purpose of occupation was to secure Iranian oil fields and ensure Allied supply lines for the USSR, and fighting against Axis

15 Nader Entessar, Kurdish Ethnonationalism, Lynne Rienner Pub, 1992, p.13.
16 Ha Quanan, History of Middle East (610-2000), Vol.1, pp.415, 421.

forces on the Eastern Front. The Shah demanded to know why they were invading his country and why they had not declared war. Both, Britain and the Soviet Union answered that it was because of "German residents" in Iran. When the Shah asked if the Allies would stop their attack if he expelled the Germans, the ambassadors did not answer. Iran resisted militarily but was weak and isolated to stop the invaders. Then, king's younger son Mohamed Reza Pahlavi replaced him. The whole territory of Iran was occupied by the British and Soviet troops. The Allies withdrew from Tehran on 17 October. However, Iran was effectively divided between Britain and the Soviet Union for the duration of World War II, with the Soviets stationed in northern Iran and the British not moving beyond Hamadan and Qazvin. The British wanted to restore the previous Qajar Dynasty to power because they had served British interests well prior to Reza Shah Pahlavi's reign.

During this period, the Iranian army was basically in complete chaos and became disintegrated. Kurdish regions of Iran was under the Soviet occupation, those Kurdish leaders who were exiled by the King to Tehran, fled back home, began to rebuild their own local forces. When the Iranian army was rapidly withdrawing and escaping from the Kurdish regions a large number of arms were left and captured by the local Kurds. Kurdish revolts became fermenting rapidly. The revolt led by the Kurdish leader Hama Rashid controlled Baneh, Sardasht and Mariwan in Western Iran and vast regions, but this revolt was suppressed in 1944 by the Iraqi government.

During this period, using the opportunity endowed by the World War II, and getting support from the Soviet Union, the Iranian Kurdish nationalist movement began to develop and established its political organizations. On September 16, 1942, the first Kurdish Iranian political organization, Komala Jiyanewey Kurdistan (abbreviated as J.K. or Komala), meaning "Rebirth of Kurdistan ", was established. This was a left-wing political party composed mainly of petty bourgeois and urban intellectuals, and strongly opposed to the feudal landlord class and tribalism, called for the expansion of Kurdish national and social rights. The party rapidly increased its support in the cities and among farmers. Qazi Muhammad was chairman of the party, and Abd-al Rahman Zabihi acted as the general secretary. This party had to a degree certain pan-Kurdish nationalist attributes, its main member stock was from the Iranian Kurds, but also had members from Iraq and Turkey.

Iraq's Kurdish party organization "Hiwa" was also represented by Mir Haji who was a close associate of Mullah Mustafa Barzani from Iraq participated the Komala's first meeting. The party journal "Nishtiman" (Motherland), was supported by the Soviet Union and distributed in the regions under the Soviet occupation. "Nishtiman" declared the Party slogan as "Long Live The Greater Kurdistan". In March 1945, Komala staged a dramatic opera titled as "Motherland" in Mahabad, content of the drama pointed to the danger of the motherland, finally the motherland was rescued after suffering from foreign humiliation, the drama was highly appreciated by the audience and was a great success for the surging nationalism.

In addition to propagating national ideology, the organization also prepared for the insurgency against the government. In May 1943, Kurdish fighters attacked the police station in Mahabad killed several policemen, and expelled all the government officials and officers from the city. In May 1944, the organization issued the Kurdish flag. And in April 1945, the committee invited Qazi Muhammad, highly respected cleric, as the party president. Getting the suggestion and support of the Soviet Union, on August 15, 1945, Qazi Muhammad and Mullah Mustafa Barzani established the Kurdish Democratic Party (PDK) later called Kurdish Democratic Party of Iran based on the heritage of Komala and Qazi Muhammad dissolved the Komala.[17]

In September 1945, Komala Jiyanewey Kurdistan announced its dissolution and it ceased activities under this name, the successor Kurdish Democratic Party inherited most of its members.[18]

The main content of the Kurdish Democratic Party's program included empowering Iranian Kurds in managing their own regional affairs and defined autonomy as the goal, within Iran; demanded Kurdish language education, Kurdish becoming the official language of the Kurdish regional government, to elect Kurdistan's provincial governance council freely, the Kurdistan regional government to assume regional governance and administration including all social affairs, government officials to be selected from among local Kurds; the rule of law, the defend legal equality for peasantry against nobility, issuing new laws to better regulate the relationships between landlords and peasants, promote agriculture and trade, promote education and health, the best use of the Kurdish region's natural resources; collecting taxes and allocate them for regional development, political freedom and national progress for the whole Iranian peoples, and upholding solidarity with Azerbaijanis. Soviet Union supported the KDP and provided economic and military assistance. The establishment of the Kurdish Democratic Party, has opened an important page and constitutes a landmark in the whole Kurdish national struggle history which. directly encouraged the development of the whole Kurdish national movement. It has been the first Kurdish nationalist party possessing modern attributes One day after its establishment Iraq's Kurdistan Democratic Party (KDP) declared its founding in Baghdad.

252

---

17 Since its foundation, this party had carried out many activities in Iran and held 15 Congresses in 1945, 1964, 1971, 1980, 1982, 1984, 1988, 1992, 1995, 1997, 2000, 2008 and 2012. Its headquarter is currently in Northern Iraq.
18 In September, 1945, Komala was disbanded and no longer carried out activities. In 1969, a new Kurdish organization was set up in Iran, and was also named Komala, but there was no relationship between the two parties.

PARTIYA DEMOKRAT YA KURDÍSTANA ÍRANÊ

Fig 4-2 Amblem of the Democratic Party Of Iranian Kurdistan (1945)

Fig 4-3 National Flag of Kurdish Republic of Mahabad

On January 10, 1946, the Azerbaijani ethnic people of Iran announced the establishment of the Azerbaijani National Government, the move was supported by the Soviet Union. Soon after Democratic Party of Iranian Kurdistan decided to follow the example of Azerbaijan people and establish the Republic of Kurdistan. On December 15, 1945, the Kurdish People's Government was established in Mahabad. A month later in January 22, 1946, Qazi Muhammad announced the establishment of the "Mahabad Republic" In February, Qazi Muhammad became the president, Haji Baba Sheikh the prime minister, Mullah Mustafa Barzani the Chief Commander of the Armed Forces of the Republic. In April, the Republic of Kurdistan concluded a treaty of alliance with the Republic of Azerbaijan. A decree ordered the Kurdish language as the official language, soon Kurdish-language newspapers have mushroomed along side with Kurdish language education including ordinary people, Kurdish freedom fighters replaced the Iranian police, Kurdish national flag was everywhere, every symbol of modern state was there, the state emblem and the Kurdish national anthem.

It can be said that the Kurdish Republic of Mahabad was established under the direct support of the Soviet Red Army. After the World War II ended, Soviet army did not withdraw its troops, although Iran government had repeatedly demanded the withdrawal of British and Soviet troops and sought US's diplomatic support to achieve its sovereignty. In January 1946, Iran filed a complaint to the UN acting secretary general which accused the Soviet Union of interfering in Iran's internal affairs, and demanded urgent Soviet withdrawal. In those days the tripartite alliance during World War II was in trouble, the Western forces had began confronting the Soviet Union, Iran's precious strategic position targeted by the competing parties had triggered further confrontation and signaled the outbreak of the Cold War. The West put multiple pressures on the Soviet Union, demanding its withdrawal from Iran. On March 2, 1946, when the deadline for the withdrawal of foreign troops was due the Britain and the US withdrew their troops from Iran, and the Soviets were still in place, thus the crisis began to develop which put Soviet Union under further pressure. On March 21, the new hawkish US President Truman sent a letter to Stalin, demanding that Soviet Union should fulfill its commitments of withdrawing troops from Iran. A major diplomatic confrontation was avoided when the Soviets announced on March 25, 1946, that they would be withdrawing their forces within six weeks.

On April 4, the Soviet Union reached a deal with the Iranian government, the Soviet Union promised to withdraw in May 6, 1946, in turn Iran gave the Soviets an oil concession, to establish joint companies to jointly develop the Iran's oil fields in northern Iran.

In May, the Soviet army retreated from Iran, which endangered the future of Kurdish Mahabad Republic and the Republic of Azerbaijan, soon after in November 1946, Iranian army attacked Azerbaijan, in December the capital Tabriz was captured which ended the newborn Republic of Azerbaijan. Next, from April to June 1946, the Iranian army attacked Mahabad, Kurds vigorously resisted. After the final surrender and occupation of Azerbaijan, the Iranian army was able to concentrate its forces to start a second large-scale attack on Mahabad. On December 15, 1946 Iranian army marched into Mahabad, and the next day president Qazi Mohammad ordered to surrender. On March 31, 1947, Qazi Mohammad and three other Kurdish leaders were hanged for treason and the Kurdish Republic was suppressed. The Iran government issued a banning order for the Kurdish newspapers, Kurdish teaching, and all the books in Kurdish books became the target of burning. In the next 2 months 1947, armed forces led by Mullah Mustafa Barzani were also completely suppressed, Barzani was forced to flee the Soviet Union, he could only return to Iraq in 1958 after 11 years.

The defeat of the Mahabad Republic was historically inevitable, the key reason being the secret deal between the Soviet Union and Iran, and the interest competition between the great powers. The Mahabad Republic was established by the machination of the Soviet Union, but under the pressure of Western forces, Soviet Union had hit a deal with Iran exchanging its withdrawal with oil concessions without seeking to secure the Kurds and letting them pay the price of the power games. Without the support of the Soviet Union, the newborn immature Kurdish Republic could not survive. The Kurds' relations with the Soviet Union had displeased the West, plus Iran's strategic importance had the West to support the Iranian government, the Iranian government had done its best to court the West against the Kurds, by labeling the Kurdish Democratic Party as a communist anti-West party.[19]

If we evaluate inherent problems and reasons of the KDPI led Kurdish movement which led to its defeat we can say the following: the political, economic, social and cultural backwardness of Kurdistan was the source and main reason of the Kurdish defeat and of the Mahabad Republic.

Secondly, the lack of unity and solidarity within the Republic and the Iran government's policy of divide and rule were also important causes of the defeat. Qazi and Mullah Mustafa Barzani were difference and contradiction, were indulged in a power struggle. Qazi government was quite weak, Qazi Muhammad's internal support eventually declined, especially among the Kurdish tribes who had supported him initially. The townspeople and the tribes had a large divide between them, and their alliance for Mahabad was crumbling. the war council of Mahabad told Qazi Muhammad that

19   Jr. Archie Roosevelt, "The Kurdish Republic of Mahabad", Middle East Journal, No. 1, July 1947, pp. 247-269.

they would fight and resist the Iranian army if they tried to enter the region. The lack of Kurdish tribal support however made Qazi Muhammad only see a massacre upon the Kurdish civilians performed by the Iranian army rather than Kurdish rebellion. This forced him to avoid war at all cost, he could not mobilize the whole people.

As the government army forces aggressively attacked, some of the Kurdish tribes that originally supported the Qazi government also retreated, and some even joined the government against the Mahabad Republic. In addition, the Kurdish leaders lacked political experience, the newly established Kurdish Democratic Party was not yet politically mature, this was one another reason for defeat. Although the territory of the Republic of Mahabad only covered 1/3 of Iran's Kurdistan, in less than a year, it had delivered a far-reaching influence in the history of the Kurdish national movement, inspiring and encouraging the Kurds.

The Mahabad Republic was the first successful Kurdish regional autonomy, it became the dream of Kurds everywhere, and no Kurdish movement has reached the height of the Mahabad Republic. Compared with the Simco uprising in Iran, this uprising had not only established a modern sense of Republic, but also bore modern Kurdish nationalist features. The leaders of the Simco revolt were mainly traditional tribal chiefs, who lacked political organizations and programs, but the Mahabad uprising was supported by a new generation composed of urban intellectuals and nobles, possessed a modern political party, modern organization and ideology.

Fig 4-4 The Territory of the Mahabad Republic in Iran

Source: http://en.wikipedia.org/wiki/File:Location Republic of Kurdistan. png.

After the fall of the Mahabad Republic, Iranian Kurdish movement entered a period of silence since the outbreak of the Iran Islamic Revolution in 1979. Kurdish parties were suppressed and went underground under the severe suppression by King Pahlavi. The government systematically began to eliminate Kurdish tribal armed forces, and suppressed the tribes. Turkey and Iraq became the main regions of the Kurdish National Movement. The number of activists in the Kurdish national movement of Iran decreased. Kurdistan Democrat Party was in a difficult situation its leadership cadres and activities had largely diminished, many of them including Aziz Yusufi, escaped and went underground.

In the 1950s, government control began to loosen, the Kurdistan Democratic Party increased its activities during 1951-1953 and began to work closely with the Communist Party of Iran (Tudeh). Pahlavi allowed Kurdish radio broadcasting, although the number of broadcasting hours and programs were limited. The government also relaxed the wearing of Kurdish national clothing, use of Kurdish language, and tribe people were allowed to carry weapons. The Iranian government proudly insisted that there was no Kurdish issue in Iran. It was also a period when democratically elected reform figure Mosaddegh became the prime minister of Iran.

In the early 1950s, in Iran it was an era of surging nationalism characterized by targeting Monarchic regime and anti-Western, anti-colonial psychology. The most prominent event in these days was the movement of oil nationalization led by Mosaddegh, who represented the national bourgeoisie. Mosaddegh aimed to transform Iran from a monarchy to a constitutional monarchy, and achieve political liberalization, equality of all citizens regardless of their ethnic or linguistic origins. Although the policies of Mosaddegh did not meet the expectations of the Kurds, his program was far more advanced than the King of Pahlavi. Consequently, the Mosaddegh government received the support of the Kurds. In August 13, 1953, Iran held a referendum, and decided limiting the power of the king, and implementation of constitutional monarchy. The Kurds had actively supported Mosaddegh in the referendum. Unfortunately, on August 15, 1953, Mosaddegh government was overthrown in a coup d'état aided by the CIA and Secret Intelligence Service of the UK supported by their respective governments. King Pahlavi enforced its dictatorship. In 1956, a Kurdish uprising occurred near Kermanshah but was soon suppressed.

In 1958, Mullah Mustafa returned back to Iraq, from exile, which had alarmed the Iranian government. The deputy prime minister of the Iranian government, Bakhtiar said: "The situation in Kurdistan is highly volatile and the Iranian government is closely following the acts of Mullah Mustafa Barzani. He visited Cairo and is currently in Baghdad, he will incite the Kurds with the support of the Soviet Union", which reflected the fear of surging national movement in Iran, by the Iranian government.[20]

20   Massoud Barzani, Mustafa Barzani and the Kurdish Liberation Movement, p. 183.

Massoud Barzani, commented on this situation: "Iranian media attacked Iraq as the center of anti-Iranian activities after Mullah Mustafa was invited back to Iraq and accused the Iraqi government for allowing Kurdish mullahs returning home."[21]

During this period, the Kurdistan Democratic Party of Iran was greatly influenced by Mullah Mustafa Barzani, whose new leaders, Abdallah Ishaqi, Ahmad Tawfiq was close to Mullah Mustafa. Consequently Democratic Party of Iran followed the political line of Iraq's Kurdistan Democratic Party and gave up its former left leaning political line, even criticized the policies and line of former leader Qazi Mohammad. However, during the 1960s and 1970s, the Iraqi Kurdistan Democratic Party led by Mullah Mustafa Barzani, in its struggle against the Iraqi government began to cooperate with King Pahlavi and supported Iran, which changed the Kurdistan Democratic Party of Iran's attitude to Mullah Mustafa Barzani.

Up to 1966, the Kurdish Democratic Party of Iran had been providing economic and human support to the Iraqi Kurdistan Democratic Party. This was also tolerated by the Shah Pahlavi, which favored the weakening of Iraq. But in 1966, King Pahlavi decided that Iran would provide direct support to the Iraqi Kurdistan Democratic Party. In return, he demanded that Mullah Mustafa Barzani should help him to suppress the Iranian Kurdish Democratic Party. Accordingly Mullah Mustafa urged the Kurds in Iran to stop fighting against the Pahlavi dynasty, emphasizing the priority of interests of the Iraqi Kurdish struggle, Iranian Kurdish struggle should be subordinated to the former. Mullah Mustafa began to expel the Iranian Kurdish fighters who fought in his ranks in Iraq and also arrested more than 40 Iranian Kurds who had fled to Iraq and handed them to the Iranian government. Mullah Mustafa's approach aroused strong dissatisfaction among Iranian Kurds, many Iranian Kurds returned to Iran, stopped supporting the Iraqi Kurds, and continued their struggle against the Pahlavi dynasty. In March 1975, Iran signed the "Algiers Agreement", with Iraq government after which Iran suspended supporting of Mullah Mustafa. Faced with increasing Iraq pressure about 90,000 Kurds fled into Iran as refugees, thus the dependence on Iran had further deepened, and finally Mullah Mustafa was forced to leave for the United States.

During this period, King Pahlavi continued to give a controlled support for Iraqi Kurds, while continued his harsh repressive policies on the Kurdish national movement of Iran. Briefly to say, Iran's Kurdish movement was greatly influence by the Iraqi Kurdish movement, but the two sides maintained a certain distance. Differences were caused by Iranian government's cooperation with the Iraqi Kurds and secondly Iranian Kurdish movement's

---

21   Ibid., pp. 183-184.

cautious attitude against traditional tribal leaders who still led the National movement in Iraq, given that the leadership of the Iranian Kurdish movement was mostly composed of Kurdish urban elite.

In January 1963, Iran's King announced the "white revolution", which included land reform, sale of some state-owned factories to finance this land reform, enfranchisement of women, nationalization of forests and pastures, formation of a literacy corps, and institution of profit sharing schemes for workers in industry, establishment of a state department representing, all aimed especially to weaken those classes that supported the traditional system. In 1966, Pahlavi further pushed the land reform. These drastic changes have had a major impact on the traditional Kurdish society. A large number of Kurds left villages to enter the urban life, tribal property increasingly disintegrated. Simultaneous with the reforms Kurdish national consciousness grew. In this period, the Kurdistan Democratic Party was rapidly changed from a small-scale underground party to a popular party with a certain mass base. In 1967, the radical left youth faction of the Party founded the Iranian Kurdistan Democratic Revolutionary Committee, and declared their support for sporadic peasant uprisings against the National Police around Mahabad and Urumiya, Baneh and Sardasht. They condemned the practices of Mullah Mustafa Barzani and Abdullah but lacking a significant social base, this new leadership of the KDPI was quickly crushed: even though the KDPI's forces managed to inflict serious losses on the Iranian army,

After 18 months of armed fighting, they were finally exterminated by the government forces, and 40 leaders of the Kurdish rebel armed forces were arrested and executed. Against this backdrop, in June 1971, the third conference of the Iranian KDP was held in Koye in Iraqi Kurdistan. During this conference Dr. Abdul Rahman Ghassemlou was elected as the General Secretary of the party, remaining in this post until he was assassinated in Vienna.[22]

Dr. Abdul Rahman Ghassemlou developed and supported the armed struggle against the Pahlavi regime, saying that the party's armed struggle was "an inevitability imposed by the Pahlavi dictatorship and that there was no room for democracy under the Pahlavi regime nor for the oppressed peoples' national rights". He also put forward the policy "Democracy for Iran and Autonomy for Kurdistan" democracy, Kurdistan autonomy". In this period the KDPI, the Iranian Communist Party and the Islamic opposition

---

22   Abdul al-Rahman Ghassemlou (1930-1989)was born in December 22, 1930 in a rich feudal tribe in the Urmiya region of western Azerbaijan. He studied in France and Czechoslovakia and was influenced by Communist ideas. In 1952, he returned to Iranian Kurdistan and devoted himself to the Kurdish national struggle. In 1971, he was elected as the General Secretary of the DPIK, in the third Congress. On July 13, 1989, he was assassinated. His main contribution was leading the DPIK to adopt the strategy and slogan of "Autonomy for Kurdistan and Democracy for the Whole Iran".

elements allied in the fight against the Pahlavi regime, but the Kurdish Democratic Party was relatively weaker in the coalition, and its revolutionary position bore several ambiguities.

In 1969, a group of left-wing Kurdish youth of students established a new Marxist Kurdish organization in Tehran called Komalah (Komełe), also known as KŞZK (Komełey Şorrişgêrrî Zehmetkêşanî Kurdistan) or its full name Komełey Şorrişgêrrî Zehmetkêşanî Kurdistanî Êran (Society of Revolutionary Toilers of Iranian Kurdistan).

Most of its members came from among urban Kurdish youth intellectuals. The organization also advocated the framework of a democratic Iran to achieve Kurdish autonomy, but chose the way of fighting similar to Turkey's PKK. Kak Foad, the leader of the Party spent most of the times studying different Marxist books and learning himself about the leftist ideas. Foad started to organize top secret meetings with the Kurdish students and started to discuss communism. He saw feudalism and tribalism of the Kurdish social existence as the main obstacles in achieving national self-determination and formulated many progressive fighting goals, including raising the status of Kurdish women, liberating women from the patriarchal oppression. Komalah also criticized Kurdish nationalism as narrow nationalism which should be surpassed. In the late 1970s, Kurdistan Democratic Party of Iran and Komalah have been the two main Kurdish political parties, which belong to secularist left-wing nationalist organizations, they cooperated at times and confronted each other, too.

Compared with the Kurdistan Democratic Party of Iran, Komalah's policies were more flexible, and creative, but also radical in organizational style. While the Kurdistan Democratic Party of Iran was heavily dependent on the Kurdish tribal elite and its resource network, the Komalah's policies emphasized the mobilization of the peasants and the urban proletariat. Komalah led underground activities, instead of open activities, till the Pahlavi dynasty was overthrown in 1978 Slemani was the main stronghold of Komalah, in turn the Iranian Kurdistan Democratic Party was mainly based in Mahabad as the center of its activity.

During the 1960s and 1970s, the Iranian economy grew rapidly due to large increases in its oil revenues. At the same time, with the strong support of the United States, Iran's military strength has increased greatly and the central government's ability to control and suppress the Kurdish national movement was greatly enhanced. Despite its arduous efforts to mobilize and publicize the Kurdish national movement has faced arrests, imprisonments or executions in the face of strong government repression. Iran's Savak, the world's one of the most ruthless and efficient intelligence agency, played an important role in the suppression of the Kurdish national movement.

Besides suppression policies, the Iran government has also implemented those policies targeting to co-opt a part of the Kurds into the governing power and offered some favors to coach them. Consequently some Kurdish tribal leaders assumed important positions in the government, were appointed as cabinet ministers, became deputies in the national assembly of Iran. As a middleman between King Pahlavi and Mullah Mustafa Barzani, the Iranian official responsible for assisting the Iraqi Kurdistan Democratic Party, General Mansurpur, was also a Kurdish figure.[23]

However, the number of senior Kurdish officials in the government was small and their proportion was quite lesser when compared with the Azerbaijanis. Another favor by the government was that, those Kurdish leaders who cooperated with the government was excluded from losing their landed property, i.e. land reform did not effect them, and their landed property was not allocated to the peasants. Overall, the King of Pahlavi's measures were quite effective, and the Kurdish national movement remained at a low ebb during this period.

At the end of the 1970s, Iran's domestic politics once again stirred up and the anti-regime discontent greatly increased. King Pahlavi's promises of improving people's livelihood was not realized, at the same time, nation-wide opposition grew against the mode of authoritarian governance, against corruption, economic deterioration and pro-US diplomacy. In 1978, a series of large-scale anti-regime protests targeting Pahlavi swept across the country, and the government's brutal repression of the protests not only was largely condemned at home and abroad, but also aroused a more intense anti-government movement. In January 16, 1979, faced with an army mutiny and violent demonstrations against his rule, Mohammad Reza Shah Pahlavi, the leader of Iran since 1941, was forced to flee the country. Fourteen days later, the famous anti-regime Shi'ite cleric, Ayatollah Ruhollah Khomeini, the spiritual leader of the Islamic revolution, returned after 15 years of exile in France and took control of Iran.

Khomeini (1902-1989), also an Islamic jurist and politician had long been engaged in the struggle against King Pahlavi and led the revolution to victory.

After the revolution and the referendum, Khomeini became the supreme leader of the country, and put forward the principle of "Neither West Nor the East- Islamic Republic" thus established in Iran Islamic jurists theocratic rule which replaced the pro-Western monarchy with an anti-Western theocracy based on the concept of Guardianship of the Islamic Jurists (or velayat-e faqih).

---

23   Iranian Foreign Affairs Research Institute, The Rise and Fall of Pahlavi Dynasty—The Secret of the Former Iranian Intelligence Director", Translated by Li Yuqi, Xinhua Publishing House, 2009, p. 328.

On February 13, a provisional revolutionary government, led by the opposition leader Mehdi Bazargan was set up, marking the end of Pahlavi dynasty. On April 1, In 1979 March, Iran voted by national referendum to become an Islamic Republic on April 1, 1979, and to approved a new theocratic-republican constitution whereby Khomeini became Supreme Leader of the country, in December 1979.

On 2-3 December 1979, the constitution of Islamic Republic of Iran was ratified by referendum. In this referendum 99.5% of Iranian voters approved the constitution and in May 1980, the first parliamentary elections were held after the revolution.

4.3 The Kurdish Issue in the Period of Iran Islamic Republic

During the upheaval of 1977 to 1979, in Iran and the Islamic revolution provided an opportunity for Kurdish national movement. Before the outbreak of the Islamic revolution, Kurdish nationalist organizations have further developed, in addition to the Kurdistan Democratic Party of Iran, there were the Revolutionary Organization of Toilers of Kurdistan, better known as Komala, and people's guerrillas, the people's Mujaheddin was fighting against the regime. Among the more active ones were the Fedaiyan-e Khalq and the Mojahedin-e Khalq (people's Mujaheddin). Most of these organizations were left-wing organizations, which supported peasant movements and made clandestine activities in the Kurdish region. They carried out socialist, nationalist and anti-king, anti-Western agitation and propaganda. In the early months of 1979, the more radical groups, the Komala and the Fedais, initiated peasant organizations. Peasants' Councils were established, and some attempts were made to distribute land among peasants around the Sanandaj and Marivan areas.

Kurds actively supported the anti-Pahlavi revolution, in which the Kurdish Democratic Party and other left-wing parties were active and played a significant role in overthrowing the Pahlavi dynasty. Only a small number of Kurdish tribal leaders who were favored by the King have opposed the revolution. Shortly after the outbreak of the revolution, Kurdish parties jointly established the Council of Kurdish People around Shaykh Izzeddin Hosseini. Hosseini joined the KDPI and other leftist organizations in their struggle against the Islamic Republic, and enjoyed a great deal of support, not only from political organizations and the tribal leadership but also, perhaps more importantly, from the Kurdish people generally.[24]

---

24 Shaykh Izzeddin Hosseini, was born in 1921. He was Kurdish Sunni leader with liberal and leftist ideas. After the failure of Kurdish uprising led by him, he fled to Sweden.

For some time, the Council negotiated on behalf of the Kurds with the central government. In January 1979, the Kurds captured military garrisons and gendarmerie outposts, and seized a considerable quantity of weapons. The revolutionary government in Tehran, which came to power in February, gave promises of support to, and respect for, the rights of minorities, which was naturally encouraging for the Kurds. In March 1979, after thirty years of underground activities, the KDPI presented the party's programme for Kurdish autonomy in Iran at a press conference. The eight points of the plan presented by the KDPI were as follows: 1. The boundaries of Kurdistan would be determined by the Kurdish people and would take into consideration historical, economic, and geographical conditions. 2. On matters of defense, foreign affairs and long-term economic planning, Kurdistan would abide by the decisions of the central government. The Central Bank of Iran would control the currency. 3. There would be a Kurdish parliament, whose members would be popularly elected. This would be the highest legislative power in the province. 4. All government departments in the province would be run locally rather than from the capital. 5. There would be a people's army, but the police and gendarmerie would be abolished and replaced by a national guard. 6. Kurdish would be the official language of the provincial government and would be taught in all schools. Persian would also continue to be an official language. 7. All ethnic minorities in Kurdistan would enjoy equal rights and would be allowed to use their own languages and observe their own traditions. 8. Freedom of speech and of the press, rights of association, and trade-union activities would be guaranteed. The Kurdish people would have the right to travel freely and choose their own occupation.[25]

If we analyze the content of the demands, the Kurdistan Democratic Party's main aspirations was still to achieve Kurdish autonomy, the implementation of democracy and equality. In addition, a new Kurdish party was established after the Islamic revolution: the Revolutionary Khabat Organization of the Iranian Kurdistan, usually called Khabat (Kurdish for "struggle") was a Kurdish nationalist opposition group in Iran which sought autonomy for Iranian Kurdistan and which still exists.

On August 27, 1980, Khabat announced the establishment of the Organization of the Nationalistic and Islamic Khabat of the Iranian Kurdistan. The party decaled: Organization Khabats' goal for Iranian Kurdistan is Self-determination and a secular democratic system in Iran. Organization Khabat is active for:

Emancipation of women in society without any discrimination; freedom for every religion and ideologies; freedom of speech and mass media; Kurdish language should be allowed at school, university and in public

25   The Times, March, 4, 1979.

and administration as a first language; Integration of all Kurdish Territory in Iranian Kurdistan; governors should be elected by Kurdish people and represent interest of Kurdish Nation; the right of the peoples of Kurdistan to self-government; religion should not be implemented for discrimination of people; democratic education system; modern infrastructure; protection of poor people financially and socially; motivate sociality for modernization of cultural attitude.[26]

The Kurds have taken an active part in the revolution, hoping to gain autonomy within the framework of the new Iran and to guarantee the Sunni Kurds' religious rights. The Kurdish demands for autonomy, and the reaction from the Islamic revolutionary camp was a complex issue. Initially, since the old regime was not yet fully suppressed and the new Islamic regime was not consolidated, during the early days after the victory of the revolution, the new government responded positively to Kurdish demands

In the meantime, the new government and the Kurds were negotiating. It was agreed that the central government would keep control over foreign policy, finance, defense, and the army. The argument with the government was over control of domestic policies and regional administration, which the Kurds felt should be left to them. However, the situation did not develop as many who had fought for the revolution had hoped. The political atmosphere was changing rapidly, and the regime curtailed democratic activities every day. It soon became clear that the government had no intention of granting autonomy to any ethnic group, and least of all to the Kurds.

Throughout the spring and summer of 1979 there were frequent clashes between the Kurds and the government forces. In August 1979 the Ayatollah Khomeini declared a holy war against the Kurds, banned all the Kurdish political organizations, cancelled Ghassemlou's membership of the Assembly of Experts and denounced Ghassemlou and Sheikh Izzeddin Hosseini as enemies of the Islamic Republic. The KDPI was called the "party of Satan". In addition to the army, a large number of pasdars (revolutionary guards) and armed hezbollahis were dispatched to the area. Helicopter gunships, Phantom jets, tanks and artillery were used to attack the towns and villages of Kurdistan. The Kurds entered the war with the weapons they had confiscated at the beginning of the revolution. The crushing of the Kurdish rebellion caused bloody scenes in many of the towns and villages of Kurdistan (Sanandaj, Naghadeh, Paveh, Marivan and Saqqiz). The revolutionary trials were held by Khalkhal the notorious Chief of Justice and scores of people were executed at the same time. It is generally believed that most of the trials did not last more than a few minutes, and that the majority of those executed were ordinary Kurds rather than peshmerges. Kurdish towns fell

26 "Khabat", http://en.wikipedia.org/wiki/Khabat.

into the hands of the government forces, but Kurdish fighters managed to keep control of the countryside. To this day, Kurdish forces still enjoyed the same degree of control and mobility.

In August 1979, the interim government announced the prohibition of the KDPI activities, the two sides continued the armed conflicts.

After bitter fighting, the government in Tehran called for a ceasefire on 2 November 1979, and a group of delegates was sent to Kurdistan for negotiations. The call for talks was welcomed by Kurdish leaders. Shaykh Izzeddin Hosseini presented the programme for Kurdish autonomy. But the Islamic government was not prepared to allow more than a limited cultural autonomy, and it refused in principle to regard the Kurds as anything other than a religious minority. This was related to Khomeini's idea of the Islamic nation and, on the other hand, Khomeini was worrisome about the multi-ethnicity of Iran, he thought that if Kurds were given autonomy other ethnic-nations would follow the suit. On December 17, 1979, Khomeini made a speech in Tehran radio station, and openly expressed opposition to the Kurdish autonomy, put forward the concept of the Islamic nation and Muslim solidarity.

Further, the government demanded full disarmament of the Kurdish region as a first condition for any solution. This alone was enough for the Kurds to abandon any hopes of an agreement, since it would have meant giving up the crucial and sole instrument of self-defense. The ceasefire failed and another round of fighting began. The cycle of calls for negotiations and resumption of fighting became a feature of this period, and continued to be so for two years.

This was related to Khomeini's idea of the Islamic nation and, on the other hand, Khomeini was worrisome about the multi-ethnicity of Iran, he thought that if Kurds were given autonomy other ethnic-nations would follow the suit. Khomeini evaluated the concept of ethnic minority contrary to the Islamic doctrines. He also accused those who do not wish Muslim countries to be united in creating the issue of nationalism among minorities. His views were shared by many in the clerical leadership

On December 17, 1979, Khomeini made a speech in Tehran radio station, and openly expressed opposition to the Kurdish autonomy, again put forward the concept of the Islamic nation (Umma) and Muslim solidarity. He declared: "Sometimes the word minorities is used to refer to people such as the Kurds, Lurs, Turks, Persians, Baluchis, and such. These people should not be called minorities, because this term assumes that there is a difference between these brothers. There is no such difference in Islam. There is no difference between Muslims who speak different languages, for instance, the Arabs or the Persians. it is very possible that such problems is that those who do not want Muslim countries to be united... They create the issues of nationalism, pan-Iranism, pan-Turkism, and such isms, which are contrary to doctrines of Islam. Their plan is to destroy Islam and Islamic philosophy."

After the clerics began to monopolize the ruling power, and started an increasingly tough Kurdish policy. This situation was similar to the Turkish national independence: during the war Mustafa Kemal had promised autonomy to Kurds but after the war was over and he consolidated his ruling power, and no more needed the Kurdish support, the Kurds were attacked.

The Kurdish leadership has repeatedly refuted the accusations that the Kurds were fighting for independence, emphasizing the desire to achieve Kurdish autonomy within a democratic new Iranian framework, with central government's control over defense, over foreign relations and the central financial management.

In the spring of 1979, the Kurdish armed forces and government engaged in armed conflicts from time to time. On March 21, Khomeini sent air forces and the Revolutionary Guards to attack the Kurdish city of Sanandaj. The government chose to attack the day before the Kurdish New Year (Newroz) on March 22, which made many Kurds feel that the Islamic government's attitude toward the Kurds could be more cruel than that of the Pahlavi dynasty.[27]

During the March referendum to decide on the name of the Republic, 85 to 90% of Iranian Kurds have resisted to participate the referendum. On August 19, 1979, Khomeini announced jihad (war) against the Kurds, announced the prohibition of all Kurdish political organizations, the banning of the Kurdistan Democratic Party and cancelled Ghassemlou's membership of the Assembly of Experts and denounced Ghassemlou and Sheikh Izzeddin Hosseini as enemies of the Islamic Republic. The KDP-Iran was labeled as the party of Satans. In addition to the army, a large number of pasdars (revolutionary guards) and armed hezbollahi fighters were dispatched to the Kurdish region. Helicopter gunships, Phantom jets, tanks and artillery were used to attack the towns and villages of Kurdistan.

The attack caused huge casualties, and a large number of Kurdish villages were destroyed, more than 10,000 people were killed, thousands of Kurds were sentenced to death by the Revolutionary Courts.[28]

---

27 Amir Hassanpour, Personal Correspondence, Dec. 9, 2001, Toronto.
28 Christopher De Bellaigue, In the Rose Garden of the Martyrs: A Memoir of Iran, Harper Books, 2005, p. 60.

The revolutionary trials were held by Khalkhali (1926-2003) the notorious Chief Justice and scores of people were executed at the same time. It was reported that most of the trials did not last more than a few minutes, and that the majority of those executed were ordinary Kurds rather than peshmerges. Kurdish towns fell into the hands of the government forces, but Kurdish fighters retreated from the city to the countryside to continue guerrilla warfare.

After bitter fighting, the government in Tehran called for a ceasefire on 2 November 1979, and a group of government delegates were sent to Kurdistan for negotiations. The call for negotiations was welcomed by the Kurdish leaders. During the talks Shaykh Izzeddin Hosseini advocated the programme for Kurdish autonomy. But the Islamic government was not prepared to allow more than a limited cultural autonomy, and regarded Kurds no more than a religious minority. Further, it demanded full disarmament of the Kurdish region as the first condition for any solution. This alone was enough for the Kurds to abandon any hopes for an agreement, and for Kurds any surrender would have meant giving up all facilities of self-defense. Consequently, this offer by the government was rejected and armed fights continued.

In November 1979, the Assembly of (clerical) Experts approved the Islamic constitution. The new constitution disappointed the minorities of Iran. In the original draft, there had been articles guaranteeing certain rights for the minorities. Article 5 of the initial draft constitution stated that "All people in the Islamic Republic of Iran....Persians, Turks, Kurds, Arabs, Baluchis, Turcomans, and others, will completely enjoy equal rights." Article 21 of the initial draft had stipulated: "The common language and script of the Iran Republic is Persian. All official texts and correspondence must be in this language and script and also free use of local languages is legitim."

But in the finally approved version of the Iran constitution, there was none of this limited concern for minority rights. All previous rhetoric related to the equality of the ethnic peoples was dropped; there was no guarantee mentioned for the religious rights of the Sunni people and as for the use of local languages, the constitution stated that local languages could be used in the press, in the mass media, and schools, but only alongside Persian, but school textbooks had to be in Persian. Thus the constitution clearly had no intention of responding to the ethnic aspirations of the minority peoples.

Soon, KDP-I boycotted the referendum for the Constitution, which further intensified the conflicts. On January 1980, the government offered another cease-fire. Khomeini agreed to add one amendment to the Constitution guaranteeing the rights of the Sunnis in the regions where they are in the majority. But this amendment was never realized and the cease-fire ended soon. The government continued to adopt military attacks to suppress the Kurdish guerrillas. On April 30, 1980, both sides reached an agreement for a cease-fire.

The Iranian President Abul Hassan Bani-Sadr announced in a statement that the Kurdistan Democratic Party's six-point plan was approved by the President. Unfortunately, the liberal democratic tendency of Abul Hassan Bani-Sadr was soon rejected by Khomeini and Abul Hassan Bani-Sadr was forced to resign. Thus the ceasefire has not been achieved.[29]

In September 1980, after the Iraqi invasion of Iran, the Iran-Iraq war broke out. During the war, Iran's Kurdistan region became an important battlefield, Kurdish villages and towns were shelled by both Iran and Iraq forces. The Iran-Iraq war seemed to be an opportunity for the Kurds within warring countries, but in reality their situation worsened and the Kurds became the tools of the warring sides. Iranian Kurds believed and aimed to use the opportunity to recover their losses. After the outbreak of the war, initially Kurdistan Democratic Party of Iran and other opposition parties have expressed their willingness to support the war against the invasion of Iraq, hoping to exchange their support for Kurdish autonomy. The Iranian authorities rejected the KDP-I's proposal, besides massively attacked Iran's Kurdistan region to prevent the Iraqis to attack north, and took full control of the Kurdish region. By 1983, all border areas were occupied and many KDP-I fighters and Kurdish guerrillas fell into the hands of the Iranian army.

In 1984, after a large-scale attack by the Irani government forces, remaining KDP-I leaders and its fighters rushed into the Iraqi territory. These Iranian Kurdish forces began to cooperate with the Iraqi government, they received weapons and material assistance. The Iraqi government was also willing to use the Iranian Kurds with two goals, to better combat the Iranian army, and to avoid Iran strike a deal with the Kurdistan Democratic Party of Iraq. Throughout the violent war, both states supported each other's Kurdish rebels. It is worth mentioning that the Iraqi Kurdish Patriotic Alliance supported the Kurdistan Democratic Party of Iran. In November 1983, when the Iraqi Kurdish Patriotic Union began negotiations with the Iraqi government, the General Secretary of the Kurdistan Democratic Party of Iran acted as a mediator. Unlike the Iraqi Kurdistan Democratic Party, the Kurdish Democratic Party of Iran maintained a distance from the KDP-Iraq, although its collaborated with the Iraqi government. During this period, despite heavy military pressure and heavy losses, the Iranian government refused to make concessions on the issue of Kurdish autonomy and

29   The first President of Islamic Republic of Iran. He was elected on February 25, 1980, and was forced to leave the office on June 22, 1981.

continued to suppress the Kurdish national movement. At the same time, in order to deal with the Kurdish Peshmerges, the Iranian government had managed to recruit some Kurds from the Shia Kurdish tribes, and formed "Islamic Peshmerges", similar to the Turkey's village guards or "Jash" fighters of Iraq. When the Iranian army attacked Kurdish region in 1982, the army helped by Shi'ite "Islamic Peshmerges" in Kermanshah.

While fighting against the Irani government, there were also some conflicts and contradictions within the Kurds. First, in the winter of 1981, the Kurdistan Democratic Party of Iran joined the National Council of Resistance of Iran (NCRI) which was based in Paris.[30]

This Council (NCRI) was a coalition against the Iran's Islamic regime, and included the Mujahideen People's Organization, (initially a left-wing student organization founded on September 5, 1965). Mujahideen People's Organization had members both from among the Iranians, and Kurds. Soon the Council was dominated by the MKO.[31]

In 1983, the KDP-Iran and the Council in Paris signed a cooperation agreement to fight for the autonomy of Iranian Kurdistan. But the cooperation between the two sides did not last long. In the summer of 1984, the KDP-Iran showed interest in negotiations with the Iranian government, but the negotiations did not make any progress, the government once again refused to discuss the issue of Kurdish autonomy. KDP-Iran's move angered the Mujahideen People's Organization, contradictions grew and the KDP-Iran withdrew from the Council. Second, the conflict between the Kurdistan Democratic Party-Iran and the more radical Komalah intensified. And Komalah, was reorganized in 1983, proclaiming itself to be part of the Communist Party of Iran, but it still retained its former name. The Komala

---

30   NCRI was anti-government political organization set up in Paris in 1981. whose main members were the Mujahedeen People's Organization (MKO), the Iranian Kurdish Democratic Party, the National Democratic Front (NDF) and so on. The organization is still present, but it is dominated by the MKO. MKO is regarded as a terrorist organization by Iran.

31   It was an Left Wing students' organization set up on September 5, 1965. Its members included Iranians, and Kurds. It was against Pahlavi Dynasty originally and joined in the Revolutionof1979. After the revolution, opposed the Khomeini's theocratic regime. It enacted vicious terrorist attacks in Iran. Under the pressure of the government, this organization was forced to move to Iraq and France. In 2001, it declared to abandon violence. This organization had been protected and supported by Saddam government and developed good relationship with the U.S and the western forces. It had passed important classified information of Iran to the US, especially its nuclear plans. After the II. Gulf War in 2003, US declined the Iranian request of extraditing the members of this organization. Currently, there are still 3.500 members in this organization in Iraq, but their conditions are worsening. Iran accuses this organization as a terrorist organization being in the service of US and Israel. US and Iran both regarded it as a terrorist organization and recently the EU also accepted it as a terrorist organization, later it was removed from the list of terrorist organizations in 2009.

criticized the Kurdistan Democratic Party of Iran for joining the National Council of Resistance (NCRI).

Komala also criticized the Kurdistan Democratic Party of Iran for seeking negotiations with the Iran government, and stressed the need to continue the armed struggle without any compromise. In the fall of 1985, hundreds of people died as a result of bloody clashes between these two opposition parties over territorial and power issues. Thirdly, since Kurdistan Democratic Party of Iran leader Abdul Rahman Ghassemlou was insistent to stop the guerrilla war, and sought to solve the issuethrough negotiations, a split has occurred in the KDP-Iran.

In April 1988, in the 8th Congress of the KDP-Iran, Ghassemlou's leadership status was faced with a strong challenge, who advocated his insistent position to disarm the party. The 15 hardliner leaders who advocated continuing the armed struggle, included one member from the Politburo- Jalil Gadani-, eight members of the Central Committee, four of the eight representatives, decided to establish the Iranian Kurdistan Democratic Party– Revolutionary Leadership.

The new organization issued a ten-point statement, which criticized Ghassemlou and his team for approaching the Western powers, and distancing from the socialist camp, and for negotiating with the Iranian government.

After the Iran-Iraq war ended, some Kurdish guerrillas continued to carry out armed struggle, but the scale was limited, and did not pose a serious threat for the government. KDP-Iran repeatedly declared that the guerrilla war would not win, and the only alternative would be holding negotiations with the government. But within the party was a small opposition, which argued that if the Iranian Islamic regime does not allow autonomy, it would be necessary to split up from Iran. Between December 1988 and January 1989, representatives of the Government of Iran and and KDP-Iran's leadership—Ghassemlou and others—held secret negotiations in Geneva. On July 13, 1989, Ghassemlou and two other Kurdish representatives were assassinated in Vienna when they were preparing for further negotiations with the representatives of the Government of Iran. The Kurds accused the Iranian government. Austrian police also pointed fingers at the Iranian agents. The Iranian government denied and rejected the request of the Austrian police for extradition of suspects.The assassination of Ghassemlou gave a heavy blow to the Iranian Kurdish Democratic Party as well as the Kurdish national movement. On 19 July 1989, Sadegh Sharafkandi took over the General Secretary post, and declared that the party did not believe in the military struggle line and would continue to seek for a political solution. On July 20, 1989, at the funeral of Ghassemlou in Paris, one of the prominent party leaders Abdullah Hasanzadeh revealed some details of the assassination and introduced the Party's general policy prospects.[32]

At the same time, a senior leader of the Party of Revolutionary Toilers of Iranian Kurdistan (Komalah Party) was assassinated in Larnaca, a port city in Cyprus, which severely damaged the organization and brought its activities to a halt in Iran.

In the 1990s, the Iranian Kurdish national movement basically did not achieve any victories, armed its guerrilla activities has basically ceased. The leadership of the Kurdistan Democratic Party, which advocated negotiations, was once again greatly damaged and the party was weakened. On September 17, 1992, Sadegh Sharafkandi general secretary of the party and other four leaders were assassinated in a hotel near Berlin. After Sadegh Sharafkandi was assassinated, the deputy general secretary Mustafa Hijri took over as the general secretary. According to the German court investigation, four suspects of the assassination were an Iranian, and three Lebanese citizens. The incident caused a tense relationship between Iran and European countries. On 10 April 1997, the German court issued an international arrest warrant for Farahiran, the Iranian intelligence minister, accussed him for ordering the assassination of Sharafkandi and other 4 leaders, the German court also condemned the Iranian leader Ayatollah Ali Khamenei and President Rafsanjani.[33]

In the 2003 elections, Kurdistan was the only province of Iran that did not give Rafsanjani a majority vote. Iran's Kurdistan Democratic Party's main stronghold was the Kurdistan region adjacent to the Turkish border centered around Mahbubad, while the Komalah Party's main stronghold was in the south, centered around Sanandaj and Saqqiz. In general, during the 1990s the 2 Kurdish parties tried to avoid confrontation with the government and did not engage in guerrilla warfare. They mainly engaged in political education and propaganda, organization and tried to develop their mass basis, membership. The reasons were, on the one hand, their power was not strong enough to confront the government; on the other hand, they believed that the guerrilla war would be responded by a strong government reaction, rather they developed the idea that political solution could be the only way out. Throughout the 1990s, the Iranian government has stationed about 200,000 troops in Kurdistan.[34]

---

32   At the funeral of Ghassemlou in Pere Lachaise Cemetery, Paris on July 20, 1989, Abdullah Hasanzadeh, leader of KDP-Iran revealed some details about the assassination and expounded on the future general direction of the party.

33   Yossi Melman, "Israel Failed to Prevent Germany Freeing Iranians", Haaretz, Apr. 2, 2008.

34   David McDowall, A Modern History of Kurds, I.B. Tauris, Third Revised Edition, 2004, p. 277.

After the Iranian Kurdish uprising was suppressed in 1991, the Iranian Kurdistan Democratic Party announced the cessation of the armed struggle against the Iranian government, defined its goal as winning Kurdish national rights under the framework of the Federal Republic of Iran, the party also stressed support for Kurdish national struggle in the other parts of Kurdistan.[35]

Following the Gulf War, the Kurdistan Democratic Party of Iran gradually shifted its bases to northern Iraq, soon after Iraqi Kurds won autonomy. After 1991, with the disintegration of the Soviet Union, Iran's Komala Party was deeply affected, negatively. Although its organization still existed and carried out some activities, its impact saw diminishing trend.

The Komalah's policy still advocates for Kurdish autonomy and its current general secretary is Abdullah Mohtadi. As of late 1990, Komala has stopped any armed activities within Iran. Abdullah Mohtadi however sent Komala fighters to the frontlines of Kirkuk in order to fight ISIS.

During the 1991 Gulf War, Iran received about 1.5 million Iraqi Kurdish refugees. Rafsanjani, Iran's president in this period, continued to covertly support the Turkish PKK fighters. Iran has repeatedly sent troops to northern Iraq, trying to manipulate Iraqi Kurds' regional affairs, and in the summer of 1996 Iran sent troops to support the Iraqi Kurdish Patriotic Alliance (PUK) against the Kurdistan Democratic Party of Iraq.

In August 1997, moderate reformist Khatami (1997-2005 the second Iranian President) won the presidential elections. In the presidential elections, the Kurdish opposition called for active participation in the elections. Khatami came to power, pursuing a relatively liberal policy, expanding civil liberties, and adopted a tolerant policy towards Kurds and other ethnic minorities.[36]

Khatami publicly praised the Kurdish cultural and historical splendor, and appointed the reformist Shiite Muslim Kurdish Abdullah Ramezanzadeh as the as the spokesman and consultant for the government.

---

35 "Brief Historical Background", www.kdppress.org/data/upimages/ brief-historical-background. pdf.
36 Born in August 23, 1954, politician, scholar and writer. In 1996, he received Ph.D. from Catholic University of Louvain, Belgium. His dissertation was on "The Domestic and External Systems of National Conflicts: Taking Iran as an Example. After, he taught in University of Tehran, participated a reformist organization, Islamic Iran Participation Front. During the Khatami period, he served as the spokesman and consultant for the government. Ramezanzadeh was arrested a few hours after the 2009 disputed presidential election. Shortly before his arrest, Ramezanzadeh released a historic speech posted on the opposition web sites and distributed throughout Iran and all over the world. He was in solitary confinement for 4 months and sentenced to 6 years jail. He is among the Iranian activists for the ethnic groups rights and the head of the Iranian Kurdish Reformists.

As governor of Iran Kurdistan region (1997-2001), the first Kurdish governor in Iran, Ramzanzadeh soon appointed a number of Sunni Kurds to senior regional government posts. President Khatami also appointed a number of Kurds as advisers to the president's office or cabinet members, allowed Kurdish publications to openly discuss national issues, Kurdish history and other issues. In February 1999, the PKK leader Ocalan was arrested in Turkey, the Iranian government allowed Iranian Kurds to hold protests for Ocalan, shouting anti-suppression, anti-American slogans. As a result, large-scale protests occurred in various Kurdish cities, such as Mahabad, Sanandaj and Urmia, demanding the release of Ocalan and finally protests turned against the Iranian government, causing clashes.

This incident not only demonstrated the trans-national, trans-teritorial and international character of the Kurdish issue, but also reflected the dissatisfaction of the Iranian Kurds towards Iran government's Kurdish policy. During Khatami's second term, his government included two Kurdish ministers, both of being Shiite Muslims. After the 6th parliamentary elections held in 2000, there was a significant increase in the number of Kurdish deputies. A group of 40 deputies from Kurdish provinces was formed in the Assembly. A Kurdish deputy demanded for more liberal Kurdish language policy in Sanandaj and Kurdish region and asked Khatami to appoint more Kurdish officials. Khatami's reform policies were strongly criticized by the conservatives of Iran. Conservative factions were fighting hard to stop him launched a series of counterattacks, Khatami was forced to concede.

In mid-February 2001, Iran held another parliament elections, 70 percent of qualified voters cast their ballots, and the country's women and younger voters—longtime supporters of reformist initiatives—turned out in record numbers. Reformist candidates routed the conservatives, claiming 70 percent of the seats. Conservative Rafsanjani finished a humiliating 30th in Tehran, barely capturing the last of the city's seats in Parliament. Kurdistan, resulting in 70% of the Kurds resisted the elections after this event, and riots occurred in a number of Kurdish cities.[37]

In April 2001, the results of the parliamentary elections in two Kurdish cities were declared void due to severe criticism from the conservative Council of Guardians, which also pointed fingers at Abdullah Ramezanzadeh, the governor of the Kurdish province. Ramezanzadeh was removed, and replaced by a non-Kurdish figure. In September 2001, the Kurdish deputies of the Iranian parliament vowed to resign so as to protest against the "media campaign discriminating Kurds and Sunnis", plus that 80% of the Kurdish population lived under poverty line, and Kurds were rarely admitted to well-established prestigious Iran universities.[38]

37   Michael M. Gunter, Historical Dictionary of the Kurds, p. 21.
38   "Ethnicity Affects Parliament", REF/RL, Oct. 15, 2001.

About half of Kurdish candidates were prohibited to participate in the parliamentary elections of February 2004. During the 2005 and 2009 presidential elections, majority of the Kurds resisted hard-line leader Ahmadinejad. In July 2009, the Kurds staged a region-wide strike to commemorate the 20th anniversary of the assassination of KDP-Iran's leader, Ghassemlou. As of September 2009, in the Iranian National Assembly there were only 18 Kurd deputies out of 290 members, thus they could not form an independent group.

In the period after the Iraq War in 2003, the establishment of the Kurdish Autonomous Region in Iraq made a significant impact on the Iranian Kurds, thus the circumstances of the Kurdish movement in Iran has changed, showing the following four prominent features.

First, the Kurdish Free Life Party (PJAK which is attached to PKK) launched armed activities, which caused clashes in the Kurdish region of Iran. Second, the Kurdish people's awareness of democracy and human rights has grown, and has led to protest, now and then. Kurdish human rights organizations and other non-governmental organizations became active in promoting the cause of human rights of Kurds, which irritated and alarmed the government. At the same time, struggle for human rights of Kurds has more and more attracted the global public. In recent years, many Iranian Kurdish human rights activists and international human rights organizations have increasingly targeted the Iranian government, criticized violations of human rights, while execution events related to Iran Kurdish political activists are more and more reported in the international media outlets and attract worldwide attention. In January 2006, the Kurdish United Front (KUF) was formed to struggle for Kurds legitimate rights and social injustice through peaceful means within the framework of the Iranian Constitution. The organization has more than 300 members, and Bahaeddin Adab, the founder of the KUF said: "Kurdish areas suffer from discrimination and [official] contempt in all political, economic, social and cultural areas of life. Kurds have no share in the distribution of power or regarding economic development; the four Kurdish provinces of our country are not developed and are deprived. They face limitations in their cultural activities, which is preventing cultural development."[39]

In September 2007, the Kurdish Democratic Party of Iran declared that about 300 Kurdish human rights activists were arrested and trialed for supporting the Kurdish political parties and that at least 200 people were imposed prison sentence of between 6 months and 20 years. According to the Amnesty International Report of 2008: "the Iranian government has long discriminated against the Kurds, and the political, economic, social and cultural rights of Iranian Kurds have been harshly suppressed."[40]

39   http://www.rferl.org/constent/article/1064384.thml.
40   http://www.amnesty.org/en/library/asset/MDE13/088/2008/en/d140767b-5e45-11dd-a592-c739f9b70de8/mde130882008eng.pdf.

The US Department of State and the International Human Rights Watch (HRW) have also criticized human rights infringements in Iran to criticize, which is an important support for Iranian Kurds.

On July 9, 2005, a Kurdish political activist, Shivan Qaderi, and two other Kurds were shot dead by security forces in Mahabad. In the next six weeks, riots and protests erupted in several cities in Kurdistan, and even spread to Balochistan. The Iranian government reacted with banning a number of Kurdish newspapers, and arrested a number of news reporters and editors.

Thirdly, after the Iraq war, and after Saddam Hussein regime was over-thrown, Kurdish region in northern Iraq became the main stronghold for the activities of Iranian Kurdish parties: Iran's Kurdistan Democratic Party, Komalah Party of Iran, Kurdish Revolutionary Freedom Organization, Kurdistan Free Life Party (PJAK) were among them. Also their training camps were located in the Iraqi Kurdish region. On 28, February 2012, the four parties met in Sulaymaniyah, called for an election boycott during the parliamentary elections of March 2012 in Iran, but the response of the boycott call in Kurdish region was unexpectedly low.

Fourth, as the conflict between Iran and the United States around the Iranian nuclear issue continues to shapen, Western support for the anti-government Kurdish parties have increased. In April 2006, Dennis Kucinich, a US congressman sent a letter to then-president George W. Bush in which he asserted that the US is likely to be supporting and coordinating with PJAK, since PJAK operates and is based in Iraqi territory under the control of the Kurdistan Regional Government. In November of the same year, journalist Seymour Hersh, writing in The New Yorker, supported this claim, further stating that the US military and Israel are giving this party, equipment, training, and targeting information in order to create internal pressures in Iran.[41]

Seymour Hersh also wrote an article criticizing the US government for supporting Iran's anti-government organizations such as the People's Mujahedin, Kurdistan Free Life Party, etc., and providing training to them and using them for information gathering on the ground, which all meant that US "targets Iran as the next war theater."[42]

41　According to the New York Times, the PJAK and PKK "appear to a large extent to be one and the same, and share the same goal: fighting campaigns to win new autonomy and rights for Kurds. The only difference is that the PJAK fights in Iran, and PKK fights in Turkey. They share leadership, logistics and allegiance to Abdullah Ocalan, the PKK leader currently imprisoned in Turkey.

42　Seymour M. Hersh, "The Next Act", The New Yorker, Nov. 20, 2006, http://www.newyorker.com/fact/content/articles/061127fa_fact.

In August 2007, the leaders of the Kurdistan Free Life Party visited the United States and soon met with US government officials. At the end of 2006, the KDP-Iran was split, the majority led by Mustafa Moloudi and some senior leaders, such as Abdullah Hassanzadeh, left the party and set up a new party the KDP-I.[43]

In 2008 September, Mustafa Hijri was reelected to the position of General Secretary in the 14th Congress of PDKI held in 14th Congress of the PDK Iran called for the implementation of federalism, and autonomous Kurdish region in Iran. He stressed: "This federalism should be based on geographical and ethnic criteria, this is the only way to resolve the frustration among various ethnic groups of Iran." Mustafa Hijri also commented that "the Kurds are ready to live in peace with the Azerbaijani people in northwestern Iran".[44]

Currently, the Mustafa Moloudi led Kurdish Democratic Party of Iran has its headquarter and is active in the Sulaymaniyah region of northern Iraq. On the other side the Mustafa Hijri led Iranian Kurdistan Democratic Party and the Komalah Party continue to maintain their armed forces, but no they longer carry out armed struggle. They are actively developing relations with the United States, with the hope of getting the US support, while United States fights to overthrow the Iranian regime. In 2006, senior leaders of the two parties, including Mustafa Hijri, visited the US and met with the senior officials of the US State Department and intelligence agencies. Mustafa Hijri expressed his willingness to accept US financial support, but opposed the use of force against the government and argued: "it would bring about many negative consequences for Kurds." On the other side Komala declared that it neither opposed nor supported a possible US military attack against Iran.

The emergence of Kurdish Free Life Party and its favor for armed struggle was a new phenomenon of this period. On March 25, 2004, the Kurdish Free Life Party was established and held its first party congress. The organization claims to be socialist, and aims to overthrow theocratic government through armed struggle, establish a democratic federal state and regional autonomy in Iran for Kurds, Baluchis, Azerbaijanis and Arabs within a federal framework. The leader is Abdul Rahman Haji Ahmadi, a former member of the Turkish PKK, who now lives in Europe. The organization claims to have 3,000 members, 40% of whom are women. The name of the armed group is

43   The Kurdistan Democratic Party (or KDP-Iran, is a Kurdish political party in Iranian Kurdistan, which seeks the attainment of Kurdish national rights within a democratic federal republic of Iran. The party split in 2006 from the Democratic Party of Iranian Kurdistan. The party was accepted a full member of the Socialist International at its November 2015 Council meeting in Luanda, Angola.
44   "Member Persective: Mustafa Hijri", UNPO, June 2010.

the "East Kurdistan Defense Force" and the women's fighting organization is named as armed with the name Yerjerika((Hêzên Parastina Jinê, in short HPJ),. The leader of HPJ is Gulistan Dogan, and it has many activists across Iran. Many experts see this Party as a branch of the Kurdish Workers' Party (PKK) in Iran. It is based mainly in northern Iraq near the Iranian border at the south hills of the Candil and the PKK is mainly based in at the west hills. The party has a common leadership with the PKK, they share logistics systems such as hospitals, and loyal Ocalan. Its leadership and organizational structure are: party congress, party chairman, leadership committee (composed of 7 leaders), the General Coordination Committee, and leads some mass organizations such as the East Kurdistan Youth Federation, East Kurdistan Women's Federation (YJRK), Federation of Democratic Press, and the Political and Diplomatic Commission. Kurdish Free Life Party has been classified as a terrorist organization by Iran, Turkey, the United States, European Union and NATO and some other countries and international organizations. Since its inception, the organization adopted guerrilla tactics similar to PKK, penetrates Iran territory to attack Iranian army and police forces.

During this period, in 2005, Iran's hard-line conservative leader president, Ahmadinejad is said to be involved in the assassination of the General Secretary Kurdistan Democratic Party-Iran. Support by the Kurds for Ahmadinejad is certainly lesser compared to reformist leader Khatami. In the 2005 and 2009 presidential elections, many Kurds boycotted. In the second round of presidential elections in June 2005, Kurdish voter turnout was only 25%, while the general voter turnout was 60%. From the outset of his tenure, Ahmadinejad did not make any visible effort to support Kurdish demands for representation and quickly rejected Kurdish appeals to place qualified Kurds in his new administration.

Summary

As we evaluate the demands of the Iranian Kurdish movement, the realization of regional autonomy is its main goal, independent state is not highlighted in its agenda. As to the means of realization, most of the Iranian Kurdish parties have shifted from armed struggle to peaceful settlement. Strictly speaking, the Kurdish issue in Iran mainly acute among a small number of intellectuals who pursue national autonomy and who struggle for the enhancing of national rights, i.e. the national autonomy is not deeply rooted in the Kurdish people across the country. Comparatively, the scale and intensity of the struggle, lags behind Turkey and Iraq. The establishment of the Kurdistan Mahabad Republic in 1946 was the culmination of the development of Kurdish nationalism in Iran, but its geographical scope was limited to the narrow region of Mahabad, and was essentially an autonomous government. In general, the Iranian Kurdish national movement and anti-government armed activities did not ascend to the level of being a major trend, nor posed a significant threat to the central government.

The central government certainly does not favour the Kurdish autonomy, this applies also for Azerbaijanis, Arabs, Baluchis and other ethnic minorities, that means it policies towards Kurdish nationalism is exceptional. Looking from the aspect of Iran's multi-ethnic identity tradition, if the Kurds were allowed for self-government, other national minorities will follow the suit, and consequently Iran will probably face a crisis of national disintegration.

Iranian Kurds have long relied on external forces. The first was the Soviet Union, then they turned to Iraq, but have been betrayed in both cases facing tragic consequences. Now the Kurds seem to be turning towards the Western forces. However, the Western forces do not indeed to support autonomy or independence demands of the Iranian Kurds, its concern for Kurdish human rights is more out of its utility against the Iranian Islamic regime, and Kurdish national forces seem to lack the necessary power and lack proper struggle experience.

Their coordinated struggle with the Iraqi Kurds also has not great utility value for the West. To some extent, I can say that the fate of the Iranian Kurds depends on the development of relations between Iran and the West. If the West insists on overthrowing the current regime of Iran, the utility value of the Kurdish issue will increase. In the event of a war similar to that of Iraq, the status of the Kurds in the future may increase, and the Iranian Kurdish autonomy under a federal state system will not be impossible to achieve. But all this is quite uncertain.

CHAPTER FIVE

Kurdish Issue in Syria

Among the Kurds residing in the four major countries, the Syrian Kurds account for the smallest number. That's why they have caught little attention from the outside world. The Syrian Kurds as a whole are not discriminated severely, the national conflicts are not protruding, and the national demands are mainly confined to the recognition of their minority status and basic citizenship rights, while the issue of stateless Kurds is the main contradiction between the Kurds and the central government. After the Iraq war in 2003, inspired by neighboring Kurds in Iraq, the Syrian Kurds began to rise up to strive for the expansion of national rights, and the dramatic changes in Syria's political situation brought about by the "Arab Spring" since 2011 also provided the Kurds an unprecedented historical opportunity to strive for national rights and national autonomy.

5.1 The Period of French Mandate

The region of Syrian Kurds, also known as West Kurdistan, covering an area of about 12,000 square kilometers, is mainly located in the northeastern region of Syria, including Aleppo and Al-Hasakah Governorate in the North, Al-Raqqah in the Northeast, and the region neighboring with Iraq and Turkey. The region of Syrian Kurds is geographically not completely linked. The Kurds are Syria's second largest ethnic group, and also the largest Syrian minority, the population of which is second only to the Arabs. As Syrian authorities do not recognize the Kurds as a national existence, the number of Kurdish population lacks of official statistics and the exact number is difficult to estimate. In 1977, Syria had a population of 7.845 million people, including about 600,000 Kurds. In 1988, the Syrian population was about 11.5 million, of which Kurds amount to about 100 million. Kurdish people are currently estimated to amount to 1 to 1.7 million, accounting for Syria's total population of 7% to 10%. Syrian Kurdish National Council (KNC) claimed that the Kurdish population was 3 million.[1] Human Rights Watch (HRW) claims that the Kurdish population is about 1.7 million, accounting for about 10% of the population.[2] The U.S State Department estimates Syria's population as 22.5 million, of which Kurds amount to 9% of Syria's total population with about 200 million people.[3] The US Peace Research Institute (USIP) estimates the Kurdish population as 1.5 million

people. But many experts who raised that the population of Syrian Kurds is about 1 million. In short, Syria's Kurdish area as well as population are by far not comparable to that of Turkey, Iran and Iraq.

In Syria, the use of Kurdish language in daily life has not been strictly limited. The Syrian Kurds mainly speak Kurmanji, and nearly 90% use Kurdish language in their daily lives. Peasants generally cannot speak Arabic. But, in the cities, many of the Kurds of younger generation cannot speak Kurdish. Of the Syrian population, 74% were Sunnis (including Sufis), whereas 13% were Shias (including 8.0% Alawites from which about 2% are called Mershdis and they are the followers of Sulayman al-Murshid, 3% Twelvers, or 1% Ismailis), 3% were Druze, while the remaining 10% were Christians. Today, most of the Kurds live in settlements, but there are also a few nomadic tribes that continue to live nomadic lives. The economy is dominated by agriculture. The main tribes are Barazi, Mendikan, Sheylanli and so on.

---

1   "Without Kurds Syria Will not Witness Stability: Ibrahim Biro", Feb. 14, 2012, http://www.ekurd.net/mismas/articles/misc2012/2/syriakurd423.htm.
2   Robert Lowe, "The Syrian Kurds: A People Discovered", Chatham House, Jan. 6 2006, http://www.chathamhouse.org.uk/files/3297_bpsyriankurds.pdf.
3   Background Note: Syria, Mar. 9, 2012, See. http://www.state.gov/r/pa/ei/bgn/3580.htm.

Syria is divided into 14 governorates: Rif Dimashq, Homs, Hama, Latakia, Idlib, Tartus, Ar-Raqqah, Deir-ez-Zor, Al-Hasakah, Daraa, As-Suwayda, Quneitra, Aleppo and Damascus. The Kurds are mainly concentrated in three regions on the border with Turkey and Iraq: the Jazire in the north-east, called Al-Hasakah governorate by Syrian authorities, the Ain al-Arab region in the north (also known as Arab-Pinar) and Afrin in the north-west [Turkish (Kurd Dagh), meaning "Kurdish mountain"].

In Jazira, Kurdish population accounts for the vast majority, about 400,000 people. In Arabic, Jazira means "island", which refers to jammed between the Euphrates and Tigris. The area of ancient Jazira was very large, and the upper reaches of Mesopotamia were called Jazira, and the lower reaches were called Iraq. After World War I, Jazira was divided, some areas were included within Turkey and Iraq. The upper regions' fertile land, planting wheat, rice and cotton, is the granary of Syria. There are about 700 Kurdish villages, five big Kurdish towns, from west to east: by Ras Al-Ain, Derbassiyeh, Amuda, Qamishli, Derek. Among them, Qamishli is the largest one with a population of 1.5 million people. The region is rich in oil resources. Contrary to other Kurdish regions, the Kurds are mainly engaged in agriculture, while the Arabs are engaged in nomadic herding. Here, many Kurds are regarded as "foreigners", non-Syrians by the Syrian authorities. Aleppo also has a large Kurdish population. Arab-Pinar has about 60,000 Kurds, also mainly engaged in agriculture. The area is very hilly, unlike the Jazira which is very plain. Afrin is the sole Kurdish mountainous area in Syria. This area is located in the most western part of Kurdistan, beginning about 60 km northeast of Aleppo, at a distance of 60 km to the Mediterranean and is connected with the Turkish mountainous area. There is abundant sun, abundant rainfall, there are plenty of rivers (mainly in the Afrin River), the land is fertile, very suitable for planting grapes, olives and other fruit trees and flowers, it is one of the most densely populated rural areas of Syria. The Kurdish population in the Afrin region is about 300,000, of which the population of the city of Afrin is about 40,000. In addition, there are a few Kurds living in Azaz, Idlib, Jalabrus and other areas. In Damascus, Aleppo and other non-Kurdish big cities, there are many Kurds. Damascus has a Kurdish population of about 70,000 to 80,000, of which about 50,000 live in the Kurdish block. These Kurds are basically integrated into the city life, where generations live. In Damascus, Aleppo, Hama and Homs, there are many influential wealthy Kurdish families.

Including the Kurdish region, the northeast of Syria is located in an important oil and gas zone, where oil and gas resources are very rich. By 1994, the region's new drilling oil and gas test wells have amounted to 184, the oil and gas fields discovered in the region amounted to 91, the proven reserves amounts to 380 million tons, natural gas reserves amounts to 141.2 billion cubic meters.[4]

Kurds have started to live in Syria a very long time ago. As early as at the end of the 11th century, Kurds started to live in the Kurdish mountainous region. There are also many Kurdish settlements in the Syrian inland region, such as al-Alawiyin, Hama and the surrounding areas. The renowned castle Krak des Chevaliers or the Knights Krak, located in the al-Alawiyin Mountains, is a castle of the Kurds built by the Kurds before the Crusades. Its Arabic name is "Hisn al-Akrad" (Castle of the Kurds). The word "Krak" may be evolved from the Arabic word Akrad or Kurd.[5] Christian crusaders coming from France garrisoned there and expanded the castle. Nowadays, there is still a cemetery of Kurdish nobles in Damascus from the time of Ayyubid dynasty.

In the Jazira region, when a Danish writer came to visit it in 1764, mentioned that there were five Kurdish tribes and one Arab tribe. These tribes still live there. In the period of the Arab Abbasid dynasty (750-1258), Syria was known as Sham (Şam) administrative region, the territory west to the east coast of the Mediterranean, east to the Euphrates River, south to the Red Sea shore of Aqaba and north to the Taurus mountains. The province of Iraq included lower Mesopotamia. From the 11th century on, the Kurdish region of Syria began to be called Kurdistan. During the Ottoman Empire, Syria was divided into four provinces: Damascus (including Palestine and Jordan), Aleppo, Tripoli and Sidon. After World War I, the Ottoman Empire collapsed. April 19-26, 1920, the Allied Conference of San Remo mandated Syria to France. Afterwards France and Turkey conducted negotiations over the Syrian-Turkish boundary. In March 1921, the two sides negotiated in London to determine the basic boundary of the territory and in 1926 determined the ultimate direction of the boundary. According to the agreement, the Kurdish-dominated regions, Afrin, Arab-Pinar and Jazira, were designated to Syria, while two Arab-dominated regions were designated to Turkey. In 1939 France officially designated Alexandretta to Turkey. June 1922, France announced the establishment of the "Syrian Federation", including the original Damascus region, Aleppo region and Allawite states. In 1936, the French authorities and the Syrian national government signed the Franco-Syrian Treaty, which incorporated Allawite states and Druze region into Syria, forming the basic prototype of modern Syria.[6]

---

4   Bai Guoping (ed.) Geographic Features of Oil and Gas Zones in Middle East, p. 8.
5   Michael M. Gunter, Historical Dictionary of the Kurds, pp.169-169.
6   Wang Xingang, General History of the Middle East: Volume of Syria and Lebanon, The Commercial Press, 2003, p. 174.

After the end of World War I, when the Sheikh Said rebellion against the Kurdish discrimination and repression policy by Turkey failed and the French rule (1920-1946) adopted a relatively tolerant policy, a large number of Turkish Kurds were prompted to flee from calamity to live in Syria. According to some scholars, the Kurds expelled from Turkey constitute the majority of the Syrian Kurds.[7]

From the French mandatory rule until the 1960s, the Syria's Arab Baath Socialist Party came to power. During this period, Kurds' living conditions were good as a whole, not subject to obvious discrimination. In October 1927, some Syrian Kurdish nationalists announced the establishment of the Kurdish nationalist organization "Khoyboun" (Independence), mainly engaged in Kurdish nationalist propaganda and struggle against Turkish government's suppression of the Kurdish national movement. It took Aleppo, Jazira and other Kurdish area as its base of action, and actively developed the organization, recruited members, trained armies, and sent them to participate in the Ararat rebellion of the Turkish Kurds. In 1928, due to the pressure of the Turkish government, the French government decided to ban the activities of the organization. The organization was one of the major Kurdish nationalist organizations of the 1920s. In 1930, French authorities promulgated the Constitution, which established a republican system of regime, which provided for the implementation of a parliamentary electoral system based on region and confession to ensure the rights of religious minorities. Between December 1931 and January 1932, the first parliamentary elections were held in Syria following the promulgation of the new constitution and three members of the organization were elected members of the parliament Khalil bey Ibn Ibrahim Pacha (Jazira province), Mustafa bey Ibn Shahin (Jarabulus), and Hassan Aouni (Kurd Dagh). The French liberally allowed Kurdish cultural activities to exist, but have not established a public Kurdish school in the country. In the 1930s and 1940s, the Kurdish-language magazine "Hawar" (Cry for Help) and the French-Kurdish bilingual magazine "Ronahi" Enlightenment appeared in Damascus and soon spread among the Kurds and played a very important role to popularize the Kurdish language and promote the development of the Syrian-Kurdish culture. During this period, a large number of Kurdish immigrants from Turkey did not have particular difficulties and basically gained Syrian citizenship. France did not encourage the Kurds to engage in any sabotage activities against Turkey in Syria, but in fact there were many Turkish Kurdish anti- government organizations in Syria hiding and carrying out activities.

---

7   Youssef M. Choueiri, A Companion to the History of the Middle East, Wiley-Blackwell, 2005, p. 475.

In the Syrian national independence movement opposing the French colonial rule, the Kurds have played an active role as "Syrians". From 1919 to 1946, France repeatedly pretended to recognize Syria's independence, but in fact Syria did not obtain an independent status. When the Syrian Republic won independence in 1932, Kurdish Muhammad Ali al-Abid became president. In addition, during the early days of the French colonization, the Kurds, Yusuf al-Azma, became the minister of war of the then Syrian government and Ibrahim Hananu was also one of the famous patriotic leaders against the French colonial rule. The Syrian Communist Party, established in 1938, played an important role in the anti-colonial struggle; its founder was the Kurd Khalid Bakdash who won a seat in the Parliament in 1954 and became deputy. Supporters of the Syrian Communist Party were mainly coming from northern Kurds and Armenians. After the arduous struggle of the Syrian nationalists, on April 17, 1946, the French army withdrew from Syria and Syria gained its true independence, so this day later became Syrian Independence Day.

Before the Syrian Kurdistan Democratic Party was founded in 1957, there was no truly independent Syrian Kurdish nationalist political organization in Syria. Although the Kurdish nationalist organization "Khoyboun" (Independence, 1927-1944), which was established in Lebanon, mainly operated within the borders of Syria, its main objective was to oppose the Turkish government. After the dissolution of the "Khoyboun", the Kurdish League (1945-1946) and similar organizations such as "Jaladat" and "Kamiran-Badrkhan" emerged. However, after the World War II, the Syrian Kurds did not take the opportunity to propose an appeal for autonomy or independence to the allies.

It is worth mentioning that, between 1932 and 1939, a small Christian-Kurdish Autonomy Movement emerged in Syria, of which the leader was the tribal leader Hajo Agha. Before the French Mandate and the mid-1950s, some Kurdish traditional tribal leaders entered the Syrian Parliament, such as Jamil, Akram Ibrahim Pasha, Hasan, Akram Hajo and son of Hassan, Sulayman Hajo. Some Kurds also joined the Syrian Communist Party.

5.2 The Kurdish Issue during the Cold War

After the end of the occupation of France in 1946, Syria entered a new stage in history. In line with the rising Arab nationalism of the Arab world in the same period, Syrian nationalism and Pan-Arabism have also developed considerably and forged ahead on a period of political upheaval. From 1949 to 1951, Syria experienced four military coups. In March 1949, Syrian army's chief of staff Husni al-Zaim launched a coup, which was Syria's first military coup in modern history and had an important impact on the historical development of Syria. It is worth mentioning that Husni al-Zaim was Kurdish. The regime led by him was overthrown in less than half a year, and he himself was executed. In 1953 the Arab Socialist Party and the Arab Baath Party merged into the Arab Baath Socialist Party and began to play an increasingly important role in Syrian politics. In February 1954, Syria experienced again a military coup, which was followed by the national parliamentary elections. The Arab Baath Socialist Party won a great victory, and joined the coalition government with al-Quwatli as president. In February 1958, Syria and Egypt merged into the United Arab Republic. This year, the Syrian government began to adopt a series of Arabization policies. The government implemented a land reform, confiscated the land of the Kurdish landlords and distributed them to the Arabs. Due to increasing differences between Egypt and Syria, on September 28, 1961, Syria announced its secession from the United Arab Republic and founded the Syrian Arab Republic.

With the rise of Arab nationalism, the fate of the Kurds began to change negatively. The main idea of the Arab Baath Socialist Party was "unity, freedom and socialism", emphasizing the unity of the Arab nation, that all peoples, tribes, religions, associations as well as regional factions, social strata should be integrated into the big melting pot of one nation (the Arab nation). In 1950, after Syrian independence the first constitution was promulgated, the new constitution stipulated that Syria was an Arab republic, emphasizing the Arab nature of Syria, that Syria should be part of the great Arab nation, all Syrians are Arabs, no ethnic-national division. According to this system of thought, the Kurds should not emphasize that they themselves are a minority nation, and should be actively integrated into the Arab nation, emphasizing the non-Arab national characteristics would threaten Syria's Arab characteristics, therefore Government vigorously implemented the policy of Arabization.

285

In this context, the Kurdish nationalist struggle in Syria began to emerge, the Kurds began to set up nationalist parties and organizations. In the early 1950s, the Society of the United Kurdish Democratic Youth in Syria (Civata Yekitiya Xortên Demokratên Kurd li Suriyê) was established in al-Qamishli, declaring its struggle to "liberate and unify the Kurds and Kurdistan." The association was a left-wing Kurdish nationalist organization, which, in addition to the Kurdish nationalist view, used a number of terms such as reactionary cliques, imperialism, etc. in its regulations, with special attention to women's issue. Its members were mostly primary and secondary school teachers and young students, such as Muhammad Mullah Ahmad, Abdul Aziz Ali Abdi, Sami Mullah Ahmad Nami and Darwish Mulla Sulayman. In 1956, a number of Kurdish nationalist activists began to prepare for the foundation of a nationalist party. Among its delegated figures were Uthman

Sabri, Abdul Hajji Darwish (law student), Hamzah Niweran and Nuruddin Zaza, members of the "Khoyboun" organization as well as the left wing organization "Society of Peace Syrians", who initially held exploratory discussions to establish the Syrian Democratic Kurd's Party (PKDS) and began drafting a party program. Jalal Talabani, who was studying in Syria at that time, also took part in the discussion.

On June 14, 1957, a group of Kurdish intellectuals, including Uthman Sabri, Daham Miró and Nur al-Din Zaza, held a congress of delegates in Aleppo and established the Kurdish Democratic Party of Syria (KDPS). Some Kurds, who left the Syrian Communist Party, joined the Syrian Kurdish Democrats and participated in the first congress of delegates such as Rashid Hammu, Muhammad Ali Khoja, Khalil Muhammad and Shawkat Hanan Nasan, also known as the "Aleppo Group". The congress was held in the apartment of Muhammad Ali Khoja in Aleppo. At that time the Syrian Communist Party did not specifically put forward to safeguard the rights of the Kurds. The delegates agreed that the new party was named the Kurdish Democratic Party in Syria and formed a seven-member Central Committee comprising of Uthman Sabri, Abdul Hajji Darwish, Hamzah Niweran as well as the leading members of the "Aleppo Group". Sabri became party chairman. At the end of 1957, Shaykh Muhammad Isa Mulla Mahmud from the Darbasiyah region joined the party and entered the Central Committee.

At the beginning of 1958, Nuruddin Zaza, who completed his studies in Switzerland, entered the Central Committee and served as the party chairman. In 1958, the Society of the United Kurdish Democratic Youth in Syria announced to join the Kurdish Democratic Party in Syria. In the same year, some of the Kurdish intellectuals from the Syrian Communist Party in the Jazira region founded the "Partiya Azadî" (Freedom Party), and subsequently joined the KDPS. The main leader of the organization and poet Mulla Shaykhmus Jigarkhwin entered the Central Committee. At this time, the Central Committee of the KDPS had reached 10 members. The goal of the Kurdish Democratic Party in Syria was to secure Kurdish language and cultural rights, develop regional economies, implement land reforms and promote political democratization in Syria. The organization had a lot of supporters among the Kurdish workers and peasants. In 1959, under the influence of the renamed Kurdistan Democratic Party-Iraq, the Kurdish Democratic Party of Syria was also renamed as Kurdistan Democratic Party in Syria, Partiya Demokrat a Kurdistani li Suriyê, and the amendment to the party constitution, proposed the goal to establish an independent and united Kurdistan. Besides the Kurdistan Democratic Party, the Syrian "Kurdistan political movement" was established in Syria in 1958, and this organization emphasized the struggle for Kurdish national rights through peaceful means.

Kurdistan Democratic Party in Syria has not been able to obtain a legal status since its inception and has engaged in underground activities. Since its founding in the mid-1960s, the party has focused mainly on developing members and building organizations, and has established branches in the Kurdish region as well as in Damascus and Aleppo. During this period, in addition to its general secretary was a Kurd and many members were also Kurds, the Syrian Communist Party actively advocated to uphold Kurdish national rights. In view of the Kurdistan Democratic Party of Iraq and of Iran's great influence and the Kurdish national movement in the two countries play an important role, the Syrian government was very vigilant about the establishment of the Kurdistan Democratic Party in Syria. In early 1959, Shawkat Hanan Nasan and Hamzah Niweran were arrested on the accusation that they were members of the Communist party. In August 1960, the Syrian government launched a large-scale crackdown on Kurdish nationalist organizations, about 120 Kurdish Democrats were arrested, including more than 20 major leaders, who were sentenced to 6 to 12 months imprisonment on charge of separatism, while hundreds of supporters were arrested. As a result of the government's crackdown on the KDPS soon split and its influence declined. In the same year, about 250 Kurdish students were burned to death in a cinema in Amouda town.

Until the early 1962, a large number of arrested Kurdish Democrats were released. In February 1962, the Kurdistan Democratic Party in Syria held a congress in Damascus and elected a new Central Committee. Since Zaza was still in prison, the congress elected Uthman Sabri as General Secretary. In November 1963, the party held a conference in al-Qamishli, elected a new Central Committee, Darwish was expelled from the party. During this period, the party has undergone a serious split, which was divided into two factions, one group was called the Sabri, the other Zaza-Darwish.

In September 28, 1961, a coup occurred in Syria, terminating the unification with Egypt, promulgating in November a provisional constitution and parliamentary elections. The new constitution once again explicitly classified Syria as an Arab Republic. Meanwhile, in neighboring Iraq a Kurdish uprising occurred. The Syrian government not only supported the Iraqi government to suppress the uprising, but also took measures in the country to combat the Kurdish movement. August 23, 1962, the Syrian government issued an order to take a census in the Jazira region. In November the same year the census work began and has been completed in one day. According to the census results, the government issued the Decree No. 93, which identified about 20% of the Kurds (around 150,000) as "illegal infiltrators" from foreign countries and as belonging to "foreigners" (ajnabis) and deprived them of their citizenship. These "foreigners" subsequently sank down to refugees, they could not work in government institutions, and could not enter schools and seek medical treatment, and could not have personal dwellings and belongings.[8]

There were also about 75,000 Kurds as well as the intermarried children of Turkish-Syrian Kurds which were included in the population census. They have no citizenship-nationality and are known as "concealed" (maktoumeen). In this context, the Syrian government for the first time launched a large-scale propaganda campaign against the Kurds, raising the slogans such as "Save Arabism in Jazira!" and "Fight the Kurdish threat!".

Colonel Mundhir al-Musalli, a former Baathist army officer, stated in his book "Arabs and Kurds: An Arab View on the Kurdish Question," that "the instigators of the Kurdish movement attacked foreign immigrants of the Kurdish region to ensure that the Kurds are in northern Syria in order to realize their evil and unjust plans to divide the nation in the future. But the approach aroused the suspicion of the Syrian authorities that, it undermined the Kurdish citizens as part of the whole nation: In fact, Kurds aroused the fear of the entire Arab nation, consequently the Syrian government has taken counter-measures against the Kurdish movement."

Another reason for Syria's suppression over the Jazira region was the then discovery of oil in the region, which the government regarded as a great asset for development. At the same time, the government sent a large number of Arab immigrants into the Jazira region and expelled Kurds from there. By 2004, population of such "foreigners" reached 200,000, and that of the "former inhabitants" had reached to 80,000-100,000.[9]

The citizenship issue of the Jazira region henceforth became a major dispute between the Kurds and the Syrian government. In February 1963, the Arab Baath Socialist Party came to power in Iraq, one month later the Arab Baath Socialist Party also came to power in Syria. On March 8, 1963, the Baath Party launched a coup, and conquered the whole Syrian state, and has been in power till today. In March 1973 the new constitution was promulgated, which declared once again that "all the people in the Syrian Arab region are part of the Arab nation."

---

8   "Syria-The Silenced Kurds", Human Rights Watch, Oct. 1996, www.hrw.org/reports/1996/Syria.htm; "Buried Alive: Stateless Kurds in Syria", Refugees International, Feb. 13, 2006, http://www.refugeesinternational.org/policy/in-depth-report/buried-alive-stateless-kurds-syria; "The Kurds in Syria: Fueling Separatist Movements in the Region?", United States Institute of Peace, Apr. 2009, pp. 3-4.
9   Harriet Montgomery, The Kurds of Syria-An Existence Denied, Europaeisches Zentrum fur Kurdische Studien, Berlin, 2005, p.80.

Mundhir al-Musalli's "Arabs and Kurds: An Arab View on the Kurdish Question" has elaborated Arab Baath Party's basic view on the Kurds. In the book, the author acknowledged that the Kurds as a nation truly existing in Syria, and moreover as a nation with own history and culture, live in Syria who felt proud of themselves for being Kurds. But he also pointed out that the Kurds should not have dual attributes as Syrians and Kurds, but either be Syrians, or Kurds.

Kurd's pursuit of the Kurdish national rights and identity should not be at the expense of the Syrian country. He stressed that Syria is not a multinational country, instead the Kurds have long been integrated to the society as Syrian Arab citizens. Consequently, the Kurds and Arabs enjoy the same rights, the evidence is that: many Kurds have been prime minister, ministers and chief of staff and other senior officials.

The Baath Party government began to adopt more radical policies of discrimination and assimilation of Kurds than the prior government. The primary content of assimilation was: It denied the existence of Kurdish nationality. It dispersed the Kurds by moving them from the original Kurdish settlements to the Arab regions and the Arabs to the Kurdish region; cunningly and artificially decreased the Kurdish population, by regarding one part as "foreigners", and deprived them of their civil rights. It restricted the social and cultural development of Kurds, did not allow them to celebrate the Kurdish New Year (Newroz), prohibited the use of Kurdish clothing, restricted the use of Kurdish language, prohibited the publication of newspapers and periodicals in Kurdish language, did not allow the establishment of Kurdish primary schools and ordered that Kurdish newborn children must be given an Arab name. In 1967, the government introduced a policy which stipulated that newborn children must carry an Arab name, otherwise would not be registered, while in school geography textbooks all references to the Kurds as a minority nationality were deleted. The names of Kurdish village and town names were changed to different irrelevant Arab names. In the use of Kurdish language, a variety of restrictive measures were taken. On May 18, 1977, the local government issued the Directive No. 15801, ordering that the Kurdish names of scores of towns and villages in the region of Afrin in the governorate of Aleppo be replaced with new Arabic names, so that they have an "Arab characteristics".[10]

---

10   "Syria-The Silenced Kurds", Human Rights Watch, www.hrw.org/reports/1996/Syria.htm.

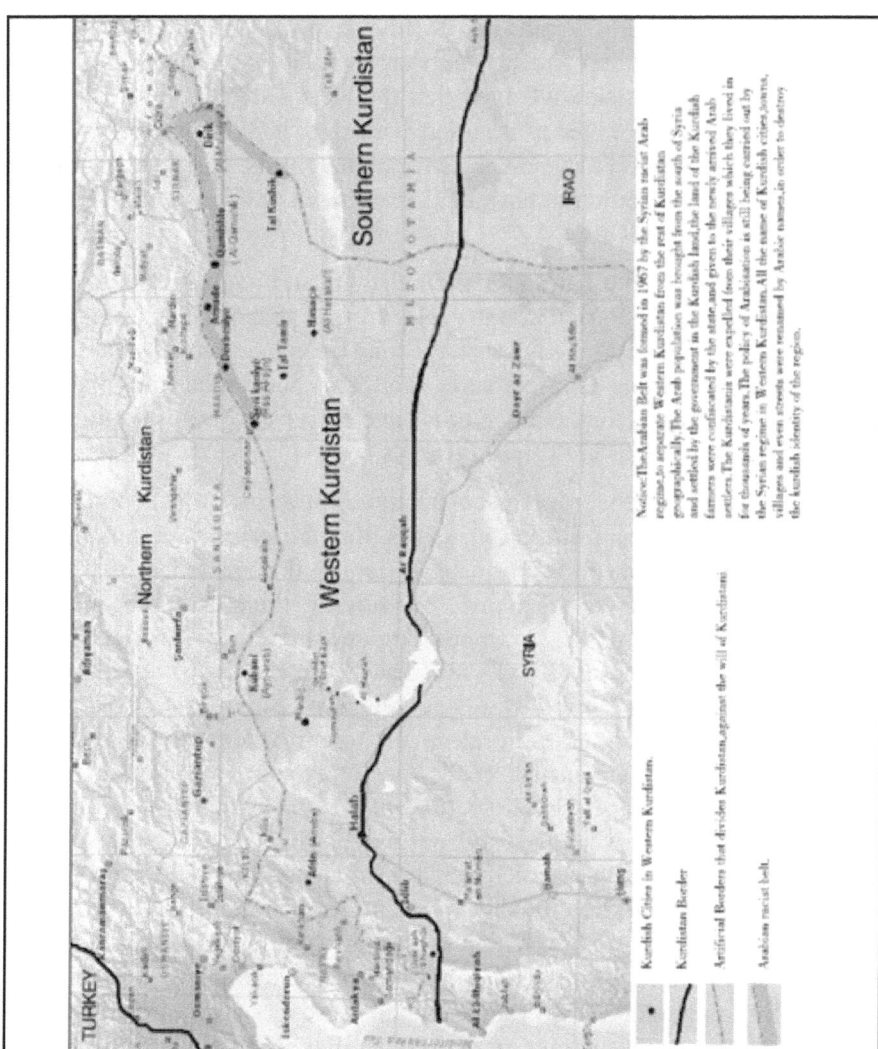

**Fig. 5-1. "Arab Belt"
Set up by the Syrian
Government**

*Source: http://www.jawadmella.
tripod.com/id13.html.*

In 1967, the Syrian government also adopted a major policy deciding to build an "Arab Belt" along the Jazira-Turkish border to isolate the Kurds on both sides of the national border, to avoid Syrian Kurds being impacted by the Kurdish nationalist movement in the neighboring Iraq and Turkey. This isolation zone was about 300 km long, 10 to 15 km wide, extending from the border with Iraq from the eastern to Ras al-Ain to the west. Syria maintained a strong military presence in the isolation zone. In the 1970s, the government's plan for the establishment of a state-run model farms in Jazira was actually still a policy of Arabization. In 1973, the plan was formally implemented, the government resettled a large number of Bedouin Arabs to this region. Meanwhile, the lands of the Kurds were confiscated for the establishment of the model farms.

According to the initial plan, about 140.000 Kurds were relocated to the southern Al-Raad region. Kurdish farmers resisted, and although their lands and homes were confiscated, they still resisted to leave their hometown. In 1975, the government has set up 41 "model farms" in the center of the Kurdish region, settling about 40,000 Arab families, there. In 1976 the Syrian government ordered to stop the construction of the "Arab belt", but the model farms remained, and the confiscated land plots of the Kurds were not returned.[11]

However, in the 1960s and 1970s, the Syrian government has appointed a number of Kurds as senior government officials in Damascus to win over the Kurds. Such as the appointment of Kurdish Sheikh Ahmad Kaftaro in 1964, as the Syrian Grand Mufti. Between 1972-1976, the Kurdish Mahmoud al-Ayyubi has been a successful, popular prime minister. There were also many Kurds in the Syrian National Assembly and among local government leading posts. The Syrian government also often cited these examples to the Kurds and the outside world that the Syrian government does not discriminate against the Kurds. In the mid-1970s, the influence of Islamism led by the Muslim Brotherhood Party in Syrian politics gradually increased and began to threaten the Baath regime. The Muslim Brotherhood actively engaged in anti-government activities, calling for the overthrow of the Baathist regime. Since 1976, due to the challenges coming from the Muslim Brotherhood and its increasing opposition against the government, the government has begun to relax the high-handed oppression over Kurds, recruited a lot of Kurds into the security agencies and the army, releases a part of arrested Kurdish politicians. Kurdish public cultural activities were tolerated. However, these reforms were still very limited, the Government still did not allow Kurdish radio broadcasting and publishing, did not solve the problem of stateless Kurds in the Jazira region. In 1982, the Syrian

11   "Group Denial: Repression of Kurdish Political and Cultural Rights in Syria", Human Rights Watch, Nov.26, 2009, www.hrw.org/sites/default/files/reports/syria109webwcover_0.pdf.

government suppressed the Muslim Brotherhood uprising in Hama, killing tens of thousands of people. Following the Hama uprising of 1982 in the wake of the wider Islamist insurgency in Syria (1979-1982), when thousands of armed insurgents and civilians were killed by the military, and the Brotherhood was effectively broken as an active political force inside Syria. With the threat of the Muslim Brotherhood weakened, the government has increased the repression of the Kurds.

In June 1963, the Iraqi government resumed war against the Kurds. The Syrian government sent troops to Iraq to help the repression, Colonel Fahd Shadz led a Syrian brigade of about 6,000 people marched into Iraqi Kurdistan passing from the Jazira region to fight against the Iraqi Kurdish militants of Mullah Mustafa Barzani.[12]

However, the Syrian expedition was unsuccessful and disastrous and troops were forced to withdraw in January 1964. On January 10, 1964, the Syrian government held a military parade in Damascus, the government praised Colonel Fahd as an "Arab national hero."

However, after the deterioration of its relations, both with Iraq and Turkey, the Syrian government has begun to support the anti-government activities of Kurds in Turkey, such as Turkey's PKK and also Iraq's Kurdish Patriotic Union (PUK). From the late 1970s to 1998, Syria has been a major supporter of the PKK and the most important activity base of Turkey's PKK. At the same time, the Syrian government also asked these Kurdish organizations to persuade the Syrian Kurds to abandon the national movement against the Syrian government, and has achieved some success. PKK leader Ocalan has repeatedly criticized the Syrian Kurds' struggle for national rights and declared agreement with President Assad that most Syrian Kurds are not native Kurds, but immigrants from Turkey and Iraq.[13]

In 1965, the Syrian Democratic Party of Kurdistan was split, two parties emerged: the Sabri-led Syrian Kurdistan Democratic Party (left-wing) and Darwish-led Syrian Kurdistan Democratic Party (right-wing). Prior to division, Darwish was re-admitted to the party in 1964 and was elected to the Central Committee. After 1969, the left-wing leader was Salah Badruddin.

In 1965 the during the party meetings, three major issues have been controversial: first, are the Syrian Kurds a nation or a minority, whether fight for the right to self-determination or just ask for cultural rights? Second, is our struggle an integral part of whole Syria's democratic movement and what should be our position on Syria's political and social problems? Third, how should the party handle the relationship with the Iraqi Kurdistan

12 P.G. Kreyenbroek, S. Sperl, The Kurds: A Contemporary Overview, Routledge, 1992, pp. 151-152.

13 "The PKK and Syria's Kurds", Terrorism Monitor, Vol. 5, Issue 3, Feb. 15, 2007. http://www.hamestown.org/terrorism/news/article.php?articleid=2370250.

Democratic Party and Kurdistan Patriotic Union, should it support Mullah Mustafa Barzani or Jalal Talabani?

From the 1980s on, the national consciousness of the Kurds in Syria has further grown. Kurdish political and cultural organizations have been established and they led clandestine activities due to suppression. But from time to time, various open and peaceful public activities and demonstrations were also held. Whereas, such activities were not prevalent in Turkey, Iraq and Iran.

On March 1986, in capital Damascus, thousands of Kurds dressed in traditional Kurdish clothing held the Kurdish New Year celebration, the police violently attacked the demonstrators, and one person was shot dead and many were wounded. In Afrin, 3 Kurds were shot dead in the New Year demonstrations.

In the al-Qamishli city, about 40,000 people participated the funeral of those Kurds killed by the police, and protested the government. However, we can say that during the 80's Syrian government's policy towards Kurds were relatively relaxed.

It is worth mentioning that the Syrian Baath government did not take heavy restrictive measures against Armenians and Assyrians and other Christian minorities, instead recognized them as ethnic-religious minorities, allowed them to use their own language, practice their religion freely, establish their various associations, clubs, and schools in their own style and languages. This reflected the Syrian government's fear coming from the Western public and Western governments. Therefore, the capital Damascus still contains a sizeable proportion of Christians, with some churches all over the city, but particularly in the district of Bab Touma (The Gate of Th omas in Aramaic and Arabic). Masses are held every Sunday and civil servants are given Sunday mornings off to allow them to attend church, even though Sunday is a working day in Syria. Schools in Christian-dominated districts have Saturday and Sunday as the weekend, while the official Syrian weekend falls on Friday and Saturday.

5.3 The Kurdish Issue since the 1990s

Since the 1990s, especially after the two Iraq wars, and after the Kurds in neighboring Iraq won autonomy, national consciousness has further grown among the Syrian Kurds.

Kurdish parties in Syria increased their activities, we observe that, Kurdish national movement in Syria is divided to many competing parties, there was about 16 parties as of May, 2012, major ones are as follows: Kurdistan Democratic National Party, the Kurdish Left Party, the Kurdish

Future Movement[14], the Democratic Progressive Party, the Kurdistan Patriotic Democratic Party, the Kurdistan People's Alliance (est.2006), the Kurdistan Democratic Movement, the Democratic Union Party[15], and the Kurdish Democratic Wifaq Party led by Nash'at Muhammad (which was split from the PYD in 2005), the Yekiti Kurdistani led by Abdul Basit Hamo. These organizations generally have small number of members, with fewer than 50 members and large ones have about a few thousand members.

These parties mainly rely on prominent individual leaders, and their two main objectives are to fight for the recognition of Kurdish national rights in Syria and achieve self-government, and they emphasize peaceful and democratic means to achieve their goals through peaceful means. None of them has publicly announced the demand for independence.

In March 2004, after the Qamishli riots, some Kurdish organizations were radicalized. On 25, April 2004, Syrian Kurdish organizations in exile in Europe met in Germany to announce the establishment of the "West Kurdistan Exile Government" with the aim of establishing an independent state in Syria.

Jawad Mella served as chairman of the government in exile, the government has five ministries: the Ministry of Foreign Affairs and External Affairs, Ministry of Internal Affairs and Organization, Ministry of Information, Ministry of National Security, Ministry of Oil.

In April 2005, the organization announced that it had established the first Kurdish-language radio station (Rojava Radio) and a television station (Rojava TV) in London, the radio station broadcasted for 24 hours a day and television station broadcasted an hour in a week. They have audiences both in Europe and the Middle East.

At the same time, the organization declared that the establishment of the "Kurdistan Government in exile" was a turning point in the history of the Kurdish people in Syria, and added: "liberation of our motherland is the prerequisite for the realization of Kurd's national rights and national recognition, and national dignity, and is the only correct path. The organization pointed out that the idea that these goals could be achieved without establishing the Kurdish state was fully wrong, and that the establishment

---

14   The Kurdish Future Movement in Syria is a liberal Syrian Kurdish political party established in 2005 by Mashaal Tammo, who in 2011 was assassinated.
15   The Democratic Union Party, is a left-wing Kurdish political party established in 2003 by Kurdish activists in northern Syria. It is a founder member of the National Coordination Body for Democratic Change, and is described by the Carnegie Middle East Center as "one of the most important Kurdish opposition parties in Syria".It is the leading political party in the Federation of Northern Syria–Rojava and its cantons. Chemical engineer Saleh Muslim became its chairman in 2010, and Asiyah Abdullah its co-chairwoman in June 2012. PYD, is closely related to the Turkey's PKK, and seen as the PKK's Syrian branch.

of the Kurdish government in exile was the first step towards the independent state.[16]

In 2006, the Kurdistan National Assembly- Syria, (KURDNAS) was established. The organization's goal was declared as to promote democracy in Syria and to guarantee the national rights of the Kurds and other ethnic minorities. At the same time, it aimed the establishment of a federal state in Syria, so as to achieve Kurdish autonomy. In March 2009, the organization sent a letter to US Vice President Joe Biden which denounced, the Assad governivent's long and systematic persecution of the Kurds, depriving the Kurds of their human rights and freedoms, thus asked the Obama administration to pay attention to Kurds faced with Syrian tyranny. The US should help Kurds, by promoting democracy and freedom in Syria. The letter added: "the Syrian government has discriminated against the Kurds for decades, and its policy has caused a disastrous life for Kurds, and 300,000 Kurds were deprived of citizenship, 500,000 Kurds were forced to migrate to other places.[17]

In addition, in October 2005, the Syrian domestic opposition parties issued a "National Declaration on Democratic Change", which proposed a fair solution to the Syrian Kurdish issue, to ensure that they have the right to do so in the Syria, full equality of rights, including national rights, cultural, national language learning and other constitutional rights.

The five-page document, unveiled at an unauthorized press conference, was signed by more than 250 "major opposition figures" as well as parties "both secular and religious, Arab and Kurdish." It was considered important that the statement included the Muslim Brotherhood group of Syria, in addition to secular groups.

Twelve members of the Damascus Declaration National Council were sentenced to two and a half years in prison in October 2008. According to a leaked March 2009 diplomatic cable, Syrian President Bashar al-Assad responded to a comment by US Senator Cardin that he could give "specific examples of citizens jailed for their political views" by saying that "we are a country in process of reform. We aren't perfect.

After the war in Iraq in 2003, the Syrian Kurds have been increasingly active. This is closely related to the substantial increase in the status of Kurds in Iraq, and the Syrian Kurds have also been stimulated and encouraged by the rise of Kurdish activities in Iran and Turkey. In June 2000, President Hafez al-Assad died and his son Bashar Assad succeeded. Young Bashar

---

16   http://.www.rojavatv.org.uk.Rojavastate.pdf.
17   "Open Letter to Joseph Biden, Vice President, From Sherkoh Abbas",
Kurdistan National Assembly, http://.democraticunderground.com/discuss/duboard.
php%3Faz%3Dview_all%26address%3D389x5332090+Kurdistan+National+Assembly+o
f+Syria+(KNAS)&cd=5&hl=zh-CN&ct=clnk&client=aff-360daohang.

came to power after the reform, the domestic political environment was relatively tolerant, and the Syrian political life breathed some freedom for a short period of time, a time which was called as the "Damascus Spring".

This provided favorable conditions for the political activities of the Kurdish national movement. Some Kurdish parties promoted the national rights movement. In December 2002, the newly established Kurdish party, "Yekiti" staged a sit-in outside parliament calling on it to "eliminate the restrictions over the Kurdish language and culture, and the recognition of the Kurdish minority within the framework democratic Syria."[18]

Police arrested two members of the Politburo, of Yekiti, Hassan Saleh and Marwan Altman, for alleged incitement of religious and ethnic separatism. The Supreme State Security Court sentenced them to 14 months' imprisonment.

On June 25, 2003, a group of Syrian Kurds held a rally outside the United Nations Children's Fund (UNICEF) office building in Damascus demanded that the Syrian Government should grant citizenship to stateless Kurds and allow Kurdish children to learn Kurdish.[19]

On March 12, 2004, security forces opened fire on an unarmed Kurdish crowd that was chanting pro-Bush slogans at a soccer match and scuffling with Arab fans (mukhabarat plants, according to some eye witnesses) in the northeastern city of Qamishli, nine people were shot dead, on the spot. This sparked eight days of Kurdish rioting that spread to other northern Kurdish cities. 40 Riots ended with people (33 Kurds and 7 Arabs) dead, more than 160 people were injured and hundreds of people were arrested."[20]

Many of the Kurdish students who participated in the protests were fired from their schools. This is the largest Kurdish casualty that has ever occurred in Syria, which made a significant impact on the Kurdish movement. After this suppression more and more protests were organized, and some Kurdish parties were more and more radicalized emphasizing the use of force to solve the Kurdish issue and demanded independent state. "Kurdish government in exile" was one among them.[21]

18 "Kurds Protest Outside Syrian Parliament Against Discrimination", Agence France-Presse, Dec. 10, 2002, http://home.cogeco.ca/-konews/11-12-02-kurds-protest-outside-syrian-parli.html.
19 "Far from Justice, Syria's Supreme State Security Court", Human Rights Watch, Feb. 24, 2009, http://www.hrw.org/en/reports/2009/02/23/far-justice, pp.43-44.
20 "Syria: Address Grievances Underlying Kurdish Unrest", Human Rights Watch, March 18, 2004, http://www.hrw.org/en/news/2004/03/18/syria-address-grievances-underlying—-Kurdish-unrest; Amnesty International, "Kurds in the Syrian Arab Republic One Year after the March 2004 Events", MDE, Feb. 24, 2005, http://www.amesty.org/en/library/info/MDE24/002/2005.
21 www.rojavatv.org.uk/Rojavastate.pdf.

The Kurdish protests were held more frequently after the "March 12" incident in 2004, while the government has passed the red line, by arresting the Kurdish political activists.

In fact the Syrian government had rarely arrested the Kurdish political leaders before. According to statistics, between 2005- 2009, there were at least 15 renown Kurdish politicians arrested, such as the spokesman Mashaal Tammo from the "Kurdish Future Movement"; some main leaders of the Yekiti party, Fuad Ali and Kazakhstan Muhammad Moussa, the General Secretary of the Kurdish Left Party, Muhammad Sayyid and Adnan Buzan, and also the leaders of the Kurdistan Democratic Party. And the government has suppressed at least 14 Kurdish public political and cultural rallies.[22]

In 2005, the famous Kurdish cleric Maashouq al-Haznawi, who often criticized the government, boldly, was murdered in Aleppo. The Kurds blamed the Syrian government, which denied any involvement.

On June 5, 2006, mourning protests for Maashouq al-Haznawi sparked clashes, police arrested dozens of Kurdish people, in al-Qamishli.

Fifty people among the protestors were trialed in the military courts. On March 20, 2006, in Aleppo, the security forces arrested dozens of people for celebrating the Kurdish New Year. On December 10, 2006, the Qamishli Kurds celebrated the International Human Rights Day and demanded the recognition of Kurdish national rights, which was also attacked by the police.

In 2006, dozens of Kurdish members of the Syrian assembly formed a dialogue with the government on the issue of stateless Kurds, living in Jazira, but no progress was achieved.[23]

In January 2007, five members of the Yekiti Party were arrested and trialed for attempting to merge part of the Syrian territory into a foreign country. Four of them were sentenced to five years' imprisonment by the Supreme State Security Court in April 2010, one of them was found innocent and released. On June 19, 2007, Syrian Security Agency arrested the leader of the Kurdistan Democratic Party Adnan Buzan. In November 2007, the Syrian Kurds in al-Qamishli and Ain-al-Arab protested the Turkish troops sent to Iraq against the PKK, Syrian security forces killed one person, wounded numerous people and arrested many, among whom 15 protesters were sent to military court. In December the same year, in Aleppo, there occurred a second protest against the Turkish army's march into Iraq to fight against the PKK, this time Syrian security forces arrested

22 "Group Denial: Repression of Kurdish Political and Cultural Rights in Syria", Human Rights Watch, Nov.26, 2009, www.hrw.org/sites/default/files/reports/syria1109webwcover_0.pdf.
23 "Syria to Tackle Kurds' Citizenship Problem", Apr. 1, 2011, www.ekurd.net.

at least 15 protesters. On February 15, 2008, in Aleppo and other places, PKK leader Ocalan's arrest day was commemorated by open air meetings, the police hindered the meetings and arrested many people. On March 8, in Ain-al-Arab the Kurds held meetings and activities to celebrate the "the Women's Day, again the police arrested 10 of the participants.

On March 20, in Qamishli, the Kurds held meetings and rallies to celebrate the Kurdish New Year, the police shot and killed 3 people. On July 19, police arrested Muhammad Moussa, general secretary of the Kurdish Left Party.

On August 15, the Syrian intelligence agency arrested the spokesman of Kurdish Future Movement.

And in May 2009 the court sentenced him to three and a half years of imprisonment on charges of "weakening national sentiments, spreading or exaggerating those news and ideas unfavorable to the nation. "

On August 26, 2007, the Syrian intelligence again arrested two leading members of the Kurdish Future Movement. On August 31, Syrian security agencies arrested Saeed, the leader of the Kurdish Democratic Party. On September 10, 2008, President Bashar Assad, issued the Decree No. 49, imposing strict restrictions on the sale and purchase of property in certain border areas, particularly the Kurdish region, which was obviously a discriminatory policy targeting Kurds.

Subsequently, the Kurdish parties began to launch protests. On November 2, 2008, the Kurds protested against the Act No. 49, in front of the Damascus parliament building, and the police arrested about 200 people. On February 28, 2009, 21 persons were arrested by the security forces in the protests against the Act No. 49 in the Jazira district.

On March 8, the Kurds organized a concert to celebrate the International Women's Day, and the police disrupted the concert and arrested the two organizers.

The authorities closed down some celebrations and arrested Faisal Sabry Na'assu, a member of the central committee of the Syrian Kurdish Democratic Party, and Fanar el-Jameel on 9 March 2009. They were immediately brought before a military court in Damascus, released on 4 April 2009, and then given three-month jail sentences on August 9, 2009, in an outright violation of the right to peaceful assembly. On March 20, 2009, security forces joined public forces in using tear gas and batons to disperse a peaceful gathering of Kurdish Syrian citizens celebrating the festival of Newroz in the Aleppo neighbourhoods of el-Sheikh Maqsoud and el-Ashrafiya. Hundreds of participants were arrested. Some were taken to custody, while the rest were released.

On March 12, students of the University of Aleppo held a rally to pay tribute to the "3/12" incident in 2004, in which dozens of protestors were arrested and 14 of them were trialed in the military courts. On April 14, 2009, the Syrian Supreme National Security Court sentenced seven members of the Kurdish Democratic Alliance, between five to seven years' of imprisonment on charges of splitting the country, and granting parts of the national territories to a foreign country.

At the same day, a military court in Damascus, charged the Yekidi party secretary Fuad Aliko and former party secretary Hassan Saleh for joining an illegal organization and incitement of riots against the government and demanded 10 years of imprisonment.

And another 22 Kurds, who participated in the November 2007, Qamishli protests against Turkey, which sent troops to suppress Kurds, were sentenced to more than one year's imprisonment.

Before and after 2005, the Syrian Kurds have established three major joint organizations: Kurdistan Democratic Alliance, the Kurdistan Democratic Front and the Coordinating Committee of Kurds. In December 2009, a new coalition was established as the Kurdish Political Congress, in which nine Kurdish political organizations, including the Kurdistan Democratic Party of Syria, was present.

5.4 The Kurdish Issue since the "Arab Spring"

In 2011, massive anti-government protests erupted in Tunisia and Egypt, known as "the Arab Spring", this wave also spread to Syria, and made great impact on Syria generally, and also changed the fate of the Kurdish national movement in this country. After the outbreak of protests in February 2011, the protests in Syria has intensified and evolved to a civil unrest and even civil war. Armed, anti-government organizations, intensified the scale of their struggles, with the support of the West in an open attempt to overthrow the Bashar government. Protests were also launched In the Kurdish region, but were smaller, in scale."[24]

When the Arab Spring broke out, Syrian protesters began consolidating numerous opposition councils. The SNC's formation was announced in the city of Istanbul, Turkey on August 23, 2011, after a succession of meetings in Turkey and elsewhere. Its intended purpose is to "represent the concerns and demands of the Syrian people." The creation of the SNC was celebrated by the Syrian protestors since the Friday protest following its establishment was dubbed as "The Syrian National Council Represents

---

24 "Syria: A Kingdom of Silence", http://www.aljazeera.com/indepth/featur es/2011/02/201129103121452395.html.

Me". Yaser Tabbara, the council's spokesman at that time, said the membership of the council would include 115 to 120 members from all Syrian opposition groups, including the now defunct National Council of Syria. It has so far unveiled the names of 71 members, mostly living outside Syria. On October 2, 2011, the council formally declared its organizational affiliations and structure, to include a General Assembly, a General Secretariat and an Executive Board.

On October 7, Mashaal Tammo, the spokesman of the Kurdish Future Movement, was killed in Qamishli, by unidentified men, leading to massive Kurdish protests. Tammo has been the founder of the Kurdish Future Movement, who has repeatedly and severely criticized the Bashar government.

Mashaal Tammo had also participated, the above October 2, meeting of the Syrian National Council, (SNC) in Istanbul.

The Kurdish Future Movement has strong relations with Kurdish youth groups, and Kurdish youth opposition groups – which include the Union of Young Kurdish Coordinating Committees in Syria, Sawa Youth Coalition (part of the Local Coordinating Committees), Avahi Coalition for the Syrian Revolution, Coordinating Committee for Brotherhood, Aleppo, Efrin Youth Coordination, and the Alind Kobani Coordination accused the Syrian government security agencies should bear the responsibility for Mashaal Tammo's assasination. On October 8, 50,000 Kurds participated the funeral meeting in al-Qamishli, and protested the government, clashes occurred with security forces, killing at least 14 people.

Britain's Daily Telegraph wrote: "The son of Tammo has asserted that assassination of his father "laid the screws on the government's coffin.".... "They made a big mistake by killing my father." Britain's Daily Telegraph added, that the assassination of Tammo has vigorously promoted the Kurdish awakening: Mr Tammo's death prompted widespread calls from senior figures in the Kurdish community to join the civilian uprising against Mr Assad, a development that could seriously weaken the president given the challenges he is already facing elsewhere in the country. Until Mr Tammo's death, the minority had only played a peripheral role in the uprising with only a handful of Kurds among the 2,900 people the UN says have been killed in Syria since protests against the regime erupted in March. "Fares Tammo, the dead man's son, urged Syria's 1.7 million Kurds to throw their support behind the revolt and predicted that their participation would prove the decisive factor in overthrowing Mr Assad."[25]

25 Adrian Blomfiled, "Thousands of Kurds Could Awaken against Syrian Regime", Oct. 9, 2011, http://www.telegraph.co.uk/news/worldnews/middleeast/syria/8816825/ Thousands-of-Kurds-could-awaken-against-Syrian-regime.html.

Since then, the Kurds began to actively participate in protests, and acted parallel with other anti-government organizations. In early 2012, protest scales by Kurds began to expand, the Government began to use tanks to suppress them, the situation further deteriorated. By August 2012, the Kurdish regions in the North was occupied and controlled by the Kurds. Montly Review praised the event as follows: demonstrations usually begin by organizers welcoming everybody from all backgrounds and declaring that Kurds do not want a war within Syria on ethnic or religious lines. "Let us praise brotherhood and comradeship between Kurds, Arabs, Muslims, Christians, Armenians, and Assyrians in Syria's Kurdistan region. The Kurdish nation condemns war on sectarian grounds because we all deserve freedom." These were the words the organizers declared in their first welcoming speech in central Qamishli on Friday, August 3, when tens of thousands of demonstrators gathered to exercise their rights, celebrate their freedom, and dance to the beats of Kurdish revolutionary music, which had been illegal until just recently. Hundreds of thousands of Kurds demonstrating on Fridays across Syria suggests that this long neglected nation is now politically awake – thus the Kurdish north is organized to the utmost for its demands on every front, like nowhere else in Syria.

With the rapid deterioration of the situation in Syria, faced with the growing strength of domestic and foreign pressures, Syrian government became quite vulnerable.

In this context, Kurdish organizations enjoyed favorable conditions, for their activities.

At present Syria has nearly 20 Kurdish political organizations. At the same time, the Kurds have gradually adjusted their strategies, strengthened their unity, actively pursued international public relations and gained the support of the international community.

Abdul Baki Yusuf, leader of the Yekiti Party, pointed out that to solve the Syrian problem, the Syrian opposition must remain united and oppose to the exclusion of the Kurds from the new constitution-making process in Syria, Kurds must have a stake in the future Syria."[26]

There is also an argument that, the Syrian Kurds must not miss the current opportunity, and it will be difficult to meet such an opportunity for a long time in the future, consequently the Syrian Kurdish parties must closely follow the situation, strengthen their unity and cooperation, and defend the fruits of democratization in Syria.[27]

---

26 "Kurdish Yekiti (Birlik) Party in Syria: Resolving the Syrian Issue Requires Unification of Opposition Forces", Feb. 26, 2012, http://www.aknews.com/en/aknews/9/292359/.
27 Minhaj Akreyi, "West Kurdistan and the Arab Awakening", Feb. 3, 2011, http://www.ekurd.net/mismas/aricles/misc2011/2/state4601.htm.

Allegedly, the Democratic Union Party (pro-PKK) has organized the armed the Revolutionary Youth of the Democratic Union Party troops to "protect the Kurdish villages and towns in the neighborhood, check the suspicious vehicles and the suspicious travelers." This has been the only Kurdish political organization with an armed force. This armed youth organization defends the "Movement of Democratic Communes" in the region.[28]

On October 26, 2011, a number of Syrian Kurdish organizations met in Qamishli and The Kurdish National Council in Syria (KNC) was established. This organization includes the Pro-Ocalan Syrian party named Partiya Yetikitiya Demokrat (PYD). On the same day, 12 pro-Barzani smaller Syrian Kurdish organizations established the Kurdish National Council (KNC or ENKS;in Arabic)in Arbil, Iraq. Masoud Barzani, the leader of the KRG of Iraq has sponsored this organization. Please notice that the names of these organizations nearly the same, only difference is the "in Syria" suffix in the first one established in Qamishli.

The main points in the political platforms of the organization are the following:

the constitutionally recognized Kurdish identity and the Kurdish people who historically lived on their own land; the abolition of discriminatory policies and laws, including the prohibition of the use of Kurdish and the creation of Kurdish schools.

And that, in keeping with the territorial integrity of Syria, the Syrian government should be politically non-centralized. The organization hopes to win the support of the West, especially the United States, and holds negotiations with the other Syrian opposition parties (SNC) to reach an agreement for the "post-Assad era" in the framework of federalism. Although the KNC has joined the Syrian National Coalition, there are key differences between the KNC and the SNC over their approach to the issue of decentralization, while the KNC presses for Kurdish autonomy, the SNC which mainly includes Arabs has rejected anything more than administrative decentralization[29]

In January 2012, the Syrian Kurdish organizations held a meeting to discuss the fate of the Syrian Kurds and the objectives of the struggle. Masoud Barzani, President of the Kurdish Regional Government of Iraq, and Saleh, Prime Minister of the Kurdistan Regional Government, attended the meeting. The main themes included: right to self-determination; to develop to protect the needs of the people of Kurdish and the establishment of a democratic Constitution in Syria. Barzani pointed out that the Syrian

302

28 "Fear of Clashes Between Kurdish Groups in Syria", http://www.rudaw.net/english/news/syria/4750.html.
29 "Without Kurds Syria will not Witness Stability: Ibrahim Biro", Feb.14, 2012, http://www.ekurd.net/mismas/articles/misc2012/2/syriakurd423.htm,

Kurds themselves must be prepared to deal with the possible challenges and decide their destiny. Barzani called for unity among the Syrian Kurds and also criticized the PYD's declaration of a federation in northern Syria as an attempt to break up Syria without previous "debate and democratic participation". He further stated that "it strictly opposes any attempt to impose federalism on the Syrian people without a preceding discussion".[30]

On June 11, 2012, the Kurdish National Council and the "People's Cuncil of Western Kurdistan"(An organization led by the Turkish PKK) held a "three-day conference related to Syrian Kurds in Hewler"

The People's Council of Western Kurdistan and the KNC formed a joint Kurdish Supreme Council and, in a supplementary agreement held on July 1, committed to the establishment of security committees as well as unarmed civilian defense forces to protect Kurdish areas.

A Carnegie Middle East Center report wrote: "These agreements, sponsored by Massoud Barzani, are an attempt to form a united Kurdish front and to reach a power-sharing solution between the KNC and the Kurdish Democratic Union Party. However, the recent behavior of the Kurdish Democratic Union Party, which has launched physical attacks against some of its Kurdish opponents in Syria, indicates that the agreement is not being implemented on the ground and explains continuing tensions between the two main Kurdish factions."

The Syrian Kurds also actively seek the support of the West. Internationally, the KNC seeks to develop close relations with the United States, the European Union, and other Western powers. On May 6, 2012 a delegation led by KNC leader Abdul Hakim Bashar visited the White House and US State Department to discuss Syrian Kurdish concerns.

The delegation also met with the President of the United States National Security Adviser Donnelon, Deputy Secretary of State for Near East Affairs, and former US Ambassador to Syria Robert Ford, former US Government Special Coordinator for Syria Fred Hoff and other US government officials. Abdul Hakim Bashar said the purpose of the visit was to explain to the US Kurds' position on the Syrian revolution.

"The invitation we received from US Department of State could be seen as a strong indication of how important the Kurdish issue has become in Syria. It is becoming one of the primary issues and a serious effort needs to be made so it is resolved on a fair basis in the post-Assad Syria. The level of legitimacy the Kurdish National Council has representing Syria's Kurds was especially illustrated by this invitation," Bashar said.[31]

---

30 "Three-day Conference of Syrian Kurds in Hewler", Jan. 31, 2012, http://en.firatnews.eu/index.php?rupel=article&nuceID=4025.
31 "Kurdish National Council of Syria KNCS Invited to US to Discuss the Kurdish Issue", May 12, 2012, http://www.ekurd.net/mismas/articles/misc2012/5/syriakurd497.htm.

It is reported that the meeting has focused on how the Kurds, together with the Syrian opposition, can push Syria's transition to a democratic pluralist state. This has been the first time in five years that the US government has officially invited Syrian Kurdish political organizations to visit the United States.[32]

On May 16, 2012, an article by Israeli Jerusalem Post wrote: Robert Ford, who left his post as US ambassador to Syria earlier this year, and Fred Hof, the administration's special coordinator on Syria, took part in this meeting. State Department Deputy Spokesman Mark Toner described its purpose as part of "ongoing efforts... to help the Syrian opposition build a more cohesive opposition to Assad."[33]

In May 2012, the Kurdish National Council leader Sherkoh Abbas called on Israel to support a federal Syria based on nationalities, which would not only help to break Syria's Iran-led Shiite crescent belt.

Sikhoun Abbas claimed: Kurds, Sunni Arabs, Allawits, and Druze are not interested in forming an alliance with Iran and will become Israel's allies. He added, "We need to break Syria into pieces," Abbas said.

The Syrian Kurdish dissident argued that a federal Syria, separated into four or five regions on an ethnic basis, would also serve as a natural "buffer" for Israel against both Sunni and Shi'ite Islamist forces.

He also criticized the US efforts which urged the Kurdish National Council to join the Syrian National Council.[34]

On May 2, 2012, the same year, the Syrian Kurdish National Council called on the Russian government to stop supporting the Bashar regime and demanded that Russia support, democratization in Syria and said that a Kurdish delegation would be visiting Russia at the invitation of the Russian Foreign Ministry and discuss the current political and security situation in Syria, with the Russian officials.[35]

---

32 "Syrian Kurdish Dissident: Break Syria into Pieces", May 16, 2012, http://www.jpost.com/MiddleEast/Article.aspx?id=270149.

33 "Syrian Kurdish National Council Visits Washington", May 13, 2012, http://yekiti-media.org/nuce.php?z=en&id=1565; http://www.state.gov/r/pa/prs/ps/2012/05/189803.htm.

34 "Syrian Kurdish Dissident: Break Syria into Pieces", May 16, 2012, http://www.jpost.com/MiddleEast/Article.aspx?id=270149.

35 "Syrian Kurds to Demand Russia to Stop Supporting Assad Regime", May 2, 2012, http://www.ekurd.net/mismas/articles/misc2012/5/syriakurd485.htm.

The sixteen Kurdish parties of the Kurdish National Council (KNC as of May 2012)

The Kurdish Democratic Party in Syria (al-Parti) led by Dr. Abdul Hakim Bashar

The Kurdish Democratic Party in Syria (al-Parti) led by Nasreddin Ibrahim

The Kurdish Democratic National Party in Syria led by Tahir Sfook

The Kurdish Democratic Equality Party in Syria led by Aziz Dawe

The Kurdish Democratic Progressive Party in Syria led by Hamid Darwish

The Kurdish Democratic Unity Party in Syria (Yekiti) led by Sheikh Ali

The Kurdish Yekiti Party in Syria led by Ismail Hamo

The Azadi Kurdish Party in Syria led by Mustafa Oso

The Azadi Kurdish Party in Syria led by Mustafa Jumaa

The Syrian Democratic Kurdish Party led by Sheikh Jamal

The Kurdish Left Party in Syria led by Muhammad Musa

Yekiti Kurdistani led by Abdul Basit Hamo

Faced with the growing Kurdish national mood and protests, the Syrian government has also taken measures to appease the Kurds, has tried to split the opposition forces and eased pressures.

On March 31, 2011, President Bashar ordered the establishment of a special Commission to address the issues raised by the 1962 Jazira Census and requested the Commission to submit a report to the President by April 15.

On April 7, President Bashar issued a decree deciding on the registration of foreigners[36] as citizens, which would gain full power by the date of publication of the decree in the state's official newspaper.

Syrian Interior Ministry was appointed to follow its implementation. He said in an interview: "Our Kurdish parties welcome this step and sees it as a sign that, the Syrian reform wheel has really started turning "

In April 2011, President Bashar announced the establishment of the Kurdish New Year as a public holiday, from 2012 on. On May 31, President Bashar issued an amnesty to release all political prisoners, including many Kurdish politicians. On June 8, Bashar invited 12 representatives of the Kurdish parties to hold talks. In addition, the government is trying to use divisions among the Kurdish Parties. In May 2012, the Democratic Union Party (pro-PKK) and Kurdish National Council supporters clashed

---

36 The Syrian law distinguishes between Kurds who are registered as foreigners (ajanib) even though their families have lived in Syria for generations and unregistered (maktoumeen) Kurds. The "foreign" Kurds cannot vote, own property, obtain government jobs and travel outside of Syria. They are, however, not exempt from compulsory army service. The "foreign" Kurds are those who couldn't prove in 1962 that they've resided in Syria since 1945.

in Qamishli. The Democratic Union Party accused the Kurdish National Council as "supporting an anti-Kurd agenda", criticizing Turkey's role for the crisis, and division among Syrian Kurds and accused the Kurdish National Council as being pro-Turkish and pro-Assad. The Kurdish National Council accused the Syrian government for manipulating the conflict, saying that the purpose of the Democratic Union Party was to prevent anti-government protests. For this reason the Kurdish National Committee is concerned about the possibility of a civil war among the Syrian Kurds.[37]

Overall, the Kurds have been cautious and careful about anti-government protests, less active and do not support extremist Arab fighters, thus Kurdish region has been relatively quiet.

As of March 10, 2012, the anti-government protests and clashes in Syria have caused 105,530 deaths, but in Kurdish region of Hasaka only 40 people were killed.[38]

There are several reasons for this. First, the Bashar government adopts a policy to keep Kurds neutral and shows some signs that he is ready to resolve the long-standing Kurdish issue. Assad's government considers the Kurdish-dominated northeast of the country strategically important because it borders Turkey and Iraq—and because it contains most of the country's limited oil supplies. The government also fears that Syrian Kurds, like Kurdish groups in neighboring states, might seek independence. All Syrian Kurdish parties currently reject separatism, however, instead demand greater rights within Syria. "The regime tried to neutralize Kurds," explained Hassan Saleh, leader of the Kurdish Yekiti Party. "In the Kurdish areas, people are not being repressed like the Arab areas. But activists are being arrested."[39]

The Christian Science Monitor says the Syrian government has succeeded in convincing many Syrian Kurds and Christians that they could live freely like the minorities of Lebanon and Iraq. The article in Christian Science Monitor has pointed out that the Bashar regime is supported by to the three main forces: Christians, Kurds, Russia.

Secondly, among the Kurds, there are differences whether to support of the overthrow of the Bashar and whether to participate in the other anti-government forces.

37 "Fear of Clashes Between Kurdish Groups in Syria", http://www.rudaw.net/english/news/syria/4750.html.
38 "Syrian Martyrs Free Syria", http://syrianshuhada.com/?lang=en&.
39 Reese Erlich, "In Syria, Kurds Split over Support for Assad Regime", Pulitzer Center on Crisis Reporting, Oct 27., 2011, http://pulitzercenter.org/reporting/syria-kurdish-groups-armed-forces-assad-controversy.

At present, the Kurdish Syrian parties are roughly divided into three factions: "The first has sought an arrangement with the Assad government in Damascus in exchange of promised concessions. The second group voices an autonomous region on similar lines to Iraqi KRG and the third group has sided with PKK of Turkey and aims to carve out a mini state of the Kurds. These developments have both concerned Iran as an extended autonomous Kurdish region would block the trade channel that Iran uses to send arms and amenities to Syria and Lebanon.

Jerusalem Post wrote: The Kurds are also divided among themselves. The KNC is dominated by the Kurdish Democratic Party in Syria, which has close links to the Kurdish Regional Government of Massoud Barzani in northern Iraq. The PKK-linked PYD, meanwhile, is, according to Abbas and others, now working in cooperation with the Assad regime.

PYD-linked sources argue that the current Syrian uprising is simply a battle between the regime and an alliance of the Turkish government and the Muslim Brotherhood. As such, they suggest, Syrian Kurds' main interest is in protecting their own areas. The bottom line, as Qubad Talabani, representative of the Kurdistan Regional Government to the US, put it in a recent speech, is that the "Syrian opposition is not talking about Kurdish issues, is not talking about the need to protect Kurdish rights or to have the Kurdish identity as part of any new Syria." For as long as this remains the case, calls for federalism, for separation, and for breaking Syria "into pieces" are likely to grow stronger.[40]

Among the 20 Syrian opposition factions, only "the Kurdish Future Movement" led by Fares Tammo, has joined in the Syrian National Committee which includes the Arab opposition groups, its representative serves as a member of the Executive Committee of the Council. Three Kurdish organizations also have joined the NDC, the National Coordinating Committee for Democratic Change.

On February 24, 2012, "Friends of Syria" meeting supported by Western powers was held in Tunisia, Kurdish National Council, the Syrian National Committee for Kurds were present at the meeting. In Tunis, even though it was not on the agenda, US Secretary of State Hillary Clinton met with the head of the KNC, Abdulhakim Bashar for the first time, along with the head of the SNC, Burhan Ghalioun, and SNC spokeswoman Basma Kodamani, to advance the calls for unification. The United States has put pressure on the SNC behind the scenes to reach an accommodation with the Kurds and recommended integrating more Kurdish opposition parties and groups into the council through meeting some of their demands.[41]

---

40 "Syrian Kurdish Dissident: Break Syria into Pieces", May 16, 2012, http://www.jpost.com/MiddleEast/Article.aspx?id=270149.

41 Ibid.

On March 17, five opposition organizations, such as the "Free National Reform Movement", "Islamic National Movement", "Liberation and Development Group", "Turkmen National Group" and "Kurdish New Life Movement", met in Istanbul and officially announced their agreement with the Syrian National Council. But, as of mid-March, the Council's structure had diverged significantly from its original charter. This has caused conflict with other SNC members who view the re-structuring as an attempt by the SNC leader Ghalioun to consolidate power. During the SNC meeting on March 28, five factions within the various blocs suspended their participation in the council until a new charter has been drafted and the Executive Committee re-structured a second time to make it more representative. This process is currently underway and the SNC began working to create a new charter as of the beginning of April.

At its inception, the SNC had 25 Kurdish members from three of the major Kurdish parties, the Kurdish Future Movement, the Kurdish Union Party in Syria, and the Kurdish Azadi Party. However, in January 2012, the Kurdish Union Party in Syria and the Kurdish Azadi Party withdrew from the SNC, leaving only representatives from the nominal Kurdish Future Movement. As a result, neither of the two major Syrian Kurdish parties were represented in the SNC as of April 2012, and the most prominent Kurdish members that do have seats are independents and are not representative of the major Kurdish political trends

308

It is clear that, Kurds are skeptical of the Syrian National Council, and it is unclear what kind of future the Kurds will face after the overthrow of the Bashar regime, the "uncertainty about their agenda". They are worrisome about the role of the Muslim Brotherhood in the Syrian National Council and its intimate relationships with Turkey. The Syrian National Council rejects the strategy of federalism pursued by Kurds and its leaders have claimed that there was no Kurdistan, and demanded that the Kurds should abandon the "useless" federalism illusions.

On March 27, held in Istanbul, Syria opposition meeting, Kurdish representative angrily left the venue, then announced his withdrawal from the Syrian National Committee, on the grounds that the organization is reluctant to adopt the Kurdish representative of the national self-determination and empowerment of local governments and other claims. Many Kurds distrust the SNC because of the strong presence of Muslim Brotherhood members in its leadership, and because of its close links to the government of Turkey.

A Kurdish representative said Turkey was behind the scenes, preventing the Kurdish National Committee from cooperating with the Syrian National Council, fearing that Syrian Kurds would put pressure over the Kurdish issue in Turkey."[42]

42 "Syrian Arab Opposition Fear Kurdish Demands", Apr. 4, 2012, http://www.ekurd. net/mismas/articiles/misc2012/4/syriakurd469.htm.

Syrian National Council spokesman commented: "some Kurdish organizations support the revolution in order to seek the realization of the Kurdish right to self-determination, but the Syrian National Committee does not accept this radical goal", stressed that the Syrian National Council aims the recognition of the Kurds as a national minority, their language and cultural rights. All acts of discrimination against different nationalities, and will enhance the role of local governments. The Syrian National Committee also exchanged views with Iraqi Kurdish regional government leaders to ensure that Kurdish rights would be guaranteed after the overthrow of the Bashar regime in order to avoid security problems and to try to bring possible Kurdish issues under its control.[43]

On December 31, 2011, the Yekiti Party issued a statement related to the Syrian National Council and the Syrian Revolution, saying that SNC's approach is the continuation of the past Syrian government which discriminated against the Kurds.

Reese Erlich wrote: "The dispute among Kurdish political parties is part of a wider division among Syrian Kurds. Many worry that that Islamist opposition parties, should they come to power, would be worse for them than the current government. Mohammad Farho, a Syrian Kurdish commentator and activist living in Erbil, Iraq, told me, "Kurds are afraid of the Arab opposition parties because their agenda is not clear."[44]

In January 2012, Azadi and Yekiti Parties announced their withdrawal from the SNC after talks failed between the KNC and SNC and remained members of the KNC only. After the withdrawal, the Azadi Party split, yet both Azadi parties are currently members of the KNC and not the SNC. Both Abdul Basit Saida and the Future Party, the other Kurdish representatives, remain on the SNC.

In February 2012, Qubad Talabani, a representative of the Iraqi Kurdish Regional Government in the United States, spoke at the joint Iraq-US conference, stating that the Syrian Kurds are in a difficult position. The Assad regime is not good for the Kurds, but the Syrian opposition will not be good to go. The Syrian opposition is not talking about the Kurdish issue now, nor does it discuss protecting the Kurds' rights or seeing the Kurds as part of the future Syria. If this situation persists, the Kurds' demands for federalism, or the division of Syria into pieces will grow."[45]

---

43 "Syrian Opposition National Council Does not 'Accept' Kurdish Right to Self-determination", http://ikjnews.com/?p=3138.
44 Reese Erlich, "In Syria, Kurds Split over Support for Assad Regime", Pulitzer Center on Crisis Reporting, Oct. 27, 2011, http://pulitzercenter.org/reporting/syria-kurdish-groups-armed-forces-assad-controversy.
45 "Syrian Kurdish Dissident: Break Syria into Pieces", May 16, 2012, http://www.jpost.com/MiddleEast/Article.aspx?id=270149."

Third, Turkey and some Arab countries in the region are deeply involved in Syria's civil war, and support anti-government organizations to over-throw the Bashar regime, and also spend efforts to isolate Kurds in Syria.[46]

On March 31, 2012, the Syrian National Council leader Khati al-Malik said in an interview with an Arabian television that, Kurdish demands in Syria were "unlawful", and it was suggested that the Council should ex-clude the Kurdish National Council from the "Friends of Syria" group.

The Kurdish Youth of Syria said the Syrian National Committee obeys the directives of Turkey, while Saudi Arabia and other countries want to arm the opposition, but the Kurds are opposed to armed opposition and hope for peaceful solution.[47]

On May 31, 2011, the Syrian anti-government factions planned a meet-ing in Antalya, Turkey Antalya: In an article published in Asharq al-Awsat, a group comprised of 12 Kurdish political parties in Syria (National Movement of Kurdish Parties in Syria) announced that they intend to boy-cott the opposition summit. The group stated that any such meeting held in Turkey can only be a detriment to the Kurds in Syria, because Turkey is against the aspirations of the Kurds, not just with regards to northern Kurdistan, but in all four parts of Kurdistan, including the Kurdish region of Syria.[48]

310

Representative of the Kurdish Leftist Party Saleh Kado echoed that con-cern saying that Turkey "has negative attitudes towards the Kurdish issue in general" and that Ankara needs to "first resolve the issue of 20 million Kurds living within their territory before seeking to bring together the Kurdish Syrian parties [in Turkey] to come to an agreement on a unified project with regards how to deal with the current events [in Syria]."

Kado stressed that "we, the Kurds in Syria, do not trust Turkey or its poli-cies, and that is why we have decided to boycott the summit." Kado also said part of the reason for the boycott was the attendance of the Muslim Brotherhood.

The Turkish government is planning to intervene in our peoples fate. Let us make it clear that if the Turkish government intervenes our West Kurdistan, the entire Kurdistan will resist to this intervention. The entire region will be a theater of war against Turkey."[49]

46   Michael Weiss, "Will Kurds Determine Syria's Fate?" New Republic, Nov. 16, 2011.
47   "Syrian Arab Opposition Fear Kurdish Demands", Apr.4, 2012, http://www.ekurd.net/mismas/articles/msc2012/4.syriakurd469.htm.
48   "Syrian Kurdish Parties Boycott Syrian Opposition Conference in Antalya, Turkey", Monthly Review, May 29, 2011, http://mrzine.monthlyreview.org/2011/kb010611.html.
49   "Kurd PKK Rebels Threaten Turkey if it enters Syrian Kurdistan", Mar. 22, 2012, http://www.ekurd.net/mismas/articles/misc2012/3/turkey3851.htm.

The Syrian National Coordinating Committee for Democratic Change, Arab nationalists and Islamic extremists, especially the Muslim Brotherhood, have cooperated with Turkey to publicize the weaknesses and division among the Kurds, who are in fact the strongest and most organized opposition group in Syria.

Turkey and Muslim Brotherhood—which includes anti-Kurdish elements—has established good relations on the basis of restricting Kurds in Syria, and reached an agreement as follows: weakening the Syrian Kurdish parties, limiting Kurdish power and Kurdish autonomy in the post-Assad era, both sides will carry out a security cooperation in the Syrian-Turkish border region against the Kurds.[50]

The position of Turkey on Syria has also difficulties: on the one hand it supports the Arab banner of democratic change, to support the armed rebels to overthrow the Bashar government, on the other hand, worried about Syrian Kurds achieving autonomy after Bashar Assad's fall, which will not only make Syria become a base for the activities of PKK activities base, but also may lead Turkey's Kurds more boldly imitate Iraq and Syria, and vigorously take the road of self-government.[51]

Looking from the current situation, the "Arab Spring" has not only provided opportunities for resolving the long-standing issues of Syrian Kurds such as the recognition of national identity, minority rights and stateless Kurds, but also provides them an opportunity for further improving their status and achieve self- government.

It is most probable that the status of Kurds in the future Syrian state will be further improved, whether or not the Baath regime will continues to be in power. And, the decisions taken by the Syrian Kurds will to a certain extent impact the Syrian revolution and even the future of Syria. There are even some comments that the Kurds will determine the fate of Syria.[52]

50   "Situation of Kurds in Syria Discussed in Belgium Senate", Mar.13, 2012, http:// www.ekurd.net/mismas/articles/misc2012/3/state5982.htm.
51   Ankara Alarmed by Syrian Kurds' Autonomy, Aug.1, 2012, http://online.wsj.com/ article/SB10000872396390443687504577563183350590066.html.
52   "Will Kurds Determine Syria's Fate?" New Republic, Nov. 16, 2011, http://www.npr. org/2011/11/16/142387417/new-republic-will-kurds-determine-syrias-fate.

Summary

Syrian Kurds and their movement for national rights have been little known to the outside world. There are many reasons for this: compared to Kurds in Turkey, Iraq and Iran, the Syrian Kurdish people are not only a small in area, population, but also the national movement is not so mature and large, nationalist organizations and the national movement has been weaker or underdeveloped.

Syrian Kurds mainly live in plains, where it is difficult to carry out armed struggle and guerrilla warfare, while the Syrian government has implemented a long-term iron rule in the region. Therefore, it is not easy to effectively confront the government forces. Syrian Kurds also live in a region at the junction of three countries, Turkey, Iraq, Syria, the location is very remote, far from main roads, thus isolated from the outside world, few foreigners have visited the region. In general, the Syrian Kurdish issue is less prominent and sharp compared to other three host countries, although occasional protests and riots have occurred in the past, their scales have not been large.

The "Arab Spring", which began in 2011, rapid deterioration of relations between the Syrian government and the West, and the weaknesses of the Syrian regime, have brought about a historic opportunity for the Syrian Kurds. Judging from the present situation, regardless of the Baath regime's maintaining its dominant position in future Syria, the uplift of the status of Kurds seems to be an inevitable trend. To effectively defend and improve the Kurdish national rights and their status, will be an important and key pillar of a democratic Syria in the future. Kurdish left party secretary Mahmoud Moussa said: Syria would not achieve a true democracy without a just and democratic solution to the Kurdish question.[53]

To which extent the Syria issue can be peacefully and fairly resolved, is still unknown. The Kurds do not believe in the current government, nor do they support the armed Syrian opposition, which is the main reason why they remain cautious and hesitant to join the current Syrian revolution and the Syrian opposition. With regard to the future of Syria, the Kurds believe that without the active participation of Kurds, Syria will not be able to achieve stability.[54]

Abdulhakim Bashar, secretary-general of the Kurdistan Democratic Party in Syria said: Federalism for the Kurds. We'll work to make this possible in Syria. I believe that if federalism isn't established in Syria the country will head toward a long-term civil war.[55]

---

53 "No Democracy in Syria without Just Solution for Kurdish Issue: Secretary of the Syrian Kurdish Left Party", Apr.20, 2012, http://www.ekurd.net/mismas/articles/misc2012/4/syriakurd480.htm.
54 "Without Kurds Syria will not Witness Stability: Ibrahim Biro", Feb. 14, 2012, http://www.ekurd.net/mismas/articles/misc2012/2/syriakurd423.htm.
55 http://www.ekurd.net/mismas/articles/misc2011/12/syriakurd398.htm.

CHAPTER SIX

Major World Powers and the Kurdish Issue

There is an old saying in the Middle East: the Kurds have no true friends. This statement not only implies the tragic fate of the Kurds, but also shows the Kurds' loneliness, hard survival circumstances in the region and in the current world. The Kurdish issue is the result of Western colonialism and imperialist power politics of great powers. Kurdish issue has not been properly handled and resolved, but has become increasingly complex and international, which is closely related with the intervention of external forces.

Kurds are the victims of great-power politics, colonialism, hegemonism. They can also be seen as an important pawn for the foreign and great powers to intervene in the affairs of the Middle East. The concern and involvement of the major world powers to the Kurdish issue is essentially selfish and self-centered. British and French colonialists have been the initiators of the Kurdish issue. And currently the U.S. is the largest external factor in the Kurdish issue. The Iraq war launched by the U.S. has directly changed the fate of the Iraqi Kurds, thus the Kurdish nation encountered with a new historical opportunity and development prospects. During the Cold War the Soviet Union was an important external force affecting the fate of the Kurds, but has declined. In the Middle East Jews and Kurds have a similar history and destiny, consequently Israel views Kurds as a potential natural ally in the region. China is a latecomer related the Kurdish issue, but China's contacts with the Kurds are developing on bona fide basis.

6.1 The U.S. and the Kurdish Issue

The United States is the key external factor to solve the Kurdish issue. The influence of the United States on the Kurdish issue has gradually increased. Before the World War II, Europe had been the key external factors affecting the Kurdish issue, during the Cold War it was the Soviet Union, in the post- Cold War era it has been the United States. Especially the two Iraq wars launched by the United States has greatly changed the fate of the Kurds and paved the way for a historical development of the Kurdish national movement of the historical development process, while the US's involvment in the Kurdish issue reached its peak.

US attitude and policies on the Kurdish issue can be divided into three stages.

The first stage (1914-1945), extends from the outbreak of World War I, to the end of the World War II.

During this period the United States began to get involved in the Kurdish issue, and has actively promoted Kurdish independence, but due to strong resistance, and rapidly gave up its concern. This stage marked by the 14 Point-principles proposed by the U.S President Wilson after the First World War, and the twelfth point in this manifest was directly related with the self-determination of the nationalities under the Ottoman Empire.

The Cold War era as the second stage (1945-1990).

During this era, utilitarianism has reached the strongest level. In its effort to respond requirements of competition between two camps of the East and West, and its pursuit for global hegemony, the United States has become more and more interested in Kurdish issue, but this didn't mean she was concerned with the Kurdish national rights, but only about her own interests. In this stage the US supported Iran's repression of the Kurdish Mahabad Republic, next she first supported, later betrayed the Iraqi Kurdish insurgency.

The post-Cold-War era is the third stage (1991 to the present).

During this period, the US involvement in the Kurdish issue has further deepened and involvement reached its peak. On the one hand, the United States launched two Iraq wars, supported the liberation of the Iraqi Kurds, helped them to realize autonomy, promoted the development of the Kurdish national movement; on the other hand, in order to maintain its global hegemony, and to defend its global interests, its strategy to this end, i.e. promotion of democracy and human rights globally, has paid increasingly more attention to the Kurdish human rights and freedom, which has objectively promoted maintenance and development of national rights and human rights for Kurds to a certain degree.

The earliest US involvement in the Kurdish issue was during the World War I. At the end of the First World War, on January 8,1918, in response to the attempt by the European powers to partition the defeated Ottoman Empire, president Wilson proposed the famous "14-point plan"[1] which mainly included: transparent diplomacy, abrogation of secret treaties; fair and impartial treatment of the colonial claims, based upon a strict observance of the principle that in determining all such questions of sovereignty the interests of the populations concerned must have equal weight with the equitable government whose title is to be determined, recognizing that the Turkish portion of the-then-Ottoman Empire should be assured a secure sovereignty, but the other nationalities which are under Turkish rule should be assured an undoubted security of life and an absolutely unmolested opportunity of autonomous development, formation of a general association of nations under specific covenants for the purpose of affording mutual guarantees of political independence and territorial integrity to great and small states alike.

According to President Wilson's idealistic blueprint, the autonomy of Kurds should be promoted. Consequently the United States proposed the establishment of an international commission of inquiry to confirm whether the subject peoples under the rule of prewar Ottoman Empire desire self-government or accept international hosting.

However, there had occurred a big gap between the position of the U.S. and Britain plus France on the partition of the Ottoman Empire as early as prewar days, consequently the US proposition for international commission of inquiry was rejected and delayed by the pressure of the latter parties.

Finally, the United States decided to form its own commission on Mandates in Ottoman Turkey. Wilson appointed Henry Churchill King the president of Oberlin College and Charles R. Crane a prominent Democrat Charles R. Crane to lead the "Inter-Allied Commission", also known as the King-Crane Commission. In 1919, the King-Crane Commission of Inquiry started to investigate the issue concerning the disposition of non-Turkish areas within the former Ottoman Empire, so as to make policy recommendations on the fate of these peoples. The commission visited the regions of Palestine, Syria, Lebanon and Anatolia and conducted an opinion survey. But the work of the Commission was has been obstructed by the British, did not proceed as intended. In 1919, before the Commission submitted its investigation report, the Paris Peace Conference made the decision to partition the Ottoman Empire, according to the "Sevres Treaty of August 1920"[2]. King-Crane Commission could only publish its findings and recommendations in 1922. The report had concluded: "since the relevant peoples of

1 See appendix part for Wilson's 14-point plan.
2 See appendix part for the Sevres Treaty.

the Middle East were not yet ready for independence, a colonial government would not serve the people well either. He recommended instead that the Americans move in to occupy the region, because only the United States could be trusted to guide the people to self-sufficiency and independence rather than become an imperialist occupier."

The report also recommended the establishment of an Armenian state, a separate Istanbul (Constantinople) state, an Anatolian state and a Kurdish state, to the Peace Conference.[3]

Although the Treaty of the Sèvres stipulated Kurdish autonomy and independence conditionally, and although Sèvres reflected the spirit of the "14-point plan", to a certain extent, most of the recommendations by the King-Crane Commission were rejected by the British and French.

In those days "isolationist trend of thought" was prevalent in the United States, consequently the US Congress refused to ratify the "Treaty of Versailles."(Paris Conference Treaty)

Moreover, after the victory of the independence war led by M. Kemal of Turkey in 1922, the Allied Powers, including Britain, France and Italy, have renounced their previous commitment of supporting the independence of the Kurds. The plan by the United States to promote the Kurdish national self-determination was not realized either.

316

It can be said that the United States policy after the World War I, which ambitiously concerned with the Kurdish issue and put forward national self-determination in support of the Kurdish independence not only reflects her dissatisfaction of the secret diplomacy followed by European great powers and her desire to establish a new world order, but also reflects Wilson's idealist anti-colonial ideas and policies. Unfortunately, the first involvement and concern by the US government of the Kurdish issue suffered a failure. From then on until the end of World War II, the United States has remained at a distance to the issue: "far less supportive and often cynically opportunistic."[4]

During the Cold War, the US interest and coaching efforts targeting Kurds has increased gradually, which was closely related to the global strategic situation and the geopolitical situation in the Middle East. During this period, the attitude of the United States on the Kurdish issue had two main characteristics. One was indifference towards Kurds in their struggle for national rights. This indifference had multiple reasons: so as to oppose and restrict the Soviet Union which positioned itself as the supporter of the

3   "Crane and King's Long-hid Report on the Near East", New York Times, Dec. 3, 1922.
4   Stephen Zune, "The United States and the Kurds: A Brief History", Foreign Policy in Focus, Oct. 25, 2007.

global nationalist movements; Kurdish nationalist parties emerging and active in the Cold War period were ideologically left and mostly believed in Marxist-Leninist left-wing ideas, and international policy they adopted was pro-Soviet Union-led socialist camp and they stood against imperialism and colonialism; thirdly those countries which were faced by the Kurdish issue, in the region were, mostly strategic allies of the West, such as the NATO member Turkey and the Iranian Pahlavi regime which undertook the task of "policing" the Gulf for the United States' overlapping geopolitical interests, which all demonstrated that the general lines of the U.S Kurdish policy during the Cold War era, was distancing from alliance.

Second, characteristic was playing the Kurdish card for the regional political interests of the United States. One most typical example was the Iraq case in the early 1970s. The Iraqi Baathist regime began to adopt the pro-Soviet policy, distancing from the West, in turn the U.S. allied with the Iran government to support the Iraqi Kurdistan Democratic Party, against Iraq. In 1975, the Iraqi Kurdistan Democratic Party was betrayed by the U.S. and Iran, after Iraq and Iran reached the Algiers Agreement, which resulted in the heavy defeat of the KDP Iraq, it leader Mullah Mustafa Barzani sadly fled to USA with the help of CIA, his health soon deteriorated and lost his life.[5]

Due to this experience Masoud Barzani and other Kurdish leaders began to approach cautiously towards the US "suggestions". In this era the US supported the Iraqi Kurds against the government under several consideration and interests: chose to ally with Iran against Iraq, since Iraq and Iran were enemies; the US targeted to frustrate Iraq since this country chose to ally with the Soviet Union, and followed anti-West policies during the Cold War; due to Iraq's hostility against Israel, the US supported the Iraqi Kurds, to alleviate the pressure over Israel by Iraq.

Kissinger later explained why the United States withdrew its support to Iraqi Kurds, saying that the United States did not want to open a new front of operation in the inhospitable mountains, just at the Soviet border, and it was hard for the US to coordinate a harmonious alliance with King Pahlavi on the issue of supporting Iraqi Kurds.[6]

---

5   In October 1974, the Vice-President of Iraq sent a cooperative message to Iran via Egypt and Algeria. In those days, also in those days the U.S. was aiming to promote a peace agreement between Egypt and Israel. Both the U.S. and Egypt wanted to gain the support of Iraq.
6   Michael M. Gunter, The Historical Dictionary of the Kurds, p.300.

William Colby, Director of the CIA (1920-1966), who led CIA between Sep. 1973-Jan. 1976, also wrote in his memoirs-"My Life in the CIA": "one of the main reasons for my dismissal by Ford in November 1975 was, the failure of CIA's covert operation to support the insurgency by the Iraqi Kurds, and the leak of covert operation information to the media." He added: "The Kurds were seeking aid from anywhere, which usually overlapped with the interests of the donor countries. Due to the Soviet Union's strengthening relationship with Iraq in 1972, both Iran and the US were worrisome about the rising communist forces in the region. The King of Iran therefore asked President Nixon to ally with the Iran's policy to support Iraqi Kurds who demand autonomy as a sign to show that the US was truly favoring joint struugle against the danger of the expansion of communist forces in the region. The CIA supported Kurds with several most secretive operations."[7]

Colby, pointed out that in March 1975, due to the increasingly unfavorable situation of the Kurdish struggle, and Iraq governments increasing successes, the King of Iran had to change his policy and approach towards Iraq, demanded from the US to cut aid for Kurds. At this time the CIA staff sent to the headquarters of a large number of telegrams content suddenly from the past requirements of the secret delivery of weapons and other military supplies into a request for assistance to refugees and exiled Kurds.[8]

318

The CIA's Tehran station director sent a telegraph to William Colby on March 10, 1975, saying: "Is headquarters In touch with Kissinger's office on this; if (the VS. government) does not handle this situation deftly In a way which will avoid giving the Kurds the impression that we are abandoning them they are likely to go public. Iran's changed behavior has not only shattered their political hopes; it endangers lives of thousands."

Mullah Mustafa Barzani also sent a telegraph to Kissinger on the same day, but the Ford administration did not answer. When Colby raised the issue to Kissinger, he was criticized sharply: "covert action should not be confused with missionary work." The Pike Commission report made it clear that the CIA had long known that once their ally, the Iranian king, reached a border agreement with his enemy Iraq, he would immediately abandon the Kurds. An important conclusion of this report was that the Kurds were are nothing more than a "trump card" for Iran and the US, the report noted: "For Iran and the U.S., Kurds were only chess pieces".[9]

---

7   William Colby (1920-1996), the Director of CIA from September 1973 to January 1976.
8   William Colby, Honorable Men: My Life in the CIA, Simon & Schuster, 1978.
9   Barry Lando, "Henry Kissinger and Iraq-Master of Treachery", Feb.4, 2010, http://blogs.alternet.org/barrylando/2010/02/04henry-kissinger-and-iraq-master-of-treachery/.

The Kurdish uprising in Iraq had resulted in 60,000 Iraqi military and civilian casualties. The Pike Commission concluded that the Kurds may have reached a peaceful resolution with the government of Iraq if the US and the Shah had not intervened and encouraged the armed insurrection. The report stated that the Kurds, at a minimum, would have gained "a measure of autonomy while avoiding further bloodshed".

During the Iran-Iraq war (1980-1988), Iran was already changed from pro-American to an anti- American Islamic regime and the containment of Iran has become the main content of the US Middle East policy. This time, Iraq became a target object for the United States that should be and won over. The United States has shifted itself to support the Iraqi government in dealing with the issue of Iraqi Kurdistan Democratic Party allying with Iran, this alliance should be broken, and the Kurds as "troublemakers" and Syria, Iran's "minions."

In 1982, the Reagan administration removed Iraq from the list of countries that supported terrorism. In February 1988, the United States and Iraq reached a secret weapon trade deal. In 1987-1988, the Iraqi government launched a suppression campaign against the Kurds, killing more than 100,000 people, also used chemical weapons causing the Halebje massacre. In these days the US, closed eyes related to Iraq's acts. The documents of the United Nations (1986-1987) show that the US government and the CIA, were aware of the use of chemical weapons by the Iraqi government to suppress the Kurds, but the Reagan administration continued to assist Iraq and helped the latter in the manufacturing of chemical weapons, and supplied chemical materials. Peter Galbraith, an expert in the US Senate Foreign Relations Committee wrote a number of reports on the Iraqi Kurds and asked the US government to halt Saddam Hussein's violent and inhuman policies.[10]

In 1988, the US Senate Foreign Relations Committee initiated the "Prevention of Genocide Act", to punish Iraq for chemical weapons attacks on the Kurds at Halabja during the Iran–Iraq War. But the bill of the Senate was defeated after intense lobbying of Congress by the Reagan-Bush White House.[11]

---

10   Peter Galbraith is regarded as one of the pro-Kurdish American diplomats. He was the first ambassador in Croatia and the vice representative of the U.N. in Afghanistan. He served as the consultant of the government in the Kurdish region after the Iraq War in 2003, he advocated the division of Iraq into "three parts" and Peter Galbraith regarded that the severe mistake of the U.S. policy was to maintain Iraq as an independent entity after the war.
11   Stephen Zune, "The United States and the Kurds: A Brief History", Foreign Policy in Focus, Oct.25, 2007.

In August 1984, PKK of Turkey, started a large-scale armed attacks, and in January 2004, it was included in the list of foreign terrorist organizations, by the US. If say that the first phase of the US's Kurdish policy and concern for Kurds was imbued rather by president Wilson's idealist approach, then we can say that in the second phase the United States' approach was imbued rather by its realistic strategic needs and self-centered interests, namely Kurdish policy was determined by its rivalry fight for global hegemony with the S.U. and its geopolitical interests in the Middle East, which demonstrated obvious selfishness.

In 1989, the Kurdish National Assembly of North America (KNC) was established to promote Kurdish human rights and Kurdish culture, KNC called on the US government to focus on Kurdish issues and help the Kurds seeking for a free Kurdistan through peaceful means.

The disintegration of the Soviet Union in 1991 marked the opening of the post-Cold War era and the third phase in the US's Kurdish policy, which was characterized as its deepest involvement in the Kurdish issue. In this era the United States began to dominate the Middle East issues including the energy issues. The most typical case reflecting the US's Kurdish policy is its changed attitude towards Iraq Kurds.[12]

In this era, the United States was trying to establish "the new world order" and launched the Gulf War to realize this goal in the Middle East, Iraq became the most important and "suitable" target of the US, but the Gulf War had failed to overthrow the Saddam Hussein regime.

In the face of worldwide condemnation and pressure, besides due to critical international public opinion, against the violent and inhuman suppression of the Kurdish uprising, the United States adopted its attitude according to this trend. Operation Provide Comfort and Provide Comfort II, as part of the Gulf War established a no-fly-zone which brought some protection, for the Iraqi Kurds, after the US military forces withdrew from the region.

Although Bush did not intend to support the Kurds, the launching of the Gulf War against Iraq and the US's decision to ally with France and UK in the establishment of the no-fly-zone, objectively promoted the Kurds marked a significant turning point, in the development of the Kurdish status.

In 1993, Bill Clinton as the candidate of the Democrats became the US president. After taking office, initially the core of Clinton's policy was to "promote peace in the Middle East, and "dual containment" of Iraq and Iran", he had no intention to overthrow the Saddam Hussein regime, he maintained policy of supporting the no-fly zone, to support the Iraqi Kurds and maintain their status.

---

12   Republican, George Bush, the 41st President from January 1989 to January 1993, also s Senior Bush.

On the other side, due to Turkey's adverse worries, Clinton did not want to increase the US support to Kurds, fearing that increasing Kurdish lead to more cleavages, disintegration and to instability in the Middle East. In those days a civil war occurred between the two Kurdish parties which took four years, with this event Clinton was disheartened, and decided to intervene for mediation, to end the bloody conflict.[13]

In the Bush administration period, intervention in Iraq and support for Kurds had significantly increased. In order to overthrow Saddam Hussein's regime and stabilize Iraq, the Bush administration basically accommodated the demands of the Kurds, supported the establishment stronger federal system in Iraq, supported Kurds to build their armed forces, thus greatly enhanced the status of Kurds in Iraq. After the new president Obama took office, he basically continued both Iraq and Kurdish policies, followed in the Bush administration period, that is "to maintain the Kurdish autonomy" but also avoid any Kurdish independence in Iraq and Middle East.[14]

In the post-Cold War era, in its handling of the Kurdish problem the US' policies contained several distinct characteristics as follows:

First, in the post-Cold War era, especially after the "9 /11" attack in 2001, promotion of human rights and democracy gained a supreme status, and became one of the core elements of the foreign policy and strategy of the United States; consequently promotion of democratization in the Middle East became an important policy. This change in the US foreign strategy has highly increased United States' concern for human survival and human rights of the Kurds. In the two wars in 1991 and 2003, the United States used military force against Iraq; one of the main reasons was that Saddam Hussein's autocratic and brutal treatment of Iraq people, especially the persecution of Kurds and Shiite Muslims.

In 1998, Turkey's Kurdish politician Leyla Zana was sentenced to imprisonment after her peaceful protest, after this event, Elizabeth Firth from the US Congress condemned Turkey as becoming a Nazi-like country, and demanded free speech for Kurds in Turkey. Abbas Manafy, a professor at the University of New Mexico, criticized Turkey for depriving the Kurds of their culture, language and traditions in a way, that does not fit any democratic standards and Turkey'politics reflects a system of apartheid that victimizes Turkey's Armenians, Kurds and Alawi Muslims believers.

Second, after the end of the Cold War, since the United States had become the world's sole hegemonic power, Kurds have lost the support of the Soviet Union, and the left-wing influence in the Kurdish national movement saw a strong decline, leading Kurdish parties to seek the US support.

---

13   US President from January 1993 to January 2001, member of the Democratic Party.
14   US President from January 2001 to January 2009, member of the Republican, known as the Junior Bush, son of the Senior Bush.

In this regard, Iraqi Kurdish leader Jalal Talabani said: "We were in need of all kinds of support from anybody in the world. When war starts, and you participate in it, you will need support from anyone. Stalin once cooperated with Hitler to keep peace with him….. you have no choice. You have to fight or surrender; if you are fighting, you have a need for help. Where does the help come from? Anywhere! You cannot ask. There is no supermarket where you can go and choose your friends in a war."

Third, "war against terrorism" has become an important element of the US' Kurdish policy.

After the "9/11" "war against terrorism" and the global war on terror, gained high priority in the US national security and foreign strategy. The relation with terrorism has become a major criterion for US when deciding and identifying the friend or the foe. Thus in 2004 the United States has classified the PKK (1984), Kurdish Freedom Eagle (2008), and Kurdistan Free Life Party (2009) as international terrorist organizations and began to impose sanctions on them.

In 1998, the United States cooperated with Turkey to capture the PKK (Kurdish Labor Party) leader Ocalan. After the Iraq war, the United States and Turkey, Iraq have also established a tripartite cooperation mechanism against the PKK, the United States promised that it will provide intelligence support to Turkey to attack PKK's military operations.

On August 28, 2006, the US State Department announced the appointment of General Joseph L. Ralston as the Special Envoy of the US government against the PKK, who would responsible from the coordination with Turkey, Iraq and the Kurdish Regional Government in Iraq.

Fourth, the two Iraqi wars launched by the United States overthrew the Saddam Hussein regime, liberated the Kurds, thus fulfilled the long-standing dream of the Iraqi Kurds–to achieve self-government. Although the persecution of the Kurds by Iraq was not the real reason behind these wars, certainly it was one of the reasons why the US has initiated the wars in foreign soil.

Fifth characteristic, while the US continued to play the Kurdish card, it has adopted multiple standards, when arranging its Kurdish policy, giving decisive priority to the self-interests of the US foreign policy.

For example, in Iran the US secretly supported the Kurdistan Free Life Party to put pressure on the Iranian government, and in order to maintain its strategic partnership with Turkey the US supported Turkey's fight against the PKK.

The U.S. Congressman Kuznetsov and well-known investigative journalist Seymour Hersh have also confirmed that the US government has secretly supported Kurdistan Free Life Party in Iran: The government consultant said that Israel is giving the Kurdish group "equipment and training." The group has also been given "a list of targets inside Iran of interest to the U.S."[15]

Resisting expert pressures, the US government did not classify the Kurdistan Free Life Party as a terrorist organization until 2009. Another example, In Iraq, during the Gulf War in 1991, US President George W. Bush had encouraged the Kurdish uprising for toppling Saddam Hussein regime, and called on the Iraqi people to "take control of their own destiny against the dictator Saddam".[16]

However, when the Kurds launched the uprising, the United States only watched quietly, when Saddam Hussein mobilized its mighty army and severely suppressed Kurds.

In those days, on the one hand, the United States did not intend to overthrow the Saddam Hussein regime, on the other hand, it was cautious that the US intervention to Iraq would not be welcomed, and could endanger the stability of Iraq and the Middle East. Therefore, only after the uprising was violently suppressed and after millions of Kurdish refugees were forced escape and gather at the border of Turkey, and after facing substantial pressure from the international public, the United States agreed to establish a no-fly zone. Ironically, the creation of a no-fly zone was first proposed by the Turkish government, not by the United States.

On April 7, 1991, in order to avoid a large number of Kurdish refugees from Iraq entering Turkey, the Turkish president Ozal, proposed the establishment of a safe area and a no-fly zone in northern Iraq.

This proposal was first well received by the British Prime Minister John Major, and later on April 16, President Bush also agreed on this proposal. After the establishment of the safe zone, the US military forces soon withdrew from Iraq – being worrisome that the US might be dragged into a long-term military engagement in Iraq. Before and during the Iraq war of 2003, the United States regarded the Kurds as the key partner in overthrowing of the Saddam Hussein regime, and the Kurds provided the valuable support to the Allies which the strategic partners of the US in the region could

15   "Kucinich questions the President on US Trained Insurgents in Iran: Sends Letter to President Bush", Apr18, 2006, http://kucinich.house.gov/News/DocumentSingle. aspx?DocumentID=42505; Seymour M. Hersh, "The Next Act", The New Yorker, Nov.20, 2006. http://www.newyorker.com/fact/content/articles/061127fa_fact.
16   "Remarks to the American Association of Advancement of Science, Feb.15, 1991", Public Papers of the President of the United States: Administration of George Bush, 1991, Book Volume 1, Washington: U.S. Government Printing Office, 1992, p.145.

not provide. The United States also regarded the Iraqi Kurds as as valuable partner in maintaining, peace and stability in post-war Iraq, strongly supported the Kurdish autonomy and the establishment of a federal state system in Iraq. But, although being "valuable partners," the United States has hindered Kurdish moves for full independence and urged the Kurds to compromise on a series of core issues such as oil revenues distribution, the status of Kirkuk, the permanent constitution, in order to achieve a US-controlled and US-led stability in Iraq.[17]

Relying on the Baker-Hamilton report of 2006, the US recommended that the Iraqi central government should centrally control and manage the oil resources, and that US should redirect its resources to a program of embedding U.S. troops in Iraqi units, and speed up the training of Iraqi security forces. In response, President Talabani expressed severe dissatisfaction and criticized the Baker-Hamilton report as "Unfair and unjust, it contains items and proposals, that devalue Iraq's sovereignty and constitution."[18]

In order to have a better understanding of the Kurdish issue, and enhancing contacts with the Kurds, the US Secretary of State, Condoleezza Rice appointed Ms. Herro K. Mustafa—a Kurdish US citizen who previously worked for National Security Council under Elliot Abrams as her special assistant, in March 2009 Vice President Joe Biden also appointed K. Mustafa as his senior adviser in the Middle East issues.

All in all, the United States' policy and approach on the Kurdish issue have the following main characteristics. First, the United States does not have a single coordinated grand strategy towards the Kurds. This is quality is firstly determined by the nature of Kurdish national movement which is split into many parties and factions, their division into four separate states; furthermore, the states in which the Kurds live are each more important for the American foreign policy interests than the Kurds themselves."[19]

---

17 In March 2006, the U.S. Congress authorized to set up the Iraq Study Group consisting from Five members from the Democratic Party and 2 from the Republican Party which was led by the former Secretary of State James Baker and Lee Hamilton the Democratic Party Congressman. After an eight-month of investigations, ISG interviewed dozens of American policy makers and key officers including intelligence agencies, prominent figures included the U.S. President George Bush, Vice President Cheney; Casey, U.S. Military Commander in Iraq; Hadley, advisor of the President's National Security; Secretary of State Condoleezza Rice; Defense Secretary who had recently resigned Donald Rumsfeld; Directors of Intelligence Agencies. ISG finally submitted a study report known as Baker-Hamilton Report in December 2006.
18 http://news.sina/com.cn/w/2006-12-12/053910741730s.shtml.
19 "U.S. Strategy Towards Kurds: Interview with Professor Michael Gunter", June 5, 2010, http://www.ekurd.net/mismas/articles/.../independentstate3404.htm.

Therefore, some experts have evaluated, the United States' policy for Iraqi Kurds as being "ambigious or ambivalent."[20]

Therefore, numerous experts have been urging the United States to develop a consistent Kurdish policy.[21]

Second, the United States has followed different and multiple policies which considered the relations with those countries where Kurds make up the minority. This has led to several consequences: the approaches and policies assumed by the United States on the Kurdish issue in different periods have been different; considering its relation with different countries (Turkey, Iraq, Iran, and Syria), the United States has adopted different policies; even towards the Kurds in the same country, the United States has adopted different policies in different periods.

Washington based, expert Kani Xulam, a native Kurdish, pointed out that Turkey and Iraq are two different countries, and United States have different interests in these two countries. How the United States views the Kurds is determined primarily through, how it values Baghdad and Ankara, not Arbil or Diyarbakir. There are plenty of well-placed bigoted Turks who still equate Kurdish gains to Turkish losses. Alas, they have powerful friends in places like Washington, Paris, London and Berlin. This alliance of Turkish bigots and Western opportunists is the source of much of the anguish that continues to exist between the Turks and the Kurds. The US policy towards Turkey's Kurds is mainly determined by the United States policy towards Turkey.[22]

325

Third, the United States given its interest in Middle East stability and human rights, the United States has come to feel that it has a certain degree of responsibility toward the Kurds. Nevertheless, the United States opposes independence for them, because this would likely lead to the partition of the states in which they live and result in unwanted instability in the Middle East. The fact that the Iraqi Kurds have achieved a greater autonomy was not the direct result of the US initiative, but rather a deliberate attempt by the United States to overthrow the Saddam regime, which severly endangered the status quo. After the 2003 war, Peter Galbraith, a US diplomat and adviser of the Kurdish regional government in Iraq, has insisted that Iraq should be "split into three" … "the reality of Iraq requires it to be divided into three states: Kurdistan, the Arab Shi'ites and an Arab Sunni state," but his proposal has was not adopted.[23]

20   Dennis P. Chapman, "Our Ambivalent Iraqi-Kurdistan Policy", Small Wars Journal, June 13, 2010.
21   John Hannah, "America Needs a Kurdish Policy", Mar.22, 2012, http://shadow.foreignpolicy.com/posts/2012/03/22america_needs_a_kurdish_policy.
22   Reina Saiki, "A Study of US Policy Towards Kurds of Iraq and Turkey",Apr.22,2012, http://www.rudaw.net/english/science/editorial/4662.html.
23   Peter Woodard Galbraith,http://en.wikipedia.org/wiki/Peter_W._Galbraith#cite_note-0.

Fourth, the use of the Kurds as a tool to be played as a Kurdish card, in this way Kurdish policy of the US was subordinated to its grand national security and foreign strategies.

If the demands and interests of the Kurds have coincided with the US strategic interests, the United States has supported the Kurds. In the case of non-coincidence, the Kurdish people were ignored. For a long period the US has turned a blind eye to the Kurds in Turkey, mainly because of its interest to maintain its strategic partnership with Turkey. The United States needed Turkey as an anti-Soviet frontier country and as a bridge to tie the Islamic world to the West. In the 1970s, when the United States cut its support for Mulla Mustafa Barzani, the United States was criticized heavily for betraying Kurds, but Henry Kissinger the renown Secretary of State, had pointed out that the US diplomacy cannot be seen as an idealist "missionary work", as was stated in a report "United States has no obligation to save Kurds."[24]

Dr. Hussein Tahiri, as an expert on the Middle East issues, said: "the United States has never had its share of the Kurds trust. It has betrayed Kurds again and again. The Kurds have served as victims of the US national interests.[25]

Fifth, US's national interest pursuit is everlasting. Themes, of democracy and human rights has increasingly occupied an important position in the US's Kurdish policy, but at the same time the status of fighting against terrorism is also elevated, the 2 aspects have a certain conflict between each other.

The Kurdish policy of the United States has many shortcomings, lack of sincerity, selfishness, multiple standards and inherent contradictions, not only in the United States has been a lot of criticism, also caused strong dissatisfaction with the Kurds, causing a lot of impact. Kurdish issues in the US foreign policy in the rise in status, and from time to time become a negative impact on US foreign policy factors. As in Turkey Kurdish human rights issues, the United States as early as 1976 on the establishment of an independent government agencies–Helsinki Commission (Helsinki Commission), specifically to monitor the OSCE.[26]

Turkey is member of the Organization for Security and Cooperation of Europe, which has criticized Turkey on the Kurdish human rights issue from time to time, and has held hearings on numerous occasions and issued critical documents and suggestions on Turkey's Kurdish issue. However, compared with Europe, the United States has not put too much pressure over Turkey on Kurdish human rights issues. The issue of the PKK has also been an important issue in Turkish-American relations, which has led to

---

24   "Pike Committee Report", The Village Voice, Feb. 16, 1976, pp.85, 87-88.
25   Hussein Tahiri, "Kurds: Victims of American National Interests", Kurdish Media, Feb. 27, 2003, http://www.kurdmedia.com/articles.asp?id=8940.
26   OSCE, Organization for Security and Cooperation, founded in 1975.

tensions between the two countries. Turkey has accused the United States of adopting double standards in fighting against terrorism and for its ineffectiveness to restrict PKK activities in Iraq, especially after the Iraq war. On the other side, some liberals in the United States have long criticized Turkey for heavily suppressing the Kurds, and approach sympathetic towards the PKK,and some members of the US Congress urge the government to stop the government sell certain weapons that it would like to use when fighting against the PKK."[27]

Previous to the US led war against Iraq in 2003, Iraq, Turkey were cautious and worrisome that if unchecked the war would lead to autonomy or independence of the Iraqi Kurds, in turn would stimulate Turkey's Kurds to be more demanding and troublemakers. The US military hoped to use the Turkish territory for the war which was in the last minute rejected by the latter which has led to the most serious crisis in the history of Turkey-US strategic alliance.

Consequently, the Pentagon of the United States was forced to shift its attack strategy and focus to South Iraq for the war operations. In addition, the Iraq issue, to fight for soil support, the United States agreed to a number of soil requirements.

But according to the original U.S. plan, the Turks were to have a major role in the 2003 war and also a major role in determining Iraq's future. Reportedly, Turkey demanded to send a large military force to establish a security arc that might permit them to enter predominantly Kurdish cities, but negotiations had failed.

In February 2003, Bush sent a special envoy to persuade the Iraqi Kurds for Turkey-US joint action in Iraq war. In order to avoid Turkey's worries, the United States also declared that the war will not use 100,000 Iraqi Kurdish armed forces. The US Undersecretary of Defense Wolfowitz also announced that, if Turkey and the US could strike a deal of all-round cooperation in the Iraq war, Turkey would enjoy abundant benefits in the end.[28]

This was in fact a green light or carrot for the Turkish offering it a free hand in Iraq. Another example is the formation of the Kurdish Autonomous Region in the north after the Iraq war, which also brought troubles to the US-Turkish relations: Turkey often sent troops into Iraq to Kirkuk and Mosul regions to attack the PKK, which not only aroused tension between Turkey and Iraq, but also seriously disturbed Iraq policies of United States. To ease this conflict, on August 28, 2006, the US State Department announced the

27   "US Threat on Turkey Arms Sales", Aug. 17, 2010, http://www.aljazeera.com/news/europe/2010/08/20108164425178581.html.
28   Hussein Tahiri, "Kurds: Victims of American National Interests", Kurdish Media, Feb. 27, 2003, http://www.kurdmedia.com/articles.asp?id=8940.

appointment of General Joseph L. Ralston as the Special Envoy, responsible for coordinating, actions against the PKK among Turkey, Iraq and Iraq Kurdistan regional government.

In 2007, when Turkey started a massive military operation entering Iraq to combat the PKK, the relations were severely deteriorated with Kurds and Iraq government in Iraq, which also led to a severe crisis between the United States and Turkey.

On July 26, 2007, the United States held a Congressional hearing on Turkey, in the hearing the famous Turkey expert Soner Cagatay, a Turkish native, testified that the current PKK issue was the most important issue in the US-Turkey relations.[29]

On October 7, 2007, President Bush said: The United States has made it clear to Turkey to send troops to Iraq and increase its garrison there will not satisfy the interests of Turkey, we said Turkey enjoys other options in the settlement of the PPK issue, more proper than sending troops into the Iraq territory."

On November 5, 2007, the US President George W. Bush held talks with visiting Prime Minister Recep Tayyip Erdogan at the White House.

Bush once again urged Turkey to be selective when sending troops to Iraq, but also stressed that the PKK is a terrorist organization, which is both an enemy of Turkey, Iraq and the United States. Bush reassured that the US is committed to cracking down on the PKK and ready to cooperate in intelligence gathering and sharing with Turkey to comfort Turkey. While the Turkish Prime Minister Recep Tayyip Erdogan responded: that, " When Turkey's national interests required, regardless of the support and opposition of other countries, Turkey will employ military action at all costs." Erdogan stressed his hope that the United States would take concrete steps in the cooperation against the PKK's terrorist acts. Bush replied: "PKK is our common enemy."[30]

Under the pressures from Turkey, the US conceded—though uncomfortably—and gave green light to Turkey's military actions. In December 2007, Turkey repeatedly delivered cross-border air strikes against the PKK targets in Iraq. Turkish military spokesman declared that the US not only provided intelligence support for Turkey, more importantly, the US also opened the northern Iraqi airspace for the Turkish warplanes. In fact, the US had supported the air strikes.[31]

29   "United States Helsinki Commission on Turkish Elections", http://www.turkishcoalition.org/in-congress/united-states-helsinki-commission-on-turkish-elections-77.htm.
30   Bush Said that the PKK was the Enemy of Both the U.S. and Turkey, Xinhua News Agency, Washington, November 5, 2007.
31   Turkey Claimed Air Attacks on North Iraq was Approved by the U.S., China News, December 17, 2007, http://news.jinghua.cn/352/c/200712/17/n585057.shtml.

On February 21, 2008, the Turkish armed forces deployed 10,000 troops into the northern Iraq, and besieged the PKK forces. In response, the United States declared: "Turkey's military operation against Kurdish rebels in Iraq is "fairly responsible" we hope the incursion to be short. "We hope that this is just a short-term incursion, and avoid harming civilians."[32]

The US and the Iraq issue

When we analyze, oil revenue, oil production and development issues, in the post-war Iraqi Kurdistan oil development issues, the United States and the Iraqi government relations are also more complex.

Initially the US government has favored the issuance of the "oil law", in the Iraqi Assembly, which to a degree centralized the oil industry, but soon afterwards the United States government adopted an ambiguous policy, after Kurdish regional government, independently signed numerous oil extraction, production contracts with the international oil companies, surprisingly the US only watched these oil deals, ignored its commitments towards the central government. Moreover some US companies also began to enter into oil deals with the Kurdish regional government by-passing the central government, which has sparked a serious conflict in US-Iraq relations.

In 2007, the Iraqi Kurdish regional government and Hunt Oil, a US based the United States, signed an oil exploration contract according to the regional decrees. After this transaction, the Iraqi government declared the deal as illegal, and Iraq's oil minister, Hussein Shahristani said: "All these contracts, that has been independently signed by Kurdish regional government should be approved by the central federal authority, and this contract was not submitted to the government for approval, so it will not have any legal effect."

On October 18, 2011, the Kurdish Autonomous Region signed a contract with Exxon Mobil, another US oil company, allowing the company to explore and develop six oil fields in the region. Iraq's prime minister, Nuri al-Maliki, declared and warned that Iraq would take "the necessary steps" if Exxon Mobil begins implement "this controversial exploration contract."[33]

On July 19, 2012, Chevron Oil, another US company, announced that it acquired 80% shares of the two exploration sites in Rovi and Sarta, at the Kurdish Autonomous Region.

On July 24, 2012, the Iraqi government announced that the Chevron Oil ignored Iraq's objections, and insisted to fulfill its contract with the Kurdish Autonomous Region, after this announcement Iraqi government suspended Chevron's ongoing projects in central and southern Iraq. The oil ministry

---

32 The US Warned Turkey to Limit the Military Action in North Iraq, http://news.cctv. com/military/20080228/101316.shtml.
33 Iraq Listed the American Chevron on the Blacklist, Xinhua News Agency, July 26, 2012.

issued a statement: "the Ministry of Petroleum announces that Chevron Oil and its affiliated companies are prohibited to fulfill any contract or agreement, unless it abandons the previously signed contract, with the KRG."[34]

At the same time, the relationship between the United States and Iraqi Kurds is quite complicated. On the one hand, both parties need each other. The Kurds need American support and protection, hoping that the United States will remain to be influential in Iraq to check the Arabs. In March 1992, the United States Senate Foreign Affairs Committee held a hearing on the Iraq's massacre against the Kurds, Jalal Talabani's representative Najmaldine Karim in the US attended this hearing, he called on the United States to support the Kurds for national self-determination. Karim said: "In the neighboring region of Turkey there is an Armenian state which lives in peace, and it has been recognized by Turkey.

And in the north of Iran, although Azerbaijanis have a sovereign state, they account for 25% of the Iran population. In Azerbaijan, in the north of the country, Azerbaijanis they account for 25 per cent of the Iraqi population. Why can't we have a Kurdish state that will allow the Kurdish people's right to national self-determination, as in the rest of the world? ... it is time for the international community to acknowledge and return to the days when President Wilson supported self-determination for the Kurds and revisit the provisions of the Treaty of the Sèvres that allowed us to build our own homeland. We request from your Committee to step forward in support of the Kurdish entity and to empower the Kurds for national self-determination."[35]

In 2009, Carnegie Endowment for International Peace, held a seminar, "Preventing Conflict Over Kurdistan", Qubad Talabani, the US representative of the Iraqi Kurdistan regional government in Washington, was invited to the seminar, Qubad Talabani pointed out: The US government should elevate the Kurdish issue to a strategic level and help solving such several key issues: the territorial dispute such as the Kirkuk problem; utilization of oil and gas resources and the distribution of oil revenues; consistent implementation of the federal state system; establishing stable and good neighbourly relations between Kurdish Region of Iraq and Turkey."[36]

In April 2012, Massoud Barzani during his visit to the US, stressed that Iraq's Kurdish regional government enjoys a special relationship with the United States; Kurds and the US allies and partners in the Middle East."[37]

---

34 Ibid.
35 Hearing of the Senate Foreign Relations Committee, "Mass Killings in Iraq", as cited by the Federal News Service, Mar. 19, 1992.
36 Carnegie Endowment For International Peace, "Preventing Conflict over Kurdistan", Feb. 9, 2009.
37 "Iraqi Kurdistan as U.S. Ally and Partner in the Middle East",Apr.12, 2012, http://www.washingtoninstitute.org/policy-analysis/view/ iraqi-kurdistan-as-u.s.-ally-and-partner-in-the-middle-east.

Kurds also tried to develop positive publicity in the United States, set up offices for this purpose and established a lobbying company. Between 2007-2010, the KRG spent $ 4.6 million for lobbying activities in the U.S. and in 2011 spent 730.000. U.S. Dollars, for its lobbying company, BRG.[38]

On the other hand, the United States also needed the support of Kurds for overthrowing Saddam and also for the post-war security and stability of Iraq, Kurds are their "best partners" in Iraq.

In May 2008, the Kurdish-American Congressional Caucus was established in the US by 23 Congress members, Barham Salih, Prime Minister of the KRG attended the establishment ceremony. The main task of this Congressional Caucus was defined as strengthening the relationships between the U.S and the Kurds. By December 2011, the Caucus members had increased to 43.[39]

But it is obvious that, the two sides do not trust each other, due to conflict of interests, and difference in strategic aims. Iraqi Kurds demand independence, but the realization of this demand will spoil the US strategy in Iraq and severely harm its interests in the Middle East region, therefore the US does not want the Kurds step into independence. After the Iraq war, a major priority for the Kurds was to ensure their own security and consolidate their semi-autonomy, while the main aim of the U.S was to ensure that Iraq would have a unified structure and maintain itself under a robust central government; which all means that there is a certain obvious contradiction between the strategic aims of two sides.[40]

The president of Iraq, Jalal Talabani has criticized the U.S. for not understanding the situation of Iraq, and said: "The most important mistake they have made is to bind the hands of Kurds and Shi'ites, they have made wrong plans, wrong strategies, and wrong policies."

In 2006, the Iraq Study Group, led by former US Secretary of State, James B. Baker and former Democratic Party Congressman Lee Hamilton, issued a report including a set of 79 recommendations of 160 pages, which proposed the centralized management of oil resources by the central government, that the United States should significantly increase the number of U.S. military personnel, including combat troops, imbedded in and supporting Iraqi Army units. that the U.S. should eventually end combat operations in Iraq and help in training Iraqi troops. The report called on the Kurds to compromise and cooperate with the central government.[41]

---

38 "Kurdistan Government Lobby in Washington: Success or Failure?", June 3,2012, http://www.ekurd.net/mismas/articles/misc2012/6/state6259.htm.
39 "Representative Tipton Joins Kurdish-American Caucus", http://www.kurdishaspect. com/doc120111KA.html.
40 "U.S.-Kurdish Relations in Post-Invasion Iraq",Dec.7, 2007, http://www.gloria-center. org/2007/12/rafaat-2007-12-07/.
41 "The Iraq Study Group Report", www.bakerinstitute.org/publications/iraqstudygroup_ findings.pdf.

The report arose huge critique and indignation among the Kurds. In this regard, President Talabani expressed strong dissatisfaction and severely criticized the contents of the report. Talabani said: "When the report suggests the increase of military personnel imbedded in and supporting Iraqi Army units, including its combat troops, it ignores whether the sovereign Iraq government would be ready to permit such an increase or accept such support." "It asks that they put foreign officers in every unit, which is a violation of Iraq's sovereignty . ...if then what will remain of our sovereignty? The report has a mentality that we are a colony where they impose their conditions and neglect our independence."

Talabani has also criticized the report's suggestion to include the former members of the Baath Party in the political process of Iraq, "such an approach would have very serious consequences."[42]

In April 2012, Massoud Barzani publicly backfired a news report which assumed that the U.S agreed to sell 36 F-16 fighter planes to the central government to help Iraq improve its air defense capability, fearing that such a move might become a tool for the government to crack down on the Kurds. Accordingly, Michael Rubin, a renowned Middle East expert wrote: "But while Iraqi Kurdistan has come far, the unreliability of its leadership makes any long-term U.S.-Kurdish alliance unwise.". ..."Despite lofty rhetoric about its suitability as an ally, Iraqi Kurdistan's actions suggest that it is far from trustworthy.". ..."the current Iraqi Kurdish leadership appears intent on replicating more autocratic models." Rubin, also criticized the Barzani leadership for "playing the terror card."[43]

6.2 The EU and the Kurdish Issue

The Kurdish issue was created by Western European colonialists. For a long time, the United Kingdom and France were the two most influential European powers to determine the Kurdish issue. Europe is also home to the largest overseas Kurdish population, and an important headquarters for the overseas Kurdish political parties and associations. In general, major European powers are sympathetic towards the Kurds, but remain cautious in supporting Kurdish autonomy or independence for practical reasons and self-interest, in turn they stress respect for Kurdish national rights, enhancement of human rights, expanding democracy, allowing them to freely express their cultural and ethnic characteristics, fight against poverty and economic development to improve their life conditions, we can say that all these are the main policy objectives and content of the EU's Kurdish policy.

42   Iraqi President Talabani Criticized the Iraqi Policy Report, http://news.sina.com. cn/w/2006-12-12/041210741487s.shtml.
43   Michael Rubin, "Is Iraqi Kurdistan a Good Ally?", AEI Middle Eastern Outlook, January 2008.

Generally, the EU lacks a unified and coordinated policy on the Kurdish issue, and embodies certain inconsistency.

The EU has the strongest factor which influences the Kurdish issues in Turkey. The EU's accession to Turkey is an important impetus for the Turkish government to continuously improve the status of Kurds, but this has also become one of the main causes and manifestations of the Turkish-European conflicts.

During the World War I, in 1915-1916, Britain, France, Russia have a series of secret treaties in order to partition the Ottoman Empire, such as the famous "Sykes-Picot Agreement". The Sykes-Picot Agreement was based on the premise that the Triple Allied Entente countries would succeed in defeating the Ottoman Empire during World War I, and decided that Kurdistan region which was under the Ottoman rule would be divided into three parts: France would get the control of west Kurdistan (Iraq), Syria and Lebanon, The British would gain the control of the territory of Iraq and South Kurdistan and North Kurdistan would remain in Turkey.

Secondly, in the Treaty of Sèvres, with the Ottoman Empire, the victorious countries had promised to allow the Kurds under the Ottoman rule to build their own state, but after the British and French forces were defeated by Mustafa Kemal led national forces, in 1922, the two major powers abandoned their commitment of supporting Kurdish independence.

During the war, British and French troops have occupied the most regions of Kurdistan under the rule Ottoman Empire, such as Kirkuk, Mosul and other regions. Among them, the oil-rich Mosul province has become the occupation target of the UK, and the UK struggled hard against France and Turkey to achieve this target. In those days, British Prime Minister Lloyd George said: Mesopotamia-Iraq should remain British otherwise I will not agree, among them the Mosul province is the most critical."

Four days after the ceasefire agreement was reached, the British forces occupied Mosul. In fact, the United Kingdom has long been occupying South Kurdistan (northern Iraq) and conducted a large number of resource surveys and found that this region possessed very rich oil resources. As early as in 1918, Britain had begun to contact and organize the local Kurdish tribes. In July 1918, Sir Cox, who later became the High Commissioner of the United Kingdom in Iraq, had met with General Muhammad Sharif Pasha, who was in Paris to represent Kurds in the Paris Peace Conference, the two had comprehensively discussed on the Kurdish autonomy or independence.[44]

---

44   Dana Adams Schmidt, Journey Among Brave Men, Boston-Toronto,1964, pp.192-193.

The British strategy was to form a new state, Iraq, which would include Mosul, Basra, Baghdad provinces, which originally belonged to the Ottoman Empire. This led to a severe tension between Britain and the newly established Turkey, thus the Mosul problem between the two states had emerged. Due to Britain's series of diplomatic activities and pressures, the Mosul Committee authorized by the League of Nations issued a survey report and suggestions, which proposed that Mosul province would belong to Iraq. Finally, the new Turkey under pressure was forced to give up the sovereignty of the Mosul province. In 1926 Mosul province was officially included in the territory of Iraq. Simultaneously France has established a new state, Syria, which included the Western Kurdistan (former Ottoman region).

From the end of the World War I, to the end of World War II, except the North Kurdistan, South and West Kurdistan had been under Anglo-French rule and control, directly or indirectly. During this period, the British abandoned the provisions of the League of Nations and ignored their own past commitments to allow the Kurdish autonomy, Kurds were not allowed to exercise autonomy.

Consequently, the Iraqi Kurds have launched vigorous revolts targeting the British colonial rule, calling for independent statehood and separation from Iraq, such as the Barzan uprising (1919-1922) led by the leaders of Barzani tribe, but it was suppressed under joint attacks by the British and Iraqi Kingdom forces. British officers have often led the repression operations of the Iraqi army, for example in 1932, British general Robinson, and in 1945 British general Renton led the repression operations.[45]

In order to repress the Kurdish revolts, the British also built the famous strategic military road—the Hamilton Highway (named after the highway engineer Hamilton from New Zealand) which extends from the Arbil city to the Iranian border.

However, the British did not support and implement the policy of Arabization in Iraq.

In Syria, the Kurds also participated in and supported the anti-colonial struggle. However, a Kurdish nationalist uprising has not occurred in Syria, which can be attributed to the relatively loose minority policy exercised by the French colonial authorities and due to smaller Kurdish population, another reason was that, in Syria nationalism has fermented later and the fact that most Kurds in Syria are Kurdish refugees who came from Turkey. The French colonial authorities sympathized with the Kurdish national movement and even embraced many Turkish and Iraqi Kurdish nationalists who

---

45 Massoud Barzani, Mustafa Barzani and the Kurdish Liberation Movement, p.178.

sought refuge in Syria and allowed Syria to be the center and haven for the Kurdish nationalist activities in the Middle East.

After the suppression of Sheikh Saed Uprising in 1925, a large number of Kurds from Turkey escaped and settled in north Syria, which is one of the reasons why, later the issue of stateless Kurds in Syria has occurred. In October 1927, the Kurdish nationalists established their political organization named Xoybün–Ciwata Serxwebuna Kurd), (or Khoybun in short) meaning oneself or being oneself in Kurdish in Bihamdun city of Lebanon, with its headquarters being in Aleppo, Syria.

This organization also received some support from Britain and France. In 1927, the organization leaders met in Syria and decided to launch the Kurdish Ararat uprising, French government had also secret officials to attend this meeting.

But later, under the strong pressure coming from the Turkish government, the French government expelled some Kurdish leaders from Syria, and some leaders were put under house arrest in the region adjacent to the Turkish border.

In 1928, the French government under the pressure of the Turkish government banned the activities of the Xoybün organization in Syria. Overall, during this period, both in Iraq and Syria, the Kurds were in a better situation, and did not face obvious ethnic discrimination, the relevant governments did not implement the policy of Arabization. However, with the end of World War II, after the British and French colonialism was overthrown in Iraq and Syria, we can see the rise and domination of Arab nationalism, thus occurred a major turning point in the fate of Kurds, being faced with the threat of Arabization and assimilation.

During the Cold War, the Western European countries have basically followed the US in the Kurdish issue, this policy served and prioritized the needs of the Cold War confrontation, which meant that Western allies, in the main were not concerned with the demands of Kurdish autonomy or independence. Before the 1991 Gulf War, France was the major supplier of weaponry to Iraq. Since the 1960s, after Europe saw a large number of Kurds emigrating to Europe, it began to pay more and more attention to Kurdish human rights.

There are many reasons for the Kurdish immigration to Europe: Europe is geographically close to the Middle East, economically developed and socially stable and generous, which has attracted Kurds. Besides in 1961, Turkey signed guest worker agreements with West Germany, Netherlands, France, Belgium to send qualified workers to these countries, nearly one million Turkish citizens including many Kurds temporarily immigrated to

European countries, but due to social and political instability in Turkey, many of the workers decided to remain as citizens in Europe.

Another Kurdish immigrant wave to Europe, after the outbreak of the Iranian revolution in 1979 and conflict between the Islamic government and Iranian Kurds. And another immigrant wave occurred—including a large number of Kurds—after the 1980 military coup occurred in Turkey. Due to 1980-1988 Iran-Iraq war, and especially after the 1991 Iraq war, when Iraqi government started a large-scale military repression and massacre targeting the Iraqi Kurds.

In 1987, Turkey formally applied in 1987 to join the EU, actually the process of Turkey's accession to the EU was started in 1961, but the process developed with zigzags due to many reasons, after 1987 Kurdish issue and EU's human rights concern was another conflict issue between EU and Turkey.

In February 1982, with the support of French President Mitterrand's wife Kurdish Institute was established in Paris. The Kurdish Institute became a legal foundation in 1993, began to receive funding from the French Ministry of Culture, the French Government's Social Action Fund and the European Union.

Currently, the EU has become an important force outside the region influencing the Kurdish issue second only to the US. especially it has the greatest influence in Turkey's Kurdish issue.

After the Cold War, the theme of democracy and human rights has increasingly become the main content and important tool in EU's foreign policy. Meanwhile, the EU has actively pushed "eastward expansion" towards Eastern Europe, Baltic countries and pushed "southward" with the Mediterranean initiative—the Union for the Mediterranean—promoted by the Barcelona Process, which includes the EU and 15 Mediterranean partner countries from North Africa, the Middle East and Southeast Europe.

In order to maintain its stake and its past relations with the Middle East countries, EU has further increased its concerns over the Kurdish issue. During the Gulf War in 1991, Britain, France and other countries actively supported the US military action against Iraq, also sent troops to establish a no-fly zone in northern Iraq, and promoted the Kurdish autonomy, we should note that in 1997, due to political reasons, France withdrew from the no-fly zone maintenance operations due to political differences among allies, especially on the issue of lifting the severe sanctions against Iraq.

In 2003 the US started the Iraq, while the major EU powers split, France and Germany was opposed due to lack of UN legitimacy, but the United Kingdom was actively involved, and the United States formed a "coalition of forces" Multi-National Force-Iraq (MNF-I), for the military operations. (United Kingdom, Australia, Spain and Poland).

After the war, EU began to involve in the reconstruction of Iraq, and restored cooperation with the United States. In June 2008, France opened a consulate in Arbil, capital of KRG. The European Court of Human Rights (ECHR) has ruled from time to time on Turkey's Kurdish human rights case after Turkey signed the European Convention on Human Rights.[46]

In March 2012, the European Parliament convened a special conference on the Kurdish massacre in Iraq. After this conference, the EU's involvement in Turkey's Kurdish issues has become increasingly deep, the issue has become an important issue in the EU-Turkey relations and the main factors affecting Turkey's accession negotiations to the EU.

EU's policies and critics targeting Turkey on Kurdish issue can be a good example to explain the EU's policy towards the Kurdish issue. The current EU policy towards Turkey on Kurdish issues mainly have three elements: first, the EU has long criticized the Turkish government for treating the Kurds in a harsh manner, depriving them of their national rights, violating their human rights and freedoms, demanding that human rights and freedoms of Kurds should be respected, and given more civil rights; that Kurds should be allowed to express their ethnic characteristics. From time to time, the European Parliament issue Turkey reports, in which violations of Kurdish human rights are underlined.

Also the European Court of Human Rights constitutes a platform where individual complaints regarding human rights infringements, freedom of expression violations are trialed, and when single cases are decided, the court judgments include many critiques and enforcements against Turkish government and Turkey's court judgments, many of which are related to human rights of Kurds. In May 1994, the International Human Rights Law Group based in Washington issued a briefing report which said: "the problem in Turkey is the Constitution is against the Kurds and the apartheid constitution is very similar to it."[47]

In September 2008, the EU foreign ministers' meeting passed a resolution which both condemned the terrorist attacks against Turkey and urged the Turkish government to respect human rights and fundamental freedoms when fighting against terrorism and demanded that Turkey amend its restrictive law on political parties in time, speed up its reform of judicial system, effective protection of civil rights, respect for freedom of speech and religion, freedom of property and property rights, protection of ethnic minorities and strengthening of their cultural rights.

---

46   Turkey joined in the European Convention on Human Rights, which to a degree restricts its acts on the Kurdish issue.

47   "Implementation of the Helsinki Accords: Criminalizing Parliamentary Speeches in Turkey", Briefing given by the International Human Rights Law Group, May 1994, Hearing before the Commission on Security and Cooperation in Europe, Washington DC, http://csce.gov/index.cfm?FuseAction=Files.Download&FileStore_id=189.

In April 2010, the European Commission Against Racism and Intolerance (ECRI) reported: "The public use by officials of the Kurdish language lays them open to prosecution, and public defense by individuals of Kurdish or minority interests also frequently leads to prosecutions under the current Criminal Code."[48]

The European Court of Human Rights has also repeatedly ruled on the unfair judgments of the Turkish courts on the Kurdish case and criticized violations of the European Convention on Human Rights. The EU has also condemned the repeated banning of Kurdish political parties in Turkey. In 2002, the European Court of Human Rights ruled a judgment on the restriction of Kurdish political parties: Turkish courts have been violating the freedom of association stipulated in article 11 of the European Convention on Human Rights. In December 2009, the European Socialist Party (PES) condemned Turkey's decision to ban the Kurdish Democratic Society Party (DTP).

In 2010, the European Court of Human Rights ruled once again that the Turkish decision was in violation of the European Convention on Human Rights. In 1994, the Turkish government arrested and prisoned 4 Kurdish political leaders—Leyla Zana, Hatip Dicle, Orhan Dogan and Selim Sadak. The EU Parliament criticized this act and urged Turkey to release the four leaders, besides European Parliament has also awarded one of the above leaders, Leyla Zana, with the Human Rights Prize. In 2004, the State Security Court of Ankara sentenced above four people to 15 years' imprisonment for "inciting separatist activities at home and abroad" in accordance with the instructions of the "terrorist" PKK. This decision was strongly condemned and opposed by the European Union and the European Parliament.[49]

The EUTCC was formed in 2004 as a mechanism to monitor the accession of Turkey to the EU, to promote respect for human rights, and promote Turkey's settlement of the Kurdish issue. This organization has been active in coaching Turkey-EU relations throughout the Turkey's accession process and it has issued several reports, which urged Turkey to respect Kurdish human rights and minority rights, and find a peaceful and democratic way in the settlement of the Kurdish issue according to Copenhagen criteria.[50]

---

48 "ECRI Report on Turkey (4th)", http://www.coe.int/t/dghl/monitoring/ecri/Country-by-country/Turkey/TUR-CBC-IV-2011-005-ENG.pdf.

49 By November 2004, the four organization were: Rafto Foundation in Norway, Kurdish Human Rights Project in Britain, Medico International in Germany, Bar Human Rights Committee in the UK.

50 The Copenhagen criteria are a series of principles to measure whether a nation is qualified to join the EU. The principles were set by the Europan Council in Copenhagen, the capital of Denmark in June 1993. Politically, it requires the candidate to have solid democratic institutions, respect for human rights, respect and protection of minority national rights; economically, it requires that the candidate nation exercises market economy.

In November 2010, the EU-Turkey Civic Commision held a special conference to discuss the Kurdish issue, the theme was "Turkey-Kurd dialogue: The Way to Peace", and invited the Turkey's Kurdish politicians and other messages were heard from Osman Baydemir, a Kurdish politician, lawyer and human rights activist and current mayor of Diyarbakir, also the conference heard from Archbishop Desmond Tutu via a video message during which he expressed his continued support for the EUTCC and saying: "until we get settlement of the Kurdish issue in Turkey and until all the stumbling blocks to Turkey's EU accession are removed."[51]

On June 15, 2011, the European Left Party made a press statement which emphasized that the Kurdish voice must be heard in the Turkish elections, and that the EU must insist that the Turkish government respect the rights of the Kurdish people and allow them to move freely in the land.

On March 22, 2012, a number of Kurdish friendly deputies of the European Parliament made a statement which condemned the Turkish government's crackdown on the Kurdish New Year celebrations (Nawroz), and said: "The Turkish government has resorted to unprecedented violent means to those who have participate in peaceful demonstrations."

Hasan Zengin, leader of the pro-Alawit Peace Democrat Party, and several hundred members of this party were injured by government, in his statement he stressed: "the EU must break the silence and condemn the excessive violence of the Turkish government."[52]

In the same month, 20 deputies of the European Parliament submitted a petition to the European Commission /the executive arm of the European Union) to put Turkey's Kurdish issue on the agenda, and underlined that the Kurdish issue and its solution is also an European. The petition said: Since 2009, the Turkish government has arrested more than 9,000 Kurds, including six Assembly members, 31 mayors, 96 journalists, 36 lawyers and 183 activists of peace and democracy."[53]

On December 1992, the European Kurdish Human Rights Project (KHRP) was established in London, as a non-governmental organization whose main task is to monitor the violations of Kurdish human rights by governments and help lodging complaints with the European Court of Human Rights.[54]

---

51   "European Parliament to Hold Kurdish Conference", Hürriyet
Daily News, Nov. 11, 2010; http://www.hurriyetdailynews.com/default.
aspx?pageid=438&n=Kurdish-conference-in-the-european-parliament-2010-11-11.
52   "EU-Kurds Friendship Group Condemns Violent Suppression of Kurdish Nawroz in Turkey", Mar.22,2012,http://www.aknews.com/en/aknews/4/297265/.
53   "Kurdish Problem Is Europe's Business Too, Says MEPs",http://en.firatnews.com/index.php?rupel=article&nuceID=4416.
54   For details, please see its website: www.khrp.org.

Its Executive, Kerim Yildiz, opposed the EU's accession negotiations with Turkey, stating that if the EU decides to start negotiations, a realistic assessment of the progress in the field of democracy and human rights in Turkey should be made. He said: "The current concessions by the Turkish government for Kurds only remain on paper, symbolic, or even false measures, none of the commitments made by the the Turkish officials to improve the status of the Kurds are implemented properly."[55]

Secondly, urging the Turkish government to solve the Kurdish issue and resolving the Kurdish issue has been set is as one of the prerequisites for Turkey's joining the EU.

In 1987, Turkey applied for the EU membership, but until 1999 it was not regarded as eligible for candidacy. On October 3, 2005, the EU decided to begin accession negotiations with Turkey. But, the negotiation process were interrupted several times. Turkey's accession negotiations include 35 policy issues which Turkey is required to adopt, as of 2012 only 12 of them were opened to negotiations, but only one of them was completed.

Negotiations with Turkey lag far behind, compared to Eastern and Southeastern European countries, although their applications were later. France, Germany, Austria and Cyprus, Greece and some other EU members resolutely oppose Turkey's accession to the EU. Although in many political, economic and social aspects Turkey has not yet met the standards required by the European Union, Kurdish issue is one of the most important explicit reasons, for the delay in Turkey's accession to EU.

Since the 1990s, the EU has repeatedly underlined, that the Turkey's approach on how to resolve the Kurdish issue would impact the country's accession to the EU. Currently the EU believes that this issue is not handled in proper way, at least human rights and freedom of Kurds are violated and Turkey does not meet the standards of accession to the EU.

In November 2008, EU's Annual Turkey Progress Report had mentioned the following: The progress of government's reform track does not meet expectations, especially in the spheres of human rights, protection of minority rights, democratization, establishment of rule of law, corruption and the influence of army in politics.

In March 2012, the European Parliament, after discussing the 2011 Annual Turkey Progress Report adopted a resolution which urged Turkey to resolve the Kurdish issue in peaceful and democratic way, and the resolution demanded: Turkey should ensure progress for the political, cultural and social rights of Kurds and ensure solid conditions for freedom of speech."[56]

---

55   Michael M. Gunter, "Turkey's Floundering EU Candidacy and Its Kurdish Problem", Middle East Policy, Mar.22, 2007.
56   "EU Urges Turkey to Find Political Solution to Kurdish Issue", Mar.31,2012,http://www.ekurd.net/mismas/articles/misc2012/3/turkey3865.htm.

In May 2012, during the Danish EU Presidency, the Danish Foreign Villy Sovndal, when visiting Turkey urged Turkey take "brave steps" in resolving the Kurdish issue, and underlined: "These steps are not just for Turkey's accession to the EU, but for its own sake," ... "We think it is important for Turkey and also important for Turkey's EU relationship to be brave on this agenda."[57]

In turn, Turkish government severely opposes, EU's attaching Turkey's accession to the Kurdish issue. In July 2009, Prime Minister Recep Tayyip Erdogan criticized some EU member states for using Turkey's accession process, as a leverage to "intervene" into its domestic politics, calling it a "totally wrong" act "which will bringing no benefits to any country."

In October 2010, in his Helsinki visit, Erdogan said that he was very disappointed with the slow progress of the accession process, "no new EU member state had experienced such a lengthy negotiation process as Turkey,"..."the accession negotiations are nearly reached a deadlock, the responsibility should be borne entirely by the EU." Erdogan, stressed that Turkey is a bridge connecting the West and the Islamic world, and EU's repeated acts of delaying the Turkish accession negotiations will only cause losses and frustration for both sides. The United States has also repeatedly expressed its dissatisfaction with the EU's repeated rejection of Turkey.

In June 2010, in his visit to London, the US Secretary of Defense Robert Gates said: "The EU delaying Turkey's accession, to a certain extent has led to Turkey's "drifting away" from the West, and to the deterioration of relations with Israel. Gates added: "I personally think that if there is anything to the notion that Turkey is, if you will, moving eastward, it is, in my view, in no small part because it was pushed, and pushed by some in Europe refusing to give Turkey the kind of organic link to the West that Turkey sought." However, Turkey insistently denies that its Western-oriented foreign policy has changed. "Adherence to the EU remains an important long-term diplomatic strategy of Turkey."[58]

Thirdly, on the issue of the PKK, while the EU shows willingness to support Turkey's fight against terrorism situation, it demands that Turkey should respect basic human rights when suppressing terrorism, and underlines that the Kurdish issue should be resolved through political means. The EU does not tolerate those Kurdish political parties engaged in terrorist activities, in its territories, and seriously restricts the PKK, and has listed it among terrorist organizations, and imposed stricter controls against its

---

57   "Danish FM Urges 'Brave Steps' in Kurdish Issue", Hürriyet Daily News,May 26,2012, http://www.hurriyetdailynews.com/danish-fm-urges-brave-steps-in-kurdish-issue. aspx?pageID=238&nid=21645
58   Turkey at the Crossroads: "Moving to West" or "Turning to East", People's Daily, July 15, 2010.

activities. In 1993, France and Germany announced banning of PKK activities in their territories. In 2004 the EU has declared Kurdistan People's Assembly (KONGRA GEL) as a terrorist organization.[59]

In November 2004, the Dutch police started an operation to arrest 29 members belonging to PKK. On August 14, 2006, Britain banned PKK activities, and freezed its financial assets and in December the same year and arrested several members of this party, and one member was deported abroad.

PKK leader Ocalan's asylum seeking efforts in European countries during February 1999, before his arrest, may clearly reflect the complex and contradictory mindset of Europe on Kurdish issues. Although Greece, Italy, Germany and other countries have expressed sympathy for Ocalan, under pressures from Turkey and the US they have refused Ocalan's request and have extradited him, finally he had the only choice to leave for Kenya where he was arrested by the Turkish security agency. After his arrest, Ocalan also publicly stated that Greece and Cyprus has supported his party. Many comments were also made by the European media, arguing that Europe should have considered the aylum issue from a humanitarian aspect, and even argued the Kurdish issue is not much different from the Kosovo issue, media also argued that the Turkish government has violated the legal proceedings when abducting Ocalan from Kenya.[60]

342

In June 1999, the State Security Court of Turkey has sentenced Ocalan to death for treason, separatist activities and ordering several massacres. Subsequently, Ocalan appealed to the European Court of Human Rights against the death penalty and demanded a fair trial, due to restricted access to his attorneys and other irregularities in the case, including the presence of a military judge.

The Court in Strasbourg asked Turkey to suspend the death penalty till its judgment would be concluded. In February 2000, the Turkish Government responded positively to the request of the European Court of Human Rights. In June 2000, the Court decided to allocate the application to the First Section of the Court which declared a judgment that "in view of the complexity and importance of the Ocalan case, and in accordance with the article 30 of the European Convention on Human Rights, the trialing will be held by "Grand Chamber", consisting of 17 judges. On June 9, 2003 the applicant, and on June 11, 2003 the Government, requested that the case be referred to the Grand Chamber in accordance with Article 43 of the Convention and Rule 73. On 9 July, 2003 a panel of the Grand Chamber

---

59   The address of the headquarters is No. 41 Rue Jean Stas, Brussels, Belgium. This address was also registered as the addresses of Kurdish National Congress and Kon-Kurd.
60   Singapore, Zaobao, February 25, 1999.

decided to refer the case to the Grand Chamber. A hearing took place in public in the Human Rights Building, Strasbourg, on June 9, 2004.

On May 12, 2005, the European Court of Human Rights, after three and a half years of trial, ruled that there was a violation of Article 5 § 4 of the Human Rights Convention. The court held by eleven votes to six that there was a violation of Article 6 § 1 of the Convention in that the applicant was not tried by an independent and impartial tribunal, and death penalty was improper and infringed the applicant's rights.

Turkey and EU also contradicted severely on the issue of Turkish troops entering into Iraq territory to fight against PKK. In 1991 August, the Turkish army marched more than 16 kilometers into the Iraq territory to attack the PKK guerillas. The Greek media criticized this military action, as "aggression", the Swiss government announced an arms-sales embargo against Turkey, the German government also protested the act.

European Commission President Jose Manuel Barroso declared that the EU shared sorrow for the victims of the terrorist attacks, but added: "The EU believes that any dispute should be resolved through dialogue, the EU demands that Turkey resolve the dispute with the PKK, in peaceful and democratic way."

During the Portuguese presidency of EU presidency Portugal Prime Minister Jose Socrates stressed that the EU condemned all terrorist activities and attacks, in which Turkish citizens became victims, and added. "The EU expresses solidarity with Turkey against terror, but any response to terror attacks "should be within the framework of international laws," ..."and should be coordinated and supplemented with diplomatic and political process."

Germany's approach on the PKK issue is the most representative. In Western Europe, Kurdish population in Germany is the largest, which has reached more than 500,000. Many Kurds in Germany sympathize with and support the PKK, and PKK is well organized in this country, and has a strong underground network. In the early 1990s, the PKK organized some violent protests across Europe, of which Germany was the most affected. The official position of the German government is to oppose terrorism, and it prohibits the organizations engaging in terrorist activities in its territory. But due to prevalent sympathy among Kurds and democratic public support for Kurdish issue in this country, Germany opts for a tolerant policy against PKK's cultural propaganda and legal activities, in turn criticizes Turkey for exporting its own "internal issue" to Germany, and urges Turkey to avoid delivering trouble to Germany.

In November 4, 1993, in Germany PKK instigated riots, violent demonstrators attacked Turkish tourism agencies, consular buildings, banks, restaurants and so on, which caused one person's death and 60 buildings belonging to Turks was damaged. Subsequently, the German government officially declared the PKK as an illegal organization, and banned its activities. Between 1996-1998, the Kohl government decided to prosecute the PKK activists who were involved in violent activities and deport them from the country. In 1999, German Chancellor Gerhard Schroeder said: "The Kurds who live in Germany are our guests, those who abide by the law and order, are welcome, but we cannot tolerate those involving in street wars in Germany."[61]

Due to the relatively loose governance policies of Germany, the number of PKK supporters in this country has kept increasing. In March 2007, the Federal Office for the Protection of the Constitution issued a report stating that the new party as the successor of PKK was "illegally collecting funds and recruiting members". German Intelligence Service has claimed that there were about 1.000 PKK supporters living in Berlin and German government ordered the closure of the ROJ- TV station and the police raided PKK related Kurdish associations, newspaper offices and organizations. In July 2008, PKK retaliated by three German mountain trekkers in eastern Turkey.

Turkish government strongly expresses dissatisfaction with EU's Kurdish and has long ignored the existence of Kurdish issue, labeling it as "terrorism" or "separatism" issue, and accuses the EU for playing on Kurds and interfering in Turkey's domestic affairs, utilizes the Kurdish card as a pretext to delay Turkey's EU accession. However, in order to join the EU as soon as possible, Turkey has also adopted a series of reform measures to speed up the process of political democratization, relaxed restrictions on Kurdish political activities, improve the basic living conditions, abolished the death penalty, Ocalan's sentence was changed to life imprisonment. In August 2002, Ecevit led government, and the Turkish National Assembly adopted a reform package in line with the EU criteria.[62]

Turkey has also begun to accept the judgments delivered by the European Court of Human Rights in many cases. On June 10, 2004, under the pressure from the European Union, the Supreme Court of Appeal in Ankara

61 Liu Zuokui, Europeanization of Turkish PKK—An Analysis of a New System, Journal of West Asia and Africa, 2009/8; Roger Cohen, "Kurds Shot Dead by Israeli Guards at Berlin Protest", The New York Times, Feb. 18, 1999.
62 In August, 2002, Turkish Parliament passed a reform plan for the integration to EU. According to the plan, Turkey revoke all death sentences except terrorism charges. On October 3, 2002, the 2nd State Security Court commuted Ocalan's death sentence penalty to life imprisonment.

overturned the convictions Leyla Zana and other 4 former Kurdish deputies, who were sentenced to 10 years in prison.

The British ambassador to Turkey, Peter Westmacott, said the Supreme Court's judgment would be "an important step" in Turkey's EU accession process. In addition, Turkey has adopted a series of reform laws that allow Kurdish parties to openly comment and debate on the Kurdish issue and allowing the use of the Kurdish language, increasing investments in the southeastern region, promoting regional economic development and increasing employment and education conditions in the region,

In 2005, the EU decided to start accession negotiations with Turkey and on 12th of August 2005 Prime Minister Recep Tayyip Erdogan gave speech in the southeastern Kurdish city, pledging "Today that the Kurdish conflict in Turkey would be resolved with more democracy."

Erdogan also noted that his government recognizes the existence of various many nationalities in Turkey, which would be treated equally. In November 2005, Erdogan made another speech which underlined his approach: "In the Republic of Turkey, "Turk" label should be an umbrella identity under which "ethnic sub-identities" like Kurds, Circassians and indeed ethnic Turks could fall and pledged that under common identity, the Kurdish people would enjoy the freedom to define themselves as a different ethnic group, you can comfortably say, I am a Kurd."

It is noteworthy that recently, the Kurds living in Europe increasingly influence EU's Kurdish policy, by stepping up lobbying and public relations activities. Currently the Kurdish people in Europe is about 1 Million, an European Commission report said there were 1.3 million Kurds in Western Europe.

Paris Kurdish Research Institute research has estimated a larger population of Kurds in Europe: 0.80 to 1 million in Germany, 0.20 million in Holland, 0.12 to 0.18 in France, 0.10 to 0.15 million in Britain, Switzerland and Sweden respectively, 0.08 to 0.10 million in Belgium, 0.05 to 0.08 million in Greece and Finland respectively, also 0.06 million in Denmark, 0.05 to 0.06 million in Austria, 0.04 to 0.06 million in Norway and 0.05 million in Italy respectively.

The largest number of Kurds live in Germany, but since population registration in the EU countries does not include ethnic identity, it is difficult to reach accurate numbers. Kurds in Europe immigrants, have become an influential force, it is estimated that more than 140 Kurdish associations are active across Europe. Kon-Kurd (European Union of Kurdish Associations) as one major federation of Kurdish organizations, include, YEK-Kom in Germany, FEYKA-Kurdistan in France, FED-BIR in UK,

FEK-BEL in Belgium, FED-Kom in Holland, FEY-Kom in Austria, FEY-Kurd in Denmark, Kurdiska Radet I Sverige in Sweden, FEKAR-Kurdistan in Switzerland and so on, as member organizations.

Turkey and the United States regard Kon-Kurd as the cover of the PKK'a illegal activities. Kurdish parties also lead a large number of Kurdish media companies and newspapers, such as the weekly Azadiya Welat, daily Özgür Politika, Medya TV, Mesopotamian TV, Kurdistan TV, Kurd-Sat TV.

PKK leads the influential MED-TV which was established in 1995, based in the UK and Belgium, mainly broadcasts in various Kurdish dialects besides Turkish and Arabic, it targets audiences in the Middle East and Europe.[63]

Later it started broadcasting under the name ROJ-TV and its center was moved to Belgium with a branch in Copenhagen Denmark. ROJ-TV employs 100 people and its annual budget is about 5 million Euros.[64]

After Ocalan was arrested in 1999, the Kurds held large-scale protests all across Europe. During the protests in German cities, also Israeli embassy was attacked, clashes occurred with the police, where in Berlin three Kurds were shot and killed.

Every time a suppression or an adverse event occur in Turkey, Iran, Iraq and Syria, against Kurds, one can see active protests in Europe. In order to seek the EU support and coach EU pressure over the Turkish government, the PKK has successfully organized public relations and publicity work, and many people believe that this violent terrorist organization has undergone a self-transformation becoming a civic organization, which has adopted peaceful and democratic ways in its struggle for Kurdish national rights and interests, consequently its positions are carefully watched and considered by the EU leaders and officials at decision-making levels.[65]

Italian scholar Nathalie Tocci has argued: EU's keen attention and concern for the Kurds in Turkey is largely influenced by the Kurdish exiles in Europe. They have achieved a capacity to attract affection on the Kurdish issue and put it on the EU agenda.[66]

---

63 The TV company name comes from the antic Medes who are believed to be the ancestor of Kurds. Following the arrest of Ocalan in 1999, the Turkish Government imposed pressure on the United Kingdom and Belgium and the MED-TV was banned on 22 March, 1999. It was soon re-opened with another name as MEDYA-TV, and soon France banned it too.

64 ROJ-TV in Kurdish "roj" means daytime.

65 Liu Zuokui, Europeanization of Turkish PKK—An Analysis of a New System, West Asia and Africa, Vol. 8, 2009.

66 Liu Zuokui, Europeanization of Turkish PKK—An Analysis of a New System, West Asia and Africa, Vol. 8, 2009; Nathalie Tocci, The EU and Conflict Resolution: Promoting Peace in the Backyard, Routledge, 2007, p.1531.

Another noteworthy point is that on the one hand, Kurds in Europe are a source causing tensions between the EU and Turkey from time to time, on the other hand their activities and influence constitute a social and security issue in Europe.

In June and November 1993, PKK supporters attacked Turkish consular buildings, Turkish travel agencies, small businesses and banks in various German cities, their violent protests ended only after Ocalan ordered them to halt, in the meantime Turkish people living in Germany, were highly alarmed. On 22 November 1993, German government decided to ban PKK activities introduced the ban on the relevant party organizations, numerous retaliatory attacks have occurred in 1994 and 1996, against the ban. In June 1995, about 70,000 Kurds organized large-scale mass rally in Cologne, calling on the German government to lift the ban on the PKK and demanded support and push for a political solution to the Kurdish issue. After the arrest of Ocalan in February 1999, there occurred 46 Kurdish demonstrations in Germany (40 of which were peaceful protests), 10 attacks against the Greek and Kenyan consular buildings in Germany, a severe attack against the Israeli embassy in Berlin, and embassy guards have shot three Kurds in defense. During the protests 27 German police officers were injured, hundreds of people were taken into police custody. To this end, 1994 German Foreign Minister Klaus Kinkel commented: the clashes were "tantamount to a declaration of war…….organizers of violent protest should be deported immediately to Turkey." He also made a speech in German Parliament, which also addressed Kurds and Turks: "Under no circumstances must this be allowed to develop into a license for them to wage violent disputes with each other here in our country."

In general, German left-wing parties and trade unions have a favorable position towards the Kurdish movement. Federal and local governments are also cautious in dealing with Kurdish political organizations in Germany. In 2008 the Interior Ministry ordered the prohibition of ROJ-TV broadcasting in Germany, but in May 2009 the German Federal Court overturned the ban. The ROJ-TV based in Denmark has also become a major diplomatic issue between Turkey and Denmark.

Turkey has been extremely disturbed by the ROJ-TV, as the mouthpiece of the PKK (Kurdistan Workers' Party) it has insistently demanded that, Denmark close the TV station. In November 2005, when Prime Minister Erdogan visited Copenhagen, he even canceled the joint press conference that he intended to hold with Danish Prime Minister Anders Fogh Rasmussen due to the fact that his Danish counterpart refused to ask the correspondent of Roj TV to leave the conference hall.

The Danish government declared: ROJ-TV does not disseminate any contents of the hatred against the Turkish government, we have not found any solid evidence between it and the PKK. In August 2010, the Danish Minister of Justice launched a new investigation into the ROJ-TV, claiming ROJ-TV has been advertising a terrorist organization and requested a Danish court to ban the channel from broadcasting. Prosecutors Anders Risager and Jakob Buch-Jepsen announced their final opinion during the 28th hearing of the trial on Wednesday. They submitted evidence of orders from PKK executives to Roj TV and photographs of Roj TV employees taken in the PKK's bases in the Kandil Mountains in northern Iraq. Buch-Jepsen said during the hearing that the evidence they put forward clearly proves that Roj TV is completely under the control of the PKK, both administratively and economically. Consequently the court decided to cancel ROJ-TV's broadcasting licence in January 2012.

Turkey welcomed the court decision and praised the government of Denmark for its responsible attitude: "We are pleased to acknowledge that the government of Denmark sticks to its international obligations in the fight against terrorism, by taking proper measures against the PKK media." Soon after, Eutelsat satellite company cancelled its service contract with the ROJ-TV, beginning from midnight 24 January, 2012.

348 In March 2010, the Belgian police also attacked ROJ-TV's studios. Belgian prosecutors said the raid was due to "very serious evidence that, in a very organised way, youngsters of Kurdish origin were recruited in western Europe, notably in Belgium". In fact Belgian prosecutors were pointing the finger at PKK. Programming was disrupted for a time but the channel returned to air.

After these developments, Kurds have heavily criticized the EU for its pressures over Turkey has been milder and milder, and that EU gives too much emphasis on cooperation with the Turkish government, in turn ignores the interests of the Kurds.

In this respect, Nazmi Gur, BDP's (Kurdish Peace and Democracy Party (BDP) in Turkey) Vice-President, who is responsible for foreign affairs and a member of the EU-Turkey Joint Parliamentary Committee, told AK news in a press conference:

"We are supporting Turkey's accession to the EU. At the same time it is very difficult to understand why the EU is not helping to find a peaceful solution to the Turkish-Kurdish conflict, but takes the side of Ankara in this conflict! "Instead of helping Turkey to change in-line with the European values, Europe will be changed according the Turkish strategy against Kurds and it will bring the Turkish-Kurdish war to Europe. "For Turkey, every Kurd who demands his fundamental right is an activist. There are already more than

7,000 Kurdish politicians, including mayors and parliamentarians, who are in prison without any proves." Ismet Kem, Chairman of KON-KURD, the Confederation of 140 Kurdish associations in Europe, said: "This proposal is not only injustice, but it's also comic, referring to the 1.5 million Kurds living in Europe. "We are not talking about a small group of politicians or activists, but about more than a 100,000 Kurdish activists in Europe. "This is a contradiction with the European values of peace and democracy".[67]

A brief summary:

All in all, the EU's Kurdish policy has the following characteristics.

Firstly, it lacks consistency and internal harmony. This nature is not only reflected in the Kurdish policy towards Turkey, but also towards Kurdish issues of Iraq and Iran. This quality also applies to the situation in the EU institutions and at the level of member states, there are quite differences in Kurdish policy among the EU institutions and member states, which reflect lack of harmony.

Second, democracy and human rights are the main contents, of EU's Kurdish policy, emphasizing respect for minority rights, protection of Kurdish human rights and freedom, maintenance and development of Kurdish culture. Non-governmental organizations supported by EU, as well as the European Parliament, the European Court of Human Rights play an increasingly important role in this regard.

Third, EU opposes terrorism and stress the need to curb and oppose excessive violence and advocate a peaceful and democratic solution to the Kurdish issue through dialogue.

Fourth, support political rights of Kurds as immigrants in Europe, requires that the host country expand political participation, but EU is cautious when it comes to autonomy or independence demands.

Fifth, EU's Kurdish policy includes playing Kurdish card, for their own interests, the degree of concern for the Kurds depends on the lucrativeness and depth of the EU's self-interests. However, compared with the US government, the EU is less selfish.

On Turkey's accession to the EU, the Kurdish issue seems to be a pretext to prevent or delay the economic and politic integration.

Sixth, policies are conflicting and contradictory. EU adopts multiple and conflicting standards for the Kurdish issue in different Middle East countries. And on the issue of PKK's armed struggle, on the one side it stresses the need to oppose violence, on the other side condones its activities.

67　"EU Urges Turkey to Find Political Solution to Kurdish Issue", Mar.31, 2012, http://www.ekurd.net/mismas/articles/misc2012/3/turkey3865.htm.

6.3 Russia and the Kurdish Issue

Kurds have been living in Russia, for hundreds of years. In the second half of the 18th century, many Kurdish tribes have moved to the Caucasus region. During the Soviet Union period, about 1 million Kurds have lived in the Soviet Union, mainly in the Soviet republics of Azerbaijan, Armenia, Georgia, Kazakhstan, Uzbekistan, Turkmenistan and Kyrgyzstan. But the exact numbers cannot be reached. After the disintegration of the Soviet Union, the Kurds currently living in the Russian Federation amount to about 400,000, they mainly live in St. Petersburg, Moscow and the Adygea Republic in Caucasus region, Krasnodar Region, Stavropol Region and Tambov city, Rostov City (Oblast), Saratov city and Nizhny Novgorod city.

The Soviet Union recognized the minority status of Kurds, allowing them to maintain and enjoy their culture, languages and traditional national customs. In the 1920s, the Soviet Union established "Red Kurdistan" (Kurdistan Okrug), also known as the "Lachin Republic". It was established in the Lachin region of the Soviet Republic of Azerbaijan, where Kurds were the majority, allowing Kurds to exercise regional ethnic autonomy and self-government, with an area of 5200 square kilometers. Schools, textbooks, radio and television freely used Kurdish language. In 1929, the autonomous republic was reduced to a Kurdish autonomous region (Kurdistan Okrug). It is said that this move was related to Soviet Union's efforts to alleviate differences with Turkey, develop better relations.[68]

In the Soviet Union, by 1937, even district-level administrative units were abolished. In the 1930s and 1940s, due to security polices related approaching war, Stalin sent more than 100,000 Kurds to the Central Asian republics and Siberia. Also, some Kurds have been assimilated into Azerbaijan national identity due to promotion of Azerbaijani nationality building. But, the Kurdish national development studies under the Oriental Institute of Baku, Azerbaijan, was maintained till the 1960s, and Kurdish research institutions in Moscow, Leningrad (Petrograd) were further continued.

Currently, Russian Kurds have more than 20 social organizations across Russia.

Also on February 17, 1995, in the Commonwealth of Independent States set up the International Union of Kurdish Public Associations; this Association maintains clise contact with the government and actively promotes Kurdish rights and interests in Russia and also supports overseas Kurds in their struggle for minority rights.[69]

---

68   In 1992, after the capture of Lachin by Armenian forces during the Nagorno-Karabakh War, the Lachin Kurdish Republic was declared in Armenia by a group of Kurds led by Wekîl Mustafayev. However, since most of the area's Kurdish population had fled along with the ethnic Azerbaijani and had found refuge in other regions of Azerbaijan.
69   Marie Mediya Badini, "Tsarist Russia-USSR-Modern Russia: Milestones in Kurdish Geopolitics—Last Part", The Kurdish Globe, July 17, 2010.

As one of the long-term hot issues in the Middle East, the Kurdish issue has been the concern of the former Soviet Union and Russia and was used as an important political card. Overall, we can see that Russia's concern and influence over Kurds and Kurdish issues has encountered a downward trend, which had reached a peak the Soviet era, during 1940-1991.

The relationship between Russia and the Kurds dates back to the Tsarist period and can be divided into three stages: the Tsarist Russia, the Soviet Union, and the Russian Federation. Three periods have different contents and characteristics.

During the Tsarist period, Kurdistan had been the target of Moscow Tsars for a long time and had instigated the Kurds to create internal troubles for the Ottoman Empire from time to time. Kurdistan has also been an important battlefield during the long wars between Russia and Ottoman Empire, Russia and Iran, becoming a war-ravaged country.

During World War I, Russia occupied Kurdistan regions of the Ottoman Empire and Iran. While the Kurds in the cracks have been Cesar as a deal with the Ottoman Empire or Iran's "savior."

During the long Russian-Ottoman Wars, especially during the Crimean War, Tsar allied with a part of Kurdish tribes to attack Ottoman Turkey and grab Kurdish Regions, Tsars also planned to recruit Kurds for the cavalry divisions as they had done with Cossacks.

351

After October 1917, with the outbreak of the Russian October Revolution, the Russian army withdrew from Kurdistan, gave up imperialist ambitions over Kurdistan.

After the founding of the Soviet Union, important changes have occurred in the foreign policy of this state: supporting socialist and national revolutions, and anti-colonialism, maintaining good relations with developing countries. Especially after the Second World War, Soviet Union strongly supported the Arab national movements and support to Kurdish national movement became an important part of the Soviet foreign policy in the Middle East, as part of its anti-imperialist camp strategy.

In those days, dozens of Kurdish nationalist organizations were active in Turkey, Iran and Iraq, the vast majority being left-wing oriented, including communist parties, left oriented national-democratic parties or worker-peasant parties, which clearly advocated Marxist socialist ideology in their party programs. Their programs included anti-imperialist, anti-colonial and anti-feudal policies and aimed to combine the cause of national liberation with socialist cause. They generally favored the methods of armed struggle, mobilizing the masses of workers and peasants, and consciously accepted the guidance of the Soviet Communist Party and cooperated with the

Soviet government to get support and assistance. The Communist Party of the Soviet Union had become a model for these Kurdish political parties, in their theories, ideological lines, organizational styles, policies and methods of struggle. As one example, we see that all these parties have established the organs and post we see in the communist parties such as the Central Committee, Politburo and General Secretary and other similar. institutions and positions.Mullah Mustafa Barzani was also known as the "Red Mullah". The Soviet intelligence agency KGB has played an important role in coaching the Kurdish struggle, and there were rumors that Mullah Mustafa worked in the KGB, with the code name Rais (meaning leader in Arabic).[70]

During World War II, the Soviet Union occupied the northern part of Iran and part of Teheran, in August 1945, and in its control area, supported the establishment of the Iranian Kurdistan Democratic Party and manipulated the establishment of the first Kurdish Republic–Mahabad Republic. However, the Republic existed for less than a year and was suppressed by the Iranian government because of the Soviet withdrawal from Iran, after a deal with the latter. The establishment of the Republic of Mahabad is a milestone in the history of the Kurdish national movement, but also its defeat was mainly caused by the Soviet Union. After the failure of the Republic, Mullah Mustafa Barzani fled exile to Moscow and stayed there until 1958, later he returned to Iraq after the Iraqi revolution where he stayed for 11 years. During the Soviet period, Mullah Mustafa and others received some preferential treatment, and was educated in the Soviet military academies and universities.

During the Cold War, the Soviet Union continued to support the Kurdish national movement, but rather aimed to utilize it as a political card. As Turkey and Iran allied the West camp, and followed anti-Soviet policies, Soviet Union supported the Kurdish national movement. Since the Kurdish parties at that time opposed imperialism, they have regarded the Soviet Union as a natural ally consciously and voluntarily, adopted Marxist-Leninist ideology and pro-Soviet policies, but in fact this was rather a political choice than an ideological choice, their grasp of Marxism-Leninism and socialism had not been deep. In Iraq, some Kurdish democratic parties have even subjectively equated themselves with the Iraqi Communist Party.

From the 1960s to the early 1970s, the Soviet Union maintained good relations with the Iraqi Kurdistan Democratic Party and the Iraqi Government, providing support for both sides, the Soviet Union mediated between the two sides when dispute occurred. However, when trying to strike a balance between the two the Soviet Union, gave more weight to Arab nationalism far more than the Kurds.

---

70 Dr. Kamal Said Qadir, "The Kurds and the KGB: "The Secret History of the Barzani Dynasty", Aug.31, 2006, http://www.antiwar.com/orig/qadir.php?articleid=9629.

When the Soviet Union's struggle for hegemony had intensified fiercely in the Middle East and Iraq had become more important, at times when the Iraqi government warned against the Kurds, the Soviet Union gradually shifted its support to Iraqi government, in turn reduced its support for the Kurds.

In the early 1970s, the Iraqi Kurds, who were disappointed with the Soviet Union policy, began to gradually turn their face towards West to seek US support. The Iraqi Kurdistan Democratic Party won Iran and United States's support during the Iraqi civil war in the early 1970s. In 1975, when Iraq and Iran reached the "Algiers Agreement", the United States and Iran betrayed Kurds and the Iraqi Kurdistan Democratic Party, Mullah Mustafa was again forced to exile, but this time to USA not to SU, he lost his life there tragically. This was caused by self-centered choice of Iran and the United States. In the Middle East, Soviet interests have been more valuable for Arabs, compared to Kurds. Since after the 1970s, the influence of the Soviet Union in the Kurdish national movement has been declining, and reached the lowest point in the late 1980s.

Although we observe selfishness and pursuit of hegemony in its Kurdish policy, generally speaking, we can comfortably say that Soviet Union has supported the Kurdish national movement, this support has objectively, played a progressive role. Besides, the Soviet Union has not only provided organizational support, cultivated and trained a large number of leading cadres for the national movement, but also promoted the deepening of the Kurdish nationalist consciousness, thus pushed the Kurdish national movement to a higher level.

353

Soviet Union's support for the Kurdish national movement was not a selfless behavior, in fact aimed to serve its foreign policy and its own interests. In the 1920s, the Soviet Union supported Mustafa Kemal and the new Turkish republic, and concluded a treaty of friendship that helped Turkey to suppress the Kurdish uprising. During the Cold War, the Soviet Union also supported the governments of Iraq and Syria, in turn accused Kurds of collaborating with "imperialism and reactionary forces", that Kurds mistakenly ignored the progressive nature of Iraq regime, also accused the West of "providing Kurdish extremists with arms and ammunition and financial support."[71]

Thus it can be said that, it gave indirect support for the suppression of Kurdish people. In Iran, Soviet Union supported pro-Soviet Kurdistan Democratic Party and the Komala (Society of Revolutionary Toilers of Iranian Kurdistan), and other Kurdish organizations that were engaged in

71   Salah Bayaziddi, "Kurdish Question and the Soviet Union (1917-1991) ", The Kurdish Globe, May 28, 2011, http://www.kurdishglobe.net/display.article.html?id=3E149 79BABDB3A4B8760D00BE15317F4.

the struggle against the Pahlavi dynasty. The Soviet Union also directly or indirectly supported the PKK and other Kurdish left-wing organizations in Turkey, which was an important country in the pro-Western camp, during the Cold War. Turkey, had a strategic position during the Cold War, to contain Soviet Union since it is located in its south wing, and among the member states of NATO, it was the only country which directly bordered the Soviet Union.

The disintegration of the Soviet Union had an important impact on the Kurdish movement in many ways: after the disintegration Iraq lost the from the Soviet Union, due to this important change, the Iraqi Kurds, with the support of U.S have achieved autonomy, this important change also led to the US' two wars targeting Iraq and to the overthrow of the Baath Party.

Secondly, the Kurdish left wing organizations have lost the support of the Soviet Union, caused by the fall, socialist ideology has seriously weakened, consequently many political parties began to change towards social democracy and liberalism and turned their faces to West. Besides in the Soviet Union, millions of Kurds were depressed and spread to the newly independent central Asian and Caucasian states, regional ethnic separatist movements grew in the Middle East and adjacent regions. Islamic revivalism and rise of Pan-Turkism was another consequent, on the other side the influence of Turkey has expanded in the region. All above has greatly affected the fate and course of the Kurdish national movement. Among them, the Russia's Chechen issue was linked with the Kurdish issue as a bargaining chip.

After the disintegration of the Soviet Union, the concern and attention of the successor state has decreased significantly, its support was basically ceased. Main reason was that, after the disintegration of the Soviet Union, its successor's political, economic and military strength has dropped significantly and lost its major role and effect in the Middle East.

On the other hand, in the decade after the disintegration, Russia's turned its face foreign policy to the West, consequently the Third World, including the Middle East was no longer its foreign policy focus.

In addition, after the disintegration of the Soviet Union, those Soviet republics which were bordered with Kurdistan such as Armenia, Georgia and Azerbaijan have all separated from the Soviet Union, and established independent states, thus Russia was no longer geographically adjacent to Kurdistan. However, Russia still has traditional strong links interests in the Middle East, therefore Russia has not completely given up its concern towards Kurds, especially toward those where Kurdish issue is more complex.

This is mainly reflected in the relations between Iraq and Turkey over the Kurdish issue. The relationship between Russia and Turkey is more complicated. Since from the time of Tsars the Russia-Turkey relations have been hostile, during the Cold War era, Turkey joined the Western camp to oppose the Soviet Union, in the post-Cold War era relations between the two countries have been relaxed, but there also remained many problems between the two sides.

In the post-Cold War era, Turkey has actively promoted Pan-Turkism, not only to benefit from Russia's weakness and try to impact Russia's sphere of influence in Central Asia, but also it aimed to build itself as a modern version of the Turkic Empire, besides Turkey has interfered in Russia's internal affairs and supported Chechen armed rebels. To this end, Russia also showed its teeth, and has supported the PKK. For quite a long time, Chechnya issue and the Kurdish issue of Turkey has become one of the sharpest conflicts in the relations between the two countries.

Russia has favored the PKK sympathetically, which has strong anti-Turkey attitude. In October 1995, Russia allowed the Kurdish Exile Parliament to convene in Russia. In 1996, the Russian Duma also allowed Kurds to hold the third conference of the Kurdish exile in Russia. Russia's internal security officials met with the PKK, and Russia announced publicly that the PKK is not a terrorist organization. At the end of 1998, under Turkey's pressure Ocalan expelled by Syria, his first option was to take refugee status in Russia asylum, many members of the Russian Duma also called for Ocalan's political asylum. However, the Russian government ultimately evaluated the overall situation of relations between Turkey and Russia, refused Ocalan. On the issue of the PKK, Russia's attitude has always been ambiguous. In 2007, Russian government declared: "We believe that the activities of the PKK Party are terroristic and we condemn it, and we believe that Turkey has the right to protect itself, but we also believe that the only way to solve the issue is dialogue."

If we would evaluate the future trends, although it seems difficult that Russia would return to the Soviet high level of influence power in the Kurdish issue, but Russia will not easily give up the Kurdish issue as an important geopolitical card in the Middle East.

The main reasons are as follows.

Firstly, since the late 1990s, especially after Putin became the president of Russia, Russia's strength has been gradually restored, and its foreign policy of turning its face towards the West, has seen a setback, thus Russia began to re-attach importance to the Middle East, decided to return to the Middle East, accordingly we see that, it embarked heated disputes with the West, on the Iraq and Iran related issues and on a series of other issues in the region.

Secondly, the Middle East region has an important global strategic position in terms of geopolitics, energy and humanitarian issues. For a long time, the Middle East region has also become a region with one of the most concentrated hotspot issues, in the world. most concentrated areas, including the Kurdish issue, which is an important hotspot over which major power diplomacies is demonstrated. Former Soviet Union and Russia have always played an important role in the Middle East issues, having traditional connections and influence. Therefore, as for the Kurdish issue, a major hot issue, which has an important impact on the fate of the region, and which involves multiple geopolitical concerns and major interests, Russia will not ignore, but pay greater attention.

Thirdly, although Russia and Kurdistan is no longer geographically adjacent, Russia has 400,000 Kurdish residents, who have multiple complex relationships with the Kurds living in the neighboring countries like Turkey, Iran and those living in countries of Caucasus, thus whether the Kurdish issue would have benign solution, will have a certain impact on Russia's ability to maintain security and integrity, stability in its territories.

6.4 Arab Countries, Israel and the Kurdish Issue

The Middle East includes five main national groups, namely Arabs, Turks, Persians, Kurds and Jews, as the Turks are the newcomers, we can say that the four nationalities among them are the natives of the Middle East for thousands of years.

Throughout thousands of years, they have formed complex relationships among themselves, before the 16th century ago, the Arabs and Persians held a dominant position, but with the 16th century, due to rise of the Turkish Ottoman Empire, the Turks and Persians gained the upper hand.

In the early 20th century, with the disintegration of the Ottoman Empire, especially after the two world wars, the Arabs have begun to rise again and established 22 states, and also the Jews have returned back to the Middle East and established a strong state, Israel,. In the 20th century Kurds also began to rise, and after the two Gulf Wars, their rise reached a historical peak, with these developments, the relationships between the five national groups and the power relations and disparities among them presents a new trend.

For a long time, in history, the Kurds living in the Middle East have not established an independent nation-state, their land has been occupied and ruled by Greeks, Romans, Mongols, Arabs in the region, Persians and Turks.

Although Kurds enjoyed a considerable degree of freedom under the rule of several Arab Empires, Ottoman Empire and Persian Empire, and although they established numerous small state-like structures, they have not establish their own nation-state, in its true sense.

After World War I, Kurdistan was divided among 4 territories under the majority rule of Arabs, Persians and Turks. Due to this subordination and constant conflicts between Kurds and others, i.e. Arabs, Turks, Persians, the relationship is rather negative, and even hostile, but their relationship with the Jews is closer.

In the earlier chapters of this book have explored the Kurdish issue in Turkey, Iraq, Iran and Syria, this section will focus on the relations of Kurds with Arab countries and Israel.

Table 6-1 Comparison of population and distribution of main ethnic groups in Middle East countries

	Population (Million)	Resident in
Arabs	300	22 Countries
Persians	50	Iran
Turks	55-60	Turkey
Kurds	30	None
Jews	12-13	Israel

Source: sorted out by the author as of 2013

In general, the 22 Arab countries in general have a "big nation" attitude towards the Kurds, and a negative position towards Kurds' demands for enhancing their national rights and pursuit for autonomy or independence.

Historically, until World War II, the relationship between the Arabs and the Kurds has been more harmonious, with no major conflict. Although Arabs have conquered the Kurdistan region in the 7th century and have forced the Kurds to convert to Islam, the Kurds rarely resisted the Arab rule for centuries.

And even the two sides have enjoyed traditional friendship and unity in the common fight against foreign enemies. Kurdish national hero Saladin Yusuf Ibn-Ayyub (Eyyubi) has led the Arabs to defeat the Crusaders coming from Europe, defended the common territories, end led the establishment the powerful Ayyubid dynasty which included Egypt and most of the Arabian Peninsula Region.

He solidified his power base in 1171 when he overthrew the Fatimid dynasty, returning Egypt to Islamic orthodoxy and becoming sole ruler there. Saladin made Egypt the major power in the Middle East. He established a stable dynasty, encouraged education, and reformed the financial structure to support the armed Kurdish and Turkish cavalry. Saladin's policies began a long period of economic prosperity, population growth, and cultural revival.

Saladin Eyyubi was not known only as the greatest national hero by the Kurds, but also by the Arabs. The contradictions and conflicts between Arabs and Kurds have begun in the late 19th and early 20th century with the formation and rise of nationalism. With the fall of the Ottoman Empire and its disintegration Arab nationalism and Kurdish nationalism have also appeared, and they sought to establish their own independent nation-states, which caused several conflicts.

But in the period between the post- World War I and the end of World War II, the contradiction between the two sides was not so serious, firstly because the real rulers of the Arab countries were the Anglo-French colonists, rather than the Arabs themselves, secondly the Arab nationalist forces have focused on the struggle against colonialism, to win national independence, and the Kurds were seen as allies. In fact, at this stage the Arabs and the Kurds fought side by side, against the British and French colonialism.

After World War II, the conflicts between the Kurds and Arabs has intensified which caused fierce clashes. And, this conflict was concentrated in Iraq.

After the World War II, especially in the 1950s and 1960s, the Arab nationalist movement has surged, after several changes and revolutions, the Arab people have won independence. Arab world has become the center of national revolutions in the Middle, and became the masters of themselves. At the same time, pan-Arabism idealism has developed continuously, holding high the banner of great Arab unity which hoped to unify the Arab world and the Middle East. The pan-Arabists came to power in various countries, especially the Baathists in Iraq and Syria, and they pursued an assimilation policy with a distinct narrow nationalist flavor.

At that time, almost all Arab countries emphasized the Arab nature of their country, stressing that their peoples, regardless of their ethnicity and religion, were part of the Arab nation.

These pan-Arabism thoughts have profoundly affected the attitude of the Arab governments and ordinary people towards the Kurds. On the other side contradictions between the Palestinian Arabs and Israel has led to the emergence of the Palestinian issue.

22 Arab countries have supported the Arab-Israeli wars to support the Palestinian Arabs, but failed in succession, a large number of Arab territories was occupied by Israel after the wars, consequently Arab world felt humiliated and the people were frustrated.

In this context, the Arabs have been particularly sensitive and cautious towards national minority movements within the Arab States, and their claims for national rights.

Under the banner of pan-Arab nationalism, almost all Arab countries have invariably advocated negative policies against those ethnic minorities such as Kurds, Berbers and some other nationalities, and have pursued a policy targeting to assimilate or integrate them into the family of Arab nation, to suppress ethnic characteristics of them.

For the Arab public and the pan-Arabs, the demands for national identity and demand for expansion of national rights by Kurds and other ethnic minorities would only lead to four consequences:

Firstly, would endanger national unity and lead to division.

Secondly, they thought Arab countries would lose Arab properties, which would endanger the great cause of reunification of the Arabs. Lebanon had largely lost its Arab identity as a result of sectarian politics between different religions and nationalities. Iraq, which would allow Kurdish autonomy and if divided between Shi'ite Arabs, Sunnit Arabs and Kurds, would not only split, but also lose its traditional Sunni Arab attributes.

Third, they thought the Palestinian tragedy may be repeated, i.e. the "second Israel threat. Israel state had occurred because the Arabs had been too tolerant against the Jewish immigration and consequently the Palestine was divided into two, which also led to humiliation in the hearts of Arab people.

Fourth, endanger the dominant position of Arabs in the Middle East. The Arabs have always regarded themselves as the true owners of the Middle East, the Turks are regarded as newcomers, the Jews are seen as the tool of Zionism supported by Western colonialists and imperialists, and outsiders, while the Persians are not seen as part of the Middle East region only located as adjacent to it.

In the current pattern, due to historical factors, the relationships between the 2 pairs, Arabs and Jews, Persians and Turks, seem to be full of incongruity and mistrust. Since the World War II to present, the relationship between Jews and Arabs has been a hostile relationship, also there continues a competition between Arabs and Persians for thousands of years, competition and hostility has not been eliminated between the two. Also Arabs are skeptical towards the Turks, not only because Ottoman Turkey had ruled the Arabs for about 600 years, and that Turks have looked down upon Arabs, but also because they are cautious about the relationships between Turkey-West and between Turkey-Israel.

Therefore, if a Kurdish state is to emerge, the relations between the five major nations will inevitably need to be re-arranged. Given the hostile attitude of the Kurds towards Arabs who have for long them, we can understand how the future of the Arab-Israeli relationship would be like. That means, if a Kurdish state is to emerge, the national relations and geopolitical situation in the Middle East will undoubtedly be more complex and difficult. This is also the important reason, why Arabs are cautious about the developing relations between Kurds and Israel.

On the Iraqi Kurdish issue, basically the policies of the Arab world includes a one-sided support for the Iraqi central government. During the Nasser period in Egypt, despite Egypt's sympathy for Kurdish nationalism, it mainly sided with Arab nationalism. Although Iraqi government had been hostile to Nasser and suppressed the pro-Nasserists in Iraq, Nasser rejected the demands of Kurds to put pressure over the Iraqi government. During the Iraqi government's crackdown on the Kurdish uprising, the Arab countries provided substantial economic and military assistance to Iraq.

In the 1960s, Syria also sent troops to assist Iraq in suppressing the Kurdish uprising. After the Gulf War, when the United States, Britain and France planned to establish a no-fly zone in the north and south of Iraq. Even pro-Western Egypt and Jordan both have expressed deep concern, saying that it would lead to a "de facto split of Iraq."

The Arab countries also expressed strong opposition and condemned Turkey for ulterior motives and infringement of Iraq's sovereignty and territorial integrity, with the pretext of fighting against PKK based in Iraq, they commented: "in fact Turkey has an eye for oil resources of Kirkuk and Mosul, and has claims over Iraqi territory".

In the 1990s, with the deterioration of the situation in Iraq, especially of the Kurds, and after Kurds used the opportunity to establish self-government with the support of the West, since in those days pan-Arabism thought was in low tide, and since democracy and human rights concerns have gradually increased the region, Arabs' understanding and attitude have undergone some changes.

In October 1996, Islamist Turkish Prime Minister Erbakan paid a visit to Libya, the Libyan leader Gaddafi suggested that Turkey should allow independence for Kurds of Turkey. After the 2003 war in Iraq, the Kurdish autonomy in Iraq, was further consolidated. In this context, the Arabs began recognize the new minority status of Kurds, and the necessity for the implementation of federalism in Iraq. They have developed a broader understanding that Iraq has to solve the long-standing Kurdish problem, and recognize Kurdish national rights.

But at the same time, Iraqi Kurds' improved status has been source of great concern in the Arab world, who fear that Iraq will split and an independent Kurdish state will probably emerge and cause the following consequences:

Firstly, with the establishment of Kurdish autonomy and federalism in Iraq, forming three parts Shiite, Sunnis and Kurds, the Arab and Sunni properties may gradually weaken and Iraq may withdraw from the Arab family, which can endanger the unity of the Arab world. This is also an important reason why Arab countries have been reluctant to deal with the Shi'ite-led pro-Shia Maliki government.

Secondly, they are afraid that the regional Sunni-Shiite balance will be disturbed, providing an opportunity for Iran to intervene in Iraq and expand its influence in the Arab world, which can trigger regional turbulence in the Middle East. All these reflect, the fear of Arabs to lose their dominant position in the region and lose their capacity in the strategic competition against the Persians, Turks, Jews and Kurds. Professor Alfred Habra, director of the Center for Strategic and Future Studies at the University of Kuwait, wrote: "These potential threats constitute the major nightmare in the Arab world."[72]

If we make a general evaluation on the current perspective of Arabs, we can say that their basic attitude on the Kurdish issue is still favors that Kurds should follow a strategy of dialogue and consultation with the central governments of the region in order to solve issue of minority rights, and should remain as part of the country, they live in. They also oppose use of armed struggle and violent means by Kurds to solve the issue.

At the same time, the Arabs have gradually begun recognize the new reality, and increased contacts with the Kurds, strengthened political and economic exchanges, seeking to expand their influence through contact in reshaping the relationship. For example, in 2011, the UAE decided to invest 6 billion Dollars in Iraq's Kurdistan region for the next three years.

Kurds and Jews as natural allies

Besides we observe that Kurds and Jews view each other as natural allies in the region, sharing "a similar history and faced by common enemies."[73]

There are mainly three reasons for such close ties, constantly increasing between Israel and Kurds: Firstly, in the ancient times both peoples lived in Mesopotamia and Jews were the first to live in the Mesopotamia, but later they were forced to migrate to Palestine. Between BC 722-586 BC, as the

---

72   Shafeeq Ghabra, "The Kurds: An Arab Perspective", http://www.american.edu/cgp/pdf/ArabKurdPerspective.pdf.

73   James Kirchick, "Another Israel", Oct.18, 2010, http://www.tabletmag.com/jewish.newsandpolitics/47651/another-israel.

neo-Assyrian and the neo-Babylonian Empires occupied Jerusalem region, a large number of Jews were forced to migrate to present-day Iraq.

Before the founding of Israel in 1948, in the Middle East there were a total of 187 Jewish communities, of which, 146 in Iraq, 19 in Iran, 11 in Turkey, and 11 in Syria and other places. The largest Jewish community was in Iraq with a population of 125,000 people.[74]

And also we see the neo-Aramaic people in Iraq, amounting to 25 to 30.000 people, among which about 22,000 of them living in Iraq's Kurdistan region who mainly speak neo-Aramean language.[75]

In the early 1950s, most of the Iraqi Jews, including the Jewish Kurds, emmigrated to Israel. At the moment there are about 50,000 Jewish Kurds in Israel. In the mid-1990s, Yitzhak Mordechai, the defense minister in the Netanyahu government, was a Kurdish who had emigrated from Iraq.[76]

Secondly, the two ethnic groups have encountered similar circumstances, which have experienced tragic historical fates and given a long-term struggle to establish a nation-state. With the dawn of first century, the Jews had fought several wars and revolts against the Romans, but were defeated.

362 The Jewish people were expelled several times from Palestine to Iraq, from Palestine to Egypt, then from Egypt to Palestine. After the first century, the Jews were almost completely expelled from the Middle East by the Romans, and world's largest diaspora community. With the early 20th century Jews began to return to Palestine, and in 1948 achieve their dream of state-building.

Although Kurds did not experience, large scale of immigration, massacre and were not forced to live as diasporas like the Jews, but they were ruled by their neighbours, and could not establish their own state and control their own destiny.

Thirdly, in the post-World War II period, in many cases, both Jews and Kurds were faced with common problems and common enemies in the region, which strategically brought them together. In this period the Arabs almost became the common enemy them. The Iranian Islamic regime founded in 1979, has also become their common enemy. Israel has pursued the "peripheral concept" to secure itself from the Arab threat and gain potential strategic allies, was certainly aware of Kurdish potential. It is said that even before the founding of Israel state, the Zionists had established certain contacts with Kurds.[77]

74 Jewish Kurds refer to the Kurds who believe in Judaism.
75 Michael M.Gunter, Historical Dictionary of the Kurds, p.149.
76 Sadi Baig, "A Clean Break for Israel", June 30, 2004, http://www.atimes.com/atimes/Middle_East/FF30Ak07.html.
77 Reuven Shiloah, 1909-1959, the first director of the Mossad, the Israeli intelligence agency, trekked through the mountains of Kurdistan and worked with the Kurds as early as 1931.

In the early 1960s, with the outbreak of civil war in Iraq, Kurdish revolts have attracted the Israeli attention, after which Israel decided to approach Kurds against Israel's "most enduring enemies"–Iraq and Syria. Israel has not only trained the Kurds but also secretly helped the Jewish Kurds living in Iraq to flee to Israel. Former Mossad, station officer Eliezer Tsafrir, who worked in North Iraq has revealed that during the Iraqi civil war of 1963-1975, Israel has provided military advisers and training to Mullah Mustafa forces and also provided small arms, anti-aircraft wepeonary and other military equipment.[78]

In 1963, Israel began to provide weapons and ammunition for the Kurds. In August 1965, Israel set up a training camp for the Kurdish military officer, the training camp was code-named as "Marvad". In 1965, one of the founders of Mossad, David Kimche, visited the Kurdish region of Iraq and met with Mullah Mustafa. Mullah asked Israel for assistance. After returning to Israel, Kimche urged the Israeli government to support the Kurds and suggested weakening the Arab encirclement by building relations with non-Arab nations and including Iran, Turkey and Kurds. Subsequently, along with the United States, Israel provided armed training for the Kurds, as well as technical assistance covering agriculture, science and technology.[79]

1966 In June, Mullah Mustafa secretly visited Israel and held talks with Israeli Prime Minister and Defense Minister. In September 1967 and September 1973, Mullah Mustafa visited Israel twice and met with Israeli Defense Minister Moshe Dayan.[80]

Israeli television has in the past broadcast photographs from the 1960s showing father (Mustafa) Barzani embracing the then Israeli defense minister Moshe Dayan.[81]

In June 1966, the Kurds defeated the government forces in the Mt.Hindarin, the help of Israeli advisers had worked. In August 1966, when an Iraqi Air Force MiG-21, flown by the Iraqi Assyrian defector Munir Redfa, landed at an air base in Israel. Israel and the United States were able to study the design of the plane, this operation was realized by the help of Iraqi Kurds. Israel has increased its aid to Kurds in 1967, amounting to nearly half a million US dollars of cash each month and provided weaponry.[82]

78   Reuters, Feb.21, 1999, Trita Parsi, Treacherous Alliance: The Secret Dealings of Israel, Iran and the U.S., Yale University Press, 2007, p.1.
79   James Kirchick, "Another Israel", Oct.18, 2010, http://www.tabletmag.com/jewishnewsandpolitics/47651/anotherisrael/.
80   Benjamin Beit-Hallahmi, The Israeli Connectoin, I.B.Tauris & Co Ltd., London, 1988, p.19.
81   http://www.atimes.com/atimes/Middle_East/FF30Ak07.html.
82   Michael M.Gunter, Historical Dictionary of the Kurds, p.147.

In the late 1960s, the Kurdish Democratic Party's intelligence agency Palastin was also established with the help of Mossad and the Iranian intelligence agency "Savak".[83]

In 1980, Israeli Prime Minister Menachem Begin has openly declared that, in addition to humanitarian aid, Israel has been secretly providing military assistance to Kurds, including delivery of weapons and sending military advisers. During the Arab-Israel War in October 1973, Israel demanded Mullah Mustafa to attack the Iraqi oil fields, and the Kurds have done it, which, to a certain extent, paralyzed the Iraqi army forces.[84]

Owing to the Israeli support of the Iraqi Kurds, sizable Syrian forces were diverted from the borders of Israel. The engagement of the Iraqi troops in the suppression of the Kurdish insurgence prevented Iraq from participating in the Israel-Arab War against Israel in 1973 since this required the withdrawal of the Iraqi army units from the home (Kurdish) front and the Iranian border.[85]

In 1975, due to US pressure, Israel has ceased aiding to Iraqi Kurds aid. And, during 1980's due to the warming of relations between the US and Saddam Hussein, Israel has followed a low profile, in its relationships with the Iraqi Kurds.

After the 1991 Gulf War, Israel began to openly support and develop relations with the Iraqi Kurds. In 1991, when the US launched the "Desert Storm" military operation, worldwide Jewish organizations began campaigns to help Iraqi Kurdish refugees, and urged the international public to act against the Iraqi government suppressing the Kurds.[86]

Israel also provided diplomatic aid to Iraqi Kurds, Israel Prime Minister Izak Shamir, when meeting with Baker, the US Secretary of State urged the US government to protect the Kurds.[87]

In 2003, after the Iraqi war overthrew Saddam Hussein's regime and when the "Kurdish Autonomous Region of Iraq" almost became an independent state, Israel's contacts with Kurds have greatly increased, and Israel further expanded its the presence in the Kurdish region of Iraq. In addition to training the Kurdish armed forces, one of the key objectives of Israel has been to use the Kurdish region soil as a base for surveillance of

---

83   Sergey Minasian, "The Israeli,Kurdish Relations", 21st Century, No.1, April, 2007, http://radioislam.org/islam/english/jewishp/iraq/israel_kurdish_relations.htm.

84   http://www.shafaqna.com/english/shafaq/item/1878-israeli-kurdish-relations-in-western-documents?.html.

85   Sergey Minasian, "The Israeli-Kurdish Relations", 21st Century, No.1, April, 2007, http://radioislam.org/islam/english/jewishp/iraq/israel_kurdish_relations.htm.

86   A.Barron, "US and Israeli Jews Express Support for Kurdish Refugees", Washington Report of Middle East Affairs, May-June,1991, p.64.

87   "Open Secrets: Israeli Nuclear and Foreign Policies",http://www.abbc.com/historia/shahak/opensec/07.htm.2003

Iran, "By aligning with the Kurds, Israel gains eyes and ears in Iran, Iraq, and Syria"…"The Turks note that the large Israeli intelligence operations in Northern Iraq incorporate anti-Syrian and anti-Iranian activity, including support to Iranian and Syrian Kurds who are in opposition to their respective governments." through the Kurdish region to the Kurdish region of Iran and Syria, and to the Kurdish region. penetration.[88]

Israeli media has reported that Israeli officials met with Kurdish political leaders Masoud Barzani and Jalal Talabani, beside Israeli Prime Minister Ariel Sharon has publicly confirmed that Israel has a good relationship with the Iraqi Kurdish region.

In 2006, Seymour Hersh, a renowned investigative journalist in the United States, pointed out that there were hundreds of IDA and Mossad personnel in the Iraqi Kurdish region who had established cooperative relations with the Kurdish armed forces to set up intelligence teams to collect nuclear intelligence related to Iran.

In September 2006, the British Broadcasting Corporation (BBC) found evidence that Israel was helping to train Kurds in Iraq's Kurdish region. The evidence confirmed that the "conspiracy theory" which has been popular in the Arab world for many years, namely, the overthrow of Saddam Hussein being the US-Israel conspiracy to eliminate the strategic threat for Israel and was the first step to redraw the Middle East map. Israel's active diplomacy to develop relations with the Iraqi Kurdish regional government is in accordance with its strategic interests.[89]

On the one hand, Israel can gather intelligence against Iran and Syria, especially against Iran's nuclear program, on the other hand, it uses the opportunity to support the Kurdish regional government as an ally against Iraqi Arabs. Israel continues to strengthen training of Kurds in fighting against terrorism, and carries out business activities with them in the fields of telecommunications technology and infrastructure.[90]

It is known that Iraqi President Talabani has made two public visits to Israel. In July 2009, the Israeli-Kurdish magazine which began publishing in the Kurdish region of northern Iraq, has caused a great shock in the Arab world. Since, the post-war Iraq has not yet established diplomatic relations with Israel, and since the central government controls Iraq's diplomacy, it is still taboo to openly mention issues related to Israel, in the post-war Iraqi media.[91]

88   Seymour M. Hersh, "Plan B", New Yorker, June 28, 2004, http://www.newyorker.com/archive/2004/06/28/040628fa_fact#ixzz1sTBsiJ3b.

89   Magdi Abdelhadi, "Israelis Train Kurdish Forces", Sept.20, 2006, http://news.bbc.co.uk/2/hi/5364982.htm.

90   Michael M.Gunter, Historical Dictionary of the Kurds, p.148.

91   "New Israel-Kurd Magazine Surprises Arab World", Aug.12, 2009, http://www.rnw.nl/english/article/new-israel-kurd-magazine-surprises-arab-world.

Although the Iraqi government does not want to established diplomatic relations with Israel, Kurdish leaders have publicly expressed their willingness to establish relations with Israel; Farah Mustafa Bakir, minister of foreign relations of the KRG, said: "There is no issue in our relationships with Israel,"…"they have not hurt us, and we cannot hate Israelis, because the Arabs hate them."

He stressed that Israel is a democratic country in the Middle East, and added "we are labeled as the second Israel." In May 2006, the President of the Kurdish Regional Government of Iraq, Masoud Barzani, during his visit to Kuwait, responded to an interview about Kurdish-Israeli relations, saying that "the Kurds cannot be blamed for establishing relations with Israel," "already many Arab countries have established relationships with Israel"… "If Baghdad establishes diplomatic relations with Israel, we would allow the opening of an Israeli consulate in Arbil."[92]

In 2007, Levi was at the Vienna International Women's Congress, sat side by side with Iraq's President Talabani's wife during the Congress and the two discussed the Middle East peace process and other issues.[93]

In 2008, at the Socialist International Congress, President Talabani and Israeli Defense Minister Barak shook hands. According to a poll conducted by the Arbil Survey Center in 2009, most of the Kurds favored good relations with Israel, which is completely opposite compared with the overwhelming majority of the people in the Middle East. The survey included the major cities of the Kurdish region–Arbil, Sulaymaniyah and also Kirkuk and Mosul where Kurds constitute the majority.[94]

Among the respondents, 87.5% said, relations between Kurds and Jews in history have been positive; 64.1% percent favored that Kurdish regional government would establish economic and cultural ties with Israel and prepare for full-fledged relations; 60% believed that Kurds should establish open relations with Israel, instead of secret contacts; 68.4% believed that, strengthening ties with Israel would produce abundant benefits for Kurds, 73.1% said KRG should establish diplomatic relations with Israel; 59.2% believed that a strategic alliance should be established with Israel, while only 9% opposed establishment of relations with Israel.

92   "The Iraqi Kurds Support Relations with Israel", Sept. 23, 2009. http://world.people. com.cn/GB/1029/42361/10106056.html.
93   Yigal Schleifer, "Mors Flow in Turkey: Kurdish Leader is a Jew", Apr.11, 2003, http://www.jweekly.com/article/full/19679/rumors-flow-in-turkey-kurdish-leader-is-a-jew/.
94   "Turkey Worried Israel's Support Waning over Kurd Issue", Dec.27, 2007, http://www.haaretz.com/news/ source-turkeyworried-israel-s-support-waning-over-kurd-issue-1.235994.

According to Dulmi, a researcher at the Arbil Research Center, commented on the reason why so many Kurds favored close relations with Israel: "they believe that Israel will remain strong forever, and be strong enough to lead the region, and will play a central role in the Middle East issues."

When it comes to Israel's relationship with Turkey and PKK, the situation is relatively more complex. In Turkey, rumors are manipulated that Massoud Barzani' ancestors were Jewish rabbis.

In the late 1990s, Turkey and Israel formed a strategic alliance, consequently the relationship between Israel and the PKK turned cold. In 1999, Israel helped Turkey in capturing Ocalan, which led to the Kurdish attacks against the Israeli Embassy in Berlin.

This shows that in the eyes of Israel, Turkey is much more important than Kurds. As the AKP led by Erdogan came to power in Turkey in 2002, Kurds' status in Iraq was already strengthened, Turkish government showed a cold response to KRG, soon the relations between Israel and KRG re-vigorated. Israel has classified the PKK as a terrorist organization, but has kept entering secret contacts with it, which caused cold relations between Israel and Turkey, besides the Israel's attitude against PKK underwent subtle changes. In December 2007, the Turkish media outlets reported that the Turkish government and Turkish military were increasingly skeptical about Israel's role in the Kurdish issue, "concerned about Israel's support for the increasingly deteriorating Kurdish issue" and that "Israeli companies were providing Iraqi Kurds with military equipment and training."[95]

In September 2010, the senior leader of PKK Murad Karayilan accepted two interviews with Israeli TV stations, and called on Israel to cease its military cooperation with the "common enemy" Turkey. "We demand that Israel, halt helping those who suppress our freedom struggle, the issue between us is the military relationship between Israel and Turkey, which hurts us deeply." "Our enemies are the enemies of Israel," and Murat Karayilan stressed: Turkey's uses the most advanced weapons in the fight against the PKK guerrillas and Kurdish civilians, bought from Israel.[96]

In another interview Murat Karayilan said: "I hope that Israel will understand and stand with us.

---

95   "PKK Leader Urges Israel to Cut Turkey Military Ties",
Sept.21, 2010, http://www.haaretz.com/news/diplomacy-defense/
PKK-leader-urges-israel-to-cut-turkey-military-ties-1.315053.
96   Othman Ali, "Possible Consequences of PKK-Israeli Alliance", Sept.18, 2011, http://www.todayszaman.com/news-257074-possible-consequences-of-PKK-israeli-unionby-othman-ali*.html.

After all, you have also experienced genocide and persecution, and now you see that the Kurdish nation is suffering the same fate. Karayilan warned Israel, saying: Turkish Prime Minister Recep Tayyip Erdogan has openly expressed his intention to further develop relations with Hezbollah and Syria, praised Hamas and embracing Ahmadinejad, do you really think he is a friend of Israel?"

There are news reports, whispering that Israel and the PKK are exchanging information and intelligence. Seymour Hersh, wrote in an article: Israel and the US are jointly supporting the armed Kurdish fighters in Iran–the Kurdish Free Life Party, which is in close relationship with the PKK, and even can be regarded as a branch of it. The WikiLeaks document, which was released in October 2010, also shows that Mossad cooperates with the PKK and that the US and Israel have been supporting the PKK. A US military document referred to the PKK as "warriors for freedom and Turkish citizens" and said the US had freed arrested PKK members. For this reason, US and Israeli officials were apprehensive about the WikiLeaks materials. Besides, many Turkish analysts and officials believe that a PKK missile attack on Iskenderun last year unquestionably bears Israeli fingerprints. Finally, the Israeli foreign minister's denial of the news about the Israeli government's increasing ties with the PKK, as mentioned in Yedioth Ahronoth last Friday, was hardly satisfactory to Turkey.

In January 2012, the Turkish and Israeli media reported that the Israeli unmanned reconnaissance plane was being used by the PKK for fixing Turkish military targets. The Jerusalem Post also wrote: an unmanned reconnaissance aircraft was shot down in Turkish borders, and it was discovered that the PKK was using it. It is known that since 2012, drones are being used by the PKK. And the news report added quoting from a Turkish newspaper: "The report also claims that Kenan Yıldızbakan – a PKK member who led an assault against a Turkish naval base in Hatay in 2010 – has visited Israel on numerous occasions, further raising suspicions of his organization's ties to the Jewish state."

More and more signs have appeared that Israel and the PKK are joining forces against the Turkish government, the article said: "If this alliance is to take place, it will have serious and far-reaching consequences for Turkey and the Kurdish question. It is our contention that the Kurds and the PKK, in particular are going to be the most adversely affected by this alliance. How and why did this union between PKK and Israel come up and what can be done to deny Israel this leverage in its conflict with Turkey? Starting in the early 1950s, the Israeli intelligence service, Mossad developed what was known as "the "periphery policy" of the Middle East in which it planned to establish ties with ethnic and religious minorities in the area in order to break the Arab embargo and the isolation Israel feels. Thus, Israel cemented close ties with some Maronites, Druze, Copts, the shah of Iran and Kurdish leaders and groups." "The story of Kurdish-Israeli ties has been detailed in "The Mossad in Iraq" by Shlomo Nakdimon. It suffices to say that the relationship was very exploitive and had harmful consequences for the Kurds. It was Zionist circles which in response to then-Egyptian President Anwar al-Sadat's request to end the war in Iraqi Kurdistan asked the shah of Iran in 1975 to cut support for the Kurdish revolution. Subsequently, Iran ceased the support and the Iraqi Kurdish movement was suppressed.

Although both Israel and the Kurds desire a deeper level of cooperation, build a strategic alliances, it is obvious that there might be many difficulties and interferences in the course, which determine that this can only be a quiet cooperation.

First of all, with the existing constitutional framework in Iraq, there can be no official and normal relations between Israel and the KRG, if not allowed by the central government, the Kurds would not by-pass this framework, without severing their relations the central government.

Secondly, for Israel, the strategic importance of Turkey is far greater than the strategic value of Kurds. Although Turkey-Israel strategic relations are faced with difficulties, it is not completely exhausted. Israel must consider the attitude of Turkey.

Thirdly, since Kurdish-Israel relations is a sensitive issue in the region, an open strategic cooperation will provoke the hostility of Arabs.

Fourthly, given the cross-border nature of Kurdish issue, affecting the territories of 4 states, Turkey, Iran, Iraq and Syria, their cooperation would disturb them with the fear of a Kurdish nation-state.

Therefore, Israel and the Kurds have repeatedly denied the existence of military cooperation between the two.

6.5 China and the Kurdish Issue

China has a long history of exchanges with Kurds, but China's involvement in the Kurdish issue is not long, compared with the US and Europe, China is a latecomer, and its involvement is not deep. Strictly speaking, China does not have a unified policy framework on the Kurdish issue. For China, the Kurdish issue is a transnational ethnic issue, which involves relevant countries, but mainly thinks the belongs to internal affairs of those countries. Therefore, China in principle does not interfere in the internal affairs of any country.

In recent years, while the Kurdish issue has increasingly become a regional hot issue, an as its influence has grown and it impacts regional affairs, and since China's interests and influence in the Middle East has expanded, its concern for the Kurdish issue has increased, consequently China has strengthened contacts and exchanges with Kurds.

China's contacts and exchanges with Kurds can be roughly divided into two stages: the first stage is from 1949 to 1990, in which the East and West confrontation between the two camps was prevalent, the Cold War climate was dominant, the Soviet Union hegemonism was prominent.

The second phase is 1991 to the present, known as the post-Cold War era.

In the 1950s and 1960s, one of the main tasks of China's diplomacy in the Middle East was to support the anti-colonial and anti-feudal national-democratic movements and socialist movements.

From the late 1960s to the late 1980s, the Chinese government and the CPC have supported anti-imperialist and anti-hegemonism policies of the nationalist and socialist movements, and also the movement for national democracy both including Arabs and Kurds

China's Kurdish policy in this period has possessed the following characteristics:

Firstly, China's concern for the Kurds was incorporated into the overall framework of China's foreign policy and regional foreign policy, actually there was no separate Kurdish policy. Secondly, the ideological emphasis was quite strong, The attitudes towards Kurds was affected by the relationship between China and the United States and the Soviet Union and by the relations between China and the Kurds, and also by China's relations with the country where Kurds lived.

On June 22, 1960, "People's Daily" published an article which wrote: In 1945-1946 Azerbaijani people of Iran and Kurds have established their local self-government, in the two regions, which mark the victory of the democratic movement, and a heavy blow to reactionaries, and which have greatly weakened the Iranian central government."[97]

But, in 1979 China has accused the Soviet Union for inciting Iranian Kurds of Iran to engage in "turmoil", and criticized the SU for supporting "insurgents" and propagating "separatism" among Kurds.[98]

Thirdly, China included the Kurdish people among the list of oppressed nations in the Middle East, but evaluated the causes of this oppression, mainly as colonialism, feudalism and imperialism, rather than big nation nationalism of the host countries.

---

97   "In Commemoration of the 40th anniversary of the Iranian Communist Party", The People's Daily, June 22, 1960.
98   "Soviet Union Manipulating Disturbance of Kurds", The People's Daily, May 7, 1979.

Fourthly, China emphasized that all nationalities, regardless of their size, are equal.

In China's policies Arab nationalist movement took precedence over the Kurdish nationalist movement, and the communist and socialist movements had priority over the nationalist movement, thus gave priority to supporting of the communist and workers' parties in the region, and emphasized the guiding role of ideology, i.e. Marxism-Leninism and Mao Zedong Thought in Kurdish people's struggle.

During this period, there were contacts with China and the Iraqi Communist Party, the Kurdistan Democratic Party, the Kurdistan Patriotic Union (PUK) and several other Kurdish left-wing organizations and nationalist organizations, and helped the training of their cadres.

In those days, many Kurdish organizations were affected by the experiences of the Chinese revolution, some even claimed, they followed the "Mao Zedong Thought" (referred to as "Maoism"), they proposed armed struggle, guerrilla warfare, mobilizing the peasant masses in the countryside to encircle the cities and finally seize the state power.

For example, the "Maoist" organizations in Turkey, during 1970s, included the communist- KAWA and "Denge Kawa" (Kawa meaning blacksmith), the Turkish Revolutionary Workers' and Peasants Party (TIIKP), TKP-ML led by Ibrahim Kaypakkaya who also established the Turkish Workers' and Peasants Liberation Army (TIKKO). and a faction of this party later established another party which was later renamed as the Maoist Communist Party (MKP)—its armed branch named as the People's Liberation Army (HKO),[99] and Iran's Kurdistan Workers' Revolutionary Organization, all of which has originated in the late 1960s. And Iran's Kurdistan Workers' Revolutionary Organization (Komala). At the same time, in the international context, including the Middle East, China gave, political and public opinion support for the national democratic movements.

The incumbent Iraqi President Talabani in 1955 as the representative of Iraqi Kurdistan Democratic Party when attended the "World University Students and Youth Day", in Warsaw, received an invitation from China, and in his first visit was received by Song Qinling.

Talabani was quite impressed by the developments in New China. China's road to national independence and revolution led by the CPC has also affected the subsequent political thoughts of Talabani.

---

99   It originates from the Turkish Communist Party–Marxist-Leninist faction (TKP-ML) formed in the late 1960s. The organization established the Turkish Workers and Peasants Liberation Army (TIKKO). In 2003, the organization changed its name to the Maoist Communist Party (MKP), and the armed organization changed its name to People's Liberation Army (HKO).

Talabani also translated the Selected Works of Mao Zedong into Kurdish for study. In April 1959, when the Iraq-China Friendship Association was inaugurated in Baghdad, Mullah Mustafa attended the inauguration ceremony.

In the post-Cold War era, China's concern over the Kurdish issue gradually increased, mainly for the following reasons: Firstly, with the rapid development of China's comprehensive national power, its general influence, including the Middle East has grown and China's concerns for the region has expanded including almost all spheres of politics, diplomacy, trade, investment, energy and other aspects. The developments in the objective situation has pushed China to pay more attention to the Middle East issues.

Secondly, with the upheaval in Iraq, Kurds' status has increased remarkably. After the Gulf War, the Iraqi Kurds have established a self-government in the no-fly zone, and became a de facto government, state in a state.

In 2003, after the Second Iraq War, Saddam Hussein regime was overthrown, on the one hand, Kurds through the establishment of Iraqi federal state, have consolidated their autonomy, and on the other hand further increased their influence in the Iraqi politics and became one of the three major political forces in Iraq. Also for the first time a Kurdish leader became the Iraqi President. Consequently, China established relations with all 3 the parties and specifically dealt with Iraqi Kurds.

Thirdly, the Kurdish issue in the region is heating up, and has become a hot issue of concern for the international community. In addition to the Iraqi Kurds' demands for independence, Turkey's PKK has become increasingly active with armed forces and armed attacks, its frequent terrorist and violent activities have brought about a certain threat to regional security and stability, as well as a threat to the national security and unity of Turkey.

All these developments, international community needs to pay more attention, on the Kurdish issue and increase positive mediation efforts.

Fourthly, as China's reliance on the energy of the Middle has grown, Iraq and Kurdistan's status in energy, has become increasingly important. In 1993, China with rapid growth in its oil imports ranked first in refined oil imports, thus the Middle East as the world's oil depot, has become the most important supplier for China.

In 2010 China imported about 500 million barrels of oil, and from in 2010, China's dependence on foreign crude oil was 53.8%, in 2011 this figure rose to 56%. According to the International Energy Agency (IEA) estimated that by 2035 China's net oil imports per day will be more than 12 million barrels. While Iraq's proven oil reserves ranks third in the world, and which is mainly concentrated in the Kurdish region. After Iraq war, has greatly disturbed its national construction, it needs to vigorously promote national construction, consequently its oil industry offers unlimited business opportunities.

Both business between China and Iraq and the Kurdish regional government, in energy trade and investment cooperation has great potential.

In 2011, China imported a total of 2.53 trillion tons of crude oil, with an increase of 6.05%. Iraq is the sixth largest source of crude oil imports of China, after Saudi Arabia, Angola, Iran, Russia and Oman. However, Chinese contracts in Iraq's oil development projects are mainly concentrated in the south and west, projects in the north (Kurdish region) are rare.

In July 2012, Wang Dongjin, deputy general manager of China National Petroleum Corporation (CNPC), said the group had invested $ 3.3 billion in the development of the Iraqi oil project and currently developing three major oil fields: First, Rumaila oil field, where Petro China and British Petroleum (BP) jointly operate the largest oilfield in Iraq, with a daily output of 1.35 million barrels per day and Al-Ahdab oilfield in Wasit province, central Iraq, with a daily output of 14 million barrels per day; the third is in Fakka in the southern Missan (Maysan) province, with oil reserves of 16 billion barrel, in July 18, 2012 the production, has been 10 million barrels per day.[100]

Energy cooperation with the Kurdish region is one of the priorities of China in the future.

Fifthly, the Kurdish issue has increasingly become a matter of concern for the Chinese people and is directly linked to the security and stability of the western regions of China. Turkey and Iran have been supporting the separatist elements who call them East Turkistan freedom fighters, the two governments condone and shield their separatist activities.

After the "7/5" incident in Xinjiang in 2009, Turkish Prime Minister Recep Tayyip Erdogan sharply criticized the Chinese government in dealing with the "7/5" incident, which was largely condemned by Chinese netizens. In internet many Chinese people demanded that the Chinese government should support Turkey's Kurds in retaliation, to fight against Turkey's support for Xinjiang separatists.[101]

---

100 "CNPC: an investment of 3.3 billion US dollars to the Iraqi oil projects", Washington Post, July 19, 2012. http://cn.wsj.com/gb/20120719/bch072339.asp
101 After the July 5th event in Xinjiang, China's major website forums were themed with demands for the Chinese government to support the Kurds to establish their own country in order to punish Turkey. Typical among them arehttp://bbs1.people.com.cn/postDetail. do?id=93253156; http://hi.baidu.com/%C3%C0%C0%F6%B5%C4%D6%ED1/blog/item/d2c0df32cedf894aad4b5fdf.html; http://q.sohu.com/forum/20/topic/52620679; http://club. china.com/data/thread/1011/2739/59/59/6_1.html; http://lt.cjdby.net/thread.916898-1-1. html; http://blog.sina.com.cn/s/blog_41381a700100e0bz.html.

Table 6-2 China's Oil imports in recent years

Year	Amount of Import (10,000 ton)	Value of Imports (10,000 US Dollar)
1994	1235	157339
1995	1709	235643
1996	2262	340655
1997	3547	545621
1998	2732	327454
1999	3661	464124
2000	7027	1486066
2001	6026	1166645
2002	6941	1275731
2003	9102	1978240
2004	12272	3391168
2005	12682	4772293
2006	14517	6641190
2007	16317	7977091
2008	17888	12930000
2009	20379	8930000
2010	23930	13493600
2011	25378	19666400

Source: Chinese General Administration of Customs

Table 6-3 Top ten crude oil suppliers of China, and their growth as of 2010

Country	Amount (10,000 ton)	Growth Rate (%)
Saudi Arabia	4464.2	6.98
Angola	3938.1	22.4
Iran	2131.9	-7.9
Oman	1586.7	35.18
Russia	1524	-0.41
Sudan	1259.9	3.36
Iraq	1123.8	56.89
Kazakhstan	1005.4	67.39
Kuwait	983	38.96
Brazil	804.7	98.32

Source: calculated from the statistics of Chinese General Administration of Customs, http://www.customs.gov.cn/tabid/7841/mid/24699/ctl/infodetail/infoid/292637/default.aspx.

Table 6-4 Top ten suppliers of China's crude oil imports in 2011

Country	Amount (10,000 ton)	Growth Rate (%)
Saudi Arabia	5027.77	12.61
Angola	3114.97	-20.9
Iran	2775.66	30.19
Russia	1972.45	29.42
Oman	1815.32	14.4
Iraq	1377.36	22.57
Sudan	1298.93	3.1
Venezuela	1151.77	52.66
Kazakhstan	1121.10	11.51
Kuwait	954.15	-2.94

Source: calculated from the statistics of Chinese General Administration of Customs, http://www.customs.gov.cn/tabid/7841/mid/24699/ctl/infodetail/infoid/353577/default.aspx

Typical comments in the internet focused on the questions such as, how to handle China-Kurdish relations, how to deal with the Kurdish issue, Kurdish issue Kurdish issue of the Chinese diplomacy, but also posits some challenges.

On the Kurdish issue, China should adopt a number of approaches in its policies.

Firstly, clarity issue. China should explicitly declare its consistent principles and position of dealing with: explain its emphasis on defending the Kurdish minority rights, its advocate of all nationalities regardless of size, are equal, its position both against big nation nationalism and ethnic discrimination policy; its advocate of resolving disputes by peaceful means; advocate of non-interference in internal affairs of a country and national affairs of a country to be decided by its own people, emphasizing both anti-terrorism, and the need to face the root of the problem, its advocate of strengthening cooperation with relevant countries in the fight against terrorism; its advocate of opposing separatism, and maintenance of national sovereignty and territorial integrity of countries.

Secondly, grasp the scale, pay attention to balanced policies, which may also include certain degree of ambiguity, our suggestion is determined by a number factors as follows: the Kurdish issue is a complex issue with its trans-border nature, which directly involves four countries and the fifth party as Kurds, and affects the security, stability and national unity of the countries concerned.

There are also other external actors which are indirectly involved in the Kurdish issue, such as the United States, Russia, the EU and some other countries which adopt a vague policy on the issue.

China has consistently upheld the principle of opposing interference in the internal affairs of other countries. In April 1991, the UN Security Council adopted a resolution on the Iraqi Kurds, and decided to set up a no-fly zone, but China abstained. During the discussion, the representative of China explained that China was sympathetic—the need to help—to the refugee issue faced by Turkey and Iraq, but it was a complex issue because it involved the internal affairs of a country and the Council should not consider and take action on the internal affairs of any sovereign country.[102]

Thirdly, China should take initiative. Objectively, whether or not admitted, China and Kurdish people are getting closer. The Kurds and the Kurdish issue are increasingly becoming important and influential in the regional and international stage. The role of Kurdish factor, is more and more affecting, China's Middle East diplomacy, bilateral relations with relevant

---

102   The People's Daily, Apr. 7, 1991.

countries such as Turkey and Iraq, relations between China and other major world powers in the region, China's energy diplomacy in the Middle East and China's frontier security (Xinjiang). Therefore, China should attach greater importance to the Kurdish issue in its foreign strategy, consequently China should take initiative, be proactive, thus strengthen contacts and exchanges with Kurds.

Fourthly, double-track approach. When developing relations with relevant countries, China should also directly contact with Kurds.

Fifthly, transactional mode. In the Kurdish issue, the adoption of a transaction of a work model, do not deliberately pursue the development of a unified Kurdish policy.

When dealing with specific cases, China should try to contact and cooperate with the relevant central government and the Kurdish regional government. Such as the anti-terrorism and security cooperation with the Turkish Government, while emphasizing the maintenance of national territorial integrity and national unity of Turkey.

And in Iraq, the Chinese Government advocates the maintenance of Iraq's sovereignty and territorial integrity, while actively supporting and participating in the post-war reconstruction of this country and the expands economic and trade cooperation. July 2004, China reopened its Embassy in Iraq.

In November, China's new ambassador to Iraq took office, Iraq's new ambassador to China has subsequently assumed office.

In 2004, the Rotating Chairman of Iraqi Interim Governing Council Muhammed Bahrululoom, Samaray the minister of Electricity, Gadamban, the Oil minister, and Zebari, the Foreign Minister Zebari visited China successively. In October 2006, Iraqi Oil Minister Hussain Shahristani visited China.

In June 2007, Iraqi President Talabani visited China. Since the establishment of diplomatic relations between China and Iraq in 1958, Talabani was the first Iraqi president who has visited China.

In February 2011, Chinese Vice Foreign Minister Zhai Jun visited Iraq. In July 2011, Iraqi Prime Minister Nouri al-Maliki made an official visit to China. Consequently, economic and trade cooperation has also made continuous progress, after these high level visits. In 2010, Iraq became China's fourth largest trading partner among the Arab countries, bilateral trade amounted to 9.86 billion US dollars, an increase of 91%. China imported 11.24 million tons of crude oil from Iraq, an increase of 56.9%. In addition, in March 2009, Petro China began to develop the Iraqi Al-Ahdab oilfield, which is estimated to have 1 billion barrels of crude oil reserves.

In June and December 2009, Petro China was awarded the bids for Rumaila and Fakka oilfield technical services respectively. At the same time, China has vigorously developed cooperation with the Iraqi Kurdish regional government, and enhanced mutual understanding.

In 2003, shortly after the war, the Chinese side invited Jalal Talabani, as chairman of the Patriotic Union of Kurdistan (PUK) and member of the Iraqi Interim Governing Council, In 2007, Talabani was again invited to China but as President Talabani to visit China. In May 2005, at the invitation of the leaders of Iraq's Kurdistan region, Chinese Ambassador to Iraq Yang Honglin and his entourage visited the oil reservoir area of the region, met with Masoud Barzani, PUK Deputy Secretary General Noshirwan Mustafa Amin, they held sincere talks and established cooperative relations. China also actively carried out exchanges at inter-party and regional government levels, the CPC, contacted with the Kurdistan Democratic Party, the Kurdistan Patriotic Union, the Kurdistan Communist Party and established exchanges and cooperation with them.

In November 2006, Ma Wenpu, vice minister of the International Department of the CPC Central Committee, led a CPC delegation to visit the Kurdish area in northern Iraq. In September 2007, the Iraqi Patriotic Union of Kurdistan cadres delegation of 10 people visited China. In June 2011, a delegation of the Patriotic Union of Iraqi Kurdistan, led by Hero Ibrahim Ahmed including a member of the Political Bureau of the PUK, together with President of Iraqi Mr. Talabani, visited China.

China has been increasing trade and energy cooperation with the Kurdish regional government and holding joint trade and investment forums. In June 2007, when President Talabani visited China, he said: "We would like to encourage more Chinese companies and enterprises coming to Iraq to invest in industry and trade cooperation, starting from the autonomous region, and gradually spreading to other parts of Iraq, this will further strengthen economic and trade exchanges between China and Iraq." In October 2007, nearly 100 Iraqi business representatives attended the First China-Iraq-Kurdistan Regional Investment and Trade Symposium, which was also attended by Iraq's Presidential Economic and Trade Assistant and several other ministers. In November 2008, the second China-Iraq Kurdistan Regional Investment and Trade Symposium and a Trade Fair was held in Sulaymaniyah.

Summary

External powers have constituted an important factor that has influenced the historical fate of Kurds and the evolution of Kurdish issue, and this reality is still prevalent.

And in different periods, the magnitude of influence by several external powers has been different, their roles and effects they have made were also different.

European powers were the first to interfere in the Kurdish issue, as external powers, and have been the initiators of the Kurdish issue. Western European colonialism has created the tragedy of the Kurds. From World War I to World War II, the influence of Western Europe on the Kurdish issue has been unmatched.

After the First World War, the United States put forward the principle of "national self-determination" and supported the independence of Kurds, but President Wilson's idealist approach suffered a cold reception by the Anglo-French colonialists, caused US to distance from the Middle East, dropped the Kurdish issue from its agenda.

During the latter part of the Second World War, the United States and the Soviet Union began to intervene in the Middle East, they occupied Iran, and the Soviet Union supported the founding of the pro-Soviet Kurdistan Democratic Party, in the Kurdish-occupied zone. During the Cold War era, the Soviet Union and the United States' effects on the Kurdish have grown greatly, and far surpassed the influence of Europe,

The influence of Europe gradually decreased, and the colonial forces were expelled from the Middle East. During this period, the influence of the Soviet Union over the Kurds have been far stronger than the United States, almost all Kurdish political organizations were left-wing socialist organizations, pro-Soviet, and followed anti-Western policies.

The United States and the Soviet Union have tried to use their Kurdish policies to serve their hegemonic policies over the Middle East, both parties, in most cases betrayed the Kurds. In the post-Cold War era, Russia's influence on the Kurdish issue has greatly diminished, due to the disintegration of the Soviet Union, and the United States became the most important external power influencing the Kurdish issue, later the two Iraq wars enabled the Iraqi Kurds to achieve true autonomy, which marked a historical turn in fate of Kurds, which also led to the development of the Kurdish issue in the neighboring countries.

In period after the Iraq War, the influence of the united European Union has strengthened, especially on Turkey's Kurdish issue, where the EU still plays a pivotal role. China is a latecomer on the Kurdish issue, but China's concern on the issue has increasingly grown, and in recent years it has gradually increased contact with the Kurds.

Due to historical and pragmatic reasons, the Kurds and Jews view each other as natural allies in the region.

The Kurdish issue becomes more and more complicated and internationalized by the intervention of the major regional powers and external forces. Whether it is Europe or the United States or the Soviet Union, their attitudes over the Kurdish issue, have mainly based on self-interests, and despite their concern over the Kurdish human rights issue, they haven't to supported the independence of them.

For them, the Kurds are just a pawn, and their the Kurdish policies are subordinated to their global and regional strategies. For a long time, the Kurds have been relying on external forces to achieve their dreams, but with a lot of painful lessons. However, due to weaknesses and scattered situation of Kurds, the intervention by international powers have also changed the situation of Kurds and to a degree have made positive reform effects, such as the Soviet Union's support for the political organization of Kurds, and the Iraq War launched by the United States has caused a great change on the fate of Kurds.

CHAPTER SEVEN

The Crux of the Kurdish Issue and the Way Out

The emergence and development of the Kurdish issue is a product of the times, and closely related to the international pattern and geopolitical changes. During the century-long development of the Kurdish issue, its development has gone through four stages of evolution. Overall, the status of Kurds has seen continuous improvement, and their conditions are gradually improving. There are many reasons why Kurdish issue was not resolved for many reasons, including their own weaknesses, the policies of relevant host countries and the intervention of external powers seems the most important factor. In the short term, as to the achievement of their dream of independence, there is still a long way to go.

7.1 International and Geopolitical Changes Surrounding the Kurdish Issue

After since the emergence, and during the evolvement of the Kurdish issue, a part of them have achieved autonomy, another part has won national rights and status, to a degree, plus the Kurdish issue has attracted more and more attention from the international community.

This is not only the inevitable result of the Kurds' long struggle for national rights and the long-term development of the Kurdish national movement, but was also closely related to the international order and the changes in the geopolitical pattern in the Middle East, and there is a strong interaction between these internal and external factors. It can be said that, if there hadn't been any changes in international and regional power distribution patterns, the Kurdish issue would not emerge and the Kurdish national movement would not be able to achieve its current status, in its development.

From the evolution of global order and international structure, every dramatic change of global order in the long history of human history, the 20th century has brought about the enormous release of nationalism in the West and East and great changes in the geopolitics of the world.

Kurdish issue is not only a trans-border national issue, but also a geopolitical problem. Its emergence and development has been closely related to the evolution of the world pattern and closely linked to the dramatic changes in the geopolitics of the region. And its future solution will not only depend on the level of Kurds' struggle, but also on the policy changes in the country where they live, as well as on the changes in the regional and global pattern.

Since modern times, the development of Western capitalism and the rise of Western Europe have dramatically changed the traditional global political pattern and power distribution, which had lasted for a millennium, consequently major world powers have encountered, great ups and downs, which can be considered as great historical changes.

By the end of the 19th century, the world's major traditional empires, such as the Ottoman Empire, Persia and China, were in decline and frustration and the global order and its power center had shifted from the old orient to West.

Since then, the global pattern has undergone three major turning points or historical events, namely, World War I, World War II and thirdly the end of the Cold War, which have caused three major re-adjustments of the global order. And these three great changes have not only completely changed the face of the world, but also produced the three global waves of nationalism, and altogether gave birth to more than 100 emerging nation-states. Kurdish issue has a history of nearly hundred years since its birth, its historical evolution and each of its historical turning points are closely related to the changes in the international order.

The World War I, 1914-1918 led directly to the formation of the Versailles-Washington system. This was the first major change in the international situation in the 20th century, which released the first global wave of nationalism. We can comfortably say that Kurdish issue is the product of European colonialism. The Ottoman Empire which was in decline since mid-19th century had long been the coveted object of Western European powers. After the World War I, the defeated Ottoman Empire has completely disintegrated, and Britain, France and Italy and other countries partitioned its territories, but also the colonial wave has triggered "nationalisms", such as Arab nationalism, Turkish nationalism and Kurdish nationalism, and led to the emergence of the first batch of emerging nations such as Yugoslavia, Turkey, Iraq, Saudi Arabia, Egypt, Syria and Yemen.

The rise of Kurdish nationalism was accompanied by the decline of the Ottoman Empire and the rise of Western European colonialism and nationalism. The disintegration of the Ottoman Empire has given Kurds the best historical opportunity for independence, but this dream was impaired by Western colonialists. After the war, the Western colonialists not only divided Kurdistan soil which was under the control of Ottoman Empire into three parts—Kurdistan under Turkey, Kurdistan, under the French mandate as Syria and Kurdistan under the British mandate, Iraq—betrayed their self-determination commitments to formerly Ottoman ruled Kurds, which completely shattered the Kurds' dream of a free nation.

If the Kurds had fought for their national rights and independence, under the declining Ottoman Empire they would probably achieve an independent state, but this was bygone, and now they were put directly under the rule of the more powerful Western colonialists (Iraq, Syria) and the nascent Turkish republic which possessed strong national ambitions, now for Kurds and their lands which were artificially split, their dream had become even more difficult to achieve. Since then, the Kurdish dream of national independence has turned into a more realistic struggle, and diminished demands, for the recognition of national rights and realization of national autonomy.

The World War II—1939-1945— broke the fragile Versailles-Washington system and established a new international pattern-the Yalta pattern, which soon after pushed the whole world into the Cold War between the two camps, led by the Soviet Union and the United States respectively.

World War II completely destroyed the Western colonial system, leading to the emergence of the second wave of global nationalism, in the post-war era, the vast regions of Asia, Africa and Latin America were freed from colonial rule, and the birth of a new batch of nation-states.

Most of the Middle East countries, such as Iraq, Syria and Iran, have achieved true independence after the World War II. Emergence of the Cold War pattern, caused by the World War II, have made an impact on the Kurdish issue in many ways.

Firstly, it greatly promoted the development and transformation of Kurdish nationalism. After the war, the Kurdish nationalism became more mature, the new nationalist political organizations were established, the Kurdistan Democratic Party in August 1946, in Iran and Iraq successively, the goals of the struggle have been more clear. Mahabad Kurdish Republic was established in 1946, as the first new nation-state established by the Kurdish nationalists, it was short-lived but far-reaching, which greatly promoted the development of the Kurdish national movement.

Secondly, the development of the global national democratic movement after the World War II, provided political space for the development of the Kurdish national movement, such as the process of democratization in Turkey in 1946, the national democratic revolution of Iran in 1953, and the anti–imperialist and anti–feudal "July Revolution" which overthrew the Faisal dynasty in Iraq. But on the other hand, here and there, a trend of big nation nationalism emerged, among them, especially the pan-Arab nationalism which took root and developed, has made a great negative impact on the Kurdish movement. After the revolution, both Iraq and Syria, actively promoted pan-Arabism and emphasized the Arab national identity for the state and people, discriminated against the Kurdish national identity, ignored the rights of ethnic minorities and took measures to assimilate Kurds with Arab attributes, i.e. assimilation or Arabization policies. This political trend coupled with the regional political instability, frequent coups and severe suppression campaigns targeting Kurds, led the Kurdish national movement to a sectarian political line which increasingly tended to separatism, violence.

Thirdly, during the Cold War, the development of the third world nationalism against imperialism and hegemonism, and the further expansion of the influence of progressive socialist ideology, marked Kurdish nationalism with a deep pro-Soviet and leftist imprint. Whether the democratic Kurdish nationalist party—such as the Kurdistan Democratic Party—, or the socialist-nationalist Kurdish party—such as the Kurdistan Communist Party, the worker and peasant parties Komala and others later PKK of Turkey – have basically adopted pro-Soviet policies, and embraced Marxism-Leninism and socialism as their guiding ideology,

As to the struggle forms, they have adopted armed struggle and mobilize the workers and peasants, emphasized anti-imperialism and anti-feudalism, promoted land reform against land lords.

Fourthly, the bi-polar cold war pattern of US-Soviet, their global hegemony pursuit has made the Kurdish issue secondary, which undermined the interests of Kurds. The United States and the Soviet Union while competing with each other, in order to safeguard/maximize their own interests and achieve their strategic objectives, in the Middle East, have played the Kurdish card, at the expense of Kurdish interests.

Typically, the United States and its Western allies have turned a blind eye to the high-handed policies adopted by the two countries—Turkey and the Pahlavi led Iran—regarding the Kurdish issue, in order to win over Turkey and the Pahlavi regime, in their fight against the S.U., since they strongly needed to keep them, as frontier guards.

For a short period the United States manipulated and supported the anti–government activities of the Iraq's Kurdistan Democratic Party, however, when its interests contradicted, and they required to abandon Kurds, as was when the United States in 1975 needed to strike a reconciliation between Israel and Egypt, Israel, and needed Iraq's support for this reconciliation, cut its support and betrayed Iraqi Kurdistan Democratic Party. Consequently, the struggle led by Iraqi Kurdistan Democratic Party was suppressed cruelly.

It was similar with the Soviet Union. After World War II, the Soviet Union initially supported the establishment of the Kurdish Mahabad Republic, but soon after it betrayed Kurds, struck a deal with Iran government, for its oil interests, which led to the collapse of the Mahabad Republic. In Iraq, the at the beginning Soviet Union supported Iraqi Kurds, but later to win Iraq to its side, to weaken US led Western camp, or because it thought, to win the hearts of the Arabs would be more advantageous for its interests, it sought double-dealing methods and finally abandoned them. This was the main reason for Mullah Mustafa's turn to the West.

In Turkey, during the Cold War period, Soviet Union supported the Turkey's Kurds, largely because, to frustrate the United States, and Turkey's access to NATO ranks, thus its support was self-centered, rather than being a genuine support for Kurdish nationalism. And, after the Cold War, Russia's support for the Kurds was directly linked to counter Turkey's support for Chechnya's separatist activities.

The drastic changes in the Soviet Union and Eastern Europe in 1989 eventually led to the disintegration of the Soviet Union, the collapse of the socialist camp, the end of the Cold War era and opening of the post-Cold War era.

An important consequence of the end of the era of bi-polar confrontation between the two camps has been the emergence of the third global nationalist upsurge.

The third global nationalist upsurge

However, the said nationalist upsurge, possessed different properties than the previous ones. The two major characteristics of the previous ones has been, anti-colonial and anti-imperialist nationalist and democratic orientation. This time rather characterized by separatist nationalism and state secessionism, which led to the disintegration of federal states like, the Soviet Union, Yugoslavia, Czechoslovakia and others, sought to incite ethnic conflicts and territorial disputes, so as to build new nation-states.

Another important consequence was that the Third World, which was originally contested by the United States and the Soviet Union, was suddenly caught in a severe power vacuum due to the end of the Cold War. The destruction, and destabilization of former established patterns in many regions, has paved the way for the upsurge of nationalist and religious extremism, causing violent bloodshed.

In the 21st century, especially after the "9/11" incident, the US national security strategy and foreign policy have undergone major changes. The fight against terrorism and the prevention of the proliferation of weapons of mass destruction have become its new priorities. In the Middle East, the United States has armed itself with the cannons of counterterrorism and democratization, accordingly, launched the war against Iraq, while it rampantly ignored the global anti-war opposition, and intensified its democratic transformation program of the Greater Middle East.

The end of the Cold War era impacted the Kurdish issue mainly in the following aspects:

Firstly, with the end of the Cold War, the Iraqi Saddam regime went out of control, and soon after launched an aggressive war targeting Kuwait war, the United States took this opportunity to build a new world order and a new order in the Middle East, consequently launched the Gulf War, — an important step after the Afghan War—and established a no-fly-zone in northern Iraq, offered protection for the Iraqi Kurds, awarding Kurds with autonomy, in true sense.

This fact has not only completely changed the balance of power between the Kurds and the Iraqi central government, but also the Kurds have achieved a true autonomy and established an independent kingdom. In the 1990s, the "double containment" policy of the United States targeting Iran and Iraq provided some opportunities for Kurds.

Secondly, in the post-Cold War era, democracy and human rights issues became increasingly important themes in the global political agenda, simultaneously the Western countries vigorously advertised democracy, democratic transformation in the Middle East. Although the eruption of of the

"Arab Spring" in 2001 was mainly caused, by people's demands for a better livelihood, and democracy, the US-led western policy of "democratic transformation", especially after the "9/11" incident, has important relationship with the "Arab Spring".

The initiation of democratic processes in the region, and the vigorous advertisement of democracy and human rights have not only increasingly raised concerns for the Kurdish human rights issue, by the international community, but also promoted a new change in the Kurdish national movement—in the new stage: Kurdish national movement increasingly adopted democracy and human rights demand (cause), in this stage of its development.

Thirdly, the two Iraq wars have completely changed the fate of the Iraqi Kurds, the Iraq became a federal system, the famous Kurdish leader became the president of Iraq and Kurds achieve autonomy, their national status reached the highest level in history.

This has greatly stimulated the Kurds in the neighboring countries, encouraged them in their fight for national rights, Kurdish region became a safe base and the headquarters for Kurds fighting in other Kurdish regions, such as the PKK, the Iranian Kurdistan Democratic Party and the Kurdistan Free Life Party and many other. Thus provided a favorable survival and activity space for their activities.

387

Fourthly, in the post-Cold War era, Europe strengthened its integration, established the EU and actively pushed its eastward expansion, absorbed new members, accepted Turkey as a candidate country (1999) and started accession negotiations with Turkey in 2005. In this context, Turkey accelerated the process of domestic democratization, began to adjust its position and policies on the Kurdish issue—both including Kurds in Turkey and in neighboring countries. Accordingly, expanded political participation of Kurds, relaxed restrictions over the Kurdish language and culture, established pragmatic cooperation and good relations with the Kurdish parties in northern Iraq and the KRG.

Fifthly, the changes in global situation have transformed the external environment for the Kurdish national struggles, significantly. With the collapse of the socialist camp, almost all the former colors—adherence to socialist ideology, and pro-Soviet stand—have changed greatly, the Kurdish parties of various countries, turned their faces to Western powers led by the US, to seek their support, secondly sought a new ideological basis for the struggle; all theis meant that United States became the most important external factor, among others, which affected the Kurdish issue.

Looking from the geopolitical pattern of view, based on the changes in the global order and the world international pattern, every change in the latter is bound to bring about the re-adjustment of the regional patterns, accordingly the emergence of the new geopolitical pattern gas brought forward new opportunities and challenges, for the Kurdish national struggle.

The great changes brought about by the first wave major changes in the global pattern had brought about a reshuffling of the geopolitical map and the former Ottoman and Iran Empires, which had ruled the Middle East for long, was divided into two dozen countries by Anglo-French powers.

The Western European colonists who led the Middle East and the Ottoman Turkey, Iran became a dominant Western Europe.

Kurdistan regions ruled by the Ottoman Empire and the region ruled by Iran was divided into four parts. The old, traditional contradictions between the Kurds and Ottoman Turkey and Persia evolved into contradictions between the Kurds, and the new colonialists such as Britain and France, plus the new rulers, Arabs, Turkey and Persia and but the contradiction between the Kurds and the new colonists was the main contradiction.

By the beginning of 50ies, the second major change brought by transformation of the global pattern, regarding Middle East was the collapse of the old colonial system in the region, secondly the national democratic movement and the socialist movement became important trends in the region, within which pan-Arab nationalist trend grew to develop and began to lead the newly born Arab states, Lastly the United States and the Soviet Union, as fierce competitors became the major hegemony seeking players in the region, and the states in the Middle East were faced with the consequences of confrontation between the two camps.

During this period, the Kurds were both under the oppression of direct rulers, (TIIS) motivated by great nationalism, but also under the oppression of the two confronting camps, led by US and Soviet Union. Under this situation, on the one hand, Kurds were not only faced with an unprecedented assimilation pressure in their history, but also obtained enormous external support. On the other hand, conditioned by fierce confrontation of the two camps, and heavy reliance on external powers has also caused Kurds to pay a heavy price, secondly their relations with the majority nations in single countries have seriously deteriorated, and they became pawns of the great powers.

In 1990s, in the post-Cold War era, the Soviet Union was out of the game in the Middle East, the United States became the determinant leading power in Middle East and ambitiously promoted the establishment of a new Middle East order.

Saddam Hussein attempted to use the power vacuum, that has occurred just after end of the Cold War, invaded Kuwait, to control the Gulf region and even intended to control the Middle East, but was forced to withdraw, after deterred by US-led international community.

For a long period of time, "containing Iran and Iraq in the east of the region and promoting Middle East peace process (Arab-Israel peace) in the west of the region," has been the main content or main topic of the US Middle East policy in the post-Cold War era.

Prior to post-Cold War era countries in the region were "members" of one camp or the other, now they have become one-sidedly pro-Western, consequently began political and economic reforms to adapt the West.

In this context, the fate of the Kurdish turned for the better, especially made a historic breakthrough, in Iraq, utilizing the opportunities brought about by the two Iraqi wars, they with the support of external forces established a self-government, a de facto state in state.

The changes and upheavals in Iraq and the achievements of the Iraqi Kurds have not only stimulated the Kurds living in neighboring countries, but also forced the relevant countries in the region to adjust their Kurdish policies.

The evolution of the Kurdish issue to date, their present status and achievements are the inevitable outcome of the Kurdish national movement, the result of long struggles by the Kurdish nationalists but the changes in the external environment, especially the changes in the international pattern and geopolitical environmental is even more critical, which is determined by the particularities of the Kurdish issue.

The scattered situation of the Kurdish national movement, its due weaknesses, the backwardness of its social formation, and the harsh reality of the split country, has been the key cause, why external powers forces have often become a key factor in boosting the development of Kurdish national movement.

In this specific process, in most cases, Kurds were coerced to move.

7.2 The Evolution and Characteristics of the Kurdish Issue

The Kurdish issue which emerged during the World War I, in its development till today can be basically divided into four stages, and each stage has its different content and characteristics.

The first stage (1914-1923), is the initial formation of Kurdish nationalism and the creation stage of the Kurdish issue.

With the defeat and disintegration of the Ottoman Empire, the post-war colonialism has carved up the Ottoman Empire, causing Kurdistan's split, and Kurds were forced to separate into four countries, their demand for national self-determination has failed to achieve, all of which caused the earliest formation of the Kurdish issue.

During this period, Kurdish nationalism was not yet fully mature, and the Kurdish national movement was still in its infancy, in terms of its ideology, organization, leadership, public opinion formation, and mass mobilization. The struggle was restricted in small circles and fragmented, as we can observe in Iraq's Sheikh Mahmud Barzanji Uprising (1919-1922) and in the Simco Uprising of Iran (1918-1920).

The struggle was tainted with strong tribalism, religious color, consequently the best opportunity—in its history—for independent nation-building was missed.

The second stage (1923-1945), has been the growth stage of the Kurdish issue. This stage is characterized by the following elements. Firstly, large-scale Kurdish rebellions erupted in Turkey, Iran and Iraq, such as the Sheikh Saed Uprising (1925), the Ararat Mountain Uprising (1927-1930), and the Dersim Uprising 1937-1938) in Turkey; Iraqi Barzani tribal uprisings (1930-1935, and 1941-1945), but all failed.

Turkey has been the center of the Kurdish movement, with the largest uprisings in size and frequency, followed by Iraq. Here we must say that Sheikh Saed Uprising occupies an important page in the history of the Kurdish national movement, which greatly promoted the regional development of the Kurdish national movement, and Turkey's Kurdish Policy, and even have a great impact on the development of Turkish air forces.

By the end of 1926, Turkey had acquired 106 aircraft. In the following years, air power was used extensively in military operations against the Kurds. Air power was an effective means by which the new Turkish republic consolidated its state power, especially against the Kurds, just as British air power was instrumental in consolidating Britain's imperial power in the post-World War I Middle East.[1]

---

1   Robert W. Olson, The Emergence of Kurdish Nationalism and the Sheikh Said Rebellion, 1880-1925, University of Texas Press, 1989, http://www.xs4all.nl/~tank/kurdish/htdocs/his/said.html.

The Kurdish movement continued to rely mainly on traditional tribal chiefs and religious leaders, but modern nationalist political parties only began to emerge in the early 1940s, such as the "Hiwa (Hope)" of Iraq and the Kurdish Revival Association of Iran.

Secondly, Turkey and Iran began to implement the Turkization and and Persianization policies, which greatly, sharpened contradictions and conflicts.

Iraq and Syria were still under the British and French mandate and control, but the Kurdish policy in Syria and Iraq was relatively loose, assimilation policy was not the implemented.

But still, both Kurds and Arabs in these two countries were faced with the common task of anti-colonialism, although there were contradictions between Kurds and Arabs, they were not not sharp.

Thirdly, except the British and French colonial mandate over Iraq and Syria, the interference of foreign forces into the Kurdish issue was not obvious during these period.

After the outbreak of the World War II, the Soviet Union and the United States began to gradually intervene in the Kurdish issue, the Soviet forces occupied Iran's Kurdistan and supported the political organization of Kurds, and the Kurdish nationalist movement.

The third stage (1946-1990), was the deepening stage of the Kurdish issue and also the full-fledged development of Kurdish national struggle.

The characteristics of this period included mainly the following elements:

Firstly, the center of the Kurdish movement has moved to Iraq, Iraqi Kurdish national movement took its largest and most intense form, reached the climax compared to other parts of the region, achieved certain important results and gained the autonomous status, nominally.

Kurdish movement, developed in full swing, including the outbreak of two long-term civil wars in Iraq 1961-70 and 1972-75, plus during Iran-Iraq War Kurds in alliance with Iran launched guerrilla wars in northern Iraq guerrilla war.

In 1950s and 1960s, Kurdish movement in Turkey began to re-active, and they led intense democratic, peaceful political movements in 1960s and 1970s, in alliance with Turkish socialists. But in the late 1970s violent struggles began. PKK was established in1978, which officially launched anti-government guerrilla warfare in 1984.

In Iran during the late 1970s and early 1980s, large-scale Kurdish national movements occurred, the Kurds participated in the movement to overthrow the Pahlavi regime, after the victory of revolution, it actively struggled and negotiated for autonomy after being rejected cunningly, launched fierce armed struggles against the new Islamic government, but failed.

Secondly, Kurdish national movement has become more mature in ideologically, organizationally and reached stable leadership structures, Kurdistan Democratic Party as the main representative of national movement Kurdish became established, which included factions adhering Kurdish nationalism, Marxist-Leninist-socialism, besides similar other part Marxist-Leninist socialism, as the main guiding ideology and weapon of struggle.

The vigorous development of the national democratic movement in the Middle East after the World War II, promoted the development of the Kurdish national movement and created a fruitful space for the Kurdish national movement: the start of the 1946 political democratization process in Turkey, the national movements in Iraq and Iran in the 1950s, the nationalist struggle led by Mossadeg in Iran in 1953, and the July Revolution by Baathists in Iraq in 1958.

But, from this national-democratic movement, emanated the great nation nationalism such as—pan-Arab nationalism and great Turkism, great Persianism—have escalated conflicts and contradictions with Kurds, which has led to the occurrence of large-scale conflicts, and even wars.

Thirdly, Third, the external forces were increasingly involved in the Kurdish issue, thus the issue became internationalized, more complex; consequently Kurds have lost the power to control their own, became pawns of external powers, utilized for their self- interests.

Kurds became, direct instruments of the hegemony struggle of the Soviet Union in the Middle East.

The influence of the Soviet Union over the Kurds peaked, the Kurdish organization generally adopted a pro-Soviet position, but in the early1970s, the Kurds began to lose confidence and turned their faces to the West began and began to rely on the United States, consequently the United States' influence over Kurdish parties began to gradually increase.

At the same time, countries in the region began to instrumentalize the Kurdish issue: Turkey, Iraq, Iran and Syria used the issue, when they had conflicts and contest with each other, but at the same time they have cooperated with each other to combat and restrict the Kurdish movement. Iran supported Iraqi Kurds to weaken the Iraqi government, the Iraqi government allied with Iran Kurds to frustrate the Iran government. Israel was also involved heavily in the Kurdish issue, seeing Kurds as a natural strategic ally in the region, and provided military assistance to Iraqi Kurds.

Fourth, it is worth mentioning that during the 1960s, Kurdish nationalist intellectuals for the first time put forward the "pan-Kurdish nationalism"— Kurdayeti—idea which later became a political thought trend. Kurdayeti, mainly promotes the idea of struggle of establishing an independent Kurdish state, in order to liberate the Kurds from the national oppression. This idea was basically secular, containing some marks of Marxism-Leninism. The development of pan-Kurdish nationalist trend was promoted by the trans-formation of rural population to settlement, the advance of urbanization, the emergence of the middle class and increase in the number educated intellectuals, the emergence of modern leaders, and was promoted by the increasing concern Kurdish issues for Kurdish issues in the international community.[2]

The fourth stage (1991- to date), is the climax stage in the Kurdish na-tional movement.

During this period the geopolitical upheaval, which has occurred in the international and Middle East levels, produced a series of major events: the two Iraq wars, Turkey's access negotiations to join the EU has started, in Turkey the Justice and Development Party took office in 2002, the Iran nuclear issue caused increasing international concerns, the United States increased democratization, counter-terrorism polices in the Middle East, in 2011 the "Arab Spring" erupted in the Arab countries, all of which made significant direct or indirect, impacts on the Kurdish issue.

The main features of the Kurdish issue at this stage include the follow-ing. Firstly, the Iraqi Kurdish movement made progress and breakthroughs, long-term suppression of the Kurds by the Arab Baath Party and Saddam Hussein regime was overthrown by the United States, Iraq established a democratic federal state system. Consequently, Kurds have not only achieved autonomy in true sense, but they also won an unprecedented po-sition in Iraq's political life. Iraqi Kurds' moves and declarations towards independent state, became a hot topic in the international community, from time to time Iraqi Kurdish leaders have made declarations, which implied that independent state would be the only way out to solve domestic power struggles and "chaos" in Iraq.

Secondly, the new status and progress achieved by the Iraqi Kurds are increasingly effecting the region, Kurds in neighboring countries increas-ingly imitate and exert great pressure on their governments. At the same time, the Iraqi Kurdistan became a de facto "state in state" and stronghold for Kurdish parties carrying anti-government activities in the neighboring countries.

---

2   Michael M.Gunter, Historical Dictionary of the Kurds, p.170.

It became an operation and logistic base for terrorist attacks in these countries, threatening the security and stability of them. Thus neighboring countries have been trying to check and arrest the Kurdish region, Turkey and Iran have repeatedly sent troops to attack Kurdish insurgents based in the region.

In Turkey, the Kurdish Workers' Party (PKK) is carrying out an increasingly intense armed struggle, which causes heavy casualties. The Kurdish issue of Turkey has not only become a prominent political and social issue, but also arouses widespread concern in the international community.

Turkey has began adjustment steps in its Kurdish policy, has gradually relaxed the ban over Kurdish language and culture, expands Kurdish political expression and participation, signals increase of investment in the Kurdish region, and has began dialogue and negotiations with PKK via Britain, and its negotiation process to join the EU has further promoted Turkey's adjustment attempts in its Kurdish policy. Iran's Kurdish policy was also adjusted to further relax the restrictions over Kurds,

At the same time, since United States has labeled Iran as an "axis of evil" state.[3]

The Iranian nuclear issue has drawn increasing attention from major powers of the world, and the conflict between Iraq and the United States has sharpened. In addition, the northern part of Iraq has become a shelter for Iran's Kurdish insurgents, and Iran enters armed clashes with the Kurdish insurgents. Kurdish Free Life Party, a radical armed organization active is supported by the United States, as a pawn to frustrate Iran, thus there occurred bloody clashes between Iranian security forces and the Kurdish Liberal Life Party, launched a fierce bloody conflict for 6 years between 2004-2011.

We can also observe that the there are some mutual promotion and influence between "Arab Spring" and "Kurdish Spring", and the Kurds in Syria seem to be faced with a unique opportunity to change their destiny.

Kurds actively use the "Arab Spring" climate to promote the "Kurdish spring" change, they organize and participate in protests, demanding recognition of their minority rights and national identity from the government. Some Kurdish parties demand autonomy or even independence. In order to relieve the Kurdish pressure, President Bashar Assad has taken a series of reform measures on the Kurdish issue, for example has solve the

---

3　Axis of Evil is a term uttered by the US President George W. Bush in January 2002 in the State of the Union Address after the 9/11event, to point finger at Iran, Iraq and North Korea, and attacked them as rogue states, which develop WMD and support terrorist activities. After the Iraqi war, Bush removed Iraq from the Axis of Evil countries list, in turn labeled Iran, North Korea, Burma, Belarus, Cuba and Zimbabwe as outposts of tyranny.

longstanding issue of 300,000 stateless Kurds and to held talks with the Kurdish parties. Assad offered recognition of Kurdish minority status, in exchange for Kurds' remaining neutral in the fight against Assad's fight against Islamic extremist opposition fighters.

All in all, the Kurdish parties have turned to the West for external support and the United States became the most influential country over the Kurdish issue, after the disintegration of the Soviet Union, the Russian influence on the Kurdish issue fell sharply, the influence of EU has gradually grown but can mainly effect in the Kurdish issue in Turkey.

Kurdish struggle for national rights and national self-determination has been going on for nearly 100 years, but in the current situation, compared with other nationalities in other regions, the Kurdish national movement has not achieved outstanding results, It is still far from achieving the goals it demands. Kurdish issue, after a hundred years of development and evolution, which has passed through the four stages above, demonstrates the following regularities main trends and characteristics:

Firstly, general national consciousness and national cohesion among Kurds are increasing, but its development in the four countries is obviously unbalanced, which determines that in each country, the level and extent of the Kurdish struggle can be deeper or shallow, higher or lower, and its scale can be smaller and larger. Because, we see different levels of economic and social development in the countries, where Kurds live, the levels of national movements are also different, besides the level of national conflicts in each of the 4 countries are different which are caused by different factors.

If we make a classification, over the host government's degree of liberal attitude towards Kurdish issue from high to low, Iraq is followed by, Iran, Syria and Turkey. As to the maturity of national development maturity, from high to low, Iraq is followed by Turkey, Iran and Syria.

As to the degree of contradictions and intensity of the struggle, from high to low, Iraq is followed by Turkey, Iran and Syria. As to the economic and social development level of Kurds, from high to low, Iraq is followed by Turkey, Iran and Syria. As to the host government's degree of control and suppression, from high to low, Turkey is followed by Iraq, Iran and Syria.

For a long time, Turkey and Syria have not recognized Kurds as a national group and prohibited their language and cultural expression, and Kurds' national demands have been suppressed, without farsightedness, but the degree of suppression by Turkey is much more severe than Syria.

Iran and Iraq allow the use of the Kurdish language, they recognize Kurdish minority identity and national identity, but Iran rejects Kurdish autonomy, while Iraq only allows limited autonomy, but does not recognize the Kurds as one of the main master of the state. In the overall evaluation, the Iraqi Kurdish movement in Iraq has reached the highest level, the largest in scale, the most mature, and its achievements are also the greatest.

Secondly, the Kurdish national movement has showed a spiral development process, but as a general trend their situation continues to improve. This is reflected in the general level of the movement and its level of maturity, but in turn we also see that, its development has experienced several ups and downs.

Among them, the movement in Iraq is the most typical example. After the uprisings in 1920s and 1930s were suppressed, there occurred a quiet phase of 40-50 years. After the "July Revolution" in 1958, the Iraqi Kurdish movement regained its vitality, and in the 1960s Kurds carried out an arduous struggle of nearly 10 years, which won a historic autonomy agreement with central government in 1970.

But soon the peace with the central government, ended and fierce struggles began, and in 1975 the Kurdish movement was dealt a devastating blow. Kurds have also rebelled during the Iran-Iraq war and the 1991 Gulf War, but were suppressed. Only after the Gulf War, when the Western powers established the no-fly zone to protect Kurds, they were able to get rid of the long yoke of suppression, and ended their evil destiny.

In Turkey, after the suppression of uprisings in the 1920s and 1930s, the Kurdish movement remained at a low ebb, and it was not until the late 1970s that the Kurdish Workers Party (PKK) started the armed struggle, followed by peaceful struggles in 1960s. In the late 90s, Turkey's war against PKK has achieved some success, in 1999 Ocalan was arrested, then PKK fell into a trouble, but after the 2003 Iraq War the PKK activities gained a new vitality, in 2004 severe clashes occurred between the two sides. We can see that the Turkish government has taken several measures to relax restrictions over the Kurds and expanded Kurdish national rights in the period after the two Iraq wars.

Thirdly, there are variations among the demands of Kurds in different countries, forms of national movements and their struggle methods also differ. Looking from the current point of view, in all the four countries, Kurdish national movements are basically inclined to fight for autonomy, but there are also differences. In Turkey, the majority of Kurdish parties demand federalism and strive to achieve Kurdish autonomy within the framework of Turkish sovereignty. Originally, the Kurdish Workers' Party fought for the realization of Kurdish independence and join the four parts, but after Ocalan was arrested it emphasized the demand for autonomy, Ocalan also put forward a unique theory of regional democratic confederalism, and subordinated PKK's Turkey strategy to it. (see Appendix part.)

In Iraq, except the early 1920s, Kurds, have demanded autonomy; and the basic goal of struggle for autonomy won victory as demanded, but today they only demand a high-degree of autonomy, which is an important source of conflict between the Kurds and the central government.

In Iran, the Kurds have a high degree of recognition by the Iran government, and only some part of Kurds demand autonomy, the Kurdish movements in Iran have never asked for independence, and the Mahabad Republic was essentially a local self-government.

In Syria, the Kurdish population is relatively small, their main goal is the recognition of national identity and national rights, they have to ask the Government to recognize its national identity and national identity, rarely demanded autonomy, and independence is not uttered. But after 2011, Syrian Kurds have begun and demand federalism and the implementation of self-government. It can be seen that, the demands of Kurds in different countries is not only different, but also change with the development of times and circumstances. As to the form of Kurdish national movements and their struggle means, due to the government's severe suppression and severe assimilation policy, except Syria, in the other three countries, mainly armed struggle is adopted.

Historically, the Kurds in Syria, have mainly resorted to peaceful means to fight against ethnic restrictions over themselves. After being suppressed, they have developed underground activities, to continue the struggle for national rights, adhered to political solution line, did not opt for violent means. Even in 2011 when Syria fell into a violent civil strife, when many anti-government organizations have formed armed militia the Kurdish people still adhered to democratic struggle methods.

In Turkey and Iraq, since Kurdish national democratic movement was heavily suppressed, the lack of legal space, armed struggle has become the main form of struggle. In Iraq, the main manifestations were guerrilla warfare and large-scale wars. In Turkey, the main manifestation of the PKK's struggle has been guerrilla war and violent terrorist activities. In Iran, the armed struggle is only an auxiliary means, subordinated to political struggle, the Kurdistan Democratic Party of Iran generally opted for negotiations with the government, and used armed struggle when severely humiliated in the negotiations, but since the 1980s it declared to abandon the armed struggle.

It is noteworthy that, in the 1990s, in order to comply with the historical trend and increase support from the general domestic public and international public and powers. the Kurdish parties have embarked on a peaceful solution course. Although PKK is still engaged in terrorist violence, it has repeatedly expressed the willingness to lay down arms and readiness for negotiations, it has declared many unilateral ceasefires, to show sincerity, and supported democratic political methods.

Fourthly, the Kurdish issue has become increasingly international, the issue has been instrumentalized both by world powers and regional powers. The current achievements of Kurdish movement, is the fruit of their long-term struggle, which has been the most important driving force, the changes in the international and regional environment should be considered as one of the most important variables which have promoted the development of the Kurdish movement, thus directly related with successes and failures.

Since its birth Kurdish issue has been a cross-border issue, but this trans-nationality can not determine its depth of internationalization.

The internationalization of the Kurdish issue was manifested in many forms:

Firstly, Kurdistan geography and Kurdish population is divided cross-regionally and cross-territorially The emergence of the Kurdish problem has been a direct consequence of colonialism by world powers;

Later, the Kurds have been major political tool in the region, by the British and French colonists and two superpowers the United States and the Soviet Union have played the Kurdish card; since their own

own powers and abilities have not been sufficient, they have generally looked around for external protectors and sponsors, with the hope of inter-nationalization of the Kurdish issue, and to arouse the concern of the inter-national community; the four governments who have ruled them, have used the Kurdish card in their power contests and also worked together to deal with the Kurdish movement when they felt an urgent threat.

Since, the emergence of the Kurdish issue to the present, the Kurdish issue has become more and more international, besides the intensity of ex-ternal involvement has also increased. This trend of internationalization, on the one hand, makes the Kurdish people unable to distance themselves from it, and makes the issue more and more complicated, and the Kurds' interests are damaged repeatedly. But on the other hand, this trend has provided a certain development space for Kurdish movement, and brought out oppor-tunities for its improvement, the United States launching two Iraq wars was such a case and played a critical role.

Fifthly, since the emergence of the Kurdish national movement, Kurds' capabilities to lead independent struggle have been weak, and this is still true, which determines that their movement and struggle are imbued with certain and passivity, consequently their self-control over their destiny, and national movement is relatively weak.

The Kurdish nationalist movement is largely dependent on external pow-ers, thus from the PKK to the Kurdistan Democratic Party, without external support, they will suffer great setbacks and will not be able survive—for a long time—easily, this means their fate is largely open to manipulation by outsiders. For the above reasons, without external intervention, it will be difficult to achieve a breakthrough for the Kurdish movement.

Thus, achievements by Kurds, are, to a large extent, determined by the conditions, brought about by global and regional changes, and Kurds belong to subjects being coerced forward. Even, the establishment of the Kurdish autonomous region in Iraq, has been the result of direct intervention by the West, whose reward has been their "autonomy."

7.3 The Attitudes of Relevant Countries on the Kurdish Issue: An Evaluation

The basic national conditions of the four countries—Iraq, Turkey, Iran and Syria—vary greatly. There are significant differences in their political system, state system, level of democratic development, the strength of their central government, the history of their nation building, the history of national unity, national structure, economic and social development level, military strength, foreign relations and others. These above, also determine their differences in political mentality, policies adopted by them, in dealing with the Kurdish issue, which produce different results.

In the following readers will find a detailed analysis of the practices of Turkish and Iraq governments and motive forces behind these practices.

After the founding of Turkey in 1923, Turkish bourgeois nationalists represented by Mustafa Kemal, have believed that, for Turkey to enhance its power, the only way would be to take the road of Westernization. The Westernization model of Turkey can be simply summarized as Kemalism, which includes, six policies of nationalism, secularism, republicanism, populism, reformism and statism, among the six, most critical one is nationalism, which determine Turkey's attitude towards Kurds and Kurdish issue.

Kemal's nationalism ideas were adopted from two sources: firstly, the Western European nationalist ideology and practices, secondly, the political practice of late Ottoman Empire, especially its internal disintegration, the lack of cohesive core, its failure to build a nation-state, which all led to its painful collapse. Mustafa Kemal, has summarized all these practices which in fact pointed to a unique nationalism: sovereignty belongs to the people (nation), all people living within the territories of the Republic, are Turks, and—embodies Turkishness; and at the core of this Turkishness is the Turkic race, but we cannot say that this new Turkishness (Turks) of Kemal, is not simply racist or does not match with parochialism of big (nation) nationalism, instead this nationalism subsumes, all races, religions, nationalities and tribes.

Kemal, believed, following this understanding, Turkey could enhance its power, and establish a solid nation-state, build a new national identity, namely the national identity of the new Turkish Republic. Based on this doctrine, all ethnic minorities including Kurds, as well as, the core cohesive nationality (genuine) Turkic people, should be instilled with the consciousness of Turkishness, which became an inevitable policy to strengthen the national identity, of the new Republic. To achieve this goal, any national consciousness or nationalism, based on race, ethnicity, religion or alternative ideology, should be absolutely, opposed. Kemal's thoughts became the guiding ideology of the Turkish state, which was also employed to deal with the Kurdish issue, and has continued to this day. Its specific policies include the following elements:

Firstly, strengthening national identity, strengthen national assimilation and fusion, the establishment of homogeneous nation-state. The Turkish government, has been implementing this policy of ethnic assimilation for a long time, and employed the methods of immigration, language restriction and manipulation, guiding religious issues in this direction, cultural and education policies, all aimed to restrict the flourishing of any separate ethnic consciousness, except Turkishness.

The content of above includes:

Completely ignoring, Kurds as a nation and labeling them "mountain Turks"[4], banning the use of Kurdish language in public places even in private sphere, prohibiting the expressions of Kurdish ethnic characteristics and cultural identity, including prohibiting the celebration of Kurdish festivals and the New Year (Newroz).

The use of Kurdish names, regarding people, places, regions, even villages and towns were banned and renamed with Turkish language.

A large number of Kurds, were forced to immigrate to other parts of the country (non-Kurdish regions), in small groups such as the Midwest Anatolia, thus demographic structure of the Kurdish region was transformed, while a large number of Turkish people forced to immigrate to the Kurdish region, to form mixed communities.

Another policy was, to re-write the national history: revision of history textbooks, deletion and modification of Kurdish history, strengthening the education of a glorified, mythic, Turkish national history; besides the education of Kurdish children was emphasized, Kurdish children in primary school age, were enrolled to special regional boarding schools, instilled with Turkishness, and Turkish language, and were forced to take Turkish names.

---

4   The ideology said, ancestors of Kurds, are in fact part of Turkic race living in remote mountainous regions.

Secondly, resolutely banning and cracking down Kurdish nationalism, separatist tendencies, and Kurdish organizations engaged in anti-government activities, and long-term high-handed oppressive policies were employed. The Turkish government has always pursued the policy of resolutely suppressing the Kurdish demands for national rights and self-government, based on "absolute ignorance", rejected any negotiation and concessions.

An "Anti-Terrorism Law" was enacted which considered "separatist speech" and deeds as separatist terror, a special national security court has been established, to trial separatists. Media and newpapers, were strictly monitored according to this law and suppressed, banned with charges as "praising separatist terrorism."

The law of "political parties" and "associations" included strict articles to ban pro-Kurdish legal and clandestine parties and organizations, such as the Kurdistan Democratic Party, Kurdistan Workers' Party, Kurdish Islamic Movement, Revolutionary Party of Kurdistan, Kurdish Freedom Eagle, the Democratic Labor Party, Democratic Party, The People's Democratic Party, The Party of Democratic Society, and dozens of other Kurdish associations, all of which were accused for supporting terrorist activities, or praising or inciting them.

The government has for a long-term, built and maintained strong military garrisons in the region, to check and deter separatist elements, and established anti-guerrilla special forces, specifically against the Kurdish guerrillas.

For many decades, martial law and state of emergency statuses have been imposed, in the governance of the region, both army chiefs and civil district governors were, super executive powers, prior to 1950s the government appointed four Inspectorate Generals to govern southeast Kurdish regions.

During the state of emergency regime, in the southeast Kurdish regions, between 1987-2002, a super governorate with extraordinary powers was established, and government issued a decree to set set up, village guard system, employing and training local peasants as anti-terror fighters; besides rival tribes were armed and bribed, to fight against those allying with PKK.

The Gendarmerie Branch of the Turkish Army, and its special security forces, which is specialized for the security of rural areas were strengthen, which also implemented covert operations.

Between, 1960-80, against Kurdish activists, the "extreme-right nationalist Gray Wolves" were used as grass-roots defense and deter militia and in 1990s, Turkey's Hezbollah, extremists were manipulated for the same purpose, they were mobilized against PKK sympathizers, and activists of legal Kurdish parties, associations, and in 1990s many assassinations were carried against them including renown Kurdish intellectuals.

In order to quell PKK activities, and eliminate their survival bases and combat support, hundreds of sympathizing villages were destroyed, forests burned, villages were either moved to controllable areas, or fully emptied and many villagers were forced to move to cities.

Turkey has fought hard, to destroy the overseas bases of PKK, hinder and stop foreign support. In 1998, under the military attack threat of Turkish government, Syria was forced to expel Ocalan, and declared that it would no longer support the PKK. Since the 1980s, Turkish troops have frequently marched into the Iraq territories to fight against the PKK, even established security zones, for this purpose.

Thirdly, Turkey took some measures to improve the livelihood and economic life of Kurds, made several moderate reforms which relaxed restrictions over, language, political and cultural expression. For a long period of time, Turkey has always curtailed the Kurdish issue as the "Eastern problem" and pinpointed to economic, social and cultural backwardness the region, and lack of investment and economic Kurdish regions area the most impoverished regions of Turkey, and economic and social development lag far behind the national average. Therefore, in 1980s, the Turkish government has started the large-scale "Southeast Anatolia Project" with an investment of total 32 billion US dollars, the core of which was to promote modern

agricultural production with improved irrigation, in the southeastern region. The project area covers the nine cities provinces, Adıyaman, Batman, Diyarbakır, Gaziantep, Kilis, Siirt, Şanlıurfa, Mardin and Şırnak, which are located in the basins of the Euphrates and Tigris and in Upper Mesopotamia. The project includes sectors such as agriculture and irrigation, hydroelectric power production, forestry, urban and rural infrastructure and uses the vigorous rivers of the region, mainly Euphrates and Tigris.

But, there is also hefty criticism, claiming that the project will not benefit the development of Southeast as advertised, instead will mostly benefit the western regions with electric power production, another critique focuses on the destruction of the cultural heritage, and flooding of the ancient city, Hasankeyf, whose history stretched back over 10.000 years and the removal of monuments such as a massive statue of Ramses and others. There are ecological concerns, too. The project has also caused some disputes with Iraq and Syria, which are severely anxious that, water volume passing to them, through Euphrates and Tigris, will decrease greatly, and negatively affect their agriculture.

Since the 1990s, the Turkish government began to acknowledge the necessity of slight reforms on the Kurdish issue, and relaxed the restrictions on Kurdish language and culture, this change was due to three factors, the need to develop relations with the EU, the improvement in the status of

Iraqi Kurds, and domestic discontent in the public, after violent bloody clashes with PKK fighters which have increased their attacks.

Fourthly, Turkey has vigorously increased publicity efforts, against the PKK at home and internationally, linking it with terrorism. After the "9/11" incident, Turkey, has highlighted, the international cooperation in the fight against terrorism, championed this cause, to benefit from the favorable international public opinion, and advertised itself as one of the victims of terrorism, with this leverage further restricted the PKK activities, at home and abroad. For a long time, the Kurdish and the Cyprus issue have been one of the most important public relations themes of the Turkish Ministry of Foreign Affairs, its embassies and consulates abroad. With vigorous diplomatic efforts of Turkey, PKK has been listed as one of the terrorist organizations, by the United States, the EU, Israel and many other countries.

Fifthly, Turkey has strengthened regional and international cooperation to contain Kurdish activities, and compressed PKK's international financial transactions and other organizational activities. It increased its efforts to find more common interest fields, including trade, investment and others, to enhance coordinated actions against Kurdish movements.

Turkey, Syria, Iran and Iraq have, historical experiences of coordination against Kurdish national movements, and suppressing its development, they have closely cooperated during several important cases.

After the outbreak of the Iraq war, in order to prevent a possible Kurdish independence, Turkey, Iran and Syria have become worrisome about the disintegration of Iraq, and increased contacts and consultation, for coordinated efforts, and have developed some countermeasures, they have repeatedly, and resolutely underlined, that "Iraq's territorial integrity and national unity, should be maintained."

In 2004, Syria and Iran have for the first time, announced their acknowledgment of the PKK as a terrorist organization, and actively sought international cooperation and engaged with the "fight against international terrorism."

Turkey has actively joined the coalition against terrorism, and cooperated with the US, EU, Israel and other countries, in many regions of the world, including the Great Middle East, and strengthened mechanism for exchange of intelligence. Turkey achieved to get the support of US and Israeli intelligence, to capture the PKK leader Ocalan.

After the Iraq war, Turkey, US and Iraq have reached a tripartite cooperation agreement against the PKK. At the same time, Turkey increased pressure over several countries to hinder their support for the PKK and even used military threats, in this respect. It launched a diplomatic offensive targeting Syria, Iraq, Iran, Armenia, Greece and Russia, urging them to stop harboring Kurdish separatist elements.

Under increasing threats by Turkey, Syria was forced to expel Ocalan, Russia, Greece, Italy, Netherlands and Germany refused Ocalan's demand as a political refugee, and extradited him, Ocalan desperately escaped to Africa, and was ultimately captured and brought to court.

Under the pressure of the Turkey, Britain and Denmark ordered the closure of Kurdish satellite TV stations. Holland, Belgium, Spain and other countries, banned the meetings of Kurdish exile parliament, on their territories.

During 1990s due to changes in its internal and external situation, namely due to increasing attention from the international community over the Kurdish issue, intensification of PKK's violent attacks, Turkish governments have made gradual adjustments in Kurdish policy: began to openly acknowledge the existence of Kurds and their demands as an internal political theme, began to allow them to use Kurdish language, increase investments in the Kurdish regions, yet guiding ideology and the basic approach, did fundamentally change, which has hindered adjustments in policies, many promising declarations were not backed with deeds.

Erdogan's "Kurdish opening policy" (Unity and Fraternity Project) which was started in 2010, could not be advanced due to various obstacles and soon failed, attacks against the PKK continued, Kurdish parties and associations kept being restricted, arrests continued.

It seems that the traditional Kemalist approach remains to be the biggest obstacle, in achieving any breakthrough. Turkey, not only needs a deeper self-reflection on Kemalism, but should also grasp the need to make adjustments in the constitutional, and judicial spheres, regarding political freedom, anti-terrorism law, political parties law, criminal law and civil law and others. Also Turkey should resolve the historical issue of—lacking common people's full sovereignty—in its political state system, which is still being influenced by the remnants of old elites, such as the military and intellectuals, thus embrace gradual and stable reforms.

Attitude and practices of Iraq government

Unlike Turkey, Iraq has long recognized the national identity of Kurds, and allowed a certain degree of autonomy, but for a long period, Iraq's approaches and practices in the handling of Kurdish issue, was determined by the two guiding ideologies of pan-Arabism and Arabism, which has stressed that Iraq is an Arab state, and its Arab character requires that all Iraqis should belong to the Arab nation. Its compromise for the Kurdish autonomy was rather accepted as a last resort.

When it has granted Kurdish autonomy in the 1970s, it has failed to satisfy the expectations of Kurds, causing sharp contradictions and intense armed clashes between the two sides, thus the Kurdish issue of Iraq has long become increasingly acute.

If we briefly expound, during the period starting with the early 1960s to 2003, when the Saddam Hussein regime has collapsed, the basic policy of the Iraqi government in dealing with the Kurdish issue has demonstrated the following features.

Firstly, the recognition of Kurds as a minority, and granting a certain degree of autonomy.

Since 1920s, the British colonial authorities and the Iraqi government have recognized the Kurdish national rights, and promised to grant autonomy, but have ultimately failed to honor this commitment, but they have granted some rights such as language usage, Kurds being appointed as government officers and some other aspects. In July 1958, Qasim led the group that identified itself as the "Free Officers", launched a state coup, and established the Republic of Iraq.

The new Iraqi government has been progressive in ideologically, promised to grant Kurds some legal rights, allowed Kurds' political participation, in some senior government posts, recognized, the legal status of the Kurdistan Democratic Party, allowed the publication of Kurdish newspapers and books, the new Iraqi government called back the Kurdish leader Mullah Mustafa and his exile was ended.

But the broader rights to self-government, as demanded by the Kurds, was rejected by the new Qasim government, thus conflicts and clashes between the two sides have started. After long fights, in 1970 the two sides reached a "March agreement" and The Iraqi government agreed to grant give autonomy to Kurds. In 1974, the Autonomy Law was promulgated, which allowed the formal implementation of the Kurdish autonomy, and establishment of Kurdish regional government and regional parliament.

But this autonomy won by Kurds and the expected, and demanded autonomy by Kurds has largely varied, Kurdistan Democrat Party, refused the new Law which led to new battles.

After the Gulf War of 1991, central government's control was weakened, Kurds took this opportunity, depended on the advantage of no-fly-zone supported by the United States and Britain, thus achieve self-government. In 1992, Kurdish Regional Council elections were held and the regional government was established.

In 2003 the war led by the United States overthrew the Saddam Hussein regime, the new constitution enabled the federal state system, which has maintained and improved the actually achieved autonomy by Kurds.

Secondly, the Arabization policy was implemented, Iraq government made efforts to assimilate the Kurdish identity, in turn Arab national identity was strengthened. The main policies were: promotion of Arabic language, restrictions on the use of Kurdish, forced migration and evacuation of Kurds, a large number of them were relocated. In turn Arab people was relocated to the Kurdish regions; Kurdish education was restricted, in turn schools teaching with Arabic language were vigorously promoted. Land reform was started to weaken the status of Kurdish tribal and religious leaders. The government promoted urbanization, so as to weaken the traditional tribal social characteristics of Kurds, thus the national or tribal attributes of them was weakened.

Thirdly, Kurds' efforts to expand autonomy or to seek independence, was resolutely suppressed, even by violent means. Iraqi Kurdistan Democratic Party, by the support of the Iranian government, launched 2 long-term civil wars, between 1961-1970, and 1972-1975. During the Iran-Iraq War (1980-1988), the Iraqi Kurds, supported by Iran, once again engaged in massive armed confrontation with the government forces, in the later phase of battles Iraqi government forces brutally repressed the Kurdish armed insurgency, even used chemical weapons, which also caused tens of thousands civil casualties. Just after the 1991 Gulf War Kurds again launched an uprising, but it was soon was suppressed by the government, caused millions of refugees who fled to Turkey and other countries.

Fourthly, Iraq government in order the suppress Kurdish movement, employed the "divide and rule policy", used anti-Barzani (Jash) Kurdish tribes to fight against the opposition parties and fighters. Iraq government also tried to use the conflict between the two Kurdish parties KDP and PUK, it generally used the Kurdish Patriotic Union against the Kurdistan Democratic Party. From time to time, Iraq government allied with the neighboring governments, to fight against Iraqi Kurds, used Iranian Kurds or Turkish Kurds to deal with domestic Kurds, the most typical was the Iran-Iraq war. While Iraq supported the Kurds of Iran, in turn Iran has supported the Iraqi Kurds.

Fifthly, Iraq government sought and entered into regional cooperation with other countries, also made diplomatic efforts to get support from international forces, so as to curb the independence demand of Kurds.

In the 1930s, Iraq, Iran, and Turkey signed a cooperation treaty, to restrict the Kurds. In the 1950s, Iraq allied closely with Turkey, Iran and other countries set up the "Baghdad Treaty Organization".

One reason behind of the Baghdad Treaty was to better deal with the Kurds.

In 1975, Iraq signed the Algiers Agreement with Iran, it did not hesitate to make territorial concessions to Iran, in exchange to stop Iran's intervention in the Kurdish issue of Iraq.

After the 2003 Iraq war, the new Iraqi government sought the support of the United States, by the United States to suppress the Kurds to ensure the unity of Iraq. Turkey and Iran have frequently made cross-border attacks against the PKK forces, although Iraqi government issued some protesting declarations against cross-border operations, in fact it kept tolerating attacks against the PKK. We observe that, the threat of Kurdish independence faced by Turkey and Iraq varies greatly. For Iraq, the threat mainly takes the form of disintegration or independence. For Turkey, the Kurdish problem is mainly a security and stability issue, it does not face a serious threat of disintegration.

There are abundant lessons to be drawn from the practice of handling the Kurdish issue: by the implementation of great nation nationalism, implementation of forced assimilation; the implementation of national discrimination, ignoring Kurds and depriving them of their national rights; long-term adherence to high-handed military suppressions, contradictions between national groups, has sharpened, imbalanced national development was caused. The economic and social development in the minority nation regions was impeded, benefits from resources has been unevenly distributed. All the above, attitudes have resulted in turmoil and disagreements, domestically and external relations of the country has deteriorated, which have not only hindered the central government to resolve the Kurdish national issue, but also provided opportunities to foreign powers, to interfere and utilize the Kurdish issue, which have brought a lot of negative effects.

To draw lessons from above, we can say that, to reinforce and maintain the stability of a country and enable a strong and unified central government, harmonious relations among all ethnic groups should be built, properly handle the relations between larger and smaller nationalities in the country. Besides, it is of great significance to resolve the problem of ethnic conflicts by using proper policies and tactics, if a country aims to establish favorable relations with neighboring countries and major world powers, and avoid negative effects from outside.

7.4 Prospects for Resolution of the Kurdish Question and Future of Kurds

The formation of the Kurdish issue has both historical and realistic sources, backgrounds, also both caused by internal and external factors.

As one of the five main subjects in the Middle East only Kurds have failed to establish their own nation-state, and they reject to admit the current status quo, refuse to yield to the rule of other nations, which constitute the most fundamental reason behind the Kurdish issue. At the same time, the Kurdish issue is also a legacy left back by the Western colonialism, and its increasing complexity is also, to a great extent, a product of imperialism and hegemonism, major world powers vainly seeking world hegemony.

Another cause is the minority status of Kurds in the host countries, who suffer from discrimination and oppression, having subordinated political status or none, backward economic and cultural development, all in all, the negligence of their national rights is the realistic reason behind Kurds' protracted struggles.

Kurdish issue has a history of nearly hundred years, but its resolve has been delayed, and an effective solution could not be found, even today, the way out is uncertain, what are the reasons behind these facts of failure?

We will point to five most important factors behind this situation as follows:

Firstly, the most important factor, is that, relevant governments of the host countries', maltreatment of Kurdish issue, their improper approaches or mistaken policies, their implementation of big nation nationalism, their denial or negligence of Kurdish national rights. is the key factor.

Secondly, the current situation is caused by the international community, especially lack of genuine concern by the Western powers, for the Kurdish issue, fate of Kurds, their indifference to a true solution of the issue. Instead, they have instrumentalized, the issue for their self-interests or as a pawn to interfere in the internal affairs of other countries. At the same time, they are worrisome that Kurdish independence will redraw the political landscape of the region, break the regional balance of powers, endanger their interests in the region, undermine their current alliances and relationships with the countries in the region.

Thirdly, the situation is caused by Kurds, namely obvious weaknesses of the Kurdish national movement itself. This includes, lack of unity in Kurdish national movement, serious internal strife, national movement is part of a relatively backward society, politically, economically and socially backward, national consciousness immature, imbued with strong tribal consciousness.

Another factor is imbalanced development of the Kurdish national movement between the four partitioned parts of Kurdistan, Kurds have not formed a joint force, their power scattered, not only they lack coordination, but contest with each other. And, this internal strife, these weaknesses are often used by external forces, consequently they are too dependent on the external forces, which often determine their destiny.

Fourthly, the relevant governments of the host countries' where Kurds reside, have the ability to cooperate with each other and have better access to international support and cooperation, so as to jointly deal with Kurds. There is an asymmetry of strength between two the two sides, in this respect.

Fifthly, during nearly a hundred years of conflicts and clashes between Kurds and the host governments, increasing mistrust and alienation between majority national group and Kurds, have strengthened the psychological cracks, contradictions have accumulated, which will need a long time to repair, or eliminate these contradictions.

However, with the 21st century, the Kurdish issue once again gained a favorable situation, especially after the two Iraq wars, which not only changed the situation in Iraq, but also effected the history of the Kurds, and once again, the Kurdish issue ascended to the forefront of the political arena in the Middle East. The rise of the status Iraqi Kurds, after the 2 wars, are the main symbols of their rise in the Middle East is one of the most important political and geopolitical changes in the region, which also brought about new changes and new development trends, for the Kurdish issue.

The Iraq wars, not only changed the fate of Kurdish issue in Iraq, but have brought new prospects for the Kurdish people in Turkey, Iran and Syria, consequently impacted, encourages and stimulated the Kurds in these countries, triggering a chain reaction. On the one hand, after the war, Iraq fell into a threat of disintegration and a prolonged turmoil, ethnic and religious sectarian conflicts have intensified, violent terrorist activities have been rampant near and in Baghdad. On the other hand, the Kurdish regional government is faced with difficult issues: it is faced by a series of issues such as the "oil law", the issue of distribution of oil revenues and oil sources, the issue of dissolution of Kurdish armed forces and the sovereignty issue of Kirkuk city and Kirkuk region, and fell into an open confrontation with the central government. It can be observed that the political reconciliation process in Iraq is showing a stagnant progress, with twists and turns.

As to the issue of oil development and production, although the central government resolutely opposes Kurdish demands, the Kurdish regional government has still insisted on signing exploration and development contracts with dozens of foreign companies.

Kirkuk city area, which is known as the "Jerusalem of Iraq" has become the focus confrontations among, Kurds Arabs and Turkmens, and the tripartite conflict may become more severe. Thus the Kirkuk issue has become a time bomb threatening the process of stabilization and political reconciliation in Iraq. In Turkey, stimulated by the new developments in Iraq, in 2004 the PKK decided to suspend its ceasefire attempts, resumed terrorist operations in the region, causing numerous deadly incidents, and casualties and property losses, consequently security threat by Turkey has increased. At the same time, Turkey is has become worrisome about the uncertain future of Iraq, and fears from the consolidation of Kurdish gains in Iraq, and from the possible independence of Iraqi Kurds, and actively lobbies in KRG region to hinder support for PKK.

To this end, in February 2008, Turkey sent large number of troops into Iraq, to attacks the PKK, air forces stroke about 300 PKK positions in Iraq, killing about 240 armed men.

These kind of operations by Turkey, aims two goals, firstly, to fight against the PKK and reduce threats from the PKK, secondly, show it power and deter Iraqi Kurds, to hinder their independence plans. Turkey, while launching heavy air strikes, pressured the United States, Iraq and the Iraqi Kurdish regional government, to increase pressure over the PKK and gain their cooperation.

At the same time, Turkey actively supports, the Iraqi Turkmens in their contest against the Kurds Besides, due to acceleration of access negotiations with the EU, since 2005, Turkey is restricted when dealing with the Kurdish issue, since it has increasingly become one of the key obstacles for its access into the EU. The EU has begun to continuously urge Turkey to improve human rights situation of Kurds,which means that Turkey has to bear a greater external pressure over the the Kurdish issue. Under the new conditions, Erdogan government has adopted the "Kurdish opening policy" In 2010, relaxed many restrictions and canceled the ban over the Kurdish language, many Kurdish place names were restored, but many other restrictions are still there.

In March 2011, affected by the outbreak of huge protests in the Arab countries, Kurdish people in Turkey led by PKK also started active protests, and initiated the "non-violent disobedience campaigns" and civil disobedience uprisings. "Kurdish opening policy" proceeded with twists and turns, yet in March 21, 2013, the Turkish government and the PKK reached a peace protocol agreement, the level of armed violence between Turkish armed forces and PKK insurgents dramatically declined thanks to Ocalan's call, during the Newroz celebrations of 21 March 2013, for the PKK to cease its armed activities in Turkey, thus the Kurdish struggle in Turkey entered into a new stage.

In Iran, the Kurdish guerillas, led by the Kurdistan Free Life Party, who were based in Iraq since 2004, have become increasingly active, they have frequently infiltrated from Iraq to engage in armed sabotage activities in Iran. Iran army forces retailed and frequently marched into Iraq, to hit guerilla bases. Inspired by the "Arab Spring", on February 28, 2012, the Iranian Kurdistan Democratic Party and other four Kurdish parties, met in in Sulaymaniyah, Iraq. A joint appeal was agreed, addressing the Iranian Kurds to boycott the parliamentary elections to be held in March 2012, Kurds in Iran have supported this boycott call, voter turnout has been low.

On August 22, 2012, the Iranian Kurdistan Democratic Party and the Komala Party (Kurdistan Workers' Revolutionary Party) signed a bi-lateral agreement of cooperation and mutual understanding, aiming to strengthen their cooperation under the new circumstances.

In Syria, since 2004, the Kurdish national movement has become increasingly active, political activities have increased and demonstrations have occurred frequently, two large-scale Kurdish riots occurred in a row. Since 2011, the "Arab Spring", the Syrian Kurds have joined the ranks of anti-government protests, took the opportunity to gain their legitimate national rights, also put forward demands for autonomy, Although the Kurdish protests have not been large scale, and although held cautious attitude to other anti-government Arab factions, they have strengthened their union, called for the establishment of federalism and realization of Kurdish autonomy, their voice is heard louder. Faced by internal and external pressures, the Syrian government was forced to take some in order to improve the situation of Kurds.

Starting from the current situation, the future development and trend of Kurdish problems may show the following trends:

Firstly, a united Kurdish state is unlikely to emerge.

This is determined by many factors, among which the following are the key factors:

1. The political and geographical realities of Kurdistan's divided situation and of the Kurdish population spread to four countries are unlikely to change in the foreseeable future.

2. The host countries where Kurds reside, will not readily allow them to establish an independent nation-state. Despite sharp contradictions, on territorial, resource based and religious issues, among the 4 host countries, and although they have used each other's Kurds to maximize their interests, against other host countries, each are in strong opposition to the establishment of an independent Kurdish state and share the same goal, and resolute attitude. Even in post-war Iraq, the Iraqi central government's stance against Kurdish independence has been resolute.

3. The Kurdish national movement has its own limitations. Its internal split and disputes continue, there are not only differences between the Turkish Kurds and the Iraqi Kurds, but also there are differences, among the Iraq Kurdish people who have been fighting for a long time, some do not desire to carry out endless struggles with the central government. In addition, the goals of Kurdish struggle in 4 countries are different, they can not form a concerted strategy. As early as August 1944, representatives of Kurdish nationalist organizations from Iran, Iraq and Turkey have met in the Dalanpur Hill, at the junction of the three countries, to discuss mutual support, resource sharing and recovery of Kurdish language and culture matters, and have signed a trilateral agreement. A Syrian delegation had also participated. Although the meeting issued a declaration that the Kurdish nation should strengthen a united voice, but after the end of the meeting, the speeches were forgotten. The establishment of an independent Kurdish state is not the common goal of all Kurds, it seems, achieving varying degrees of self-government within the framework of their respective countries is the primary goal of the Kurds.

4. Western major powers do not support Kurds, to establish an independent Kurdish state. Although Kurdish situation has aroused widespread sympathy, in the West, especially in Europe, and gained the support of some politicians and parties, NGO's organizations, the West starting from the realities of the Middle East, is unwilling to change the status quo in the region. They have a negative attitude towards the independence demand. Especially the United States-led Western countries on the surface sympathy with Kurds but we should note that, behind sympathy with the Kurds, seen on the surface, the US led Western countries, in fact, aim to instrumentalize the Kurdish issue to intervene in the Middle East affairs and the internal affairs of the countries concerned, to seek their self-interests.

Second, in the future, the settlement of Kurdish issues will be characterized by diversified solutions, proceed in multi-speed and will contain various contents and demands.

As the basic national conditions of 4 countries differ, the situation faced by Kurds are faced also different, this determines that the Kurdish national movements have various magnitudes and depth, being relatively strong or relatively weaker, their demands are also not the same.

Departing, from the current situation, we see that the demands of Kurds vary widely, the Iraqi Kurds have achieved autonomy and the next step may be independent state.

Turkey's Kurds are still in the stage of struggles for recognition of national rights, they demand autonomy, but also voice the demand of independence, but even the autonomy is rejected by the Turkish government. Most of the Kurds in Iran are basically satisfied with the status quo, opt to compromise with the reality of Iran's abundant multi-ethnic situation and do not particularly pursue autonomy or independence. Even the Iran's Kurdistan Democratic Party and other parties have only asked for autonomy.

In Syria, the population of Kurds are smaller, the main objective of the struggle is to win the status of national recognition and national minority status, but since 2011 there has been a political turbulence after Syrian Kurds, call for autonomy, but yet, independent state demand is absent.

The so-called multi-speed development of the national movements, refers to the speed of national Kurdish movements, resolving of Kurdish issues will not achieve the same speeds. Some will develop faster, others slower. While the various natures refers that the demands of Kurdish movements will vary in different periods, this reality does not only depend on the level of development of the Kurdish national movement and its own strengths, but will also depend on changes in the external environment. For example, Turkey's PKK, in the post-Cold War era, after the end of the Iraq war, especially after 2003 proposed the national self-government slogan, within the framework of Turkey. Another example, while Iraqi Kurds, demanded true autonomy in the Saddam Hussein era, after they have won this goal, now there have appeared demands for independence.

Third, there are a great number of uncertainties about the solution and development of the Kurdish issue. This is determined by a number of uncertainties as listed below.

1. There are great number of uncertainties in the development of the international situation. At present, the international pattern of one super power accompanied with other major world powers, and the trend of multi-polariazation is still undergoing further changes.

The economic powers of United States and the West see a trend of weakening, and "BRICS" (Brazil, Russia, China, India and South Africa) as the representative of emerging developing countries sees an ascending trend, economically, with other developing countries.

The ability of the West to dominate the Middle East affairs is challenged, but hegemonism, power politics and big-nation nationalism is still strong. Terrorism, non-proliferation, energy security, climate change and other issues have become common new global issues.

The Middle East has been brewing upheavals, geopolitical changes, which have promoted great uncertainties, such as the Iraq wars, United States' Greater Middle East strategy, to transform the region, later has erupted the "Arab Spring".

Thus, the Middle East's strategic pattern, geopolitical relations in the region, plus contests among various political forces and their relative powers have seen encountered major changes, this transformation is still in a development process, consequently there are uncertain trends in the region. Especially, the ongoing "Arab Spring", may not only dramatically change the Arab world, but may also have a significant impacts on the regional pattern and may affect the relationships between the Arab, Turkish, Persian, Kurdish and Jewish peoples.

2. The future development of host countries where Kurds reside is still uncertain.

The developments in Iraq has become a key factor in determining the future of the Kurds. Whether Iraq can get out of the current crisis as quickly as possible and maintain the existence of a strong and complete sovereign state will have a crucial impact on the future fate of Kurds. If Iraq cannot overcome the prevalent long-term turbulences, and if ethnic, sectarian contradictions are not well resolved, the likelihood of an independent state by Kurds will increase.

Currently, domestic political struggles, among the ruling class parties of Turkey are sharp, the reforms by ruling AKP government seriously impacts the traditional Kemalism, leading to serious conflicts with secular forces and the military establishment.

414

But, at the same time, Turkey's process of joining the EU in the future is still uncertain, although it seems that Turkey's access in the short term is difficult, but its gradual access into the Europe is still a remarkable trend. It is imperative that Turkey will need to start more democratization reforms, and we can predict that EU will go on putting more stringent demands, related to the Kurdish issue. If Turkey achieves the desired democracy, then we cannot rule out the possibility of a Kurdish autonomy in this country, and of the PKK problem, a possible referendum may decide the decision on Kurdish autonomy.

Iran's current situation is also extremely complex.

On the one hand, there is an intense domestic political struggle going on, conservative groups have temporarily gained an upper hand, on the other side, inside the conservative camp, contradictions between Ahmadinejad and supreme leader Khamenei have become increasingly obvious, the reformists and the "Green Movement"[5] has have encountered a setback.

---

5   The Iranian Green Movement refers to a political movement that arose after the 2009 Iranian presidential election, in which protesters demanded the removal of Mahmoud Ahmadinejad from office. Green was initially used as the symbol of Mir Hossein Mousavi's campaign, but after the election it became the symbol of unity and hope for those asking for annulment of what they regarded as a fraudulent election.

The process of reform to improve Kurdish rights is interrupted, but the covert struggle between the factions in the Iranian state is still going on, also the West has been increasingly and openly supporting the Iranian democratization movement. On the other hand, since the negotiations on Iranian nuclear issue is not solved yet, Iran continues to develop its nuclear technology and vigorously tries to infiltrate into Iraq and other Arab countries and this infiltration causes tensions between, Saudi Arabia-led Sunni Arab countries which ally with the West and Iran. Also the United States and Israel from time to time threatens Iran with military attacks. All in all, the fate of domestic political struggles in Iran, the fate of the Iranian nuclear negotiations and the US-Iranian relations seem uncertain. If Iran faces a similar foreign strike, like the Iraq war in 2003, Iran's future political system and its state system may be re-arranged, ethnic relations will also face restructuring, thus its national integrity and territorial unity will face serious challenges.

Syria is currently in a critical situation. Bashar government is facing the biggest challenge since Bashar took office in 2000, anti-government demonstrations have evolved into direct armed resistance, a large-scale civil war has erupted, the armed opposition forces gradually grow, and get the support of the Western countries, also Turkey and Saudi Arabia and other Arab countries support tha armed groups.

The future of Syria may face the following several options: the Bashar regime may collapse, thus Baath party may collapse. Secondly, there could be a reconciliation, through international coordination, consequently a national reconciliation government may be formed, but when implementing democratization, this time sectarian type of politics and atomization of political forces may occur, and this may lead Syria into long-term chaos or disintegration. No matter which of the above-mentioned options prevail, it will have a great impact on the fate of Kurds, it is difficult to predict whether the positive or negative impact will prevail. Kurds are dissatisfied with the Bashar government, but also do not trust the opposition, This is also the main reason why they hesitate to participate in the anti-government protests.

3. Uncertainties regarding the Kurdish people's demands.

Kurdish people's demands, in different eras, different periods, different stages of development, and in different countries, have shown and will show differences, this shows a dynamic evolution. Kurdish people's demands will not only depend on their own program and ideological motives, but will also depend on the international and regional situation and political

---

Mir Hossein Mousavi and Mehdi Karroubi are recognized as political leaders of the Green Movement. Hossein-Ali Montazeri was also mentioned as spiritual leader of the movement.

changes in the host country they reside. For example, the Iraqi Kurds now focus on strengthening and increasing their autonomy, but once the Iraqi central state gets stronger, it is likely that they will raise demands for independence. In Syria, the Kurds have long struggled for the recognition and respect for the minority rights, but in the context of the current state of turbulence and civil war, they have put forward the demand for autonomy.

Fourthly, the resolution of the Kurdish question will be a long process. Kurdish issue has a history of nearly a hundred years, and in the short term signs of a complete solution are still not there, it seems long-term development is one of its important features.

The three characteristics of the Kurdish issue, such as the complexity, trans-border nature and internationalized nature, determine that its solution will bear a long-term nature. And the solution of the Kurdish issue will depend on the following several long-term factors:

The democratization and modernization of the host country where Kurds reside will be a long and gradual process. For example, Turkey has achieved the most successful democratization in the Islamic world, but to achieve true democracy, it still needs a long way to take. For a long time, Turkey has been indulged in acute struggles between secular and religious factions, also the struggle between dictatorship and democracy has been acute. Iraq has established democracy after the 2003 war, but its democracy is very fragile, there are severe splits among several ethnic and religious groups, also sectarian politics is serious, thus the country is in turmoil, there are no signs that it will achieve stability in the short term. Syria and Iran are accused of being dictatorships by the West, the two countries are faced with the difficult task of achieving democratic transformation, but also faced by huge pressures coming from the West, which raises the risk of instability, in particular, Syria is currently under the risk of Iraqization.

Both the economic and social development levels of the Kurds and secondly, full-fledged the development of their national consciousness will be a long-term and gradual process, which determine that its solution will bear a long-term nature.

Fifthly, the contradiction between Kurds fighting for autonomy and interference of external powers will not be resolved in the short term.

The solution of the Kurdish issue is closely linked with the development of the international and regional situation, consequently Kurds need to cooperate with the outside forces, it will be difficult to achieve their goals, by solely relying on their own powers. Since their weaknesses are prevalent in the current the current situation, and since their forces cannot be united and coordinated, seeking support of and resorting to external sponsorship will continue to be an important means of struggle for Kurds. As the Kurdish issue further heats up, and its forces and capabilities increase, those actors which have the ability to determine the International and regional patterns and geopolitical trends, will also accelerate adjustments in their policies, regarding the Middle East and Kurds. Consequently, the external forces, especially countries in the region and the Western major powers will not easily give up instrumentalizing Kurds and their demands, so as to serve their self-interests.

Sixthly, the development of the situation in Iraq will be a key factor affecting the development of the Kurdish issue in the next period.

At present, Kurdish region in Iraq, enjoys the highest degree of political, economic and social development among all other Kurdish regions. Its development is outstanding. But the situation in Iraq continues to remain volatile, the contradiction between the central government and the Kurdish region, especially core issues have not been resolved. Kurds are increasingly dissatisfied with the central government, there centrifugal tendencies are obvious. The new generation of Kurds do not identify themselves with the Iraqi state, and feel aleniated to Arabs, lack of national identity and feelings of Iraq, Kurdish identity and Kurdish national consciousness are on the rise. Therefore, we cannot not rule a move for independence by Iraq Kurds in the near future.

In November 2011, Barham Salih, prime minister of the Kurdistan Regional Government (KRG), said: "You can never say never, and every Kurd deep down yearns for independence," said Barham Salih, prime minister of the Kurdistan Regional Government (KRG). "But I live in that neighborhood. The reality of politics, the reality of the region has certain obligations on one as you make your decisions. "I genuinely believe that a democratic, federal Iraq may well represent a very viable option for the Kurds of Iraq," he said. "So far, we have proven that to be the case."[6] Masoud Barzani, the president of the Kurdish regional government, in a threatening tone has argued that Kurds will seek independence, due to their deepening contradictions with the central government, and claimed: "the partnership that had built the national unity government in the country is now "completely non-existent and has become meaningless."[7] In the same month, Kosrat Rasul the vice-chairman of the Kurdish regional government, also delivered a speech in parliament, and emphasized self-determination.[8]

---

6 "Independent Kurds Can Live Within Iraq, Leader Says", The Washington Times, Nov.9, 2011.

7 www.ekurd.net/mismas/articles/misc2012/3/state6017.htm. "Iraqi Kurdistan Threatens to Declare Independence", Mar. 22, 2012.

8 "Iraq's Kurdistan Vice President: Kurds Have Right to Self-determination", Mar.30th, 2012.

Summary

The evolution of the Kurdish issue is the greatly affected by the evolution of international and regional patterns. Since the 20th century, the evolution of international and regional patterns showed three

changes evolving into the fourth, they have not only brought not only the Kurdish problem, but also affected the deepening and development of the Kurdish problem, which determined different characteristics of the Kurdish national movement in these 4 stages. Thus the fate of the Kurds has also fluctuated with the development of the international and regional politics. The two have encountered a close interaction.

The development of Kurdish issue can be divided into four stages regarding international and regional patterns, each stage has different characteristics, but the development of Kurdish issue also has its own self-evolution, due to its inner dynamics: generally speaking, the level of Kurdish national movement and struggle has continuously improved and continued to progress, Kurdish national consciousness has increased and still increasing.

On the other side, the development of the national movement is unbalanced, yet its process is ascending in spiral path; its overall strength is still weak and its forces seem scattered, consequently national movements seek to rely on external forces, and may often become a tool of external forces.

Iraq and Turkey, are the countries where the Kurdish issue is most prominent, the methods these two governments employ in dealing with the Kurdish issue is also the most typical.

In approaching and resolving the Kurdish issue, the two governments have a lot in common, which can be summarized as the big nation chauvinism, ruthlessly suppression of the national resistance movements. Their assimilation policy through causing Kurdish immigration in many ways has become also very important.

The reasons why Kurdish issue is not resolved is manifold, determined the following characteristics of this national movement: its trans-border character, complexity, its internationalized character till the beginning, the Kurdish peoples' own weaknesses and many other factors. The future development of the Kurdish issue is still quite uncertain, and the development and solution path of the Kurdish issue still seems to take long path, the movement will encounter a diversified path and its development speed in different regions will be unbalanced. In the foreseeable future, a unified Kurdish national state will not emerge, but I do not rule out the possibility of Iraq Kurds deciding for an independent state. The development of Kurdistan Regional government in Iraq will become an important benchmark for the development of the Kurdish issue in the future.

CONCLUSION

As one of the five major ethnic-national groups in the Middle East, the Kurds are the only nation, not ever established their own nation-state. The Kurdish issue is the consequence of colonialism. And it is quite complicated to explain why the issue remains unresolved for so long, since today. Despite the fact that the Kurds have their own weaknesses, the reason should also be attributed to complex regional and international factors, such as the everlasting cautious conservative policies adopted by the nations concerned and also the lack of sincere understanding by the international community.

In general, over the past century, the Kurdish issue has undergone through arduous struggles and was effected by the development and changes of the times. Thus Kurds have witnessed continuously improving status and have largely promoted their situations. The Kurds and the Kurdish issue have become increasingly important in the region and around the world. The emergence and development of the Kurdish issue shows that although the Kurds have not yet fully controlled their own destiny, this ability of them is growing and there exists great possibility for them to do so. However, for achieving their long-cherished national aspirations, Kurds do not only need to develop and expand their own strengths, their achievement also depends on the progress of modernization, democratization and policy adjustments of the relevant countries in the region, the changes in the international and regional patterns, as well as the Kurds relations with the outside world.

Kurdish issue continues to get more intense and the growing tension not only affects the fate of the Kurds, but also exerts profound influence on the development of a wide range of international and regional developments. From a regional perspective, regional geopolitical map is being rewritten, the relations, strength and conflicts between the five main ethnic nations— Arabs, Persians. Turks, Kurds Jews—are taking new forms, which further changes inter-state relations and geopolitical patterns, triggering the reconstruction of the relationship and balance of power between the five major nations of the region.

If we look from a global perspective, global politics, global security, diplomacy, antiterrorism, and global energy issues also have certain impact on the Kurdish issue. In addition, the Kurdish oil has become an important factor affecting the international energy security issue. The rising of Kurds' status may bring forward a new wave of ethnic-national separatism, can impact the existing nation-state system, and may pose an international and regional security threat. It turns out to be an urgent task for the international community, especially for the world's major powers, to develop an unified policy for the Kurds.

Nationalism since its birth has always been a double edged sword. As being determined and the product of times and of history, the principles of nationalism and national self-determination could be either progressive or reactionary at different times. National autonomy, ethnic division or independent national state cannot be the master key to resolve the national problem, nor the only way for the development of a nation or nationalism. What serves the best, to the interests of a nation? How to evaluate the overall interests and the particular interests, in the national issue? These are theoretical issues worth of consideration.

The general direction of the development of Kurdish nationalism is winning respect for their national rights, the recognition and development of their own national languages and cultural rights, the right to self-determination and winning equal rights to participate fully in the domestic issues regarding political, economic and social development.

In the light of the positive experiences of many countries around the world when addressing the issue of nationalism, the key to solve the Kurdish issue lies in the elimination of ethnic discrimination, in the realization of national equality, and the abandonment of big-nation chauvinism.

To solve the Kurdish problem, the following seven principles: democracy principle, equality principle, autonomy principle, peaceful solution principle, mutual benefit principle, coexistence principle and balancedness principle, should be followed. Only by eliminating the discrimination against ethnic minorities, respecting the Kurdish national identity and national rights, giving the Kurds the right to manage their own affairs and rights to participate in the management of state affairs on an equal footing, equitably sharing the resources and achievements of the country, Kurdish issue can be solved amply and well. Consequently, human destiny can achieve historic change.

Kurdish issue, as a cross-border ethnic-national issue, with its centuries-old development history, with its experiences and lessons, the experiences and lessons of relevant countries, offer some valuable reference, which can be important for China's understanding and handling of national problems, that can summarized as the following:

1. Big-nation chauvinism should be resolutely abandoned, and the principle of equality and democracy for all nationalities should be upheld.

2. The solution to national problems requires a comprehensive solution, other partial policies hard-line approach or soft approach, left or right approaches, all will have some costs to pay. Ethnic-national issues have never been merely a matter of national equality, not just a matter of poverty, nor simply an issue of anti-terrorism or security, therefore, the solution to the issue needs a multi-pronged and an integrated approach. As a multi-ethnic country China's current ethnic issues are largely related to social social contradictions conflicts generated in transitional period or largely related to great social transformation it is faced with.

3. The interference from the external forces should be eliminated and restrained to the largest extent, particularly that from the Western countries with ulterior motives.

4. Given the cross-national nature of the relevant ethnic groups and considering the reality that most of them live in the border areas, their relations with the neighboring countries should be properly handled.

5. As mankind enters the 21st century, in the era of globalization, a new type of ethnic relations should be built, we should strengthen national identity, accelerate the building of the civil society, dilute the national consciousness and national attributes.

6. Our historical tradition of multi-ethnic unity should be vigorously promoted, national security and common national prosperity should be maintained, consequently the stability of the central government should be retained. It is necessary to take a clear-cut stand against separatism and terrorism.

7. The nationalities policy, should be long-term and stable, but it should also pay to keep up with, adjust itself to current changes and new social developments, and accordingly timely and realistic adjustments should be made.

8. Concepts such as nationalism and national self-determination are all products of history which evolve with the changes of the times, may be progressive in a certain period of time, and may be reactionary in another certain period; it may be progressive for a group or a country, but in turn it may be reactionary for another country or group.

It is always an ongoing progress to seek solutions to the ethnic problems. Even those countries where the nationality issues seem to be absent or better addressed, do not rule out problems that may grow in the future. Therefore, in the construction of nationality policies, we should avoid the pursuit of perfectionism and once-for-all solutions; nationality issues never have best solution, there are only time suited optimal solutions.

Postscript

I can still recall, the fall of 1998, when I had just graduated from the Peking University and soon after began to work for the CICIR (China Institute of Contemporary International Relations), just in those days, a series of events occurred in the Middle East which attracted me to the Kurdish issue ever since: in October the same year, under the pressure of 100 thousand Turkish troops, which had gathered and stationed on the Syrian border, the latter was forced to expel the PKK leader Öcalan, who had hidden for long in Syria. A few months later, Öcalan fled to Europe, seeking political refugee from many countries of the World. But eventually his claim was refused and later he was cornered and captured by the Turkish National Security Agency in Kenya, on February, 16th, 1999, by the help of US intelligence. I was then in charge of reporting on Turkey events. So, naturally I was ordered to closely track this hot event. Since, the leaders of the central government were also very concerned about this incident, and made instructions to provide information and material, this had been also the first internal report, I had prepared after getting the job. Perhaps it is because of this first task that my interest in the Kurdish issue has never diminished for years, later I have written numerous articles on the subject. In my PhD study, I directly chose Kurdish issue as the topic of my doctoral dissertation and made an in-depth study. Today, with the support of my instructors and friends, I have finished this manuscript of more than 400,000 words.

Fifteen years have passed so quickly. Although my job changed from the Oriental Wind to the Zhang Zizhong Road Nr. 3, my research passion of the Middle East issues has remained intact. There are numerous people who deserve my gratitude, in those so many years along the way. First of all, thanks will go to my doctoral dissertation supervisor Prof. Li Shaoxian. In the decade when I worked with the Oriental Wind, I was honored to have the opportunity to follow his valuable instructions from scholarship to life, which I benefited a lot. Special thanks should also go to my former leader and former dean of the China Institute of Contemporary International Relations, Prof. Lu Zhongwei, who has always been kind to me. Despite being very busy with multiple tasks all the time, it was touching that, he gave his time to be personally involved in the whole process of my doctoral dissertation including the defense phase.

In addition, my fellow research colleagues, Zhao Guozhong, Li Rong, Zhang Xiaodong, Wang Linggui, Wang Jinglie and Niu Xinchun and other experts have also made a number of valuable suggestions to the manuscript, which I would like to express my sincere gratitude for.

The publication of this book owes greatly to the efforts of Prof. Yang Guang, head of the Institute of West Asia and Africa attached to Chinese Academy of Social Sciences, and my other fellow colleagues working in the Academic Committee of the Institute of West Asia and Africa. It is with their strong recommendations that this book was granted the publication fund from the Chinese Academy of Social Innovation Project. And, my gratitude has been beyond description, when Prof. Yang confirmed to write the preface for the book, although he was very busy then. And I also want to extend my gratitude to Ms. Gao Mingxiu, at the Social Sciences Academic Press, who has worked for the editing and publication of the book for months.

Finally, I would like to dedicate this book to my wife Ms. Song Yingying, without her support for my academic researches and considerate care of my life, this book would never have been possible.

Tang Zhichao

Early summer, 2013

Appendix 1

Chronology

Around 1000 BC, The word "Kurd" was officially recorded in the Assyrian literature, Assyrians called those living near the Lake Kul as Kurti people.

850 BC, Kurds began to speak an Indo-European language.

Around 700 BC, Deioces founded the Kingdom of the Medes.

Around the mid-7th century BC, Zoroaster (628 BC-551 BC) founded Zoroastrianism, later becoming the state religion of the Persian Empire, and the main religion of Kurds.

550 BC, The kingdom of Cyrus ended the Kingdom of the Medes, and founded the Persian Empire (550 BC-330 BC).

401 BC, The Persians were defeated by the Greeks in the war near present-day Baghdad.

330 BC, Persian Empire disintegrated.

226, Sassanid Dynasty was established.

610, Sticking to apocalyptic tradition Prophet Muhammad has founded and began to spread Islam.

632, Arab Empire began to expand its territories while spreading Islam.

637, Kurds faced with the northward Arab invaders for the first time. Arabs conquered the Kurdish region and Kurds began to be convert to Islam.

650, Sassanid dynasty disintegrated.

9th century, Muslim Kurdish writer-theologian Al-Dinawari (Ibn Qutaybah) Persian origin (828-889) wrote the book named as Kurdish Ancestry and many other works. His studies included Qur'anic exegesis, hadith, theology, philosophy, law and jurisprudence, grammar, philology, history, astronomy, agriculture and botany.

Around 1150, The Seljuk Sultanate ordered the formation of a Kurdistan Province.

1171-1250, The Kurdish Salahaddin Ayubbi built the powerful Ayyubid Dynasty.

1299, The Ottoman Empire (1299-1922) founded.

13th century, Mongol troops came into Kurdistan, followed by the establishment of Ilhan Dynasty.

1370, Timurid dynasty (1370-1507) conquers Ilhani land.

1502, Ismail I founded Safavid Dynasty (1502-1736), declaring Shia Islam as the national religion.

1514, Chaldiran War broke out between the Ottoman Empire and the Safavids. The Ottoman Empire Army captured Tabriz, the capital of the Safavid dynasty together with a part of Kurdistan and Azerbaijan.

1639, Safavids and the Ottoman Empire signed the Treaty of Qasr-e Shirin; that most part of Kurdistan regions were given to the Ottoman Empire, while other part of about 20,000 square kilometers remained under the Safavid Rule. Thus, Kurdistan was divided into two.

1736, The Safavid Army forced Ottoman Empire to sign the Treaty of Constantinople, the Ottoman Empire returned the western territories of Kurdistan after decades of occupation. Borders returned to the border lines decided as in theTreaty of Qasr-e Shirin.

1806-1808, A rebellion took place in the Ardalan region and the city of Senna led by Abdul Rahman Baban. The city of Suleymaniyah was founded by Baban prince Mahmud Pasha in 1781.

1811, Mevlana Khalidi Baghdadi started to form the Naqshbandi Sect as a part of Sufi Islamic belief in the Kurdish Region of northern Iraq.

1831, Facing the growing threat of separatism, the declining Ottoman Empire began to enhance central authority in the Kurdish region to strengthen its control. The Mohammad uprising broke out in the Kurdish Sorani region.

1840s, Barzani tribe began to migrate permanently to the Barzan region.

1843, The Colemerg (Hakkari) uprising.

1843, The first Botan and the Bedr Khan Bey uprisings against the Ottoman Empire. Ottoman Empire and Qajar Dynasty signed the second "Erzurum Treaty". Bothsides re-arranged their territories in the Kurdish region. Iran Qajar Dynasty gave up its claims one Sulaymaniyah; the Ottoman Empire left Zohab.

1855, Yezdan Sher uprising against the Ottoman rule.

1870, Ottoman Empire Military academies began enrolling Kurdish students.

Aug. 31, 1876, "Despotic Sultan" Hamid II (1842-1918) rises to power.

1880-1881, Shaikh Ubeydullah uprising against the Qajar Dynastyin the Nehri Region.

Nov. 1890, Hamid II. followed the model of Russian Cossack cavalry to form a predominantly Kurdish cavalry, or the Hamidiye Cavalries.

1898, Midhad Bedir Khan founded the first Kurdish magazine named Kurdistan.

Nov.1905-1911, The unsuccessful Constitutional Revolution in Iran.

July 1908, Coup by Young Turks in Turkey. The Ottoman Empire began to draw a Constitution for the second time.

1908, Sheik Abdul Kadir founded the Kurdi Taawin Jamiyyati, meanwhile Kurdistan Revival and Development Association was also founded (Kürt Teali Cemiyeti).

1910, Several Kurdish students and intellectuals set up the secret Kurdish political organization Hewa (Hope) in Istanbul.

Oct. 29, 1914, Ottoman Empire jointed the WWI. Meanwhile, the Empire deported and executed a large number of Kurds in the East.

March 1916, The first Kurdish Dersim rebellion

May 16, 1916, Britain and France reached the Sykes-Picot Agreement to divide and share the Ottoman Empire.

June 1916, The Arab uprising began.

Oct. 1917, The Russian October Revolution. The Soviet government announces the unequal secret treaties the Tsarist Russia signed with Ottoman Empire and Iran.

1918, Society for the Rise of Kurdistan was founded in Istanbul.

May 1918, British troops occupied Kirkuk.

Jan. 8, 1918, US President Wilson proposes the famous Fourteen Points.

Oct.30, 1918, Ottoman Empire unconditionally surrenders and signs the Mudros cease-fire agreement.

Nov. 1918, British troops occupies Mosul.

Dec.1, 1918, The Iraqi Kurdish leaders held a meeting with Sir Arnold Wilson, the British ambassador to Iraq, demanded an independent and unified Kurdistan with the support of UK.

May 11, 1919, Kurdish Ali Batti (Elike Bette) Kurdish uprising in Dersim Turkey.

May 22, 1919, Mahmud Barzanji, uprising.

427

1919-1922, The Ismail Simko Kurdish uprising in Iran.

Apr. 29-26, 1920, Conference of San Remo put Syria under French mandate, and Iraq under British mandate.

July 1920, 62 Iraqi Kurdish leaders demanded Kurdish independence under a British mandate.

Aug.10, 1920, Treaty of Sèvres is signed, dividing Ottoman Empire among western major powers which placed Syria under French mandate, Iraq under British mandate, and granting independence for the Turkish Kurds.

1920, The Koçgiri (West Dersim) uprising in Turkey.

March 7, 1920, Syrian National Assembly declares the foundation of independent Syria.

Nov. 1920, The Government of Iraq is formed, with 21 cabinet members from Basra, Baghdad and Mosul provinces.

1921, Turkey's Kurdish Koçgiri uprising was suppressed by Mustafa Kemal. Reza Khan Pahlavi coup in Iran.

Aug. 1921, British supported Faisalas the King of Iraq. The Kingdom of Iraq was founded.

1922, Turkey wins the Independence War, and allies agreed to repeal the Treaty of Sèvres, and re-opened the peace talks in Lausanne, Switzerland. The British and Soviet Army withdrew from Iran, ending the long-term occupation.

Oct. 1922, British Government and Faisal dynasty signs the "Iraqi-British Treaty of Alliance," establishing the British control over Iraqi politics, economy and Army.

Oct. 10, 1922, Sheikh Mahmoud Barzanji announces the foundation of the Kurdish Kingdom and appoints himself as ruler in Iraq.

Dec. 24, 1922, Britain and Iraq issues in a joint declaration, the establishment of an autonomous Kurdish government in Iraq.

Dec. 1922, Colonel Soureya Bedir Khan Bey, Yusuf Ziya and Halit Bey founded the Kurdish Independence Committee in Erzurum, Turkey.

July 1923, Sheikh Mahmoud Barzanji reached an agreement with the Iraqi government, accepting the Iraqi-British Joint Declaration. The Government agrees to Kurdish autonomy under a united Iraq.

July 24, 1923, Turkey signs the "Treaty of Lausanne", abolishing provisions including the Kurdish autonomy and independence in the Sevres.

Oct. 29, 1923, Republic of Turkey founded.

March 3, 1924, Turkish Government announces the abolition of Caliphate institution.

July 16, 1924, League of Nations forms the International Committee of Survey on Mosul.

Sept. 4, 1924, The Kurdish Hakkari-Beytüşşebap uprising in Turkey.

1925, Iraq held its first Assembly elections.

Jan.-March 1925, the International Committee of Survey on Mosul conducts the field investigations in Mosul.

Feb. 14-May 31, 1925, Sheikh Said uprising in Turkey.

March 3, 1925, Turkish Grand National Assembly passes the Public Security Maintenance Law to empower government with the special powers to suppress the Kurdish rebellion.

June 10, 1925, The Nehrî Kurdish uprising in Iran.

June 30, 1925, Sheikh Said and other 52 insurgents were hanged in Diyarbakir.

July 16, 1925, International Committee of Inquiry on Mosul reveals its investigation report in Geneva, suggesting Iraq's sovereignty on Mosul.

Oct. 16, 1925, League of Nations formally includes Mosul to Iraq.

Aug. 7, 1925-1926, The Kurdish Raman-Reşkotan Kurdish uprising in Turkey.

1926, Iraqi government issues the Local Language Law, allowing the schools in the Kurdish region to carry out primary education in Kurdish.

Jan. 21, 1926, The second Simko Shikak Kurdish uprising broke out.

Apr. 1926, Reza Khan Pahlavi was officially crowned, resulting in the foundation of Pahlavi Dynasty.

May 16-June 17, 1926, The Kurdish Agiri (Ağrı) Kurdish uprising in Turkey.

June 5, 1926, Britain, Turkey and Iraq signs the Treaty of Ankara, Turkey gave up its claims of sovereignty over Mosul.

Oct. 7, 1926, The Kurdish uprising in Turkey, provinces included Palu and Malatya, Lice, Bingöl, south of Erzurum, Mardin, Beyazid.

1926-1927, The Second Sheikh Mahmoud Barzanji uprising.

1927-1930, The Kurdish Ararat (Ağrı) uprising in Turkey.

May 26-Aug.25, 1927, The Kurdish Mutkî uprising in Turkey.

June 25, 1927, The Turkish Grand National Assembly passes the law No. 1164, establishing the organ of the Inspectorate General in the Kurdish Region.

Aug. 1927, Kurdish nationalists of Turkey participated a meeting in Lebanon to form the National Kurdish League, to prepare for the II. Ararat uprising.

Sept. 13, 1927, The second Kurdish Agri uprising in Turkey.

Oct. 1927, Pan-Kurdish nationalist organization Khoybun founded. The Sason-Perwarî-Kozluk Kurdish uprising in Turkey.

Nov. 1928, Turkey announces the adoption of Latin alphabet and begins a language campaign to promote the Turkish language.

May 22-Aug. 3, 1929, The Kurdish Zîlan uprising in Turkey.

July 6, 1929, The Kurdish Asi-Resul uprising in Turkey.

1929, The KurdishTendǔrek uprising in Turkey.

May 26, 1929, The Kurdish Savur uprising in Turkey.

June 20, 1930, The Kurdish Zeylan uprising in Turkey.

July 21, 1930, The Kurdish Oramar uprising in Turkey.

Sept. 7-14, 1930, The third Kurdish Agri uprising in Turkey.

Sept. 1930, Iraqi Mahmoud Barzamji launches another uprising.

Oct. 24, 1930, The Kurdish Pülümür uprising in Turkey.

1931, A group of Iraqi Kurdish nationalists issues a petition to the League of Nations, demanding the establishment of an independent Kurdistan.

429

Nov.1931, the Kurdish Shaikh Ahmed Barzani uprising in Iraq.

March 21, 1931-July 16, 1938, The second Kurdish Dersim uprising in Turkey, in the same year Turkish Language Association was founded to promote Turkish language.

May 5, 1932, Turkish Government passes the Forced Migration Law.

1933, Iranian Government implements the compulsory settlement policy, forcing nomad Kurdish tribes to permanent settlement.

1934-1935, The Mustafa Barzani tribe uprising in Iraq.

1934, The Iraqi Communist Party (ICP) is founded with many Kurdish members, the party announced recognition of the Kurdish national rights and its support for the Kurdish national cause.

June 13, 1934, The Turkish Grand National Assembly passes the Resettlement Law.

1935, Shah Reza Pahlavi officially changes the country's name from Persia to Iran.

Dec. 25, 1935, Turkey passes the law No. 2884, or the Tunceli Province Administration Law, changing the name of Dersim toTunceli.

1937-1938, The third Kurdish Dersim uprising in Turkey.

July 8, 1937, Iraq, Turkey and Iran sign the Saadabad Pact which also included coordinated actions against Kurds.

Aug. 11, 1937, Iraqi Kurdish politician Imam Qasim and Ismaili Hakki appeals both to the Iraqi Government and the foreign governments to prevent Turkey's extermination policy against Kurds.

1938, Lyrics of the Kurdish national anthem Hey, Enemy (Ey Raqip) were written.

Nov. 10, 1938, Mustafa Kemal, the founding father of the Modern Turkey passes.

1941, Iraqi Kurdish political organization Hiwa founded.

1941-1944, Kurdish uprising in Baneh erupted in Iran led by Hama Rashid.

June 8, 1941, Commander of the Free French Forces, General Georges Catroux promises Syria and Lebanon "freedom and independence" and ending of the French Mandate. But three months later Syria declared independence on Aug. 25, 1941, United Kingdom and Soviet Union invades Iran simultaneously, subsequently Tehran was occupied. Shah Reza Khan Pahlavi was forced to abdicate, his son Muhammad Reza Pahlavi becomes his successor.

Sept.16, 1942, Iran's first Kurdish political organization is founded, by the name of Komala Jiyanewey Kurdistan.

June 1943, Mullah Mustafa Barzani escapes house arrest. After he arrives home Barzani launches another uprising.

July 1943, Kurdish uprising led by Said Biroki in the eastern border of Turkey.

Aug. 1944, Kurdish nationalists in Turkey, Iraq, Iran and Syria held a meeting in Dhahranto discuss the plans for a united national struggle.

1945, Rizgari Kurd, the Kurdish branch of Iraqi Communist Party, is founded.

Jan. 15, 1945, Mullah Mustafa Barzani leads the formation of the Freedom Committee.

Aug.-Oct. 1945, Mullah Mustafa uprising in Iraq.

Aug. 15, 1945, The Kurdistan Democratic Party of Iran is founded.

Aug. 16, 1945, The Kurdistan Democratic Party of Iraq is founded.

Dec. 15, 1945, The Kurdish People's Government is founded in Mahabad, Iran.

Jan. 22, 1946, The Republic of Mahabad, The first Kurdish Republic founded led by Qazi Muhammed.

Apr. 4, 1946, The Soviet Union reaches an agreement with the Iranian Government, on the withdrawal of Soviet troops from Iran on May 6, 1946, and promises not to interfere in Iran's internal affairs. A joint Soviet-Iranian company is founded for the development the oil fields in Northern Iran.

Apr. 17, 1946, French troops withdraws from Syria. Syria becomes independent, this day began to be celebrated as Independence Day.

Dec. 15, 1946, Iranian Army attacks Mahabad.

March 31, 1947, Iranian Kurdish leader Qazi Mohammed and other three Kurdish leaders were hanged on charges of treason. The Republic of Mahabad ended in failure.

Apr. 1947, Arab Baath Party is formally founded.

June 1947, Mullah Mustafa Barzani and some remnants fled to the Soviet Union.

Apr. 4, 1948, PKK leader Abdullah Ocalan is born.

May 1950, The first multi-party Turkish election held. The long-ruling CHP (RPP) lost the election while the Democratic Party rises to power. Syria issues its first post-independence Constitution, defining Syria as a Democratic Arab Republic. Constitution stresses the Arab characteristic of Syria and declares Syria as part of the Arab nation.

1951, Baghdad radio station begins broadcasting in Kurdish.

Jan. 1953, KDP of Iraq holds its Second Congress. Hamza Abdullah was expelled, Hamza Abdullah formed the Kurdistan Democratic Party Progressive Front.

Apr. 1952, Syrian Government orders the dissolution of all political parties and groups, and arrests BJP Assemblyarians and cabinet members.

1953, The Arab Socialist Party of Syria and the Arab Baath Party merged into pan-Arab Baath Party

Dec. 1953, The anti-dictatorship and anti-imperialist movement erupts in Syria.

1955, Iraq, Iran and Turkey forms the pro-Western Baghdad Pact, mainly targeting Soviet Union, and coordinate actions against Kurds. The Kurdish leader Sheikh Mahmoud Barzanji passes.

1957, A number of Kurdish intellectuals including Osman Sabri, Daham Miro and Muheidin Zaza founded the Kurdistan Democratic Party of Syria.

Feb. 1, 1958, Syria and Egypt announces their merger and the founding of the United Arab Republic.

July 14, 1958, July Revolution, Iraq. Faisal dynasty is overthrown led by a military coup led by General Abdul Karim Qasim. Republic of Iraq is founded.

July 16, 1958, KDP issues the Declaration to the Kurdish People, welcoming the deposition of the corrupt dynasty and demands autonomy.

July 17, 1958, A delegation led by general secretary of the Iraqi KDP, Ibrahim meets with General Abdul Karim Qasim, demanding Kurdish autonomy, but refused.

Sept. 2, 1958, Qasim replies the telegram and letter of the exiled leader Mullah Mustafa Barzani, accepting his appeal to return back to Iraq.

Oct. 6, 1958, Mullah Mustafa Barzani returns to Baghdad from the Soviet Union via Romania.

Nov.10, 1958, the Iraqi KDP reaches an agreement with Iraqi Communist P,arty, they form the National High-ranking Committee for a bi-party cooperation.

Feb. 1959, Iraq and Soviet Union signs a seven-year economic and technical cooperation agreement.

March 1959, Mosul Rebellion. Mullah Mustafa Barzani supports suppression by the government.

March 24, 1959, Iraq announces its withdrawal both from the Baghdad Pact and the Sterling currency zone.

Apr. 4, 1959, the newspaper Hope Struggle of the Iraqi Kurdish National Front was allowed for publishing.

July 1959, armed conflicts erupted between Kurds and Turkmens in Kirkuk. President Qasim accuses ICP for manipulation and bans the ICP (Iraqi Communist Party). The Iraqi KDP quits the alliance with the ICP, suspending the cooperation agreement.

1960, Turkey's Forced Resettlement Law comes into effect (Decree No. 105).

Jan. 6, 1960, political Party Law is passed in Iraq. The Kurdistan Democratic Party obtains legal status.

May 27, 1960, military coup in Turkey, Democratic Party government ousted.

May 5-10, 1960, The Iraqi KDP held its fifth Congress, Mullah Mustafa re-elected as party chairman and Ahmed Ibrahim as general secretary.

Nov. 1960, Mullah Mustafa was invited to Soviet Union, he participated the October Revolution celebrations.

1961, Turkish TIP (Workers Party) is founded, becoming Turkey's first socialist party that achieves to get into the Turkish Assembly. A large number of Kurds join the Party.

Feb. 1961, Clashes broke out between Barzani and the pro-government Kurdish tribe Shekak in Iraq.

March 9, 1961, Iraqi Government orders the arrest of KDP General Secretary Ahmad Ibrahim.

March 22, 1961, Iraqi Government bans KDP party newspaper Struggle.

Aug. 1961, KDP issues an ultimatum to President Qasim, demanding the end to dictatorship and the acknowledgment of the Kurdish autonomy.

Sept. 11, 1961, Iraqi Government takes military action against the KDP, the revolt which the Kurds called September Revolution, breaks out.

Sept. 13, 1961, Qasim orders the Air Force to strike Barzan area.

Sept. 23, 1961, Iraqi Government officially bans KDP.

Sept. 28, 1961, Syria announces its withdrawal from the United Arab Republic and the, founding of the Syrian Arab Republic.

Nov. 16, 1961, Iraqi KDP Central Committee sent a letter to the UN Secretary General, accusing Iraqi Army of massacre and demanded the establishment of an international committee to conduct field investigations on the matter.

March 1962, Iraqi Kurds launches the spring offensive against government troops.

July 1962, Sheikh Ahmed Barzani (Mustafa Barzani's brother) holds unsuccessful secret negotiations with President Qasim.

Aug. 23, 1962, Syrian Government issues a decree for a census to be held in Jazira region. About 20 percent of the Kurds were identified as illegal infiltrators, or Ajanib, thus were deprived of citizenship.

Feb. 8, 1963, Military Coup in Iraq. President Qasim was arrested and executed. Abdul Salam Muhammad Arif becomes President. Kurds begin to negotiate with new Iraqi Government.

March 8, 1963, Syrian Baath Party successfully launches the White Revolution, or the bloodless coup, and rises to power.

June 10, 1963, Iraq launches a massive military offensive against the Kurdish Region. The war breaks out. Turkish KDP is founded.

Feb. 1964, Iraq President Arif and Mullah Mustafa meet and reach a cease-fire agreement. Bothsides declared a ceasefire, which resulted in a split in KDP.

Apr. 1964, Syria issues the Interim Constitution, defining Syrian rule as an Arab Democratic Socialist Republic.

June 1964, Ibrahim Ahmed, Jalal Talabani and 14 other members are expelled from KDP. The Soviet Union and Iraq signes a military agreement where Soviet Union pledges to provide a large number of weapons and military equipment to Iraq.

1965, Syrian Government decides to establish an Arab Belt population along the border between Jazira and Turkey.

March 4, 1965, Iraqi Government army launches the Spring Offensive against the Kurds.

Feb. 23, 1966, Deputy Secretary of the Syrian Baath Party, Salih Jadidi and Hafez al-Assad overthrew Amin Hafiz government by a coup and captured the leadership of the Syrian Baath Party. They immediately denounced the 1964 Interim Constitution, dissolve the Revolutionary Committee, and begin implementing social and economic reforms.

Apr 13, 1966, Iraqi President Abdul Salam Arif passes in a helicopter crash.

May 1966, Kurdish fighters defeat the Iraqi Army in the mountainous region of Handlin.

June 15, 1966, Iraqi government announces cease-fire and the 12-Point Peace Plan.

1967, Syrian government issued a new decree ordering that the newborn babies must given Arabic names. Otherwise they will not be registered.

July 17, 1968, Iraqi Baath Party coup headed by Ahmed Hassan al-Bakr.

1969, DDKO, Eastern Revolutionary and Cultural Center is founded in Turkey. Turkey's special forces are established, known as Kommandos, to fight with Kurdish insurgents. Society of Revolutionary Toilers of Iranian Kurdistan, or Komalah, founded.

May 1969, Soviet Union and Iraqi Government signed a new military aid agreement. The Soviet Union continued to provide weapons and military facilities for Iraq and send military advisers to train the Iraqi army.

March 11, 1970, KDP of Iraq and the Iraqi government signs the March Declaration, Iraqi Government allows the Kurdish autonomy, through a four-year transition period.

July 1970, Iraqi Government declares the Interim Constitution, which stipulates that the Republic of Iraq is composed from Araband the Kurdish nations, while aiming to achieve the Arab unity and Socialism.

Nov. 13, 1970, Baathist officer, defense minister and air force commander Assad launches the "Corrective Movement" to reorganize the Syrian Baath Party's regional leadership and government, while appointing himself as Defense and Prime Minister.

1971, DDKO is banned by the Turkish government. The Revolutionary Democratic Cultural Association, or DDKD, becomes its successor.

March 12, 1971, Turkish Military coup, Martial law is declared in 11 provinces, and all left-wing political parties and Kurdish organizations are banned. Hafız Assad is elected as the Syrian President.

Sept. 29, 1971, Mullah Mustafa narrowly escapes an assassination attempt while meeting with a delegation of the Iraqi Government, which worsens the relationship between Kurds and the Iraqi government.

Nov. 1971, Mullah Mustafa accuses the Iraqi Government for trying to Arabize Kirkuk, stressed that Kirkuk has always been a Kurdish city.

1972, Mullah Mustafa resumes relations with Iran, establishes contacts with the United States, while distances from the Soviet Union. Iraqi Government issues a decree to announce the nationalization of foreign oil companies.

Apr. 9, 1972, Soviet Union and Iraq signs the 15-year Soviet-Iraqi Friendship and Cooperation Treaty.

May 30, 1972, US President Richard Nixon visits Iran. Shah requests support from the United States for Iraqi Kurds.

1974, Abdullah Ocalan and 6 other activists set up an independent Marxist-Leninist organization, nicknamed as Apoists (Apocular) group.

Feb. 1974, Iraqi government unilaterally introduced the regional autonomy law. Iraqi government expellslarge number of Kurds from Kirkuk.

Feb. 24, 1974, Iraqi Revolutionary Command Council issues the Decree No.176, banning all political organizations, including KDP, those who refused to join the People's Progressive Front.

March 11, 1974, Iraqi government unilaterally issues the Kurdistan Autonomy Law (No. 33). The government gives a 15-day ultimatum to Mullah Mustafa, requiring them to accept the law.

Apr. 1974, Iraqi government begins to implement the Autonomy Law. President Bakr appoints former Kurdish diplomat Taha as vice president, forming the Kurdish Regional Government.

June 6, 1974, Iraqi KDP submits a report on the Kurdish issue to UN Secretary-General.

Aug. 1974, Iraqi troops march into the Kurdish mountainous areas and war breaks out.

Oct. 5, 1974, Assembly of the Iraqi Kurdish Autonomous Region is inaugurated.

March 6, 1975, Iran and Iraq sign the Algiers Agreement. Iraq gives concessions on the Shatt-ül-Arab river border demarcation in exchange to Iran's ceasing support to Iraqi Kurds. Iraqi Government launches a massive offensive, which leads to the failure of the Kurdish Uprising.

March 18, 1975, KDP held an enlarged meeting of the political bureau and military leaders and announced cease-fire and retreats to Iran. Mullah Mustafa is exiled to Iran.

June 1, 1975, Jalal Talabani announces the foundation of Patriotic Union of Kurdistan or PUK, in Damascus, Syria.

June 1975, Iraqi Revolutionary Command Council passes a resolution to carry outland reform in the North, and promotes the peasants' cooperative associations.

May 18, 1977, Syrian government issues the decree No. 15801, ordering name changes of all Kurdish-villages and towns from Kurdish to Arabic in the Afrin forest areas of Aleppo Province, to promote Arabization.

Nov. 27, 1978, Ocalan founds the PKK.

Jan. 1979, Islamic Revolution in Iran. Shah Pahlavi fled, Kurdistan Islamic Party is founded in Turkey. Iranian Kurds revolt against the Iran Islamic government.

March 1979, Referendum in Iran, adopts the name Iran Islamic Republic. The KDP-I holds a public rally for the first time, and declares its eight guiding principles.

March 1, 1979, Mullah Mustafa Barzani dies from lung cancer in the United States.

July 16, 1979, Bakr resigns due to illness. Saddam Hussein takes over the Iraqi Presidency.

Aug. 1979, Khomeini announces Jihad against Kurds, bans all the Kurdish political organizations.

Oct. 1979, Massoud Barzani assumes the chairmanship of the KDP. Iraq government issues the Election Law for the Kurdish Autonomous Region.

Sept. 1980, Elections in the Iraqi Kurdish Region.

Sept. 12, 1980, military Coup in Turkey. PKK and other legal Kurdish organizations are banned and attacked.

Sep 22, 1980, Iraq sends troops to Iran. The Iran-Iraq War begins.

July 1981, PKK held its first congress and decides to form a united front. Turkey's new constitution prohibits the establishment of ethnic based political parties, and the use of Kurdish and other non-Turkish languages. The Reagan administration removes Iraq from the list of countries supporting terrorism.

Aug. 20-25, 1982, PKK held its second congress develops a three-phase strategy: the defensive, stalemate and offensive phases, and launches guerrilla war in Turkey against military, police, economic and civilian targets.

Nov. 1982, the new Turkish constitution is drawn, including a large number of discriminative clauses against the Kurds.

1983, Turkey issues a new Political Party Law. The Islamist Welfare Party is founded.

May 26, 1983, 15,000 Turkish troops march 40 kilometers deep in Iraq against PKK, with the help of the Iraqi army.

July 1983, Mullah Mustafa Barzani agrees to cooperate with PKK and permits PKK activities in Northern Iraq.

435

Oct. 1983, Turkey passes The Law (Decree No. 2932) on Foreign Language Education and Teaching which excluded Kurdish.

Jan. 1984, Iraqi Government and the Kurdish Patriotic Union (PUK) reaches a cease-fire agreement.

Aug. 15, 1984, PKK raids Siirt (Eruh) and Hakkari provinces. Attacks marks the beginning of guerrilla warfare and the long-term civil war in the eastern Turkey.

Oct. 1984, Turkey and Iraq reaches an agreement, to coordinate and control Kurdish population in their respective territories, while allowing each other's troops into the territory of the other to suppress the rebels. Turkish army launches the cross-border "Sun Action" to combat the PKK in Iraq.

Nov. 15, 1984, Turkish Government amends and passes the Population Registration Law, prohibiting the naming of newborn babies in Kurdish.

Dec 15, 1984, PKK, the Turkish Communist Labor Party, Revolutionary Path, the Socialist Party of Turkish Kurdistan and Socialist Workers Party of Turkey and the Turkish Labourers' Party and other left parties declare the formation of United Revolutionary Front Against fascism in Turkey.

March 1985, PKK establishes a separate military branch, Kurdish National Liberation Front, or ERNK, specifically to carry out military operations. Turkish Government builts a barbed wire wall along the Syrian to block the PKK infiltration.

1985, PKK clashes in Hakkari, results in the deaths of 60 Turkish soldiers, plus PKK members and civilians, causing a nationwide shock.

Apr. 1985, Turkish Government amends the Village Law to allow the government to form and maintain temporary village guards, to arm the local Kurds against PKK. In Turkey, Social Democratic Party and People's Party merges to form the Social Democratic People's Party, or SHP.

March 1986, Thousands of Kurds wear traditional Kurdish attires to celebrate the Kurdish New Year in Damascus. Police opens fire causing one death and many injuries.

Aug. 1986, Assembly elections Iraqi Kurdistan.

Aug. 15, 1986, Turkish Air Force strikes northern Iraq, while Turkish special forces penetrates into Iraq to fight against the PKK.

Oct. 1986, PKK establishes the Kurdistan People's Liberation Army, or ARGK.

1987-1988, Iraqi government embarks on the Anfal campaign against the Kurdish fighters and civilians causing a mass massacre.

March 4, 1987, Turkish Army bombed the PKK targets in Iraq with 30 jet-fighters, resulting in 170 injuries.

Apr. 14, 1987, Turkey's formal application to EU.

May 1987, KDP, PUK and other Kurdish parties decides to establish Iraqi-Kurdistan Front to cooperate against the Iraq government.

July 19, 1987, Turkey imposes nationwide martial law, issues the Decree 285, and declares state of emergency across the southeast region of Turkey.

Feb. 9, 1988, PKK prisoners started a long term hunger strike in Diyarbakır prison.

Feb. 11, 1988, The US State Department's annual report on the worldwide human rights requires that Turkey should acknowledge Kurds' minority status, and severely criticizes the serious phenomenon of torture in Turkey.

Feb. 18, 1988, Turkish Prime Minister Ozal allows prisoners' use of Kurdish language and promises to improve the prison conditions.

Feb. 23, 1988-Apr. 23, 1989, Iraq mobilizes the 200.000 troops for a large-scale military operation against the Kurdish region.

March 16, 1988, Halabja massacre shocks the world, chemical weapons were used. Around 5000 Kurds were killed and 10,000 injuries.

May 1988, PKK and PUK reach an agreement. The Iraqi Kurdistan Front (IKF) is formally built

June 10, 1988, 8 Kurdish organizations of Turkey held a press conference in Brussels, announcing the formation of the United Front of Kurdistan Liberation Movement, or TEVGER, and declares armed struggle in Kurdistan.

Aug. 1988, Iraq and Iran announces to recognize the UN Security Council Resolution No. 598 of cease-fire, which ended the eight-year long Iran-Iraq War.

July 13, 1989, General secretary of the KDP-Iran Abdul Rahman Ghassemlou was assassinated in Vienna.

Sept. 1989, PKK announces 13 Kurdish tribes (families) as the enemies of the nation in Turkey. Assembly Elections held in KRG of Iraq.

Nov. 1989, Turkey's Motherland Party chairman Ozal elected as the 8th Turkish president.

1990, Ocalan cancels the order to attack 13 hostile Kurdish families.

Apr. 1990, Turkish government issues Decree No. 413, giving the regional state governor limitless authorities. Ocalan claims that PKK would not demand Kurdish independence from Turkey.

June 1990, Pro-Kurdish People's Labor Party (HEP) founded in Turkey.

Aug. 2, 1990, Iraq invades Kuwait.

Sept. 5, 1990, The Turkish Assembly passes the decree authorizing the government to deploy and send troops to Iraq, according to the decree Turkey would allow foreign troops to be stationed in or pass through Turkish soil for a possible attack against Iraq.

Nov. 29, 1990, UN Security Council passes the Resolution No. 678 authorizing the UN member countries to use all means to force Iraq to withdraw from Kuwait.

1991, Mesopotamian Cultural Center, founded in Istanbul.

Jan. 17, 1991, US-led United Nations multinational forces launches the "Operation Desert Storm" in Iraq. The Gulf War begins

Feb. 25, 1991, Iraq retreats and the Gulf War ends.

Feb. 1991, The Turkish president Ozal asks the Turkish National Assembly to allow the use of the Kurdish language except in the broadcasting, publishing and education systems, and accordingly amend the Decree No. 2932.

March 1991, Kurdish rebellion in Iraq. The revolt was promptly and violently repressed by the Iraqi Army, causing millions of refugees. PKK spokesman hints a welcome to the possibility of federal autonomy solution in Turkey.

March 11, 1991, the Turkish president Ozal announced that the Turkish officials and Iraqi Kurdish leaders were holding talks.

Apr. 5, 1991, UN Security Council passes the Resolution No. 688, condemning the suppression against the Iraqi Shi'ites and Kurdish civilians and decided to establish a no-fly Zone in Iraq. Turkey announces to opening its borders for refugees.

Apr. 10, 1991, Turkish Army enters into Iraq to control the large-scale refugee wave.

Apr. 12, 1991, Turkey officially issues a new anti-terror law, expanding the definition of terrorism.

Apr. 17, 1991, The US ground forces enters northern Iraq, followed by the British and French troops, a Kurdish safe zone was established.

May 1991, Turkish troops march 50 km deep into Iraq to combat PKK.

Aug. 1991 Government of Iraq and the Kurds agrees to start negotiations based on the March 1970 agreement.

Aug. 2, 1991, PKK kidnaps 10 German tourists in south east Turkey. The Turkish Army marches 16 km deep into Iraq to combat PKK. The Iraqi Kurds condemn Turkey's aggression, but demand PKK not to use their territory to attack Turkey.

Oct. 1991, Turkey launches another military action, and bombs Kurdish villages in northern Iraq. General Elections in Turkey, True Path Party led by Mr Demirel wins the elections with 27.3% of the vote and forms a coalition Government with SHP. In the elections pro-Kurdish HEP and the SHP make an election coalition, Kurds gain 22 seats in the Assembly.

437

October 23, 1991, Iraqi Government and state's administrative bodies unilaterally withdraw from Iraq's Kurdish region.

Nov. 1991, In an interview Ocalan expresses his willingness to accept federal autonomy solution. Demirel becomes prime minister of Turkey, saying that Turkey recognizes the Kurdish reality.

Dec. 1991, Turkey allows the publication of the first Kurdish newspaper Rojname.

1992, Kurdish Institute is founded in Istanbul.

Apr. 1992, Turkey partly lifts the ban on the Kurdish language and allows of Kurdish in the radio and television broadcasting. Also schools are allowed to use Kurdish as a second language.

May 19, 1992, Council elections of the Iraqi Kurdish Region, KDP and PUK respectively won 51 and 49 seats, a coalition government is formed by the two victorious parties.

June 1992, Coached ad promoted by United States, Iraqi anti-government factions founded an umbrella organization, the Iraqi National Congress, to fight against Saddam Hussein's rule KDP and PUK join the Iraqi National Congress and become its major forces.

June 4, 1992, Iraqi Kurdish Regional Assembly is founded.

July 4, 1992, Iraqi Kurdish regional government, or KRG, is founded.

Sept. 1992, PKK kills 40 village guards in Van province, attacks Turkish Army in Tasdelen, killing 20 soldiers. The Democratic Party of Turkish Kurdistan or Bakur faction was founded. Its original name was Hevgırtın-PDK.

Sept. 17, 1992, General Secretary of KDP-Iran Sadegh Sharafkandi and three others was assassinated in Berlin.

Oct. 4, 1992, Iraqi Kurdish Regional Assembly declares Kurdistan to be a federal region of Iraq. Turkey, KDP, PUK jointly attacks PKK in northern Iraq.

Oct. 5-Nov.15, 1992, Turkish Army attacks PKK in Northern Iraq.

Oct. 27, 1992, INC (Iraqi National Congress) is formally founded.

Nov. 14, 1992, Turkish, Iraqi and Iranian leaders and officials meet in Istanbul, they confirmed commitment to maintain the territorial integrity of Iraq and respect Iraq's sovereignty.

March 17, 1993, Ocalan declares a unilateral cease-fire from March 21 to April 15.

Apr. 17, 1993, Turkish President Ozal suddenly dies.

May 1993, In Turkey, Members of the Turkish People's Labor Party, (HEP), establishes the Democratic Party, (DEP). Demirel, a hardliner, center-right leader elected as the Turkish president.

May 24, 1993, PKK declares the suspension of the unilateral ceasefire, attacks a military vehicle in Bingol province, 35 soldiers were killed.

July 1993, HEP is banned by the Turkish Constitutional Court.

Dec. 1993, PUK and Islamic extremists engage military clashes in the northern Iraq.

1994-1998, The 2 main partners of the government in the Iraqi Kurdish region. KDP and PUK engage a mutual war and deterrence. March 1994, 13 Kurdish deputies were deprived of their legal immunity rights in Turkey.

June 16, 1994, Turkish Constitutional Court out laws pro-Kurdish Democratic Party (DEP), and several party members were arrested., several HEP deputies established the People's Democratic Party, (HADEP).

Dec 1994, Six former Kurdish deputies sentenced to 15 years in prison.

1995, Leyla Zana, former Kurdish deputy was awarded the 1995 Sakharov Prize by the European Assembly.

March 1995, Turkey mobilizes 35.000 troops to attack PKK in Iraq. Intense Kurdish protests in Istanbul.

Kurds launch a series of attacks against Turkish embassies and business buildings in Europe. The INC of Iraq fails as CIA withdraws its support.

Apr. 12, 1995, Turkey's some former Kurdish deputies and Kurdish fugitives in Europe initiates the establishment of the Kurdish Assembly in exile.

Apr. 14, 1995, Security Council passes the Resolution No. 986 to implement the Oil for Food Program for Iraq which allowed Iraq to export a certain amount of oil in order to buy essential medicals and food supplies. Kurds would get 13% of the oil export revenues according to this program.

May 1995, Kurdish television station MED-TV began broadcasting targeting Turkish Kurds.

July 1995, Turkey mobilizes 30.000 troops to fight PKK in Iraq.

Aug. 1995, PKK attacks KDP in Northern Iraq.

Oct. 1995, under internal and external pressures, Turkey amends the 8th clause of the Anti-terror Law 8 concerning anti-government propaganda.

Dec. 1995, HADEP participates in the Turkish general elections, becoming the first Kurdish party participating in the election.

Dec. 15, 1995, PKK declares unilateral cease-fire.

May 1996, PKK suspends cease fire.

Aug. 31, 1996, Iraq Army enters into the Kurdish region to help KDP fighting against the KPU, captures and executes many INC members.

Dec. 1996, UN's Oil for Food program officially begins.

Jan.1, 1997, Operation Northern Watch Northern Observation Operation by the western allies, replaces the Operation Provide Comfort, in Northern Iraq.

Apr.1997, Kurdish Assembly in exile passes the resolution to acknowledge the evil role Kurds had played during Armenian and Assyrian massacres in the late Ottoman era; speaker declared: Kurdish cavalry was an accomplice of the Ottoman empire.

Apr. 10, 1997, A German court issues an international arrest warrant of the then incumbent Iranian intelligence minister Farah Sheeran, court has ruled that he had given the order for the assassination of KDP-Iran's leader Sadegh Sharafkandi and other leaders.

May 1997, Turkish troops attack PKK guerrillas in northern Iraq.

June 1997, Turkish Military launches a soft coup. The Islamic Welfare Party coalition government collapses.

Aug. 1997, Moderate reformist cleric Mohammad Khatami selected as the president of Iran, Sept. 1997, Turkish troops enter northern Iraq.

Oct. 1997, Turkey announces its support for the establishment of the no-fly zone in Northern Iraq.

Oct. 24, 1997, Democratic People's Party, (DEHAP,) founded in Turkey.

Jan. 1998, Turkish Constitutional Court bans the Islamist Welfare Party.

Feb. 20, 1998, UN Security Council passes the Resolution No. 1153 to increase the Iraqi oil export quotas.

May 1998, some former members of the Welfare Party founds the Islamist Moral Party.

Aug. 1, 1998, Ocalan declares unilateral cease-fire.

Sept. 17, 1998, with the mediation of United States, KDP and PUK reaches an agreement in Washington.

Oct. 1998, Turkey stations large number of troops at the Syrian border to force Syrian government to expel Ocalan and close PKK camps. Syria expels Ocalan under pressure. The US Congress passes the Iraqi Liberation Law, granting 97 Million US Dollars to support the Iraqi opposition parties including Kurdish parties.

Oct.-Nov. 1998, Turkish troops cross the border into Iraq for several military operations against PKK. Nov. 1998-Feb. 1999, Ocalan flees Syria for Europe. He issues a statement through his lawyer, condemning terrorism and violence and proposes the Seven-point Peace Plan.

Feb. 1999, Clinton administration decides to fund 7 Iraqi opposition groups, including the KDP, PUK, and the Iraqi Kurdish Islamic Movement party.

Feb. 15, 1999, with the help of US and Israeli intelligence agencies, Ocalan is captured by the Turkish Special Forces in Kenya. Subsequently, massive Kurdish protests held in Europe and the Middle East.

Apr. 1999, HADEP participates in the Turkish general elections, winning 4.75% of the total votes.

May 1999, Pro-PKK Kurdish National Congress (KNC/KNK) is established to replace the Kurdish Assembly in exile.

May 31, 1999, Turkish State Security Court began the formal trial of Abdullah Ocalan. Ocalan expressed his repentance for PKK's past actions and his willingnes to dedicate himself to the peace process.

June 29, 1999, Ocalan sentenced to death by the Turkish court on the charge of treason.

July 1999, Kurdish television station MEDYA-TV began broadcasting targeting Turkey.

Sept. 1, 1999, Ocalan declares a cease-fire from prison, calls on PKK to cease the armed struggle, and withdraw armed forces from the Turkish territory.

Jan. 2000, Turkish government announces the postponement of Ocalan's death penalty, due to pressure from the, European Court of Human Rights.

Jan. 17, 2000, Turkish police raided several houses and arrested the leaders of Sunni-Islamist Hezbollah-Turkey, Hezbollah leader captured dead.

June 2000, President Hafez al-Assad dies. His son, Bashar al-Assad succeeded him. The Morality Party banned by the Turkish Constitutional Court. Some former members founded the Islamic Saadet Party.

Sept. and Dec. 2000, PUK attacks the PKK fighters in northern Iraq.

Dec. 15, 2000, European Court of Human Rights accepts Ocalan's appeal.

Feb. 18, 2001, a Christian politbüro member of the Iraqi KDP Francis Hariri assassinated by an Islamist extremist organization.

Aug. 14, 2001, pro-Islamic Turkish Justice and Development Party (AKP) is founded by Tayyip Erdogan.

Sept. 2001, armed conflicts began between PUK and Islamic extremists.

Feb. 2002, PKK changes its name as the Kurdistan Freedom Democratic Congress, (KADEK), consequently, announced to halt guerilla warfare and its new strategy to achieve political goals through peaceful means.

Aug. 2002, Ecevit led coalition government in Turkey introduces new decrees allowing the use of non-Turkish languages in radio and television broadcasting. A new decree allows private schools to teach non-Turkish languages. The Turkish National Assembly amends the Criminal Law including the abolition of the death penalty. US government invites Massoud Barzani, Jalal Talabani, and the INC President Ahmed Chalabi and other three Iraqi opposition group leaders to meet in Washington to draw up a strategy for overthrowing Saddam.

Sept. 2002, Turkey officially announces the abolition of the death penalty.

Oct. 5, 2002, Iraqi Kurdish Regional Assembly resumes its works after years of suspension, in the first meeting the Assembly reaffirms to maintain the Kurdish Federal Autonomous Region.

Oct. 2002 Turkish court changes Ocalan's death sentence to life imprisonment.   441

Nov. 3, 2002, General elections in Turkey, AKP gains landslide victory winning nearly two-thirds of the total seats, achieves to form a single-party government, thus the Turkey's coalition government period since 1987 ends. Pro-Kurdish DEHAP wins 6% of the votes.

Nov. 30, 2002, Turkey announces the abolition of state of emergency status in the Southeastern cities.

Dec. 14-17, 2002, the Iraqi opposition holds a meeting in London to discuss the post-war political arrangements in Iraq, the meeting announced that the post-war Iraq would become a democratic federal republic.

March 2003, AKP chairman Recep Tayyip Erdogan becomes the prime minister of Turkey.

March 1, 2003, Turkish Assembly rejects the NATO motion to allow the US troops to use Turkish territory to attacks Iraq.

March 12, 2003, European Court of Human Rights,rules Ocalan's trial as unfair.

March 13, 2003, Turkish Constitutional Court outlaws DEHAP.

March 17, 2003, US President George W. Bush issues a 48-hours ultimatum to Saddam demanding to step down.

March 18, 2003, Saddam refused the US ultimatum.

March 20, 2003, US and British forces launches the so-called "Operation Iraqi Freedom". The II. Iraq War begins. The Iraqi Kurdish militants actively cooperate with the US forces and carry out operations in northern Iraq.

March 28, 2003, UN Security Council passes the resolution to reform the implementation and adjustment of the oil-for-food program in Iraq.

Apr. 9, 2003, Saddam Hussein's rule was overthrown. The pro- Kurdish retired American lieutenant general Jay Garner is appointed as the chief civilian executive officially responsible for overseeing Iraq's post-war political and economic reconstruction.

May 5, 2003, General Garner meets with Massoud Barzani, Jalal Talabani, and other Iraqi opposition leaders.

May 6, 2003, US President George W. Bush formally appoints former US diplomat Paul Bremer as the presidential envoy to replace Jay Garner.

July 13, 2003, The Interim Management Committee, agency responsible for the temporary management of state affairs in Iraq is established. 25 members include Talabani, Massoud Barzani and other three independent Kurds. Talabani and Barzani were among the nine members of the executive governing body, which will implement a monthly-rotating presidency.

Aug. 5, 2003, Turkish Assembly passes the Reintegration Law, issuing amnesty for possible surrendering PKK members.

Oct. 2003, Kurdish Democratic Freedom Congress Party announces its dissolution, and the party is given a new name Kurdish People's Assembly (KONGRA-GEL).

Nov. 2003, Paul Bremer, American chief executive official for the Iraqi Administrative Affairs, and Jalal Talabani, as the rotating president of the Iraqi Interim Executive Management Committee agree on the schedule to transfer of power in Iraq, agreement specifically clarifies Iraq's political transition process.

Dec. 2003, United Nations HCR issues the human rights Assessment Report for Turkey.

Dec. 13, 2003, Saddam Hussein is captured. The Kurdish television station ROJ-TV begins broadcasting.

Feb. 2004, Unofficial referendum held in Iraqi Kurdistan. Kurds almost unanimously agree on the independence of the Kurdish Region.

March 2004, Local elections in Turkey. The AKP wins getting the 42.18% of the votes; AKP wins 1.750 local municipalities.

March 8, 2004, US-led Iraqi Transitional Government Law, also known as the Interim Constitution of Iraq was issued, defining a federal Iraq state. The Law recognized Kurds' regional autonomous rights and endowed them with veto rights in the enactment of the permanent constitution.

March 12, 2004, Protests and armed conflicts in the Syrian city of Qamishli during a football match between Kurdish and Arab football clubs, causing nine civil deaths. Riots in Syria spread to other northern Kurdish cities, causing 65 deaths and 160 injuries, hundreds were arrested.

March 24, 2004, Iranian Kurdistan Free Life Party, or PJAK (attached to Ocalan's PKK), was founded and held its first congress meeting.

April 2004, Ankara State Security Court sentences former deputies Leyla Zana, Hatip Dicle, Orhan Dogan and Selim Sadak to a 15-years imprisonment on the charges of implementing the instructions of PKK, and inciting separatist activities home and abroad, the four had already been in prison for 10 years.

Apr. 25, 2004, Syrian Kurdish political organizations exiled in Europe held a meeting in Germany, announcing the establishment of the West Kurdistan government in exile.

June 2004, Turkish Prime minister Recep Tayyip Erdogan declared Turkey would insist opposing the Kurdish autonomy in Northern Iraq and claimed Turkey's Kurdish minority policy will not change. The Kurdish Hoshyar Zebari appointed as the Iraqi Foreign Minister.

June 1, 2004, PKK announces the suspension of the cease-fire.

June 7, 2004, Turkish State Television TRT officially begins broadcasting programs in Kurdish.

June 9, 2004, According to an ECHR verdict, Turkey's Supreme Court of Appeal releases Leyla Zana and other three Kurdish politicians.

July 8, 2004, The second Chief of Staff of Turkey's Armed Forces Ilker Basbug claimed: "as long as PKK armed forces are active in Northern Iraq, Turkey will not withdraw its troops."

Sept. 1, 2004, Iraqi Interim National Assembly founded, composed of a total of 100 seats, including 40 Shi'ite seats and 25 seats for the Sunni Arabs and Kurds respectively.

Jan. 2005, The European Court of Human Rights awarded Zana and each of the other defendants €9000 from the Turkish government condemning Turkey for violating Zana's right to free speech.

Jan. 30, 2005, The first post-war elections in Iraq. The Democratic Patriotic Alliance of Kurdistan, wins 75 seats out of the 275 seats in the National Assembly.

March 2005, Ocalan releases his "Kurdistan Democratic Confederation Manifesto".

Apr. 2005, Iraqi Transitional National Assembly elects one Speaker and two Deputy Speakers. A Sunni deputy was elected as the Speaker, two Deputy Speakers came from Kurds and Shiites. The West Kurdistan (Syria) Government in exile announces the establishment of the first Kurdish radio and television stations in London. Rojava Radio begins broadcasting 24 hours a day, ROJ-TV begins broadcasting one hour per week.

Apr. 6, 2005, PUK President Talabani, elected as President of Iraq, becomes the first Kurdish President in the Iraqi history.

June 2005, In the Assembly elections in the Iraqi Kurdistan Region, Massoud Barzani elected as the President of the KRG.

June 14, 2005, Abdullah Demirbaş, mayor of Sur district in Diyarbakır city is dismissed for providing multilingual services to the citizens.

Aug. 11, 2005, Iraqi Shi'ite leader and President of the Supreme Islamic Council of Iraq (SIIC) Abdul Hakim proposes the establishment of Federal district governments in the southern Shi'ite regions.

Aug. 17, 2005, Kurdish political movement Democratic Society Movement,(DTH), and the DEHAP party merge to form the Democratic Society Party (DTP).

Aug. 25, 2005, Prime Minister Recep Tayyip Erdogan acknowledges the Kurdish issue in Turkey, declares "a serious error was made in the past which needs to be resolved with more democracy" in order to "democratize Turkey". He was the first Turkish prime minister who admitted that Turkey had made mistakes on the Kurdish issue.

Oct. 2005, Iraqi Permanent Constitution approved by 78% of the votes in the referendum, establishing federal system and autonomy in the Kurdish Region.

Oct. 3, 2005, Turkey starts EU entry negotiations.

Oct. 15, 2005, Iraqi Permanent Constitution approved, stipulating the federal system. The Article 140 stipulated a referendum to decide the sovereignty over Kirkuk region.

Dec. 2005, The Hague-based International Tribunal rules Anfal Campaign as genocide.

Dec. 15, 2005, Based on the new Iraqi constitution, Iraq held its first official National Assembly Election, among which Kurdish Coalition List composing from KDP and PUK and others win 53 seats in the 275 seat Assembly. The formation of the Iraqi KSG completed. Massoud Barzani's nephew Idris Barzani becomes the Regional prime minister.

2006, Iranian Kurdish United Front, founded, advocating to achieve Kurdish rights through peaceful means. Senior leaders of the KDP-Iran and the Kurdistan Workers' Revolutionary Organization (Komalah) visit United States. The Syrian Kurdish Assembly in Exile, or the KNAS, founded.

Jan. 2006, KDP and PUK agrees to strengthen their cooperation on the basis of partnership, equality and consensus, reunify the KRG and relevant agencies to promote political, economic and social development in the Kurdish region.

March 8, 2006, Turkey allows the private radio stations to broadcast in Kurdish.

March 17, 2006, Protests in the Iraqi Kurdistan district of Halabja against the corruption of KRG.

Apr. 22, 2006, Jalal Talabani re-elected as the Iraqi President. The Kurdish leader Hoshyar Zebari remains as the Foreign Minister, while Kurdish leader Barham Salih becomes the deputy prime minister.

May 7, 2006, Existing sub-regional governments in Iraqi Kurdistan begin to merge, with the exceptions of four sub-provinces. Idris Barzani sworn as the regional Prime Minister after the reunification.

May 20, 2006, Nouri al-Maliki was elected as the Iraqi Prime Minister, with the support of the Kurds.

July 2006, Iraqi Kurdistan Assembly passes the Investment Law.

Aug. 28, 2006, US State Department announces the appointment of General Joseph Ralston as the US government special envoy to communicate with the PKK, responsible for the coordination with Turkey, Iraq and KRG.

Oct. 1, 2006, PKK announces the 5th ceasefire.

Dec. 2006, Former Iraqi President Saddam Hussein trialed for the Anfal massacre, and sentenced to death on the charges of genocide. The Iraq Study Group, led by former US Secretary of State and Republican member of the US Senate James Baker, as well as former Democratic member of the Senate Lee Hamilton, publishes the policy report on Iraq, calling on the Kurds to compromise and cooperate with the Iraqi central government.

Dec. 6, 2006, Senior leader of PUK, Nashirwan Mustafa criticizes the corruption and monopoly of the KRG and PUK, and quits PUK to found the Gorran Movement.

June 2007, Turkish troops cross the border into Iraq to strike the PKK militants and bombs their camps. Former Iraqi officials Majid and two others were charged with war crimes, crimes against humanity and genocide, sentenced to death.

July 22, 2007, General elections in Turkey, AKP wins 341 seats and independently forms a cabinet. The Democratic Society Party (DTP) wins 27 seats, becoming the first pro-Kurdish political party in the National Assembly since 1994, and becomes the third largest opposition party.

Sept. 2007, Iraqi Kurdish Regional Assembly passes the Oil and Gas Law.

Oct. 7, 2007, PKK ambushes a Turkish army patrol in Hakkari province, killing 15 and wounding 3. In retaliation, Turkish Assembly renews the decree to allow the Turkish army to cross the border into the Iraqi territory to combat the PKK.

Oct. 21, 2007, PKK attacks a Turkish army checkpoint, killing 12, wounding 17, and capturing 8 Turkish soldiers. Subsequently, Turkish Army retaliates by killing 32 PKK guerillas.

Oct. 24, 2007, Turkish Army shells PKK camps in northern Iraq.

Dec. 16, 2007, Turkish Army launches continuous air strikes against PKK camps in northern Iraq.

Dec. 31, 2007, Kirkuk referendum indefinitely postponed.

Feb. 21, 2008, Turkish Army launches a large-scale military operation code-named "Sun" against the PKK across the Iraqi border.

Apr. 2008, Leyla Zana sentenced to 2 years in prison for mentioning Ocalan, Massoud Barzani and Talabani as the three Kurdish leaders in her speech. 445

Aug. 2008, Iraqi Kurdish armed forces clashes with the pro-government Kurdish militia.

Sept. 10, 2008, Syrian President Bashar Assad issues the Decree No. 49, which further restricts the sale of properties in some border areas, including the Kurdish regions. Kurds regard this move as another discrimination.

Oct. 14, 2008, Kurdish Assembly passes the resolution that accuses Turkey for genocide in the Dersim uprising.

2009, Bilgi University in Istanbul opened Kurdish courses. The Artuklu University in Mardin became the first university to offer postgraduate programs on the Kurdish language.

Jan. 1, 2009, The Turkish government allows the TRT-6 to broadcast in Kurdish for 24 hours a week.

Jan. 31, 2009, Provincial Elections in Iraq, except the Kurdish Region and Kirkuk.

March 2009, Syrian Kurdish Assembly in Exile sent a letter to US Vice President Joe Biden, condemning Syrian government's long-term and systematic persecution of the Kurds, the denial of Kurdish rights and requesting Obama administration to focus on the persecuted Kurds, and demanded US Government's help in promoting democracy in Syria.

March 29, 2009, Local elections in Turkey. The Democratic Society Party (DTP) wins 5.4% of the vote, increasing their mayor posts from 4 to 8, the number of mayors from 32 to 51, including 9 big cities. Osman Baydemir was re-elected as the Mayor of Diyarbakır city.

Apr. 2009, UN report recommends the temporary suspension of the Iraqi Constitution Article 140, and suggests postponing of the Kirkuk referendum.

Apr. 13, 2009, PKK declares a ceasefire. Ocalan calls on the PKK to stop guerilla operations paving the way for peace.

May 2009, Turkish Head of State Abdullah Gul says: "Whether you call it terrorism or not, southeastern Anatolia issue or the Kurdish issue, this is a priority for Turkey, and the most pressing problem. Now Turkey is faced with a historical opportunity to solve the problem."

June 2009, Iraqi Kurdish Regional Assembly approves the Kurdistan Regional Constitution.

July 2009, Erdogan government launches the "solution process" for the resolution of the Kurdish issue.

July 25, 2009, Legislative and Regional presidential elections held in the Iraqi Kurdistan. Massoud Barzani re-elected as president with nearly 70% of the votes, while PUK Barrhamm Saleh becomes the regional prime minister.

Aug. 2009, Prime Minister Nouri al-Maliki visits Arbil (Kirkuk), his first official visit to the Kurdish Autonomous Region since he took office.

Aug. 15, 2009, Ocalan announces a comprehensive peace proposal at the 25th anniversary of the Kurdish uprising.

Sept. 2009, Turkish Radio and Television control institution decides to further relax the restrictions on private radio and television stations which broadcast in Kurdish. Under the new regulations, private televisions could broadcast Kurdish programs 24 hours likeTRT-6.

Sept. 2009, Iranian Army starts military operation against PJAK (pro-PKK), and PJAK declares cease-fire.

Oct. 2009, Erdogan re-elected as AKP chairman.

Oct. 6, 2009, Turkish Grand National Assembly passes the proposal submitted by the government to extend the time limit of the cross-border operations, with 452 to 23 votes.

Dec. 11, 2009, Turkish Constitutional Court decides to outlaw the Democratic Society Party, (DTP). Large number of party members were arrested. Kurdish protests broke out in many Turkish cities.

Dec. 2009, The south-eastern municipal authorities decide to use Kurdish language together with the Turkish in water bills, marriage certificates, building and road signs, first aid, social and cultural notifications. Kurdish also began to be used in Imam's Friday Prayers sermon and in price tags.

March 4, 2010, Belgian police raids ROJ-TV and arrests its staff members.

March 7, 2010, National Assembly elections in Iraq. The Kurdish coalition list mainly composed of KDP and PUK receives equal votes with the Arab-Turkmen alliance in Kirkuk elections.

Apr. 11, 2010, Turkey amends Political Party Law, allowing the political parties to use non-Turkish propaganda materials in the elections.

May 2010, Turkish Assembly passes a package of constitutional amendments.

May 1, 2010, PKK announces the suspension of cease-fire and attacks Dersim province.

May 31, 2010, Ocalan announces that the efforts to seek reconciliation through dialogue has failed declaring "PKK has a free hand now".

June 29, 2010, the Turkish Assembly passes new Anti-terror Law to prohibit the prosecution of minors under the age of 18 and decreases the punishments on the illegal demonstrations and rallies.

July 21, 2010, PKK leader Murat Karayılan announces: "if the government is willing to resolve the Kurdish issue through dialogue, PKK is ready to lay down the arms; otherwise we will continue the fight for a free Kurdistan".

Aug. 12, 2010, PKK declares a unilateral ceasefire during Ramadan.

Sept. 12, 2010, The constitutional amendment referendum proposed by Erdogan was held and was approved with 58.2 % of the votes.

Oct. 2010, Turkish Government confirmed that a dialogue was being held between the Turkish government representatives and Ocalan

Nov. 2010, Jalal Talabani re-elected as President of Iraq.

2011, School of Oriental Languages founded in the Kurdish language and literature department of the Artuklu University, becoming the first undergraduate Kurdish teaching unit in Turkey.

Feb. 28, 2011, Three PKK guerillas were shot to death while attempting to enter Turkey across the border from northern Iraq, causing massive protests in Turkey.

March 2011, A Turkish court ruled that the suppression of the Kurdish Dersim uprising event was not a genocide.

March 14, 2011, PKK guerilla funerals in the Turkish city of Nusaybin grew into a large-scale riot, many people were injured, 700 people under custody.

March 31, 2011, Syrian President Bashar al-Assad ordered the establishment of a special committee to resolve the problems caused by the 1962 Jazira census, requesting the Commission to submit a report to President before April 15.

March 24, 2011, Pro-Kurdish Peace and Democracy Party publicly announced immediate civil disobedience protests in Turkey.

Apr. 2011, Syrian President Bashar al-Assad announced that the Kurdish New Year would be listed as a public holiday from 2012 on.

Apr. 7, 2011, Syrian President Bashar al-Assad issued a decree, granting the people of Eastern Hasaka region the Syrian nationality, which fundamentally solved the issue of stateless Kurds in Syria.

Apr. 19, 2011, Turkish Supreme Electoral Council disqualified 12 Kurdish politicians from being candidates in the coming general elections. This decision triggered widespread protests.

June 26, 2011, Large-scale protests in Istanbul against the Supreme Electoral Council's decision disqualifying the newly elected Kurdish deputy, Hatip Dicle. Protests have escalated to violent clashes.

Aug. 17, 2011, Turkish army launched multiple attacks on PKK camps in northern Iraq, bombed 132 targets.

Oct. 19, 2011, PKK simultaneously launched eight attacks in the (Colemerg) Hakkari province, killing 26 soldiers and wounding 18. Prime minister Recep Tayyip Erdogan urges for retaliation.

Oct. 20, 2011, Turkish Army deployed 22 battalions to wipe out PKK in 5 regions on the border areas between Turkey and Iraq.

Oct. 26, 2011, 11 Kurdish organizations founded the Syrian Kurdish National Committee (KNC).

Nov. 2011, Turkish Prime Minister Recep Tayyip Erdogan publicly apologized for the Kurdish victims of the Dersim massacre on behalf of the state.

March 19, 2012, Over 100,000 Kurds celebrated the Kurdish New Year in Turkey, clashes occurred between the protestors and the police, numerous people were injured.

Apr. 2012, President of the KRG Massoud Barzani publicly criticized Iraqi Prime Minister Nouri al-Maliki for constructing a dictatorship.

May 6, 2012, By the invitation of US State Department, a senior delegation of the Syrian Kurdish National Committee visited Washington.

July-Aug. 2012, Syrian Kurds establish control in the Kurdish region. Syrian troops withdrew.

Dec. 2013, Turkish Prime Minister Recep Tayyip Erdogan publicly admits that the Government has been secretly negotiating with PKK leaders.

March 21, 2013, Turkish Government and PKK leader Ocalan reaches a peace agreement plan after secret negotiations, announcing the withdrawal of PKK.

May 8, 2013, The first batch of PKK guerillas began to withdraw from Turkey to Northern Iraq.

May 14, 2013, The first batch of 13 PKK guerillas entered into Iraq fulfilling the promise.

Appendix 2

1. Main Points of the Treaty of Sèvres (abridged translation)

The Treaty of Sèvres was signed on August 10, 1920, between the defeated Ottoman Empire by its Prime Minister Rıza Tevfik, the grand vizier Damat Ferid Pasha, and ambassador Hadi Pasha, and the minister of education Reşid Halis, who were endorsed by Sultan Mehmed VI. Sir George Dixon Grahame signed for Great Britain, Alexandre Millerand for France, and Count Lelio Bonin Longare for Italy. The treaty solidified the partitioning of the Ottoman Empire, in accord with secret agreements among the Allied Powers. Thrace (Trakya), up to the Chatalja line, islands of Imbros and Tenedos, and the islands of Marmara was ceded to Greece. The sea line of these islands was declared international and left to administration of "Zone of (water) Straits." According to the provisions of the Treaty, Smyrna (Izmir) in the Western Anotolia (Minor Asia) was to be administered by a local parliament and it also gave the people of Smyrna the chance of a plebiscite after five years (in 1925) on whether they wished to join Greece as opposed to remaining in the Ottoman Empire. This plebiscite would be overseen by the League of Nations. Italy was confirmed in the possession of the Dodecanese Islands (Aegean islands) which were already under Italian occupation since the Italo-Turkish War of 1911-1912.

The Ottoman Army was to be restricted to 45000 men. Italy was confirmed in the possession of the Dodecanese Islands (Aegean islands) which were already under Italian occupation since the Italo-Turkish War of 1911-1912, Allied Powers would not seize Constantinople (Istanbul) which would be the capital of Turkey (Ottoman state).

This treaty altogether consisted of 433 articles, among which many involve the Kurdish nation, the treaty also recognized self-determination right of the Kurdish nation. Treaty of Sèvres was the first important international convention which recognized the Kurdish question.

The 27th article of the Treaty defined the Turkish (Ottoman) borders. Point 1 defined the European borders of Turkey (Ottoman). Point 2 defined the Asia boundaries of Turkey (Ottoman) as follows: (Ottoman) in Asia.

a) On the West and South: From the entrance of the Bosphorus into the Sea of Marmora to a point described below, situated in the eastern Mediterranean Sea in the neighbourhood of the Gulf of Alexandretta near Karatash Burun the Sea of Marmora, the Dardanelles, and the Eastern Mediterranean Sea; the islands of the Sea of Marmora, and those which are situated within a distance of 3 miles from the coast, remaining Turkish....

b) Border with Syria

c) Border with Mesopotamia: Thence in a general easterly direction to a point to be chosen on the northern boundary of the vilayet of Mosul, a line to be fixed on the ground; thence eastwards to the point where it meets the frontier between Ottoman Turkey and Persia, the northern boundary of the vilayet (province) of Mosul, modified, however, so as to pass south of Amadia.

d) Borders on the East and the North East:

From the point above defined to the Black Sea, the existing frontier between Turkey and Persia, then the former frontier between Turkey and Russia.

Section III of the Sevres Treaty deals with Kurdistan under the Article Nr. 62.

The Article Nr. 62 stipulates a Commission sitting at Constantinople (capital Istanbul) and composed of three members appointed by the British, French and Italian Governments respectively. This commission shall draft within six months from the coming into force of the present Treaty a scheme of local autonomy for the predominantly Kurdish areas lying east of the Euphrates, south of the southern boundary of Armenia as it may be hereafter determined, and north of the frontier of Turkey with Syria and Mesopotamia, as defined in Article 27, II (2) and (3). The draft (scheme) shall contain full safeguards for the protection of the Assyro-Chaldeans and other racial or religious minorities within these areas, and with this goal a Commission composed of British, French, Italian, Persian and Kurdish representatives shall visit the region to examine and decide what rectifications, if any, should be made in the Turkish frontier where, under the provisions of the present Treaty, that frontier coincides with that of Persia.

The Article Nr. 63 says: The Turkish (Ottoman) Government hereby agrees to accept and execute the decisions of both the Commissions mentioned in the Article 62 above within three months from their communication to the said Government.

The Article Nr. 64 says: If within one year from the coming into force of this present Treaty the Kurdish peoples within the areas defined in Article 62 shall address themselves to the Council of the League of Nations in such a manner as to show that a majority of the population of these areas desires independence from Turkey, and if the Council of the League of Nations then considers that these Kurdish peoples are capable of such independence and recommends that it should be granted to them, (Ottoman) Turkey hereby agrees to execute such a recommendation, and accepts to renounce all rights and title over these areas.

The detailed provisions for such renunciation by Turkey will form the subject of a separate agreement between the Principal Allied Powers and Turkey.

If and when such renunciation takes place, no objection will be raised by the Principal Allied Powers to the voluntary adhesion to such an independent Kurdish State of the Kurds inhabiting that part of Kurdistan which has hitherto been included in the Mosul vilayet (province).

2. President Woodrow Wilson's Fourteen Points

The speech made by President Woodrow Wilson on January 8, 1918 mainly covers the following:

It will be our wish and purpose that the processes of peace, when they are begun, shall be absolutely open and that they shall involve and permit henceforth no secret understandings of any kind. The day of conquest and aggrandizement is gone by; so is also the day of secret covenants entered into in the interest of particular governments and likely at some unlooked-for moment to upset the peace of the world. It is this happy fact, now clear to the view of every public man whose thoughts do not still linger in an age that is dead and gone, which makes it possible for every nation whose purposes are consistent with justice and the peace of the world to avow nor or at any other time the objects it has in view.

We entered this war because violations of right had occurred which touched us to the quick and made the life of our own people impossible unless they were corrected and the world secure once for all against their recurrence. What we demand in this war, therefore, is nothing peculiar to ourselves. It is that the world be made fit and safe to live in; and particularly that it be made safe for every peace-loving nation which, like our own, wishes to live its own life, determine its own institutions, be assured of justice and fair dealing by the other peoples of the world as against force and selfish aggression. All the peoples of the world are in effect partners in this interest, and for our own part we see very clearly that unless justice be done to others it will not be done to us. The programme of the world's peace, therefore, is our programme; and that programme, the only possible programme, as we see it, is this:

I. Open covenants of peace, openly arrived at, after which there shall be no private international understandings of any kind but diplomacy shall proceed always frankly and in the public view.

II. Absolute freedom of navigation upon the seas, outside territorial waters, alike in peace and in war, except as the seas may be closed in whole or in part by international action for the enforcement of international covenants.

III. The removal, so far as possible, of all economic barriers and the establishment of an equality of trade conditions among all the nations consenting to the peace and associating themselves for its maintenance.

IV. Adequate guarantees given and taken that national armaments will be reduced to the lowest point consistent with domestic safety.

V. A free, open-minded, and absolutely impartial adjustment of all colonial claims, based upon a strict observance of the principle that in determining all such questions of sovereignty the interests of the populations concerned must have equal weight with the equitable claims of the government whose title is to be determined.

VI. The evacuation of all Russian territory and such a settlement of all questions affecting Russia as will secure the best and freest cooperation of the other nations of the world in obtaining for her an unhampered and unembarrassed opportunity for the independent determination of her own political development and national policy and assure her of a sincere welcome into the society of free nations under institutions of her own choosing; and, more than a welcome, assistance also of every kind that she may need and may herself desire. The treatment accorded Russia by her sister nations in the months to come will be the acid test of their good will, of their comprehension of her needs as distinguished from their own interests, and of their intelligent and unselfish sympathy.

VII. Belgium, the whole world will agree, must be evacuated and restored, without any attempt to limit the sovereignty which she enjoys in common with all other free nations. No other single act will serve as this will serve to restore confidence among the nations in the laws which they have themselves set and determined for the government of their relations with one another. Without this healing act the whole structure and validity of international law is forever impaired.

VIII. All French territory should be freed and the invaded portions restored, and the wrong done to France by Prussia in 1871 in the matter of Alsace-Lorraine, which has unsettled the peace of the world for nearly fifty years, should be righted, in order that peace may once more be made secure in the interest of all.

IX. A readjustment of the frontiers of Italy should be effected along clearly recognizable lines of nationality.

X. The peoples of Austria-Hungary, whose place among the nations we wish to see safeguarded and assured, should be accorded the freest opportunity to autonomous development.

XI. Rumania, Serbia, and Montenegro should be evacuated; occupied territories restored; Serbia accorded free and secure access to the sea; and the relations of the several Balkan states to one another determined by friendly counsel along historically established lines of allegiance and nationality; and international guarantees of the political and economic independence and territorial integrity of the several Balkan states should be entered into.

XII. The Turkish portion of the present Ottoman Empire should be assured a secure sovereignty, but the other nationalities which are now under Turkish rule should be assured an undoubted security of life and an absolutely unmolested opportunity of autonomous development, and the Dardanelles should be permanently opened as a free passage to the ships and commerce of all nations under international guarantees.

XIII. An independent Polish state should be erected which should include the territories inhabited by indisputably Polish populations, which should be assured a free and secure access to the sea, and whose political and economic independence and territorial integrity should be guaranteed by international covenant.

XIV. A general association of nations must be formed under specific covenants for the purpose of affording mutual guarantees of political independence and territorial integrity to great and small states alike.

In regard to these essential rectifications of wrong and assertions of right we feel ourselves to be intimate partners of all the governments and peoples associated together against the Imperialists. We cannot be separated in interest or divided in purpose. We stand together until the end.

For such arrangements and covenants we are willing to fight and to continue to fight until they are achieved; but only because we wish the right to prevail and desire a just and stable peace such as can be secured only by removing the chief provocations to war, which this programme does remove. We have no jealousy of German greatness, and there is nothing in this programme that impairs it. We grudge her no achievement or distinction of learning or of pacific enterprise such as have made her record very bright and very enviable. We do not wish to injure her or to block in any way her legitimate influence or power. We do not wish to fight her either with arms or with hostile arrangements of trade if she is willing to associate herself with us and the other peace- loving nations of the world in covenants of justice and law and fair dealing. We wish her only to accept a place of equality among the peoples of the world, the new world in which we now live, instead of a place of mastery.

3. National Anthem of Republic of Mahabad in Iran (Republic of Kurdistan in Iran) 453

Short lived Republic of Mahabad was declared in 1946 and its total destruction occurred in 1947. Ey Reqip is the Kurdish national anthem of Republic of

Mahabad in Iran. Later this anthem has widely spread in Kurdish regions and was used officially, by many Kurdish Political parties. It was written by the Kurdish poet and political activist, Dildar in 1938, while in jail. "Ey Reqîb" means "Oh, Enemy" or "Hey Enemy", in reference to the jail guards in the prison where Dildar was held and tortured and who also symbolized the occupying countries of Turkey, Iraq and Syria "Ey Reqîb" has been adopted by the Iraqi Kurdistan Regional Government as the official national anthem of the federal south Kurdistan.

Hey Enemy (Ey Reqip)

I

Oh, enemy! The Kurdish people live on,
They have not been crushed by the weapons of any time
Let no one say Kurds are dead, they are living
They live and never shall we lower our flag

II

We are descendants of the red banner of the revolution
Look at our past, how bloody it is
Let no one say Kurds are dead, they are living
They live and never shall we lower our flag

III

The Kurdish youth rise bravely,
With their blood they colored the crown of life
Let no one say Kurds are dead, they are living
They live and never shall we lower our flag

IV

We are the descendants of the Medes and Cyaxares
Kurdistan is our religion, our credo,
Let no one say Kurds are dead, they are living
They live and never shall we lower our flag

V

The Kurdish youth are ready and prepared,
To give their life as the supreme sacrifice
Let no one say Kurds are dead, they are living
They live and never shall we lower our flag.

4. Algiers Agreement (Accord) between Iran and Iraq – signed in March 6, 1975 (abridged translation)

During the convocation of the during the OPEC Summit Conference in the Algerian capital and upon the initiative of President Houari Boumedienne, Mohammed Reza Pahlavi and Saddam Hussein (Vice-Chairman of the Revolution Command Council) met twice and conducted lengthy talks on the relations between Iraq and Iran. These talks, attended by President Houari Boumedienne, were characterized by complete frankness and a sincere will from both parties to reach a final and permanent solution of all problems existing between the two countries in accordance with the principles of territorial integrity, border inviolability and non-interference in internal affairs. The agreement includes the following articles:

The two esteemed Parties have decided to:

1) Carry out a final delineation of their land boundaries in accordance with the Constantinople (Istanbul) Protocol of 1913 and the Proceedings of the Border Delimitation Commission of 1914. (protocol of Constantinople)

2) Agree to Demarcate their river boundaries according to the Thalweg line [meaning the median course of the Shatt al-Arab waterway].

3) Both parties will accordingly, shall restore security and mutual confidence along their joint borders. They shall also commit themselves to carry out a strict and effective observation of their joint borders so as to put an end to all infiltrations of a subversive nature wherever they may come from.

4) Both parties have also agreed to consider the aforesaid arrangements as inseparable elements of a comprehensive solution. Consequently, any infringement of one of its components shall naturally contradict the spirit of the Algiers Accord. The two parties shall remain in constant contact with President Houari

Boumedienne who shall provide, when necessary, Algeria's brotherly assistance whenever needed in order to apply these resolutions.

5) The two parties have decided to restore the traditional ties of good neighbourliness and friendship, in particular by eliminating all negative factors in their relations and through constant exchange of views on issues of mutual interest and promotion of mutual co-operation.

The two parties officially declare that the region ought to be secure from any foreign interference.

5. Security Council Resolution Nr 687 of the United Nations

On April 3, 1991, the UN Security Council adopted the No. 687 resolution, the content mainly included the following:

Iraq should unconditionally remove and destroy all chemical and biological weapons and ballistic missiles with a range greater than 150km. As part of this demand, the Council requested Iraq submit, within 15 days, a report declaring all locations of all the aforementioned weapons and agree to urgent, on-site inspections. It then established the United Nations Special Commission relating to inspections and set provisions for it, and asked Iraq to abide by its obligations under the Nuclear Non-Proliferation Treaty, agreeing not to develop nuclear weapons and submitting a report to the Secretary-General and International Atomic Energy Agency. Resolution 687 forced Iraq to repatriations and compensation, stating that Iraq is liable for any loss, damage, and injury inflicted upon Kuwait, further demanding that Iraq hand over any remaining property seized from Kuwait during the Persian Gulf War.

The full text is given below:

Resolution Adopted by the Security Council at its 2981st meeting, on 3 April 1991

The Security Council, Recalling its resolutions 660 (1990) of 2 August 1990, 661 (1990) of 6 August 1990, 662 (1990) of 9 August 1990, 664 (1990) of 18 August 1990, 665 (1990) of 25 August 1990, 666 (1990) of 13 September 1990, 667 (1990) of 16 September 1990, 669 (1990) of 24 September 1990, 670 (1990) of 25 September 1990, 674 (1990) of 29 October 1990, 677 (1990) of 28 November 1990, 678 (1990) of 29 November 1990 and 686 (1991) of 2 March 1991,

Welcoming the restoration to Kuwait of its sovereignty, independence and territorial integrity and the return of its legitimate Government,

Affirming the commitment of all Member States to the sovereignty, territorial integrity and political independence of Kuwait and Iraq, and noting the intention expressed by the Member States cooperating with Kuwait under paragraph 2 of resolution 678 (1990) to bring their military presence in Iraq to an end as soon as possible consistent with paragraph 8 of resolution 686 (1991), Reaffirming the need to be assured of Iraq's peaceful intentions in the light of its unlawful invasion and occupation of Kuwait,

Taking note of the letter sent by the Minister for Foreign Affairs of Iraq on 27 February 1991 and those sent pursuant to resolution 686 (1991),

Noting that Iraq and Kuwait, as independent sovereign States, signed at Baghdad on 4 October 1963 "Agreed Minutes Between the State of Kuwait and the Republic of Iraq Regarding the Restoration of Friendly Relations, Recognition and Related Matters", thereby recognizing formally the boundary between Iraq and Kuwait and the allocation of islands, which were registered with the United Nations in accordance with Article 102 of the Charter of the United Nations and in which Iraq recognized the independence and complete sovereignty of the State of Kuwait within its borders as specified and accepted in the letter of the Prime Minister of Iraq dated 21 July 1932, and as accepted by the Ruler of Kuwait in his letter dated 10 August 1932,

Conscious of the need for demarcation of the said boundary, Conscious also of the statements by Iraq threatening to use weapons in violation of its obligations under the Geneva Protocol for the Prohibition of the Use in War of Asphyxiating, Poisonous or Other Gases, and of Bacteriological Methods of Warfare, signed at Geneva on 17 June 1925, and of its prior use of chemical weapons and affirming that grave consequences would follow any further use by Iraq of such weapons,

Recalling that Iraq has subscribed to the Declaration adopted by all States participating in the Conference of States Parties to the 1925 Geneva Protocol and Other Interested States, held in Paris from 7 to 11 January 1989, establishing the objective of universal elimination of chemical and biological weapons,

Recalling also that Iraq has signed the Convention on the Prohibition of the Development, Production and Stockpiling of Bacteriological (Biological) and Toxin Weapons and on Their Destruction, of 10 April 1972,

Noting the importance of Iraq ratifying this Convention,

Noting moreover the importance of all States adhering to this Convention and encouraging its forthcoming Review Conference to reinforce the authority, efficiency and universal scope of the convention,

Stressing the importance of an early conclusion by the Conference on Disarmament of its work on a Convention on the Universal Prohibition of Chemical Weapons and of universal adherence thereto,

Aware of the use by Iraq of ballistic missiles in unprovoked attacks and therefore of the need to take specific measures in regard to such missiles located in Iraq,

Concerned by the reports in the hands of Member States that Iraq has attempted to acquire materials for a nuclear-weapons programme contrary to its obligations under the Treaty on the Non-Proliferation of Nuclear Weapons of 1 July 1968,

Recalling the objective of the establishment of a nuclear-weapons-free zone in the region of the Middle East,

Conscious of the threat that all weapons of mass destruction pose to peace and security in the area and of the need to work towards the establishment in the Middle East of a zone free of such weapons,

Conscious also of the objective of achieving balanced and comprehensive control of armaments in the region,

Conscious further of the importance of achieving the objectives noted above using all available means, including a dialogue among the States of the region,

Noting that resolution 686 (1991) marked the lifting of the measures imposed by resolution 661 (1990) in so far as they applied to Kuwait,

Noting that despite the progress being made in fulfilling the obligations of resolution 686 (1991), many Kuwaiti and third country nationals are still not accounted for and property remains unreturned,

Recalling the International Convention against the Taking of Hostages, opened for signature at New York on 18 December 1979, which categorizes all acts of taking hostages as manifestations of international terrorism,

Deploring threats made by Iraq during the recent conflict to make use of terrorism against targets outside Iraq and the taking of hostages by Iraq,

Taking note with grave concern of the reports of the Secretary-General of 20 March 1991 and 28 March 1991, and conscious of the necessity to meet urgently the humanitarian needs in Kuwait and Iraq,

Bearing in mind its objective of restoring international peace and security in the area as set out in recent resolutions of the Security Council,

Conscious of the need to take the following measures acting under Chapter VII of the Charter,

1. Affirms all thirteen resolutions noted above, except as expressly changed below to achieve the goals of this resolution, including a formal cease-fire;

A

2. Demands that Iraq and Kuwait respect the inviolability of the international boundary and the allocation of islands set out in the "Agreed Minutes Between the State of Kuwait and the Republic of Iraq Regarding the Restoration of Friendly Relations, Recognition and Related Matters", signed by them in the exercise of their sovereignty at Baghdad on 4 October 1963 and registered with the United Nations and published by the United Nations in document 7063, United Nations, Treaty Series, 1964;

3. Calls upon the Secretary-General to lend his assistance to make arrangements with Iraq and Kuwait to demarcate the boundary between Iraq and Kuwait, drawing on appropriate material, including the map transmitted by Security Council document S/22412 and to report back to the Security Council within one month;

4. Decides to guarantee the inviolability of the above-mentioned international boundary and to take as appropriate all necessary measures to that end in accordance with the Charter of the United Nations;

B

5. Requests the Secretary-General, after consulting with Iraq and Kuwait, to submit within three days to the Security Council for its approval a plan for the immediate deployment of a United Nations observer unit to monitor the Khor Abdullah and a demilitarized zone, which is hereby established, extending ten kilometres into Iraq and five kilometres into Kuwait from the boundary referred to in the "Agreed Minutes Between the State of Kuwait and the Republic of Iraq Regarding the Restoration of Friendly Relations, Recognition and Related Matters" of 4 October 1963; to deter violations of the boundary through its presence in and surveillance of the demilitarized zone; to observe any hostile or potentially hostile action mounted from the territory of one State to the other; and for the Secretary-General to report regularly to the Security Council on the operations of the unit, and immediately if there are serious violations of the zone or potential threats to peace;

6. Notes that as soon as the Secretary-General notifies the Security Council of the completion of the deployment of the United Nations observer unit, the conditions will be established for the Member States cooperating with Kuwait in accordance with resolution 678 (1990) to bring their military presence in Iraq to an end consistent with resolution 686 (1991);

C

7. Invites Iraq to reaffirm unconditionally its obligations under the Geneva Protocol for the Prohibition of the Use in War of Asphyxiating, Poisonous or Other Gases, and of Bacteriological Methods of Warfare, signed at Geneva on 17 June 1925, and to ratify the Convention on the Prohibition of the Development, Production and Stockpiling of Bacteriological (Biological) and Toxin Weapons and on Their Destruction, of 10 April 1972;

8. Decides that Iraq shall unconditionally accept the destruction, removal, or rendering harmless, under international supervision, of:

(a) All chemical and biological weapons and all stocks of agents and all related subsystems and components and all research, development, support and manufacturing facilities;

(b) All ballistic missiles with a range greater than 150 kilometres and related major parts, and repair and production facilities;

9. Decides, for the implementation of paragraph 8 above, the following:

(a) Iraq shall submit to the Secretary-General, within fifteen days of the adoption of the present resolution, a declaration of the locations, amounts and types of all items specified in paragraph 8 and agree to urgent, on-site inspection as specified below;

(b) The Secretary-General, in consultation with the appropriate Governments and, where appropriate, with the Director-General of the World Health Organization, within forty-five days of the passage of the present resolution, shall develop, and submit to the Council for approval, a plan calling for the completion of the following acts within forty-five days of such approval:

458

(i) The forming of a Special Commission, which shall carry out immediate on-site inspection of Iraq's biological, chemical and missile capabilities, based on Iraq's declarations and the designation of any additional locations by the Special Commission itself;

(ii) The yielding by Iraq of possession to the Special Commission for destruction, removal or rendering harmless, taking into account the requirements of public safety, of all items specified under paragraph 8 (a) above, including items at the additional locations designated by the Special Commission under paragraph 9 (b) (i) above and the destruction by Iraq, under the supervision of the Special Commission, of all its missile capabilities, including launchers, as specified under paragraph 8 (b) above;

(iii) The provision by the Special Commission of the assistance and cooperation to the Director-General of the International Atomic Energy Agency required in paragraphs 12 and 13 below;

10. Decides that Iraq shall unconditionally undertake not to use, develop, construct or acquire any of the items specified in paragraphs 8 and 9 above and requests the Secretary-General, in consultation with the Special Commission, to develop a plan for the future ongoing monitoring and verification of Iraq's compliance with this paragraph, to be submitted to the Security Council for approval within one hundred and twenty days of the passage of this resolution;

11. Invites Iraq to reaffirm unconditionally its obligations under the Treaty on the Non-Proliferation of Nuclear Weapons of 1 July 1968;

12. Decides that Iraq shall unconditionally agree not to acquire or develop nuclear weapons or nuclear-weapons-usable material or any subsystems or components or any research, development, support or manufacturing facilities related to the above; to submit to the Secretary-General and the Director-General of the International Atomic Energy Agency within fifteen days of the adoption of the present resolution a declaration of the locations, amounts, and types of all items specified above; to place all of its nuclear-weapons-usable materials under the exclusive control, for custody and removal, of the International Atomic Energy Agency, with the assistance and cooperation of the Special Commission as provided for in the plan of the Secretary-General discussed in paragraph 9 (b) above; to accept, in accordance with the arrangements provided for in paragraph 13 below, urgent on-site inspection and the destruction, removal or rendering harmless as appropriate of all items specified above; and to accept the plan discussed in paragraph 13 below for the future ongoing monitoring and verification of its compliance with these undertakings;

13. Requests the Director-General of the International Atomic Energy Agency, through the Secretary-General, with the assistance and cooperation of the Special Commission as provided for in the plan of the Secretary-General in paragraph 9 (b) above, to carry out immediate on-site inspection of Iraq's nuclear capabilities based on Iraq's declarations and the designation of any additional locations by the Special Commission; to develop a plan for submission to the Security Council within forty-five days calling for the destruction, removal, or rendering harmless

as appropriate of all items listed in paragraph 12 above; to carry out the plan within forty-five days following approval by the Security Council; and to develop a plan, taking into account the rights and obligations of Iraq under the Treaty on the Non-Proliferation of Nuclear Weapons of 1 July 1968, for the future ongoing monitoring and verification of Iraq's compliance with paragraph 12 above, including an inventory of all nuclear material in Iraq subject to the Agency's verification and inspections to confirm that Agency safeguards cover all relevant nuclear activities in Iraq, to be submitted to the Security Council for approval within one hundred and twenty days of the passage of the present resolution;

14. Takes note that the actions to be taken by Iraq in paragraphs 8, 9, 10, 11, 12 and 13 of the present resolution represent steps towards the goal of establishing in the Middle East a zone free from weapons of mass destruction and all missiles for their delivery and the objective of a global ban on chemical weapons;

D

15. Requests the Secretary-General to report to the Security Council on the steps taken to facilitate the return of all Kuwaiti property seized by Iraq, including a list of any property that Kuwait claims has not been returned or which has not been returned intact;

E

16. Reaffirms that Iraq, without prejudice to the debts and obligations of Iraq arising prior to 2 August 1990, which will be addressed through the normal mechanisms, is liable under international law for any direct loss, damage, including environmental damage and the depletion of natural resources, or injury to foreign Governments, nationals and corporations, as a result of Iraq's unlawful invasion and occupation of Kuwait;

17. Decides that all Iraqi statements made since 2 August 1990 repudiating its foreign debt are null and void, and demands that Iraq adhere scrupulously to all of its obligations concerning servicing and repayment of its foreign debt;

18. Decides also to create a fund to pay compensation for claims that fall within paragraph 16 above and to establish a Commission that will administer the fund;

19. Directs the Secretary-General to develop and present to the Security Council for decision, no later than thirty days following the adoption of the present resolution, recommendations for the fund to meet the requirement for the payment of claims established in accordance with paragraph 18 above and for a programme to implement the decisions in paragraphs 16, 17 and 18 above, including: administration of the fund; mechanisms for determining the appropriate level of Iraq's contribution to the fund based on a percentage of the value of the exports of petroleum and petroleum products from Iraq not to exceed a figure to be suggested to the Council by the Secretary-General, taking into account the requirements of the people of Iraq, Iraq's payment capacity as assessed in conjunction with the international financial institutions taking into consideration external debt service, and the needs of the Iraqi economy; arrangements for ensuring that payments are made to the fund; the process by which funds will be allocated and claims paid; appropriate

procedures for evaluating losses, listing claims and verifying their validity and resolving disputed claims in respect of Iraq's liability as specified in paragraph 16 above; and the composition of the Commission designated above;

F

20. Decides, effective immediately, that the prohibitions against the sale or supply to Iraq of commodities or products, other than medicine and health supplies, and prohibitions against financial transactions related thereto contained in resolution 661 (1990) shall not apply to foodstuffs notified to the Security Council Committee established by resolution 661 (1990) concerning the situation between Iraq and Kuwait or, with the approval of that Committee, under the simplified and accelerated "no-objection" procedure, to materials and supplies for essential civilian needs as identified in the report of the Secretary-General dated 20 March 1991, and in any further findings of humanitarian need by the Committee;

21. Decides that the Security Council shall review the provisions of paragraph 20 above every sixty days in the light of the policies and practices of the Government of Iraq, including the implementation of all relevant resolutions of the Security Council, for the purpose of determining whether to reduce or lift the prohibitions referred to therein;

22. Decides that upon the approval by the Security Council of the programme called for in paragraph 19 above and upon Council agreement that Iraq has completed all actions contemplated in paragraphs 8, 9, 10, 11, 12 and 13 above, the prohibitions against the import of commodities and products originating in Iraq and the prohibitions against financial transactions related thereto contained in resolution 661 (1990) shall have no further force or effect;

23. Decides that, pending action by the Security Council under paragraph

22 above, the Security Council Committee established by resolution 661 (1990) shall be empowered to approve, when required to assure adequate financial resources on the part of Iraq to carry out the activities under paragraph 20 above, exceptions to the prohibition against the import of commodities and products originating in Iraq;

24. Decides that, in accordance with resolution 661 (1990) and subsequent related resolutions and until a further decision is taken by the Security Council, all States shall continue to prevent the sale or supply, or the promotion or facilitation of such sale or supply, to Iraq by their nationals, or from their territories or using their flag vessels or aircraft, of:

(a) Arms and related materiel of all types, specifically including the sale or transfer through other means of all forms of conventional military equipment, including for paramilitary forces, and spare parts and components and their means of production, for such equipment;

(b) Items specified and defined in paragraphs 8 and 12 above not otherwise covered above;

(c) Technology under licensing or other transfer arrangements used in the production, utilization or stockpiling of items specified in subparagraphs (a) and (b) above;

(d) Personnel or materials for training or technical support services relating to the design, development, manufacture, use, maintenance or support of items specified in subparagraphs (a) and (b) above;

25. Calls upon all States and international organizations to act strictly in accordance with paragraph 24 above, notwithstanding the existence of any contracts, agreements, licences or any other arrangements;

26. Requests the Secretary-General, in consultation with appropriate Governments, to develop within sixty days, for the approval of the Security Council, guidelines to facilitate full international implementation of paragraphs 24 and 25 above and paragraph 27 below, and to make them available to all States and to establish a procedure for updating these guidelines periodically;

27. Calls upon all States to maintain such national controls and procedures and to take such other actions consistent with the guidelines to be established by the Security Council under paragraph 26 above as may be necessary to ensure compliance with the terms of paragraph 24 above, and calls upon international organizations to take all appropriate steps to assist in ensuring such full compliance;

28. Agrees to review its decisions in paragraphs 22, 23, 24 and 25 above, except for the items specified and defined in paragraphs 8 and 12 above, on a regular basis and in any case one hundred and twenty days following passage of the present resolution, taking into account Iraq's compliance with the resolution and general progress towards the control of armaments in the region;

29. Decides that all States, including Iraq, shall take the necessary measures to ensure that no claim shall lie at the instance of the Government of Iraq, or of any person or body in Iraq, or of any person claiming through or for the benefit of any such person or body, in connection with any contract or other transaction where its performance was affected by reason of the measures taken by the Security Council in resolution 661 (1990) and related resolutions;

G

30. Decides that, in furtherance of its commitment to facilitate the repatriation of all Kuwaiti and third country nationals, Iraq shall extend all necessary cooperation to the International Committee of the Red Cross, providing lists of such persons, facilitating the access of the International Committee of the Red Cross to all such persons wherever located or detained and facilitating the search by the International Committee of the Red Cross for those Kuwaiti and third country nationals still unaccounted for;

31. Invites the International Committee of the Red Cross to keep the Secretary-General apprised as appropriate of all activities undertaken in connection with facilitating the repatriation or return of all Kuwaiti and third country nationals or their remains present in Iraq on or after 2 August 1990;

H

32. Requires Iraq to inform the Security Council that it will not commit or support any act of international terrorism or allow any organization directed towards

commission of such acts to operate within its territory and to condemn unequivocally and renounce all acts, methods and practices of terrorism;

I

33. Declares that, upon official notification by Iraq to the Secretary-General and to the Security Council of its acceptance of the provisions above, a formal ceasefire is effective between Iraq and Kuwait and the Member States cooperating with Kuwait in accordance with resolution 678 (1990);

34. Decides to remain seized of the matter and to take such further steps as may be required for the implementation of the present resolution and to secure peace and security in the area.

6. Abdullah Öcalan's Democratic Confederation Solution Declaration for Kurdistan (Turkey) (full translation)

To The Kurdish People and The International Community

We are in an historical era which is affording mankind both immense opportunities for development and great dangers. The Middle East is going through a period of conflicts and chaos in what has been deemed the Third World War and at the centre of these conflicts and contradictions is Kurdistan. Despite attempts to maintain the former political status quo and the endeavours of the forces of global capital to find solutions in line with their own interests, the peoples seek the development of their own democratic systems based on freedom and to overcome the current situation of chaos and conflict. Here is a rough summary of the main points:

1. The basis for all development of humanity in the 19th century was the agricultural revolution which originated in the ecological system of the Zagros mountains. The 19th century ushered in the second big revolution, the industrial revolution. This second revolution played an important role in the development of nation states. The system of nation states, however, has become a serious barrier to the development of society and democracy and freedom since the end of the 20th century.

2. The right of self-determination of nations was interpreted as the right to establish a nation state.

The model of the United Nations based on nation states is not working. The nation state is an obstacle to its development. The Gulf War and the current situation in Iraq stand as proof of this.

3. The only way out of this situation is to establish a democratic confederal system that will derive its strength directly from the people, and not from globalisation based on nation states. Neither nation states nor globalisation which supersedes them are sustainable. Imperialism fails to develop a serious alternative model. Consequently the crisis of the system is deepening.

4. For this reason, the only alternative is democratic confederalism, which is a pyramid-like model of organisation. Here it is the communities who talk, debate and make decisions. From the base to the top the elected delegates would form a kind of loose co-ordinating body. They will be the elected representatives of the people for one year.

5. A system of democratic confederalism would be the model for the resolution of the problems of the Middle East. Neither the capitalist system nor the pressure of imperialist forces will lead to democracy; except to serve their own interests. The task is to assist in developing a grass-roots based democracy. Democratic confederalism is a system which takes into consideration the religious, ethnic and class differences in society.

6. For Kurdistan, however, democratic confederalism is a movement which does not interpret the right to self determination to establish a nation state, but develops its own democracy in spite of political boundaries. A Kurdish structure will develop through the creation of a federation of Kurds in Iran, Turkey, Syria and Iraq. And by uniting on a higher level they will form a confederal system.

7. Within Kurdistan democratic confederalism will establish village, towns and city assemblies and their delegates will be entrusted with the real decision-making, which in effect means that the people and the community will decide.

Current events throughout the world, including the Middle East, and the situation in Kurdistan have led to the conclusion that to develop and establish democratic confederalism is an unavoidable historical duty. To start to develop, promote and establish democratic confederalism on a new Newroz day is historically seen as a progressive, exciting and liberating step.

Democratic confederalism of Kurdistan is not a state system, but a democratic system of the people without a state. With the women and youth at the forefront, it is a system in which all sectors of society will develop their own democratic organisations. It is a politics exercised by free and equal confederal citizens by electing their own free regional representatives. It is based on the principle of its own strength and expertise. It derives its power from the people and in all areas including its economy it will seek self-sufficiency.

Kurdish democratic confederalism draws its strength from the historical roots of its people, and the deep-rooted, rich cultural identity of Mesopotamia. It is based on the democratic communal structure of natural society. Throughout their whole history Kurds have favoured Clan systems and tribal confederations and struggled to resist centralised governments. Democratic confederalism is based on the reality of the patriotic people, the free life and the vast experience of democratic organisation and structures which the PKK has fought for for over 30 years in all areas of the struggle, in particular in prisons and in the mountains with its thousands of martyrs.

Democratic confederalism aims and struggles to press for deep-rooted reforms in order to open the road to democracy; and to remove any barriers facing democratisation. From now on, three laws will be applied in Kurdistan: EU Law, the law of the national government and the democratic confederal law. So long as the national governments of Iran, Iraq, Turkey and Syria respect the democratic confederal laws the Kurdish people will observe their laws and thereby common ground will be sought.

Democratic confederalism is based on the principle of the recognition, and preservation of all cultural identities as well as the promotion of the right to freedom of expression. To this end, it seeks as its main task the resolution of the Kurdish question by democratic means, the recognition of the Kurdish identity on all levels and the development and furtherance of the Kurdish language and culture.

The principle of democratic confederalism promotes an ecological model of society. It is opposed to all forms of sexual oppression and aims to overcome it through the liberation struggle of the women. It seeks the establishment of democracy in all spheres of life of Kurdish society which is based on ecology and equality of the sexes and struggles against all forms of reaction and backwardness. It conjoins individual rights and freedoms with the development of democracy.

Democratic confederalism seeks the resolution of society's problems without resorting to violence and thus it is based on a policy of peace. It will use the right to legitimate self-defence against any attacks on its country, its people, its freedoms and against any violation of its rights.

Democratic confederalism is the movement of the Kurdish people to establish their own democracy and system of society. It is the expression of a democratic society and transcends all national structures. It is based on the freedoms of political, social, economic, cultural, sexual and ethnic rights. It strives for the unity of the different ecological and communal organisations and at the same time represents the governing organisation as an expression of organised society. On this premise, I am calling upon all sectors of society, in particular all women and the youth, to set up their own democratic organisations and to govern themselves.

465

Democratic confederalism is the expression for the democratic unity of the Kurds who are spread in four countries and scattered throughout the world. It seeks the resolution of the internal problems of the Kurdish nation through democratic unity. It views the tendency to create a nation state based on nationalism as a continuation of an outdated understanding of the nation state. As these models will neither resolve the Kurdish question nor assist the Kurdish people in the development of Kurdish society I call on these forces to be open to democratisation and to join the confederation on the basis of democratic national unity.

Democratic confederalism is based on a deep-rooted democratic understanding and sense of freedom, it makes no difference between peoples and defends the equality and freedom of all peoples. It replaces the centralist nation state based on borders. It is the basis for the unity of the peoples and democratic forces of the Middle East. It establishes its relationships with neighbouring countries on the basis of equality and freedom of political, social and cultural rights. To that end, I call on all regional peoples to unite within the democratic confederation and I call on the neighbouring countries to adopt a democratic position.

Democratic confederalism is opposed to global imperialism and seeks the global democracy of peoples. It is a system in which all peoples and all humanity should be living in the 21st century. This will pave the way for global democratic confederalism and a new era. I call on humanity to create a new world under the umbrella of a global democratic confederalism.

I believe by announcing the formation of the KOMA KOMALEN KURDISTAN (KKK), as the expression of democratic confederalism and the unity of the Kurdish people, on this Newroz (spring) day 2005 we have established a new philosophy and way of life for our people. I call on all our people to establish their own democracy, to unite and to govern themselves under their own flag (on green background a yellow sun with a red star). I will carry this flag proudly and I will continue to carry out my duties as a leader. On this day of spring, a day closer to freedom than the days of springs in the past, I wish our people and the regional peoples a Happy Newroz. With kind regards.

Abdullah Acalan (Öcalan)

Koma Komalen Kurdistan

20 March 2005

7. The Party Program of the Kurdish Workers' Party (PKK), promulgated in 5th Party Congress (abridged translation)

Date January 24, 1995

Chapter Three: The Revolution In Kurdistan

The Characteristics of the Revolution In Kurdistan

The revolution in Kurdistan, which is led by our party, is a national and a democratic revolution whose most important characteristics can be described as follows:

A) The national contradiction is the main contradiction and determines the solution for the other social contradictions. If the national contradiction is not resolved, there is no possibility to solve the remaining social contradictions on their own. The first steps which were taken in the name of the revolution were primarily national in character and they placed Kurdistan in a phase of extensive revolutionary development. The second aspect of our revolution is democratic. The democratic revolution aims to defeat the remaining social contradictions which have been in place since the Middle Ages... As soon as these contradictions are solved, the society will take on a democratic character.

B) Another characteristic of the revolution in Kurdistan lies in the problem of leadership. The national and democratic revolution displays two types of leadership: firstly, that of class, and secondly, the leadership in the various geographical regions. The leadership which will bring victory is the ideological, political, and organizational leadership of the working class. The leading forces of the other classes are steadily losing their power, and they can no longer pose a serious threat to colonialism. On the other hand, there has been a steady development in the leadership of the working class, which is embodied in our party.

The leadership in Northwest Kurdistan, whose struggle has been directed against the Turkish Republic, has been characterized by gained and lasting achievements.

The revolutionary socialist leadership provided by our party will continue to lead the national and democratic revolution, according to the line of the working class, on a socialist path, without interruption.

The third characteristic of our revolution is the long-term vision of the struggle and the broad mobilization of popular forces. This has manifested itself in praxis in the form of a protracted people's war.

The fourth fundamental characteristic of our revolution is that it is not limited to Kurdistan, rather it has an influence on its surroundings and on the entire region. That shows the universalism of our revolution. This characteristic of our revolution can be explained by the fact that it is a social revolution with a broad base, and that it continues to grow stronger despite being in a world situation where there are developments aimed against it. It affects the interests of all the nations in the region due to the fact that

Kurdistan is divided. This characteristic gives life to our revolution and exerts an influence on the entire region; if things continue to develop in this direction, our revolution will have an influence at the global level as well.

The Tasks of The Revolution In Kurdistan

The revolution will realize the following tasks:

A) An end to Turkish colonialism and all forms of imperialist domination over Kurdistan. In order to do this, the following must be achieved.

Conflicts between the various population groups, which are continually fueled by the colonialists and their local agents, must be stopped. Those tendencies which aim at purely local or nationalist organizing must be defeated.

We must create our own institutions of economics, culture, health, and education in order to stop diseases and to fight against the other forms of destruction of nature and people which have been brought about by about by colonialism.

B) Revolution must establish, a national, independent, democratic society, ruled by the people, must be established. In order to do this, the following must be achieved:

The nationalization of all institutions, including factories, farms, and other establishments, belonging to the colonialists. Land reform must be carried out in the interest of the working class. As part of the democratization of the society, all hindrances to the organization of working people in the economic, political, and cultural spheres must be eliminated, and such organizations must be granted legal status. New employment possibilities must be created for the workers, bearing in mind that the physical and mental development of workers is of great importance. Furthermore, the work day shall be 8 hours long.

C) An independent economic structure must be built up. In order to do this, the following must be achieved:

The economy will be centrally planned. Farmers will be encouraged to form collectives and they will be supported in this effort.

D) In place of colonialist education and culture, a national educational and cultural system must be established. All dialects of the Kurdish language will be allowed to develop, although one will be made into the national language. With respect to the Kurdish language, literature, and history, intensive research will be carried out, and to aid in this, research institutes will be created. The entire population will be able to learn to read and write.

E) For revolution and unity in Kurdistan, the following are needed:

The revolution in the various parts of Kurdistan is primarily the task of the people living in those regions. Efforts must be made to increase the support and solidarity between the revolutionary forces in the different parts of Kurdistan. The democratic rights of Kurdish people spread out across the countries of the world must be guaranteed. Kurds living abroad should join with progressive humanity and with the struggle in Kurdistan. Preparations should be made to facilitate these people's return home to Kurdistan.

F) With respect to relations with neighboring peoples and international questions, we must apply the principles of proletarian internationalism. In order to do this, the following must be achieved : Due to the division of Kurdistan between different countries, all relations with revolutionary forces among neighboring peoples will be based on the assumption that all revolutionary movements are themselves responsible for the revolution in their own country ; on this basis, different forms of joint struggle at various levels must be developed.

Unity with neighboring peoples must be based on the notion that all peoples are independent and free. All forced unities which are not based on this notion must be resisted. Relations with neighboring peoples, in particular with the people of Turkey, will be developed within our vision of a "Federation of the Middle East". Relations with independent countries and their national liberation movements, cooperation with movements of the working class and revolutionary forces across the world, and solidarity with democratic, anti-fascist, environmental, and humanitarian circles must be built up.

January 24, 1995

5th Congress, Kurdistan Workers Party (PKK)

8. The Iraqi Kurdistan Democratic Party (KDP) Party Programme and Constitution

The program and Bylaws of the Iraqi Kurdistan Democratic Party was promulgated in the 13th Congress on December 11-18, 2010. The program includes altogether 271 articles. On the other hand the party constitution (Bylaws) includes 33 articles The abridged translation is given below:

Iraqi Kurdistan Democratic Party Programme

Section 1 includes the Introduction part and Section 2 includes the goals (tasks) of the party. Section 3 includes the Principles and the Strategies of the Party.

Article (2): Mission Statement

The KDP is a patriotic and democratic party based on a fundamental commitment to human rights, individual freedom, and national rights for the Kurds and other nations as regards self-determination. The KDP believes in achievement through systematic programs and democracy which has originated from the roots of the historical and national Kurdish liberation movement along with Mustafa Barzani's patriotic experience.

Section 2. The Goals of the Party

Part 1: National Goals

Article (3): To improve and develop respectful relationships and exercise co-existence with all other parties; cooperating and supporting democratic peace-oriented organizations and the Kurdish Diaspora in order to achieve Kurdish national and lawful rights peacefully, in order to expand tolerance through dialogue within Kurdish homes while diminishing violence.

Article (4): To struggle to internationalize the Kurdish cause within the framework of international and regional organizations, where the Kurdish liberation movement must have the role of observer status to defend Kurdish national and patriotic rights.

Article (5): To return all of the disputed territories to the border of the Kurdistan Region in accordance with the methods mentioned in Article (140) of the Iraqi Constitution, and then to finalize the Region's borders.

Part 2: Patriotic Goals

Article (7) To work towards building a civil society that offers rule of law and equal opportunities, where everybody can live under a transparent and fair authority, and also where pluralism and peaceful devolution of power are applied.

Article (8) To verify and confirm a democratic, parliamentarian federal system in Iraq that provides full citizenship for all Iraqis while protecting Iraq's international position and guaranteeing liberty and independence.

Article (9) To protect and develop all national, political, cultural and economic gains and achievements which were attained by a historical struggle and were fundamentally the result of martyrs' blood and sacrifices for our people, which were undoubtedly the reflection of a true, brave and free ambition.

Article (10) To verify and confirm national unity in the Kurdistan Region and Iraq; to strive to find just solutions for internal issues between the KRG and Iraqi government in accordance with the Iraqi Constitution.

Article (11) To develop a parliamentary, federal system and guarantee the participation of all Iraqi components in the Constitutional institutions.

Article (12) To guarantee the participation of the Kurdish people in making political decisions in Iraq by participating in Iraqi government agencies.

Article (13) To respect the federal Constitution by implementing its articles, and considering it sacred, as it is the direct expression of Iraq's will and also the only guarantee for the unity of Iraq and its territories.

Article (14) To guarantee national, cultural, and administrative rights for Turkmen, Chaldeans, Assyrians, Syriacs and Armenians.

Article (15) To secure the rights of any religious and sectarian component (in carrying out their rituals and establishing their council) to improve, organize, and develop their cultural and social affairs inside the Kurdistan Region.

Article (16) To establish good relations with parties that work in Kurdistan and Iraq and believe in the Constitution's commitment to democracy, human rights, federalism, national brotherhood, and recognition of the Kurds' right to self-determination.

Article (17) To strengthen principles of co-existence and tolerance among all national, ethnic, and religious groups of people.

Article (18) To ensure that Iraq lives up to its international obligations and follows all international protocol and pacts, especially those which deal with human rights, the rights of minorities, and the rights of self-determination.

Part 3: Regional and International Goals

Article (19) To strengthen peaceful relationships between the Region and neighboring countries in accordance with the principles of common interest, mutual respect, good neighboring, non-intervention, and solving problems and miscommunication by way of general international law and peace.

Article (20) To commit to the United Nation's goals and principles, and to respect those international agreements and protocols that do not oppose the interests of the Kurdish people.

Article (21) To support the efforts of friendly countries, governmental and non-governmental organizations that participate in the political, economical, and cultural development of the Kurdistan region, facilitating their work in proper and legal ways.

Article (22) To initiate an international campaign to encourage countries and international organizations, especially the United Nations, to defend nations who have suffered international crimes, and to support them in gaining political freedom and economical development.

Article (23) To strengthen relations with nations, parties, and organizations who support the Kurdish nation.

Article (24) To encourage and strengthen the diplomatic relations of the Kurdistan Regional Government through the opening of KRG representation offices in countries all over the world, in accordance with the recent Iraqi constitution, while also encouraging these countries to open their offices and consulates in the Kurdistan Region.

Article (25) To gain observer status for the Kurdish liberation movement in the United Nations and other professional agencies, so as to guarantee a peaceful life for the Kurdish people, free from oppression and another genocide.

Article (26) To strengthen and develop the KRG's relations with the UN and other international organizations and to find proper mechanisms for the involvement of the Region's representatives in international conferences and UN commissions, organizations, and professional agencies.

Article (27) To seek material and moral support for the party's organization abroad for the purpose of below goals: Establishing optimum relations with political parties in the country, especially those who believe in democracy and human rights and recognize the Kurds' right to self-determination. Caring for the Party's members and supporters abroad. To become helpful to the KRG offices abroad in strengthening relations and providing support for Kurdish immigrants outside of Iraq.

Section 3: The Principles and the Strategies of the Party

Part 1: Political System & Governing Issues includes the articles from 28 to 41

The Party believes that the political system in Kurdistan must express the ambitions of the people and work for the approval of citizens' rights and freedoms, and to encourage them to play their positive role in a political system that preserves democracy, human rights, rule of law, and the separation of authorities.

Part 2: Judicial System includes the articles from 42 to 47

The Party believes that there is no higher authority than a just law and an independent judge with the final authority to determine the law. In order to enable him to do his crucial job.

Part 3: Administrative System includes the articles from 48 to 54

As the role of administration and management is critical for achieving humanitarian, political, economic and social developmen.

Part 4: Economic & Financial Policies includes the articles from 55 to 67

The Party pays special attention to economic and financial policies, since they have a crucial role in the development of society and standards of living. Thus, the Party tries to develop a financial policy that is compatible with the great changes in the world and serves the interests of Kurdistan Region.

Part 5: Educational and Higher Educational System includes the articles from 68 to 82

The Party deems it necessary that a public and transparent philosophy for education must emerge for the purpose of framing a united and national policy. It should include a new and modern vision for erasing the effects of old, negative, racist and chauvinistic educational policies of the past Iraqi authorities.

Part 6: On Scientific Research includes the articles from 83 to 86

Scientific research is a critical factor in the development of a vibrant civil society and healthy governmental institutions in the Kurdistan Region. Academics and scholars must be encouraged and the Kurdistan Academy must be expanded and promoted in line with its international counterparts.

Part 7: Health System includes the articles from 87 to 92

Since the health system is critically important for building a healthy and productive society, the Party believes that there must be efforts for the following goals...

Part 8: Civil Society principle includes the articles from 93 to 107

As Kurdish society undergoes dramatic development, the Party carefully works to implement an advanced social system through the application of the following principles...

Part 9: Peshmergas (The Army Organization) principle includes the articles from 108 to 116

Since the advent of the Great September Revolution, the "Peshmergas" have been the true protector of the people of Kurdistan and its borders. Through their brave sacrifices, our nation was able to overcome difficult political situations and achieve most of its goals. The Party proudly commemorates and appreciates the Peshmergas' role in history and also its recent role as an important component of the Iraqi army...

Part 10: Internal Security Forces principle includes the articles from 117 to 120

Security at both the 'individual' and 'community' level is a basic right. The Party believes that those tasked with providing internal security have an important role to play in protecting the security and freedom of citizens, defending the achievements of our nation, upholding the rule of law, implementing justice, and protecting human rights.

Part 11: Communications System principle includes the articles from 121 to 124

In the last few years, the Kurdistan Region has taken a dramatic step forward in modern communication technologies and devices, and being of crucial importance.

Part 12: Transportation & Infrastructure principle includes the articles from 125 to 130

Transportation and infrastructure are fundamental pillars of a healthy economy, and since Kurdistan is one of the international gateways to Iraq, they have a crucial importance. Thus, the Party works for the following goals:

Part 13: Environment Protection principle includes the articles from 131 to 137

As everybody has the right to live in a clean environment, protecting the environment and re-greening Kurdistan is a national, patriotic, and humanitarian mission.

Part 14: Natural Resources principle includes the articles from 138 to 150

The Party works for the development and protection of natural resources in the Kurdistan Region in the interest of the Region's citizens and future generations, through the following: First: Oil & Gas, Second: Minerals Third: Water Resources

Part 15: Agriculture, Construction & Trading includes the articles from 151 to 173

Part 16: Construction & Housing principle includes the articles from 174 to 182

In accordance with the fact that the establishment and maintenance of a proper house is every citizen's right.

Part 17: Municipalities & Public Services principle includes the articles from 183 to 186

The Party pays special attention to municipalities because they have a pivotal role in providing public services.

Part 18: Developing Tourism principle includes the articles from 187 to 192

Part 19: Media & Broadcasting principle includes the articles from 193 to 199

The Party believes in the importance of the freedom of media and broadcasting in Kurdistan (through print, television, radio, and the internet), believing that they play an important role in educating the community, revealing facts, declaring weak points in governmental and non-governmental institutional performance, suggesting resolution, deepening the values of democracy and patriotism, and calling attention to our national cause abroad.

Part 20: Culture principle includes the articles from 200 to 206

Part 21: Religion Affairs principle includes the articles from 207 to 215

Religion is one of the main pillars of life. It is crucial for the organization and direction of human relations, and the KDP supports promoting tolerance, co-existence, and freedom of religious beliefs. The Party pays attention to religion and works for the following goals:

Part 22: Women, Students, Youth & Sport Affairs principle includes the articles from 216 to 244

Part 23: Non-governmental Organizations principle includes the articles from 245 to 251

Public and professional organizations, unions, syndicates, communities, centers and clubs... etc., have had a historical and ongoing role in our nation's liberty movement and in defending the principles of democracy. The Party strongly believes in this role, and thus works for the following goals:

Section 4: Victims of Genocide & Crimes Against Humanity.

A look into Iraq's recent history reveals the damage that has affected the Kurdish individual in every aspect of life, especially their national rights. Kurds have encountered many hardships and faced dramatic oppression that violated their God-given, natural rights. The oppression of the Kurds is clearly shown through the use of deadly chemical weapons against them, embodied in the Anfal operations, Arabization and forced deportations, and in the many other racist crimes classified as genocide and mass murder. From mass executions to attempts to erase Kurdish culture, the aim was ultimately to have the Kurdish identity be extinguished.

Part 1: Rights of Victims & Their Families principle includes the articles from 252 to 261

Part 2: Legislation (Law making) principle includes the articles from 262 to 265

The Iraqi Council of Representatives should legislate to define mass murder as crimes, demanding serious punishments for those violate international agreements regarding the punishment of such crimes...

Part 3: Other Internal & International issues principle includes the articles from 266 to 271

Party Constitution of the Kurdistan Democratic Party

Section One: Some Basic Definitions of the Party Constitution

Article 1: The Definition of the KDP in terms of its organization.

The Kurdistan Democratic Party is a patriotic and democratic party. The KDP has benefitted from the positive experiences of other democratic nations and uses them as a prime example to follow in the Kurdistan Region.

Article 2: The Name of KDP and its Abbreviation

In Kurdish written in Arabic alphabet

In Latin: Partiya Demokrata Kurdistane

In English: Kurdistan Democratic Party.

Article: 3 The Motto and symbols of the KDP

Article: (4) KDP Flag

The color of the flag is yellow with a red circle in the middle with the abbreviation of KDP inside.

Article: (5) KDP Media

The mouthpiece of the party is the Khabat ("struggle") newspaper, which is published in Kurdish, and the "Al-Taekhi" ("brotherhood) website published in Arabic.

Section Two: Organizational Principles of the Kurdistan Democratic Party KDP.

Article: (6) The KDP has been founded on the following organizational principles:

1- Implementing confidential voting for the elections of committees.
2- Low-level members will obey the instructions and decisions of high-level members.
3- Individuals have no right to engage in decisions that are under the authority of the committee's organizations, however, the individual is responsible for not violating the principles.
4- Implementing the principles of consultation and the exchange of ideas among KDP organizations.
5- Practicing constructive criticism within the KDP organization, but veering away from defamation, libel, and abuse.
6- Abiding by equal opportunity principles.

Section Three: Membership in the KDP includes articles from 7 to 9

Section Four: Organizational Components of the KDP includes articles from 10 to 22

Section Five: Committees and Boards of Conferences includes articles from 23 to 25

Section Six: Election of Representatives for Conferences and KDP Organizations includes articles from 26 to 27

Section Seven: KDP's Finance includes the article Nr 28

Section Eight: KDP's System and Discipline includes articles from 29 to 33

9. The Patriotic Union of Kurdistan (PUK) Party Programme and Constitution (the Party under the leadership of Mr. Talabani)

PUK is a socialist democratic party, striving to establish peace and promote the values of freedom, democracy, citizenship, human rights and self-determination. The PUK believes in a culture of equality and tolerance. And the party restricts its activities in the Kurdistan Region of Iraq, separated areas, other areas of Iraq and outside of the country.

The Party believes that these principles should become the foundation of civil rights in our present age. the establishment of PUK was in response to the end of the previous Kurdish revolt, known as the Aylul Revolution, after the Iraqi government withdrew from the peace plan and autonomy accord that had been signed with the Kurdish people on March 11, 1970.

A- General Objectives of the PUK

1- Establish peace, democracy, freedom, tolerance, the principles of the market economy, social justice, prosperity, the rule of law, the rights of citizenship, the precepts of a civil society, self-determination, a secular system of government, freedom of conscience, protection of the environment, peaceful coexistence and stability of all nations on the basis of mutual respect for the rights and will of others. At the same time, the PUK will struggle against dictatorship, war, invasion, oppression, poverty, corruption, discrimination on the bases of race, sex, religion or sect, violations of human rights, chauvinism, ignorance and terrorism. 2- Show commitment to the Universal Declaration of Human Rights and all other international human rights instruments and treaties. 3- Achieve right to self-determination for the Kurdish people in a democratic manner. 4- Maintain and promote the democratic, federal and parliamentary systems of Iraq. 5- Reintegrate Kirkuk, Khanaqin, Shengal, Makhmour, Mandeli, Badra, Jassan and all other separated areas into the Kurdistan region. 6- Uphold all legal and constitutional rights of the Kurdish people as given in the Iraqi constitution. 7- Express commitment to the constitutional rights of all other ethnic and religious groups such as Turkmens, Arabs, Armans, Chaldeans, Assyrians, Ezidies, Christians, Saebi-Mandani, Kakeyees, and Shabak people in Kurdistan and Iraq. 8- Apply the principles and views of social democratic society to build a prosperous and modern community. 9- Establish peace and security in Iraq and in Kurdistan in particular, and across the Middle East and the world on the basis of being a friendly neighbor, our mutual interests, and peaceful coexistence according to international laws. 10- Enforce those international agreements related to the prohibition of weapons of mass destruction and their use. 11- Establish the mass killings of Anfal and chemical bombardments as crimes of genocide and ethnic cleansing within Kurdistan and Iraqi and as well as the international level and make all efforts to compensate the victims of those crimes. 12- Provide job opportunities and educational services to those Kurds who have come from the other parts of Kurdistan and lived under the control of the Kurdistan Regional Government as well as to their families and provide opportunities for cultural, sporting and other activities. 13- Provide political, economic, cultural and economic opportunities for all social groups in the wish to give them a better life. 14- Promote the idea of Kurdish individuals as citizens with political, social and economic rights in a civil and modern society. 15- Promote the peaceful coexistence of all people of various religious and sectarian backgrounds. To achieve this, the PUK seeks to form a political system on the bases of democracy and secularism. 16- Support the political struggles of Kurds in all countries of the region in a move to find peaceful and democratic solutions suitable to conditions in the real world so that they may attain their legitimate rights. 17- Remove landmines planted in the region and ameliorate the impacts these weapons have had. The PUK also seeks to compensate the victims of mine explosions. 18- Make efforts toward economic reform and promote the growth of the economy in all aspects. 19- Normalize the social situation in Kurdistan and heal the wounds of the past destructive civil wars and address remaining problems through legal, political and social means. 20- Make efforts to remove weapons of mass destruction and support those international treaties that prohibit such weapons. 21- Honor the struggles of political prisoners and make efforts to compensate them and their tribe members according to law No. 4 that was passed in 2006. 22- Organize the political system in Kurdistan to regulate relations between various parties and the government in a way that suits the needs of the Kurdish people. 23- Make efforts to create support for a draft constitution for the Kurdistan region by placing it before the people in a referendum in a bid to win the trust of the majority of people.

B- Political Objectives of the PUK

1- Complete the process of separation of powers for the legislative, judicial and executive bodies and protect the independence of the courts. Also, establish the fourth power, the media, which should be used to serve freedom and democracy. 2- Commit to the peaceful exchange of political power at all levels in Kurdistan as a result of elections or other democratic processes. 3- Provide legal grounds for a democratic and civil life through provisions of freedom in religion and sects, personal expression, in the media and in residency, and in the freedom to form political organizations, unions and civil society organizations. 4- Provide the freedom to express disagreement through hunger strikes, protests or demonstrations for all people as according to law. 5- Consider the supreme interests of the Kurdistan region when making local and international alliances.

On the Question of Nationalism

The lack of a democratic solution to the Kurdish national question was among the primary reasons for the ongoing instability of Iraq beginning with the formation of the country in 1921 and continuing until the collapse of Saddam Hussein's regime on April 9, 2003. The pro-Kurdish liberation movement was a democratic movement but the Iraqi authorities had had always taken an undemocratic stance on the issue of Kurdish nationalism. At the beginning of the1980s, the PUK made a radical change in the pro-Kurdish liberation movement's objectives, shifting from a call for genuine autonomy to one of self-determination. Following the Uprising, the strategy of self-determination became the primary means within the Kurdistan parliament for establishing a democratic and federal state for Kurdistan within Iraq. Later, self-determination was embodied in the Iraqi constitution after the fall of the dictatorial Baath regime. The PUK believes that a democratic solution to this problem is appropriate for Iraq and for Kurdistan. Thus, it regards the development of a federal system in Iraq as paramount and wishes for the implementation of constitutional rights for the separated areas, therefore ensuring the continuity of the constitution. The constitution is the primary tool for stability, security and peaceful coexistence in Iraq and throughout the region.

C- Economic Objectives of the PUK

The PUK seeks to provide a suitable environment for the establishment of a market economy as regulated by law. Thus, the economy of Kurdistan will recover from its suffering by means of plans and programs that generate prosperity for its people. However, transformation into a market economy requires strong political will and the passage or amending of numerous laws.

Economic Objectives part of the program includes 9 principles or policies as below:

First, Agricultural sector

Second, Industry and Energy

Third, Financial industry

Fourth, the Administrative sector

Fifth, Private sector Sixth, Micro projects

Seventh, Tourism

Eighth, Environment

Ninth, Combating corruption

D- Social Objectives of the PUK includes 11 principles or policies

First, Humanitarian development

Second, youth

Third, sports

Fourth, Women

Fifth, Education

Sixth, Health

Seventh, Residence (Housing issues)

Eighth, Culture

Ninth, Relatives of martyrs relative and victims of Anfal massacre and chemical weapons

Tenth, Political prisoners

Eleventh, Disabled Peshmarga (army figters) veterans, political prisoners and people with special needs

10. Democratic Party of Iranian Kurdistan — Party Programme and Constitution

Programme and Internal Regulations of the Party were adopted in the XIIIth Congress (3-7 July 2004) which altogether includes a Preamble and 7 chapters with 48 articles. On the other hand the Party constitution includes altogether 13 Articles and their sub rules. The main contents include the following:

Part I of the Programme

Preamble:

After the war of 1514 A.D. between the two Safawid and Ottaman empires in Chalderan, Kurdistan was practically partitioned between these two empires, and in the year 1639 with the signing of a treaty between King Abas Safawi and Soltan Morad Osmani, the partition became official. The liberation struggle of Sheikh Obidolla Nahri (1880) was the birth of Kurdish national struggle against occupiers for an independent Kurdistan. The early years of 20th Century witnessed a burgeoning national liberation movement where numerous Kurdish political movements emerged across Kurdistan; however, due to regional powers' plans and bargain with the world powers, each one of them failed.

When the Second World War started, the struggle of the free-willing nations against reactionism and fascism advanced. Concurrently, a historical necessity was felt to establish a political organization in the Iranian part of Kurdistan that could lead liberation struggle of the Kurdish nation. With the annexation of Iran by the allied forces and the downfall of Reza Shah's two decades of tyranny in Iranian Kurdistan, conditions to carry on the struggle forward were favourable. The Kurdish leaders took advantage of this historic opportunity and formed Democratic Party of Kurdistan in August 16, 1945. But this (Mahabad) Republic lasted only eleven months, and after setback of the movement of the Iranian people, military dictatorship was once again imposed on all Iranian Kurdistan. However, the Kurdish people did not give up the fight, and still continued their struggle to realize their inveterate ideas.

Democratic Party of Iranian Kurdistan (PDKI) has left behind 59 years of difficult struggle, full of obstacles, and filled with sacrifices. It is evident that our Party in this period has become more competent, and has earned experiences from the Kurdish people and other nations' struggles.

In the second half of the 20th century, scientific and technological advancements and high-speed communication networks have altered the image of the world... In general, the oppressed nations and those social forces who are able to control their destiny and advance their society, are witnessing a brighter optimism to establish a more humane, developed and free society.

After the demise of the former Soviet Bloc in 1991, two important issues have gained prominency in the global dimension, and revealed their real value: first, national issue and the necessity to accommodate the national rights of oppressed people of the world. Even though it had been claimed for 70 years that there was not an issue such as national question in the socialist countries, still, when the

Soviet system was demolished, and an appropriate opportunity was brought about for the people in these countries, we observed how these people stepped into the centre of struggle and established their national governments.

Second, it was the issue of democracy. This issue that was opposed in major parts of the world under the banner of protecting and defending workers' interests, finally proved its necessity in a way that resulted in the overthrowing of many dictatorial regimes, and many others fearing that they might fall into an uncertain destiny, opened their gates to democracy, and adapted themselves to modern conditions.

Economically as well as socially, Iranian Kurdistan is considered as an underdeveloped region within an underdeveloped country. Although Kurdistan is rich in natural and mineral resources, in many aspects it is regarded as one of the most underdeveloped regions of Iran. Social and economic developments, especially industrial are well below national average. In medical and cultural aspects, there has been little or no improvement in the livelihood of Kurdistan inhabitants. The standards of living remains extremely low, and the farmers and workers live in an abject poverty and misery, and the countryside is practically without any form of health and medical services.

In order to free Iran from oppression of dictatorship, PDKI deems it necessary to establish a federal democratic system, which will heed the rightful claims of the peoples of Iran instead of the unpopular and reactionary regime of the clerics…

Our Party believes that for the democratic movement in Iran not once again find itself without a program, and its achievements become plundered, the democratic and progressive forces of Iran must from now on agree on a common platform for the country's future.

To obtain such a union, our Party also fights against the Iranian chauvinism, which denies the existance of the Kurdish people, and against the narrow-minded nationalism of those Kurds who make no distinction between the central dictatorship and the peoples of Iran. Iranian chauvinism and the narrow-mined Kurdish nationalism are both the enemies of the union of the peoples of Iran. At the same time, our Party believes that the danger of arrogant Iranian chauvinism to be a major threat at present times.

It is more than 25 years that PDKI has led the Kurdish people's uprising against the savage aggression of the clerical regime with competence and skilfulness. The struggle, resistance and sacrifices of our heroic members, supporters and sympathizers have increased the respect and influence of our Party among the masses. PDKI currently has not only been the most widely respected political party in Iranian Kurdistan, but it has also gained the respect of other nationalities of Iran, and of the progressive organizations within Iran and abroad.

PDKI presents this Programme to the people of Kurdistan, and request from all those who live in Kurdistan consisting of workers, farmers, urban and rural toilers, intellectuals, students, civil servants, craftsmen, traders and all patriots of every social stratum to strive for the realization of its objectives. Party members and sympathizers are to circulate the Programme among the Kurdish masses and expound the Party views on political, social, economic and cultural issues. It is necessary that the peoples of other regions in Iran become informed of the Kurdish and our Party's essential claims.

PDKI is the main political force in Iranian Kurdistan that has the support of the majority of the Kurdish population; therefore, we must do all we can to mobilize the considerable forces of our people to carry out objectives that have been put into our Party's Programme. In such a case the Party will become a powerful material force, and will be able to fulfil the legitimate rights of the Kurds in Iran within the framework of a democratic federal Iran.

Chapter I- The General Objectives of the Party:

1- PDKI is the pioneer party of the people of Iranian Kurdistan, and together with the progressive forces all over Iran struggles to safeguard Iran's independence, and establish a democratic regime in Iran to obtain the rights of the Kurdish people in Iranian Kurdistan to self-determination.

2- The long-term objective of PDKI is to establish a democratic socialist society.

3- The strategic motto of PDKI is the establishment of a democratic federal Iran and the attainment of Kurdish national rights in Iranian Kurdistan.

4- PDKI considers the oppressed nationalities of Iran as its strategic allies, and supports their national struggle to attain their national rights.

5- Support for the national-democratic struggle of Kurdish people in other parts of Kurdistan is the leading principle of PDKI.

6- PDKI supports the liberation struggle of all the people of the world, and supports peace and friendship of the people in all the countries.

Chapter II-Principles of Kurdistan Regional Government

7- Kurdistan is one of the regional governments of democratic federal Iran.

8- The regional government comprises of the whole territory of Iranian Kurdistan. The geographical dimension of the regional government of Kurdistan will be defined by taking into account the geographic and economic factors, and the demand of the majority of the people living in every region inhabited by Kurds.

9- In the autonomous region of Kurdistan, the power in its totality is derived from the people, and will be exercised through their representatives at the Kurdish parliament and the regional governmental bodies.

10- Affairs concerning international relations (political and economic), national defence (the army), long-term economic planning and the monetary system will be the prerogatives of the Federal government. Aside from the mentioned cases, the legitimacy of administrating the governmental institutions in Kurdistan is under the supervision of the Kurdistan Regional Government. The people of the autonomous region of Kurdistan and their compatriots throughout Iran will take part legally and without any discrimination in the administration of the country's affairs.

11- Kurdistan Region has its own national anthem, flag and festivities. In Kurdistan region, the flag of federal Iran will be flying along side the Kurdistan flag.

12- Federal Supreme Court will be formed equally of all the experts of all the nations of Iran. It will review all the legal conflicts between the federal government and the regional governments.

13- The Parliament of Kurdistan is the highest legislative authority in the autonomous region of Kurdistan. The representatives are elected by direct suffrage, secret ballot and equal vote.

14- The Parliament of Kurdistan designates the KRG, which will be answerable to the Parliament of Kurdistan.

15- Internal order and security are in the hands of the Peshmergas and other law enforcing institutions in the autonomous region. The army is responsible to defend the country's sovereignty and national borders, and does not have the right to interfere in maintaining internal security and internal law enforcing affairs.

16- The Kurdish language is the official language of education and correspondence within internal administration in the autonomous region of Kurdistan. Persian language will also be the official language of the region, as well as other regions of Iran, and will be taught in schools along with Kurdish.

17- The administrative correspondence between the autonomous region of Kurdistan and the federal government, and other regional administrations related to the federal government will take place in the Persian language.

18- All the non-Kurdish inhabitants of the autonomous region of Kurdistan will be provided with resources to promote their own culture, and study in their own language.

481

Chapter III Rights of the Kurdistan Region's Inhabitants includes the articles (19 to 22)

Chapter IV Economic and Social Policy includes the articles (23 to 36)

Chapter V Cultural and Health Policies includes the articles (37 to 41)

Chapter VI Characteristic of the Federal Republic of Iran, includes the articles (42 to 45)

Article 42-All the nations of Iran without any discrimination based on race, religion, ethnicity and gender will participate in the forming of the Federal Republic of Iran, and this must be entrenched in the constitution of the Federal Republic.

Article 43-The Constitution of the Federal Republic of Iran must be drawn up in accordance with the international standards of human rights and other international covenants, where the national rights of Iranian nationalities will be recognized within their geographic and ethnic borders.

Article 44- The Constitution of the Federal Republic of Iran must grant jurisdiction to the regional administrations over the areas of their concern.

Article 45- The federal Republic of Iran will not join any pact that advocates aggression against other countries.

Chapter VII Foreign Policy includes the articles (46 to 48)

Party constitution of the Democratic Party of Iranian Kurdistan

Article I: Name and Identity of the Party

1- The Party's name is: "Democratic Party of Iranian Kurdistan" (PDKI).

2- PDKI is the progressive Party of the people of Iranian Kurdistan that particularly absorbs workers, farmers, and progressive intellectuals into its ranks.

Article II: Party Membership

All citizens residing in Iranian Kurdistan and all the Iranian Kurds have the right to become members of PDKI on the following conditions: Not to be less than eighteen years old. To accept the Party's Programme and Internal Regulation. To be a patriotic and progressive citizen of certified good character. None-Iranian Kurds are entitled to join organizations and associations affiliated with PDKI, and if they reside in Iranian Kurdistan for more than 5 years they become eligible for membership.

Article III: Terms of Admission of membership

For one to be granted membership, one must:be sponsored by two Party members.Go through a probationary period of at least six months. Not to be member of another party or any other political organization. Be accepted with the approval of the majority of the members of a cell or a higher organ of the Party.Members who have obtained residency abroad, and are recognized as official citizen of that country, can become members of organizations of their residing country.

Article IV: Duties of a Party Member—Pay membership fee and rules included. Individuals who are not in a position to perform the full duties of a member, but have organizational ties with the Party and support its policies are called "sympathizers".

Article V: Rights of a Party Member—A Party member has the right to: Express viewpoints, ask questions or submit proposals to any Party organ via organizational method. Lodge complaints against any organ to a higher authority. Be present at any meetings of her/his organ that analyses her/his political and Party activeness, and decides about her/him.

Article VI: Punishment of a Member

Article VII: The Organizational Structure of the Party- A lower level organ must carry out the decisions of a higher organ. From top to bottom in the hierarchy, decisions are taken collectively. Self-centredness and egotism is condemned in the Party.

Article VIII: Party Congress:

1- The Congress is the most supreme organ of the Party.
2- The Congress convenes every four years. It comprises of main members, alternate and advisory members of the Central Committee, and the delegates of other Party members according to the proportion that the Central Committee determines.
3- Extraordinary Congress will be held provided the Central Committee or two thirds of the full time personnel of the Party requests it.

4. The duties and the powers of the Congress are as follows: Discussing the Central Committee's report, and make decisions about it. Determining the Party's general, political, strategic and tactical policies. Ratification of the Party's Programme and Internal Regulation, and its amendment if necessary. Electing main and alternate members of the Central Committee.

Article IX: Party Conference

Article X: Central Committee

1- The Central Committee is the highest authority during the period between the two Congresses, and conducts the Party affairs.

2- The responsibilities and the prerogatives of the Central Committee are as follow: Convenes cessions at least three times a year. The alternate and advisory members of the Central Committee participate in the meetings of the Central Committee with consultive vote.–No one can be elected to the office of Secretary-general for more than two consecutive terms.

Article XI: Political Bureau: During the period between the two meetings of the Central Committee, the Political Bureau takes over the Central Committee's duties and is responsible for the implementation of its resolutions. The Political Bureau convenes based on necessity and submits reports on its activities to the Central Committee.

Article XII: Organizational Structure of the Party

1- The basis of Party organization is cell. The number of members of a cell should not be less than three.

2- The Party's organization is led by the village committee for the village, the district committee for the district, the regional committee for the region, the town committee for the town, and the provincial committee for the province.

3- It is the responsibility of the cell, village, district, regional, town, and provincial committees to advertise the Party policies among the masses, and to implement the Central Committee's resolutions and to administer the Party's affairs.

4- The Committee of each organ will be elected by the organ's members or their representatives.

5- The highest authority of each organ is the organ's Conference, which must be held at least once every two years, comprised of the delegates of all the Party members of the concerned organ. Under certain circumstances, the Central Committee can adopt other appropriate methods for the Party structures.

Article XIII: Party Income

Bibliography & Names

Chinese literature

1. Anthony C. Lobaido "The Kurds of Asia", translated by Zheng Xinyang, Chinese Water Conservation and Electricity Publishing house, 2004.

2. Philip Khuri Hitti, "The History of Arabs", translated by Ma Jianyi, New World Press Agency, 2008.

3. "Iran Travel Guide", translated by Ye Yiliang, World Culture Publishing House, 2000.

4. "The Ethnic and Religion Question in the Global Age", China University of Politics and Law Publishing house, 2011.

5. Jin Tao, "National Relations. An Introduction", Central University of Nationalities publishing house, 1996.

6. "The General History of the Middle East countries. Volume on Iraq", Commercial Press, 2002.

7. "The History of the Middle East (610-2000)", Tianjin Peoples Publishing House, 2010.

8. "Political Democratization Advancement Research on Republic of Turkey", Shanghai San Lien Book Store, 2010.

9. "Iraq", Social Sciences Literature Publishing House, 2007.

10. "Cold War Bay Area's International Relations", Social Sciences Literature Publishing House, 2002.

11. Li Yifu, Chief Editor Zhao Jinyuan "Introduction to Nationalities", Central University of Nationalities Publishing House, 1993.

12. Chief Editor Peng Shuzhi "The History of the 20th century Middle East" (Second Edition), Higher Education Publishing house, 2001.

13. "The General History of the Middle East countries. Volume on Syria and Lebanon", Commercial Press, 2003.

14. "The General History of the Middle East countries. Volume on Iran", Commercial Press, 2002.

15. The Historical Exploration of the "Contemporary Middle East Issue: Religions and Traditions", People's Publishing Agency, 2000.

16. The Historical Heritage and The Wind of the Times and the Cloud of Relations, Forest Publishing House, 1999.

17. "Middle East Issue And The American Middle East Policy", Current Affairs Press, 2006.

18. Zhao Guozhong (Chief Editor), "Persian Gulf War Middle East Pattern", China Social Sciences Publishing House, 1995.

19. China Institute of Contemporary International Relations Nationality and Religious Research Center (compilor), "World Nationality Requires Big Focus", Current Affairs Press, 2001.

Chinese Academic Papers

1. "The Kurdish Question", "Knowledge of the World" in 1979 the 15th issue.

2. "Straddling of zones National issue under Security, social Angle of view–Takes Kurdish Question as Example", "Nation" in 2009 the 4th issue.

3. "Potential Threat to a Stable Middle East – The Kurdish Question", "West Asia Africa" in 1992 the 2nd issue.

4. "Intravenous Injection into the Kurdish Culture", "Arab world" in 1984 the 4th issue.

5. "The Question of the Kurdistan Workers' Party of Its Effect on the Turkish Domestic and Foreign Policy", "West Asia-Africa" in 1995 the 4th issue.

6. Hussein, "Turkey's Kurdish Question", "Nationality" in 1985 the 2nd issue.

7. "Turkey Kurd Question Research Narration", "Nation" in 2010 the 4th issue.

8. "A Brief Analysis of Turkey's Kurdish Question", "Nation" in 2008 the 3rd issue.

9. "Long and Short History of the Kurdish Question", "Modern International Relations" in 1996 the 10th issue.

10. "The Puzzle of Middle East Kurdish Question", "International Data intelligence" in 2004 the 3rd issue.

11. "A Politics Investigation on the Kurdish Question and the Middle East", "Northwest University Journal (Philosophy and Social Sciences Version)" in 1994 the 4th issue.

12. "Kurdistan Workers' Party "Europe" Forbidden by Turkey–One New System Principle Analysis", "West Asia Africa" in 2009 the 8th issue.

13. " Investigation on the Relations between the Soviet Union and Iraqi and the Kurds in 1921-1979", "Journal of Harbin Institute of Technology (Social Sciences Version)" in 2005 the 2nd issue.

14. "The Differences and Contradiction between the US and Turkey in the Iraqi-Kurdish Question", "Hexi Institute Journal" in 2007 the 1st issue.

15. "The Investigation of the US Factor in the Iraqi-Kurdish Question After Saddam's Times", "Chongqing Science and Technology Institute Journal (Social Sciences Version)" in 2008 the 11th issue.

16. "Kurds Question's Effect on Turkish Foreign Relations at the End of the 20th Century", "Langfang Normal School Journal (Social sciences Version)" in 2011 the 2nd issue.

17. "The Welcome Ceremony of the Kurds", "Culture Translation Press" in 1984 the 3rd issue.

18. "New Changes and Prospects of the Iraqi-Kurdish Question", "Nation" in 2010 the 4th issue.

19. "The History, Present and Prospects of the Kurdish Question", "Modern International Relations" in 1999 the 11th issue.

20. "Why the Kurd Want Independence?", "Nanfang Weekly" on November 1, 2007.

21. "The Development Process and Prospects of the Kurdish Question", "Nation" in 1998 the 1st issue.

22. "The Emergence, Development and Geopolitical Influence of the Kurdish Question", "World Geography Research" in 1998 the 1st issue.

23. "The Puzzle of Multi-national Kurdish Question", "West Asia Africa" in 1994 the 5th issue.

24. "Turkey Join into the European Union Advances the Kurdish Question", "International Observation" in 2010 the 4th issue.

25. "The Construction of the Iraqi Federal system and the Kurdish Question", "Nation" in 2006 the 3rd issue.

26. "Post-war Change and Development of the Separatist Movement of the Iraqi-Kurds", "Arab World Research" in 2006 the 5th issue.

27. "Fragments of the Islamic World–Kurdish Question Analysis", "West River Financial College Newspaper" in 2006 the 4th issue.

28. "US and Turkish Countermeasure to Iraqi Border Crisis", "West Asia Africa" in 2008 the 6th issue.

29. "Kurdish Nationality's Tragedy", "Nationality Translation Press" in 1981 the 1st issue.

30. "The Analysis of the Kurdish National Issue", "West Asia Africa" in 1982 the 5th issue.

31. "Europe-Kurds Migration and International Relations", "Yunnan School of Administration Journal" in 2009 the 1st issue.

32. "West Asian Kurd and Soviet Kurds", "Foreign National Question Research" in 1991 the 3rd issue.

33. "Kurd's Misery", "Nationality Translation Press" in 1984 the 2nd issue.

34. "The Kurdish Question from Angle of Turkey's Application To Join European Union", "West Asia Africa" in 2011 the 9th issue.

35. "The Origin of the Kurdish Question", "World History" in 1992 the 5th issue.

International Literature

1. Abdul Rahman Ghassemlou, Kurdistan and the Kurds, Publishing House of Czechoslovok Academy of Sciences, Prague, 2005.

2. Aliza Marcus, Blood and Belief: The PKK and the Kurdish Fight for Independence, New York University Press, 2007.

3. Ismet G. Imset, The PKK: A Report on Separatist Violence in Turkey (1973-1992), Ankara: Turkish Daily News Publications, 1992.

4. Brendan O'Leary, John McGarry, Khaled Salih, The Future of Kurdistan in Iraq, University of Pennsylvania Press, 2006.

5. Cecil J. Edmonds, Kurds, Turks and Arabs: Politics, Travel and Research in North-Eastern Iraq, 1919-1925, London, 1957.

6. David McDowall, A Modern History of the Kurds, I. B. Tauris, 3 Revised Edition, 2004.

7. David Romano, The Kurdish Nationalist Movement: Opportunity, Mobilization and Identity, Cambridge University Press, 2006.

8. David Kenneth Fieldhouse, Kurds, Arabs and Britons: The Memory of Wallace Lyon in Iraq 1918-1944, I. B. Tauris, 2002.

9. Denise Natali, The Kurdish Quasi-state: Development and Dependency in Postgulf War Iraq, Syracuse University Press, 2010.

10. Edgar O'Balance: The Kurdish Revolt: 1961-1970, Archon Books, 1973.

11. Faleh A. Jabar, Hosham Dawood, The Kurds: Nationalism and Politics, Saqi Books, 2007.

12. Gareth R. V. Stansfield, Iraqi Kurdistan: Political Development and Emergent Democracy, Routledge, 2003.

13. Gérard Challand, The Kurdish Tradedy, Zed Books Ltd.

14. Gérard Chaliand, A People Without a Country: The Kurds and Kurdistan, Interlink Publishing Group, 1993.

15. "Terrorism: Middle Eastern Groups and State Sponsors, Kurdistan Workers Party (PKK)", Global Security CRS Report, August 27, 1998.

16. G.S. Harris, Ethnic Conflict and the Kurds, Annals of the American Academy of Political and Social Science, 1977.

17. Henri J. Barkey, Graham E. Fuller, Turkey's Kurdish Question, Rowman & Littlefield Publishers, Inc., 1998.

18. Harriet Montgomery, The Kurds of Syria: An Existence Denied, Europaeisches Zentrum für Kurdische Studien, Berlin, 2005.

19. Ismet G. Imset, The PKK: A Report on Separatist Violence in Turkey (1973-1992), Turkish Daily News Publications,1992.

20. Jordi Tejel, Syria's Kurds: History, Politics and Society, Routledge, 2009.

21. Kerim Yildiz, The Kurds in Iraq: The Past, Present and Future, Pluto Press, Second Edition, 2007.

22. Kevin Mckiernan, The Kurds: A People in Search of Their Homeland, St. Martin's Press, 2006.

23. Kemal Kirişçi, Gareth M. Winrow, The Kurdish Question and Turkey: An Example of a Trans-State Ethnic Conflict, London: Frank Cass Publishers, 1997.

24. Lokman I. Meho, The Kurdish Question in U.S. Foreign Policy: A Documentary Sourcebook, Greenwood Publishing Group, 2004.

25. Massoud Barzani, Mustafa Barzani and the Kurdish Liberation Movement, Palgrave Macmillan, 2003.

26. Mahir A. Aziz, The Kurds of Iraq: Ethnonationalism and National Identity in Iraqi Kurdistan, I.B.Tauris, 2011.

27. Marianna Charountaki, The Kurds and US Foreign Policy: International Relations in the Middle East Since 1945, Routledge, 2011.

28. Michael M.Gunter, Historical Dictionary of the Kurds, Scarecrow Press, 2011.

29. Michael M.Gunter, The Kurds Ascending: The Evolving Solution to the Kurdish Problem in Iraq and Turkey, Palgrave Macmillan, 2007.

30. Michael M.Gunter,The Kurds and the Future of Turkey, Palgrave Macmillan, 1997.

31. Philip G. Kreyenbroek, Christine Allison (Editor), Kurdish Culture and Identity, Zed Books, 1996.

32. PKK Terrorism, Ministry of Foreign Affairs, Ankara, 1998.

33. Philip G. Kreyenbroek (Editor), Stefan Sperl (Editor), The Kurds: A Contemporary Overview, Routledge, 1991.

34. P.G. Kreyenbroek, S. Sperl, The Kurds: A Contemporary Overview, Routledge, 1992.

35. Quil Lawrence, Invisible Nation: How the Kurds: Quest for Statehood is Shaping Iraq and the Middle East, 2008.

36. Robert W. Olson, The Emergence of Kurdish Nationalism and the Sheikh Said Rebellion, 1880-1925, University of Texas Press, 1989.

37. Susan Meiselas, Kurdistan: In the Shadow of History, University of Chicago Press, 2008.

38. Trita Parsi, Treacherous Alliance: The Secret Dealings of Israel, Iran and the U.S., Yale University Press, 2007.

39. The Kurdistan File, The Kurdish Institute at Brussels, 1989.

40. Vera Eccarius, Kelly, The Militant Kurds: A Dual Strategy for Freedom, Praeger, 2010.

41. Wadie Jwaideh, The Kurdish National Movement: Its Origins and Development, Syracuse University Press, 2006.

42. William Eagleton Jr., The Kurdish Republic of 1946, Oxford University Press, 1963.

Name Index

Ismail Agha Simko
Qazi Muhammad
Abdul al-Rahman Ghassemlou
Sadegh Sharaf Kandi
Mustafa Hejri
Abdul Rahman Haji Ahmedi
Gulistan Dogan
Dr. Abdollah Ramezanzadeh
Bahaeddin Adab
Shaykh Izzeddin Hosseini
Ahmad Tawfiq
Mustafa Kemal Atatürk
Mustafa Ismet Inönü
Celal Bayar
Adnan Menderes
Cemal Gürsel
Alparslan Türkeş
Tansu Ciller
Kamran Inan
Kenan Evren
Turgut Özal
Süleyman Demirel
Abdullah Gül
Mustafa Bülent Ecevit
Ahmet Mesut Yılmaz
Recep Tayyip Erdogan
Nuri as-Said
Abd al-Karim Qasim
Abdul Salam Mohammed Arif
Abdul Rahman Arif
Ahmed Hassan al-Bakr
Saddam Hussein
Nouri al-Maliki
Alī Hasan al-Majīd
Ahmad Chalabi
Reza Khan Pahlavi
Mohammad Rezā Shāh Pahlavī
Mohammad Mosaddegh
Abulhassan Banisadr
Ayatollah Ruhollah Mussavi Khomeini
Ayatollah Sayyed Ali Khamenei
Seyyed Mohammad Khatami
Mahmoud Ahmadi-Nejad
Hafez al-Assad
Bashar al-Assad
Sarafettin Elci
Deniz Gezmis

Mahir Cayan
Kemal Burkay
Abdullah Öcalan
Osman Öcalan
Murat Karayılan
Mahmud Osman
Bakr Sidqi
Hhalid Bakdash
Ibrahim Ahmad
Hamaza Abdullah
Fuad Masum
Hoshyar Zibari
Lahur Talabani
Barham Salih
Nurettin Demirtas
Mazlum Korkmaz
Duran Kalkan
Mustafa Karasu
Ali Haydar Kaytan
Zübeyir Aydar
Cemil Bayik
Sir Arnold Talbot Wilson
Sir Percy Zachariah Cox
Gertrude Bell
Henry Churchill King
Charles R. Crane
Woodrow Wilson
Richard Milhous Nixon
Henry Alfred Kissinger
William Colby
Peter Galbraith
Joseph Ralston
Herro K. Mustafa
Ronald Wilson Reagan
George Herbert Walker Bush
George Walker Bush
William Jefferson Clinton
Barack Hussein Obama
Paul Bremer
Houari Boumedienne
Gamal Abdel Nasser
Joseph Stalin
Yitzhak Mordechai
Moshe Dayan
Menachem Begin
Maurizio Garzoni
Ibrahim Pasha
Kerim Yildiz

www.ingramcontent.com/pod-product-compliance
Lightning Source LLC
Chambersburg PA
CBHW020427130626
46549CB00001B/23